PEDAGOGY IN ANCIENT JUDAISM
AND EARLY CHRISTIANITY

EARLY JUDAISM AND ITS LITERATURE

Rodney A. Werline, Editor

Editorial Board:
Esther Glickler Chazon
Kelley N. Coblentz Bautch
Maxine L. Grossman
Jan Joosten
James S. McLaren

Number 41

PEDAGOGY IN ANCIENT JUDAISM AND EARLY CHRISTIANITY

Edited by
Karina Martin Hogan, Matthew Goff, and Emma Wasserman

SBL PRESS

Atlanta

Copyright © 2017 by SBL Press

All rights reserved. No part of this work may be reproduced or transmitted in any form or by any means, electronic or mechanical, including photocopying and recording, or by means of any information storage or retrieval system, except as may be expressly permitted by the 1976 Copyright Act or in writing from the publisher. Requests for permission should be addressed in writing to the Rights and Permissions Office, SBL Press, 825 Houston Mill Road, Atlanta, GA 30329 USA.

Library of Congress Cataloging-in-Publication Data

Names: Hogan, Karina Martin, editor. | Goff, Matthew J., editor. | Wasserman, Emma, editor.
Title: Pedagogy in ancient Judaism and early Christianity / edited by Karina Martin Hogan, Matthew Goff, and Emma Wasserman.
Description: Atlanta : SBL Press, [2017] | Series: Early Judaism and its literature ; number 41 | Includes bibliographical references and index.
Identifiers: LCCN 2016056512 (print) | LCCN 2016056867 (ebook) | ISBN 9781628371659 (pbk. : alk. paper) | ISBN 9780884142089 (hardcover : alk. paper) | ISBN 9780884142072 (ebook)
Subjects: LCSH: Education in the Bible. | Jewish ethics—Biblical teaching. | Wisdom literature—Criticism, interpretation, etc.
Classification: LCC BS1199.E38 P43 2017 (print) | LCC BS1199.E38 (ebook) | DDC 221.8/37—dc23
LC record available at https://lccn.loc.gov/2016056512

Printed on acid-free paper.

For Ellen Aitken of blessed memory

> But you have come to Mount Zion and to the city of the living God, the heavenly Jerusalem, and to innumerable angels in festal gathering, and to the assembly of the firstborn who are enrolled in heaven, and to God the judge of all, and to the spirits of the righteous made perfect. (Heb 12:22–23 NRSV)

Contents

Acknowledgments ix
Abbreviations xi

Introduction
    Karina Martin Hogan 1

Part 1. Pedagogy in Second Temple Judaism: From *Musar* to Paideia

Ancient Israelite Pedagogy and Its Survival in Second Temple
Interpretations of Scripture
    James L. Kugel 15

Wisdom and Torah
    John J. Collins 59

Would Philo Have Recognized Qumran *Musar* as Paideia?
    Karina Martin Hogan 81

Kyropaideia versus *Paideia Kyriou*: The Semantic Transformation
of Paideia and Cognates in the Translated Books of
the Septuagint
    Patrick Pouchelle 101

Paideia and the Gymnasium
    Robert Doran 135

Part 2. Sapiential and Apocalyptic Perspectives on Ancient Jewish Pedagogy

Reading Proverbs in Light of Torah: The Pedagogy of 4QBeatitudes
    Elisa Uusimäki 155

Gardens of Knowledge: Teachers in Ben Sira, 4QInstruction,
and the Hodayot
Matthew Goff 171

Paideia: A Multifarious and Unifying Concept in the Wisdom
of Solomon
Jason M. Zurawski 195

Job and the "Mystic's Solution" to Theodicy: Philosophical
Paideia and Internalized Apocalypticism in the Testament
of Job
Andrew R. Guffey 215

PART 3. HELLENISM AND PAIDEIA IN EARLY CHRISTIANITY

The Mysteries of Paideia: "Mystery" and Education in Plato's
Symposium, 4QInstruction, and 1 Corinthians
C. Andrew Ballard 243

Mosaic Torah as Encyclical Paideia: Reading Paul's Allegory of
Hagar and Sarah in Light of Philo of Alexandria's
Jason M. Zurawski 283

Wily, Wise, and Worldly: Instruction and the Formation of
Character in the Epistle to the Hebrews
Ellen Bradshaw Aitken 309

Paideia and Polemic in Second-Century Lyons: Irenaeus
on Education
D. Jeffrey Bingham 323

Why Did Christians Compete with Pagans for Greek Paideia?
Raffaella Cribiore 359

Contributors...375
Ancient Sources Index..377
Modern Authors Index...396

Acknowledgments

The majority of the chapters in this volume were presented in sessions of the Wisdom and Apocalypticism section at the Annual Meetings of the Society of Biblical Literature between 2012 and 2014. Two of the volume's editors, Karina Martin Hogan and Matthew Goff, were cochairs of the section, and the third, Emma Wasserman, joined the steering committee in 2014. We are grateful to the members of the steering committee during that period for their contributions to planning and presiding at the sessions and for the responses they provided in these sessions: Ellen Aitken (McGill University), Robert Doran (Amherst College), Matthias Henze (Rice University), Judith Newman (University of Toronto), Larry Wills (Episcopal Divinity School), and Benjamin Wright (Lehigh University). Thanks are due, moreover, to the Society of Biblical Literature for its support of the work of this section, and to SBL Press for its assistance in publishing it. In particular, we are grateful to Rod Werline, the editor of the Early Judaism and Its Literature Series, and to Nicole Tilford, Production Manager of SBL Press, for their patient assistance.

As explained further in the introduction, the inspiration for this volume was a suggestion by Ellen Aitken, a former chair of the Wisdom and Apocalypticism section and a member of the steering committee until shortly before her untimely death in 2014. Hence the volume is dedicated to her memory. Thanks are due to Gütersloher Verlagshaus for allowing us to republish an essay of hers entitled "Wily, Wise, and Worldly: Instruction and the Formation of Character in the Epistle to the Hebrews," originally published in the volume *The Changing Face of Judaism, Christianity and Other Greco-Roman Religions in Antiquity*, edited by Ian H. Henderson and Gerbern S. Oegema. We are grateful to Robert Doran, Samuel Williston Professor of Greek and Hebrew in the Department of Religion at Amherst College, and to Patrick Pouchelle, Member of the Faculty of Theology at the Centre Sèvres, Paris, for contributing essays to round out the volume.

Finally, several doctoral students assisted in the preparation of this volume: Elizabeth Pyne (Fordham University), Kyle Roark (Florida State University), Steven Payne (Fordham University), and M Tong (Fordham University); special thanks are due to Blake Jurgens (Florida State University) for efficiently compiling the chapter bibliographies and volume indices. The editors are appreciative of their respective institutions, Fordham University, Florida State University, and Rutgers University, for supporting their research and publication projects. We are also very grateful to our families for their support and encouragement in this work.

Abbreviations

Primary Sources

1 En.	1 Enoch (Ethiopic Apocalypse)
1QH^a	1QHodayot^a or Thanksgiving Hymns^a
1QS	Rule of the Community
1QSa	Rule of the Congregation (appendix A to 1QS)
2 En.	2 Enoch (Slavonic Apocalypse)
3 En.	3 Enoch (Hebrew Apocalypse)
4QM	Milḥama or War Scroll
4QMMT	Miqṣat Ma'aśê ha-Torah
Abr.	Philo, *De Abrahamo*
Ab urbe cond.	Livy, *Ab urbe condita*
Aet.	Philo, *De aeternitate mundi*
Ag.	Aeschylus, *Agamemnon*
Agr.	Philo, *De agricultura*
Aj.	Sophocles, *Ajax*
Alc.	Plutarch, *Alcibiades*
Anach.	Lucian, *Ancharsis*
Ant.	Josephus, *Jewish Antiquities*; Sophocles, *Antigone*
Apoc. Ab.	Apocalypse of Abraham
Apoc. Zeph.	Apocalypse of Zephaniah
Ascen. Isa.	Martyrdom and Ascension of Isaiah 6–11
Ath. pol.	Aristotle, *Athēnaiōn politeia* (*Constitution of Athens*)
Avot R. Nat.	Avot of Rabbi Nathan
Bab.	John Chrysostom, *De sancto hieromartyre Babyla*
Bell. Cat.	Sallust, *Bellum catalinae*
Bib. hist.	Diodorus Siculus, *Bibliotheca historica*
b. Ta'an.	Babylonian Talmud, Ta'anit
Caes.	Aurelius Victor, *De Caesaribus*

C. Ap.	Josephus, *Contra Apionem*
Cat. Maj.	Plutarch, *Cato Major*
Caus. plant.	Theophrastus, *De causis plantarum*
CD	Cairo Genizah copy of the Damascus Document
Cels.	Origen, *Contra Celsum*
Cher.	Philo, *De cherubim*
Cod. Theod.	Codex Theodosianus
Comp.	Dionysius of Halicarnassus, *De compositione verborum*
Congr.	Philo, *De congressu eruditionis gratia*
Contempl.	Philo, *De vita contemplativa*
Decal.	Philo, *De decalogo*
Decl.	Choricius of Gaza, *Declamation*
Deipn.	Athenaeus, *Deipnosophistae*
De or.	Cicero, *De oratore*
Dial.	Tacitus, *Dialogus de oratoribus*
Diatr.	Epictetus, *Diatribai* (*Dissertationes*)
Dio	Synesius of Cyrene, *Dio, sive de suo ipsius instituto*
El.	Propertius, *Elegiae*
Ench.	Epictetus, *Enchiridion*
Ep.	Diogenes, *Epistle*; Jerome, *Epistulae*; John Chortasmenos, *Epistle*; Julian, *Epistle*; Libanius, *Epistulae*; Lysias, *Epistle*; Optimus, *Epistle*; Pliny the Younger, *Epistulae*; Seneca the Younger, *Epistulae morales*
Epid.	Irenaeus, *Epideixis tou apostolikou kērygmatos*
Epit.	Alcinous, *Epitome doctrinae platonicae* (*Didaskalikos*)
Ep. Pyth.	Epicurus, *Epistle to Pythocles*
Eq.	Xenophon, *De equitande ratione*
Eth. nic.	Aristotle, *Ethica nicomachea*
Ezek. Trag.	Ezekiel the Tragedian
Flor.	Stobaeus, *Florilegium*
Fug.	Philo, *De fuga et inventione*
Gen. Rab.	Genesis Rabbah
Gen. Socr.	Plutarch, *De genio Socratis*
Geogr.	Strabo, *Geographica*
Gig.	Philo, *De gigantibus*
GV	*Gnomologium Vaticanum*
Gymn.	Philostratus, *De gymnastica*
Haer.	Irenaeus, *Adversus haereses* (*Elenchos*)
Hekh. Rabb.	Hekhaloth Rabbati

Her.	Julian, *Contra Heraclium*
Her.	Philo, *Quis rerum divinarum heres sit*
Hist.	Herodotus, *Historiae*
Hist. eccl.	Socrates Scholasticus, *Historia ecclesiastica*
Hist. eccl.	Sozomen, *Historia ecclesiastica*
Inst.	Quintilian, *Institutio oratoria*
Iph. taur.	Euripides, *Iphigenia taurica*
Is. Os.	Plutarch, *De Iside et Osiride*
Jul.	Gregory of Nazianzus, *Contra Julianum*
LAB	Pseudo-Philo, Liber antiquitatum biblicarum
Leg.	Philo, *Legum allegoriae*; Plato, *Leges*
Legat.	Philo, *Legatio ad Gaium*
Let. Aris.	Letter of Aristeas
Lex	Hippocrates, *Lex*
Lib. ed.	Pseudo-Plutarch, *De liberis educandis*
LXX	Septuagint
Mart. Ascen. Isa.	Martyrdom and Ascension of Isaiah
m. Avot	Mishnah Avot
Med.	Marcus Aurelius, *Meditations*
Mek.	Mekilta
Mem.	Xenophon, *Memorabilia*
Metaph.	Aristotle, *Metaphysica*
Migr.	Philo, *De migratione Abrahami*
Mor.	Plutarch, *Moralia*
Mos.	Philo, *De vita Mosis*
MT	Masoretic Text
Mut.	Philo, *De mutatione nominum*
Nat. d.	Cicero, *De natura deorum*
Opif.	Philo, *De opificio mundi*
Or.	Julian, *Oration*; Libanius, *Orations*
Or. Bas.	Gregory of Nazianzus, *Oratio in laudem Basilii*
PapyCol	Papyrologica Coloniensia
Phaedr.	Plato, *Phaedrus*
Phil.	Plutarch, *Philopoemen*
Phorm.	Terence, *Phormio*
Pol.	Aristotle, *Politica*
Post.	Philo, *De posteritate Caini*
Pref.	Preface (to each book of Irenaeus, *Adversus haereses*)
Prob.	Philo, *Quod omnis probus liber sit*

Prog.	Aphtonius, *Progymnasmata*
Prol.	Prologue (to Sirach)
Prot.	Plato, *Protagoras*
Protr.	Galen, *Protrepticus*
Pss. Sol.	Psalms of Solomon
P.W.	Thucydides, *History of the Peloponnesian War*
Pyr.	Sextus Empiricus, *Pyrrhoniae hypotyposes*
Quo. adol.	Plutarch, *Quomodo adolescens poetas audire debeat*
Res gest.	Ammianus Marcellinus, *Res gestae*
Resp.	Plato, *Respublica*
Rust.	Columella, *Res rustica*
Sacr.	Philo, *De sacrificiis Abelis et Caini*
Sat.	Horace, *Satires*
Sat.	Juvenal, *Satires*
Sent.	Menander, *Sententiae (Gnomai)*; Pseudo-Phocylides, *Sentences*
Sept.	Aeschylus, *Septem contra Thebas*
Sib. Or.	Sibylline Oracles
Silv.	Statius, *Silvae*
Sir	Sirach/Ecclesiasticus
Sobr.	Philo, *De sobrietate*
Somn.	Philo, *De somniis*
Spec.	Philo, *De specialibus legibus*
Strom.	Clement of Alexandria, *Stromateis*
T. Ab.	Testament of Abraham
Tg. Neof.	Targum Neofiti
Tg. Ps.-Jon.	Targum Pseudo-Jonathan
Th.	Theodotion
Theaet.	Plato, *Theaetetus*
Them.	Plutarch, *Themistocles*
Ti. C. Gracch.	Plutarch, *Tiberius et Caius Gracchus*
Tim.	Aeschines, *In Timarchum*
T. Job	Testament of Job
T. Levi	Testament of Levi
Tri. Trac.	I 5 Tripartite Tractate
Var. hist.	Aelian, *Varia historia*
Vesp.	Aristophanes, *Vespae*
Virt. mor.	Plutarch, *De Virtute Morali*
Vit. Apoll.	Philostratus, *Vita Apollonii*

Vit. Phil.	Diogenes Laertius, *Vitae Philosophorum*

Secondary Sources

AB	Anchor Bible
ABD	Freedman, David Noel, ed. *Anchor Bible Dictionary*. 6 vols. New York: Doubleday, 1992.
ABRL	Anchor Bible Reference Library
ACW	Ancient Christian Writers
AGJU	Arbeiten zur Geschichte des antiken Judentums und des Urchristentums
AJP	*American Journal of Philology*
ANRW	Temporini, Hildegard, and Wolfgang Haase, eds. *Aufstieg und Niedergang der römischen Welt: Geschichte und Kultur Roms im Spiegel der neueren Forschung*. Part 2, *Principat*. Berlin: de Gruyter, 1972–.
AncSoc	*Ancient Society*
ApBS	T&T Clark Approaches to Biblical Studies
ASP	American Studies in Papyrology
AT	Aegyptiaca Treverensia
ATANT	Abhandlungen zur Theologie des Alten und Neuen Testaments
ATDan	Acta Theologica Danica
AuBib	Autour de la Bible
BA	La Bible d'Alexandrie
BCT	*The Bible and Critical Theory*
BDAG	Danker, Frederick W., Walter Bauer, William F. Arndt, and F. Wilbur Gingrich. *Greek-English Lexicon of the New Testament and Other Early Christian Literature*. 3rd. ed. Chicago: University of Chicago Press, 2000.
BETL	Bibliotheca Ephemeridum Theologicarum Lovaniensium
BFCT	Beiträge zur Förderung christlicher Theologie
BGU	*Aegyptische Urkunden aus den Königlichen Staatlichen Museen zu Berlin, Griechische Urkunden*. 15 vols. Berlin: Weidmann, 1895–1937.
BHQ	Schenker, Adrian, et al., eds. *Biblia Hebraica Quinta*. Stuttgart: Deutsche Bibelgesellschaft, 2004–.
BHT	Beiträge zur historischen Theologie

Bib	*Biblica*
BibInt	Biblical Interpretation Series
BibTS	Biblica: Testi e Studi
BJRL	*Bulletin of the John Rylands University Library of Manchester*
BJS	Brown Judaic Studies
BLS	Bible and Literature Series
BNP	Cancik, Hubert, ed. *Brill's New Pauly: Encyclopaedia of the Ancient World*. 22 vols. Leiden: Brill, 2002–2011.
BNTC	Black's New Testament Commentaries
Brenton	Brenton, Lancelot Charles Lee. *The Septuagint Version of the Old Testament and Apocrypha*. London: Bagster & Sons, 1870.
BRPC	Brill's Paperback Collection
BRS	Biblical Resource Series
BSGRT	Bibliotheca Scriptorum Graecorum et Romanorum Teubneriana
ByzZ	*Byzantinische Zeitschrift*
BZAW	Beihefte zur Zeitschrift für die alttestamentliche Wissenschaft
BZNW	Beihefte zur Zeitschrift für die neutestamentliche Wissenschaft
CBC	Cambridge Bible Commentary
CBQ	*Catholic Biblical Quarterly*
CBQMS	Catholic Biblical Quarterly Monograph Series
CdE	*Chronique d'Égypte*
CJA	Christianity and Judaism in Antiquity
ClAnt	*Classical Antiquity*
CollLing	Collection linguistique (Société de linguistique de Paris)
CP	*Classical Philology*
CrStHB	Critical Studies in the Hebrew Bible
DCLS	Deuterocanonical and Cognate Literature Studies
DJD	Discoveries in the Judaean Desert
DP	Les dix paroles
DSD	*Dead Sea Discoveries*
EBib	Etudes bibliques
ECDSS	Eerdmans Commentaries on the Dead Sea Scrolls
ECF	Early Church Fathers
ECL	Early Christianity and Its Literature

EDEJ	Collins, John J., and Daniel C. Harlow, eds. *Eerdmans Dictionary of Early Judaism*. Grand Rapids: Eerdmans, 2010.
EDNT	Balz, Horst, and Gerhard Schneider, eds. *Exegetical Dictionary of the New Testament*. 3 vols. Grand Rapids: Eerdmans, 1990–1993.
EJL	Early Judaism and Its Literature
ExpTim	*Expository Times*
FAT	Forschungen zum Alten Testament
FRJS	Fontes ad res Judaicas spectantes
FRLANT	Forschungen zur Religion und Literatur des Alten und Neuen Testaments
GRBS	*Greek, Roman, and Byzantine Studies*
HBM	Hebrew Bible Monographs
HNT	Handbuch zum Neuen Testament
HSCP	*Harvard Studies in Classical Philology*
HSM	Harvard Semitic Monographs
HThKAT	Herders Theologischer Kommentar zum Alten Testament
HTR	*Harvard Theological Review*
HTS	*Harvard Theological Studies*
HUCM	Monographs of the Hebrew Union College
IBC	Interpretation: A Bible Commentary for Teaching and Preaching
ICC	International Critical Commentary
IEJ	*Israel Exploration Journal*
IGUR	Moretti, Luigi, ed. *Inscriptiones graecae urbis Romae*. 4 vols. Rome: Istituto italiano per la storia antica, 1968–1991.
IOSCS	International Organization for Septuagint and Cognate Studies
IOSOT	International Organization for the Study of the Old Testament
JAAR	*Journal of the American Academy of Religion*
JAJ	*Journal of Ancient Judaism*
JBL	*Journal of Biblical Literature*
JCMAMW	Jews, Christians, and Muslims from the Ancient to the Modern World
JEOL	*Jaarbericht van het Vooraziatisch-Egyptisch Gezelschap*

	"Ex Oriente Lux" / *Annuaire de la Société Orientale "Ex Oriente Lux"*
JETS	*Journal of the Evangelical Theological Society*
JJS	*Journal of Jewish Studies*
JJTPSup	Journal of Jewish Thought and Philosophy Supplements
JNES	*Journal of Near Eastern Studies*
JPS	Jewish Publication Society
JQR	*Jewish Quarterly Review*
JR	*Journal of Religion*
JSCS	*Journal of Septuagint and Cognate Studies*
JSHRZ	Jüdische Schriften aus hellenistisch-römischer Zeit
JSJ	*Journal for the Study of Judaism*
JSJSup	Journal for the Study of Judaism Supplement Series
JSOT	*Journal for the Study of the Old Testament*
JSOTSup	Journal for the Study of the Old Testament Supplement Series
JSP	*Journal for the Study of the Pseudepigrapha*
JSPSup	Journal for the Study of the Pseudepigrapha Supplement Series
Kaibel	Kaibel, Georg. *Athenaei Naucratitae dipnosophistarum libri xv*. 3 vols. Leipzig: Teubner, 1887–1890. Repr., Stuttgart: Teubner, 1961–1965.
KJV Webster	*The Holy Bible Containing the Old and New Testaments in the Common Version with Amendments of the Language*, by Noah Webster
Klio	*Klio: Beiträge zur Alten Geschichte*
KTU	Dietrich, Manfried, Oswald Loretz, and Joaquín Sanmartín, eds. *Die keilalphabetischen Texte aus Ugarit*. Münster: Ugarit-Verlag, 2013. 3rd enl. ed. of *KTU: The Cuneiform Alphabetic Texts from Ugarit, Ras Ibn Hani, and Other Places*. Edited by Manfried Dietrich, Oswald Loretz, and Joaquín Sanmartín. Münster: Ugarit-Verlag, 1995.
KUSATU	*Kleine Untersuchungen zur Sprache des Alten Testaments und seiner Umwelt*
LCL	Loeb Classical Library
LD	Lectio Divina
LHBOTS	Library of Hebrew Bible/Old Testament Studies
LSJ	Liddell, Henry George, Robert Scott, and Henry Stuart

	Jones. *A Greek-English Lexicon*. 9th ed. with revised supplement. Oxford: Clarendon, 1996.
LSTS	Library of Second Temple Studies
MEFR	*Mélanges d'archéologie et d'histoire de l'École française de Rome*
Meghillot	*Meghillot: Studies in the Dead Sea Scrolls*
ML	Medical Life
MnemosyneSup	Mnemosyne Supplement Series
MS(S)	manuscript(s)
MVAW	Münchner Vorlesungen zu Antiken Welten
NA²⁸	*Novum Testamentum Graece*, Nestle-Aland, 28th ed.
Neot	*Neotestamentica*
NETS	Pietersma, Albert, and Benjamin G. Wright, eds. *A New English Translation of the Septuagint*. Oxford: Oxford University Press, 2007.
NIB	Keck, Leander E., ed. *The New Interpreter's Bible*. 12 vols. Nashville: Abingdon: 1994–2004.
NJPS	*Tanakh: The Holy Scriptures: The New JPS Translation according to the Traditional Hebrew Text*
NLH	*New Literary History*
NovT	*Novum Testamentum*
NovTSup	Supplements to Novum Testamentum
NRSV	New Revised Standard Version
NS	New Series
NTOA	Novum Testamentum et Orbis Antiquus
NTR	New Testament Readings
NTS	*New Testament Studies*
OBO	Orbis Biblicus et Orientalis
OCD	Hornblower, Simon, and Antony Spawforth, eds. *The Oxford Classical Dictionary*. 4th ed. Oxford: Oxford University Press, 2012.
OPA	Les oeuvres de Philon d'Alexandrie
OTE	*Old Testament Essays*
OTL	Old Testament Library
OTP	Charlesworth, James H., ed. *Old Testament Pseudepigrapha*. 2 vols. New York: Doubleday, 1983, 1985.
PIASH	Proceedings of the Israel Academy of Sciences and Humanities
PRSt	*Perspectives in Religious Studies*

PSC	Protocol Series of the Colloquies of the Center for Hermeneutical Studies in Hellenistic and Modern Culture
PSI	*Papiri della Società italiana.* Florence: Istituto papirologico G. Vitelli, 1912–.
PVTG	Pseudepigrapha Veteris Testamenti Graece
Rahlfs	Rahlfs, Alfred, ed. *Septuaginta: Id est Vetus Testamentum graece iuxta LXX interpretes.* 2 vols. Stuttgart: Württembergische Bibelanstalt, 1935.
RBPH	*Revue belge de philologie et d'histoire*
REJ	*Revue des études juives*
RevQ	*Revue de Qumran*
RGRW	Religions in the Graeco-Roman World
RTAM	*Recherches de théologie ancienne et médiévale*
RVV	Religionsgeschichtliche Versuche und Vorarbeiten
SBFCM	Studium Biblicum Franciscanum Collectio Maior
SBLDS	Society of Biblical Literature Dissertation Series
SBLSP	Society of Biblical Literature Seminar Papers
SBLTT	Society of Biblical Literature Texts and Translations
SC	Sources chrétiennes
ScBib	Sciences bibliques
ScrB	*Scripture Bulletin*
SCS	Septuagint and Cognate Studies
SEC	*Semitica et Classica*
SEP	*Studi di egittologia e di papirologia*
SGU	Acta Universitatis Upsaliensis: Studia Graeca Upsaliensia
SH	*Studia Hellenistica*
SHR	Studies in the History of Religions (supplemens to Numen)
SJOT	*Scandinavian Journal of the Old Testament*
SNTSMS	Society for New Testament Studies Monograph Series
SPhiloA	*Studia Philonica Annual*
SSEJC	Studies in Scripture in Early Judaism and Christianity
SSH	Le Sycomore: Série Horizon
SSLL	Studies in Semitic Languages and Linguistics
StAC	Standorte in Antike und Christentum
StBibLit	Studies in Biblical Literature
STDJ	Studies on the Texts of the Desert of Judah

StPatr	Studia Patristica
StSp	*Studies in Spirituality*
StudMor	Studia Moralia
StudNeot	Studia Neotestamentica
SUNT	Studien zur Umwelt des Neuen Testaments
SVF	Arnim, Hans Friedrich August von, ed. *Stoicorum Veterum Fragmenta*. 4 vols. Leipzig: Teubner, 1903–1924.
SVTG	Septuaginta: Vetus Testamentum Graecum
Symp.	Plato, *Symposium*
SymS	Symposium Series
TA	*Tel Aviv*
TBN	Themes in Biblical Narrative
TCSup	Trends in Classics Supplements
TDNT	Kittel, Gerhard, and Gerhard Friedrich, eds. *Theological Dictionary of the New Testament*. Translated by Geoffrey W. Bromiley. 10 vols. Grand Rapids: Eerdmans, 1964–1976.
TDOT	Botterweck, G. Johannes, and Helmer Ringgren, eds. *Theological Dictionary of the Old Testament*. Translated by John T. Willis et al. 8 vols. Grand Rapids : Eerdmans, 1974–2006.
TLOT	Jenni, Ernst, and Claus Westermann, eds. *Theological Lexicon of the Old Testament*. Translated by Mark E. Biddle. 3 vols. Peabody, MA: Hendrickson: 1997.
TOB	Traduction oecuménique de la Bible
TrGF	Snell, Bruno, ed. *Tragicorum Graecorum fragmenta*. vols. Göttingen: Vandenhoeck & Ruprecht, 1971–2004.
TSAJ	Texte und Studien zum antiken Judentum
TSK	*Theologische Studien und Kritiken*
TTH	Translated Texts for Historians
TU	Texte und Untersuchungen
UALG	Untersuchungen zur antiken Literatur und Geschichte
VC	*Vigiliae Christianae*
VT	*Vetus Testamentum*
VTG	Vetus Testamentum Graecum
VTSup	Supplements to Vetus Testamentum
WAW	Writings from the Ancient World
WBC	Word Biblical Commentary

WLAW	Wisdom Literature from the Ancient World
WMANT	Wissenschaftliche Monographien zum Alten und Neuen Testament
WSC	Wisconsin Studies in Classics
WUNT	Wissenschaftliche Untersuchungen zum Neuen Testament
YAB	Yale Anchor Bible
YJS	Yale Judaica Series
Ziegler	Ziegler, Joseph, et al., eds. *Septuaginta: Vetus Testamentum graecum auctoritate Societatis litterarum Gottingensis editum.* Göttingen: Vandenhoeck und Ruprecht, 1931–
ZNW	*Zeitschrift für die neutestamentliche Wissenschaft und die Kunde der älteren Kirche*
ZPE	*Zeitschrift für Papyrologie und Epigraphik*
ZWT	*Zeitschrift für wissenschaftliche Theologie*

Introduction

Karina Martin Hogan

The genesis of this volume was a suggestion made by our late colleague Ellen Aitken, to whose memory this book is dedicated. At the 2011 Annual Meeting of the Society of Biblical Literature in San Francisco, in a steering committee meeting for the Wisdom and Apocalypticism in Early Judaism and Early Christianity section, which she had chaired from 2002 to 2009, she observed that a great many of the texts with which our group has dealt over the years are concerned with paideia, a concept that encompasses education, enculturation, and character formation. Yet this concept had not been explored much in our group, or in the broader academy, in the study of wisdom or apocalyptic literature. Ellen suggested that we take up this theme in one or more of our sessions for several years in a row, should it prove to be a fruitful one for us.

It did indeed prove fruitful. We held a series of excellent sessions on the theme of paideia: "Paideia and 'Internalized Apocalypticism'" (2012, Chicago); "Paideia with an Eschatological Horizon," "Late Antique Paideia," and "Pedagogical Concepts and Techniques" (2013, Baltimore); and "Teachers, Torah and Paideia in Early Judaism" (2014, San Diego). Ellen's untimely death fell between the 2013 and 2014 annual meetings. Matthew Goff and Karina Martin Hogan, the co-chairs of the section at the time, had the idea of collecting essays from those three years of sessions on paideia into a volume in Ellen's memory. To round out the volume, we solicited two more chapters that had not been presented as papers in our sessions and obtained permission to reprint a published essay of Ellen's on pedagogy that had originally been presented in a Wisdom and Apocalypticism session at the 2002 annual meeting.[1] We invited a member of our steering committee, Emma Wasserman, to edit the chapters on early Christianity.

---

1. Ellen Bradshaw Aitken, "Wily, Wise, and Worldly: Instruction and the Forma-

The essays collected in this volume for the most part bear the stamp of the Wisdom and Apocalypticism section, which was formed as a consultation in 1994 with the goal of bringing together scholars of Second Temple Judaism with scholars of the New Testament and early Christianity to examine the relationship between sapiential and apocalyptic literature. The group's founders believed that these two discourses had much more in common than had been recognized by scholarship at that time. The Wisdom and Apocalypticism section succeeded in breaking down the boundaries between these two overlapping bodies of literature and the scholars who studied them, as a volume published in 2005 demonstrates.[2] It is no longer unusual for scholars to point to sapiential themes in apocalypses or apocalyptic tendencies in Hellenistic-period wisdom literature. Ellen's involvement in and leadership of the section during its first decade was instrumental in moving the discussion of the interplay of sapiential and apocalyptic themes into the field of early Christianity.

The topic of paideia challenged the Wisdom and Apocalypticism section to look beyond the chronological boundaries within which it has traditionally worked, looking backward to the pedagogical significance of the book of Proverbs and the torah of Moses and forward to the development of Christian pedagogy in late antiquity. The topic of early Christian pedagogy has been fairly extensively studied, at least since Werner Jaeger followed his magisterial three-volume work on ancient Greek paideia with a series of lectures on the influence of Greek paideia on early Christianity.[3] The early Christian authors themselves were conscious of developing a distinctive pedagogy under the influence of the classical education that most of them had received. To give just one example, the title of Clement of Alexandria's major work *Paedagogus* refers to Christ as the teacher of all humankind, but it also draws extensively on examples from the curriculum of Greek paideia, especially Homer. Indeed, the allegorical interpreta-

---

tion of Character in the Epistle to the Hebrews," in *The Changing Face of Judaism, Christianity, and Other Greco-Roman Religions in Antiquity*, ed. Ian H. Henderson and Gebern S. Oegema, JSHRZ (Gütersloh: Gütersloher Verlagshaus, 2006), 296–307.

2. Benjamin G. Wright and Lawrence M. Wills, *Conflicted Boundaries in Wisdom and Apocalypticism*, SymS 35 (Atlanta: Society of Biblical Literature, 2005).

3. Werner Jaeger, *Paideia: The Ideals of Greek Culture*, trans. Gilbert Highet, 3 vols. (New York: Oxford University Press, 1939–1944). His Carl Newell Jackson lectures, delivered at Harvard University in 1960, were first published as *Early Christianity and Greek Paideia* (Cambridge: Harvard University Press, 1961).

tion of Homer, which was developed in Alexandria in the third century BCE in response to the centrality of Homer in the Greek curriculum, was almost certainly the model for the allegorical interpretation of scripture.[4] It is Clement and his student Origen who are responsible for introducing allegorical exegesis into Christian theology, but they were following in the footsteps of Philo of Alexandria, the most prolific Jewish practitioner of allegorical interpretation of scripture. A number of scholars have studied the relationship of Philo's classical education to his innovative approach to the interpretation of scripture.[5]

With the exception of Philo, there is less evidence for the influence of classical paideia on ancient Judaism than on early Christianity, and until recently the topic of a distinctively Jewish paideia in the Second Temple period had not been much explored. This is surprising because the pedagogical function of wisdom literature (especially the element of moral formation) has long been recognized. There was a proliferation of textual production that could be considered sapiential in the Second Temple period, but wisdom literature offers only hints about the contexts in which education took place, the extent to which it was limited to the elite, and its relationship to scribalism.[6] David Carr has argued that biblical texts in general gained their status as scripture by being used to educate and enculturate young Israelite men and that studying the use of scripture in the literature of Second Temple Judaism offers a window into educational practices of that period.[7] If these arguments hold, the field for exploration of the phenomenon of education-enculturation (as Carr refers to it) or paideia in ancient Judaism is quite broad. Nevertheless, with a few isolated

---

4. See Robert Lamberton, *Homer the Theologian: Neoplatonist Allegorical Reading and the Growth of the Epic Tradition* (Berkeley: University of California Press, 1989).

5. For a recent summary, see Erkki Koskenniemi, "Philo and Classical Education," in *Reading Philo: A Handbook to Philo of Alexandria*, ed. Torrey Seland (Grand Rapids: Eerdmans, 2014), 102–28.

6. Recent scholarship has tended to construe the category of "wisdom" broadly in the Second Temple period and even to call into question the existence of a distinct wisdom genre. See Hindy Najman, Jean-Sébastien Rey, and Eibert J. C. Tigchelaar, eds., *Tracing Sapiential Traditions in Ancient Judaism*, JSJSup 174 (Leiden: Brill, 2016). On the limitations of wisdom literature for answering questions about its social context, see James L. Crenshaw, *Education in Ancient Israel: Across the Deadening Silence*, ABRL (New York: Doubleday, 1998).

7. David M. Carr, *Writing on the Tablet of the Heart: Origins of Scripture and Literature* (New York: Oxford University Press, 2005).

exceptions, the literature of Second Temple Judaism had not been examined through that lens.

The present volume aims to address that lacuna in the scholarship by offering a variety of perspectives on ancient Jewish pedagogy, as a preliminary contribution to a broader discussion of this important topic. The volume also includes essays on early Christian sources, reflecting the commitment of the Wisdom and Apocalypticism section to considering early Christianity alongside ancient Judaism from a variety of methodological perspectives. Part 1, "Pedagogy in Ancient Judaism: From *Musar* to Paideia," lays the groundwork for future considerations of ancient Jewish pedagogy by first examining the pedagogical assumptions of Proverbs and other wisdom writings in Hebrew, including the assumptions of ancient sages about the pedagogical function of the torah. Second, this section explores the impact of the introduction of the term παιδεία as the equivalent of מוסר (discipline or instruction) in the Septuagint (LXX) of Proverbs. It ends with a consideration of why Greek paideia was perceived as a threat to Jewish identity in Jerusalem at the time of the Maccabean Revolt.

James L. Kugel's essay, "Ancient Israelite Pedagogy and Its Survival in Second Temple Interpretations of Scripture," adroitly reviews and unpacks an extensive array of sayings that are preserved in the book of Proverbs. He demonstrates that these sayings are often enigmatic and were designed to be pondered over time in order to be understood. Kugel argues that the pedagogical function of Proverbs is crucial for understanding the development of scripture and the interpretative traditions surrounding it. He reviews the interpretations of scriptural texts found in numerous late Second Temple texts. These writings, he demonstrates, were composed by authors who understood scripture as an enigmatic text that requires careful reflection and interpretation. This is analogous to the mindset evident in the older sapiential sayings preserved in Proverbs. The exegetes of the late Second Temple period, Kugel concludes, can be understood as the direct descendants of the earlier sages whose teachings are reflected in Proverbs.

John J. Collins, in "Wisdom and Torah," examines the relation of the term *torah* to wisdom and how it changed from the biblical wisdom literature to wisdom texts of the later Second Temple period. He shows that while Deuteronomy draws themes and language from the wisdom tradition, playing on the root meaning of torah, "instruction," it sets in motion a process by which the term torah comes to refer to the torah of

Moses. Whereas some scholars have read Prov 1–9 as alluding to the Deuteronomic understanding of torah as Israel's inheritance, Collins argues that Proverbs and even the later Qoheleth show no interest in the torah of Moses and continue to use torah in its more universal, pedagogical sense. The earliest sapiential text to identify the torah of Moses as a source of wisdom is Ben Sira (Sir 24:23), but even Ben Sira acknowledges other paths to wisdom. In Ben Sira and the wisdom texts from Qumran, the torah of Moses functions as an icon for a wise way of life, rather than referring to a collection of specific commandments.

The chapter by Karina Martin Hogan addresses the question "Would Philo Have Recognized Qumran *Musar* as Paideia?" The root יסר in Proverbs is almost always translated in the LXX by forms of the word παιδεύω, suggesting that the translators understood these Hebrew and Greek terms as compatible. In Proverbs מוסר often denotes verbal rebuke and bodily punishment, which were considered important aspects of the process of education that allows one to acquire wisdom and long life. While in the Dead Sea Scrolls מוסר usually connotes a specifically sectarian program of education, some Qumran texts, in particular the wisdom writings, often show a range of meanings of מוסר that is similar to that of Proverbs. Although Philo's conception of paideia is shaped by Greek philosophy, another important source for him is the LXX text of Proverbs. Philo, Hogan argues, likely would have recognized the מוסר practiced by the Dead Sea sect as a kind of paideia, in part because both Philo and the authors of the wisdom texts from Qumran were shaped by the study of Proverbs and the torah.

Patrick Pouchelle's contribution, "*Kyropaideia* versus *Paideia Kyriou*: The Semantic Transformation of Paideia and Cognates in the Translated Books of the Septuagint," is a thorough investigation of the phenomenon that prompted Hogan's inquiry: the systematic translation of the root יסר and cognates with παιδεύω and cognates in the LXX. Pouchelle summarizes the results of his dissertation research to explain that curious decision by the translators of the LXX. He shows that while the semantic fields of יסר and παιδεύω are not identical, they overlap in carrying the sense of oral rebuking. This nuance, which may reflect a more popular usage, develops rather late for παιδεύω, appearing in documentary papyri in the Common Era. The nuance of oral rebuke for יסר is common in classical Hebrew, especially in the wisdom literature, whereas in Late Biblical Hebrew it develops a nuance of education, similar to the classical meaning of παιδεύω. Pouchelle concludes that the translators of the LXX version of the Torah may have chosen to translate יסר with παιδεύω to connote a relationship of authority between God and Israel, while παιδεία in some of the later books of the LXX connotes "a sapiential way of life."

Robert Doran, in his "Paideia and the Gymnasium," examines the extensive evidence for education in Greek that took place in Ptolemaic Egypt as a parallel that may shed light on the nature of education in Jerusalem in the Hellenistic period. He argues that before Jason had the gymnasium built, it is likely that there was already an educational system in Jerusalem that taught Greek. If this was the case, Doran asks, why would the construction of the gymnasium and the beginning of an ephebate have been controversial? The function of the ephebate was to produce good citizens who observed the religious traditions of their city and were trained to defend it from attack. It is not clear that people in Jerusalem would have disliked training of this sort. There are examples from antiquity of cities that refused to introduce the common ephebate system, such as Sparta. This case helps Doran argue that 1 and 2 Maccabees reject the institutions of the gymnasium and the ephebate because of the importance education plays in the formation of cultural identity. These texts testify to an effort to establish Jewish identity as different from that of the Greeks.

Part 2 of the volume, "Sapiential and Apocalyptic Perspectives on Ancient Jewish Pedagogy," exemplifies the kind of work that the Wisdom and Apocalypticism section has been doing for over twenty years to push forward the scholarly conversation on the intersection of sapiential and apocalyptic discourses. Most of the texts examined in these chapters are broadly sapiential, but all of them contain motifs not present in the biblical wisdom literature, such as torah piety, appeals to examples from scripture, apocalyptic eschatology, belief in the immortality of the soul, reflections on the role of teachers, and allusions to philosophical training and mystical transformation.

Elisa Uusimäki, in her "Reading Proverbs in Light of Torah: The Pedagogy of 4QBeatitudes," focuses on one of the better-preserved sapiential texts of the Dead Sea Scrolls, 4QBeatitudes (4Q525). While scholarship on the text has generally focused on the composition's sequence of beatitudes, Uusimäki examines not only this material but also other key features of the composition. The text of 4QBeatitudes draws heavily from the book of Proverbs and is written by a teacher who exhorts students to be ethical and righteous. Uusimäki's basic argument is that 4QBeatitudes extensively reworks material from Proverbs in order to emphasize torah piety. Like Ben Sira, 4QBeatitudes attests a combination of the sapiential and covenantal traditions. It also incorporates eschatological themes to motivate obedience to the torah. Uusimäki shows that the pedagogy of 4QBeatitudes encourages one not only to be pious and righteous but also to be a dedicated student of the ancestral texts of Judaism.

Matthew J. Goff, in his "Gardens of Knowledge: Teachers in Ben Sira, 4QInstruction, and the Hodayot," examines how teachers constructed their authority in the late Second Temple period. This trope is important for understanding how teachers presented the knowledge they conveyed as important and worthy of transmission. Ben Sira and the Hodayot (col. XVI) provide important examples of a teacher emphasizing his own importance as a source of knowledge. These texts and 4QInstruction, interestingly, describe the pedagogical space they inhabit with their students as gardens. All three texts also utilize imagery from the description of the garden of Eden in Gen 1–3 to make this point. Goff concludes that this scriptural appeal not only provides legitimacy to the knowledge that teachers wish to transmit; it also helps present their teachings as divinely revealed, giving authority and legitimacy to the knowledge they convey to their students.

Jason M. Zurawski's "Paideia: A Multifarious and Unifying Concept in the Wisdom of Solomon" contains an insightful discussion of the theme of paideia in the deuterocanonical Wisdom of Solomon. The theme of the education of humankind by God and by personified wisdom runs throughout the composition. The Wisdom of Solomon endorses a comprehensive mode of education that ultimately does not privilege a particular ethnic group but rather encourages the cultivation of wisdom and righteousness through which anyone can attain the immortal life of the soul. The content of the education fostered by the text, which includes a profound knowledge of humankind and the cosmos, is deeply shaped by Hellenistic culture (Wis 7:15–22). With regard to the means of attaining such knowledge, the paideia of the Wisdom of Solomon is often quite different from classical Greek conceptions of education. The composition highlights the themes of divine retribution and corporal punishment as key means of education. This reflects Hebrew traditions of מוסר that were available in Greek through the LXX. Zurawski demonstrates that the paideia of the Wisdom of Solomon represents a synthesis of biblical and classical educational traditions.

Andrew R. Guffey, in "Job and the 'Mystic's Solution' to Theodicy: Philosophical Paideia and Internalized Apocalypticism in the Testament of Job," argues that the Testament of Job seeks to resolve the tensions in the biblical book of Job over theodicy by appealing both to philosophical training and to mystical transformation, or internalized apocalypticism. In the Testament of Job, Job's ordeals are cast as an *agōn* (athletic contest), which is an opportunity for philosophical training in impassibility (ἀπάθεια), imperturbability (ἀταραξία), or, to use the term preferred by the author of the testament, patience (μακροθυμία). Job's mastery of the Cynic-Stoic ideal of patient detachment is not the end of the story in Testament of Job, however. The second half of the book offers a very different solution to the problem of Job's undeserved suffering, one based on a direct experience of the divine and participation in a heavenly existence while still alive—in other words, the type of mystical experience that April DeConick has referred to as "internalized apocalypse." The mythical pattern of the book of Job, Guffey concludes, is replaced by a mystical pattern in the Testament of Job.

Part 3 of the volume, "Hellenism and Paideia in Early Christianity," reflects the interests of the Wisdom and Apocalypticism section in situating New Testament and early Christian texts in a larger context, especially with an eye to their interaction with sapiential and apocalyptic discourses. In this section, as in the first two, the theme that connects the chapters is paideia. There are pedagogical implications to Paul's use of mystery language in 1 Corinthians and in his allegory of Sarah and Hagar in Galatians; the Epistle to the Hebrews is also rich in pedagogical language and themes. The final two chapters examine the development of a Christian form of paideia by Irenaeus of Lyons and the common ground between pagan and Christian paideia in the fourth century CE.

C. Andrew Ballard, in his "The Mysteries of Paideia: 'Mystery' and Education in Plato's *Symposium*, 4QInstruction, and 1 Corinthians," explores the pedagogical functions of mystery language. Focusing on the three texts mentioned in the title of his article, he argues that the authors of these compositions describe their teachings with mystery terminology to distinguish their pedagogical techniques from other forms of education. He also suggests that, in the varying cultural and historical contexts of each composition, the mystery language they utilize has similar functions—to legitimate the authority of the instructor, to lead the student on a path to acquire esoteric knowledge, and to encourage the student to experience some sort of transformative vision. By exploiting the multivalent term *mystery*, Ballard argues, Paul was able to legitimate his esoteric paideia to his highly educated critics in Corinth.

Jason M. Zurawski's second contribution to this volume, "Mosaic Torah as Encyclical Paideia: Reading Paul's Allegory of Sarah and Hagar in Light of Philo of Alexandria's," takes a fresh look at Paul's much-studied allegorical reading of the story of Sarah and Hagar as a tale of two covenants (Gal 4:21–5:1). Although recent scholarship has moved away from viewing this allegory as an example of supersessionism or anti-Jewish rhetoric, it has largely overlooked the connection between Paul's reading of the Sarah and Hagar story and Philo's, which supports a more sympathetic reading of Paul's allegory. Paul and Philo both belonged to a Hellenized Jewish intellectual environment in which the Mosaic torah was seen as a source of paideia in competition with Greek encyclical paideia. Whereas Philo uses the story of Sarah and Hagar to argue that the lover of wisdom must leave behind encyclical paideia, as Abraham sent away Hagar at Sarah's behest, Zurawski argues that Paul collapses encyclical paideia with the Mosaic law, which he calls a παιδαγωγός (Gal 3:24–25). Just as Philo allows that preliminary paideia lays the groundwork for the pursuit of wisdom, Paul believes that the torah prepared the Jewish people for salvation, but that it must be set aside now that salvation is freely given through Christ to Jews and gentiles alike.

The chapter by Ellen Bradshaw Aitken, "Wily, Wise, and Worldly: Instruction and the Formation of Character in the Epistle to the Hebrews," looks at the practices of instruction in Hebrews, noting how sapiential and apocalyptic motifs function together to form the character of the audience. Participation in the community is seen as crucial to character formation and the suffering of the community is presented as having a pedagogical purpose. Jesus is a model learner of obedience through suffering, rather than a teacher, and the audience is addressed as Jesus's "brothers," rather than "sons" as in typical wisdom instructions. The goal of the instruction is envisioned in apocalyptic terms in Heb 12:18–29: a kingdom that cannot be shaken in the tumult of the last days. Although at times Hebrews suggests that its addressees are not as mature as they might be in their interpretation of scripture (Heb 5:12), it clearly expects them to be able to follow a complex argument and to pick up on double entendres. Aitken concludes that Hebrews can be read as inculcating resourcefulness and versatility in the interpretation of scripture so that they will be able to endure their present suffering by reading scripture through the lens of Jesus's suffering and glory.

"Paideia and Polemic in Second-Century Lyons: Irenaeus on Education" by D. Jeffrey Bingham offers a reassessment of the level of Irenaeus's classical education and examines the ways in which he deployed it in the service of his polemical theology. Irenaeus presents human history as a type of paideia, a process through which humanity is educated and perfected. The idea of God as father/teacher is based on Greco-Roman ideas about the role of fathers in education, but Irenaeus makes it the basis of his distinctively Christian pedagogy in which love establishes boundaries for knowledge. Irenaeus's emphasis on moral virtue as the goal of education is shared with the elite Greco-Roman discourse on paideia, but he makes humility, love for God, and adherence to Christian doctrine the primary virtues. Irenaeus's appreciation for the classical curriculum contrasts with the negative assessment of paideia by his opponents, the Carpocratians and Valentinians. Bingham argues that Irenaeus exploits the classical education he received in Smyrna to deride his opponents, to explicate the rule of faith, and to inculcate an enduring love for God.

Raffaella Cribiore addresses the question "Why Did Christians Compete with Pagans for Greek Paideia?" with reference to the fourth century CE. At this time, there were competing systems of education, but the study of literature was a mandatory prerequisite for any advanced study. Since most Christians (the exception being Coptic Christians) did not have separate schools for general education, pupils were exposed to pagan myths in school, even while identifying themselves as Christian by means of symbols on their written exercises. Beyond the elementary stage of schooling, however, the classics of Greek literature and rhetoric were considered a "neutral ground" by Christians. At this time, Cribiore argues, both Christian and pagan identities were fluid, malleable, and context dependent. The sophist Libanius is an example of a pagan whose religious identity was context dependent. Like his Christian friends and students, who included John Chrysostom, Basil of Caesarea, and Gregory of Nyssa, Libanius sometimes ridiculed the Greek myths and encouraged his students to refute them, but nevertheless considered them an inevitable part of traditional paideia. The emperor Julian's edict of 362 CE forbidding Christians to teach the pagan classics may have targeted "lukewarm" pagans like Libanius as well as it targeted Christians. In the fourth century CE, Cribiore concludes, educated pagans and Christians had a common cultural heritage.

By publishing a collection of essays on the topic of pedagogy in ancient Judaism and early Christianity with SBL Press, we hope to encourage other sections of the Society of Biblical Literature to take up this important theme. To be sure, there is already a healthy discussion of pedagogy going on within the Society of Biblical Literature, but mainly from the perspective of teachers of biblical literature reflecting on best practices. As important as it is for us as a community of teachers to take the opportunity to reflect on our own pedagogical practices, as biblical scholars we are also in a position to ask what the texts we study have to say about pedagogy and how they might have been used as pedagogical tools. The apparently close relationship between the development of an educational curriculum and the formation of a cultural and religious canon suggests that scholars who are interested in the function of biblical texts as scriptures should take a closer look at ancient pedagogy. A more historical approach to the topic of pedagogy would not only complement the Society of Biblical Literature's already strong consideration of contemporary pedagogical practices, but it would also challenge us to integrate our work as scholars and teachers.

Bibliography

Aitken, Ellen Bradshaw. "Wily, Wise, and Worldly: Instruction and the Formation of Character in the Epistle to the Hebrews." Pages 296–307 in *The Changing Face of Judaism, Christianity, and Other Greco-Roman Religions in Antiquity*. Edited by Ian H. Henderson and Gebern S. Oegema. JSHRZ. Gütersloh: Gütersloher Verlagshaus, 2006.

Carr, David M. *Writing on the Tablet of the Heart: Origins of Scripture and Literature*. New York: Oxford University Press, 2005.

Crenshaw, James L. *Education in Ancient Israel: Across the Deadening Silence*. ABRL. New York: Doubleday, 1998.

Jaeger, Werner. *Early Christianity and Greek Paideia*. Cambridge: Harvard University Press, 1961.

———. *Paideia: The Ideals of Greek Culture*. Translated by Gilbert Highet. 3 vols. New York: Oxford University Press, 1939–1944.

Koskenniemi, Erkki. "Philo and Classical Education." Pages 102–28 in *Reading Philo: A Handbook to Philo of Alexandria*. Edited by Torrey Seland. Grand Rapids: Eerdmans, 2014.

Lamberton, Robert. *Homer the Theologian: Neoplatonist Allegorical Reading and the Growth of the Epic Tradition*. Berkeley: University of California Press, 1989.

Najman, Hindy, Jean-Sébastien Rey, and Eibert J. C. Tigchelaar, eds. *Tracing Sapiential Traditions in Ancient Judaism*. JSJSup 174. Leiden: Brill, 2016.

Wright, Benjamin G., and Lawrence M. Wills. *Conflicted Boundaries in Wisdom and Apocalypticism.* SymS 35. Atlanta: Society of Biblical Literature, 2005.

Part 1
Pedagogy in Second Temple Judaism: From *Musar* to Paideia

Ancient Israelite Pedagogy and Its Survival in Second Temple Interpretations of Scripture

James L. Kugel

Ancient sages often sought to transmit their insights in enigmatic form, challenging their readers to discover the hidden meaning of a proverb or saying. In the following, I wish to give some examples of this pedagogical technique, particularly as found in two biblical books, Proverbs and Ecclesiastes. Following this, I wish to explore how some of the same assumptions that listeners/readers brought to the reading of ancient proverbs came to characterize the interpretation of scripture in Second Temple times: a law in Leviticus, a story about Abraham in Genesis, and the Israelites' departure from Egypt in Exodus were likewise assumed to carry some hidden meaning beyond the plain sense of the text. Before getting to these, however, I wish to mention a few more general propositions about the pursuit of wisdom in ancient Israel.

The Great, Underlying Plan

"Wisdom" (חכמה and its synonyms) is many things in the book of Proverbs. Typically, commentators have focused on its human manifestations: the sage (חכם) is possessed of prudence and good judgment, practical know-how, and the like. At the same time, Israelite wisdom has an ethical side and is, as one scholar recently noted, "never merely instrumental"; much of it thus consists of moral instruction, the proper path for a person to follow in life. Indeed, in view of its various aspects, חכמה might be described overall as "essentially a high degree of knowledge and skill in any domain."[1]

---

1. These observations are from a particularly thoughtful presentation of this side of wisdom, Michael V. Fox's introductory essay in his *Proverbs 1–9: A New Translation with Introduction and Commentary*, AB 18A (New York: Doubleday, 2000), 3–43.

Furthermore, it should be stressed that, while חכמה can sometimes refer to a person's ability to understand things (comparable to our use of the word *wisdom*), the Hebrew term often refers to *things known*. Thus, for example, the assertion that Solomon's wisdom "was greater than the wisdom of the people of the east, and all the wisdom of Egypt" (1 Kgs 5:10, in some versions 4:30) is not comparing his power of understanding to that of the sages of other nations but rather refers to the greater body of learning that Solomon had acquired.[2] (For this reason, the text goes on to specify what that body of learning consisted of: three thousand proverbs, a thousand and five songs, plus a knowledge of plants, animals, birds, reptiles, and fish [1 Kgs 5:12–13].) So, similarly, toward the end of the biblical period, when Qoheleth speaks of his having acquired חכמה, he is referring not to his potential for understanding, but to an actual body of learning: "I had gotten more and greater wisdom than all who ever ruled before me over Jerusalem, and my mind had come to know much wisdom and knowledge" (Eccl 1:16).[3] The book of Daniel reports that "God made all four of these young men intelligent and proficient in

---

2. Please note that translations of biblical verses herein are usually my own, although sometimes (as in this citation) I have followed that of either the NRSV or the NJPS.

3. Similarly, when the book of Proverbs commands people to "buy" or "acquire" wisdom—"Acquire wisdom, acquire discernment" (Prov 4:5)—it is not talking about acquiring a capacity of the mind or a trait of character, but acquiring as much as possible of that great body of discrete insights that make up חכמה. Hence acquiring bits of wisdom is often contrasted to acquiring gold or silver. Also, "How much better to acquire wisdom than gold" (Prov 16:16); "What good is money in the hand of a fool to acquire wisdom, if he has no mind for it?" (Prov 17:16)—that is, why should he spend his money on learning a lot of proverbs when he lacks the capacity to internalize them (see also Prov 26:9)? Likewise, "Acquire truth and never sell it, [nor] wisdom, discipline, and understanding" (Prov 23:23). See also Prov 4:7; 8:10–11. Clearly, חכמה is sometimes also used in the sense of wise conduct in general or the application of the "lessons of life" (e.g., Jer 49:7; Ps 37:30; 111:10; Prov 3:13; etc.) of the sort that one accumulates fully only in old age (with a few exceptions: Ps 119:99–100; Job 32:6–9). Nevertheless, Biblical Hebrew sometimes explicitly distinguishes between חכמה in the sense of "things known" and the mental capacity that we call wisdom or intelligence; the latter two may be more specifically called רוח חכמה (Exod 28:3; Deut 34:9; Isa 11:2), לב חכם (1 Kgs 3:12; Prov 16:23; Eccl 8:5, 10:2), or חכמת לב (Exod 35:35). A good example of the distinction is found in regard to the designing of the desert tabernacle: God fills every person whose mind has the *capacity* of wisdom (כל חכם לב) with the know-how (חכמה) to design it (Exod 28:3; 36:1–2).

all writings and *wisdom*" (Dan 1:17), that is, in the great body of learning acquired through study.

A further point: the *things known* that constituted חכמה are not comparable to our modern conception of knowledge as an ever-expanding body of facts and insights. Rather, wisdom in the ancient Near East was conceived to be an altogether static and finite body of knowledge, one that had been established of old by the gods.[4] Indeed, this circumstance highlights what is the most basic premise underlying the *pursuit* of wisdom. Reality is not random or the result of mere chance, no matter how things may seem; rather, there are rules that govern all that happens. The pursuit of wisdom was thus the attempt to establish these rules and to live in accordance with them.

In fact, these rules themselves were sometimes referred to collectively in ancient Israel by the word חכמה. Thus, when the psalmist says, "How great are your works, O LORD, you have made them all *with wisdom*" (Ps 104:24), he is not praising the manner in which God created things; rather, this verse is an assertion that there was, and is, an order to all of created reality, that all things are governed by "wisdom," the world's great, underlying set of plans. Similarly: "*By wisdom* the LORD founded the earth, by understanding He established the heavens" (Prov 3:19). Moreover: "How great are your works, O LORD, *so very deep are your plans*: a simpleton cannot know, nor a foolish man understand this" (Ps 92:6-7).[5]

This great, underlying set of plans is said to have preceded the very creation of the world (Prov 8:22-31; Sir 1:4; see also Wis 8:1; 9:1-2; Tg. Neof. Gen 1:1; John 1:1-2).[6] Certainly some of those plans, the rules by which reality operates, belong to what we would describe as early scientific lore: thus, it is simply a rule that the light of the moon waxes and wanes

---

4. In this connection, see Richard J. Clifford, *Proverbs: A Commentary*, OTL (Louisville: Westminster John Knox, 1999), 8. Note also Gerhard von Rad, *Wisdom in Israel* (Nashville: Abingdon, 1972), 144-76; Roland E. Murphy, "Wisdom: Theses and Hypotheses," in *Israelite Wisdom: Theological and Literary Essays in Honor of Samuel Terrien*, ed. John G. Gammie et al. (Missoula, MT: Scholars Press, 1978), 35-39. The theme of the world's creation has been held to play a central role in wisdom writings; see Hans-Jürgen Hermisson, "Observations on the Creation Theology of Wisdom," in Gammie, *Israelite Wisdom*, 43-57; see also R. B. Y. Scott, *The Way of Wisdom in the Old Testament* (New York: Macmillan, 1971), 3-10.

5. Von Rad, *Wisdom in Israel*, 155.

6. On these last two, see Gary A. Anderson, "The Interpretation of Genesis 1:1 in the Targums," *CBQ* 52 (1990): 21-29.

according to a fixed pattern and that the rainy winter is always followed by the dryness of summer. But beyond such obvious insights were other phenomena that attested to the existence of this great set of divinely ordained plans, both in the natural world and in the realm of human behavior.[7] In this sense, all of wisdom ultimately originated with God the creator.

Discovering the rules by which the world operated was no easy undertaking because much of the divine plan was hidden from view. In fact, as various texts suggest, God had *intentionally* hidden the rules by which the world worked, leaving it up to this or that sage to discover individual pieces of the puzzle:

> It is the glory of God to conceal things, and the glory of kings to find them out. (Prov 25:2)

> If only God would speak, if only he would open His lips to you, then He would tell you the secrets of wisdom, [reveal] understanding twice over.... But can *you* grasp God's insights? Can you probe to the Almighty's limit? (Job 11:5–7)

> Where does wisdom come from? And where is the place of understanding? She is hidden from the sight of all the living, and concealed from the birds of the sky.... God [alone] knows the path to her, yes, he knows her place. (Job 28:20–23)

But even if the whole of חכמה could not be discovered, individual aspects of this great body of knowledge certainly could be, and had been, uncov-

---

7. Examples of regularities involving the natural world include the following: if a tree is chopped down to its stump, it may seem to be dead, but sometimes it regenerates itself; "at the scent of water" it may bud anew (Job 14:9). Ostriches lay their eggs on the ground, "letting them warm in the dirt" and apparently caring little for their survival (Job 39:14–16), while storks build their nests in the highest fir trees (Ps 104:17–18). The hymn to wisdom in Job 28 celebrates all that humans have discovered about the natural world even as it bemoans our inability to find wisdom itself/herself; contrast von Rad, *Wisdom in Israel*, 144–48. Regularities involving human behavior include such things as the proper way to behave in the royal court (e.g., Prov 14:35; 19:12; 23:1–2; 25:6–7; Eccl 10:20), the proper way for parents to behave toward their children (e.g., Prov 13:24; 23:13–14), and the proper way for the young to treat their elders (Sir 3:1–16). In general, modesty and the via media are the right path: "Better a dry piece of bread eaten in peace than a house full of abundance that is consumed in strife" (Prov 17:1; see also m. Avot 6:4).

ered; since each individual insight constituted part of the puzzle, each one represented a little square on the divine graph paper that could now be counted as filled in.

That is why the most common literary form for the imparting of wisdom was the *anthology*, the collection of pithy sayings whose individual insights might, taken all together, fill in at least a good part of the rules.[8] For this reason, ancient Near Eastern sages did not seek to "start from zero" and compose whole treatises of wisdom on their own, even though book titles sometimes seem to attribute an entire tome to a single teacher: "The Instructions of Ptah-hotep," "The Instruction of the Scribe Kheti," "The Sayings of Qoheleth," "The Wisdom of Ben Sira," and so forth. The very overlap of insights from one collection to the next suggests that this literature was by nature anthological (and one in which the modern virtue of originality was not particularly prized—quite the contrary). To be a sage meant mastering the wisdom of the past, and the basic unit of wisdom, in biblical Israel and elsewhere, was the two-part wise saying, the משל; sages therefore collected such sayings, sometimes rewording and rearranging them, and thus preserved them for posterity.[9]

INCULCATION

We do not know much about the identity or the social niche of the ancient figures who composed or collected individual proverbs (save perhaps for Ben Sira's famous description of the sage, 38:24–39:11); nor can we know for whom their collections of sayings were intended.[10] (The common asser-

---

8. James L. Kugel, "Wisdom and the Anthological Temper," *Prooftexts* 17 (1997): 9–32.

9. That wisdom is acquired through the pondering of ancient proverbs is the point of Prov 1:1–6; see also 1 Kgs 10:7; Prov 10:31; 30:2–3; Eccl 1:16. Note that the expression דעת חכמה (Prov 1:2; Eccl 7:12) refers specifically to the activity of learning (and/or teaching) wise sayings. On this expression, see James L. Kugel, "Qohelet and Money," *CBQ* 51 (1989): 32–49, esp. 40–44.

10. See Benjamin G. Wright, "Putting the Puzzle Together: Some Suggestions Concerning the Social Location of the Wisdom of Ben Sira," in *Conflicted Boundaries in Wisdom and Apocalypticism*, ed. Benjamin G. Wright and Lawrence M. Wills, SymS 35 (Atlanta: Society of Biblical Literature, 2005), 133–49; also Samuel L. Adams, *Wisdom in Transition: Act and Consequence in Second Temple Instructions*, JSJSup 125 (Leiden: Brill, 2008), 68–87. Ideas about the *Sitz im Leben* and addressees of wise proverbs have gradually broadened in recent research, not only with regard to writings

tion of earlier scholars that such proverbs were the work of sages attached to the royal court, whose duties must have included imparting wisdom to the children of courtiers and other members of the ruling class, is plausible but lacks reliable support from the texts themselves.)[11] One thing does, however, suggest itself from a consideration of the biblical book of Proverbs: this collection, or collection of collections, was probably not so much intended to be read as to be *inculcated*. (Here I mean to evoke the English word's Latin antecedent, *inculcare*, "to pound in, to grind down.") The same themes appear again and again: wisdom is good, folly is bad; listen to the teachings of your elders and take them to heart; tread the straight and narrow path and be content with your lot; beware of hypocrites and false friends; there are two kinds of people, the righteous and the wicked (or their equivalents, the wise and the foolish), and a world of difference separates them; watch out for the wiles of women; speak little, since fools talk too much.

How many times can these same ideas be reformulated and rearticulated? If they were indeed imparted time and again, in fact, repeated here and there with only slight variation or even none at all, it seems probable that the author/editor's purpose was not merely to impart information, but to pound it in.[12] These texts may have been intended for the education of others or for self-inculcation, a kind of litany of wisdom's truths.[13] In either case, repeating the same idea in different formulations seems to

---

about wisdom in ancient Israel but in Mesopotamia as well. See Paul-Alain Beaulieu, "The Social and Intellectual Setting of Babylonian Wisdom Literature," in *Wisdom Literature in Mesopotamia and Israel*, ed. Richard J. Clifford, SymS 36 (Atlanta: Society of Biblical Literature, 2007), 3–19. Beaulieu concludes, "It is obvious from this survey that in the Mesopotamian view, wisdom occupied a considerably wider sphere than we intuitively ascribe to it" (Beaulieu, "Social and Intellectual Setting," 18).

11. The "royal court" hypothesis was defended by (among others) Hans-Jürgen Hermisson, *Studien zur israelitischen Spruchweisheit*, WMANT 28 (Neukirchen-Vluyn: Neukirchener Verlag, 1968), 113–36, but it has been subsequently questioned by Claus Westermann and others; see Fox, *Proverbs 1–9*, 7–12. Note also von Rad, *Wisdom in Israel*, 15–23.

12. The phenomenon of actual repetition within the book of Proverbs has been treated by various authors; see recently Daniel C. Snell, *Twice-Told Proverbs and the Composition of the Book of Proverbs* (Winona Lake, IN: Eisenbrauns, 1993). He asserts that Proverbs repeats sayings far more than other ancient Near Eastern collections (Snell, *Twice-Told Proverbs*, 11).

13. Ps 119, whose associations with Israelite wisdom have been frequently cited, seems to be such a litany. See the review of recent scholarship in Kent Aaron Reynolds,

have served as a form of indoctrination, pounding in wisdom's basic doctrines with only slightly different variations until they came to be accepted without question.

Riddles to Ponder

There is, however, a disadvantage to this sort of inculcation: it cannot long sustain a listener's interest.[14] This, I believe, was the principal pedagogical problem facing the ancient teacher of wisdom, and one apparent solution was to formulate things in such a way as to challenge his listeners' (or readers') ingenuity and so keep their attention.[15] This is the quality of "sharpness" that some proverbs exhibit.[16] Certainly not always, but often, a משל seems to have been deliberately formulated as a kind of riddle whose meaning was not immediately apparent.[17] Such is the case, for example, with Eccl 7:1:

טוב שם משמן טוב ויום המות מיום הולדו
A name is better than precious oil, and the day of death than the day of one's birth.

Torah as Teacher: The Exemplary Torah Student in Psalm 119, VTSup 137 (Leiden: Brill, 2010), 21–28.

14. This point was stated clearly in Richard J. Clifford, "Your Attention Please! Heeding the Proverbs," *JSOT* 29 (2004): 155–63.

15. Such challenging sayings and maxims are definitely in the minority within a given collection, but I believe that their very existence helped to create an attitude of close consideration of the precise wording of *all* proverbs in a given collection. It may thus be no accident that, within Prov 10–31, many such proverbs are clustered in chap. 10, which appears to be the beginning of a new collection. Michael V. Fox has described such proverbs as "disjointed" because of the apparent lack of connection of part A and part B. See his "The Rhetoric of Disjointed Proverbs," *JSOT* 29 (2004): 165–79; also James L. Kugel, "Solomon's Riddles," in *The Great Poems of the Bible: A Reader's Companion with New Translations* (New York: Free Press, 1999), 160–80.

16. The comparison of proverbs to sharp objects appears in Prov 26:9; Eccl 12:11; and Sir 19:12 (see below); see also Deut 28:37; 1 Kgs 9:7; etc. Perhaps the sharpness of proverbs is connected with their being used as a goad to action. See further James L. Kugel, *The Idea of Biblical Poetry* (New Haven: Yale University Press, 1981), 12.

17. For the explicit connection of משל with חידה ("riddle"), see Ezek 17:2; Hab 2:6; Pss 49:5; 78:2; Prov 1:6. Many previous writers have sought to catalogue the different forms and functions of biblical proverbs. See, inter alia, von Rad, *Wisdom in Israel*, 25–40; Scott, *The Way of Wisdom*, 59–71; and above, nn. 14 and 15.

Here is the usual, two-part form of the משל, and part A is, in the world of wisdom, quite unarguable: one's name (not only one's reputation, but a kind of abstract essentialization of a person's life summoned up by his name) is more valuable than any material possession, even those expensive oils that served as perfumes for men and women.[18] But who could agree with part B? The day of a person's death is almost always a sad occasion, whereas a baby's birth is usually the opposite—how can the former be "better"? Here indeed was a riddle.

But it is a general principle that the two parts of a משל are inevitably related. Part A is always to be understood in the light of part B, or vice versa. So here, the "precious oil" is not mentioned in part A merely because it costs a lot of money. As everyone knew, precious oil was fragile; it was kept in sealed vials to preserve its scent, and as Qoheleth himself mentions later, "if a fly dies [in it], the perfumer's ointment turns fetid and putrid; so a little folly outweighs great wisdom" (Eccl 10:1).[19] But no matter how well it was preserved from the elements, precious oil eventually did go bad or was simply used up; either way, now nothing was left of what had once been so valued. In this way, the oil was like the human body; it lasts for a while, but no matter how it is cared for, a human's physical existence eventually comes to an end.

All this explains the apparent riddle of part B of the משל. The day of a child's birth may be a happy occasion, but the child does not yet have that other aspect of human existence, a name—certainly not in the sense of a reputation or essentialization of his being. That kind of name takes years to develop, indeed, the process is only finished when life is over and a person's name is all that remains. On that day, the physical body has, like the precious oil, been spent; this may be a sad day, but precisely because a person's name is more valuable than any oil (part A), so the day on which the making of that name is at last complete must be counted as *better* (not happier, but better nonetheless) than the day of one's birth (part B).

There are many such riddles among biblical משלים. Here is another:

מחזיק באזני־כלב עבר מתעבר על־ריב לא־לו

---

18. See also Prov 22:1, "A name is preferable to great wealth." On expensive oils in biblical times, see the survey article by Victor H. Matthews, "Perfumes and Spices," *ABD* 5:226–28.

19. Note that Abraham is compared in Gen. Rab. 39:2 to a "vial of *foliatum* with its lid closed tight," which prevents any of the perfume from escaping.

One who grabs a dog's ears, a passerby who meddles in a dispute not his own. (Prov 26:17)[20]

What do part A and part B have in common? Someone who seizes a dog by the ears may do so with the best of intentions (to prevent the dog from biting someone else or to hold him back from another dog). But now that he is holding both ears, the person cannot let go; if he does, the dog is likely to turn on him, and even if he lets go of only one ear, the dog may still whirl around and bite the hand holding the other ear.[21] Similarly, someone who intervenes in a dispute between two people may be seeking only to help, but once he has entered the fray, he may find that one or both of the disputants will turn on him.

כחמץ לשנים וכעשן לעינים כן העצל לשלחיו
As vinegar to the teeth or smoke to the eyes, so is the sluggard to those who send him. (Prov 10:26)

That the lazy are consistently disparaged in Proverbs is not a particularly obscure point, but one might still ask about the intended sense of these two juxtaposed clauses: why *is* a lazy man like vinegar or smoke? The key here is the word שלחיו, "those who send him." This particular sluggard is a messenger of some sort, hired by his employers to deliver something; but—since he is a sluggard—instead of leaving he is still hanging around, and like vinegar to the teeth or smoke to the eyes, the more he stays put, the more his presence irritates and burns.

כקול הסירים תחת הסיר כן שחק הכסיל

---

20. The meaning of מתעבר has been the subject of debate. Some have suggested that it refers to someone given to fits of anger, but this hardly fits the context; see Bruce K. Waltke, *The Book of Proverbs: Chapters 15–31* (Grand Rapids: Eerdmans, 2005), 358 ("hothead"); also Clifford, *Proverbs*, 233. The MT and LXX may reflect an early scribal error for מתערב ("intervene, meddle") or it may represent a metathetical variation of that word; see Michael V. Fox, *Proverbs 10–31: A New Translation with Introduction and Commentary*, AB 18B (New Haven: Yale University Press, 2009), 579, 799; and the comments on Prov 14:16 in Fox, *Proverbs: An Eclectic Edition with Introduction and Textual Commentary* (Atlanta: SBL Press, 2015), 220–21. Clearly the word עבר ("passerby") echoes the sound of מתעבר and may be the reason for the latter's use.

21. The same predicament was expressed in the Latin saying cited by the Roman playwright Terence (*Phorm.* 506) *auribus teneo lupum* ("I hold a wolf by the ears").

> Like the sound of thorns under a pot, so is the laughter of a fool. (Eccl 7:6)

Certainly the crackling of thorns and the cackling of a fool may sound somewhat similar, but is that all there is to this משל? The pot (סיר) is mentioned not merely because it resonates with the word for thorns (סירים), but because it plays a crucial role in the overall sense of this proverb. Someone who puts a pot of food on the fire needs some real wood to warm it up. Thorns underneath the pot will warm nothing at all; they may make a lot of noise, but they are altogether useless to the purpose at hand and can thus be disregarded. Such is the laughter of a fool.

> מכסה שנאה שפתי־שקר ומוצא דבה הוא כסיל
> One who covers up hatred—lying lips; and a slanderer—he's a fool. (Prov 10:18)

Again, the overall sense of parts A and B is clear, but what is intended by their juxtaposition? Both halves of the verse seem to be quite independent assertions; true, they both have to do with improper speech, but the two are in some sense opposites. In part A, the person's "lying lips" are the result of his covering up his hatred—*not* speaking what he really feels—whereas in part B the fool is proclaiming his slander out loud, presumably to anyone who will listen. In truth, however, parts A and B are conjoined because they are talking about the same person. Someone who hides his hatred from his enemy is indeed a hypocritical liar, but that same person, having concealed his true feelings in part A, cannot then help but blurt them out to others: he becomes the foolish slanderer of part B. This is a slight variant of Prov 26:26, "He who hides his hatred in guile, his wickedness is [later] revealed in a crowd" (see also Prov 26:24 and the prohibitions in Lev 19:16–17).

> בטוב צדיקים תעלץ קריה ובאבד רשעים רנה
> The city rejoices in the goodness of the righteous, and when the wicked disappear there is jubilation. (Prov 11:10)

This seems like the most obvious truism: of course the city is happy to have righteous citizens in its midst, and just as obviously, the death of its wicked inhabitants is a cause for celebration. But if this were the only point, it might have been driven home more directly by saying something like: "In the *lives* of its righteous the city rejoices, and in the *death* of its wicked there is jubilation." It is precisely the nonparallelism of "goodness" in part A, along with the word "disappear" in part B, that suggests a somewhat different meaning. Actually, everyone in this saying is already dead. The "goodness" of the righteous is the legacy (material and otherwise) that they leave behind, whereas the wicked not only leave behind nothing at all, but they themselves actually "disappear" (that is, they do not just "die"); not even their name will survive (see above).

> ארח לחיים שומר מוסר ועוזב תוכחת מתעה
> Keeping discipline—the path of life; disregarding reproof—leads astray. (Prov 10:17)

Here is another, crucial nonparallelism: someone who "keeps discipline"— that is, someone who has been chastened and retains the lesson he has learned—is on the path of life. But the person who disregards reproof not only leaves the "path of life" to wander about aimlessly himself, but he also leads others astray, making his offense still worse.

> באין אלפים אבוס בר ורב־תבואות בכח שור
> When there are no oxen, the food trough is empty, but a multitude of harvests comes by the strength of an ox. (Prov 14:4)

This משל centers on a kind of paradox. Oxen have to be fed, so in not having them around, you do not have to fill their trough—an apparent saving. But of course, if you want to have any food at all you have to have oxen to plow your fields, and you must therefore "invest" in feeding them. The food you put in their trough will eventually yield a plentiful harvest for you. So, more generally, sometimes one has to invest a little (whether money or effort) in order to gain much.[22]

> עשיר ורש נפגשו עשה כלם ה'
> Rich man and poor man meet; the LORD made them all. (Prov 22:2)

"Meet where?" the wisdom instructor asks. The rich and the poor do sometimes cross paths—perhaps most commonly when the poor man comes begging at the rich man's door.[23] But then the assertion of part

---

22. That is, "benefits have cost." See Clifford, *Proverbs*, 143.
23. Fox, *Proverbs 10–31*, 695, lists no fewer than seven possible places in which

B, "the Lord made them all," makes little sense. In truth, such a reading ignores what is, in the world of wisdom, the *preordained* meeting place of all human beings, namely, the grave, which is similarly termed by Job "the meeting place of all the living" (Job 30:23). The same God who created humanity (part B) has thus decreed that all humans will end up in the same place: "Rich man and poor man [will all eventually] meet" (part A). Qoheleth similarly laments: "Everyone meets the same end.... How can the sage die in the same way as the fool?" (see also Eccl 2:14, 16). Death is the crucial element in this riddle, unstated but left to be figured out by the listener.

חוח עלה ביד־שכור ומשל בפי כסילים
A thistle got stuck in a drunkard's hand, and a proverb in the mouth of a fool. (Prov 26:9)

Biblical drunkards are often depicted as staggering and falling (Isa 19:14; 24:20; Ps 107:27; Job 12:25, etc.). In this proverb, a drunkard has fallen to the ground and in the process of his groping around, a thorn has accidentally gotten stuck in his hand. Similarly, you may now and then hear a fool quoting a משל, but he has acquired it not through any devotion to wisdom, but quite by chance. Especially since a proverb is sometimes conceived as proverbially sharp,[24] it may well get "stuck" in his mouth—he will repeat it at every opportunity. But his citing it means nothing.

"You Know A, Therefore Accept B"

Apart from such "riddles," some Hebrew proverbs make sense only (or most fully) in the light of certain conventions of wisdom sayings. One of these has already been glimpsed: Eccl 7:1 ("A name is better than precious oil...") takes the form "You agree with part A; now you must admit part B as well." A number of such proverbs exist in the biblical store of wisdom:

נאמנים פצעי אוהב ונעתרות נשיקות שונא
Long-lasting are the wounds of a friend, and profuse the kisses of an enemy. (Prov 27:6)

---

this meeting might take place; alas, he does not mention the final encounter intended here.

24. See above, n. 16.

Once again, the listener is challenged to see the precise relationship between parts A and B. Part A is quite unarguable: when a friend criticizes you or otherwise causes you hurt, the pain does not disappear quickly, that is, "long-lasting are the wounds of a friend."[25] By the same token, this proverb then says, you must realize that the opposite of such wounds—namely, the "kisses of an enemy"—are *not* of any weight: they are mere flattery or hypocrisy. Therefore, just as you agree with part A, you must likewise realize the truth of part B: no matter how profuse they may be, an enemy's "kisses" are of no substance and should be disregarded.

עשיר ברשים ימשול ועבד לוה לאיש מלוה
The rich man rules over the poor; the man who borrows is the lender's slave. (Prov 22:7)

Anyone can borrow money, rich or poor. But just as you agree with part A, that the rich do indeed rule over the poor, so you must accept part B: the minute you (whether you are rich or poor) become a borrower, you become the lender's "slave," forever subservient until you can pay back the money.[26]

דרך אויל ישר בעיניו ושמע לעצה חכם
The path of a fool seems fine to him; the wise man heeds counsel. (Prov 12:15)

No great subtlety here, nevertheless: just as you will agree that the stereotypical fool proceeds without seeking anyone's advice—his "path" seems fine to him—so you, if you wish to be the wise opposite of him, must seek out counsel, no matter how good your own judgments may seem to you.

שאול ואבדון נגד ה' אף כי־לבות בני־אדם
Sheol and Abaddon lie before the Lord—so too people's minds. (Prov 15:11)

The underworld ("Sheol and Abaddon") is inaccessible to the living, but somehow God is able to penetrate its depths and know what goes on there

---

25. Such wounds may also be in the more conventional sense of "faithful"; that is, since the criticism comes from a friend, it may be relied upon.

26. So Fox, *Proverbs 10–31*, 699: "As surely as the rich subjugate the poor, so does the lender soon subjugate the buyer."

(part A). How much more so, then, are the hearts of human beings open to divine inspection (part B)—after all, we are right here, on the surface of the earth.

> טוב אחרית דבר מראשיתו טוב ארך־רוח מגבה־רוח
> Better is the end of a thing than its beginning; better a patient spirit than a haughty one. (Eccl 7:8)

Part A is obvious: the finished product is always superior to the thing as it existed in the preliminary stages—thus, for example, the completed building far surpasses what was the initial blueprint, or even the putting down of the building's cornerstone. But if you accept part A, then you must also agree with part B: a patient spirit is able to wait for the project to be completed, whereas a haughty one (not merely an impatient one, but an arrogant spirit which demands results *now*) always loses sight of the ultimate goal.

> גם אויל מחריש חכם יחשב אטם שפתיו נבון
> Even a fool who keeps quiet is considered a sage; the sage seals his lips. (Prov 17:28)

Again: you know part A is true; recognize that part B is true as well. If even a fool can seem wise simply by dint of not speaking, then certainly one who is truly a sage will seal his lips, speaking only when his speech is called for, and only then with restraint.

Lips and Heart

A number of other proverbs can be fully understood only in the light of certain conventional truths. For example, wisdom sayings prioritize what is *inside* a person over what is *outside*; hence, speech is not what counts, but thoughts, and the body parts associated with the exterior (lips, tongue, face) are axiomatically inferior to those associated with the inside (heart, innards). This point is easily missed in such appositions as:

> חכם־לב יקח מצות ואויל שפתים ילבט
> The wise of *heart* accepts commandments; the foolish of *lips* will come to grief. (Prov 10:8)

It is not merely the contrast between "wise" and "foolish" that operates here, but also that of "heart" and "lips." Likewise:

כסף סיגים מצפה על־חרש שפתים דלקים ולב־רע
Like shiny glaze[27] on a clay pot, effusive *lips* and an evil *heart*. (Prov 26:23)

Again, it is not merely the contrast between "effusive" and "evil" that carries the message, but the automatic associations of "lips" and "heart." Similarly:

חכמים יצפנו־דעת ופי־אויל מחתה קרבה
The wise *hide* knowledge, but the fool's *mouth* [means] destruction is nigh. (Prov 10:14)

It goes without saying that, in the world of wisdom, a person hides his true feelings and thoughts in his *inside*; these can be positive or negative, as, for example, hatred (Prov 26:24–25; see also Lev 19:17) or, here, knowledge.

Sometimes, however, the normal superiority of heart over lips is deliberately reversed, and this surprise is another source of sharpness in a proverb:

שפתי חכמים יזרו דעת ולב כסילים לא־כן
The *lips* of the wise spread forth knowledge; the *heart* of fools is not so. (Prov 15:7)

That is, even the normally discounted lips are, in the case of a sage, highly valued because they spread knowledge. With a fool, however, the opposite is true: the usually valued heart contains nothing worthwhile. Similarly:

לאדם מערכי־לב ומה' מענה לשון
A person has his *heart's* assessments [that is, his hidden plans and ideas], but from the LORD comes the *tongue's* reply. (Prov 16:1)

---

27. The reading of the first two words in the MT as a single word that is improperly divided was first proposed by H. L. Ginsberg in light of Ugaritic *sfsg*, "glaze." See Baruch Margalit, *The Ugaritic Poem of Aqht: Text, Translation, Commentary*, BZAW 182 (Berlin: de Gruyter, 1989), 316–19. Some have subsequently questioned the emendation *sfsg*, wrongly to my mind: כסף סגים makes little sense—normally, the סגים (dross) are a part of the silver, not silver a part of the dross! Moreover, no clay pot overlaid with dross silver has, to my knowledge, been unearthed; finally, none of this would suit the overall message, a common one in Proverbs: flattery or hypocrisy often hides the evil that lies beneath them.

That is, God always has the last word; so also Prov 19:21, "Many are the plans in a man's *heart*, but the *counsel* of the LORD is what prevails."

> כסף נבחר לשון צדיק לב רשעים כמעט
> The *tongue* of the righteous man is choice silver, the *heart* of the wicked is of little worth. (Prov 10:20)

> שפתי צדיק ירעו רבים ואוילים בחסר־לב ימותו
> The *lips* of the righteous man sustain many, while fools die by mindlessness (lit., "lack of *heart*"). (Prov 10:21)

Another way of playing with these conventional opposites is the frequent assertion that the wise/righteous are characterized by equally good insides and outsides, both thoughts and speech:

> לחכם־לב יקרא נבון ומתק שפתים יסיף לקח
> The wise of *heart* is called discerning; the sweetness of [his] *speech* adds [to his] teaching. (Prov 16:21)

> לב חכם ישכיל פיהו ועל־שפתיו יסיף לקח
> The *heart* of the wise man makes his *speech* enlightening; by his *speech* he increases *learning* [which is stored in the heart]. (Prov 16:23)

> לב נבון יקנה־דעת ואזן חכמים תבקש־דעת
> The *heart* of the wise will obtain knowledge; the *ears* of sages seek out knowledge. (Prov 18:15)

A similar sort of reversal occurs in one place with regard to another of wisdom's truths, the one already seen in Eccl 7:1: while people die physically, their "name" goes on forever (see also Prov 22:1: "A name is more precious than great wealth"). Significant, then, is the wording of another wise saying:

> זכר צדיק לברכה ושם רשעים ירקב
> A righteous man's name will be for a blessing, but the name of the wicked will rot. (Prov 10:7)

As we have already seen, some sages held that a person's "name" lives after him;[28] thanks to this, people may recall a long-departed soul in blessing a newborn or a young person, "May you live to be like So-and-so!" This is the convention. But part B of the proverb cited above carries an additional sting: not only will the wicked physically rot in the grave, but their supposedly undying names will rot there too.

Striking Comparisons

One common use of the two-part משל is the implied or explicit comparison: "Just as A, so B." Some "sharp" examples have been examined above.[29] But even without their requiring particularly close consideration on the listeners' parts, such proverbs can often present a vivid, or even shocking, image that will jar those listening and that may, arguably, be remembered long after. Here are but a few well-known examples:

נזם זהב באף חזיר אשה יפה וסרת טעם
Gold ring in pig's snout: a beautiful woman of errant sense. (Prov 11:22)

The onlooker first sees the beautiful gold ring; only then does he become aware of its incongruous surroundings, a pig's snout. So similarly with a beautiful woman: he may be struck by her beauty at first, but soon he realizes its incongruity with her behavior.

תפוחי זהב במשכיות כסף דבר דבר על־אפניו
Golden apples in silver settings: a word spoken in the proper circumstances. (Prov 25:11)

If a person has wise insights, they should not be spouted out under any circumstances but, like a certain kind of jewelry, should be reserved for the proper setting.

כצפור לנוד כדרור לעוף כן קללת חנם לא תבא
Like a sparrow that flits and a swallow that flies, an undeserved curse will not enter. (Prov 26:2)

---

28. This truth was not uncontested: Ps 41:6; Eccl 1:11; 2:16; 6:4; on this last verse, see Kugel, "Qohelet and Money," 39–40.

29. See also Clifford, "Your Attention Please!," and William P. Brown, "The Didactic Power of Metaphor in the Aphoristic Sayings of Proverbs," *JSOT* 29 (2004): 133–54.

Curses were certainly capable of harming those cursed (hence the law of Lev 19:14), penetrating their being to do them harm. But an undeserved curse, precisely because it is undeserved, can harm no one; rather, like a little bird flapping its wings this way and that, it will never really go anywhere, and perhaps not even get off the ground.

ככלב שב על־קאו כסיל שונה באולתו
Like a dog turning in his own vomit, so a fool repeats his folly. (Prov 26:11)

This one hardly requires comment, but it certainly presents a memorable image.

באפס עצים תכבה־אש ובאין נרגן ישתק מדון
Without wood the fire goes out, and without a [third-party] slanderer, the quarrel is quieted. (Prov 26:20)

When two people quarrel, they should be left alone to solve their dispute (see also Prov 25:9–10). It is only when a third party gets involved that complications ensue; his intervention is comparable to adding wood to a fire that was on its way to going out.

דלף טורד ביום סגריר ואשת מדינים נשתוה
A constant dripping on a rainy day: an argumentative wife is like this. (Prov 27:15)

Again, no comment required, but certainly this proverb presents a striking image.

ברזל בברזל יחד ואיש יחד פני־רעהו
Iron grows sharp with iron; so does one man sharpen his fellow. (Prov 27:17)

Discussion and debate between friends serve to sharpen their wits, just as one blade may whet another.[30]

---

30. Translators since the LXX, the Vulgate, and the Syriac version have understood part A in this sense, as have numerous later commentators. Fox rightly objects that a whetstone is what normally sharpens iron, but certainly two blades striking one another are also used for that purpose. The phrase יחד פני־רעהו in part B remains a

Pedagogy in Late Second Temple Times

Following the mention of these various features of the classic Hebrew משל, it may be appropriate here to briefly examine the imparting of wisdom in late Second Temple times. In general, it seems that some of the stylistic and thematic features mentioned above survived to some extent into the first or second centuries BCE. If one takes the book of Ben Sira as the closest relative of the book of Proverbs in this period, elements of continuity certainly can be found.[31] Thus, the striking comparison of the "just as A, so B" sort, seen above in Proverbs and Qoheleth, is in evidence in Ben Sira as well. Here are a few examples:

βέλος πεπηγὸς ἐν μηρῷ σαρκός, οὕτως λόγος ἐν κοιλίᾳ μωροῦ.
Like an arrow lodged in a person's thigh, a word[32] in a fool's innards. (Sir 19:12)

In context (Ben Sira has been warning of the dangers of repeating something one has heard), this refers to the fool's inability to *not* report on what he has heard. Like an arrow shot into the thigh, the fool feels that what he has heard must be taken out, no matter how bloody and painful the process.[33]

---

problem, however: can someone *sharpen* another's face? One possible solution might be to see here an alternative root, חד"ה, "gladden." Note that "gladdening the face" is close to a similar expression, "sweetening the face" (חלה את פני), that is, "seeking the favor of" someone: Prov 19:6; Job 11:19; Dan 9:13; and many more. Still, my guess would be that the *Urtext* was simply miscopied: it read יחד פי־רעהו, "sharpens the mouth of his friends." The cutting edge of a sword is called its "mouth" (פה) in Hebrew, and the assertion that striking one "mouth" against the other will hold as true of human mouths as of swords makes sense.

31. Patrick W. Skehan and Alexander A. Di Lella, *The Wisdom of Ben Sira*, AB 39 (New York: Doubleday, 1987), 43–45; Adams, *Wisdom in Transition*, 155–59.

32. The NRSV and other translators have rendered the Greek λόγος in this verse contextually as "gossip," but this has no lexicographical support; more to the point, since the original Hebrew most probably read דבר, then this word ought to be understood in the simple sense of "word" or "matter."

33. But if so, the image does not fit the overall message: after all, wouldn't anyone want to remove an arrow shot into the thigh? This hardly makes the fool in question foolish! For this reason, it seems that this משל may once have had an independent existence before being located here. Considering the words alone, outside their present context, דבר might be understood in the sense of "word[s] of wisdom," "proverb"

כחותם על כיס זהב שיר[ת] אל על משתה יין
Like a seal on a golden purse, so is the praise of God at a wine feast. (Sir 35:5 [MS B])

The "praise" referred to here is a prayer or hymn of thanksgiving that ends the feast, properly "sealing" it. The point is that, like a purse, a wine feast that has not been properly closed in this fashion is incomplete; indeed, it may lose its valuable contents.

βαπτιζόμενος ἀπὸ νεκροῦ καὶ πάλιν ἁπτόμενος αὐτοῦ, τί ὠφέλησεν ἐν τῷ λουτρῷ αὐτοῦ; οὕτως ἄνθρωπος νηστεύων ἐπὶ τῶν ἁμαρτιῶν αὐτοῦ καὶ πάλιν πορευόμενος καὶ τὰ αὐτὰ ποιῶν· τῆς προσευχῆς αὐτοῦ τίς εἰσακούσεται; καὶ τί ὠφέλησεν ἐν τῷ ταπεινωθῆναι αὐτόν;
One who washes after [touching] a dead body and touches it again, what use was his washing? So a man fasts for his sins, and then once again goes and does the same thing: who will listen to his prayer, and what has he gained by humbling himself [i.e., fasting]? (Sir 34:25–26 [30–31])

This is certainly a striking comparison: the point is that fasting to atone for a sin is worthless unless the sinner casts off the sin and does not repeat it. The connection between ritual and moral purification is evoked in many texts;[34] note the similar comparison in t. Ta'an. 1:8: "If someone held a source of impurity in his hand, even if he bathed in the Siloam and all the waters of creation, he will never be purified; but if he cast the impurity from his hand, bathing in the [minimal amount of] forty *seahs* would be counted as a [purifying] immersion."

πληγὴ μάστιγος ποιεῖ μώλωπας, πληγὴ δὲ γλώσσης συγκλάσει ὀστᾶ.
A blow from a whip leaves a welt, but a blow from the tongue smashes bones. (Sir 28:17)

Rather the opposite of the English saying, "Sticks and stones may break my bones, but names can never hurt me." On the contrary, according to Ben Sira: words can do far more damage than a physical blow.

---

as used, inter alia, by Ben Sira himself (Sir 11:15; 16:24; 36:3; 37:20; 46:15; 51:30). This would make the proverb a bit like Prov 26:9 (treated above). Presumably, a sage had aimed his דבר at the fool to correct him. The sage hit the mark, but all the fool can do is resist correction: he pulls and tugs at what the sage has said, denying any wrong.

34. This issue is studied in detail in Jonathan Klawans, *Impurity and Sin in Ancient Judaism* (New York: Oxford University Press, 2004).

Ben Sira is likewise familiar with the classic oppositions of outside/inside or lips/heart:

בשפתיו יתמהמה צר ובלבו יחשוב מהמרות עמוקות
וגם אם בעיניו ידמיע אויב אם מצא עת לא ישבע דם

With his *lips* an enemy hems and haws, while in his *heart* he is planning deep traps.
Though a foe may weep tears in his *eyes*, given a chance he will never have enough of [your] *blood*. (Sir 12:16)

The "you know A, therefore accept B" pattern is also found in Ben Sira:

τί φωτεινότερον ἡλίου; καὶ τοῦτο ἐκλείπει· καὶ πονηρὸν ἐνθυμηθήσεται σὰρξ καὶ αἷμα.

What is brighter than the sun—yet it is eclipsed; and [still,] flesh and blood devise to do evil. (Sir 17:31)

Everyone knows that even the light of the sun, despite all its brightness, can be darkened (by God, through an eclipse, or perhaps every evening by sunset);[35] realize, then, how much more is this true of the petty little evils devised by men. (This would fit well with the next verse, "God holds accountable the hosts of highest heavens, while all humans are dust and ashes.")

Torah and Wisdom

While such lines of wisdom's continuity into the late Second Temple period are clear, so are the differences. As many scholars have observed, the late Second Temple period marked a change in the very idea of pursuing wisdom. Wisdom herself explains what happened in a famous passage from Ben Sira:

> Wisdom praises herself, and tells of her glory in the midst of her people. In the assembly of the Most High she opens her mouth, and in the presence of his hosts she tells of her glory: "I came forth from the mouth of the Most High, and covered the earth like a mist. I dwelt in the highest heavens, and my throne was in a pillar of cloud. Alone I compassed the

---

35. Moshe T. Segal, *The Complete Book of Ben Sira* (Jerusalem: Bialik Institute, 1953), 108.

> vault of heaven and traversed the depths of the abyss. Over waves of the sea, over all the earth, and over every people and nation I have held sway. Among all these I sought a resting place; in whose territory should I abide? Then the Creator of all things gave me a command, and my Creator chose the place for my tent. He said, 'Make your dwelling in Jacob, and in Israel receive your inheritance.'" (Sir 24:1–8)

Wisdom thus took up her residence among the people of Israel—and lest there be any doubt about what Ben Sira was alluding to, he makes it explicit in the verses that follow:

> All this is the book of the covenant of the Most High God, the law that Moses commanded us, as an inheritance for the congregations of Jacob. (Sir 24:23–24)

Similarly, the apocryphal book of Baruch reports:

> He [God] found the whole way to knowledge, and gave her to his servant Jacob, and to Israel, whom He loved.... She is the book of the commandments of God, and the law that endures forever. (Bar 3:36–4:1)

In short, Wisdom came to dwell on earth in the form of the Torah, "the law that Moses commanded us," "the law that endures forever."[36] As a result,

---

36. On the relation of Wisdom and Torah there is a vast and ever-growing scholarly literature, without much agreement over the past few decades: see thus von Rad on Ben Sira in his *Wisdom in Israel*, 240–62 ("It is certainly not, therefore, the case that the specific functions of wisdom have been replaced among teachers of Torah," 245); see also Martin Hengel in his *Judaism and Hellenism: Studies in Their Encounter in Palestine during the Early Hellenistic Period*, trans. John Bowden, 2 vols. (Philadelphia: Fortress, 1974), 1:157–75 (inter alia); Moshe Weinfeld, *Deuteronomy and the Deuteronomic School* (New York: Oxford University Press, 1972); Gerald T. Sheppard, "Wisdom and Torah: The Relationship of Deuteronomy Underlying Sirach 24:23," in *Biblical and Near Eastern Studies: Essays in Honor of William Sanford LaSor*, ed. Gary Tuttle (Grand Rapids: Eerdmans, 1978), 166–76; John J. Collins, *Jewish Wisdom in the Hellenistic Age*, OTL (Louisville: Westminster John Knox, 1997), 42–61; Jack T. Sanders, "When Sacred Canopies Collide: The Reception of the Torah of Moses in the Wisdom Literature of the Second Temple Period," *JSJ* 32 (2001): 121–36; Jessie Rogers, "'It Overflows Like the Euphrates with Understanding': Another Look at the Relationship between Law and Wisdom in Sirach," in *Ancient Versions and Traditions*, vol. 1 of *Of Scribes and Sages: Early Jewish Interpretation and Transmission of Scripture*, ed. Craig A. Evans, LSTS 50, SSEJC 9 (London: T&T Clark, 2004), 114–21; Friedrich Vin-

sages would no longer devote their attention exclusively to pondering the riddles and wise sayings of their predecessors.[37] Now they had something else to ponder, the words of sacred scripture.[38] To be sure, sapiential texts from the late Second Temple period are not monochromatic; there was still much more to the pursuit of wisdom than the interpretation of ancient scripture. But it is striking nonetheless how much of such interpretation is to be found in texts from the closing two centuries BCE and the first century CE.[39]

A Transitional Figure

Ben Sira is something of a transitional figure. As seen above, he seeks to pursue traditional forms of wisdom instruction; indeed, his terse, epigrammatic style is at one with that of earlier sages in Israel and elsewhere, and he takes evident pleasure in transmitting all that he and his predecessors have discerned about the ways of the world. Yet as was seen above, he is also the sage who proclaimed that supernal Wisdom had come down to earth and made her home in Israel as "the book of the covenant of the Most

---

cenz Reiterer, "The Interpretation of the Wisdom Tradition of the Torah within Ben Sira," in *The Wisdom of Ben Sira: Studies on Tradition, Redaction, and Theology*, ed. Angelo Passaro and Giuseppe Bellia, DCLS 1 (Berlin: de Gruyter, 2008), 209–31; and the essays recently collected in Bernd U. Schipper and D. Andrew Teeter, eds., *Wisdom and Torah: The Reception of "Torah" in the Wisdom Literature of the Second Temple Period*, JSJSup 163 (Leiden: Brill, 2013). On the relation of Torah and Wisdom specifically in the Dead Sea Scrolls, see Matthew J. Goff, *Discerning Wisdom: The Sapiential Literature of the Dead Sea Scrolls*, VTSup 116 (Leiden: Brill, 2007), 89–92, 130–34, 165–72, 298–300; John Kampen, *Wisdom Literature*, ECDSS (Grand Rapids: Eerdmans, 2011), esp. 307, 309–10.

37. See above, n. 9.

38. This is explored extensively in Gerald T. Sheppard, *Wisdom as a Hermeneutical Construct: A Study in the Sapientializing of the Old Testament*, BZAW 151 (Berlin: de Gruyter, 1980).

39. I collected some of these in *Traditions of the Bible* (Cambridge: Harvard University Press, 1998), a book of some 1,055 pages, to which much more could be added now, thanks to the subsequent full publication of the Qumran texts as well as the availability of better manuscripts of other, contemporaneous texts, plus the existence of previously unavailable search tools and similar aids. See also my essay, "Some Instances of Biblical Interpretation in the Hymns and Wisdom Writings of Qumran," in *Studies in Ancient Midrash*, ed. James L. Kugel (Cambridge: Harvard University Press, 2001), 155–69.

High God." That book could hardly be irrelevant to his pursuit of wisdom, and indeed, Ben Sira shows himself to be no stranger to scripture, nor—just as significant—to some of the already-established interpretations of scriptural stories or individual verses.[40] He knows, for example, that "arrogance" or "pride" was the great sin of Lot's neighbors in Sodom (Sir 16:8), even though this fault is not mentioned in the Genesis story (it comes, rather, from Ezek 16:49–50);[41] he is also apparently aware of the exegetical tradition that held that Moses actually ascended into heaven (Sir 45:1–2).[42] Moreover, Ben Sira knows that God's angels were created sometime during the first six days of creation, apparently even before God "filled it [the earth] with its stores" on the third day (Sir 16:26–30), although their creation is not mentioned in Genesis; he is likewise aware of the interpretation according to which human mortality was the punishment for Eve's sin in the Garden of Eden (Sir 25:24), even though this is never stated in Genesis.[43] These and numerous other passages (including, but hardly limited to, his great catalogue of biblical heroes in chapters 44–50), show Ben Sira to be a new sort of sage, one who seeks where possible to connect his words to scripture and its interpretive traditions.[44] Moreover, his "Praise of

---

40. Ben Sira's relation to scripture has recently been examined by Benjamin G. Wright, "Biblical Interpretation in the Book of Ben Sira," in *A Companion to Biblical Interpretation in Early Judaism*, ed. Matthias Henze (Grand Rapids: Eerdmans, 2012), 363–88. Wright's study makes many good points, and at times he is appropriately cautious about attributing to Ben Sira too detailed a knowledge of the text of ancient scripture. Overall, however, I believe his caution is overdone and, indeed, refuted by the very evidence that he cites; moreover, this study often seems to assume that Ben Sira wrote in an exegetical vacuum, ignoring the widespread evidence from roughly contemporaneous texts that reflect on the same scriptural passages. See next note, as well as Wright's other examples presented in "Biblical Interpretation," 377–84.

41. Kugel, *Traditions of the Bible*, 333–34; see on this Wright, "Biblical Interpretation," 377. About the story of Sodom and Gomorrah alluded to in Sir 16:8, Wright is reluctant to conclude that Ben Sira even had the Genesis account in mind: "The most we can say is that Ben Sira is alluding to events that Genesis also narrates" ("Biblical Interpretation," 377).

42. Kugel, *Traditions of the Bible*, 544–45; 635–36.

43. Ibid., 49, 96.

44. Note Ben Sira's many reflections on biblical passages and/or exegetical traditions, among them those cited in Kugel, *Traditions of the Bible*, 49, 81, 96, 101, 112, 117, 118, 127, 131, 143, 174, 177–78, 182, 186, 194, 205, 207, 210, 237, 298, 308, 333, 342, 361, 545, 549, 552, 567, 585, 602, 627, 628, 635, 649, 652, 664, 683, 701, 703, 706, 714, 715–16, 723, 725, 726, 728, 751, 754, 769, 779, 790, 811, 824.

the Fathers of Old"⁴⁵ (chapters 44–50) is a prime example of how ancient historical accounts came to be reinterpreted in Second Temple times and turned into *exempla*, little lessons of moral instruction. While it is not altogether unprecedented, this transformation in Ben Sira was an interpretive shift of the greatest importance: it gave these ancient texts an immediate relevance to today's world, saving them from being of merely antiquarian interest. And beyond this overall approach, Ben Sira's book is dotted with specific bits of interpretation that betray a new way of looking at scripture.⁴⁶

---

45. This is the Hebrew title that appears in MS B; for עולם in the sense of "of old," "of yore," as in "days/years of old," see James L. Kugel, *A Walk through Jubilees*, JSJSup 156 (Leiden: Brill, 2012), 18 n. 22.

46. See, for example, Sir 19:13–17 and 44:16, discussed in my "Ancient Biblical Interpretation and the Biblical Sage," in *Studies in Ancient Midrash*, ed. James A. Kugel (Cambridge: Harvard University Press, 2001), 1–26. About the former passage, Wright asserts that the "close mapping of Sir 19:13–14 onto Lev 19:17 does not pan out, since the verse [in Sirach] really does not enjoin two separate warnings" (Wright, "Biblical Interpretation," 381). This conclusion would be altogether justified if only the Greek text could be equated with the original Hebrew one. However, in this case the Syriac offers a different translation of the original: it has the reprover reproving his friend in advance, "lest he do any wrong," and then reproving after he has committed the offense "lest he continue." While (typically) expansive in adding the word "wrong," the Syriac seems to reflect what was the Hebrew original: see Segal, *Complete Book of Ben Sira*, 115–16. This before-and-after reproof, repeated in the next verse, seems to have been prompted by the "doubled" verb הוכח תוכיח in Lev 19:17, a stylistic feature which, at least since the time of the LXX, had been a focus of interest for translators and commentators. See J. A. L. Lee, *A Lexical Study of the Septuagint Version of the Pentateuch*, SCS 14 (Chico, CA: Scholars Press, 1983), 17. (Thus, the LXX translates the "doubled" verbs הוכח תוכיח in Lev 19:17 as ἐλεγμῷ ἐλέγξεις τὸν πλησίον.) Apparently, however, the Greek translator of Sir 19:13–17 found the idea of reproving someone even before an act was committed to be illogical, prompting him to change the text from "Reprove a friend *lest* he do" to "Reprove a friend, *perhaps* he did not do." This best accounts for the difference between the Syriac and Greek versions; if the Greek represented the Hebrew original, there would be no explanation for the Syriac text's deviation from it, as there is for the deviation in the Greek text. Another striking feature of Ben Sira's treatment of reproof (not mentioned in my article) is this passage's suggestion that such reproof take place between friends: "Reprove a *friend* lest he do…. Reprove a *friend*, for often it is false gossip." Nothing in Lev 19:17 suggests that such reproof should take place specifically between friends, but this idea is widespread in Second Temple Judaism; thus "[the Torah] holds sway over relations *among friends*, [so that] one reproves them for having acted badly" (4 Macc 2:13). This notion is attested at Qumran as well; see 1QS IX, 16–17. Note further that two other Qumran texts, CD IX, 7 and 1QS V, 24, cite Lev 19:17, but substitute the word

The Wisdom of Solomon

Another wisdom-imbued text with clear connections to the emerging interpretive tradition is the apocryphal Wisdom of Solomon. The exegetical traditions reflected in, especially, chapter 10 of that book have been studied in detail, but a brief sample may serve to illustrate the whole.[47] In its own review of biblical heroes (all of them unnamed, referred to simply as "a righteous man" and the like), the Wisdom of Solomon says the following about Abraham:

> αὕτη καὶ ἐν ὁμονοίᾳ πονηρίας ἐθνῶν συγχυθέντων ἔγνω τὸν δίκαιον καὶ ἐτήρησεν αὐτὸν ἄμεμπτον θεῷ
> And when the nations in wicked agreement had been confounded, she [Wisdom] recognized the righteous man and kept him blameless before God. (Wis 10:5)

The "wicked nations" mentioned here are the builders of the Tower of Babel (Gen 11:1-9), who are said to have been "confounded" (συγχυθέντων), echoing God's "confounding" their speech in the Genesis narrative. Of course, the story of the Tower of Babel makes no mention of Abraham. His name appears for the first time in Genesis fully twenty-five verses

---

"friend" (רע) for the more neutral term "fellow" (עמית). This may represent a different textual tradition from that of the MT and the LXX, but more likely it was an attempt to tilt this law in Leviticus in the direction of reproving friends only. For reproof in another wisdom-related text, see 4Q417 2 I, 1-5 (here too, reproach seems to take place between friends or family members). In light of all this, Ben Sira's twofold use of "friend" further suggests his acquaintance with this exegetical tradition attached to Lev 19:17. See further on Lev 19:17 Florentino García Martínez, "Brotherly Rebuke in Qumran and Mt 18:15-17," in *The People of the Dead Sea Scrolls*, ed. Florentino García Martínez and Julio Trebolle Barrera (Leiden: Brill, 1995), 221-32; John Kampen, "Communal Discipline in the Social World of the Matthean Community," in *Common Life in the Early Church: Essays Honoring Graydon F. Snyder*, ed. Julian Victor Hills and Richard B. Gardner (Harrisburg, PA: Trinity Press International, 1998), 158-74; and Menahem Kister, "Divorce, Reproof, and Other Sayings in the Synoptic Gospels," in *Text, Thought, and Practice in Qumran and Early Christianity: Proceedings of the Ninth International Symposium of the Orion Center*, ed. Ruth A. Clements and Daniel R. Schwartz, STDJ 84 (Leiden: Brill, 2009), 195-229.

47. See Peter Enns, *Exodus Retold: Ancient Exegesis of the Departure from Egypt in Wis 10:15-21 and 19:1-9*, HSM 57 (Atlanta: Scholars Press, 2001); and David Winston, *The Wisdom of Solomon*, AB 43 (New York: Doubleday, 1979).

later, at the end of a genealogical list of Shem's descendants (Gen 11:26); Abraham's story proper does not begin until Gen 12. Here, however, the "righteous man" Abraham is said to have been "kept blameless" from the evil deeds being perpetrated by the builders of the tower.

How exactly Abraham became involved with them is not specified in the Wisdom of Solomon, but the author seems to have been familiar with one or more traditions that place Abraham at the scene, cast into a fiery furnace, or otherwise persecuted for his virtuous refusal to join in with the building of the tower.[48] If so, the author of the Wisdom of Solomon is not simply alluding to the pentateuchal narrative but as well to some of the exegetical traditions surrounding it. This is true even of the reference to the builders as being "in wicked agreement." The Genesis narrative had said that "the whole earth had the same language and the same words" (Gen 11:1), but it said nothing about any "agreement" of the builders as to their plans or ideas. However, the apparently pleonastic formulation "the same language and the same words" in Gen 11:1 came to be recast by ancient interpreters as their being of "one speech and of *one counsel*," that is, "in wicked agreement."[49] Finally, it is to be noted that God's words to Abraham in Gen 17:1, "Walk in my ways and be blameless" are here retrojected to the Tower of Babel incident; it was personified Wisdom who kept Abraham blameless even at this early stage.

Later in the same chapter, the author briefly recounts the exodus from Egypt:

διεβίβασεν αὐτοὺς θάλασσαν ἐρυθρὰν καὶ διήγαγεν αὐτοὺς δι' ὕδατος πολλοῦ· τοὺς δὲ ἐχθροὺς αὐτῶν κατέκλυσεν καὶ ἐκ βάθους ἀβύσσου ἀνέβρασεν αὐτούς. διὰ τοῦτο δίκαιοι ἐσκύλευσαν ἀσεβεῖς καὶ ὕμνησαν, κύριε, τὸ ὄνομα τὸ ἅγιόν σου τήν τε ὑπέρμαχόν σου χεῖρα ᾔνεσαν ὁμοθυμαδόν·ὅτι ἡ σοφία ἤνοιξεν στόμα κωφῶν καὶ γλώσσας νηπίων ἔθηκεν τρανάς.

She [Wisdom] brought them over the Red Sea, and led them through deep waters; but she drowned their enemies, and cast them up from the depth of the sea. Thereafter the righteous plundered the ungodly; they sang hymns, O Lord, to your holy name, and praised with one

---

48. See Enns, *Exodus Retold*, 18–22; Winston, *Wisdom of Solomon*, 214; Kugel, *Traditions of the Bible*, 258; Chaim Milikowsky, *Seder Olam: Critical Edition, Commentary, and Introduction*, 2 vols. (Jerusalem: Yad Ben Zvi, 2013), 2:5.

49. Enns, *Exodus Retold*, 23, in addition to Pseudo-Philo's LAB, see also Tg. Neof. Gen 11:1; Tg. Ps.-Jon. Gen 11:1; Gen. Rab. 18:4; etc. Consult further Kugel, *Traditions of the Bible*, 236–37, 239–40.

accord your defending hand; for Wisdom opened the mouths of those who were mute, and made the tongues of infants speak clearly. (Wis 10:18–21 NRSV)

Here too, what looks like a straightforward summary of the Exodus story actually addresses a number of exegetical questions. Thus the second line, "she drowned their enemies, and *cast them up* from the depths of the sea," derives from an exegetical motif intended to explain an inconsistency in the text. While the book of Exodus in one place says of the Egyptians that "the floods covered them, they went down into the depths like a stone.... The sea covered them; they sank like lead in the deep waters" (Exod 15:5, 10), elsewhere it says that the Israelites "saw the Egyptians dead on the shore of the sea" (14:30). How did the Egyptians get from being sunk in the watery depths to being visible on the shore? The passage cited above recounts that, after drowning the soldiers, Wisdom "cast them up from the depths of the sea" so that they would be visible to the Israelites.[50] (Apparently, Wisdom's purpose was to allow the Israelites to "plunder the ungodly," specifically, by removing the weapons of war that the Israelites seem to have been equipped with shortly afterwards, in their war against Amalek in Exod 17.)[51]

After recounting these miraculous events, the Wisdom of Solomon says that the Israelites "sang hymns, O Lord, to your holy name, and praised *with one accord* (ὁμοθυμαδόν) your defending hand" (Wis 10:20). The indicated word might seem altogether unnecessary, but it actually addresses another exegetical issue. The hymn of praise sung by the Israelites in Exod 15 is introduced by the phrase, "Then Moses and the Israelites sang this song to the LORD" (Exod 15:1). But how did they know the words? They had just now been saved from the Egyptians and miraculously crossed the sea; how could they all spontaneously sing a song of praise recounting what had just happened? True, Moses, as God's prophet, might indeed have sung the song on the spot with the aid of prophetic inspiration, but what about the others? Various answers were proposed by ancient interpreters.[52] In saying that the Israelites sang "with one accord," the Wisdom

---

50. For a reflection of this same motif in Philo and Tg. Neof., see Kugel, *Traditions of the Bible*, 592–93.

51. Ibid., 608.

52. Note that while the verb "sang" appears in the MT as a singular verb (ישיר), the subject governing it is in the plural, "Moses and the Israelites." This led some inter-

of Solomon seeks to dispel any doubt about the matter: *all* the Israelites must have been gifted with some sort of divine inspiration at that moment (see below), because they all sang this hymn of praise together, "with one accord," along with Moses.

Finally, Wisdom is said to have "opened the mouths of those who were mute, and made the tongues of infants speak clearly" (Wis 10:21). These two assertions are likewise reflections of ancient exegesis. "Those who were mute" were the Israelites whom Moses rebuked just before the crossing of the Red Sea. Having heard their cowardly complaints, Moses told the Israelites: "Have no fear; stand firm and see the Lord's salvation.... The Lord will fight for you, but as for you, *hold your peace!*" (Exod 14:13–14). Thus chastised, did the Israelites really remain silent—and for how long? This author's answer is that the Israelites did indeed obey Moses: they spoke not a word until singing the hymn of praise in Exod 15. It was in this sense that they were "those who were mute."[53]

As for Wisdom causing "the tongues of infants [to] speak clearly," this seems to reflect yet another exegetical concern (attested in numerous sources as well).[54] When the Israelites beheld God's miraculous deeds at the Red Sea, they are said to have exclaimed, "This is my God, and I will praise him, the God of my father, and I will exalt him" (Exod 15:2). The first part of this verse is altogether understandable: the Israelites, having just witnessed God's saving hand with their own eyes, might well proclaim, "This is my God, and I will praise him." (Indeed, an old rabbinic motif suggests that, in so saying, the least of the Israelites at that moment gave proof of their having been elevated to the rank of prophet, since by saying "*this* is my God" they indicated that they actually beheld God in front of them.)[55] But how did they know that this God, whom they now saw face-to-face, was the same God whom their ancestors had known, that is, "the God of my father, and I will exalt him." Surely he was not wearing a sign identifying himself as the God of Abraham, Isaac,

---

preters to suppose that Moses began each verse on his own and that the Israelites either repeated each verse after him or sang a single verse time after time, as a refrain, after each line. See Enns, *Exodus Retold*, 75–82.

53. Ibid., 82–88.
54. Ibid., 88–95.
55. Indeed, they showed thereby that they were at a level of prophecy even greater than that of Isaiah and Ezekiel, who only saw a likeness or image of God; see Mek. of R. Ishmael, *Beshallah* 3.

and Jacob! The somewhat whimsical answer to this conundrum was to divide the speakers of this verse into two groups. The fathers among the Israelites sang the words "This is my God, and I will praise him"; hearing this, their children then chimed in, "the God of my father, and I will exalt him."

4QInstruction

Among wisdom-inspired compositions found at Qumran, 4QInstruction has been the subject of much recent research.[56] The longest sapiential text found at Qumran, it is a strange amalgam of a number of traditional wisdom themes and expressions (advice to the would-be adept [מבין], formulated in the imperative), along with striking apocalyptic elements, a dualistic view of humanity characteristic of other writings found at Qumran, and more. Does 4QInstruction demonstrate an interest in ancient interpretation? While it is certainly not a major concern of its author, the meaning of scriptural passages is inevitably addressed here and there in the text. One example comes in a brief bit of counsel on the subject of poverty (a major theme in 4QInstruction):[57]

> Honor your father in your poverty, and your mother in your tough straits, for as God is to man, so is his father, and as the deity[58] is to man,

---

56. In addition to the major sections in 4Q415–418 and 4Q423, 1Q26 has been identified as belonging to this text, parts of the text overlapping with 4Q423; see further Matthew J. Goff, *4QInstruction*, WLAW 2 (Atlanta: Society of Biblical Literature, 2013), 3. Major contributions to the study of this text include Armin Lange, *Weisheit und Prädestination: Weisheitliche Urordnung und Prädestination in den Textfunden von Qumran*, STDJ 18 (Leiden: Brill, 1995); Daniel J. Harrington, *Wisdom Texts from Qumran* (London: Routledge, 1996); Eibert J. C. Tigchelaar, *To Increase Learning for the Understanding Ones: Reading and Reconstructing the Fragmentary Early Jewish Sapiential Text 4QInstruction*, STDJ 44 (Leiden: Brill, 2001); Matthew J. Goff, *The Worldly and Heavenly Wisdom of 4QInstruction*, STDJ 50 (Leiden: Brill, 2003); Benjamin G. Wold, *Women, Men, and Angels: The Qumran Wisdom Document Musar leMevin and Its Allusions to Genesis Creation Traditions*, WUNT 2/101 (Tübingen: Mohr Siebeck, 2005); Jean-Sébastien Rey, *4QInstruction: Sagesse et eschatologie*, STDJ 81 (Leiden: Brill 2009); Kampen, *Wisdom Literature*, 36–190.

57. I have dealt with this passage at greater length in "Some Instances of Biblical Interpretation," 165–69.

58. The text reads וכאדונים, which might suggest a plurality of divine beings, that is, angels—perhaps the angels implied by Gen 1:26; see Wold, *Women, Men, and*

so is his mother. For they are the furnace of your creation, and since he gave them to rule over you, and created (you?) upon the(ir) spirit [ויצר על הרוח], so serve them. And as he opened your ear to (i.e., gave you to understand) the secret of existence [רז נהיה], honor them for the sake of your own honor. (4Q416 2 III, 15–18)[59]

As elsewhere in 4QInstruction, the speaker of this passage is speaking to an impoverished addressee. Poverty was not a minor concern in real life, and it had ramifications for, among other things, the Torah's injunction to honor one's father and mother (Exod 20:12). Modern readers tend to forget that this commandment was understood to involve not only treating parents with deference and respect, but—in an age when there were no pensions or social security—supporting them in their old age.[60] The duty to do so is precisely the point of this passage: even though you are poor and in "tough straits," it says, you must not scrimp on this filial duty.

The explanation for this requirement is, however, rather odd. Another writer might have simply said that honoring (supporting) one's parents is one of the Ten Commandments, perhaps even quoting it, and left things at that. Our author, however, suggests that it is the parents' *resemblance to God* that justifies their being supported: "for as God is to man, so is his father, and as the deity is to man, so is his mother." The idea, apparently, is that since the addressee respects and honors God, so he should respect, honor, and even support his parents—despite his poverty. But if so, there seems to be something missing in this argument: Who ever said that a parent is like God?

The answer, at least in the context of ancient Judaism, goes back to a long-standing *crux interpretum*. The Decalogue was, by the Torah's account, written on two tablets. Presumably, this division had some significance (since all ten could easily fit on a single tablet), and indeed, ancient interpreters saw it as a thematic one: the first tablet concerned items between God and man, the second between man and his fellow.[61]

Angels, 149–55. On balance, however, it seems more likely that this is a "plural of abstraction" intended as synonymous with "God" in the preceding clause.

59. For textual issues in this passage, see Goff, *Worldly and Heavenly Wisdom*, 74 n. 164.

60. On this aspect of the commandment, see Gerald J. Blidstein, *Honor Thy Father and Mother: Filial Responsibility in Jewish Law and Ethics* (New York: Ktav, 2005), 60–74.

61. Kugel, *Traditions of the Bible*, 651–52, 692–93.

There was only problem with this idea: if the commandments were split symmetrically, five and five, this would leave the commandment to honor one's parents on the first tablet. But surely honoring one's parents was a matter between human beings and thus belonged on the second tablet, spoiling the five-and-five symmetry.

To answer this objection, ancient interpreters sought to claim that this fifth commandment was transitional: a person's parents were in some respects godlike, so that the commandment to honor them properly belonged as the last commandment on the first tablet, standing on the border between the man-and-God commandments and the man-and-man ones:

> After giving the commandment concerning the seventh day, he [Moses] gives a fifth commandment concerning the honoring of parents, putting it on the borderline between the two sets of five. For it is the last of the first set, in which laws of the sacred are given, and yet it is connected as well to the second set, which deals with duties of man to man. I believe the reason to be this: the very nature of parenthood places it on the borderline between the immortal and the mortal, the mortal because they [that is, parents] belong to [the class of] men and other animals through the perishability of the body; the immortal because the act of generation assimilates them to God, the parent of all. (Philo, *Decal.* 106–107)[62]

It is noteworthy that Philo justifies his equation of parents with God by means of the same argument as that found in 4QInstruction: the latter had said "For they are the furnace of your creation," whereas Philo says that "the act of generation assimilates them to God."

The second explanation for honoring parents found in 4QInstruction is somewhat harder to unscramble: "and since he gave them to rule over you, and created (you?) upon the(ir) spirit, *so serve them*." While the text and meaning of the second clause (ויצר על הרוח) are somewhat obscure, the first seems to connect parents to God on the simple matter of authority: just as God rules over humanity, so parents were given the authority to rule over their children; as a consequence, children must also *serve* their parents (that is, support them) just as they *serve* God (through worship and sacrifice). The same argument is found in Ben Sira: "Whoever fears the Lord will honor his father, and will *serve* his parents as masters" (Sir

---

62. See also Philo, *Her.* 171–172; *Spec.* 2.225.

3:7). Moreover, the last justification in the passage from 4QInstruction, "honor them for the sake of your own honor," is likewise found in Ben Sira:

> The honor of his father is a man's own honor, and he who curses his mother commits a great sin. (Sir 3:11)

Beyond these specific arguments, the connection of honoring parents to honoring God seems to have been a commonplace in Second Temple period writings:[63]

> Honor God foremost, and afterward your parents. (Pseudo-Phocylides, *Sent.* 8 [Horst])

> They [the Jews] honor only the Immortal who always rules, and then their parents. (Sib. Or. 3.593–594 [Collins])

> The Torah ranks the honoring of parents second only to that of God.... It requires respect to be paid by the young to all their elders because God is the most ancient of all. (Josephus, *C. Ap.* 2.206)

> It says, "Honor your father and mother," while elsewhere it says, "Honor the Lord with your wealth" (Prov 3:9). Honoring one's father [and mother] is thus equated with honoring God. (Mek. of R. Shim'on bar Yoḥai)[64]

WISDOM AND THE INTERPRETATION OF SCRIPTURE

In considering Ben Sira and the anonymous authors of the Wisdom of Solomon and 4QInstruction, a reader might rightly point out that the texts cited above are not of equal weight with regard to the role of scriptural interpretation in Second Temple wisdom. Ben Sira's discourse on Lev 19:17 certainly seems like exegesis proper, whether or not it is Ben Sira's own:[65] he, or some source of his, has taken the "doubled" verb הוכח תוכיח

---

63. But does the commandment to support one's parents take precedence over the need to support one's own family? For the answer of 4QInstruction, see Kugel, "Some Instances of Biblical Interpretation," 168–69.

64. See the edition of Jacob N. Epstein and Ezra Z. Melamed, *Mekilta de Rabbi Shimon bar Yoḥai* (Jerusalem: Makor, 1979), 152.

65. See above, n. 46.

as an indication that the Torah is actually referring to two separate acts of reproof, before and after the offense is committed. Moreover, he has offered his own explanation of what the unspecified "sin" to be avoided in Lev 19:17c consists of ("growing angry" and/or "threatening") as well as the remedy if reproof has not worked (take the matter to court). As for the first passage treated from the Wisdom of Solomon (10:5), it may simply reflect the author's familiarity with a popular exegetical expansion that placed Abraham at the site of the building of the Tower of Babel. Certainly, evidence of this or similar motifs is both widespread and relatively early; perhaps, then, he was just repeating a theme in wide circulation. The same cannot be said, however, of this author's brief summary of the exodus from Egypt (Exod 10:18–21), nor of numerous other passages in the Wisdom of Solomon. Nearly every word in this passage seems to summarize in precise fashion motifs that developed out of exegetical questions raised by the scriptural text. This author may not have originated any of the motifs that he cites, but as we have seen, each of them was apparently devised to answer a specific exegetical query: "Where *were* the corpses of the Egyptian soldiers?"; "How did all the Israelites know what to sing?"; "How long did the Israelites have to follow Moses' order to keep silent?"; and "How did the Israelites know that the God who saved them at the Red Sea was the God of their fathers?" Finally, what can be said of the author of 4QInstruction? There is rather little scriptural interpretation in his work: the similarity of parents to God may simply have been a Jewish motif that was "in the air" and adopted by him without his knowing its origin in the exegesis of the Decalogue. As for the similarity of his passage specifically to two verses in Ben Sira, this may simply illustrate the author's familiarity with Ben Sira, without the necessity of his peering behind Ben Sira's words to the questions raised by Exod 20:12.

But there is a broader point to be made in considering these examples. Whether one or another of the sages of the Second Temple period was himself devoted to interpreting scripture (as other writers such as the author of the book of Jubilees or Philo of Alexandria unquestionably were) or simply a transmitter (sometimes even an inadvertent one) of exegetical motifs created by others, scriptural interpretation was now part of the pursuit of wisdom.[66] Soon, the old-fashioned sort of sage seen

---

66. See Gabriel Barzilai, "Offhand Exegesis: Passing Allusions to Interpretation of the Book of Genesis as Found in the Dead Sea Scrolls" (PhD diss., Bar Ilan University, 2002). Benjamin G. Wright has put it well: "By the second century BCE, the sages had

earlier, the maker of pithy epigrams, would cede his place to the full-fledged *Schriftgelehrter* and his insights into specific verses and phrases in sacred scripture.

In this connection, it is important to note the extent to which ancient interpreters of scripture were the direct descendants of old-style sages, such as the authors/editors of Proverbs and Qoheleth. At first glance, the ancient interpreters seem a highly diverse group: what did Ben Sira have in common with his contemporary, the anonymous author of Jubilees, and how might either of them be compared to the author of the Genesis Apocryphon or Philo of Alexandria? But one thing they all share is the conviction that the words of scripture need to be probed for their hidden meaning, since when the Torah says *x*, what it often means is *y*. This is certainly not an assumption that readers bring to most texts, but as we have seen above, such does appear to be the attitude adopted by ancient sages to the wisdom collected in proverbs: only by the careful sifting of its words can the true meaning of "A name is better than precious oil..." or "One who grabs a dog's ears..." or "Like the sound of thorns under a pot..." be understood. That *all* ancient interpreters shared this basic assumption about scripture—its cryptic nature—betrays their genealogy: they are all descendants of the ancient Israelite sages, who probed the "riddles" of ancient wisdom.

The same is true of other aspects of ancient scriptural interpretation—for example, the whole approach of ancient sages to the phenomenon of contradictions in the text.[67] The book of Proverbs hardly shrinks from contradictions; in fact, at times it seems to revel in them:

> Do not answer a dullard in keeping with his foolishness, lest you be compared to him. (Prov 26:4)

> Answer a dullard in keeping with his foolishness, lest he consider himself a sage. (Prov 26:5)

Similarly:

---

to incorporate into their teaching a Torah that had become authoritative for them." See his "Conflicted Boundaries: Ben Sira, Sage and Seer," in *Congress Volume Helsinki 2010*, ed. Martti Nissinen, VTSup 148 (Leiden: Brill, 2012), 229–54.

67. While its definition of "contradiction" seems overly broad, some further examples are found in Peter T. H. Hatton, *Contradictions in the Book of Proverbs: The Deep Waters of Counsel* (Burlington, VT: Ashgate, 2008).

> I find woman more bitter than death: she is all traps, her hands are fetters, and her heart is snares. (Eccl 7:26)

> Enjoy life with the woman whom you love all the fleeting days of life that have been granted to you. (Eccl 9:9)

Or:

> Anger is better than laughter. (Eccl 7:3)

> Anger abides in the breast of fools. (Eccl 7:9)

Such contradictions posed a practical problem for the ancient sage: "What am I being told to do or to think?" Someone who studied—and especially someone who sought to teach—such conflicting proverbs no doubt looked for a way to reconcile them: "Under such-and-such circumstances do *x*, under other circumstances observe *y*," or the like. Viewed from a distance, the imperative to resolve contradictions is not terribly different from the approach of scriptural exegetes who sought to explain that the bodies of the Egyptian soldiers were *first* at the bottom of the sea but *later* were spat out on the shore, or that Moses and the Israelites all sang the song of Exod 15 together, "of one accord," in the sense that Moses sang each verse and the Israelites joined in with a refrain (or else, as in the Wisdom of Solomon, that all the Israelites *somehow* knew what to sing and sang everything with one voice).[68]

A third assumption shared by ancient exegetes hardly needs to be pointed out. Many of the texts that these interpreters were expounding had been written centuries before; why should anyone care about laws that had originated in a very different society, or seek to learn lessons of life from narratives that belonged to the ancient past (and in some cases, hardly seemed to agree with later notions of morality or proper conduct)? But the fundamental assumption of books like Proverbs or Ecclesiastes was that wisdom in general was part of the great set of plans underlying reality and was thus essentially timeless. So too for scripture: its laws (properly interpreted, of course) applied perfectly to today and its narratives always had something to teach us not only about the past, but about the present as well.

---

68. See above, n. 52.

For some time it has been observed that narratives such as the biblical story of Joseph, the apocryphal book of Tobit, and the tale of Ahiqar are primarily devoted to the imparting of ancient wisdom values and themes.[69] Whatever genre is assigned to such compositions, there can be little doubt that their wise sayings and the lessons imparted by their twists of plot were expounded by sages and teachers. How natural, then, that the narratives that ultimately became the Joseph story's canonical neighbors—namely, the tales of Israel's patriarchs in Genesis—should be read in precisely the same way, not simply as history, but as history with a point, tales of moral instruction. True, this was not always an easy task. What ethical lessons could one learn from the story of a man who sought to pass his wife off as his sister, or of someone who cheated his brother out of his birthright and paternal blessing and later managed to walk off with most of his uncle's flocks? The fact that ancient biblical interpreters opted for such a moralizing reading of Genesis seems to demonstrate further the extent to which their reading habits had been influenced by the inheritance of other, wisdom-imbued tales.[70]

Finally, ancient wisdom was, as mentioned earlier, essentially authorless. Individual sages may have taken the time to collect proverbs from different sources into a single composition, no doubt sometimes rewording them or expanding on their themes. But precisely because wise sayings

---

69. With regard to the Joseph story, see Gerhard von Rad's 1953 essay "The Joseph Narrative and Ancient Wisdom" in Gerhard von Rad, *The Problem of the Hexateuch and Other Essays* (London: SCM, 1966), 292–300. The subject has been taken up by other scholars, sometimes in disagreement: see James L. Crenshaw, "Method in Determining Wisdom Influence upon 'Historical' Literature," *JBL* 88 (1969): 129–42; Crenshaw, *Old Testament Wisdom: An Introduction*, rev. and enl. ed. (Louisville: Westminster John Knox, 1998), 29–30; Donald B. Redford, *A Study of the Biblical Story of Joseph*, VTSup 20 (Leiden: Brill, 1970), 100–105; George W. Coats, "The Joseph Story and Ancient Wisdom: A Reappraisal," *CBQ* 35 (1973): 285–97; J. P. H. Wessels, "The Joseph Story as a Wisdom Novelette," *OTE* 2 (1984): 39–60; and Michael V. Fox, "Wisdom in the Joseph Story," *VT* 51 (2001): 26–41. For Tobit, see the recent exploration of wisdom themes in Francis M. Macatangay, *The Wisdom Instructions in the Book of Tobit*, DCLS 12 (Berlin: de Gruyter, 2011), 179–216; for Ahiqar, consult Jonas Greenfield, "The Wisdom of Ahiqar," in *Wisdom in Ancient Israel: Essays in Honour of J. A. Emerton*, ed. John Day, R. P. Gordon, and Hugh G. M. Williamson (Cambridge: Cambridge University Press, 1995), 43–52.

70. James L. Kugel, "Jubilees, Philo, and the Problem of Genesis," in *The Hebrew Bible in Light of the Dead Sea Scrolls*, ed. Nóra Dávid et al., FRLANT 239 (Göttingen: Vandenhoeck & Ruprecht, 2012), 295–311.

were all deemed to be part of the great set of truths underlying all of reality, they were all simply wisdom that had existed from time immemorial, the world's operating instructions that began with (indeed, according to some, preceded) the creation of the world.[71] Similarly, scripture itself had no author, at least no human author. Of course, this or that sentence may have been *spoken* by Moses or Isaiah, but soon enough all of scripture was held to be of divine origin, so that even the psalms spoken by David and addressed *to* God came to be attributed to God's own authorship.[72] Interesting in this connection is a passage from the first-century CE Martyrdom of Isaiah:

> And all these things, behold they are written in the Psalms, in the parables of David the son of Jesse, and in the Proverbs of Solomon his son, and in the words of Korah and of Ethan the Israelite, and in the words of Asaph, and in the rest of the psalms *which the angel of the spirit has inspired*, (namely) in those which have no name written. (Mart. Ascen. Isa. 4:21–22 [Knibb, emphasis added])

Ultimately, all of scripture had to come from God; if parts of it were attributed to one of his divinely inspired prophets or sages, that was certainly sufficient, but even those parts of scripture that seemed to be anonymous had, of necessity, to be attributed to divine authorship, namely, the "angel of the spirit."

All this is to say that the transition from the old-time sage to the late Second Temple period interpreter was crucial to the whole career of scripture. Without its wisdom background, ancient biblical interpretation would have certainly been of a different character. Indeed, scripture itself might well have come to be considered antiquated, full of contradictions, and therefore altogether irrelevant, were it not for the ancient Israelite sages who preceded those earliest interpreters.

Bibliography

Adams, Samuel L. *Wisdom in Transition: Act and Consequence in Second Temple Instructions*. JSJSup 125. Leiden: Brill, 2008.

---

71. See above, n. 6.

72. James L. Kugel, "David the Prophet," in Kugel, *Poetry and Prophecy: The Beginnings of a Literary Tradition* (Ithaca, NY: Cornell University Press, 1990), 45–55.

Anderson, Gary A. "The Interpretation of Genesis 1:1 in the Targums." *CBQ* 52 (1990): 21–29.

Barzilai, Gabriel. "Offhand Exegesis: Passing Allusions to Interpretation of the Book of Genesis as Found in the Dead Sea Scrolls." PhD diss., Bar Ilan University, 2002.

Beaulieu, Paul-Alain. "The Social and Intellectual Setting of Babylonian Wisdom Literature." Pages 3–19 in *Wisdom Literature in Mesopotamia and Israel*. Edited by Richard J. Clifford. SymS 36. Atlanta: Society of Biblical Literature, 2007.

Blidstein, Gerald J. *Honor Thy Father and Mother: Filial Responsibility in Jewish Law and Ethics*. New York: Ktav, 2005.

Brown, William P. "The Didactic Power of Metaphor in the Aphoristic Sayings of Proverbs." *JSOT* 29 (2004): 133–54.

Clifford, Richard J. *Proverbs: A Commentary*. OTL. Louisville: Westminster John Knox, 1999.

———. "Your Attention Please! Heeding the Proverbs." *JSOT* 29 (2004): 155–63.

Coats, George W. "The Joseph Story and Ancient Wisdom: A Reappraisal." *CBQ* 35 (1973): 285–97.

Collins, John J. *Jewish Wisdom in the Hellenistic Age*. OTL. Louisville: Wesminster John Knox, 1997.

———. "Sibylline Oracles: A New Translation and Introduction." Pages 317–472 in *Apocalyptic Literature and Testaments*. Vol. 1 of *The Old Testament Pseudepigrapha*. Edited by James H. Charlesworth. New York: Doubleday, 1983.

Crenshaw, James L. "Method in Determining Wisdom Influence upon 'Historical' Literature." *JBL* 88 (1969): 129–42.

———. *Old Testament Wisdom: An Introduction*. Rev. and enl. ed. Louisville: Westminster John Knox, 1998.

Enns, Peter. *Exodus Retold: Ancient Exegesis of the Departure from Egypt in Wis 10:15–21 and 19:1–9*. HSM 57. Atlanta: Scholars Press, 2001.

Epstein, Jacob N., and Ezra Z. Melamed. *Mekilta de Rabbi Shimon bar Yohai*. Jerusalem: Makor, 1979.

Fox, Michael V. *Proverbs: An Eclectic Edition with Introduction and Textual Commentary*. Atlanta: SBL Press, 2015.

———. *Proverbs 1–9: A New Translation with Introduction and Commentary*. AB 18A. New York: Doubleday, 2000.

———. *Proverbs 10–31: A New Translation with Introduction and Commentary*. AB 18B. New Haven: Yale University Press, 2009.

———. "The Rhetoric of Disjointed Proverbs." *JSOT* 29 (2004): 165–79.
———. "Wisdom in the Joseph Story." *VT* 51 (2001): 26–41.
García Martínez, Florentino. "Brotherly Rebuke in Qumran and Mt 18:15–17." Pages 221–32 in *The People of the Dead Sea Scrolls*. Edited by Florentino García Martínez and Julio Trebolle Barrera. Leiden: Brill, 1995.
Goff, Matthew J. *4QInstruction*. WLAW 2. Atlanta: Society of Biblical Literature, 2013.
———. *Discerning Wisdom: The Sapiential Literature of the Dead Sea Scrolls*. VTSup 116. Leiden: Brill, 2007.
———. *The Worldly and Heavenly Wisdom of 4QInstruction*. STDJ 50. Leiden: Brill, 2003.
Greenfield, Jonas. "The Wisdom of Ahiqar." Pages 43–52 in *Wisdom in Ancient Israel: Essays in Honour of J. A. Emerton*. Edited by John Day, R. P. Gordon, and Hugh G. M. Williamson. Cambridge: Cambridge University Press, 1995.
Harrington, Daniel J. *Wisdom Texts from Qumran*. London: Routledge, 1996.
Hatton, Peter T. H. *Contradictions in the Book of Proverbs: The Deep Waters of Counsel*. Burlington, VT: Ashgate, 2008.
Hengel, Martin. *Judaism and Hellenism: Studies in Their Encounter in Palestine during the Early Hellenistic Period*. Translated by John Bowden. 2 vols. Philadelphia: Fortress, 1974.
Hermisson, Hans-Jürgen. "Observations on the Creation Theology of Wisdom." Pages 43–57 in *Israelite Wisdom: Theological and Literary Essays in Honor of Samuel Terrien*. Edited by John G. Gammie, Walter A. Breuggemann, W. Lee Humphreys, and James M. Ward. Missoula, MT: Scholars Press, 1978.
———. *Studien zur israelitischen Spruchweisheit*. WMANT 28. Neukirchen-Vluyn: Neukirchener Verlag, 1968.
Horst, Pieter Willem van der. "Pseudo-Phocylides: A New Translation and Introduction." Pages 565–82 in *Expansions of the "Old Testament" and Legends, Wisdom and Philosophical Literature, Prayers, Psalms, and Odes, Fragments of Lost Judeo-Hellenistic Works*. Vol. 2 of *The Old Testament Pseudepigrapha*. Edited by James H. Charlesworth. New York: Doubleday, 1985.
Kampen, John. "Communal Discipline in the Social World of the Matthean Community." Pages 158–74 in *Common Life in the Early Church:*

Essays Honoring Graydon F. Snyder. Edited by Julian Victor Hills and Richard B. Gardner. Harrisburg, PA: Trinity Press International, 1998.

———. *Wisdom Literature.* ECDSS. Grand Rapids: Eerdmans, 2011.

Kister, Menahem. "Divorce, Reproof, and Other Sayings in the Synoptic Gospels." Pages 195–229 in *Text, Thought, and Practice in Qumran and Early Christianity: Proceedings of the Ninth International Symposium of the Orion Center.* Edited by Ruth A. Clements and Daniel R. Schwartz. STDJ 84. Leiden: Brill, 2009.

Klawans, Jonathan. *Impurity and Sin in Ancient Judaism.* New York: Oxford University Press, 2004.

Knibb, Michael A. "Martyrdom and Ascension of Isaiah: A New Translation and Introduction." Pages 143–76 in *Expansions of the "Old Testament" and Legends, Wisdom and Philosophical Literature, Prayers, Psalms, and Odes, Fragments of Lost Judeo-Hellenistic Works.* Vol. 2 of *The Old Testament Pseudepigrapha.* Edited by James H. Charlesworth. New York: Doubleday, 1985.

Kugel, James L. "Ancient Biblical Interpretation and the Biblical Sage." Pages 1–26 in *Studies in Ancient Midrash.* Edited by James L. Kugel. Cambridge: Harvard University Press, 2001.

———. *The Idea of Biblical Poetry.* New Haven: Yale University Press, 1981.

———. "Jubilees, Philo, and the Problem of Genesis." Pages 295–311 in *The Hebrew Bible in Light of the Dead Sea Scrolls.* Edited by Nóra Dávid, Armin Lange, Kristin De Troyer, and Shani Tzoref. FRLANT 239. Göttingen: Vandenhoeck & Ruprecht, 2012.

———. *Poetry and Prophecy: The Beginnings of a Literary Tradition.* Ithaca, NY: Cornell University Press, 1990.

———. "Qohelet and Money." *CBQ* 51 (1989): 32–49.

———. "Solomon's Riddles." Pages 160–80 in *The Great Poems of the Bible: A Reader's Companion with New Translations.* New York: Free Press, 1999.

———. "Some Instances of Biblical Interpretation in the Hymns and Wisdom Writings of Qumran." Pages 155–69 in *Studies in Ancient Midrash.* Edited by James L. Kugel. Cambridge: Harvard University Press, 2001.

———. *Traditions of the Bible.* Cambridge: Harvard University Press, 1998.

———. *A Walk through Jubilees.* JSJSup 156. Leiden: Brill, 2012.

———. "Wisdom and the Anthological Temper." *Prooftexts* 17 (1997): 9–32.

Lange, Armin. *Weisheit und Prädestination: Weisheitliche Urordnung und Prädestination in den Textfunden von Qumran.* STDJ 18. Leiden: Brill, 1995.

Lee, J. A. L. *A Lexical Study of the Septuagint Version of the Pentateuch.* SCS 14. Chico, CA: Scholars Press, 1983.

Macatangay, Francis M. *The Wisdom Instructions in the Book of Tobit.* DCLS 12. Berlin: de Gruyter, 2011.

Margalit, Baruch. *The Ugaritic Poem of Aqht: Text, Translation, Commentary.* BZAW 182. Berlin: de Gruyter, 1989.

Matthews, Victor H. "Perfumes and Spices." *ABD* 5:226–28.

Milikowsky, Chaim. *Seder Olam: Critical Edition, Commentary, and Introduction.* 2 vols. Jerusalem: Yad Ben Zvi, 2013.

Murphy, Roland E. "Wisdom: Theses and Hypotheses." Pages 35–42 in *Israelite Wisdom: Theological and Literary Essays in Honor of Samuel Terrien.* Edited by John G. Gammie, Walter A. Breuggemann, W. Lee Humphreys, and James M. Ward. Missoula, MT: Scholars Press, 1978.

Rad, Gerhard von. *The Problem of the Hexateuch and Other Essays.* London: SCM, 1966.

———. *Wisdom in Israel.* Nashville: Abingdon, 1972.

Redford, Donald B. *A Study of the Biblical Story of Joseph.* VTSup 20. Leiden: Brill, 1970.

Reiterer, Friedrich Vincenz. "The Interpretation of the Wisdom Tradition of the Torah within Ben Sira." Pages 209–31 in *The Wisdom of Ben Sira: Studies on Tradition, Redaction, and Theology.* Edited by Angelo Passaro and Giuseppe Bellia. DCLS 1. Berlin: de Gruyter, 2008.

Rey, Jean-Sébastien. *4QInstruction: Sagesse et eschatologie.* STDJ 81. Leiden: Brill 2009.

Reynolds, Kent Aaron. *Torah as Teacher: The Exemplary Torah Student in Psalm 119.* VTSup 137. Leiden: Brill, 2010.

Rogers, Jessie. "'It Overflows Like the Euphrates with Understanding': Another Look at the Relationship between Law and Wisdom in Sirach." Pages 114–21 in *Ancient Versions and Traditions.* Vol. 1 of *Of Scribes and Sages: Early Jewish Interpretation and Transmission of Scripture.* Edited by Craig A. Evans. LSTS 50; SSEJC 9. London: T&T Clark, 2004.

Sanders, Jack T. "When Sacred Canopies Collide: The Reception of the Torah of Moses in the Wisdom Literature of the Second Temple Period." *JSJ* 32 (2001): 121–36.

Schipper, Bernd U., and D. Andrew Teeter, eds. *Wisdom and Torah: The Reception of "Torah" in the Wisdom Literature of the Second Temple Period.* JSJSup 163. Leiden: Brill, 2013.
Scott, R. B. Y. *The Way of Wisdom in the Old Testament.* New York: Macmillan, 1971.
Segal, Moshe T. *The Complete Book of Ben Sira.* Jerusalem: Bialik Institute, 1953.
Sheppard, Gerald T. "Wisdom and Torah: The Relationship of Deuteronomy Underlying Sirach 24:23." Page 166–76 in *Biblical and Near Eastern Studies: Essays in Honor of William Sanford LaSor.* Edited by Gary Tuttle. Grand Rapids: Eerdmans, 1978.
———. *Wisdom as a Hermeneutical Construct: A Study in the Sapientializing of the Old Testament.* BZAW 151. Berlin: de Gruyter, 1980.
Skehan, Patrick W., and Alexander A. Di Lella. *The Wisdom of Ben Sira.* AB 39. New York: Doubleday, 1987.
Snell, Daniel C. *Twice-Told Proverbs and the Composition of the Book of Proverbs.* Winona Lake, IN: Eisenbrauns, 1993.
Tigchelaar, Eibert J. C. *To Increase Learning for the Understanding Ones: Reading and Reconstructing the Fragmentary Early Jewish Sapiential Text 4QInstruction.* STDJ 44 Leiden: Brill, 2001.
Waltke, Bruce K. *The Book of Proverbs: Chapters 15–31.* Grand Rapids: Eerdmans, 2005.
Weinfeld, Moshe. *Deuteronomy and the Deuteronomic School.* New York: Oxford University Press, 1972.
Wessels, J. P. H. "The Joseph Story as a Wisdom Novelette." *OTE* 2 (1984): 39–60.
Winston, David. *The Wisdom of Solomon.* AB 43. New York: Doubleday, 1979.
Wold, Benjamin G. *Women, Men, and Angels: The Qumran Wisdom Document* Musar leMevin *and Its Allusions to Genesis Creation Traditions.* WUNT 2/101. Tübingen: Mohr Siebeck, 2005.
Wright, Benjamin G. "Biblical Interpretation in the Book of Ben Sira." Pages 363–88 in *A Companion to Biblical Interpretation in Early Judaism.* Edited by Matthias Henze. Grand Rapids: Eerdmans, 2012.
———. "Conflicted Boundaries: Ben Sira, Sage and Seer," Pages 229–54 in *Congress Volume Helsinki 2010.* Edited by Martti Nissinen. VTSup 148. Leiden: Brill, 2012.
———. "Putting the Puzzle Together: Some Suggestions Concerning the Social Location of the Wisdom of Ben Sira." Pages 133–49 in *Con-*

flicted Boundaries in Wisdom and Apocalypticism. Edited by Benjamin G. Wright and Lawrence M. Wills. SymS 35. Atlanta: Society of Biblical Literature, 2005.

Wisdom and Torah

John J. Collins

The word תורה (*torah*) means simply "instruction." It is used in the Priestly tradition for specific instructions, such as "the torah of the burnt offering" (Lev 6:9) or "the torah of the Nazirite" (Num 6:13, 21).[1] It is also used for sapiential instruction.[2] The association of the term with the torah, or law, of Moses is first found in Deuteronomy, where we first read of "the book of the torah" (Deut 17:19-20; 28:58; 29:19; 31:11-12). In the Deuteronomistic History, we find "the book of the torah of Moses" (Josh 8:31; 23:6; 2 Kgs 14:6). By the late Second Temple period, the association of torah with Moses was practically universal.

Deuteronomy

Torah is also associated with wisdom in Deuteronomy: "I now teach you statutes and ordinances for you to observe in the land that you are about to enter and occupy. You must observe them diligently, for this will show your wisdom and discernment to the peoples, who, when they hear all these statutes, will say, 'Surely this great nation is a wise and discerning people'" (Deut 4:5-6 NRSV).[3] Moreover, the content and phraseology of Deuteronomy shows numerous points of contact with Israelite and other

---

1. Gunnar Östborn, *Tora in the Old Testament: A Semantic Study* (Lund: Ohlsson, 1945), 89-111; Moshe Weinfeld, *Deuteronomy 1-11: A New Translation with Introduction and Commentary*, AB 5 (New York: Doubleday, 1991), 17-18. All translations are my own unless noted otherwise.

2. Östborn, *Tora*, 112-26.

3. On this passage see Thomas Krüger, "Law and Wisdom According to Deut 4:5-8," in *Wisdom and Torah: The Reception of "Torah" in the Wisdom Literature of the Second Temple Period*, ed. Bernd U. Schipper and D. Andrew Teeter, JSJSup 163 (Leiden: Brill 2013), 35-54.

Near Eastern wisdom traditions.[4] Moshe Weinfeld argued that the book took shape among scribes at the Judean court. There is evidently some relationship between Deuteronomy and the kind of traditions that underlie the book of Proverbs.

In fact, it is not inappropriate to refer to the kind of material we find in Deuteronomy as a kind of wisdom. It is now increasingly recognized that the collections of laws in the ancient Near East, including Israel, did not function as positive law, but were rather akin to wisdom instruction, that could form character and sensibility without serving as binding precedents. The king, rather than a law code, was the source of legal authority. As Martha Roth has noted, "whether or not the king was always himself an active participant in the administration of the legal system, he was always its guardian, for the application of justice was the highest trust given by the gods to a legitimate king."[5] Judges relied on their sense of the mores of a community rather than on written law. Written laws are never cited as decisive in trial scenes, and sometimes cases are decided in contradiction of what is written.[6] Law collections were descriptive rather than prescriptive. They may have been "an aid for applying the law, but not a rule."[7] Bernard Jackson has even referred to the laws of the book of the covenant in Exodus as "wisdom laws."[8] In the case of Deuteronomy, it is likely that some form of the core of the book dates from the time of Josiah. But the book as we know it must have received its shape in the exile, in a context in which it had primarily hortatory value, and may not have been very different from a book like Proverbs in the way it would have functioned.

But while Deuteronomy may have been akin to wisdom in some respects, it offered a distinct form of wisdom. The tradition of proverbial

---

4. Moshe Weinfeld, *Deuteronomy and the Deuteronomic School* (Oxford: Oxford University Press, 1972; repr., Winona Lake, IN: Eisenbrauns, 1992), 244–81; Karin Finsterbusch, *Weisung für Israel: Studien zu religiösem Lehren und Lernen im Deuteronomium und in seinem Umfeld*, FAT 44 (Tübingen: Mohr Siebeck, 2005).

5. Martha T. Roth, *Law Collections from Mesopotamia and Asia Minor*, 2nd ed., WAW 6 (Atlanta: Scholars Press, 1997), 5.

6. Michael LeFebvre, *Collections, Codes, and Torah: The Re-characterization of Israel's Written Law*, LHBOTS 451 (New York: T&T Clark, 2006), 35.

7. Jan Assmann, *Herrschaft und Heil: Politische Theologie in Ägypten, Israel und Europa* (Munich: Hanser, 2000), 179; Konrad Schmid, *The Old Testament: A Literary History*, trans. Linda M. Maloney (Minneapolis: Fortress, 2012), 97.

8. Bernard S. Jackson, *Wisdom-Laws: A Study of the Mishpatim of Exodus 21:1–22:16* (Oxford: Oxford University Press, 2006).

wisdom has much in common with the scribal wisdom of the ancient Near East, especially Egypt. On the whole, this was practical, pragmatic wisdom. In principle, it was based on empirical observation, even if hardened into dogma on occasion. It was not based on distinctively Israelite traditions. In the words of James Crenshaw:

> Within Proverbs, Job, and Ecclesiastes one looks in vain for the dominant themes of Yahwistic thought: the exodus from Egypt, election of Israel, the Davidic covenant, the Mosaic legislation, the patriarchal narratives, the divine control of history, and movement toward a glorious moment when right will triumph. Instead, one encounters in these three books a different world of thought, one that stands apart so impressively that some scholars have described that literary corpus as an alien body within the Bible.[9]

David Carr argues, plausibly, that the absence of torah in this material is due to the fact that it originated before the torah attained its central importance:

> In the beginning, there were various forms of textual "wisdom" in which Torah is either not reflected at all or is reflected in very subtle ways.... Just as Mesopotamian and Egyptian [educational] systems began with proverbs, instructions, and hymns as their foundational texts, it is likely that Israel ... likewise started with some of the texts we now see in Proverbs and Psalms, these texts serving as foundational texts for the rest of the curriculum.[10]

Deuteronomy borrowed some themes and phraseology from this tradition, but it placed them in a new context. Its torah, or instruction, was addressed specifically to Israel, in light of its supposed history. Proverbial wisdom had assumed a chain of act and consequence that made it advisable to follow the advice of the sages. Deuteronomy cast its advice as commands, structured like an ancient Near Eastern treaty, with curses and

---

9. James L. Crenshaw, *Old Testament Wisdom: An Introduction*, rev. and enl. ed. (Louisville: Westminster John Knox, 1998), 21.

10. David M. Carr, "The Rise of Torah," in *The Pentateuch as Torah: New Models for Understanding Its Promulgation and Acceptance*, ed. Gary Knoppers and Bernard M. Levinson (Winona Lake, IN: Eisenbrauns, 2007), 43. See also Carr, *The Formation of the Hebrew Bible: A New Reconstruction* (New York: Oxford University Press, 2011), 403–31; Carr, *Writing on the Tablet of the Heart: Origins of Scripture and Literature* (Oxford: Oxford University Press, 2005), 111–73.

blessings attached. This too was wisdom, but wisdom in a more peremptory mode. Rather than provide, as proverbial wisdom did, a platform to unite Israel and its neighbors, Deuteronomy was a nationalistic document, which aimed to underline the distinctiveness of the people and its God.[11]

The Ancestral Law

The torah of Moses acquired new status in the Persian period when it was accepted as the official ancestral law of Judah. This development is credited in the Hebrew Bible to the intervention of Ezra. Whatever historical problems the book of Ezra entails, and they are legion, it is clear that Judeans were thought to live according to the law of Moses by the beginning of the Hellenistic period, as we can see from the account of Hecataeus of Abdera.[12] A century later, Antiochus III graciously allowed the people of Judea to live according to their ancestral laws. These were the laws that were in dispute in the time of the Maccabees.[13] Ezra is also said to have wisdom (Ezra 7:25), but his wisdom is of a narrow, coercive kind, that focuses on a few aspects of the torah of Moses that could serve as identity markers, to distinguish Judeans from their neighbors. (In fact, he appeals to the authority of the torah even in cases where it does not correspond, or correspond fully, to the measures he wants to impose).[14] The so-called Passover Papyrus from Elephantine shows an attempt to impose standard practice on the Judeans of the Egyptian Diaspora (although they apparently did not have a copy of the torah of Moses).

---

11. See Carly L. Crouch, *The Making of Israel: Cultural Diversity in the Southern Levant and the Formation of Ethnic Identity in Deuteronomy*, VTSup 162 (Leiden: Brill, 2014), 105–224.

12. Hecataeus of Abdera, *apud* Diodorus Siculus, *Bib. hist.* 40.3. See Menahem Stern, *Greek and Latin Authors on Jews and Judaism*, 3 vols., FRJS, PIASH (Jerusalem: Israel Academy of Sciences and Humanities, 1976), 1:26–34.

13. See Robert Doran, "The Persecution of Judeans by Antiochus IV: The Significance of 'Ancestral Laws,'" in *The "Other" in Second Temple Judaism: Essays in Honor of John J. Collins*, ed. Daniel C. Harlow et al. (Grand Rapids: Eerdmans, 2010), 423–33.

14. See Joachim Schaper, "Torah and Identity in the Persian Period," in *Judah and the Judeans in the Achaemenid Period: Negotiating Identity in an International Context*, ed. Oded Lipschitz, Gary N. Knoppers, and Manfred Oeming (Winona Lake, IN: Eisenbrauns, 2011), 27–38.

Proverbs

We should not suppose, however, that all Judeans immediately accepted the torah of Moses, as it was brought back from Babylon and interpreted by Ezra, as the standard by which their Judean identity should be measured. The books of Proverbs and Qoheleth do not explicitly acknowledge the torah of Moses at all. At least in the case of Qoheleth, we have to assume that an independent wisdom tradition, with no explicit acknowledgement of torah, persisted into the Hellenistic period.

This situation changed in the second century BCE, when Ben Sira famously declared that all wisdom is "the book of the covenant of the Most High God, the law that Moses commanded us" (Sir 24:23 NRSV). By this time the torah was incorporated into the educational curriculum of the sages as an important source of wisdom.[15] The association of wisdom and torah is also attested in the Dead Sea Scrolls in 4Q525.[16] Even 4QInstruction, which does not thematize torah, clearly draws on it.[17] It should be said that Ben Sira uses the torah as a source of wisdom rather than law, but he clearly accords the torah of Moses iconic status as an expression of the traditional Judean way of life.

Some scholars find the fusion of wisdom and torah already in the later stages of the book of Proverbs. Bernd U. Schipper notes the echoes of Deuteronomy in Prov 6:20–23:[18]

---

15. See John J. Collins, *Jewish Wisdom in the Hellenistic Age*, OTL (Louisville: Westminster John Knox, 1997), 42–61.

16. Matthew J. Goff, *Discerning Wisdom: The Sapiential Literature of the Dead Sea Scrolls*, VTSup 116 (Leiden: Brill, 2007), 198–229.

17. Matthew J. Goff, *The Worldly and Heavenly Wisdom of 4QInstruction*, STDJ 50 (Leiden: Brill, 2003), 116–23; Goff, *4QInstruction*, WLAW 2 (Atlanta: Society of Biblical Literature, 2013) 22; Lawrence H. Schiffman, "Halakhic Elements in the Sapiential Texts from Qumran," in *Sapiential Perspectives: Wisdom Literature in Light of the Dead Sea Scrolls*, ed. John J. Collins, Gregory E. Sterling, and Ruth A. Clements, STDJ 51 (Leiden: Brill, 2004), 89–100.

18. Trans. of Bernd U. Schipper, "When Wisdom Is Not Enough! The Discourse on Wisdom and Torah and the Composition of the Book of Proverbs," in Schipper and Teeter, *Wisdom and Torah*, 58. On echoes of Deuteronomy in the passage, compare already Michael A. Fishbane, "Torah and Tradition," in *Tradition and Theology in the Old Testament*, ed. Douglas A. Knight (Philadelphia: Fortress, 1977), 275–300, esp. 284.

(6:20) Keep, my son, your father's מצוה, forsake not your mother's תורה.
(21) Bind them always upon your heart, tie them about your neck.
(22) When you walk about it will guide you, when you lie down it will watch over you, when you wake up it will converse with you,
(23) for the מצוה is a lamp, and the תורה is a light, and disciplinary reproof is a way to life.

Similar echoes of Deuteronomy can be found in the wisdom instructions in Prov 3 and 7: "The three wisdom instructions share a number of terms like תורה in 3:1; 6:20; 7:2; מצוה in 3:1; 6:20; 7:1 and the ideas to bind the Torah upon the heart (6:21), to 'inscribe on the tablet of the heart' (verbally in 3:3, and 7:3) or 'to tie them about your neck' (3:3 and with the exact the same [sic] wording in 6:21)."[19] These and other observations support the view that Proverbs is alluding to Deuteronomy. Schipper concludes: "The crucial point is that by this intertextual allusion, the מצוה of the father and the תורה of the mother comes [sic] close to the תורה and מצות of God. Even if they appear in the textual strategy of Proverbs as a parental instruction, this instruction refers to the will of YHWH."[20] Wisdom has become "a hermeneutic of Torah." Schipper even claims that Prov 6 prioritizes torah over wisdom. Similarly, Stuart Weeks argues that Proverbs is "trying to assert some sort of connection between proper Instruction and the Law."[21]

In fact, however, Proverbs refers neither to the torah of Moses nor to the torah of YHWH, but to the teaching and instructions of the parents (or the sage in loco parentis). As Michael V. Fox has noted, the terms תורה and מצוה in Proverbs refer to authoritative injunctions, not suggestions or recommendations, but do not refer to law or legally enforceable ordinances.[22] It is authoritative teaching, but its authority derives from human teachers, not from divine law given on Sinai. Insofar as Proverbs uses lan-

---

19. Schipper, "When Wisdom Is Not Enough," 59.

20. Ibid., 60. Compare Bernd U. Schipper, *Hermeneutik der Tora: Studien zur Traditionsgeschichte von Prov 2 und zur Komposition von Prov 1–9*, BZAW 432 (Berlin: de Gruyter, 2012), 297 (English summary), and compare also Scott L. Harris, *Proverbs 1–9: A Study of Inner-biblical Interpretation*, SBLDS 150 (Atlanta: Scholars Press, 1995).

21. Stuart Weeks, *Instruction and Imagery in Proverbs 1–9* (Oxford: Oxford University Press, 2007), 105.

22. Michael V. Fox, *Proverbs 1–9: A New Translation with Introduction and Commentary*, AB 18A (New York: Doubleday, 2000), 142–43.

guage derived from Deuteronomy, this means, in the words of Fox, "only that terms of honor learned from the one book are used in the other."[23] It is noteworthy that the sages were familiar with Deuteronomy, but they do not invoke it as divine revelation. Rather, they claim for their own תורה or teaching what Deuteronomy claims for its torah. No doubt, in rabbinic times, or perhaps even in the period of the Dead Sea Scrolls, the use of words like תורה and מצוה would evoke the torah of Moses,[24] but this was not necessarily the case in the circles in which Proverbs was composed.

Qoheleth

The relation of Qoheleth to the torah has also been a matter of controversy. Many scholars see an allusion to Gen 2–3 in Qoh 3:20: "All go to one place; all are from the dust, and all turn to dust again" (NRSV),[25] or to Deut 23:22–24 in Qoh 5:3–4, which warns that one should fulfill a vow without delay.[26] But while Qoheleth may know Genesis and Deuteronomy, he hardly treats them as torah or acknowledges them as authoritative. As Bernard Levinson has commented, "While Qoh 5:3–4 cites Deuteronomy's law of vows, it does not do so because of the authority of Scripture as much as because of the law's reasonableness."[27] As Weeks has commented,

---

23. Ibid., 79.
24. As argued by Weeks, *Instruction and Imagery*, 104–5.
25. See Carolyn J. Sharp, *Irony and Meaning in the Hebrew Bible* (Bloomington: Indiana University Press, 2009), 209–10; Thomas Krüger, *Qoheleth*, Hermeneia (Minneapolis: Fortress, 2004), 92. More generally, Krüger holds that "the main features of his view of the relationship of God and humankind seem, however, to be indebted to the essence of the Torah and more precisely to the so-called primal history in Genesis 1–11" (*Qoheleth*, 25).
26. Krüger, *Qoheleth*, 25; Bernard M. Levinson, *A More Perfect Torah: At the Intersection of Philology and Hermeneutics in Deuteronomy and the Temple Scroll*, CrStHB1 (Winona Lake, IN: Eisenbrauns, 2013), 54–61; Jennie Barbour, *The Story of Israel in the Book of Qohelet: Ecclesiastes as Cultural Memory* (Oxford: Oxford University Press, 2012), implausibly finds pervasive allusions to the history of Israel in Qoheleth.
27. Levinson, *More Perfect Torah*, 56. Compare Thomas Krüger, "Die Rezeption der Tora im Buch Kohelet," in *Das Buch Kohelet: Studien zur Struktur, Geschichte, Rezeption und Theologie*, ed. Ludger Schwienhorst-Schönberger, BZAW 254 (Berlin: de Gruyter, 1997), 303–25, repr. in Krüger, *Kritische Weisheit: Studien zur weisheitlichen Traditionskritik im Alten Testament* (Zurich: Pano, 1997), 173–93.

until the closing verses of the book, Qoheleth shows no obvious interest in the torah at all.[28]

The main controversy about Qoheleth's attitude to the torah concerns the epilogue in Qoh 12:13, "The end of the matter; all has been heard. Fear God, and keep his commandments; for that is the whole duty of everyone" (NRSV). Most scholars regard the epilogue as a corrective coda added by an editor, not as a summary of the sage's teaching.[29] Even Fox, who argues that it was part of the original composition, sees the epilogue as an attempt to win acceptance for the book by a gesture toward conventional piety.[30] It is true that this epilogue does not contradict the sayings of Qoheleth, since he never disparages the keeping of commandments.[31] Yet, as C. L. Seow has noted, it puts a different spin on Qoheleth's work by associating the fear of God with keeping the commandments.[32] In the words of Weeks,

> To fear and obey God is to act in a way that characterizes almost any ancient piety, but the specific formulation here, "keep his commandments," is so quintessentially Deuteronomic (see, for instance Deut 4:40; 7:9;13:5; 26:18) that it could hardly but have been read by early Jewish readers as a reference to the Torah, and the author of the verses must surely have been aware of these connotations. Although Qohelet might allow the possibility of divine communication and commands, it is very doubtful that his thought has any place for the concept of a Torah, or its many implications.[33]

The late Gerald Sheppard argued that the epilogue finds its closest parallels in Ben Sira and is therefore a secondary addition to the book.[34] In contrast,

---

28. Stuart Weeks, "'Fear God and Keep His Commandments': Could Qohelet Have Said This?," in Schipper and Teeter, *Wisdom and Torah*, 101–18.

29. *Pace* Sharp, *Irony and Meaning*, 196–220, who regards the epilogue as the true message of the book and "Qoheleth" as an ironic persona. Brevard S. Childs, *Introduction to the Old Testament as Scripture* (Philadelphia: Fortress, 1981), 584, says that "the most obvious sign of canonical shaping appears in the epilogue."

30. Michael V. Fox, *A Time to Tear Down and a Time to Build Up: A Rereading of Ecclesiastes* (Grand Rapids: Eerdmans, 1999), 373–74.

31. This point is emphasized by C. L. Seow, *Ecclesiastes: A New Translation with Introduction and Commentary*, AB 18C (New York: Doubleday, 1997), 395; Krüger, *Qoheleth*, 213.

32. Seow, *Ecclesiastes*, 395.

33. Weeks, "Fear God," 112.

34. Gerald T. Sheppard, *Wisdom as a Hermeneutical Construct*, BZAW 151

Thomas Krüger argues that one can also interpret Qoh 12:13 as "a purely pragmatic recommendation to all people in daily life to hold 'undogmatically' to the religious and cultural norms that they find in their particular living environment."[35] In that case, however, it would no longer bespeak a torah-centered piety at all.

The wisdom tradition, at least before Ben Sira, is not an attempt to formulate Judean identity. We simply do not know whether the sages and their students were circumcised and kept the Passover. It would be hasty to infer that they did not. Nonetheless, it is significant that a whole area of instruction in the Second Temple period could proceed without reference to the torah. The torah was not the only possible framework for teaching fear of the Lord. Crenshaw is surely right that the canonical wisdom books exhibit a worldview that is quite different from that of the torah, and as such represent a different construal of "Judaism" from what we find in Maccabees or even in the wisdom literature itself from the second century BCE on.

Torah as Icon

Already in the case of Ezra, it has been noted that the authority of the torah is invoked even for measures that do not actually correspond to the text of the Pentateuch as it has come down to us. Stipulations regarding the Feast of Booths "according to the law" (Neh 8:13–18) are different from what we find in the torah. The prohibitions against intermarriage go beyond Deuteronomy (Neh 10:31), and making purchases on the Sabbath is not actually prohibited in the Pentateuch (Neh 10:32). The institution of an annual temple tax and of a wood offering (also in Neh 10) lack scriptural support. In the words of Joachim Schaper, "some [texts] that refer to torah, in fact *refer to no known (quasi)-canonical or otherwise authoritative text.*"[36] The use of the formula ככתוב, "as it is written," testifies to the new authority of written scripture as a point of reference for Judean practice in the mid to late fifth century BCE.[37] Again, although Antiochus III declared

---

(Berlin: de Gruyter, 1980), 127; Sheppard, "The Epilogue to Qoheleth as Theological Commentary," *CBQ* 39 (1977): 182–89.

35. Krüger, *Qoheleth*, 215.

36. Schaper, "Torah and Identity," 32, emphasis original.

37. Lars Hänsel, "Studien zu 'Tora' in Esra-Nehemiah und Chronik: Erwägungen zur Bezugnahme auf חוק, מצוה, דבר, משפט, תורה in Esra-Nehemia und Chronik im

that the people of Judea should conduct their affairs in accordance with their ancestral laws (Josephus, *Ant.* 12.142), his decree is mainly concerned with the upkeep of the temple. One of his provisions restricted access to the temple and banned the flesh of certain animals from Jerusalem. As E. J. Bickerman noted, there is no precept excluding foreigners from the temple in the law of Moses.[38] Neither is the prohibition of the flesh or hides of certain animals explicit in the torah. In these and other cases the torah is assumed to extend to customs that are not actually found in it. (This is still true of Josephus.) The torah of Moses had taken on an iconic status whereby it stood for the entire Judean way of life, whether specific provisions were actually found in the text or not.

The iconic character of the torah is also in evidence in some of the psalms from the Second Temple period. Psalm 119 uses the word *torah* twenty-five times, a usage that Jon Levenson described as "like a mantra,"[39] and also uses several terms such as משפט and מצוה as rough equivalents.[40] Yet, Levenson argues, "the psalmist's Torah lacks a constant identity."[41] It can variously refer to received tradition, to cosmic or natural law, or to unmediated divine teaching.[42] The psalmist declares his love for the torah and says that "your commandment makes me wiser than my enemies" (Ps 119:98 NRSV), but he gives no examples of the specific commandments.

Horizont frühjüdischer Texte" (PhD diss., Leipzig University, 1999), cited by Schaper, "Torah and Identity," 32, finds that this formula is only used with reference to the Torah and that the references in Chronicles, unlike those in Ezra-Nehemiah, correspond to the Torah as it is known to us.

38. E. J. Bickerman, "A Seleucid Proclamation Concerning the Temple in Jerusalem," in Bickerman, *A New Edition in English Including* The God of the Maccabees, vol. 1 of *Studies in Jewish and Christian History*, ed. Amram D. Tropper, BRPC (Leiden: Brill, 2011), 1:363.

39. Jon D. Levenson, "The Sources of Torah: Psalm 119 and the Modes of Revelation in Second Temple Judaism," in *Ancient Israelite Religion: Essays in Honor of Frank Moore Cross*, ed. Patrick D. Miller, Paul D. Hanson, and S. Dean McBride (Philadelphia: Fortress, 1987), 566.

40. Kent Aaron Reynolds, *Torah as Teacher: The Exemplary Torah Student in Psalm 119*, VTSup 137 (Leiden: Brill, 2010), 109–21; Karen Finsterbusch, "Yahweh's Torah and the Praying 'I' in Psalm 119," in Schipper and Teeter, *Wisdom and Torah*, 123–28.

41. Levenson, "Sources of Torah," 565.

42. Reynolds, *Torah as Teacher*, 128, denies that it refers to unmediated revelation.

In the words of Kent Reynolds, torah is "greater than the sum of the parts."[43] It is a comprehensive expression for the will and revelation of God.[44]

In Psalm 19, which draws some of its terminology from Ps 119, this comprehensive concept of torah becomes an object of praise:

> The Torah of the LORD is perfect, reviving the soul;
> the decrees of the LORD are sure, making wise the simple;
> the precepts of the LORD are right, rejoicing the heart....
> More to be desired are they than gold, even much fine gold;
> sweeter also than honey, and drippings of the honeycomb. (Ps 19:7–8a, 10 NRSV [modified]).

Anja Klein has noted that the praise of torah here has a close parallel in the self-praise of the Lady Wisdom in Prov 8, notably in the comparison with gold, but also in their general terminology.[45] Klein refers to this as a sapiential interpretation of torah: "Drawing on the portrayal of wisdom in Proverbs 8, the Torah from Psalm 119 is set as an absolute and attracts both characteristics and predications of classic wisdom."[46] Torah is analogous to personified wisdom as an abstraction that represents a whole way of life. The way of life summed up in the torah is somewhat different from that described in Proverbs, since it affirms the specifically Israelite laws of the Pentateuch, but the Psalm is not concerned with the details. Rather, it uses the torah as an icon, which is treated with great respect and deference but not examined for the specificity of its commandments.

BEN SIRA

Klein also notes affinities between Ps 19 and Ben Sira, notably in the praise of God as lord of creation in Sir 42:15–43:33. Ben Sira famously identifies

---

43. Ibid., 183.

44. See also David Noel Freedman, *Psalm 119: The Exaltation of the Torah* (Winona Lake, IN: Eisenbrauns, 1999), 91–92; Erich Zenger, "Torafrömmigkeit: Beobachtungen zum poetischen und theologischen Profil vom Psalm 119," in *Freiheit und Recht: Festschrift für Frank Crüsemann zum 65. Geburtstag*, ed. Christof Hardmeier, Rainer Kessler, and Andreas Ruwe (Gütersloh: Kaiser, 2003) 380–96, esp. 387.

45. Anja Klein, "Half Way between Psalm 119 and Ben Sira: Wisdom and Torah in Psalm 19," in Schipper and Teeter, *Wisdom and Torah*, 148–49; compare Alexandra Grund, *'Die Himmel erzählen die Ehre Gottes": Psalm 19 im Kontext der nachexilischen Toraweisheit*, WMANT 103 (Neukirchen-Vluyn: Neukirchener Verlag, 2004), 235–40.

46. Klein, "Half Way," 149.

wisdom with the torah of Moses. The praise of wisdom as a cosmic force in creation in chapter 24 concludes, rather counterintuitively, by saying that "all this is the book of the covenant of the Most High God, the law that Moses commanded us as an inheritance for the congregations of Jacob" (Sir 24:23 NRSV). The force of the identification is endlessly debated. Does it mean that the torah is all the wisdom you need or that all wisdom is ipso facto torah?[47] Klein writes that "the law comes into play as a way of practicing wisdom" and that "the encompassing quality of wisdom manifests itself in the guidelines of the law."[48] But as Benjamin Wright observes in the same volume, Ben Sira never explicitly cites material from the torah, and torah is only one of several sources of wisdom.[49] Wright grants that references to law, commandments, statutes, and so forth should be read as references to the Mosaic torah, but he is unsure just what that encompasses. In any case, performance of the law is not the only way that wisdom can be actualized. The sapiential tradition and the created order are also sources of wisdom.[50]

But while I would argue that Ben Sira subsumes torah under wisdom, rather than vice versa, his understanding of wisdom is distinctly different from that of Proverbs or Qoheleth. The very fact of acknowledging the torah of Moses as a source of wisdom brought him closer to the orbit of the Deuteronomic tradition. Entailed in that acknowledgement was an affirmation of the election and special status of Israel.[51] The great figures of Israel's history were recast as examples of wisdom in action, but they were given a role that had no precedent in the older wisdom tradition. Ben Sira does not take over the treaty framework of Deuteronomy, and does not invoke curses on those who fail to follow his teachings. The *Tun-Ergehen Zusammenhang* of traditional wisdom was enough to constitute a general similarity of outlook with the Deuteronomic tradition. Whether Ben Sira can be said to exemplify "covenantal nomism" in the manner of E. P.

---

47. For the literature, see Benjamin G. Wright, "Torah and Sapiential Pedagogy in the Book of Ben Sira," in Schipper and Teeter, *Wisdom and Torah*, 157–86, esp. 157–58.

48. Klein, "Half Way," 152–53. She also says that in Ben Sira the balance has shifted in favor of wisdom, but this seems hard to reconcile with the view that the law is the enactment of wisdom.

49. Wright, "Torah and Sapiential Pedagogy," 159.

50. Ibid., 169.

51. See Greg Schmidt Goering, *Wisdom's Root Revealed: Ben Sira and the Election of Israel*, JSJSup 139 (Leiden: Brill, 2009).

Sanders, however, is debatable.⁵² Despite his great respect for the torah of Moses, he does not cast his teaching in a covenantal context. It is still presented as teaching for individuals, even, perhaps, for an elite segment of Judean society.

Wright is probably correct that "the increasing authority of the Torah and the growing importance of Torah-piety in … Second Temple Judaism worked to make the Torah an indispensible source of wisdom for a sage like Ben Sira."⁵³ Even the authors of non-Mosaic writings, such as Qoheleth and the Book of the Watchers, drew on the writings of the torah in various ways. Where Ben Sira differed from these writers was in his explicit acknowledgement of the status of the torah. In this, I suspect, he was influenced by his social location. His admiration for the High Priest Simon suggests that he was a retainer who enjoyed and depended on the patronage of the priestly establishment in Jerusalem in a way that Qoheleth and the Enochic writers did not. Consequently, he had to acknowledge the wisdom of the official "ancestral laws" of Judah more explicitly than some of his contemporaries.

But Ben Sira's use of the torah still seems to be largely iconic. It is a formal acknowledgement of the superiority of Mosaic wisdom, but it is far removed from the kind of obsession with the details of Mosaic law that we find in 4QMMT and some other Dead Sea Scrolls. Halakhic Judaism, the view that Judaism is defined primarily by Mosaic law, as law, had not yet become dominant in Judah when Ben Sira wrote. Even covenantal nomism, the view that one's standing in the people of Judea depended on conformity to Mosaic law, which had been propounded for centuries in the Deuteronomic history, was not yet the default understanding of Judean identity. This situation would change, to a great degree, with the Maccabean revolt.

Wisdom Texts in the Scrolls

I would like to conclude with a few comments on wisdom texts in the Dead Sea Scrolls.⁵⁴ The sectarians evidently read wisdom texts, just as they

---

52. E. P. Sanders, *Paul and Palestinian Judaism: A Comparison of Patterns of Religion* (Philadelphia: Fortress, 1977), 70.

53. Wright, "Torah and Sapiential Pedagogy," 166.

54. The fullest and best introduction to the wisdom literature of the Scrolls is that of Goff, *Discerning Wisdom* (see n. 16 above).

read other religious literature, but wisdom texts found among the scrolls are not necessarily sectarian compositions. The relation of several of these texts to the sectarian movement is unclear.

The text of 4QInstruction certainly has much in common with the Hodayot and with the Instruction on the Two Spirits, but it may have been a source on which the sectarian authors drew rather than a sectarian composition. The other wisdom texts that are most immediately relevant to our subject, 4QBeatitudes (4Q525) and 4Q185 also lack clear indication of sectarian origin, although they are not incompatible with sectarian provenance either.

The text of 4QInstruction, as already noted, draws on the torah implicitly at various points, but does not acknowledge it at all. The idea that it refers to the torah as רז נהיה must be regarded as improbable: why should the torah be regarded as a mystery?[55] The relation of 4QInstruction to the torah is not significantly different from that of Prov 1–9 or Qoheleth.

The most explicit acknowledgement of the torah in the wisdom texts from the Scrolls is found in 4Q525.[56] This text echoes Ps 1, which praises those who meditate on the law of the Lord, but it correlates that with the pursuit of wisdom: "Blessed is the man who attains Wisdom, and walks in the law of the Most High" (4Q525 2 II, 3).[57] The passage that follows may apply equally to wisdom and torah: "and directs his heart to her ways, and is constrained by her discipline and alwa[ys] takes pleasure in her punishments.... For he always thinks of her, and in his distress he meditates [on her]."[58] William Tooman construes this to mean that "the written Torah

---

55. *Pace* Armin Lange, "Wisdom Literature and Thought in the Dead Sea Scrolls," in *The Oxford Handbook of the Dead Sea Scrolls*, ed. Timothy H. Lim and John J. Collins (Oxford: Oxford University Press, 2010), 464, who holds that the רז is the sapiential order of the cosmos but was revealed to Israel as the torah.

56. Goff, *Discerning Wisdom*, 198–99.

57. Translations of 4Q525 are those Florentino García Martínez and Eibert J. C. Tigchelaar, eds. *The Dead Sea Scrolls Study Edition*, 2 vols. (Leiden: Brill; Grand Rapids: Eerdmans, 1997–1998), 2:1053–55.

58. William Tooman, "Wisdom and Torah at Qumran," in Schipper and Teeter, *Wisdom and Torah*, 211, says that the Torah is the antecedent of these phrases, but in fact both wisdom and Torah are antecedents. See Elisa Uusimäki, "Turning Proverbs towards Torah: 4Q525 in the Context of Late Second Temple Wisdom Literature" (PhD diss., University of Helsinki, 2013), 244; now published as *Turning Proverbs towards Torah: An Analysis of 4Q525*, STDJ 117 (Leiden: Brill, 2016).

is the source of wisdom and Torah piety is its sign and substance."⁵⁹ Similarly, George Brooke relates the language of "walking in her ways" to the concept of halakah: "The halakhah is based on practical advice for everyday living which is the application of various of the principles underlying the torah, rather than the application of individual rulings (משפטים) or statutes (חקים)."⁶⁰ Brooke is certainly right that the text does not refer to individual rulings or statutes, but for that reason it is misleading to refer to it as "halakhic exegesis."⁶¹ Rather, 4Q525 uses torah as an "ideological sign," in the phrase of Carol Newsom, interchangeably with "wisdom."⁶² The term "righteousness" is a similar "ideological sign" that signifies an approach to life, that may be construed quite differently by different groups. As Hindy Najman has put it: "Torah was not limited to a particular corpus of texts but was inextricably linked to a broader tradition of extrabiblical law and narrative, interpretation, and cosmic wisdom."⁶³ This remains what I am calling an "iconic" use of torah, where the idea of Torah, like personified Wisdom, signifies an approach to life but is not analyzed in detail. The language of 4Q525 is much more heavily indebted to Proverbs than to the laws of the Pentateuch, but by identifying wisdom with torah it claims for the wisdom tradition the authority of God's revelation to Moses on Mount Sinai.

Another wisdom text from Qumran, 4Q185, does not refer to torah as such, but urges its readers to "draw wisdom from the [p]ower of our God, remember the miracles he performed in Egypt" (4Q185 1–2 I, 14).⁶⁴ As Tooman puts it, "the excerpt is a complex conflation of locutions from scriptural poems that recite the history of Israel for pedagogic purposes, texts like Ps 78, 105, and 106."⁶⁵ It also refers to "[the way which he commanded to J]acob and the path which he decreed to Isaac" (4Q185 1–2

---

59. Tooman, "Wisdom and Torah," 212.
60. George J. Brooke, "Biblical Interpretation in the Wisdom Texts from Qumran," in *The Wisdom Texts from Qumran and the Development of Sapiential Thought*, ed. Charlotte Hempel, Armin Lange, and Hermann Lichtenberger, BETL 159 (Leuven: Peeters, 2002), 209.
61. Uusimäki, "Turning Proverbs," 247.
62. Carol A. Newsom, *The Self as Symbolic Space: Constructing Identity and Community at Qumran*, STDJ 52 (Leiden: Brill, 2004), 10–11.
63. Hindy Najman, "Torah and Tradition," *EEDJ* 1316.
64. Translations of 4Q185 are those of García Martínez and Tigchelaar, *The Dead Sea Scrolls Study Edition*, 1:379. On the passage, see Goff, *Discerning Wisdom*, 122–45.
65. Tooman, "Wisdom and Torah," 216.

II, 4). Tooman infers: "wisdom, in so far as this author is concerned, is the proper possession of Israel."[66] Here the reference is not specifically to the laws revealed at Sinai, but rather to the Pentateuchal narratives. It does not necessarily follow that "worldly wisdom of the international type is surely excluded," as Tooman assumes.[67] But at least in the fragments that have survived, the torah found in the Pentateuch appears to be the primary source of wisdom. There is no reason to regard 4Q185 as a sectarian composition.

Conclusion

Torah was already viewed as a kind of wisdom in Deuteronomy, but the kind of wisdom it represented was significantly different from that found in Proverbs, Job, and Qoheleth, primarily in its particularist focus on Israel as the locus of wisdom. It is apparent that this approach to wisdom was not universally accepted. The writers of Prov 1–9 and Qoheleth were acquainted with the content of the torah, but they do not acknowledge it all. This is still true of 4QInstruction. By the early second century BCE the torah of Moses was increasingly regarded as an important source of wisdom. In some texts, such as Ps 19 and 4Q525, torah functions as an icon, or ideological sign, analogous to personified wisdom, as a general signifier of a way of life, rather than as a collection of specific commandments. Both 4Q185 and Ben Sira look to the narrative books as sources of wisdom, although Ben Sira also identifies the torah with Wisdom in an iconic sense. What we do not yet find in the wisdom literature, down to the early second century BCE, is a clear claim that the revelation to Moses is the only source of wisdom, or a systematic subordination of wisdom to halakhic exegesis. In the sectarian scrolls, however, wisdom is increasingly overshadowed by the legal demands of the torah, and this is more broadly true of the sectarian disputes that arose in the wake of the Maccabean revolt.

Bibliography

Assmann, Jan. *Herrschaft und Heil: Politische Theologie in Ägypten, Israel und Europa.* Munich: Hanser, 2000.

---

66. Ibid.
67. Ibid.

Barbour, Jennie. *The Story of Israel in the Book of Qohelet: Ecclesiastes as Cultural Memory*. Oxford: Oxford University Press, 2012.
Bickerman, E. J. *A New Edition in English Including* The God of the Maccabees. Vol. 1 of *Studies in Jewish and Christian History*. Edited by Amram D. Tropper. BRPC. Leiden: Brill, 2011.
———. "A Seleucid Proclamation Concerning the Temple in Jerusalem." Pages 357–75 in *A New Edition in English Including* The God of the Maccabees. Vol. 1 of *Studies in Jewish and Christian History*. Edited by Amram D. Tropper. BRPC. Leiden: Brill, 2011.
Brooke, George J. "Biblical Interpretation in the Wisdom Texts from Qumran." Pages 201–20 in *The Wisdom Texts from Qumran and the Development of Sapiential Thought*. Edited by Charlotte Hempel, Armin Lange, and Hermann Lichtenberger. BETL 159. Leuven: Peeters, 2002.
Carr, David M. *The Formation of the Hebrew Bible: A New Reconstruction*. New York: Oxford University Press, 2011.
———. "The Rise of Torah." Pages 39–56 in *The Pentateuch as Torah: New Models for Understanding Its Promulgation and Acceptance*. Edited by Gary Knoppers and Bernard M. Levinson. Winona Lake, IN: Eisenbrauns, 2007.
———. *Writing on the Tablet of the Heart: Origins of Scripture and Literature*. Oxford: Oxford University Press, 2005.
Childs, Brevard S. *Introduction to the Old Testament as Scripture*. Philadelphia: Fortress, 1981.
Collins, John J. *Jewish Wisdom in the Hellenistic Age*. OTL. Louisville: Westminster John Knox, 1997.
Crenshaw, James L. *Old Testament Wisdom: An Introduction*. Rev. and enl. ed. Louisville: Westminster John Knox, 1998.
Crouch, Carly L. *The Making of Israel: Cultural Diversity in the Southern Levant and the Formation of Ethnic Identity in Deuteronomy*. VTSup 162. Leiden: Brill, 2014.
Doran, Robert. "The Persecution of Judeans by Antiochus IV: The Significance of 'Ancestral Laws.'" Pages 423–33 in *The "Other" in Second Temple Judaism: Essays in Honor of John J. Collins*. Edited by Daniel C. Harlow, Karina Martin Hogan, Matthew J. Goff, and Joel S. Kaminsky. Grand Rapids: Eerdmans, 2010.
Finsterbusch, Karin. *Weisung für Israel: Studien zu religiösem Lehren und Lernen im Deuteronomium und in seinem Umfeld*. FAT 44. Tübingen: Mohr Siebeck, 2005.

———. "Yahweh's Torah and the Praying 'I' in Psalm 119." Pages 119–35 in *Wisdom and Torah: The Reception of "Torah" in the Wisdom Literature of the Second Temple Period*. Edited by Bernd U. Schipper and D. Andrew Teeter. JSJSup 163. Leiden: Brill, 2013.

Fishbane, Michael A. "Torah and Tradition." Pages 275–300 in *Tradition and Theology in the Old Testament*. Edited by Douglas A. Knight. Philadelphia: Fortress, 1977.

Fox, Michael V. *Proverbs 1–9: A New Translation with Introduction and Commentary*. AB 18A. New York: Doubleday, 2000.

———. *A Time to Tear Down and a Time to Build Up: A Rereading of Ecclesiastes*. Grand Rapids: Eerdmans, 1999.

Freedman, David Noel. *Psalm 119: The Exaltation of the Torah*. Winona Lake, IN: Eisenbrauns, 1999.

García Martínez, Florentino, and Eibert J.C. Tighchelaar. *The Dead Sea Scrolls Study Edition*. 2 vols. Leiden: Brill; Grand Rapids: Eerdmans, 1997–1998.

Goering, Greg Schmidt. *Wisdom's Root Revealed: Ben Sira and the Election of Israel*. JSJSup 139. Leiden: Brill, 2009.

Goff, Matthew J. *4QInstruction*. WLAW 2. Atlanta: Society of Biblical Literature, 2013.

———. *Discerning Wisdom: The Sapiential Literature of the Dead Sea Scrolls*. VTSup 116. Leiden: Brill, 2007.

———. *The Worldly and Heavenly Wisdom of 4QInstruction*. STDJ 50. Leiden: Brill, 2003.

Grund, Alexandra. *"Die Himmel erzählen die Ehre Gottes": Psalm 19 im Kontext der nachexilischen Toraweisheit*. WMANT 103. Neukirchen-Vluyn: Neukirchener Verlag, 2004.

Hänsel, Lars. "Studien zu 'Tora' in Esra-Nehemia und Chronik: Erwägungen zur Bezugnahme auf חוק, מצוה, דבר, משפט, תורה in Esra-Nehemia und Chronik im Horizont frühjüdischer Texte." PhD diss., Leipzig University, 1999.

Harris, Scott L. *Proverbs 1–9: A Study of Inner-biblical Interpretation*. SBLDS 150. Atlanta: Scholars Press, 1995.

Jackson, Bernard S. *Wisdom-Laws: A Study of the Mishpatim of Exodus 21:1–22:16*. Oxford: Oxford University Press, 2006.

Klein, Anja. "Half Way between Psalm 119 and Ben Sira: Wisdom and Torah in Psalm 19." Pages 137–55 in *Wisdom and Torah: The Reception of "Torah" in the Wisdom Literature of the Second Temple Period*. Edited by Bernd U. Schipper and D. Andrew Teeter. JSJSup 163. Leiden: Brill, 2013.

Krüger, Thomas. *Kritische Weisheit: Studien zur weisheitlichen Traditionskritik im Alten Testament*. Zurich: Pano, 1997.

———. "Law and Wisdom According to Deut 4:5-8." Pages 35-54 in *Wisdom and Torah: The Reception of "Torah" in the Wisdom Literature of the Second Temple Period*. Edited by Bernd U. Schipper and D. Andrew Teeter. JSJSup 163. Leiden: Brill, 2013.

———. *Qoheleth*. Hermeneia. Minneapolis: Fortress, 2004.

———. "Die Rezeption der Tora im Buch Kohelet." Pages 303-25 in *Das Buch Kohelet: Studien zur Struktur, Geschichte, Rezeption und Theologie*. Edited by Ludger Schwienhorst-Schönberger. BZAW 254. Berlin: de Gruyter, 1997.

Lange, Armin. "Wisdom Literature and Thought in the Dead Sea Scrolls." Pages 455-78 in *The Oxford Handbook of the Dead Sea Scrolls*. Edited by Timothy H. Lim and John J. Collins. Oxford: Oxford University Press, 2010.

LeFebvre, Michael. *Collections, Codes, and Torah: The Re-characterization of Israel's Written Law*. LHBOTS 451. New York: T&T Clark, 2006.

Levenson, Jon D. "The Sources of Torah: Psalm 119 and the Modes of Revelation in Second Temple Judaism." Pages 559-74 in *Ancient Israelite Religion: Essays in Honor of Frank Moore Cross*. Edited by Patrick D. Miller, Paul D. Hanson, and S. Dean McBride. Philadelphia: Fortress, 1987.

Levinson, Bernard M. *A More Perfect Torah: At the Intersection of Philology and Hermeneutics in Deuteronomy and the Temple Scroll*. CrStHB 1. Winona Lake, IN: Eisenbrauns, 2013.

Najman, Hindy. "Torah and Tradition." *EEDJ* 1316-17.

Newsom, Carol A. *The Self as Symbolic Space: Constructing Identity and Community at Qumran*. STDJ 52. Leiden: Brill, 2004.

Östborn, Gunnar. *Tora in the Old Testament: A Semantic Study*. Lund: Ohlsson, 1945.

Reynolds, Kent Aaron. *Torah as Teacher: The Exemplary Torah Student in Psalm 119*. VTSup 137. Leiden: Brill, 2010.

Roth, Martha T. *Law Collections from Mesopotamia and Asia Minor*. 2nd ed. WAW 6. Atlanta: Scholars Press, 1997.

Sanders, E. P. *Paul and Palestinian Judaism: A Comparison of Patterns of Religion*. Philadelphia: Fortress, 1977.

Schaper, Joachim. "Torah and Identity in the Persian Period." Pages 27–38 in *Judah and the Judeans in the Achaemenid Period: Negotiating Identity in an International Context*. Edited by Oded Lipschitz, Gary N. Knoppers, and Manfred Oeming. Winona Lake, IN: Eisenbrauns, 2011.

Schiffman, Lawrence H. "Halakhic Elements in the Sapiential Texts from Qumran." Pages 89–100 in *Sapiential Perspectives: Wisdom Literature in Light of the Dead Sea Scrolls*. Edited by John J. Collins, Gregory E. Sterling, and Ruth A. Clements. STDJ 51. Leiden: Brill, 2004.

Schipper, Bernd U. *Hermeneutik der Tora: Studien zur Traditionsgeschichte von Prov 2 und zur Komposition von Prov 1–9*. BZAW 432. Berlin: de Gruyter, 2012.

———. "When Wisdom Is Not Enough! The Discourse on Wisdom and Torah and the Composition of the Book of Proverbs." Pages 55–79 in *Wisdom and Torah: The Reception of "Torah" in the Wisdom Literature of the Second Temple Period*. Edited by Bernd U. Schipper and D. Andrew Teeter. JSJSup 163. Leiden: Brill, 2013.

Schmid, Konrad. *The Old Testament: A Literary History*. Translated by Linda M. Maloney. Minneapolis: Fortress, 2012.

Seow, C. L. *Ecclesiastes: A New Translation with Introduction and Commentary*. AB 18C. New York: Doubleday, 1997.

Sharp, Carolyn J. *Irony and Meaning in the Hebrew Bible*. Bloomington: Indiana University Press, 2009.

Sheppard, Gerald T. "The Epilogue to Qoheleth as Theological Commentary." *CBQ* 39 (1977): 182–89.

———. *Wisdom as a Hermeneutical Construct*. BZAW 151. Berlin: de Gruyter, 1980.

Stern, Menahem. *Greek and Latin Authors on Jews and Judaism*. 3 vols. FRJS; PIASH. Jerusalem: Israel Academy of Sciences and Humanities, 1976.

Tooman, William. "Wisdom and Torah at Qumran." Pages 203–32 in *Wisdom and Torah: The Reception of "Torah" in the Wisdom Literature of the Second Temple Period*. Edited by Bernd U. Schipper and D. Andrew Teeter. JSJSup 163. Leiden: Brill, 2013.

Uusimäki, Elisa. *Turning Proverbs towards Torah: An Analysis of 4Q525*. STDJ 117. Leiden: Brill, 2016.

———. "Turning Proverbs towards Torah: 4Q525 in the Context of Late Second Temple Wisdom Literature." PhD diss., University of Helsinki, 2013.

Weeks, Stuart. "'Fear God and Keep His Commandments': Could Qohelet Have Said This?" Pages 101–18 in *Wisdom and Torah: The Reception of "Torah" in the Wisdom Literature of the Second Temple Period.* Edited by Bernd U. Schipper and D. Andrew Teeter. JSJSup 163. Leiden: Brill, 2013.

———. *Instruction and Imagery in Proverbs 1–9.* Oxford: Oxford University Press, 2007.

Weinfeld, Moshe. *Deuteronomy and the Deuteronomic School.* Oxford: Oxford University Press, 1972. Repr., Winona Lake, IN: Eisenbrauns, 1992.

———. *Deuteronomy 1–11: A New Translation with Introduction and Commentary.* AB 5. New York: Doubleday, 1991.

Wright, Benjamin G. "Torah and Sapiential Pedagogy in the Book of Ben Sira." Pages 157–86 in *Wisdom and Torah: The Reception of "Torah" in the Wisdom Literature of the Second Temple Period.* Edited by Bernd U. Schipper and D. Andrew Teeter. JSJSup 163. Leiden: Brill, 2013.

Zenger, Erich. "Torafrömmigkeit: Beobachtungen zum poetischen und theologischen Profil vom Psalm 119." Pages 380–96 in *Freiheit und Recht: Festschrift für Frank Crüsemann zum 65. Geburtstag.* Edited by Christof Hardmeier, Rainer Kessler, and Andreas Ruwe. Gütersloh: Kaiser, 2003.

Would Philo Have Recognized Qumran *Musar* as Paideia?

Karina Martin Hogan

Would Philo have recognized Qumran מוסר as παιδεία? When I first asked myself that question, as someone who regularly teaches about both the Dead Sea Scrolls and Philo's works in the context of a graduate introduction to Second Temple Judaism but does not consider herself by any means an expert in either corpus, my initial answer was "of course not." What Philo means by παιδεία is a philosophical education, beginning with training in the liberal arts and aiming at individual wisdom and virtue as its highest goals, whereas מוסר in the Qumran sectarian texts usually means discipline or chastisement, aimed at training members of the יחד (*yahad*, "community") to curb their inclinations and to live according to the regulations of the community. What prompted me to ask the question was discovering that nearly every instance of מוסר and the related verb יסר in Proverbs is translated in the LXX by παιδεία and παιδεύω, respectively.[1] To the translator(s) of Proverbs into Greek, then, these terms must have seemed functionally equivalent, or at least their semantic fields overlapped

---

1. The LXX version of Proverbs is not anomalous within the LXX in the regularity with which it uses παιδεία and παιδεύω to translate מוסר and יסר. In Proverbs, מוסר is translated with παιδεία or its cognate verb in twenty-seven out of thirty instances, and יסר is translated with παιδεύω in all five instances. Taking the nominal and verbal forms together, the equivalency rate is 91 percent. Of the twenty-two occurrences of מוסר in the rest of the Hebrew Bible, fourteen are translated with παιδεία, while of the thirty-seven occurrences of יסר outside of Proverbs, thirty-four are translated with παιδεύω. If the nominal and verbal forms are combined, the rate of equivalency is 81 percent, which is not so different from the rate in Proverbs.

considerably.² So how could these words have come to mean such different things to the Qumran sectarians and to Philo?

I decided to begin my investigation by interrogating the equivalency of מוסר and παιδεία and their cognate verbs in Proverbs. I discovered that the distinction between "discipline" and "instruction" exists more in the mind of the English translator than in either the MT or LXX of Proverbs. There are some verses in which one nuance or the other is clearly dominant, but others in which it is very hard to decide which translation to use. When I turned to the Dead Sea Scrolls, I found a fairly consistent, almost technical usage of מוסר and יסר in the sectarian rule texts (Rule of the Community, Damascus Document, and Rule of the Congregation), but even so, it was hard to decide whether the process of initiation or enculturation that these terms designate should be translated "discipline" or "instruction." The difficulty of determining the nuance of מוסר and יסר was even more pronounced in the wisdom texts discovered at Qumran. Not surprisingly, the usage of מוסר and יסר in these nonsectarian wisdom texts was similar to Proverbs and less specific than the usage in the sectarian rule documents.

The surprise came when I began to investigate the meaning of παιδεία for Philo, focusing on the work in which he discusses παιδεία most extensively, *On Mating with the Preliminary Studies* (Περὶ τῆς πρὸς τὰ προπαιδεύματα συνόδου, the traditional Latin title being *De Congressu quaerendae eruditionis gratia*). Although the concept of παιδεία with which Philo begins the work is clearly a Greek philosophical one (in particular, a Platonic one), as the work progresses he gives several indications that the LXX usage of παιδεία, particularly that of Proverbs, has also contributed to his own understanding of παιδεία. Hence, my admittedly incomplete examination of Philo's understanding of παιδεία forced me to rethink my initial answer that Philo would not have recognized Qumran מוסר as παιδεία. If Philo had been able to read the wisdom literature from Qumran, he would likely have recognized its concept of מוסר as a form of παιδεία, via the common background of παιδεία in the LXX of Proverbs.

---

2. See now the study by Patrick Pouchelle, *Dieu éducateur: Une nouvelle approche d'un concept de la théologie biblique entre Bible Hébraïque, Septante et littérature grecque classique*, FAT 2/77 (Tübingen: Mohr Siebeck, 2015), especially part 2 on the difficult translation of the root יסר in the Hebrew Bible and other Semitic languages, and part 4, on the usage of παιδεία and its cognates in the LXX. For a summary, see the chapter by Pouchelle in this volume.

While the narrower sectarian usage of מוסר has less in common with Philo's use of παιδεία, it is possible that Philo would have recognized the initiation into the way of life of the Qumran sectarians as fitting into his own broad concept of παιδεία.

Musar and Paideia in Proverbs

First, a word about the translation technique of the LXX version of Proverbs is in order. Johann Cook, the leading scholar of the LXX of Proverbs, characterizes it as "an exegetical writing" and describes the translation technique as "remarkably free … in some respects."[3] Those respects include a large number of "double translations," meaning additional, exegetical phrases with no counterpart in the MT. At the same time, he concludes that "the bottom line of [the translator's] approach can be defined as the drive to make the intention of the parent text, *as he understood it*, evident to his readers."[4] In a recent essay, Michael V. Fox concurs with the latter assessment but considers the translator's technique so flexible that it is "almost impossible to characterize the translation as a whole in quantifiable terms."[5] Patrick Pouchelle points out that the almost slavish consistency in translating מוסר and its cognates with παιδεία and its cognates is an exception to the general flexibility of the LXX of Proverbs; he discusses a few variations from this equivalency that seem deliberate, including Prov 1:3, discussed below.[6]

In Proverbs, the meaning of מוסר ranges from instruction leading to wisdom, to verbal correction, to corporal punishment—but in all (or nearly all) cases as part of a regimen of discipline for the sake of improving the future prospects of the one being disciplined. A few examples will have to suffice to illustrate the range of meanings captured by מוסר in Proverbs and translated with παιδεία in the LXX of Proverbs.

---

3. Johann Cook, *The Septuagint of Proverbs: Jewish and/or Hellenistic Proverbs? Concerning the Hellenistic Colouring of LXX Proverbs*, VTSup 69 (Leiden: Brill, 1997), 35–36.

4. Ibid., 316 (emphasis is Cook's).

5. Michael V. Fox, "A Profile of the Septuagint Proverbs," in *Wisdom for Life: Essays Offered to Honor Prof. Maurice Gilbert, SJ on the Occasion of His Eightieth Birthday*, ed. Núria Calduch-Benages, BZAW 445 (Berlin: de Gruyter, 2014), 5.

6. Pouchelle, *Dieu éducateur*, 237–40.

The prologue of Proverbs (Prov 1:1–7) includes the word מוסר three times. In Prov 1:2 it appears in parallelism with חכמה and hence has a noetic nuance (as also in Prov 1:7): "For learning about wisdom and instruction, for understanding perceptive sayings" (אמרי בינה).[7] The next verse specifies a more ethical content to the instruction: "for gaining מוסר in wise dealing, righteousness, justice, and uprightness."[8] The LXX has παιδεία in Prov 1:2 and 1:7, but not in Prov 1:3. In this case, I think Cook is right to assume that the parent text had מוסר in both Prov 1:2 and 1:3, and the LXX translator chose to interpret the second usage with another expression, στροφὰς λόγων, which seems to refer to rhetorical or hermeneutical skill: either the inventive use of language or an understanding of the nuances of words.[9] Cook draws a comparison with Sir 6:22 (MS A), "For מוסר is like her name; she is not straightforward to many (ולא לרבים היא נכוחה), which implies the derivation of מוסר from סור."[10] It is possible that the Greek translator was puzzled by the phrase מוסר השכל and substituted στροφὰς λόγων because it flowed naturally from λόγους φρονήσεως at the end of the previous verse.

Proverbs 1:7, the final verse of the prologue, is the first example of a verse that is greatly expanded in the LXX, in this case by the addition of two additional half-lines. But the fourth half-line in the Greek is a literal rendering of the second half-line in the MT: "fools despise wisdom and מוסר." The second additional half-line in the Greek intensifies the association of wisdom and instruction with "fear of the Lord" in the Hebrew by introducing the term εὐσέβεια ("piety"). The verse in Prov 1:7 in the LXX makes clear that the παιδεία of Proverbs has a moral and religious purpose, a point that might have been lost due to the omission of παιδεία from Prov 1:3.

The abstract, almost mystical, sense of מוסר as the pursuit of wisdom recurs several more times in Proverbs after the prologue, at times being closely associated with personified Wisdom.[11] The injunction in Prov 4:13,

---

7. My translation; unless otherwise indicated, biblical translations are my own.

8. Following NRSV; the first half-line could also mean "for acquiring the discipline for success" (JPS) or even "une correction éclairée" (Pouchelle, understanding השכל as an adjective, in *Dieu éducateur*, 238).

9. Pouchelle (*Dieu éducateur*, 238–39) points out that in the other three occurrences of the noun στροφή in the LXX (Wis 8:8; Sir 39:2; Pss. Sol. 12:2) it is associated with interpretation or complexity.

10. Cook, *Septuagint of Proverbs*, 49–50.

11. See Prov 8:10, 33.

"Keep hold of instruction [החזק במוסר], do not let go; guard her, for she is your life" recalls the famous description of Wisdom in Prov 3:18, "She is a tree of life to those who keep hold of her" (למחזיקים בה)). The LXX, in keeping with the context of a paternal speech (introduced in Prov 4:1) personalizes the injunction: "Take hold of my παιδεία, do not let it go; keep it for yourself, for your life." In doing so, it lends more concreteness to παιδεία: it is not some abstract quality that the addressee is to adhere to, but his own father's teaching. A similar tendency can be observed in the translation of Prov 19:20, which is rather abstract in the Hebrew: "Listen to advice [עצה] and accept מוסר, that you may become wise for your future" (למען תחכם באחריתך). In the same verse in the LXX, παιδεία is personalized and concretized: "Listen, son, to the παιδεία of your father, in order that you may become wise toward your end" (ἵνα σοφὸς γένῃ ἐπ' ἐσχάτων σου).

Many of the occurrences of מוסר in Proverbs have a more disciplinary nuance, however. In nine verses it is associated with תוכחת ("reproof").[12] For example, Prov 12:1 asserts bluntly, "Whoever loves מוסר loves knowledge, but whoever hates reproof is stupid." Here מוסר clearly refers to an aspect of education that includes reproof or reprimand, so "discipline" is an appropriate translation. The same can be said for παιδεία in the LXX version of this verse, which is very close to the Hebrew. The term מוסר/παιδεία in the disciplinary sense sometimes takes the form of corporal punishment. A famous example is Prov 13:24, "The one who spares his rod hates his son; the one who loves [his son] is intent on disciplining him." The Greek translation is again very faithful: "The one who spares the rod hates his son; but the one who loves carefully disciplines"—using the verb παιδεύω for "disciplines."

The association of מוסר with "life" that connects it with Wisdom in Prov 4:13 is also found in Prov 6:23, where מוסר has a clear disciplinary nuance: "For the commandment is a lamp and the teaching a light, and the reproofs of discipline are the way of life." In the MT, the "commandment" and the "teaching" refer back to Prov 6:20, "My son, keep your father's commandment, and do not forsake the teaching of your mother." The LXX translation of Prov 6:23 is free with respect to the syntax, transforming the first half of the verse from a comment on parental instruction to one on the torah of Moses: "For the commandment of the law [ἐντολὴ νόμου]

---

12. See Prov 3:11; 5:12; 6:23; 10:17; 12:1; 13:18; 15:5, 10, 32.

is a lamp and a light, and reproof and discipline [ἔλεγχος καὶ παιδεία] the way of life." Much could be said about how this transformation changes the meaning of the verse, but for present purposes I am interested in the association of מוסר/παιδεία in the disciplinary sense with the "way of life." Proverbs 6:23, in both Hebrew and Greek, shows that it is impossible to distinguish between מוסר/παιδεία as instruction leading to wisdom and the disciplinary sense of those terms. In both Hebrew and Greek Proverbs, physical punishment and verbal rebuke are part of the same educational process that leads to wisdom and "life."

One more example will suffice to illustrate this conclusion: מוסר occurs in both Prov 23:12 and 23:13, apparently in different senses: "Apply your mind [לבך] to מוסר"—I would translate "instruction" here—"and your ear to words of knowledge" (Prov 23:12); and "Do not withhold מוסר"—here, "discipline"—"from a child [or better, 'from a youth'; מנער]; if you beat him with a rod, he will not die" (Prov 23:13). The following verse clarifies that the expression "he will not die" does not just mean "it will not kill him": "[If] you beat him with a rod, you will save his life from Sheol" (Prov 23:14). The LXX adds a verb to the second half-line of Prov 23:12 and uses the verb παιδεύω rather than the noun in 23:13, but neither change substantially alters the meaning of the two verses. So in both the MT and the LXX versions of Prov 23:12–13, we see the full range of meanings of מוסר/παιδεία and how the noetic and disciplinary senses of these terms both aim at the same goal: "life," in the shorthand of Proverbs. Not only do they aim at the same goal, but since they are indistinguishable verbally, the distinction between instruction and discipline is one that we modern readers and translators impose on Proverbs.

Qumran *Musar*

The noun מוסר and the verb יסר are not terribly frequent in the sectarian texts from Qumran, but they are used in a consistent and almost technical sense to refer to the process of indoctrination or enculturation into the distinctive regulated life of the sect. For example, the Rule of the Community describes a person who is not worthy to enter the יחד as follows (1QS II, 25–III, 1; III, 5–6):[13]

---

13. Unless otherwise noted, I follow the translations of Florentino García Martínez and Eibert J. C. Tighchelaar, *The Dead Sea Scrolls Study Edition*, 2 vols. (Leiden: Brill; Grand Rapids: Eerdmans, 1997–1998).

II, 25 And anyone who declines to enter [26] [the covenant of Go]d in order to walk in the stubbornness of his heart shall not [enter the Com]munity of his truth, since [III, 1] his soul loathes the disciplines of knowledge of just judgments [כי געלה נפשו ביסורי דעת משפטי צדק]. He has not the strength to convert his life and shall not be counted among the upright.... [5] Nor shall he be purified by all the water of ablution. Defiled, defiled shall he be all the days he spurns the decrees [6] of God, without allowing himself to be taught by the Community of his counsel [לבלתי התיסר ביחד עצתו].

The root יסר is used twice in this passage (1QS III, 1, 6) to designate a distinctly sectarian form of "discipline" or "instruction." The nominal form, מוסר, occurs in the Rule of the Community in a similar context involving someone's worthiness to enter the community (1QS VI, 13–15):

VI, 13 And anyone from Israel who freely volunteers [14] to enroll in the council of the Community, the man appointed at the head of the Many shall examine him with regard to his insight and his deeds [... ידורשהו לשכלו ולמעשיו]. If he suits [or: "attains to"] the discipline [ואם ישיג מוסר], he shall let him enter [15] into the covenant so that he can revert to the truth and shun all injustice, and he shall teach him all the precepts of the Community.

The translation "the discipline," despite the lack of a definite article on מוסר, suggests that the translators recognize it as a technical term, referring to the period of probation and instruction required to become a member of the "council of the community," as described in the following lines (1QS VI, 15–23). The verb יסר also occurs near the end of a passage in the Rule of the Community explaining the raison d'être of the *yahad* (1QS IX, 3–11). The final lines read:

IX, 9 They should not depart from any counsel of the law in order to walk [10] in complete stubbornness of their heart, but instead shall be ruled by the first directives which the men of the Community began to be taught [ונשפטו במשפטים הרשונים אשר החלו אנשי היחד לתיסר בם] [11] until the prophet comes, and the Messiahs of Aaron and Israel.

It is not entirely clear whether the verb לתיסר, to be construed as a *hithpael*, should be translated as a passive ("to be taught") or a reflexive ("to discipline themselves") here, since there is no mention in this passage of a teacher, and in the remainder of the pericope the men of the community are the subject of active verbs. There are two passages in the Damascus Document, however, that use the verb יסר in the *hithpael* stem in a similar context, looking back to the founding of the community. The first is CD IV, 6–10:

> IV, 6 They were the forefathers [הם הרא[שונים]], for whom 7 God atoned, and who declared the just man as just and declared the wicked as wicked, and all those who entered after them 8 in order to act according to the exact interpretation of the law in which the forefathers were instructed [לעשׂות כפרוש התורה אשר התוסרו בו הראשנים] until 9 the period of these years is complete. According to the covenant which God established with the forefathers, in order to atone 10 for their iniquities, so will God atone for them.

The other passage is in the B text of the Damascus Document (CD XX, 27–34):

> XX, 27 But all those who remain steadfast in these regulations [וכל המחזיקים במשפטים האלא], [co]ming and going in accordance with the law, and listen to the Teacher's voice …30 and they do not raise their hand against his holy regulations and his just 31 judgments and his truthful stipulations; and they are instructed in the first ordinances [והתיסרו במשפטים הראשונים] 32 in conformity with which the men of the Unique One were judged; and they lend their ears to the voice of the Teacher of Righteousness …34 and God will atone for them, and they shall see his salvation, for they have taken refuge in his holy name.

The verb יסר in the *hithpael* refers in the first of these passages to the founders of the sect (הראשונים) being instructed in sectarian interpretation of the torah, and in the second to being instructed in the "first ordinances" (משפטים הראשונים), which are associated with the Teacher of Righteousness. Although both passages locate this sectarian "instruction" in the past, they also imply that the current members of the sect live their lives in accordance with the regulations established at the beginning, and hence that the instruction is ongoing. It is less clear than in the Rule of the Community that the instruction functions as an initiation into the sect, but it clearly includes sectarian halakah.

In the Rule of the Congregation, the noun מוסר is used for the education of a child born into the community, prior to his being enrolled in the congregation (1QSa I, 6–8):

1, 6 And this is the rule for all the armies of the congregation, for all native Israelites. From his yo[uth] 7 [they shall edu]cate him in the book of Hagy, and according to his age, instruct him in the precept[s of] the covenant, and he will [receive] 8 his [ins]truction in their regulations [ול]קחת] [מו]סרו במשפטיהמה]; during ten years he will be counted among the children.

It is clear from the previous lines (1QSa I, 4–5) that the congregation includes women and children and that they are to be instructed in "all the precepts of the covenant" (כ]ול חוקי הברית]) and "in all their regulations" (בכול משפטיהמה); the מוסר in view here is a specifically sectarian education. The Damascus Document also refers in passing to the education of children; in the case of parents who divorce, the Inspector of the camp (המבקר למחנה) "shall inst[ruct [ייסר] their children] ... [and their small children with a spirit of] modesty and compassionate love" (CD XIII, 17–18 // 4Q269 10 II, 2). In this case there is no indication of the content of the instruction, though presumably it included sectarian halakah, but the emphasis on a compassionate mode of instruction is noteworthy.

Given how prevalent the noun מוסר and its cognates are in Proverbs, it is surprising how rarely they occur in the wisdom texts discovered at Qumran. Even in 4QInstruction, which takes its name from the title assigned by the editors, *musar lemebin*, "Instruction for the Understanding One," מוסר is not a key term. It occurs only four times (two of them identical, from overlapping fragments, and one doubtful) and the verb יסר not at all (according to the *Dead Sea Scrolls Concordance*).[14] By contrast, מבין occurs at least sixteen times.[15]

Only in the instance of the two overlapping fragments is there enough context to determine the sense in which מוסר is being used:

[12] You are poor; do not say, I am poor and (therefore) I can no[t] [13] seek knowledge. Apply your shoulder to all *musar* [בכל מוסר הבא שכמכה], and with all ... refine (?) your heart, and with abundance of understanding, [14] your thoughts.

---

14. Martin G. Abegg, James E. Bowley, Edward M. Cook, eds., *The Dead Sea Scrolls Concordance*, 3 vols. (Leiden: Brill, 2003–2010), listing 4Q416 2 III, 13 // 4Q418 9+9a–c 13; 4Q418 169+170 3; 4Q418 297 1 (doubtful).

15. See John Kampen, *Wisdom Literature*, ECDSS (Grand Rapids: Eerdmans, 2011), 51 n. 63.

Here the idiom "apply your shoulder to" can be illuminated by comparison with other instances of the construction הביא + body part + ב + object[16] and other metaphorical uses of "shoulder"[17] in biblical Hebrew to determine that מוסר is being conceptualized metaphorically as a burden, or more literally as a task that requires effort. On the other hand, the context is rich in noetic terminology: knowledge (דעת), understanding (בינה), and "your thoughts" (מחשבותיכה).[18] Hence, either "discipline" or "instruction" would be an appropriate translation here, since the difficulty and effort involved is conveyed by the idiom "apply your shoulder." This usage is entirely consistent with Proverbs, which assumes that מוסר is something that is frequently rejected or neglected.[19]

There is a possible occurrence of מוסר in 4Q412, Sapiential-Didactic Work A, but it is more plausibly read as מוֹסֵר ("bond"), in keeping with the metaphorical context: "Place a bond on your lips and for your tongue (place) doors of protection."[20] Although מוסר is probably attested once in Mysteries (4Q299 30 4), there is too little context to determine its nuance. By contrast, 4Q424 (titled Instruction-like Composition B), provides a good deal of context for its single attestation of מוסר. Near the end of fragment 3, there is a list of the distinguishing habits of various types of virtuous men, parallel to the advice about negative types in fragment 1 and earlier in fragment 3.

> [7] A man of intelligence (or prudence) accepts instruction [איש שכל יקבל
> מוס]ר]. A man of knowledge obtains wisdom [איש ידע יפיק חכמה]....
> [8] A man of uprightness takes delight in justice. A man of truth re[joices in a prov]erb. A man of substance is zealous for ... [9] [and h]e is an adver-

---

16. E.g., Neh 3:5; Jer 27:12; Prov 23:12. See also 4Q438 3 3, "I have submitted my neck to your yoke and *musar*."

17. E.g., Gen 49:15; Isa 9:3; 10:27; 14:25.

18. Moreover, it is likely that the word that is missing after "and with all" is "wisdom," given how frequently חכמה appears in combination with מוסר, בינה, and דעת in Proverbs and in the Qumran wisdom texts. I am grateful to my colleague Sarit Kattan Gribetz for pointing this out to me.

19. E.g., Prov 3:11; 5:12; 8:33; 13:18; 15:5, 32; 19:27.

20. This is Annette Steudel's interpretation, in Torleif Elgvin et al., eds., *Qumran Cave 4.XV: Sapiential Texts*, part 1, DJD 20 (Oxford: Clarendon, 1997), 164–65. Matthew Goff prefers to read it as *musar*; see his *Discerning Wisdom: The Sapiential Literature of the Dead Sea Scrolls*, VTSup 116 (Leiden: Brill, 2007), 271.

sary to all who "move the boundary." A man of generosit[y perfo]rms charity for the poor.[21]

As Matthew Goff has noted, the ethic of 4Q424 is entirely compatible with Prov 10–31.[22] The association of intelligence or prudence with accepting מוסר recalls, for example, Prov 19:20: "Listen to advice and accept instruction, that you may gain wisdom for your future." It appears that the nuance of מוסר in 4Q424 is noetic, as in Prov 1:2; but just as Prov 1:3 mentions justice, righteousness, and equity as objects of מוסר along with "wise dealing" or prudence (השכל), 4Q424 quickly transitions from intelligence and knowledge to moral virtues. If the order in which the virtues are mentioned is significant, one could infer that the ultimate goal of accepting מוסר and obtaining wisdom is to become a defender of justice and someone who "performs charity for the poor."

The extremely fragmentary 4Q425 (Sapiential-Didactic Work B) includes the word מוסר in the first line of the text's longest passage, a combination of fragments 1 and 3. There is enough context to determine the nuance; the first line has been reconstructed to read כו[ל] מוסר תועבה דב]ר ה[מב]קר] ("[eve]ry correction of abomination is a mat[ter of the] Inspec[tor])." Although the reconstruction of the line as a whole is uncertain, the words מוסר תועבה are complete and legible, and assuming they belong together in construct, it seems safe to say that מוסר has a disciplinary nuance and "correction" or "discipline" is the best translation.

Fragment 1 of 4QBeatitudes (4Q525), which may preserve the beginning of the work, resembles the opening verses of Proverbs so much that מוסר can be reconstructed with great confidence in line 2 from its first two letters:

> [1] [which he has sai]d with the wisdom God gave him [2] ... [in order to kn]ow wisdom and disci[pline] [[לדע]ת חוכמה ומו[סר] ...]], in order to understand (להשכיל) ... [3] in order to increase kn[owledge] (להוסיף [ד]עת)

---

21. Trans. of Sarah Tanzer in Stephen J. Pfann and Philip S. Alexander, eds., *Qumran Cave 4.XXVI: Cryptic Texts and Miscellanea*, part 1, DJD 36 (Oxford: Clarendon, 2000), 343.

22. Goff, *Discerning Wisdom*, 196–97.

There is not much more to say about this usage of מוסר than that it is apparently an allusion to Prov 1:2. Hence, the nuance of מוסר is noetic and it should be translated "instruction."

Most of the attestations of the verb יסר in the Qumran texts are found in fragments of the Damascus Document and Rule of the Community, considered above. There happens to be only one surviving usage in a wisdom text, in 4QWays of Righteousness (4Q421 1a I, 6). There has been a move away from classifying this composition as a wisdom text and toward considering it a rule book, due to the presence of stipulations similar to those in the Damascus Document and Rule of the Community.[23] Nevertheless, many of the fragments contain wisdom sayings, and the fragment containing יסר begins with several wisdom terms in the second line: "his wisdom, his knowledge, and his insight" (חכמתו ודעתו ובינתו), followed (less clearly) by וטובו, "and his goodness" or "and his good things." Then in 4Q421 1a I, 5 we find "our words will be approved/carefully observed" ([י]תישרו אמרינו), followed in line 6 by [...]תו ליסרו. The following lines are unfortunately missing, so the interpretation must be based on the preceding lines 3 and 4, which read לסרך הכול איש לפני רע[הו] ("to arrange/rank everyone, one before the other"), and [יצ]א הגורל הרישון וכן יצאו ("the first lot will fall/go out and thus they will go out"). Based on similar passages in the Rule of the Community that discuss ranking members of the community hierarchically (1QS V, 23) and by lot (e.g., 1QS VI, 21–22), Elgvin persuasively argues that the topic of this fragment is "sectarian organization."[24] Therefore, based on the usage of יסר in the sectarian scrolls, the best translation of ליסרו in 4Q421 1a I, 6 is "to discipline him" or "to train him," in the technical sense of initiating him into the ways of the community.[25]

Thus, although the sample size is small, this survey of the usage of מוסר and יסר in the Qumran wisdom texts shows a similar range of meanings to Proverbs. In fact, the usage of these terms is clearly informed by Proverbs in some cases. As with Proverbs, while some usages could be classified as clearly either noetic or disciplinary, others could go either way, showing that this distinction is foreign to the texts and is only of concern to the

---

23. Goff, *Discerning Wisdom*, 160–61.
24. Elgvin, *Sapiential Texts*, 186; Goff, *Discerning Wisdom*, 174–75.
25. According to Elgvin (*Sapiential Texts*, 187), "In this text the Piʻel form indicates that a superior member disciplines another member." He cites as parallels CD IV, 8; VII, 5, 7–8; and 1QS IX, 10.

modern translator. Even in the sectarian rule documents, where the usage is fairly consistent, the translator is hard-pressed to choose a consistent translation, since מוסר in the ways of the יחד includes both instruction and discipline.

Philo's Understanding of Paideia in *On Mating with the Preliminary Studies*

Philo's understanding of παιδεία, both as a process and as a goal, is shaped by many Greek philosophical ideas, but the Platonic influence is the most pronounced, as Hindy Najman has argued in her essay "Text and Figure in Ancient Jewish *Paideia*."[26] Philo pronounces Plato "most holy" (ἱερώτατος), an adjective he otherwise reserves for Moses (*Prob.* 13).[27] Philosophical education, for Philo as for Plato, aims at knowledge of a truth that transcends the reality available to sense perception, and its goal is wisdom and virtue. But Philo, like Plato (in book 7 of the *Republic*), recognized the need for a course of "preliminary studies" in the liberal arts as a foundation for a philosophical education.[28] It was something of a commonplace among Hellenistic philosophers that most people who attempt a philosophical education fail, and like Penelope's failed suitors in the *Odyssey*, satisfy themselves with the handmaidens of philosophy, the liberal arts (Pseudo-Plutarch, *Lib. ed.* 7D).[29] In keeping with this maxim, Philo discusses both the benefits and the pitfalls of the liberal arts in his allegorical interpretation of the story of Abraham's relationships with Sarah and Hagar in Gen 16, *On Mating with the Preliminary Studies*.[30]

For Philo, several of the heroes of the Pentateuch serve as models of wisdom to be imitated, but Abraham is the prime example of the educational

---

26. This essay is available in Hindy Najman, *Past Renewals: Interpretive Authority, Renewed Revelation and the Quest for Perfection in Jewish Antiquity*, JSJSup 53 (Leiden: Brill, 2010), 243–56.

27. See also *Aet.* 52 and *Contempl.* 57. Cited by Maren Niehoff, *Philo on Jewish Identity and Culture*, TSAJ 86 (Tübingen: Mohr Siebeck, 2001), 138.

28. Alan Mendelson, *Secular Education in Philo of Alexandria* (Cincinnati: Hebrew Union College Press, 1982), xxiii–xxiv.

29. Cited by Peder Borgen, *Philo of Alexandria: An Exegete for His Time*, NovTSup 86 (Leiden: Brill, 1997), 163. Mendelson (*Secular Education*, xxiii) attributes the same maxim to Ariston of Chios.

30. See Jason Zurawski's second chapter in this volume, "Mosaic Torah as Encyclical Paideia: Reading Paul's Allegory of Hagar and Sarah in Light of Philo of Alexandria's."

model, because he alone progresses from the status of a "heaven-born" man to become a "man of God."[31] In *On the Giants* (60–63), Philo explains that there are three types of people: the earth-born, the heaven-born, and the God-born.[32] The earth-born are only interested in the pleasures of the body, and at the other extreme:

> The men of God are priests and prophets who have refused to accept membership in the commonwealth of the world and to become citizens therein, but have risen wholly above the sphere of sense-perception and have been translated into the world of the intelligible and dwell there registered as freemen of the commonwealth of Ideas, which are imperishable and incorporeal. (*Gig.* 61)[33]

Isaac is an example of the God-born, and also of the self-taught (αὐτομαθὲς) type, who do not have to perfect their virtue by learning or practice because they are virtuous by nature.[34] The middle category of the heaven-born, to which Abram belonged before his name was changed (*Gig.* 62–63), is defined by devotion to education:

> The heaven-born are the votaries of the arts [τεχνῖται] and of knowledge, the lovers of learning. For the heavenly element in us is the mind, as the heavenly beings are each of them a mind. And it is the mind which pursues the learning of the schools [τὰ ἐγκύκλια] and the other arts one and all, which sharpens and whets itself, and trains and drills itself solid in the contemplation of what is intelligible by mind.

Philo describes the process by which Abram was perfected and became a man of God via an allegorical interpretation of Gen 16 in *On*

---

31. Mendelson, *Secular Education*, 47–54, 62–64.
32. Loren T. Stuckenbruck points out some intriguing parallels between Philo's interpretation of Gen 6:1–4 in *On the Giants* and both the Book of the Watchers (esp. 1 En. 15–16) and the Treatise on the Two Spirits in the Community Rule (1QS III, 13–IV, 26); see Stuckenbruck, "To What Extent Did Philo's Treatment of Enoch and the Giants Presuppose a Knowledge of the Enochic and Other Sources Preserved in the Dead Sea Scrolls?," *SPhiloA* 19 (2007): 131–42.
33. All translations of Philo herein are by F. H. Colson and G. H. Whitaker, *Philo*, 10 vols., LCL (Cambridge: Harvard University Press, 1949–1962).
34. *Congr.* 35–36; see also *Abr.* 50–54. See also Mendelson, *Secular Education*, 106 n. 92.

*Mating with the Preliminary Studies.*³⁵ Sarah or Sarai, whose name Philo interprets to mean "sovereignty of me" (ἀρχή μου), represents every virtue of the individual (*Congr.* 2). She is barren only in relation to Abraham, "for we are not capable as yet of receiving the impregnation of virtue unless we have first mated with her handmaiden, and the handmaiden of wisdom is the culture gained by the primary learning of the school course" (ἡ διὰ τῶν προπαιδευμάτων ἐγκύκλιος μουσική; *Congr.* 9). So Sarai gives Abram her handmaiden, Hagar, who represents an "all-around" (ἐγκύκλιος) course of studies: grammar, geometry, astronomy, rhetoric, and music are mentioned in *Congr.* 11, and dialectic, "the sister and twin ... of rhetoric," in *Congr.* 18.³⁶ Philo compares these school subjects to the "simple and milky foods of infancy ... while the virtues are grown-up food, suited for those who are really men" (*Congr.* 19). Toward the end of the treatise, he explains why Abram puts Hagar in Sarai's hands, calling her "the servant-girl" (ἡ παιδίσκη) to denote both immaturity and servitude (Gen 16:6): "while what is implied by the slave belongs to the domain of the hands in the bodily sense, since the school subjects require the bodily organs and faculties, what is implied by the mistress reaches to the soul, for wisdom and knowledge and their implications are referred to the reasoning faculties" (*Congr.* 154–55).

Although Abram is certainly not young in Gen 16, Philo goes on to compare Abram's mating with Hagar while remaining married to Sarai with his own experiences "in early youth" of studying grammar, geometry and music, while never losing sight of his "lawful wife" and the mistress of these handmaids, Philosophy (*Congr.* 73–76). He contrasts his own experience (and Abraham's) with those who, having grown old, "have been ensnared by the love lures of the handmaids and spurned the mistress" (*Congr.* 77). At the end of this passage, he lays out most clearly the path from preliminary studies to wisdom (*Congr.* 79):³⁷

---

35. An abbreviated version of the allegory can be found in *Leg.* 3.244–45.

36. The translation "all-around" for ἐγκύκλιος is suggested by Hent de Vries (following L. M. DeRijk) in his "*Philosophia Ancilla Theologiae*: Allegory and Ascension in Philo's *On Mating with the Preliminary Studies* (*De Congressu Quarendae Eruditionis Gratia*)," trans. Jack Ben-Levi, *BCT* 5 (2009): 41.7.

37. See also *Spec.* 2.230, where, in enumerating the benefits that parents confer on their children, Philo speaks of the school subjects as leading to philosophy and hence to a vision of heaven and reliance on God (cited by Niehoff, *Philo on Jewish Identity*, 181). Niehoff notes the elite and male-oriented biases of Philo's discourse on education (ibid., 181–85).

And indeed just as the school subjects [τὰ ἐγκύκλια] contribute to the acquirement of philosophy, so does philosophy to the getting of wisdom. For philosophy is the practice or study of wisdom, and wisdom is the knowledge of things divine and human and their causes. And therefore just as the culture of the schools [ἡ ἐγκύκλιος μουσική] is [the servant] of philosophy, so must philosophy be the servant of wisdom.

The timing of Abram's mating with Hagar, ten years after coming to Canaan from Egypt, is associated with reaching the proper age for the encyclical studies, since Philo identifies Egypt with childhood, the senses and the passions, and Canaan with adolescence and the vices (*Congr.* 83–85).[38] As he does frequently, Philo universalizes Abram's experience (*Congr.* 88; see also 121):

> So then ten years after our migration to the Canaanites we shall wed Hagar, since as soon as we have become reasoning beings we take to ourselves the ignorance and indiscipline [ἀπαιδευσίας] whose nature is to be mischievous and only after a time and under the perfect number ten do we reach the desire for the lawful discipline [νομίμου παιδείας] which can profit us.

Not surprisingly to those who know Philo, this comment gives rise to a lengthy excursus on the "perfect number ten" (*Congr.* 89–120). One example from this excursus, *Congr.* 94, is highly relevant to our subject and lends support to the translation of παιδεία with "discipline" in the previous quotation:

> Furthermore, everything that comes "under the rod" [ὑπὸ τὴν ῥάβδον], meaning discipline [λέγω δὲ τὴν παιδείαν], that is every tame and docile creature, has a tenth set apart from it which by the ordinance of the law becomes "holy" [Lev 27:32], that so through many reminders we may learn the close connection of ten with God and nine with our mortal race.

The identification of a rod or shepherd's staff with παιδεία is quite common in Philo's works, occurring in at least four other places: in *Leg.*

---

38. See also *Her.* 295–296, where Philo establishes a connection between adolescence (youth) and sinfulness based on Gen 8:21. See Maren Niehoff's discussion of "Transforming New-Born Children into Jewish Adults" in Niehoff, *Philo on Jewish Identity*, 162.

2.89–90 in connection with Moses's staff in Exod 4:3; in *Sacr.* 63 in reference to the Passover commandment to eat standing up with a staff in one's hand (Exod 12:11); in *Post.* 97, again with reference to Lev 27:32; and in *Fug.* 150, in reference to Judah's staff in Gen 38:18.[39] Although Philo never explains why a rod or staff symbolizes παιδεία, it seems quite likely that the association was suggested by Proverbs, perhaps particularly Prov 22:15, "Folly is bound up in the heart of a youth (נער), but the rod of discipline (שבט מוסר) drives it far away from him." In the LXX version of this verse, the endorsement of corporal punishment is not quite as strong, but the association is still present: "Folly is attached to the heart of a youth, but the rod and discipline [ῥάβδος δὲ καὶ παιδεία] are far from him." Compare also the association of the rod with discipline in Prov 13:24 and 23:13, discussed above.

The disciplinary connotation of παιδεία recurs at the end of the treatise, where Philo attempts to justify Sarai's affliction of Hagar by giving several biblical examples of beneficial afflictions. He concludes, "Let us not, then, be misled by the actual words, but look at the allegorical meaning that lies beneath them, and say that 'afflicted' [ἐκάκωσε] is equivalent to 'disciplined and admonished and chastened'" (ἐπαίδευσε καὶ ἐνουθέτησε καὶ ἐσωφρόνισε; *Congr.* 172). Acknowledging that slavery is the most humiliating form of affliction (*Congr.* 175), Philo nevertheless claims that it can be a blessing, since Isaac "blessed" Esau with being a slave to his brother (*Congr.* 176). Is Philo implying that Hagar should have been grateful to be afflicted by Sarah? I think so, because he goes on to quote Prov 3:11–12 LXX, "My son, despise not the discipline [παιδείας] of God, nor faint when you are rebuked by him, for whom the Lord loves he rebukes [ἐλέγχει], and scourges [μαστιγοῖ] every son whom he receives" (*Congr.* 177).[40] Further, Philo imagines Moses explaining his strange expression in Exod 22:22, "If you afflict them with evil" (ἐὰν δὲ κακίᾳ κακώσητε αὐτούς) as follows: "I know that one may be rebuked by virtue [ὑπὸ ἀρετῆς ἐλεγχόμενον] and disciplined by wisdom [καὶ ὑπὸ φρονήσεως παιδευόμενον], and therefore I do not hold all afflicting … to be blameworthy" (διόπερ οὐ πᾶσαν κάκωσιν ἐν αἰτίᾳ τίθημαι; *Congr.* 179).

Philo's allegorical treatment of Gen 16 as an account of Abraham's education and perfection in virtue upholds a very lofty view of the goal

---

39. Georg Bertram, "Παιδεύω κτλ.," *TDNT* 5:614.
40. The word order in Philo's quotation differs a bit from the present LXX, and interestingly, he has ἐλέγχει in Prov 3:12, where the LXX has παιδεύει.

of παιδεία. At the same time, Philo shares with Proverbs an understanding of παιδεία as discipline, which he is able to incorporate into his account of Abraham's education via the subordinate status of Hagar as a slave and an Egyptian.[41] Because Philo associates Egypt with childhood, the body, and the senses, it is not surprising that he would understand Sarai "afflicting" Hagar in a pedagogical sense, even though, to a modern reader, that element of the story seems hard to reconcile with an allegorical reading in which Hagar represents the liberal arts. But Philo's understanding of παιδεία, which is informed as much by Proverbs as by Plato, includes both the disciplinary and noetic nuances of מוסר in Proverbs. Therefore, in spite of his allegorical approach to interpretation and his own highly Hellenized education, I think Philo would have recognized מוסר in the Qumran wisdom texts, and perhaps even in the sectarian rule texts, as a kind of παιδεία. Besides the common heritage of Proverbs, the Qumran texts and Philo share a set of values rooted in the commandments of the torah, so in a broad sense, they are oriented toward similar understandings of virtue and piety.[42]

BIBLIOGRAPHY

Abegg, Martin G., James E. Bowley, and Edward M. Cook, eds. *The Dead Sea Scrolls Concordance*. 3 vols. Leiden: Brill, 2003–2010.
Bertram, Georg. "Παιδεύω κτλ." *TDNT* 5:596–625.
Borgen, Peder. *Philo of Alexandria: An Exegete for His Time*. NovTSup 86. Leiden: Brill, 1997.

---

41. It clearly serves Philo's ends in this treatise to emphasize Hagar's Egyptian origins and slave status, rendering her "disposable" because she represents a stage of paideia that the philosopher must leave behind. In another context, however, Philo seeks to minimize those very traits. In *Abr.* 251, where Sarai is persuading Abram to father a child with Hagar, Sarai describes Hagar as "outwardly a slave, inwardly of free and noble race … an Egyptian by birth, but a Hebrew by her rule of life." Alan Mendelson opines that "this elevation of Hagar is not warranted by Scripture (cf. Gen 16 and 21)" in *Philo's Jewish Identity*, BJS 161 (Atlanta: Scholars Press, 1988), 72. That judgment is open to question, however; see Tikva Frymer-Kensky's sympathetic reading of Hagar as "the archetype of Israel" in *Reading the Women of the Bible: A New Interpretation of Their Stories* (New York: Schocken Books, 2002), 225–37.

42. As observed by John J. Collins, "Philo and the Dead Sea Scrolls: Introduction," *SPhiloA* 19 (2007): 81–83.

Collins, John J. "Philo and the Dead Sea Scrolls: Introduction." *SPhiloA* 19 (2007): 81–83.

Cook, Johann. *The Septuagint of Proverbs: Jewish and/or Hellenistic Proverbs? Concerning the Hellenistic Colouring of LXX Proverbs.* VTSup 69. Leiden: Brill, 1997.

Elgvin, Torleif, Menachem Kister, Timothy C. Lim, Bilhah Nitzan, Stephen J. Pfann, Elisha Qimron, Lawrence H. Schiffman, and Annette Steudel, eds. *Qumran Cave 4.XV: Sapiential Texts.* Part 1. DJD 20. Oxford: Clarendon, 1997.

Fox, Michael V. "A Profile of the Septuagint Proverbs." Pages 3–17 in *Wisdom for Life: Essays Offered to Honor Prof. Maurice Gilbert, SJ on the Occasion of His Eightieth Birthday.* Edited by Núria Calduch-Benages. BZAW 445. Berlin: de Gruyter, 2014.

Frymer-Kensky, Tikva. *Reading the Women of the Bible: A New Interpretation of Their Stories.* New York: Schocken Books, 2002.

García Martínez, Florentino, and Eibert J. C. Tighchelaar. *The Dead Sea Scrolls Study Edition.* 2 vols. Leiden: Brill; Grand Rapids: Eerdmans, 1997–1998.

Goff, Matthew J. *Discerning Wisdom: The Sapiential Literature of the Dead Sea Scrolls.* VTSup 116. Leiden: Brill, 2007.

Kampen, John. *Wisdom Literature.* ECDSS. Grand Rapids: Eerdmans, 2011.

Mendelson, Alan. *Philo's Jewish Identity.* BJS 161. Atlanta: Scholars Press, 1988.

———. *Secular Education in Philo of Alexandria.* Cincinnati: Hebrew Union College Press, 1982.

Najman, Hindy. *Past Renewals: Interpretive Authority, Renewed Revelation and the Quest for Perfection in Jewish Antiquity.* JSJSup 53. Leiden: Brill, 2010.

Niehoff, Maren. *Philo on Jewish Identity and Culture.* TSAJ 86. Tübingen: Mohr Siebeck, 2001.

Pfann, Stephen J., and Philip S. Alexander, eds. *Qumran Cave 4.XXVI: Cryptic Texts and Miscellanea.* Part 1. DJD 36. Oxford: Clarendon, 2000.

Philo. Translated by F. H. Colson and G. H. Whitaker. 10 vols. LCL. Cambridge: Harvard University Press, 1949–1962.

Pouchelle, Patrick. *Dieu éducateur: Une nouvelle approche d'un concept de la théologie biblique entre Bible Hébraïque, Septante et littérature grecque classique.* FAT 2/77. Tübingen: Mohr Siebeck, 2015.

Stuckenbruck, Loren T. "To What Extent Did Philo's Treatment of Enoch and the Giants Presuppose a Knowledge of the Enochic and Other Sources Preserved in the Dead Sea Scrolls?" *SPhiloA* 19 (2007): 131–42.

Vries, Hent de. "*Philosophia Ancilla Theologiae*: Allegory and Ascension in Philo's *On Mating with the Preliminary Studies* (*De Congressu Quaerendae Eruditionis Gratia*)." Translated by Jack Ben-Levi. *BCT* 5 (2009): 41.1–19.

Kyropaideia versus Paideia Kyriou: The Semantic Transformation of Paideia and Cognates in the Translated Books of the Septuagint

Patrick Pouchelle

Any study of pedagogy in early Judaism raises the question of its relationship with Greek paideia, whose influence may well have been very important throughout the Hellenistic kingdoms. In that respect, the decision of translators of the Septuagint (LXX) to use a word of the family of παιδεύω to translate the Semitic root יסר, probably at the time of translating the Pentateuch, is striking. The correspondence between the root יסר and words of the family of παιδεύω is so strong that of around one hundred occurrences of the root יסר in the Masoretic Text (MT), only twelve do not correspond to παιδεύω and cognates in the LXX, including six occurrences with no correspondence at all.[1]

Among the ancient translations of the Hebrew Bible, only the Targum Neofiti is as systematic as the LXX in the translation of the root יסר. To take one example, in the Pentateuch, the Vulgate uses *erudio*, "to educate" (Deut 8:5); *correptio/corriptio*, "to rebuke" (Lev 16:18, 28); *doceo*, "to teach" (Deut 4:26); *coerceo*, "to rebuke" (Deut 21:18); and *verbero*, "to chastise" (Deut 22:18).[2] In the LXX, the only exception is the Old Greek of Job, which renders יסר with νουθετέω and cognates, similarly

---

[1]. Jer 10:8, Jer 30:11, and Prov 8:33 are verses with no parallel in the LXX. For the LXX of Hos 7:15, Ezek 5:15, and Job 36:10, where there is nothing corresponding to the root יסר, see Patrick Pouchelle, *Dieu éducateur: Une nouvelle approche d'un concept de la théologie biblique entre Bible Hébraïque, Septante et littérature grecque classique*, FAT 2/77 (Tübingen,: Mohr Siebeck, 2015), 234–35. As for the occurrences of יסר that correspond to a Greek word other than παιδεύω and cognates, see ibid., 235–43.

[2]. Even the Peshitta, which systematically renders יסר by רדא, makes an exception for Deut 4:36, with אלף.

to Josephus, whereas the asterisked material of Job follows the LXX with παιδεύω and cognates.³

The choice of the LXX is a systematic rendering, but the semantic fields of the Hebrew and the Greek terms are not identical. To take just one example, Deut 22:18 deals with the punishment of a young man who gives a false testimony:

ולקחו זקני העיר־ההוא את־האיש ויסרו אתו
The elders of that town shall take the man and punish him. (NRSV)

καὶ λήμψεται ἡ γερουσία τῆς πόλεως ἐκείνης τὸν ἄνθρωπον ἐκεῖνον καὶ παιδεύσουσιν αὐτόν.
And the council of elders of that city shall take that man and discipline him. (NETS)

In the frame of the "interlinear paradigm," which constitutes the organizational pattern of the *New English Translation of the Septuagint* (NETS),⁴ the replacement of "punish" by "discipline" is problematic. There is only one reason why here NETS dares to change NRSV: the lexical choice of the NRSV to represent the Hebrew differs significantly from that of the

---

3. See Pouchelle, *Dieu éducateur*, 240–45.

4. The aim of NETS was to produce a translation based on the NRSV according to the so-called interlinear paradigm that focuses on the text "as produced" rather than the text "as received" (NETS, xiv–xvi). In other words, when the Greek corresponds to the MT exactly, then the translation of NRSV is kept. The introduction of NETS gives many reasons for NETS being different from NRSV. When we apply these reasons to our verse, we observe that the presence of καί corresponding to ו (which was left untranslated by NRSV, as the form ולקחו was a *wayyiqtol*) may reflect reason no. 2 as listed in NETS—the Greek was "hyper-literalistic, where the NRSV is not"—and the replacement of "the man" by "that man" may reflect reason no. 4—the Greek "apparently rendered a text at variance with MT" (here, the presence of ההוא in the *Vorlage*, a variant also attested in the Samaritan Pentateuch). The three other differences could only be justified by reason no. 1—"The lexical choice of the NRSV to represent the Hebrew differs significantly from that of the Greek translator's even though either rendering, independently, might be regarded as an adequate translation of the same Hebrew" (NETS, xvi). Obviously, γερουσία, "council of elders," is not an exact rendering of זקנים, "elders," even if both terms denote an assembly of elders, and it would be debatable to keep here the wording of NRSV. More problematic is the case of πόλις, which renders עיר. The correspondence between עיר and πόλις seems to be very systematic, such that it could be questioned whether "town" may have been kept.

Greek translator's, even though either rendering, independently, might be regarded as an adequate translation of the same Hebrew text.

The interlinear paradigm asserts that the LXX was produced so as to bring the Greek readers to the Hebrew text and not the opposite. In this context, a Greek lexeme that consistently renders a Hebrew one is to be understood as a pointer. It loses its Greek semantic field to adopt that of the Hebrew lexeme and should be considered as a symbol of that Hebrew lexeme and translated accordingly. However, NETS has chosen to replace "punish" by "discipline." Two reasons could be given: (1) παιδεύω really points to יסר, and there is no reason to alter NRSV except to correct it; in this case, the difference is not due to the Greek translator but to the modern assessment of what יסר should mean here (i.e., a nuance of discipline more than punishment); (2) παιδεύω points to a part of the semantic field of יסר only; in this case the systematic rendering of יסר by παιδεύω reveals a semantic shift between the Hebrew and the Greek text: the Greek conveys a more pedagogic nuance, owing to the meaning of παιδεύω in Classical Greek.

The second reason is probably correct, since all the occurrences of παιδεύω and παιδεία corresponding to יסר have been rendered in the NETS by the unique lexeme "discipline."[5] The NETS considers that παιδεύω and cognates convey a more pedagogical nuance than יסר.[6] However, in this case, why has the Greek translator chosen to render the root יסר by a cognate of παιδεύω even in the less pedagogic occurrences of יסר, when the Greek Jewish literature had already begun to use παιδεύω in the Greek classical sense?

Apart from Georg Bertram, there were no systematic studies of that question until I published my dissertation in French.[7] The aim of this chapter is to present the state of research and to study the root יסר in Classical Hebrew and παιδεύω and cognates in classical and Hellenistic

---

5. In Deut 32:10, NETS translates by "to educate." Here, παιδεύω does not correspond to יסר but to בין, "to understand" or "to take care."

6. It should be clear enough that these arguments are neither intended to contradict the "interlinear paradigm" nor to discredit NETS, but only to show that the systematic rendering of יסר by παιδεύω poses a problem. In this regard, the translation of Brenton is probably closer to the assumptions of the NETS, as his is very close to that of KJV: "and the elders of that city shall take that man, and shall chastise him" (Brenton), to be compared to: "And the elders of that city shall take that man and chastise him" (KJV Webster). The only difference is the appearance of a second "shall" in the Brenton translation, maybe for stylistic reasons.

7. Georg Bertram, "παιδεύω κτλ.," TDNT 5:608–11 Pouchelle, Dieu éducateur.

literature as well as in papyri and inscriptions, in order to try to answer the aforementioned question by studying the use of παιδεύω and cognates in the translated books of the LXX.[8]

Status Quaestionis

It seems that the first modern scholar to deal with this problem is Hermann Cremer.[9] Assuming the specificity of a Greco-Jewish language, he simply states that παιδεύω and cognates are synonyms of יסר and do not convey the classical meaning of the term before Acts 7:22. Cremer was influenced by the theory of a Greco-Jewish language, which has been abandoned since the publication of the studies of Adolf Deissmann.[10] Indeed, Deissmann demonstrates that many specific meanings of the LXX could be found in the nonliterary works of Hellenistic era. In this context, the nuance of punishment and discipline found in the LXX use of παιδεύω and cognates may well be found in the papyri and in the Greek Koine, as presumed by Paul Harlé and Didier Pralon.[11] In this case, its use in the LXX and in the New Testament (esp. Luke 23:16) would simply be a normal usage in the contemporary Greek.

---

8. In other words, in all the books with a counterpart in the MT, as well as the translated deuterocanonical texts. This chapter does not present a comprehensive study of all occurrences of these terms. In particular, the coverage of Sirach's usage of παιδεύω and cognates, despite the importance of these terms in his book, will not be exhaustive.

9. Hermann Cremer, *Biblisch-theologisches Wörterbuch des neutestamentlichen Griechisch*, 11th ed. (Gotha: Klotz, 1923), s.v. παῖς.

10. Adolf Deissmann, *Bibelstudien: Beiträge, zumeist aus den Papyri und Inschriften, zur Geschichte der Sprache, des Schrifttums und der Religion des hellenistischen Judentums und des Urchristentums* (Marburg: Elwert, 1895); and Deissmann, *Neue Bibelstudien: Sprachgeschichtliche Beiträge, zumeist aus den Papyri und Inschriften, zur Erklärung des Neuen Testaments* (Marburg: Elwert, 1897).

11. See Paul Harlé and Didier Pralon, *Le Lévitique: Traduction du texte grec de la Septante, introduction et notes*, BA 3 (Paris: Cerf, 1988), 207. However, they do not present a single example.

However, Bertram does not follow that path.[12] For him, the Hebrew language does not have any pedagogical terms.[13] The root יסר especially denotes a coercive relationship between a person having authority (God, a father, a teacher) and a subordinate (the people, a son, a pupil). During the Hellenistic era, discipline was more and more understood as "education" through a "psychologization" of Jewish thought. Hence, a "pedagogical" nuance comes into the Jewish culture and conversely, παιδεύω gained a nuance of discipline and punishment, absent from the classical Greek.[14] The theory of Bertram is clearly biased, however. His anti-Semitism leads him to consider the LXX as the first step toward the de-Judaizing of the Jewish religion, the first entrance of classical Greek culture into Jewish religious belief. According to him, this step paved the way to Jesus and Christianity, considered as the second step toward de-Judaizing. Although this theory is never expressed as such in his academic writings, they are clearly permeated with these ideas, like those of many others of his colleagues.[15] Hence, the idea that Hebrew does not develop any pedagogical vocabulary is highly debatable and contradicted by Bertram himself when he wrote that:

> The Heb. OT has a whole series of words for teaching and direction, for chastisement and correction, but only the one word יסר and the derived מוסר can denote "to educate," "education."[16]

Despite its great biases, the theory of Bertram concerning παιδεύω and cognates still exerts great influence on scholars. Gerhard Schneider

---

12. Georg Bertram, "Der Begriff der Erziehung in der griechischen Bibel," in *Imago dei: Beiträge zur theologischen Anthropologie, Gustav Krüger zum siebzigsten Geburstage am 29. Juni 1932 dargebracht*, ed. Heinrich Bornkamm (Giessen: Töpelmann, 1932), 33–51; and Bertram, "παιδεύω," 5:595–625.

13. "If the substance of education is in some sense present, there is no psychological exposition or development. Hence no pedagogic vocabulary is formed" (Bertram, "παιδεύω," 5:603).

14. Ibid.

15. This is one of two main problems in using the *TDNT* today; see Tobias Nicklas, "The Bible and Anti-Semitism," in *The Oxford Handbook of the Reception History of the Bible*, ed. Michael Lieb, Emma Mason, and Jonathan Roberts (Oxford: Oxford University Press, 2013), 267–80. The other problem is mixing words and concepts. This bias was notoriously shown by James Barr, *The Semantics of Biblical Language*, 2nd ed. (Oxford: Oxford University Press, 1962), 206–62.

16. Bertram, "παιδεύω," 5:604.

asserts that the unique character of παιδεύω and παιδεία could be found in the LXX.[17] Isac Leo Seeligmann, despite his critiques of Bertram, thinks that the LXX does promote an educative ideal based on its use of παιδεία.[18] Martin Rösel holds a similar position.[19] Leo Prijs and Knut Usener nuance these theories by stating that the ideal promoted by the LXX is Jewish education in the torah.[20]

A few scholars attempt to contradict Bertram. Werner Jentsch suggests that יסר does have a pedagogic nuance and that, in fact, it shares the same semantic field as παιδεύω.[21] Nevertheless, he observes that παιδεύω and cognates have lost most of their Greek meaning. On the contrary, James A. Arieti asserts that παιδεύω and cognates are deliberately used in a way different from their classical and "philosophical" sense, whereas Staffan Olofsson explicitly doubts the thesis of Bertram.[22] Developing similar ideas, Dorothea Betz observes that the verb παιδεύω conveys more a nuance of discipline and chastisement in the LXX than a nuance of "education."[23]

---

17. Gerhard Schneider, "παιδεία, κτλ.," *EDNT* 3:3.

18. Isac Leo Seeligmann, "Problems and Perspectives in Modern Septuagint Research," in Isac Leo Seeligmann, *The Septuagint Version of Isaiah and Cognates Studies*, ed. Robert Hanhart and Hermann Spieckermann, FAT 40 (Tübingen: Mohr Siebeck, 2004), 73; trans. from Seeligmann, "Problemen en Perspectieven in het Moderne Septuaginta Onderzoek," *JEOL* 7 (1940): 359–90, 763–66.

19. Martin Rösel, "Theologie der griechischen Bibel: Zur Wiedergabe der Gottesaussagen im LXX-Pentateuch," *VT* 48 (1998): 49–62, at 50–51; Rösel, "Towards a 'Theology of the Septuagint,' " in *Septuagint Research: Issues and Challenges in the Study of the Greek Jewish Scriptures*, ed. Wolgrant Kraus and R. Glenn Wooden, SCS 53 (Atlanta: Society of Biblical Literature, 2006), 249.

20. Leo Prijs, *Jüdische Tradition in der Septuaginta* (Leiden: Brill, 1948), xiv–xvi, 64; and Knut Usener, "Die Septuaginta im Horizont des Hellenismus: Ihre Entwicklung, ihr Charakter und ihre sprachlichkulturelle Position," in *Studien zur Entstehung und Bedeutung der Griechischen Bibel*, vol. 2 of *Im Brennpunkt: Die Septuaginta*, ed. Siegfried Kreuzer and Jürgen Peter Lesch, BWANT 161 (Stuttgart: Kohlhammer, 2004), 111–12.

21. Werner Jentsch, *Urchristliches Erziehungsdenken: Die Paideia Kyriu im Rahmen der hellenistisch-jüdischen Umwelt*, BFCT 45.3 (Gütersloh: Bertelsmann, 1951), 81–91.

22. James A. Arieti, "The Vocabulary of Septuagint Amos," *JBL* 93 (1974): 346; Staffan Olofsson, "The Crux Interpretum in Ps 2,12," *SJOT* 9 (1995): 195.

23. Dorothea Betz, "Gott als Erzieher im Alten Testament: Eine semantisch-traditionsgeschichtliche Untersuchung der Begrifflichkeit *jsr/musar* (*paideuo/paideia*) mit Gott als Subjekt in den Schriften des AT" (PhD diss., Universität Osnabrück, 2007), 317–21.

To sum up, the possible explanations of the relationship between יסר and παιδεύω and cognates could be summarized this way: (1) יסר means "to chastise" and παιδεύω "to educate"; the Greek translators chose παιδεύω to denote the difference between Greco-Jewish thought and Hebrew-speaking Judaism (Bertram, but also with important differences and nuances, Seeligmann, Rösel, Prijs, and Usener); (2) יסר and παιδεύω mean to educate; the choice of the LXX was obvious (Jentsch); (3) יסר means "to chastise" and παιδεύω "to chastise," especially in the papyri and inscriptions; the choice of the LXX was also obvious (Harlé and Pralon); and (4) Παιδεύω was used deliberately used in a way different from its Greek background (Arieti).

In my book on God as an educator, I argue that the semantic field of יסר and of παιδεύω and cognates are not fully identical, but they share the nuance of oral rebuking. When corresponding to יסר, παιδεύω and cognates are to be understood as denoting discipline, as received by the scribes. However, the systematic rendering of יסר by παιδεύω leads the Greek lexeme to develop a nuance of punishment that is absent from the ancient Greek but does survive in modern Greek. Conversely, the LXX also witnesses uses of παιδεύω that convey some classical Greek nuances, especially when not corresponding to יסר.

Classical and Hellenistic Greek

Educating

It is obvious that παιδεύω (and cognates) means "education" in classical and Hellenistic Greek. Many famous monographs have been published to deal with the importance of παιδεία in Greek culture and in Greek identity.[24] It seems, however, that this widely attested usage eclipsed some other nuances.

---

24. The most famous one is Werner Jaeger, *Paideia: The Ideals of Greek Culture* (Oxford: Oxford University Press, 1939–1944; repr., Oxford: Oxford University Press, 1967–1971). But see also Henri Irénée Marrou, *History of Education in Antiquity*, trans. George Lamb, WSC (London: Sheed & Ward, 1956); trans. of *Histoire de l'éducation dans l'antiquité*, 3rd ed. (Paris: Seuil, 1948); and more recently Graham Anderson, "The *pepaideumenos* in Action: Sophists and Their Outlook in the Early Empire," *ANRW* 33.1:80–208; and Anderson, *The Second Sophistic: A Cultural Phenomenon in the Roman Empire* (London: Routledge, 1993).

Etymologically deriving from παῖς, the basic meaning of παιδεύω is "to act toward someone as if he or she is a child."[25] Non-Homeric, this word is not particularly ancient. The substantive παιδεία is the verbal noun of παιδεύω. Its earliest occurrences, mingled with παιδία, denote the youth of someone,[26] explaining why παιδεία gained the important nuance of "education" or "culture." Indeed, having spent one's youth somewhere is also having been educated in a specific manner of life.[27] From there, these terms gained the primary nuance of "education" and "culture," especially under the influence of philosophers like Plato, Aristotle, and Isocrates. Some linguistic markers that point to such a meaning can be enumerated: (1) the use of the verb in the passive voice, with the dative or the preposition ἐν indicating the subject taught;[28] (2) the substantive usage of the passive perfect participle πεπαιδευμένος, denoting a person who has finished his educative *cursus*; (3) the triple characterization of a person as being born (γεννάω), nurtured (τρέφω), and educated (παιδεύω) somewhere; (4) the *nomen rectum* of παιδεία denoting the person who received the education, and never the one who provided it; for instance, it is Chiron who educated Hercules, as well as many other heroes, but Chiron is never employed as the *nomen rectum* of παιδεία; accordingly, the Cyropaedia of Xenophon describes the education received by Cyrus the Persian king; and (5) the noun παιδεία denoting education or culture in the abstract but never the subject taught; there is never any mention of παιδεία "in" a particular subject.

But more basically, the verb is also employed as a synonym of τρέφω. In a fragment of Sophocles, it means "to rear" or "to nourish" (*TrGF* 4.648). This nuance is rare but attested until Hellenistic times. For instance, Theophrastus uses it to denote the growth of a plant (*Caus. plant.* 3.7.4.), and Athenaeus, that of fishes (*Deipn.* 7).

---

25. Hélène Perdicoyianni, *Étude lexicologique des familles de* δαῆναι, *de* διδάσκειν *et* παιδεύειν *d'Homère à Hippocrate* (Athens: Perdicoyianni, 1994), 81.

26. Aeschylus, *Sept.*18. See also Euripides, *Iph. taur.* 205–207, in which ἐξ ἀρχᾶς λόχιαι στερρὰν παιδείαν Μοῖραι συντείνουσιν θεαί means that the destiny of Iphigenia is cruel: her youth was just finished when she had to be sacrificed. See also Pouchelle, *Dieu éducateur*, 164–65.

27. Pouchelle, *Dieu éducateur*, 165.

28. E.g., music, with a simple dative: Plato, *Resp.* 430A; with ἐν: Plato, *Crito* 50E.

Rebuking

Neither παιδεύω nor παιδεία seems to adopt the nuance of violent rebuking. Such nuances are expressed by words like κολάζω, τιμωρέω, ἐπιτρίβω, τύπτω, δέρω, and νουθετέω, but never with παιδεύω. The closest example may be found in Aristophanes, who compares παῖς to παίω:

τί δ' ἐστίν, ὦ παῖ; παῖδα γάρ, κἂν ᾖ γέρων, καλεῖν δίκαιον ὅστις ἂν πληγὰς λάβῃ. (Aristophanes, Vesp. 1297)
Why, what's the matter, my child? For, old as he may be, one has the right to call anyone a child who has let himself be beaten. (O'Neill and Oates)

The fact of being educated somewhere also means that a child is acquainted with a specific way of life, even if this way if life is hard, like that of the Athenian. In that context, παιδεύω may have developed a nuance of "to be trained":

τήν τε ψυχὴν ἐπαίδευσε καὶ τὸ σῶμα (Xenophon, Mem. 1.3.5)
He schooled his body and soul (Marchant, LCL)

Furthermore, Xenophon also uses παιδεύω to denote the training of a horse:

ἃ δ' ἂν ὑπὸ τοῦ τραχέος παιδευθῇ (Xenophon, Eq. 10.6)
what he has been trained to do with the aid of the rough one. (Marchant, LCL)

To obtain the obedience of a slave is similar to taming a horse.[29] However, it is hard to say whether παιδεύω is here synonymous with "rebuking" a horse in order to tame it. Indeed, the metaphorical use of παιδεύω to denote the taming of a horse also means that the taming is a long process that leads the horse to be useful:

ἐρωτηθεὶς τίνι διαφέρουσιν οἱ πεπαιδευμένοι τῶν ἀπαιδεύτων, ἔφη, ᾧπερ οἱ δεδαμασμένοι ἵπποι τῶν ἀδαμάστων. (Diogenes Laertius, Vit. Phil. 2.69)

---

29. See also Yun Lee Too, *A Commentary on Isocrates' Antidosis* (Oxford: Oxford University Press, 2008), 194–95.

To the question how the educated differ from the uneducated, he replied, "Exactly as horses that have been trained differ from untrained horses." (Hicks, LCL)

It is only later that παιδεύω is used as a synonym of "to chastise," in *Vita Aesopi* G.61 and in Libanius:

παίδευε δὲ αὐτοὺς μήτε θανάτοις μήτε πληγαῖς, ἀλλ' ἀρκείτω δεσμός. (Libanius, *Or.* 26.10)
Don't punish them by death or by chastisement, but may a bond suffice. (my translation)

Neither *Vita Aesopi* nor Libanius may be used a witness for such a meaning in the non-Jewish and non-Christian Greek culture, as they may well be influenced by the LXX owing to their lateness. Therefore, in classical and Hellenistic Greek, παιδεύω is not attested as meaning "to punish."

However, a clear nuance of rebuking is conveyed when παιδεύω is used with an adult as an object. This metaphorical usage usually denotes an action or a discourse whose aim is to change the mind or the behavior of someone. This nuance is attested from Sophocles onward. In his *Ajax*, the hero gets angry and thereafter wishes to die. When his partner, Tecmessa, tries to dissuade him from committing suicide, Ajax replies:

Μῶρά μοι δοκεῖς φρονεῖν, εἰ τοὐμὸν ἦθος ἄρτι παιδεύειν νοεῖς. (Sophocles, *Aj.* 595)
You have foolish hope, I think, if you plan so late to begin schooling my temper. (Jebb)

In this semantic field, the verb could be used with the preposition ἐν indicating the event that caused the behavior to be altered:

παιδεύοντας δ' ἐν τοῖς τῶν τεθνεώτων ἔργοις τοὺς ζῶντας (Lysias, *Ep.* 3)
and finding in the achievements of the dead so many lessons for the living. (Lamb, LCL)

In his *Funeral Oration*, Lysias asserts that after a war the living people are "educated," or more precisely, "exhorted," by the examples of the dead. Claudius Aelianus relates a story which recalls Deut 21:18. A father has seven sons and the last one is disrespectful:

Καὶ τὰ μὲν πρῶτα ἐπειρᾶτο αὐτὸν ὁ πατὴρ παιδεύειν, καὶ ῥυθμίζειν λόγῳ
(Aelian, *Var. hist.* 1.34)
And firstly, the father attempted to exhort him and to correct him by words. (my translation)

Once the father fails to discipline his son, he asks judges to sentence him to death. In this meaning, παιδεύω is used together with νουθετέω. The two terms occur together also in a statement attributed to Apollonius, who exhorts his brother to rebuke him as their recently deceased father used to do:

ὃς ἐπαίδευέ τε ἡμᾶς καὶ ἐνουθέτει (Philostratus, *Vit. Apoll.* 1.13)
He who admonishes and rebukes us. (my translation)

The fact that Philostratus and his brother are adults whose father has passed away and the fact that the verb παιδεύω is conjugated in present and not in perfect indicate that the meaning here is "to rebuke" more than "to educate."

It is noteworthy that this meaning only belongs to the verb. The noun παιδεία seems to belong to the semantic field of education only and is never used to denote the process of rebuking.

Gnomic Wisdom

Gnomic wisdom is hard to date and to identify. These collections of sayings were made long after the lifetimes of the speakers, and a gnomic sentence is frequently attributed to three or more authors.[30] However, these sentences are worth studying because they associate παιδεύω more closely with violence without using it as a synonym for "to chastise."[31] See, for example, the well-known sentence of Menander:[32]

---

30. See, for example, the sentence: Ἡ παιδεία εὐτυχοῦσι μέν ἐστι κόσμος, ἀτυχοῦσι δὲ καταφύγιον, attributed to Democritus (frag. 180) by Stobeaus, *Flor.* 2.31.58, to Aristotle by *GV* 50, and finally to Socrates by John Chortasmenos, *Ep.* 23.

31. See also Dennis Michael Searby, *Aristotle in the Greek Gnomological Tradition*, SGU 19 (Uppsala: Uppsala University Press, 1998), 166; and John T. Fitzgerald, "Proverbs 3:11–12, Hebrews 12:5–6, and the Tradition of Corporal Punishment," in *Scripture and Traditions: Essays on Early Judaism and Christianity in Honor of Carl R. Holladay*, ed. Patrick Gray and Gail R. O'Day, NovTSup 129 (Leiden: Brill, 2008), 314–15. For other examples, see Pouchelle, *Dieu éducateur*, 191–92.

32. See also Βακτηρία γάρ ἐστι παιδεία βίου (Menander, *Sent.* 122), "And the rod is the education of life" (author's translation).

Ὁ μὴ δαρεὶς ἄνθρωπος οὐ παιδεύεται (Menander, *Sent.* 573).
The man who is not thrashed is not educated. (my translation)

More than emphasizing the hardness of the education, gnomic wisdom also praises παιδεία. It is the most precious thing for humanity:

Κάλλιστόν ἐστι κτῆμα παιδεία βροτοῖς (Menander, *Sent.* 384)
The best of the possessions for mortals is education. (my translation)

Or:

ἡ παιδεία εὐτυχοῦσι μέν ἐστι κόσμος, ἀτυχοῦσι δὲ καταφύγιον (Stobaeus, *Flor.* 2.31.58)
Education is for the fortunate an ornament and for the unfortunate a refuge. (my translation)

That is to say, a person does not owe his or her beauty to good fortune (*tychē*) but to "education." Education leads to real wisdom and is sometime used as warning against encyclopedic knowledge. Hence, the Tabula of Cebes distinguishes between false and true paideia. False paideia is technical education, while the true one is a conversion to wisdom. Such a description may well be influenced by the myth of the cave of Plato, who also sees paideia not as knowledge but as a conversion.[33]

This conception interestingly resonates with the semantic evolution of the passive perfect participle πεπαιδευμένος. Whereas during the classical period it denotes a person perfectly integrated into the city for acting toward the common good (e.g., Aristotle, *Eth. nic.* 1180b2), during the Hellenistic era this person becomes a gentleman whose main characteristic is his correct and moderate behavior (e.g., Plutarch, *Dion* 1.4).[34]

The Contribution of the Papyri

In the documentary papyri, the nuance of education is widely attested.[35] Some rare nuances could be expressed, however. Two documents are of special interest.

---

33. Pouchelle, *Dieu éducateur*, 213–18.
34. See also Pouchelle, *Dieu éducateur*, 171–76.
35. In inscriptions this seems the only attested meaning, apart from one attesta-

The first example is a papyrus from Arsinoe, which dates to the third century CE. The papyrus *BGU* 3.846 is a letter from Antonius to his mother. Antonius is ashamed for having done something bad, revealed to his mother by one of his relatives, Postumus. Accordingly, his mother has decided to cut him off from her support. This letter is an attempt by Antonius to sway his mother.

> Παιπαίδδευμαι, καθ' ὃν δὶ τρόπον (*BGU* 3.846, line 11)
> I admonish myself that it was my fault. (my translation)

According to George Milligan,[36] the verb here means "to punish." However, in the papyrus, this verb is flanked by two occurrences of οἶδα, so the context implies a meaning close to the metaphoric usage of παιδεύω.[37]

The second papyrus, *PSI* 8.972, was found in Oxyrhynchus and dates to the fourth century CE. This is a complaint from Antoninos, a Christian, to his boss, Gonatas. Antoninos quarreled with Tithoes and was thrashed by Pantheros. These two people must be known to Gonatas because Antoninos states that he did not respond to the attack, but warns that he will:

> Γνῶτι οὖν ὅτι δύναμε αὐτῷ πεδεύσω (*PSI* 8.972, lines 18-19)
> Know then that I can, I will thrash him. (my translation)

Pace John R. Rea,[38] it seems improbable that the meaning intended here is the metaphoric one, "to rebuke." The context implies a harsher meaning, "to beat."

Both documents are characterized by their incorrect grammar and orthography. They were written by less-educated people. The first one witnesses a meaning of rebuking, the second one a meaning of chastisement. This last nuance is probably influenced by the LXX, as the author is Christian.

---

tion of παιδεία in the plural meaning "training" in the epitaph of a gladiator (*IGUR* 3.1243, line 7, unknown date, Rome).

36. George Milligan, *Selections from the Greek Papyri* (Cambridge: Cambridge University Press, 1910), 94-95.

37. See also Régis Burnet, *L'Égypte ancienne à travers les papyrus: Vie quotidienne* (Paris: Pygmalion, 2003), no. 210.

38. John R. Rea, "Two Christian Letters: PSI VII 831 and VIII 972," *CdE* 45 (1970): 357-68.

Classical Hebrew

The Masoretic Text

The basic meaning of the root יסר is not easy to determine for two main reasons. First, this root is composed of a weak consonant, י, and an alveolar consonant, ס, both subject to alteration. Second, the root is hardly attested outside the Hebrew language.

Two mutually exclusive theories try to explain the root יסר. The first one is formulated by R. D. Branson.[39] This root originally meant "to educate." Owing to the coercive pedagogical methods of that period, especially in the influential Egyptian culture, the root יסר developed the nuance of coercive punishment, losing completely its pedagogic character even before the writing of the biblical texts.[40] The speculative nature of this hypothesis, associated with a doubtful reference to Akkadian, weakens the theory of Branson.[41] Yet, a major argument could be made from the presence of this root in a few texts from Ugarit. However, it is attested only four times, and the meaning of this root in the Ugaritic corpus is largely based on its meaning in the Hebrew Bible, so it is hard to draw clear-cut conclusions. Only one occurrence may be used to strengthen the thesis of Branson:

> You are great, O El, so very wise [ḥkmt]; The gray hair of your beard so instructs you [tsrk]. (KTU 1.4 V 4 [Smith and Pitard])

Here *tsrk*, presumably derived from *ysr*, is used in parallel with "to be wise." However, the use of *ysr* with an inanimate subject, here "the gray hair of your beard," is rare (only attested in Ps 16:7). Moreover, could we convincingly base a theory on a single form which may possibly derive from other roots containing /s-r/?[42]

---

39. R. D. Branson, "יָסַר," *TDOT* 6:127–34.

40. On Egyptian influence, see See Nili Shupak, *Where Can Wisdom be Found? The Sage's Language in the Bible and in Ancient Egyptian Literature*, OBO 130 (Göttingen: Vandenhoeck & Ruprecht, 1993), for whom the Egyptian lemma *sbꜣ* means both "to educate" and "to chastise," but see also Pouchelle, *Dieu éducateur*, 68–77. On the development of the term, see Branson, "יָסַר," 6:128.

41. Branson, "יָסַר," 6:127–28; see Pouchelle, *Dieu éducateur*, 56–58.

42. See, for instance, the discussion of Mark S. Smith and Wayne T. Pitard, *Introduction with Text, Translation and Commentary of KTU/CAT 1.3–1.4*, vol. 2 of The

The second theory is developed by Magne Sæbø.⁴³ For this scholar, the etymology of this root is unknown. It could be an Akkadian loanword.⁴⁴ Its principal meaning is related to punishment and fines (Deut 22:18; 2 Kgs 12:11, 14). Later, it develops the nuance of a disciplinary measure when it was applied to the relationship between a father and his son (Deut 21:18) or a teacher and his pupils (Prov 5:12). Finally, the root denotes the results of this coercive process: an obedient son.⁴⁵

The main argument to be advanced for discerning between the theory of Branson and that of Sæbø is to note that, although there are some occurrences of the root יסר without any pedagogic nuances (Deut 22:18; 2 Kgs 12:11, 14; Hos 5:2; Prov 7:22), the occurrences associated with education always link an authoritative person with a subordinate in a coercive context.⁴⁶ Hence, Branson is forced to make the assumption that the root יסר developed all of its nuances before the writing of the biblical text. This assumption weakens his theory because his etymological study is based on too few occurrences.

To take one example, even in Deut 4:36 such a coercive nuance is at stake, even if some deny it:⁴⁷

Ugarit Baal Cycle, VTSup 114 (Leiden: Brill, 2008), 691, for the form *ystrn* in KTU 1.4 VII 48.

43. Magne Sæbø, "ysr, to chastise," *TLOT* 2:548–51.

44. According to Hayim Tawil, "Hebrew יסר, Akkadian *esuru*: A Term of Forced Labor," in *Teshûrôt LaAvishur: Studies in the Bible and the Ancient Near East, in Hebrew and Semitic Languages; Festschrift Presented to Prof. Yitzhak Avishur on the Occasion of His 65th Birthday*, ed. Michael Heltzer and Meir Malul (Tel Aviv: Archeological Center Publications, 2004), 185*–90*. Furthermore, the disciplinary nuance sometimes conveyed by למד, close to the basic meaning of יסר (A. S. Kapelrud, "לָמַד," *TDOT* 8:4–5), may be an indicator of this loan: יסר may have supplanted למד in its nuance of discipline.

45. G. Gerleman, "Bemerkungen zum alttestamentlichen Sprachstil," in *Studia Biblica et Semitica: Theodoro Christiano Vriezen qui munere professoris theologiae per XXV annos functus est, ab amicis, collegis, discipulis dedicata*, ed. W. C. van Unnik and A. S. van der Woude (Wageningen: Veenman, 1967), 112, and Gerhard von Rad, *Theologie des Alten Testaments*, 2 vols. (Munich: Kaiser, 1957), 1:429.

46. See Pouchelle, *Dieu éducateur*, 139–40; and Wendy L. Widder, *"To Teach" in Ancient Israel: A Cognitive Linguistic Study of a Biblical Hebrew Lexical Set*, BZAW 456 (Berlin: de Gruyter, 2014), 193.

47. Although the Peshitta translates with אלף and the Vulgate with *doceo*, and *pace* Karin Finsterbusch, *Weisung für Israel: Studien zu religiosem Lehren und Lernen im Deuteronium und seinem Umfeld*, FAT 44 (Tübingen: Mohr Siebeck, 2005), 157–58.

מִן־הַשָּׁמַיִם הִשְׁמִיעֲךָ אֶת־קֹלוֹ לְיַסְּרֶךָּ

From heaven he made you hear his voice to discipline you. (NRSV)
Out of heaven he made thee to hear his voice, that he might instruct thee. (KJV)

Indeed, *pace* KJV, God's voice relates to the law and the commandments that God addresses to the people as a warning to adopt the correct behavior:

> So acknowledge today and take to heart that the LORD is God in heaven above and on the earth beneath; there is no other. Keep his statutes and his commandments, which I am commanding you today for your own well-being and that of your descendants after you, so that you may long remain in the land that the LORD your God is giving you for all time. (Deut 4:39–40 NRSV)

This kind of oral rebuke is frequently attested in the sapiential literature and in some prophetic oracles (Prov 3:11; 4:1; Ps 50:17; Jer 7:28 with מוּסָר). The verb יסר introduces in Prov 31:1 such a discourse of admonition from a mother to her son, Lemuel (Prov 31:2–9). The link made between this root and the law in Ps 94:10 may be understood this way:

> Happy are those whom you discipline, O LORD, and whom you teach out of your law. (NRSV)

The warning, rebuke, or discipline of God to the believers is based on the law he gave.

The verb יסר is mainly used in the *piel* stem.[48] The disciplinary nuance is emphasized by the construction of the verb with the preposition בּ, which always denotes the means by which someone is disciplined. Hence, it is never used to denote intellectual or technical teaching, even if a few occurrences are sometimes translated according to this hypothesis:

וְיִסְּרוֹ לַמִּשְׁפָּט אֱלֹהָיו יוֹרֶנּוּ

For they are well instructed; their God teaches them. (Isa 28:26 NRSV)

וְיִסַּרְתִּיךָ לַמִּשְׁפָּט

---

48. See Pouchelle, *Dieu éducateur*, 92 n. 103; and Widder, "*To Teach*," 166, who observe that since the verb is used almost exclusively in the *piel* stem, it is unsafe to draw conclusions regarding the potential difference with the *qal*.

I will chastise you in just measure. (Jer 30:11 NRSV; see also Jer 46:28)[49]

The NRSV, according to most scholars, interprets Jer 30:11 as assuring the people that their correction will not exceed measure.[50] The same Hebrew construction in Isa 28:26 is interpreted differently: God instructs the farmer about how to deal with his field. However, this interpretation raises some questions, such as the separation of the verb and its subject (אלהיו). Another interpretation, promoted by Joseph Blenkinsopp and Dorothea Betz, suggests that the subject is the farmer and that the object of the verb is the plotted land or the grain.[51]

> For he[52] will chastise [or: "thresh"] him[53] in just measure; his God teaches him.[54] (my translation)

The text draws a comparison between the people and the grain and between God and the farmer. Indeed, this comparison is clear in Isa 28:27–28, where the grains are crushed but not destroyed.

The verbal noun מוסר also expresses the importance of the person who has authority over someone else. Accordingly, the *nomen rectum* is the person who originates the discipline and never the one who endures it. The word מוסר, then, expresses the process of disciplining or chastising, hence "punishment" (e.g., Prov 13:24; 22:15; 23:13), but also the results of this process, hence "good behavior," "good education." This nuance is confirmed by the use of מוסר with verbs expressing reception, like לקח "to

---

49. Contrast the French translation TOB: "Je t'apprends à respecter l'ordre."
50. So, Georg Fischer, *Jeremia*, 2 vols., HThKAT (Freiburg im Breisgau: Herder, 2005), 2:118, 129; Gerald L. Keown, Pamela J. Scalise, and Thomas G. Smothers, *Jeremiah 26–52*, WBC 27 (Waco, TX: Word, 1995), 94; Jack R. Lundbom, *Jeremiah 21–36: A New Translation with Introduction and Commentary*, AB 21B (New York: Doubleday, 2004), 392; and Finsterbusch, *Weisung*, 65.
51. For the argument that the subject is the plotted land, see Joseph Blenkinsopp, *Isaiah 1–39: A New Translation with Introduction and Commentary*, AB 19 (New York: Doubleday, 2000), 396. However, the land (אדמה) is feminine, whereas the object of the form ויסרו is masculine. For the argument that the object is the grain, see Betz, "Gott als Erzieher," 228.
52. The farmer (החרש); see Isa 28:24.
53. The grain, "dill" (קצח), or "cart" (כמן), mentioned in Isa 28:25 and 28:27, treated as singular collective masculine, according to Betz, "Gott als Erzieher," 228.
54. Blenkinsopp suggests here another nuance of the verb ירה, "to water."

take" (e.g., Jer 2:30; 5:3; Song 3:2, 7; Prov 1:3; 8:10), or acceptance/rejection, like נאץ "to despise" (Prov 15:5).[55] Another nuance is denoted by the collocation with שמע "to hear": מוסר is an oral discourse whose aim is to rebuke someone.[56]

Therefore, in accordance with Michael Carasik and Wendy L. Widder, it is more accurate to state that the root יסר basically conveys a negative nuance of rebuking and then to follow Sæbø and to schematize the evolution of the semantic field of יסר as follows:

chastisement → corporal discipline → oral rebuke → result of the discipline/rebuke.[57]

Late Classical Hebrew

Even if the MT does not attest a meaning for יסר close to the meaning "education" for παιδεύω and cognates, it is possible that such nuances occurred in Late Biblical Hebrew and particularly in Ben Sira and Qumran. In particular, E. J. Bickerman, basing his assertion on Ben Sira, stated that the concept of paideia entered Jerusalem during the third century BCE.[58]

Indeed, Ben Sira attests a shift in the use of מוסר.[59] First, the *nomen rectum* may refer to the person who receives the discipline rather than the one who gives it (Sir[B, M] 42:8). Second, it can denote the content of an oral

---

55. For other Hebrew verbs, see Pouchelle, *Dieu éducateur*, 98–100.
56. A good example of such discourse is given by Prov 31:1–9.
57. Michael Carasik, *Theologies of the Mind in Biblical Israel*, StBibLit 85 (New York: Lang, 2006), 148–49; Widder, "*To Teach*," 194–95; Sæbø, *TLOT* 2:548–51. However, Widder nuances her position by taking into account verses she considers to have a more pedagogical nuance, like Deut 4:36 and Isa 28:26.
58. See E. J. Bickerman, *The Jews in the Greek Age* (Cambridge: Harvard University Press, 1988), 171. A few pages earlier (166), he states the interesting hypothesis that, during the Hellenistic Era, the Hebrew term חכמה could have gained something of the semantic field of παιδεία, that is to say, "culture." This article will not aim to assess this hypothesis further.
59. One should not neglect the difficulty of dealing with the Hebrew manuscripts of Ben Sira. Even though the discovery of the Masada manuscript has shown that the Cairo Genizah manuscripts are not a retranslation into Hebrew of the Syriac or the Greek, we cannot exclude such marginal corrections, errors or even retranslation; see W. Th. van Peursen, *The Verbal System in the Hebrew Text of Ben Sira*, SSLL 41 (Leiden: Brill, 2003), 9–26.

discourse (Sir^B 31:11, Sir^B, M 41:15). Indeed, in Ben Sira, מוסר becomes increasingly a sapiential term. It seems difficult to prove, however, that the idea of παιδεία permeated Jewish thought in Jerusalem, because the traditional meanings of chastisement, discipline, and rebuking still exist for some occurrences of מוסר (e.g., Sir^B, M 42:8),[60] and, in my opinion, for all the occurrences of יסר.[61]

In Qumran and in the Damascus Document, a more spectacular shift occurs. The verb is used in the *hithpael* stem with the preposition ב. However, although in the MT this preposition introduces the means of discipline—mainly the rod—here it introduces the law or the commandments:

ואלה הם[שפטים א]שר ישפטו [בם כל המתיסרים] (4Q270 7 I, 15)
[And these are the reg]ulations by which [shall be ruled] all those disciplined.[62]

Although it is still possible that this usage corresponds to a basic meaning of יסר attested only in Qumran, the close parallel to the Greek construction of the passive participle with ἐν may be an indication of a possible influence of the relationship between יסר and παιδεύω in the LXX.[63] Hence, in Qumran Hebrew, יסר may have gained the semantic field of the Greek παιδεύω. Such influences of the Greek on Qumran Hebrew have been noticed by some scholars but are still an open field to explore.[64]

---

60. As for the wordplay in Sir^A 6:22, please refer to Núria Calduch-Benages, "A Wordplay on the Term *mûsar* (Sir 6:22)," in *Weisheit als Lebensgrundlage: Festschrift für Friedrich V. Reiterer zum 65. Geburtstag*, ed. Renate Egger-Wenzel, Karin Schöpflin, and Johannes Friedrich Diehl, DCLS 15 (Berlin: de Gruyter, 2013), 13–26.

61. See Pouchelle, *Dieu éducateur*, 109–12. The only exception would be Sir^A, C 7:23, in which an injunction to "discipline" one's son is associated with his marriage. Such an injunction is close to that of Sir 30:13 or of Prov 19:18; 29:17, but there the context more clearly indicates the meaning of "discipline." The Hebrew text of Sir^A, C 7:23 could hardly be the *Vorlage* of either the Greek or the Syriac version. For Patrick W. Skehan and Alexander A. Di Lella, *The Wisdom of Ben Sira*, AB 39 (New York, Doubleday, 1987), 204, this is a late gloss, whereas Charles Mopsik, *La Sagesse de Ben Sira*, DP (Lagrasse: Verdier, 2003), 109–10 n. 5, considers it to be authentic.

62. Trans. by Florentino García Martínez and Eibert J. C. Tigchelaar, eds., *The Dead Sea Scrolls Study Edition*, 2 vols. (Leiden: Brill; Grand Rapids: Eerdmans, 1997–1998).

63. Illustrated, for instance, by Aristotle: πεπαιδευμένοι ἐν τῇ πολιτείᾳ (*Pol.* 1310A 14).

64. For more detail, please refer to Patrick Pouchelle, "The Contribution of 1QS and CD to the Lexicography of יסר," *KUSATU* 19 (2015): 225–236.

The Septuagint

When παιδεύω and cognates correspond to יסר, the LXX attests a grammatical usage that is unknown to non-Jewish and non-Christian Greek and that corresponds exactly to the grammatical usage of יסר: (1) the rection of παιδεύω with the preposition ἐν or with the dative denotes the means by which someone disciplines someone else and not the discipline taught;[65] contrary to the metaphorical usage,[66] the means is not an event but a material tool, like a bond (3 Kgms 12:11 LXX), or a divine quality, like anger (Ps 6:2); (2) the *nomen rectum* of παιδεία expresses the person who disciplines and not the one who endures it; that is, the παιδεία κυρίου: the discipline of the Lord (e.g., Deut 11:2); and (3) the substantive παιδεία is used with ἀκούω. Hence, παιδεία is a discourse to be heard, which is never the case in non-Jewish and non-Christian Greek.[67]

Such usages clearly show that παιδεύω was indeed a pointer to יסר and means "to discipline." Another argument for giving to παιδεύω the meaning of יסר is the LXX of Deut 8:5:

וידעת עם־לבבך כי כאשר ייסר איש את־בנו יהוה אלהיך מיסרך
Know then in your heart that as a parent disciplines a child so the LORD your God disciplines you. (NRSV)

καὶ γνώσῃ τῇ καρδίᾳ σου ὅτι ὡς εἴ τις παιδεῦσαι ἄνθρωπος τὸν υἱὸν αὐτοῦ, οὕτως κύριος ὁ θεός σου παιδεύσει σε
And you shall know in your heart that as a certain person might discipline his son, so the Lord your God will discipline you. (NETS)

The main difference between the MT and LXX is the tense of יסר and παιδεύω when God is the subject. In MT the form is a participle, which denotes simultaneity: God disciplines his people during the wandering in the desert. On the contrary, the LXX uses the future tense: God will discipline his people later. This tense better fits the contents of a discourse that warns the people to keep God's commandments when they will enter the

---

65. E.g. Pss 6:2; 37:2 LXX (Ps 38:2 MT); Prov 29:19, with dative; and 3 Kgms 12:11, 14; 2 Ch 10:11, 14, with ἐν.

66. See above, "Rebuking," under the heading "Classical and Hellenistic Greek."

67. This is not the case for the association of παιδεία with verbs of prehension and acceptation that can be found in Greek: with δέχομαι, Plato, *Leg.* 832D; with λαμβάνω, Aeschines, *Tim.* 11; with ὀλιγωρέω, Plutarch, *Gen. Socr.* 579C.

promised land. Therefore, the discipline here evoked is the chastisement promised to the people if they do not obey God's commandments. Such a future tense in a similar context also occurs in Lev 26:18, 26, 28 LXX.

The cause of this difference is difficult to determine. I would be inclined to think that the LXX witnesses a different *Vorlage* from the MT. This *Vorlage* may well be more ancient, but it is difficult to prove. However, this difference clearly shows that the nuance conveyed by the verb παιδεύω is not a nuance of "education" but of "discipline," in line with the meaning of יסר.

This thesis is not contradicted by other differences that occur when the use of παιδεύω and cognates literally corresponds to that of the root יסר.[68] Accordingly, παιδεύω and cognates could be considered more or less as a pointer to יסר.[69]

The Development of the Septuagintal Meaning

Leaving aside textual variants,[70] the LXX sometimes uses παιδεύω and cognates when the MT does not have the root יסר. Generally speaking, the meaning is close to that of יסר. This is particularly true in Psalms:

δράξασθε παιδείας, μήποτε ὀργισθῇ κύριος καὶ ἀπολεῖσθε ἐξ ὁδοῦ δικαίας (Ps 2:12)
Seize upon instruction, lest the Lord be angry and you will perish from the righteous way. (NETS)

The corresponding verse in the MT has the *crux interpretationis* נשקו־בר, literally "kiss a son." Many scholars have attempted to resolve the link between the MT and the LXX. The simple solution is probably that the

---

68. Of course, there are some differences between the MT and the LXX that are of some interest, for example the use of παιδευτής in Hos 5:2. This choice probably denotes that the translators conceive of God as the one who disciplines his people in the desert (see also Pss. Sol. 8:29). See Eberhard Bons, "'Je suis votre éducateur' (Os 5:2 LXX): Un titre divin et son contexte littéraire," in *Mélanges offerts à Raymond Kuntzmann*, vol. 1 of *Le jugement dans l'un et l'autre Testament*, ed. Eberhard Bons, LD 197 (Paris: Cerf, 2004), 191–206.

69. For example, a *niphal tolerativum* is translated by a passive form that does not convey such a nuance. See particularly the difference between Jer 31:18 MT and Jer 38:18 LXX; see also Pouchelle, *Dieu éducateur*, 243–44.

70. See Pouchelle, *Dieu éducateur*, 278–84.

translator has freely translated a difficult Hebrew form and that he indicated his difficulty by using a rare Greek word, here δράσσομαι, used only here with παιδεία.[71]

The book of Psalms offers other examples in which the MT conveys a nuance of humiliation and oppression, and the LXX does introduce the concept of παιδεία in its disciplinary nuance. An example among others is Ps 89:10 LXX (Ps 90:10 MT):[72]

ὅτι ἐπῆλθεν πραΰτης ἐφ' ἡμᾶς, καὶ παιδευθησόμεθα
Because meekness came upon us, and we shall become disciplined. (NETS)

Here καὶ παιδευθησόμεθα does not correspond to the MT, ונעפה, which has a different meaning ("to fly").[73] Either the *Vorlage* contained the root יסר or the Greek translator read the idea of discipline into the verse.[74]

Two occurrences in Psalms have been interpreted as introducing a more classical meaning of παιδεύω and cognates: Ps 118:66 LXX (Ps 119:66 MT) and Ps 104:22 LXX (Ps 105:22 MT):

χρηστότητα καὶ παιδείαν καὶ γνῶσιν δίδαξόν με (Ps 118:66 LXX)
Kindness and discipline and knowledge teach me. (NETS)

τοῦ παιδεῦσαι τοὺς ἄρχοντας αὐτοῦ ὡς ἑαυτόν (Ps 104:22 LXX [Ps 105:22 MT])
to educate his officials to be like himself. (NETS)

However, in Ps 104:22 LXX, the meaning of παιδεύω is not incompatible with that of יסר in its usage in Proverbs. In the first place, it corresponds to לאסר, a form in the MT that could have been interpreted as deriving from יסר; and secondly, the verb παιδεύω does not share some of the characteristics common to classical Greek: the officials are not children and we know nothing about their origins. Another way to interpret this verse is that it is claiming that Joseph has the same authority over the officials that a master has over his pupils, as described in Proverbs.

---

71. Such a metaphorical usage is sometimes attested in classical Greek literature; see, for example, Sophocles, *Ant.* 235.

72. See also Ps 17:36 LXX (Ps 18:36 MT), or Ps 140:5 LXX (Ps 141:5 MT).

73. NRSV: "and we fly away."

74. See Pouchelle, *Dieu éducateur*, 287–88.

The same could be said about Ps 118:66 LXX (Ps 119:66 MT), which is far from the MT. In classical Greek, παιδεία is neither heard nor taught. In line with the evolution of מוסר from Proverbs to Ben Sira, παιδεία could mean here a rebuking discourse which evolves into a sapiential one.

According to this interpretation, there are three occurrences in the LXX where a prophet is described as announcing the παιδεία κυρίου: Amos 3:7; Hab 1:12; and Ezek 13:9. All these occurrences have in common that they contain the two letters סד deriving either from the word סוד or the verb יסד. It could be argued that the *Vorlage* contains a form associated with the root יסר; however, this is debatable.[75] The main idea of these passages, to which we may add Isa 50:4,[76] is to identify God's action as a rebuking discourse to his people. The divine action in history is conceived as discipline announced by the prophets.

The Appearance of the Classical Meaning

Another argument to deny to παιδεύω and cognates the classical meaning is to observe that this meaning appears in the LXX in some occurrences when παιδεύω and cognates do not correspond to the root יסר. In these occurrences, the context as well as the grammatical use of παιδεύω and cognates implies such a meaning.

The first case is in Ezek 28:3:

μὴ σοφώτερος εἶ σὺ τοῦ Δανιηλ; ἢ σοφοὶ οὐκ ἐπαίδευσάν σε τῇ ἐπιστήμῃ αὐτῶν;
Surely, you are not wiser than Daniel? Or did wise ones not discipline you with their knowledge? (NETS)

The first part of the verse follows more or less the MT: the second part, however, departs from it:

הנה חכם אתה מדנאל כל־סתום לא עממוך
You are indeed wiser than Daniel; no secret is hidden from you. (NRSV)

No link can be drawn between the MT and the LXX, which is here probably a free rendering. It is noteworthy that παιδεύω does not corre-

---

75. See ibid., 297–302.
76. See ibid., 302–3.

spond to יסר and that the grammatical construction perfectly fits classical Greek usage, with the dative denoting the discipline taught.⁷⁷ This usage is unique in the LXX. Tyre is here praised for having been educated in all knowledge and for being wiser than Daniel.

Daniel contains, in fact, virtually all the occurrences of παιδεύω and cognates with the meaning of "education."⁷⁸ In Dan 1:5 LXX the unique compound ἐκπαιδεύω⁷⁹ corresponds to the Hebrew verb גדל:

καὶ ἐκπαιδεῦσαι αὐτοὺς ἔτη τρία
and to educate them for three years. (NETS)

The context precludes interpreting ἐκπαιδεύω with a nuance of rebuking. According to R. Glenn Wooden, the rendering of גדל with a verb linked to education is unique in the LXX.⁸⁰ In fact, we can note the rendering of this verb with τρέφω in Dan 1:5 LXX (Th.) and in Num 6:5. Both τρέφω and (ἐκ)παιδεύω belong in their classical meaning to the semantic field of education, with the meaning "to rear." Such a nuance can also be found in Dan 1:20 LXX:

---

77. See above, "Educating," under the heading "Classical and Hellenistic Greek."
78. There is also Esth 2:7 LXX, in which Mordechai is said to train Esther "for himself as a wife" (NETS). The construction of παιδεύω with εἰς expressing the end or final product does not occur in the LXX (Jer 37:11 LXX [Jer 30:11 MT] is a literal rendering of its *Vorlage*) and the use of the verb παιδεύω to describe the education of women is attested in classical Greek (see Pouchelle, *Dieu éducateur*, 314–16). A last occurrence is noteworthy: Deut 32:10. The presence of παιδεύω does not fit the context if it conveys the meaning of יסר, *pace* Marguerite Harl, "Le grand cantique de Moïse en Deutéronome 32: Quelques traits originaux de la version grecque des Septante," in *La langue de Japhet: Quinze études sur la Septante et le grec des chrétiens* (Paris: Cerf, 1992), 137 n. 29. Corresponding to יבוננהו, it was probably chosen for etymological reasons, as the complex Hebrew form may have not been interpreted as deriving from בין but from בנן, like the Samaritan tradition (see *BHQ*), with a probable nuance of "sustenance." Such a nuance is rarely but clearly attested in classical Greek; for more detail, see Pouchelle, *Dieu éducateur*, 164. In this context, the best way to interpret παιδεύω is probably to see it as a synonym of τρέφω, "nourish," with Deut 32:10 referring here to the manna (see Pouchelle, *Dieu éducateur*, 316–20).
79. Unique in the LXX, this compound is frequently used in Classical Greek.
80. R. Glenn Wooden, "The Recontextualization of Old Greek Daniel 1," in *Ancient Version and Traditions*, vol. 1 of *Of Scribes and Sages: Early Jewish Interpretation and Transmission of Scripture*, ed. Craig A. Evans, LSTS 50; SSEJC 9 (London: T&T Clark, 2004), 58.

καὶ ἐν παντὶ λόγῳ καὶ συνέσει καὶ παιδείᾳ, ὅσα ἐζήτησε παρ' αὐτῶν ὁ βασιλεύς, κατέλαβεν αὐτοὺς σοφωτέρους δεκαπλασίως ὑπερφέροντας τῶν σοφιστῶν καὶ φιλολόγων[81] ἐν πάσῃ τῇ βασιλείᾳ

And in every topic and understanding and education, which the king inquired of them, he took them to be ten times wiser, surpassing the savants and scholars that were in the whole kingdom. (NETS)

According to Usener,[82] παιδεία, corresponding here to בינה, "understanding," conveys its classical meaning. Indeed, this verse shows some semantic associations unknown to the LXX but frequent in classical and Hellenistic literature: παιδεία and λόγος, παιδεία and σύνεσις, and the presence of sophists and philologists.[83] The text of Daniel is not only translated but actualized so as to present the wise Daniel as wiser than the wise people of the time of the translator, that is to say the πεπαιδευμένοι, as Wooden perfectly stated,[84] even if the word itself is not used in the LXX of Daniel.

This participle, frequent in the non-Jewish and non-Christian literature, is very rare in the LXX. Sirach contains almost all of its occurrences.[85] Interestingly, whereas παιδεύω and παιδεία correspond to the root יסר (when the Hebrew counterpart is available), only one occurrence of πεπαιδευμένος corresponds to the root יסר.[86] On the contrary, the participle rather corresponds to Hebrew words or a group of words denoting wisdom or moderation.[87] The same could be said of the occur-

---

81. Rahlfs: ὑπὲρ τοὺς σοφιστὰς καὶ τοὺς φιλοσόφους. For textual criticism, see Wooden, "Recontextualization," 53–54.
82. Usener, "Septuaginta im Horizont des Hellenismus," 111–12.
83. Or philosophers; see n. 81 above.
84. Wooden, "Recontextualization," 54–55, 58–59.
85. Prov 10:4, υἱὸς πεπαιδευμένος σοφὸς ἔσται, τῷ δὲ ἄφρονι διακόνῳ χρήσεται, has no correspondence in the MT. In my opinion, the future sense ἔσται precludes interpreting πεπαιδευμένος as meaning "to be educated," and the form πεπαιδευμένος should here be interpreted as the perfect participle of παιδεύω so as to express an efficient action and not an accomplished one; see Pierre Chantraine, Histoire du parfait grec, CollLing 21 (Paris: Champion, 1927). Psalm 89:12 LXX (Ps 90:12 MT) is controversial, as some manuscripts read πεπεδημένους. Tobit 4:14 is in line with the interpretation of Sirach: the πεπαιδευμένος is the one who masters his or her passion.
86. In Sir 40:29, πεπαιδευμένος could correspond to the verbal noun יסור. However, the Hebrew text is corrupt, and this form occurs in the margin only in a Hebrew sentence that considerably differs from the Greek text; see Patrick Pouchelle, "On the use of πεπαιδευμένος in Greek Sirach," JSCS 47 (2014): 64–65.
87. Sir^C 21:23, איש מזמות, "a man of discretion"; Sir 26:14 has no counterpart but

rence of παιδευτής,[88] which corresponds to the *niphal* of חכם. Moreover, the use of παιδεία in the translator's prologue conveys the classical meaning, whereas its use in the translated text corresponds to the meaning of יסר.[89] It is therefore possible to conclude that, whereas he acknowledges of the association of יסר and παιδεύω, the translator may well have felt free to choose πεπαιδευμένος or παιδευτής as the best rendering in Greek of different Hebrew expressions, emphasizing that the wise person promoted by Greek Sirach is a good challenger to the wise person offered by Greek culture, that is to say the πεπαιδευμένος.[90]

Concluding Remarks

When corresponding to the root יסר, παιδεύω and cognates do not convey the nuance of classical Greek education, that is to say a process that trans-

---

Sir[C] 26:15, which is a doublet of Sir 26:14, contains פה לצרורת, "chastity in mouth" denoting someone who speaks modestly; Sir 34:19 (Sir[B] 31:19), נבון, "intelligent person," and Sir[B] 42:8, זהיר "prudent person."

88. For the occurrence of παιδευτής in Hos 5:2, see above, n. 68.

89. See also Alexander A. Di Lella, "Ben Sira's Doctrine on the Discipline of the Tongue: An Intertextual and Synchronic Analysis," in *The Wisdom of Ben Sira: Studies on Tradition, Redaction, and Theology*, DCLS 1 (Berlin: de Gruyter, 2008), 233–52. Some verses clearly show a "Septuagintal" meaning of παιδεύω, like Sir 6:32. Even some more ambiguous verses could be explained this way. Sirach 10:1, Κριτὴς σοφὸς παιδεύσει τὸν λαὸν αὐτοῦ, could refer to Job 4:3 MT or even to 3 Kgms 12:11, 14 LXX (see also Sir 37:23). Sirach 18:13 associates παιδεύω with ἐλέγχω and διδάσκω in a probable allusion to Ps 93:10, 12 LXX (Ps 94:10, 12 MT), Moreover, ἐπιστρέφω shows a process of conversion (see Deut 30:2 LXX) more than of acquiring knowledge. However, some verses are more problematic, like Sir 30:2, which opens the so-called discourse on education. However, in Sir 30:13, which closes the discourse, παιδεύω, which is frequently translated "to educate," is better interpreted as meaning "to discipline." Indeed, being associated with ἐργάζομαι, the occurrence of παιδεύω here points to a more "tactile" definition of "education," to say the least. However, most of these passages could also be interpreted according to the classical meaning of παιδεύω. Accordingly, we should make the distinction between the text "as translated" and the text "as received," without totally rejecting the idea that Sirach may have merged the two meanings. As for παιδεία, its whole semantic range seems to be represented, from wisdom (Sir 1:27; see also this association in Prov 1:2) to harsh discipline (Sir 4:17 or 21:19).

90. This is perfectly in line with the evolution of πεπαιδευμένος in the Hellenistic period. This person is less the one who is educated to be a good citizen than the one who adopts wise and moderate behavior (see above). See also Pouchelle, "On the Use of πεπαιδευμένος," 68–69.

forms a child into a citizen or a virtuous person. Moreover, the Greek translators made their choice with regard to a more popular meaning of παιδεύω: "to rebuke" an adult so that he would change his behavior.[91] This fact is proven by the context as well as by the grammatical use of these words: when the classical meaning is present, some characteristic features are also detected.[92]

The presence of this more popular nuance may be an indication that the Greek translators of the Pentateuch were not part of the Hellenistic system of education.[93] In this regard, a comparison with the nonasterisked material of Job shows that this translator (who probably knows Homer) does not use παιδεύω and cognates to render the root יסר but instead uses νουθετέω and cognates, which were a better choice so that the translation could be understood by non-Jewish Greeks.[94] By contrast, the translator of the LXX version of Proverbs, who also seems to have a good knowledge of Hellenistic culture, maintains the relationship between παιδεύω and the root יסר.

---

91. "More popular" means here that this nuance is absent from the works of the best philosophers and present in papyri written by less educated people, as discussed above.

92. Such as the construction with the dative of the discipline taught or the association with some keywords like σύνεσις.

93. Of course, it is possible to assert like Arieti, "Vocabulary of Septuagint Amos," 346, that the Greek translators deliberately chose this nuance as a reaction against the Hellenistic culture. But it seems hard to prove. Moreover, some scholars argue against this hypothesis, mainly with the help of the Letter of Aristeas; see for example Sylvie Honigman, *The Septuagint and Homeric Scholarship in Alexandria: A Study in the Narrative of the Letter of Aristeas* (London: Routledge, 2003). For a similar opinion, see Natalio Fernández Marcos, "The Greek Pentateuch and the Scholarly Milieu of Alexandria," SEC 2 (2009): 81–89. Jan Joosten, "Le milieu producteur du Pentateuque grec," REJ 165 (2006): 349–61, has noted the use of military terms where the Hebrew does not justify such words. He then suggests that the LXX was produced in a milieu influenced by the Jewish soldiers in Egypt. The question is still open, and it is worth asking why the translated books of the LXX relatively rarely use words of great importance in Greek educated culture, like ἀρετή. A related question is why the main usage of παιδεύω in the LXX is so far away from the classical meaning.

94. See Pouchelle, "The Use of νουθετέω in the Old Greek," in *XV Congress of the International Organization for Septuagint and Cognate Studies: Munich, 2013*, ed. Wolfgang Kraus, Michaël N. van der Meer, and Martin Meiser, SCS 64 (Atlanta: SBL Press, 2016), 437–54.

This close relationship is very intriguing. In my opinion, in the Pentateuch, it implies that the root יסר was not interpreted as denoting chastisement only, but always a relationship between a person having authority and a person submitted to it, even in its less pedagogic occurrences, like Deut 22:18. This interpretation, in line with the use of יסר in the book of Proverbs, may indicate that the translators were scribes who were attached to their master, even if he beat them, precisely because a master beats his disciples for their own good.[95] Moreover, these translators interpret the relationship between God and his people as such: God disciplines his people so that they will not die but live. The close relationship of Deut 8:5 and Lev 26:18, 21, 28 is best understood in this context. Accordingly, παιδεύω and cognates were preferred to νουθετέω and cognates in the LXX because the latter may fail to express this relationship between the master and his people and because the word παιδεία, more than νουθεσία, was used in Greek culture, and mainly in gnomic wisdom, as a precious treasure to keep.

Of course, the relationship of παιδεύω and cognates to the root יסר should not be pressed too hard in an attempt to prove the identification of the translators with bilingual scribes who did not belong to the Hellenistic education system. In this respect, the comparison with gnomic wisdom that is close to the LXX in many aspects, like the hardness of education and the praise of παιδεία, may be interesting to pursue and could lead to the speculative hypothesis of a Jewish interpretation of a wisdom-like Hellenistic παιδεία.[96]

---

95. The article by Arie van der Kooij, "The Septuagint and Scribal Culture," *XIV Congress of the International Organization for Septuagint and Cognate Studies, Helsinki, 2010*, ed. Melvin K. H. Peters, SCS 59 (Atlanta: Society of Biblical Literature, 2013), 33–39, is a starting point for a renewal of studies on the scribes and the LXX. See also Emanuel Tov, "Les traducteurs des Écritures grecques et leur approches des Écritures," in *Traduire la Bible hébraïque: De la Septante à la Nouvelle Bible Segond / Translating the Hebrew Bible: From the Septuagint to the Nouvelle Bible Segond*, ed. Robert David and Michael Jinbachian, ScBib 15 (Montreal: Médiaspaul, 2005), 122–26, and M. Rösel, "Schreiber, Übersetzer, Theologen: Die Septuaginta als Dokument der Schrift-, Lese-, und Übersetzungskulturen des Judentums," in *Die Septuaginta: Texte, Kontexte, Lebenswelten; Internationale Fachtagung veranstaltet von Septuaginta Deutsch (LXX.D), Wuppertal 20.–23. Juli 2006*, ed. Martin Karrer and Wolfgang Kraus, WUNT 219 (Tübingen: Mohr Siebeck, 2008), 98.

96. Even if the gnomic collection is very hard to date.

Such a hypothesis would need to be grounded on firmer arguments. However, it is harder to assert now, as Bertram did, that the translators of the LXX deliberately chose παιδεύω and cognates to introduce new educational thoughts or new pedagogical concepts into the Hebrew texts. On the contrary, it is παιδεύω and cognates that develop nuances of pure chastisement absent from the non-Jewish Greek texts, whereas it is only in some sectarian documents of Qumran that יסר really does develop nuances of education to law, perhaps under the influence of παιδεύω and cognates. The LXX texts of Ezekiel, Daniel, and Sirach clearly show, however, that their translators were aware of a Hellenistic concept of παιδεία, that is to say a sapiential way of life.

Bibliography

Anderson, Graham. "The *pepaideumenos* in Action: Sophists and Their Outlook in the Early Empire." *ANRW* 33.1:80–208.

———. *The Second Sophistic: A Cultural Phenomenon in the Roman Empire.* London: Routledge, 1993.

Arieti, James A. "The Vocabulary of Septuagint Amos." *JBL* 93 (1974): 338–47.

Balz, Horst, and Gerhard Schneider, eds. *Exegetical Dictionary of the New Testament.* ET. 3 vols. Grand Rapids: Eerdmans, 1990–1993.

Barr, James. *The Semantics of Biblical Language.* 2nd ed. Oxford: Oxford University Press, 1962.

Bertram, Georg. "Der Begriff der Erziehung in der griechischen Bibel." Pages 33–51 in *Imago dei: Beiträge zur theologischen Anthropologie, Gustav Krüger zum siebzigsten Geburstage am 29. Juni 1932 dargebracht.* Edited by Heinrich Bornkamm. Giessen: Töpelmann, 1932.

———. "παιδεύω κτλ." *TDNT* 5:596–625.

Betz, Dorothea. "Gott als Erzieher im Alten Testament: Eine semantisch-traditionsgeschichtliche Untersuchung der Begrifflichkeit *jsr/musar* (*paideuo/paideia*) mit Gott als Subjekt in den Schriften des AT." PhD diss., Universität Osnabrück, 2007.

Bickerman, E. J. *The Jews in the Greek Age.* Cambridge: Harvard University Press, 1988.

Blenkinsopp, Joseph. *Isaiah 1–39: A New Translation with Introduction and Commentary.* AB 19. New York: Doubleday, 2000.

Bons, Eberhard. "'Je suis votre éducateur' (Os 5:2 LXX): Un titre divin et son contexte littéraire." Pages 191–206 in *Mélanges offerts à Raymond*

Kuntzmann. Vol. 1 of *Le jugement dans l'un et l'autre Testament*. Edited by Eberhard Bons. LD 197. Paris: Cerf, 2004.

Branson, R. D. "יָסַר." *TDOT* 6:127–34.

Burnet, Régis. *L'Égypte ancienne à travers les papyrus: Vie quotidienne*. Paris: Pygmalion, 2003.

Calduch-Benages, Núria. "A Wordplay on the Term *mûsar* (Sir 6:22)." Pages 13–26 in *Weisheit als Lebensgrundlage: Festschrift für Friedrich V. Reiterer zum 65. Geburtstag*. Edited by Renate Egger-Wenzel, Karin Schöpflin, and Johannes Friedrich Diehl. DCLS 15. Berlin: de Gruyter, 2013.

Carasik, Michael. *Theologies of the Mind in Biblical Israel*. StBibLit 85. New York: Peter Lang, 2006.

Chantraine, Pierre. *Histoire du parfait grec*. CollLing 21. Paris: Champion, 1927.

Cremer, Hermann. *Biblisch-theologisches Wörterbuch des neutestamentlichen Griechisch*. 11th ed. Gotha: Klotz, 1923.

Deissmann, Adolf. *Bibelstudien: Beiträge, zumeist aus den Papyri und Inschriften, zur Geschichte der Sprache, des Schrifttums und der Religion des hellenistischen Judentums und des Urchristentums*. Marburg: Elwert, 1895.

———. *Neue Bibelstudien: Sprachgeschichtliche Beiträge, zumeist aus den Papyri und Inschriften, zur Erklärung des Neuen Testaments*. Marburg: Elwert, 1897.

Di Lella, Alexander A. "Ben Sira's Doctrine on the Discipline of the Tongue: An Intertextual and Synchronic Analysis." Pages 233–52 in *The Wisdom of Ben Sira: Studies on Tradition, Redaction, and Theology*. DCLS 1. Berlin: de Gruyter, 2008.

Diogenes Laertius. *Lives of Eminent Philosophers*. Translated by R. D. Hicks. 2 vols. LCL. Cambridge: Harvard University Press, 1959–1970.

Fernández Marcos, Natalio. "The Greek Pentateuch and the Scholarly Milieu of Alexandria." *SEC* 2 (2009): 81–89.

Finsterbusch, Karin. *Weisung für Israel: Studien zu religiosem Lehren und Lernen im Deuteronium und in seinem Umfeld*. FAT 44. Tübingen: Mohr Siebeck, 2005.

Fischer, Georg. *Jeremia*. 2 vols. HThKAT. Freiburg im Breisgau: Herder, 2005.

Fitzgerald, John T. "Proverbs 3:11–12, Hebrews 12:5–6, and the Tradition of Corporal Punishment." Pages 291–317 in *Scripture and Traditions: Essays on Early Judaism and Christianity in Honor of Carl R. Holladay*.

Edited by Patrick Gray and Gail R. O'Day. NovTSup 129. Leiden: Brill, 2008.
García Martínez, Florentino, and Eibert J. C. Tigchelaar. *The Dead Sea Scrolls Study Edition*. 2 vols. Leiden: Brill; Grand Rapids: Eerdmans, 1997–1998.
Gerleman, G. "Bemerkungen zum alttestamentlichen Sprachstil." Pages 108–14 in *Studia Biblica et Semitica: Theodoro Christiano Vriezen qui munere professoris theologiae per XXV annos functus est, ab amicis, collegis, discipulis dedicata*. Edited by W. C. van Unnik and A. S. van der Woude. Wageningen: Veenman, 1967.
Harl, Marguerite. *La langue de Japhet: Quinze études sur la Septante et le grec des chrétiens*. Paris: Cerf, 1992.
Harlé, Paul, and Didier Pralon. *Le Lévitique: Traduction du texte grec de la Septante, introduction et notes*. BA 3. Paris: Cerf, 1988.
Honigman, Sylvie. *The Septuagint and Homeric Scholarship in Alexandria: A Study in the Narrative of the Letter of Aristeas*. London: Routledge, 2003.
Jaeger, Werner. *Paideia: The Ideals of Greek Culture*. 3 vols. Translated by Gilbert Highet. Oxford: Oxford University Press, 1939–1944. Repr., Oxford: Oxford University Press, 1967–1971.
Jenni, Ernst, and Claus Westermann, eds. *Theological Lexicon of the Old Testament*. Translated by Mark E. Biddle. 3 vols. Peabody, MA: Hendrickson: 1997.
Jentsch, Werner. *Urchristliches Erziehungsdenken: Die Paideia Kyriu im Rahmen der hellenistisch-jüdischen Umwelt*. BFCT 45.3. Gütersloh: Bertelsmann, 1951.
Joosten, Jan. "Le milieu producteur du Pentateuque grec." *REJ* 165 (2006): 349–61.
Kapelrud, A. S. "לָמַד." *TDOT* 8:4–10.
Kayser, C. L., ed. *Flavii Philostrati Opera auctiora*. 2 vols. Leipzig: Teubner: 1870–1871.
Keown, Gerald L., Pamela J. Scalise, and Thomas G. Smothers. *Jeremiah 26–52*. WBC 27. Waco, TX: Word, 1995.
Kooij, Arie van der. "The Septuagint and Scribal Culture." Pages 33–39 in *XIV Congress of the International Organization for Septuagint and Cognate Studies, Helsinki, 2010*. Edited by Melvin K. H. Peters. SCS 59. Atlanta: Society of Biblical Literature, 2013.
Lundbom, Jack R. *Jeremiah 21–36: A New Translation with Introduction and Commentary*. AB 21B. New York: Doubleday, 2004.

Lysias. Translated by W. R. M. Lamb. LCL. Cambridge: Harvard University Press, 2014.

Marrou, Henri Irénée. *History of Education in Antiquity*. Translated by George Lamb. WSC. London: Sheed & Ward, 1956. Translation of *Histoire de l'éducation dans l'antiquité*, 3rd ed. Paris: Seuil, 1948.

Milligan, George. *Selections from the Greek Papyri*. Cambridge: Cambridge University Press, 1910.

Mopsik, Charles. *La sagesse de Ben Sira*. DP. Lagrasse: Verdier, 2003.

Nicklas, Tobias. "The Bible and Anti-Semitism." Pages 267–80 in *The Oxford Handbook of the Reception History of the Bible*. Edited by Michael Lieb, Emma Mason, and Jonathan Roberts. Oxford: Oxford University Press, 2013.

Olofsson, Staffan. "The Crux Interpretum in Ps 2,12." *SJOT* 9 (1995): 188–99.

O'Neill, Eugene, Jr., and Whitney J. Oates. *The Complete Greek Drama: All the Extant Tragedies of Aeschylus, Sophocles and Euripides, and the Comedies of Aristophanes and Menander*. New York: Random House, 1963.

Perdicoyianni, Hélène. *Étude lexicologique des familles de δαῆναι, de διδάσκειν et de παιδεύειν d'Homère à Hippocrate*. Athens: Perdicoyianni, 1994.

Peursen, W. Th. van. *The Verbal System in the Hebrew Text of Ben Sira*. SSLL 41. Leiden: Brill, 2003.

Pouchelle, Patrick. "The Contribution of 1QS and CD to the Lexicography of יסר." *KUSATU* 19 (2015): 225–36.

———. *Dieu éducateur: Une nouvelle approche d'un concept de la théologie biblique entre Bible Hébraïque, Septante et littérature grecque classique*. FAT 2/77. Tübingen: Mohr Siebeck, 2015.

———. "On the Use of πεπαιδευμένος in Greek Sirach." *JSCS* 47 (2014): 59–68.

———. "The Use of νουθετέω in the Old Greek." Page 437–54 in *XV Congress of the International Organization for Septuagint and Cognate Studies: Munich, 2013*. Edited by Wolfgang Kraus, Michaël N. van der Meer, and Martin Meiser. SCS 64. Atlanta: SBL Press, 2016.

Prijs, Leo. *Jüdische Tradition in der Septuaginta*. Leiden: Brill, 1948.

Rad, Gerhard von. *Theologie des Alten Testaments*. 2 vols. Munich: Kaiser, 1957.

Rea, John R. "Two Christian Letters: PSI VII 831 and VIII 972." *CdE* 45 (1970): 357–68.

Rösel, Martin. "Schreiber, Übersetzer, Theologen: Die Septuaginta als Dokument der Schrift-, Lese-, und Übersetzungskulturen des Judentums." Pages 83–102 in *Die Septuaginta: Texte, Kontexte, Lebenswelten; Internationale Fachtagung veranstaltet von Septuaginta Deutsch (LXX.D), Wuppertal 20.–23. Juli 2006*. Edited by Martin Karrer and Wolfgang Kraus. WUNT 219. Tübingen: Mohr Siebeck, 2008.

———. "Theologie der griechischen Bibel: Zur Wiedergabe der Gottesaussagen im LXX-Pentateuch." *VT* 48 (1998): 49–62.

———. "Towards a 'Theology of the Septuagint.'" Pages 239–52 in *Septuagint Research: Issues and Challenges in the Study of the Greek Jewish Scriptures*. Edited by Wolfgang Kraus and R. Glenn Wooden. SCS 53. Atlanta: Society of Biblical Literature, 2006.

Searby, Denis Michael. *Aristotle in the Greek Gnomological Tradition*. SGU 19. Uppsala: Uppsala University Press, 1998.

Seeligmann, Isac Leo. "Problemen en Perspectieven in het Moderne Septuaginta Onderzoek." *JEOL* 7 (1940): 359–90, 763–66.

———. "Problems and Perspectives in Modern Septuagint Research." Pages 230–80 in Isac Leo Seeligmann, *The Septuagint Version of Isaiah and Cognates Studies*. Edited by Robert Hanhart and Hermann Spieckermann. FAT 40. Tübingen: Mohr Siebeck, 2004.

Shupak, Nili. *Where Can Wisdom be Found? The Sage's Language in the Bible and in Ancient Egyptian Literature*. OBO 130. Göttingen: Vandenhoeck & Ruprecht, 1993.

Skehan, Patrick W., and Alexander A. Di Lella. *The Wisdom of Ben Sira*. AB 39. New York: Doubleday, 1987.

Smith, Mark S., and Wayne T. Pitard. *Introduction with Text, Translation and Commentary of KTU/CAT 1.3–1.4*. Vol. 2 of *The Ugarit Baal Cycle*. VTSup 114. Leiden: Brill, 2009.

Sophocles. *The Ajax of Sophocles*. Translated by Richard C. Jebb, with commentary by A. C. Pearson. Cambridge: Cambridge University Press, 1912.

Tawil, Hayim. "Hebrew יסר, Akkadian *esuru*: A Term of Forced Labor," Pages 185–90 in *Teshûrôt LaAvishur: Studies in the Bible and the Ancient Near East, in Hebrew and Semitic Languages; Festschrift Presented to Prof. Yitzhak Avishur on the Occasion of His 65th Birthday*. Edited by Michael Heltzer and Meir Malul. Tel Aviv: Archeological Center Publications, 2004.

Too, Yun Lee. *A Commentary on Isocrates' Antidosis*. Oxford: Oxford University Press, 2008.

Tov, Emanuel. "Les traducteurs des Écritures grecques et leur approches des Écritures." Pages 103–26 in *Traduire la Bible hébraïque: De la Septante à la Nouvelle Bible Segond / Translating the Hebrew Bible: From the Septuagint to the Nouvelle Bible Segond*. Edited by Robert David and Michael Jinbachian. ScBib 15. Montreal: Médiaspaul, 2005.

Usener, Knut. "Die Septuaginta im Horizont des Hellenismus: Ihre Entwicklung, ihr Charakter und ihre sprachlichkulturelle Position." Pages 78–118 in *Studien zur Entstehung und Bedeutung der Griechischen Bibel*. Vol. 2 of *Im Brennpunkt: Die Septuaginta*. Edited by Siegfried Kreuzer and Jürgen Peter Lesch. BWANT 161. Stuttgart: Kohlhammer, 2004.

Widder, Wendy L. *"To Teach" in Ancient Israel: A Cognitive Linguistic Study of a Biblical Hebrew Lexical Set*. BZAW 456. Berlin: de Gruyter, 2014.

Wooden, R. Glenn. "The Recontextualization of Old Greek Daniel 1." Pages 47–68 in *Ancient Version and Traditions*. Vol. 1 of *Of Scribes and Sages: Early Jewish Interpretation and Transmission of Scripture*. Edited by Craig A. Evans. LSTS 50; SSEJC 9. London: T&T Clark, 2004.

Xenophon. *Memorabilia and Oeconomicus*. Translated by E. C. Marchant. LCL. Cambridge: Harvard University Press, 1965.

Paideia and the Gymnasium

Robert Doran

In his discussion of the interaction between traditional Egyptian education and Greek education in the Hellenistic period, Bernard Legras notes how the first two centuries of the Roman period marked the height of literary and religious production in Demotic.[1] He observes in particular the statements of Diodorus Siculus on Egyptian education, not mentioned in Henri Marrou's classic *A History of Education in Antiquity*:

> In the education of their sons the priests teach them two kinds of writing, that which is called "sacred" and that which is used in the more general instruction. Geometry and arithmetic are given special attention. For the river, by changing the face of the country each year in manifold ways, gives rise to many and varied disputes between neighbors over their boundary lines, and these disputes cannot be easily tested out with any exactness unless a geometer works out the truth scientifically by the application of his experience. And arithmetic is serviceable with reference to the business affairs connected with making a living and also in applying the principles of geometry, and likewise is of no small assistance to students of astrology as well.... As to the general mass of

---

1. Bernard Legras, "Entre grécité et égyptianité: La fonction culturelle de l'éducation grecque dans l'Égypte hellénistique," in *Que reste-t-il de l'éducation classique? Relire "le Marrou" Histoire de l'éducation dans l'Antiquité*, ed. Jean-Marie Pailler and Pascal Payen (Toulouse: Mirail University Press, 2004), 135–36: "les deux premiers siècles de l'empire romain constituaient l'apogée de la production littéraire et religieuse démotique." Here Legras relies on the work of Karl-Heinz Zauzich, "Demotische Texte römischer Zeit," in *Das römisch-byzantinische Ägypten: Akten des internationalen Symposions 26.–30. September 1978 in Trier*, ed. Günter Grimm, Heinz Heinen, and Erich Winter, AT 2 (Mainz: von Zabern, 1983), 77–80. Note also Henri Irénée Marrou, *A History of Education in Antiquity*, trans. George Lamb, WSC (London: Sheed & Ward, 1956).

the Egyptians, they are instructed from their childhood by their fathers or kinsmen in the practices proper to each manner of life as previously described by us; but as for reading and writing, the Egyptians at large give their children only a superficial instruction in them, and not all do this, but for the most part only those who are engaged in the crafts. In wrestling and music, however, it is not customary among them to receive any instruction at all; for they hold that from the daily exercises in wrestling their young men will gain, not health, but a vigor that is only temporary and in fact quite dangerous, while they consider music to be not only useless but even harmful, since it makes the spirits of the listeners effeminate. (Diodorus Siculus, *Bib. hist.* 1.81.1–7 [Oldfather])

The elite, the sons of the priests, preserved the traditional sacred learning of the Egyptians. Yet some Greeks did learn Demotic, as evidenced by the case of two brothers, Ptolemais and Apollonios, sons of the Macedonian Glaukias, who understood and spoke the language, although they may not have been able to read or speak it.[2] In another letter, a mother (?) congratulates her son on learning the Egyptian language.[3] Legras reports the findings of Wolja Erichsen, who published a Demotic papyrus of the Ptolemaic period which outlines a course of studies.[4] At the first level, young children went to an elementary school located near the temple. There they were taught by scribes from the temple writing, grammar, and the formulas used in writing letters. At a second level, the students learned to transcribe Demotic texts written in hieratic script or in hieroglyphs. Was Greek taught in these schools? In a group of buildings near an Egyptian temple were found seven ostraca geared to education in Greek: an alphabet for the students to copy; the names of Zeus, Sarapis, and Ammon (an interesting combination of Greek and Egyptian divinities); problems of geometry; and moral maxims.[5] For Legras, this shows that Greek was taught in Egyptian schools,

---

2. Ulrich Wilcken, *Urkunden der Ptolemäerzeit (Ältere Funde)*, 2 vols. (Berlin: de Gruyter, 1927), 1:116.

3. Claire Préaux, "Lettres privées grecques d'Egypte relatives à l'éducation," *RBPH* 8 (1929): 767–69.

4. Legras, "Grécité et égyptianité," 139–40; Wolja Erichsen, *Eine ägyptische Schulübung in demotischer Schrift* (Copenhagen: Munksgaard, 1948).

5. Rosario Pintaudi and Pieter J. Sijpesteijn, "Ostraka di contenuto scolastico provienti da Narmuthis," *ZPE* 76 (1989): 85–92.

which led to the high level of Greek as the language of administration and legal proceedings.[6]

This penetration of learning Greek in Egyptian schools could serve as an analogy to what was happening in Jerusalem prior to Antiochus IV. Benjamin Wright, in two well-argued essays, has laid out the arguments for education in reading and writing in Greek in pre-Antiochus IV Jerusalem.[7] Drawing on the work of previous scholars, Wright holds that several passages of Ben Sira show "a remarkable similarity to sayings of the Greek poet Theognis"; that Ben Sira "knows and adapts Hellenistic genres"; that he uses his own name, which suggests his imitation of a Greek sense of authorship; and finally, that Ben Sira states that he traveled and stressed the importance of this experience (Sir 34:10–12). When this evidence from Ben Sira is coupled with evidence for Jews in Jerusalem writing in Greek, such as, for example, Eupolemus and possibly Theodotus and Philo the Epic Poet, Wright is led to ask:[8]

> Was there some type of educational institution in Jerusalem before Jason built his *gymnasium* that trained young scribal bureaucrats for professional careers as scribes/sages who would be required to interact with the imperial power whose language was Greek and that would have little interest in learning the language of its client state? If there were such an institution, would it be connected with the temple, as we see in the training of scribal bureaucrats in late Ptolemaic Egypt?[9]

Where Wright is tentative, I would be much more affirmative. The analogy of the schools in Ptolemaic Egypt, as outlined above by Legras,

---

6. Legras, "Grécité et égyptianité," 140–41. See also Gilles Gorre, *Les Relations du clergé égyptien et des Lagides d'après les sources privées*, SH 45 (Leuven: Peeters, 2009), for priests who are royal scribes.

7. Benjamin G. Wright, "What Does India Have to Do with Jerusalem? Ben Sira, Language, and Colonialism," in *Jewish Cultural Encounters in the Mediterranean and Near Eastern World*, ed. Mladen Popovic, Myles Schoonover, and Marijn Vandenberghe (Leiden: Brill, 2017), 136–56; Wright, "Ben Sira and Hellenistic Literature in Greek," in *Tracing Sapiential Traditions in Ancient Judaism*, ed. Hindy Najman, Jean-Sébastien Rey, and Eibert J. C. Tigchelaar; JSJSup 174 (Leiden: Brill, 2016), 71–88. I thank Ben for sending me advance copies of these two articles.

8. Wright, "Ben Sira and Hellenistic Literature," 76–79, also points to the existence of Greek manuscripts in the Qumran corpus, as well as the possibility that writings such as Tobit, Judith, and Qoheleth may "reflect knowledge of Greek literature."

9. Ibid., 87.

shows that leaders of a traditional religion could accommodate their training of priestly scribes to interact with the ruling power. It is interesting, for example, that we know that Eupolemus came from the priestly house of Hakkoz (1 Macc 8:17) mentioned in the list of priestly ancestral houses (1 Chr 24:10). Judea was firmly under Ptolemaic rule for roughly a century (301–198 BCE), and there is no reason why the same process of accommodation, which entailed the elites learning Greek, should not have taken place in Jerusalem, as in the temple cities of Egypt as part of the regular curriculum of children of the priests.

The Gymnasium and the Ephebate

If Greek was being taught in Jerusalem before Antiochus IV, what was all the fuss about the building of a gymnasium and the introduction of an ephebate? The lurid poetic statement of 1 Macc 1:15—"they made foreskins for themselves" (ἐποίησαν ἑαυτοῖς ἀκροβυστίας)—comes, as I have shown elsewhere, within a concentrated mass of biblical allusions, whereby the author forged a new metaphor to invoke how his opponents had rejected God's covenant (see Gen 17:4).[10] Those who participated in the gymnasium did not have to be naked or uncircumcised. What was it, then, that aroused such horror, as in 2 Macc 4:11–17, at the institution of the gymnasium and the ephebate in Jerusalem? We find lists of Jewish ephebes, from a later period of course, but there seems to be no problem with their attending the gymnasium.[11] There is also the statement of Josephus that Seleucus I (312–281/280 BCE) allowed those Jews who did not want to use foreign oil to "receive a fixed sum of money from the gymnasiarchs to pay for their own kind of oil" (*Ant.* 12.120 [Marcus, LCL]). So there was no problem with their participating in the gymnasium in Josephus's eyes. What was the problem in Jerusalem?

---

10. Robert Doran, "Jason's Gymnasium," in *Of Scribes and Scrolls: Studies on the Hebrew Bible, Intertestamental Judaism, and Christian Origins Presented to John Strugnell*, ed. Harold W. Attridge, John J. Collins, and Thomas H. Tobin (Lanham, MD: University Press of America, 1990), 106–8.

11. Margaret H. Williams, *The Jews among the Greeks and Romans: A Diasporan Sourcebook* (Baltimore: Johns Hopkins University Press, 1998), 107–8, 113–14.

The Ephebate

Andrzej Chankowski has shown how the system of education known as the ephebate had its beginning at a precise moment in Athens and that it spread from there to other Greek cities on the mainland, on the Aegean islands and in Asia Minor.[12] He has shown, through an exhaustive analysis of the terminology, that

> le terme ἔφηβος/ἔφηβοι n'est jamais utilisé à l'époque classique (et longtemps à l'époque hellénistique) hors du context institutionnel.... Ce mot, précis et univoque, appartient à la terminologie institutionnelle de la communauté civique, et ne désigne, jusqu'à une époque relativement tardive, que celui qui exerce un service d'entraînement civique dans un cadre prescript par la cité.[13]

It designated the period prior to becoming an adult in the social and legal practice of the Greek cities, and it was for this reason that the term ἔφηβος/ἔφηβοι was invented at Athens.[14] The Athenians

> décidèrent de ritualiser l'aboutissement des jeunes gens, à dix-huit ans, à cette *hèbè* qui, du point de vue de la cité, était la plus importante.... Cette ritualization consistait à les obliger à accomplir non pas, comme cela faisait dans les phratries, un rite ponctuel, mais tout un service qui avait pour but à la fois de leur inculquer des aptitudes pratiques (en particulier dans le domaine militaire) et de leur confier, pendant cette période transitoire, un rôle culturel particulier, joué traditionnellement, dans les sociétés grecques, par ceux qui se trouvaient au moment du passage entre l'âge d'enfant et l'âge adulte.[15]

Chankowski dates the institution of the ephebate to after the Peloponnesian War.[16]

---

12. Andrzej S. Chankowski, *L'éphébie hellénistique: Étude d'une institution civique dans les cités grecques des îles de la Mer Égée et de l'Asie Mineure* (Paris: de Boccard, 2010).
13. Ibid., 135.
14. Ibid., 137–38.
15. Ibid., 139.
16. Ibid., 140.

The ephebes were trained in military exercises, as the list from a second century BCE Babylonian inscription shows.[17] Chankowski insists that these exercises did not degenerate into purely sporting games. They did not train someone to be a member of the royal forces, but they showed the youths of the city how to use weapons. These young men were being trained to defend their city in local skirmishes and engagements with their neighboring cities, with whom jealousies and frictions remained, even as they were under the same imperial rule:

> Les exercices pratiqués dans les gymnases avaient pour but de transmettre aux jeunes gens des aptitudes physiques générales et des capacités militaires adaptées à de petits conflits locaux plutôt qu'à de grandes guerres menées par les rois. Des patrouilles sur le territoire pour intervenir contre des actes de violence ponctuels ou pour les prévenir constituaient probablement des taches assumées par ces milices locales beaucoup plus fréquemment que des batailles régulières avec des voisins.[18]

John Ma has insightfully analyzed these conflicts in Asia Minor.[19] However, during their training, the ephebes probably did not participate in these military activities; rather, they did so once they had completed their ephebate. The ephebes were on the way to becoming citizens.

Finally, Chankowski has underlined how the ephebes were part of the processions and cultic ceremonies of a city. He writes:

> Manifestement, ce groupe [des jeunes gens] est conçu par les citoyens non pas, ou non pas exclusivement, comme le groupe de ceux qui deviendront citoyens, mais comme un groupe faisant déjà partie de la communauté ét constituant un élément indispensable à son image et à son ordre sacral.... De même que les magistrats et les prêtres symboli-

---

17. Bernard Haussoulier, "Inscriptions grecques de Babylone," *Klio* 9 (1909): 352–63.

18. Chankowski, *L'éphébie hellénistique*, 380. See also Chankowski, "L'éphébie à l'époque hellénistique: Institution d'éducation civique," in Pailler and Payen, *Que reste-t-il de l'éducation classique?*, 271–79; Chankowski, "L'entraînement militaire des éphèbes dans les cités grecques d'Asie Mineure à l'époque hellénistique: Nécessité pratique ou tradition atrophiée?," in *Les cités grecques et la guerre en Asie Mineure à l'époque hellénistique*, ed. Jean-Christophe Couvenhes and Henri-Louis Fernoux (Tours: Université François-Rabelais, 2004), 55–76.

19. John Ma, "Fighting *poleis* of the Hellenistic World," in *War and Violence in Ancient Greece*, ed. Hans van Wees (London: Duckworth, 2000), 175–86.

sent la pérennité civique, de même la jeunesse symbolize la renovation permanente de la cite.... En outre, ces cérémonies avaient une function educative importante. Les fêtes publiques auxquelles participaient les éphèbes étaient, en effet, toujours liées à un événement important, soit du passé mythique ou historique, soit du present. Une procession ou une cérémonie d'accueil permettait de la sorte aux éphèbes de perpétuer ou de vivre la tradition de leur communauté.[20]

The education that the ephebes received was therefore not primarily literary. Saskia Hin has shown how infrequently intellectual activities are mentioned during the ephebate, while most ephebic inscriptions report athletic activities.[21] The education was geared primarily to physical and military training, and to becoming an active member of the civic community:

> There is no or only very meagre evidence that ephebes took courses in other sciences, such as medicine and music; intellectual disciplines are not found on the list of victors in the gymnasium. One must assume that this instruction, if it took place at all, was provided outside the structure of the *ephebeia*, most likely through private education by home tutors and in private schools. Young men could also attend lectures by itinerant scholars in the gymnasium.... However, the *ephebeia* was not all about physical training. Considerable attention was also paid to developing the social skills and the proper conduct of the ephebes. They were trained in endurance (*philoponia*), in bodily harmony or fitness (*euexia*), and in discipline or orderly behaviour (*eutaxia*).... [These skills] were first and foremost regarded as integral to the proper conduct of the citizen in the *polis*.[22]

What's the Problem?

If the ephebate was geared to turning out good citizens, who participated in the city's religious actions and who were prepared to defend the city from attack, why then was its institution in Jerusalem so vigorously opposed in writings such as 1 and 2 Maccabees? The ephebes no doubt learned Greek, but their literary and intellectual formation seems to have

---

20. Chankowski, *L'éphébie hellénistique*, 426–27.
21. Saskia Hin, "Class and Society in the Cities of the Greek East: Education during the *Ephebeia*," *AncSoc* 37 (2007): 155–57.
22. Christian Laes and Johan H. M. Strubbe, *Youth in the Roman Empire: The Young and Restless Years?* (Cambridge: Cambridge University Press, 2014), 114, 117.

taken place outside the gymnasium. As in Ptolemaic Egypt, this education in Greek would have occurred alongside traditional scribal training around the temple.

As regards the age of the ephebes, the *Athenian Constitution*, an important source for understanding the political structure of ancient Athens, has the following:

> The present state of the constitution is as follows. The franchise is open to all who are of citizen birth by both parents. They are enrolled among the demesmen at the age of eighteen.... Under the charge of these [chosen] persons the youths first of all make the circuit of the temples; then they proceed to Piraeus, and some of them garrison Munichia and some the south shore. The Assembly also elects two trainers, with subordinate instructors, who teach them to fight in heavy armor, to use the bow and javelin, and to discharge a catapult. The guardians receive from the state a drachma apiece for their keep, and the youths four obols apiece. Each guardian receives the allowance for all the members of his tribe and buys the necessary provisions for the common stock (they mess together by tribes), and generally superintends everything. In this way they spend the first year. The next year, after giving a public display of their military evolutions, on the occasion when the assembly meets in the theatre, they receive a shield and spear from the state; after which they patrol the country and spend their time in the forts. For these two years they are on garrison duty, and wear the military cloak, and during this time they are exempt from all taxes. They also can neither bring an action at law, nor have one brought against them, in order that they may have no excuse for requiring leave of absence; though exception is made in cases of actions concerning inheritances and wards of state, or of any sacrificial ceremony connected with the family. When the two years have elapsed they thereupon take their position among the other citizens. Such is the manner of the enrollment of the citizens and the training of the youths. (Aristotle, *Ath. pol.* 42 [Kenyon])

Here the ephebe is eighteen years old, and the training lasts for two years. Chankowski has gone over in great detail the difficulties entailed in calculating exact age when there is no birth registry and also how the length of the ephebate varied over time and place. By the early second century BCE, it would only have lasted a year at Athens.[23] According to the *Constitution of Athens*, an ephebe would begin the ephebate at eighteen

---

23. Chankowski, *L'éphébie hellénistique*, 235–317.

years old, and after two years would take on the responsibilities of a citizen. One might note how this resonates with Jewish tradition:

> The Lord spoke to Moses: "When you take a census of the Israelites to register them, at registration all of them shall give a ransom for their lives to the LORD, so that no plague may come upon them for being registered.... Each one who is registered, from twenty years old and upward, shall give the LORD's offering." (Exod 30:11-12, 14 NRSV)

> Take a census of the whole congregation of Israelites, in their clans, by ancestral houses, according to the number of names, every male individually; from twenty years old and upward, everyone one in Israel able to go to war. (Num 1:2-3 NRSV)

The same time frame is also found in 1Q28a (1QSa):

> And this is the rule for all the armies of the congregation, for all native Israelites. From [his] infancy, [they shall edu]cate him in the book of Hagy, and according to his age, instruct him in the precept[s of] the covenant, and he will [receive] his [ins]truction [מו[סרו]] in their regulations; from the age of ten years he will enter among the youth [reading בטף instead of בטב]. At the age of twenty ye[ars, he will transfer to] those enrolled to enter the lot among his fam[il]y and join the holy community. (1Q28a I, 6-9)[24]

The age of twenty thus seems to have been the traditional Jewish age for entering into full membership in the community, and no different from that of the Athenian community as described in the *Constitution of Athens*.

Setting aside a special time for military training is not mentioned in the literature just cited. However, those residing in Jerusalem did have some pesky neighbors to the north. Josephus records their hostility to the Jews

---

24. I have basically followed the translation of Florentino García Martínez and Eibert J. C. Tigchelaar, *The Dead Sea Scrolls Study Edition*, 2 vols. (Leiden: Brill; Grand Rapids: Eerdmans, 1997-1998), 1:101. However, there seems to be a progression in age status from נער to טף and on the age of twenty years, and so I have modified the translation accordingly. At line 8, I follow Jean Carmignac in thinking that one should insert בן before שנים עשר. See his "Règle de la Congrégation," in *Les Textes de Qumran: Traduits et Annotés*, ed. Carmignac et al., 2 vols., AuBib (Paris: Letouzey et Ané, 1961-1963), 2:19 n. 20.

in the time of Darius (*Ant.* 11.114). When Antiochus the Great controlled the area, "the Samaritans, who were flourishing, afflicted [ἐκάκωσαν] the Judeans greatly, laying waste their land and carrying off slaves" (*Ant.* 12.156 [Marcus, LCL, modified]). During the Maccabean period, Josephus notes how the Samaritans had been only too happy to inflict injury on the Judeans and their allies (*Ant.* 13.275). With such a troublesome neighbor to the north, the Judeans needed to have their young men undergo military training and preparedness.

So what is the problem with introducing the ephebate?

Issues of Identity

Chankowski has also explored those cities that did not accept the ephebate system. Foremost among these is Sparta, which had its own system of military training. In Lucian's *Anacharsis*, where Solon, the Athenian lawgiver, is explaining to the Scythian Anacharsis the Spartan system of training, Anacharsis asks why Solon did not imitate the system set up by the Spartan Lycurgus. Solon replies: "Because we are content, Anacharsis, with these exercises which are our own [οἰκεῖα]; we do not much care to copy foreign customs" (τὰ ξενικά; *Anach.* 39 [Harmon, LCL, modified]). Here the distinction between the two systems is clearly shown. It is also seen in the actions of the Achaean leader Philopoemen against Sparta in 188 BCE, and the Spartan reaction to them. Plutarch reports:

> Now, glutting his anger at the Lacedaemonians and unworthily trampling upon them in their misery, he treated their constitution [τὴν πολιτείαν] in the most cruel and lawless [παρανομώτατον] fashion. For he took away and abolished the system of training which Lycurgus had instituted [τὴν Λυκουργεῖον ἀγωγήν], and compelled their boys and their young men to adopt the Achaean in place of their ancestral discipline [τῆς πατρίου παιδείας], being convinced that while they were under the laws of Lycurgus they would never be humble.
>
> For the time being, then, owing to their great calamities, the Spartans suffered Philopoemen to eat away, as it were, the sinews of their city, and became tractable and submissive; but a while afterwards, having obtained permission from the Romans, they abandoned the Achaean polity [τὴν Ἀχαικὴν πολιτείαν] and resumed and reestablished that which had come down from their fathers [τὴν πάτριον], so far as was possible

PAIDEIA AND THE GYMNASIUM   145

after their many misfortunes and ruin. (Plutarch, *Phil.* 16.5–6 [Perrin, LCL, modified])[25]

Here the training and discipline established by Lycurgus is seen as fundamental to the Spartans' sense of who they were, and what distinguished them from the Athenian system. Chankowski also shows how there is no evidence for the ephebate system at Rhodes. As he comments: "L'attachement des Rhodiens à leur propre identité est, en tout cas, un phénomène bien connu."[26] He also notes the absence of the ephebate system modeled on the Athenian at Delos and Korissia on the island of Kea. Chankowski suggests that Delos while it was independent may not have wanted a system of military training because of the reputation of its sacred sanctuary, while Korissia already had in place its own system of military training.[27]

In all these negative cases, then, the cities did not want to follow the Athenian model of training but to maintain their own identity vis-à-vis the civic training of their young men.

The Case in Jerusalem

If Jason the high priest of Jerusalem received permission to install a gymnasium and the ephebate system soon after Antiochus IV took power in September 175 BCE (2 Macc 4:9), it would take some time for Jason to build a gymnasium with all its attendant facilities. So one can assume that, at the earliest, the gymnasium would have been operational by the end of 174 BCE. Until the rebuff of Antiochus IV by the Roman legate Popillus Laenas in July 168 BCE and Antiochus's subsequent plundering of the Jerusalem temple and his change of the city's ancestral laws (2 Macc 5:11–6:1), the activity in the gymnasium seems to have taken place without any rejection by the people in Jerusalem. In fact, if the gymnasium was built on the unpopulated area of the western hill of Jerusalem, the gymnasium would have filled in empty space and provided jobs for the local community.[28] We have laid out above the reasons why there should have been no outcry against the implementation of the ephebate and the gymnasium

---

25. See also Livy, *Ab urbe cond.* 38.34.
26. Chankowski, *L'éphébie hellénistique*, 232.
27. Ibid., 206–9, 210–14, 232–33.
28. Benjamin Mazar and Hanan Eshel, "Who Built the First Wall of Jerusalem?,"

in Jerusalem. What were the reasons in favor? For all its rhetorical edge, the author of 1 Maccabees is on to something when he states that "they yoked themselves [ἐζευγίσθησαν] to the gentiles" (1 Macc 1:15).[29] It would seem that Jason wasted no time in making these connections. The games at Tyre mentioned at 2 Macc 4:18 were probably held in 174 BCE.[30] As I have argued elsewhere, the host city holding games usually sent out invitations to those connected to the city by συγγένεια (kinship).[31] The games at Tyre were celebrated in honor of Heracles, long connected with Sparta, and Jason claims kinship with the Spartans (2 Macc 5:9).

Jason the high priest seems to have been a person of great ambition for Jerusalem. He would have seen the economic advantages that Jerusalem had received by going over to the side of Antiochus III in his campaigns against the Ptolemies. In response, Antiochus had provided the means for the temple and city to be rebuilt, had given tax relief to restart the economy, and in many ways showed his *philanthropia* towards the city and the way reciprocity worked (Josephus, *Ant.* 12.133–153).[32] By founding a gymnasium in Jerusalem, he joined Jerusalem to a select group of cities in Syria. There were gymnasia at Laodicea and Babylon, and no doubt in the Phoenician cities of Sidon, Tyre, and Babylon. Jerusalem would now be able to pursue economic and other ties with these cities, and to increase its prosperity. As I have noted above, there was no reason why there should not be a system of military training for young men in Jerusalem, and the emphasis on participation in the rituals of the city would only enhance what was already taking place. That young men entered the adult stage at age twenty was already part of the traditional lore of Judeans.[33] One might

---

IEJ 48 (1998): 268. See also Bezalel Bar-Kochva, *Judas Maccabaeus: The Jewish Struggle against the Seleucids* (Cambridge: Cambridge University Press, 1989), 447 n. 7.

29. My translation.

30. Robert Doran, *2 Maccabees*, Hermeneia (Minneapolis: Fortress, 2012), 107.

31. Robert Doran, "The High Cost of a Good Education," in *Hellenism in the Land of Israel*, ed. John J. Collins and Gregory E. Sterling, CJA 13 (Notre Dame: University of Notre Dame Press, 2001), 108–9.

32. See the fine discussion of this notion in John Ma, *Antiochus III and the Cities of Western Asia Minor* (Oxford: Oxford University Press, 1999), 179–242. Consult also Rolf Strootman, "Babylonian, Macedonian, King of the World: The Antiochus Cylinder from Borsippa and Seleukid Imperial Imagination," in *Shifting Social Imaginaries in the Hellenistic World: Narrations, Practices and Image*, ed. Eftychia Stavrianopolou, MnemosyneSup 363 (Leiden: Brill, 2013), 67–91.

33. Some would object if the Judean ephebes exercised naked. But there is no

also raise the question of how many young men per year would have been ephebes in Jerusalem. No doubt older men would have also taken part in the exercises in the gymnasium, but one needs to ask what the population of Jerusalem would have been at this time. Hillel Geva has estimated the population of pre-Maccabean Jerusalem to be between two thousand five hundred and three thousand.[34] How many ephebes would such a city produce? Christian Laes and Johan Strubbe state: "A small city such as Apollonis [in Lydia] would typically have had a population of around five thousand. On this basis, one would expect there to have been around fifteen aristocratic boys of ephebic age at any one time."[35] The inscriptional evidence, however, shows that there were fifty-six ephebes, and Laes and Strubbe surmise that some public funds were available for boys from less wealthy families. They also speculate: "It is possible that, in very small cities, there were not enough young men available to organize the *ephebeia* every year."[36] Given these figures, how many ephebes could Jerusalem, a city half the size of Apollonis in Lydia, have mounted each year? Eight? Or, if funds were available, twenty-six? Would this have upset the life of the city that much?

Here one comes back to the reasons why Sparta and other cities rejected the ephebate model—for reasons of maintaining their own identity. Wright has noted how Ben Sira, though he knew Greek, nevertheless wrote in Hebrew, and has concluded: "Thus, Ben Sira's choice to write in Hebrew both witnesses to and likely made a significant contribution to the trend in the Second Temple period to fashion Hebrew as a marker of Jewish identity."[37] I have noted elsewhere how the language of 2 Macc 4:10–17, where the author speaks of the disastrous effects of the gymnasium on the *politeia* of Jerusalem, reflects the way in which Greek authors emphasize that the educational system is an integral part of each culture's

---

mention of their having done so, and, since the ephebate was a civic institution, each city controlled what was done in the ephebate. Thucydides had noted how "many foreigners, especially in Asia, wore loincloths for boxing matches and wrestling bouts" (*P.W.* 1.6). J. P. Thuillier held that Roman athletes were not naked. See his "Denis d'Halicarnasse et les jeux romains (*Antiquités romains* VII, 72–73)," *MEFR* 87 (1975): 563–81.

34. Hillel Geva, "Jerusalem's Population in Antiquity: A Minimalist View," *TA* 41 (2014): 143.

35. Laes and Strubbe, *Youth in the Roman Empire*, 110.

36. Ibid., 110 n. 17.

37. Wright, "What Does India Have to Do with Jerusalem?," 151.

politeia, and especially with what Philopoemen did to Sparta.[38] The attack on the gymnasium in 1 Macc 1:11–15 is also a passage devoted to character assassination of the Maccabean opponents.[39] The discussion of the gymnasium in both authors is thus part of a rhetorical strategy to establish a Jewish identity clearly separate from that of "the Greeks."

Conclusion

What I have tried to suggest is that there were no practical reasons why there should not have been military training of the young men and their enculturation into the ritual life of the Jerusalem community. There is no indication of any protest from the founding of the gymnasium till the attack of Antiochus IV on Jerusalem. Second Maccabees reflects a rhetorical effort to establish a Jewish identity distinct from the Greeks, and the negative portrayal of the gymnasium and the ephebate reflects this effort.

Bibliography

Aristotle. *The Athenian Constitution*. Translated by Sir Frederic G. Kenyon. *The Internet Classics Archive*. Daniel C. Stevenson, Web Atomics. http://tinyurl.com/SBL3548a.

Bar-Kochva, Bezalel. *Judas Maccabaeus: The Jewish Struggle against the Seleucids*. Cambridge: Cambridge University Press, 1989.

Carmignac, Jean. "Règle de la Congrégation." Pages 9–27 in vol. 2 of *Les Textes de Qumran: Traduits et Annotés*. Edited by Jean Carmignac, Pierre Guilbert, Édouard Cothenet, and Hubert Lignée. 2 vols. AuBib. Paris: Letouzey et Ané, 1961–1963.

Chankowski, Andrezej S. "L'entraînement militaire des éphèbes dans les cités grecques d'Asie Mineure à l'époque hellénistique: Nécessité pratique ou tradition atrophiée?" Pages 55–76 in *Les cités grecques et la guerre en Asie Mineure à l'époque hellénistique*. Edited by Jean-Christophe Couvenhes and Henri-Louis Fernoux. Tours: Université François-Rabelais, 2004.

———. "L'éphébie à l'époque hellénistique: Institution d'éducation civique." Pages 271–79 in *Que reste-t-il de l'éducation classique? Relire "le*

---

38. Doran, "Jason's Gymnasium," 103–6.
39. Ibid., 106–8.

Marrou" *Histoire de l'éducation dans l'Antiquité.* Edited by Jean-Marie Pailler and Pascal Payen. Toulouse: Mirail University Press, 2004.

———. *L'éphébie hellénistique: Étude d'une institution civique dans les cités grecques des îles de la Mer Égée et de l'Asie Mineure.* Paris: de Boccard, 2010.

Diodorus Siculus. *Bibliotheca historica.* Translated by Charles Henry Oldfather, Charles Lawton Sherman, Francis R. Walton, and C. Bradford Welles. 12 vols. LCL. Cambridge: Harvard University Press, 1933–2014.

Doran, Robert. *2 Maccabees.* Hermeneia. Minneapolis: Fortress, 2012.

———. "The High Cost of a Good Education." Pages 94–115 in *Hellenism in the Land of Israel.* Edited by John J. Collins and Gregory E. Sterling. CJA 13. Notre Dame: University of Notre Dame Press, 2001.

———. "Jason's Gymnasium." Pages 99–109 in *Of Scribes and Scrolls: Studies on the Hebrew Bible, Intertestamental Judaism, and Christian Origins Presented to John Strugnell.* Edited by Harold W. Attridge, John J. Collins, and Thomas H. Tobin. Lanham, MD: University Press of America, 1990.

Erichsen, Wolja. *Eine ägyptische Schulübung in demotischer Schrift.* Copenhagen: Munksgaard, 1948.

García Martínez, Florentino, and Eibert J. C. Tigchelaar. *The Dead Sea Scrolls Study Edition.* 2 vols. Leiden: Brill; Grand Rapids: Eerdmans, 1997–1998.

Geva, Hillel. "Jerusalem's Population in Antiquity: A Minimalist View." *TA* 41 (2014): 131–60.

Gorre, Gilles. *Les relations du clergé égyptien et des Lagides d'après les sources privées.* SH 45. Leuven: Peeters, 2009.

Haussoulier, Bernard. "Inscriptions grecques de Babylone." *Klio* 9 (1909): 352–63.

Hin, Saskia. "Class and Society in the Cities of the Greek East: Education during the *Ephebeia.*" *AncSoc* 37 (2007): 141–66.

Josephus. Translated by Henry St. J. Thackeray, Ralph Marcus, and Louis H. Feldman. 10 vols. LCL. Cambridge: Harvard University Press, 1926–1965.

Laes, Christian, and Johan H. M. Strubbe. *Youth in the Roman Empire: The Young and Restless Years?* Cambridge: Cambridge University Press, 2014.

Legras, Bernard. "Entre grécité et égyptianité: La fonction culturelle de l'éducation grecque dans l'Égypte hellénistique." Pages 133–41 in

Que reste-t-il de l'éducation classique? Relire "le Marrou" Histoire de l'éducation dans l'Antiquité. Edited by Jean-Marie Pailler and Pascal Payen. Toulouse: Mirail University Press, 2004.

Lucian. Translated by A. M. Harmon, K. Kilburn, and M. D. MacLeod. 8 vols. LCL. London: Heinemann; New York: Macmillan, 1913–1967.

Ma, John. *Antiochus III and the Cities of Western Asia Minor*. Oxford: Oxford University Press, 1999.

———. "Fighting *poleis* of the Hellenistic World." Pages 175–86 in *War and Violence in Ancient Greece*. Edited by Hans van Wees. London: Duckworth, 2000.

Marrou, Henri Irénée. *A History of Education in Antiquity*. Translated by George Lamb. WSC. London: Sheed & Ward, 1956.

Mazar, Benjamin, and Hanan Eshel. "Who Built the First Wall of Jerusalem?" *IEJ* 48 (1998): 265–68.

Pintaudi, Rosario, and Pieter J. Sijpesteijn. "Ostraka di contenuto scolastico provienti da Narmuthis." *ZPE* 76 (1989): 85–92.

Plutarch. *Lives*. Translated by Bernadotte Perrin. 11 vols. LCL. London: Heinemann; New York: Macmillan, 1914–1926.

Préaux, Claire. "Lettres privées grecques d'Egypte relatives à l'éducation." *RBPH* 8 (1929): 757–800.

Strootman, Rolf. "Babylonian, Macedonian, King of the World: The Antiochus Cylinder from Borsippa and Seleukid Imperial Imagination." Pages 67–91 in *Shifting Social Imaginaries in the Hellenistic World: Narrations, Practices and Image*. Edited by Eftychia Stavrianopolou. MnemosyneSup 363. Leiden: Brill, 2013.

Thuillier, J. P. "Denis d'Halicarnasse et les jeux romains (*Antiquités romains* VII, 72–73)." *MEFR* 87 (1975): 563–81.

Wilcken, Ulrich. *Urkunden der Ptolemäerzeit (Ältere Funde)*. 2 vols. Berlin: de Gruyter, 1927.

Williams, Margaret H. *The Jews among the Greeks and Romans: A Diasporan Sourcebook*. Baltimore: Johns Hopkins University Press, 1998.

Wright, Benjamin G. "Ben Sira and Hellenistic Literature in Greek." Pages 71–88 in *Tracing Sapiential Traditions in Ancient Judaism*. Edited by Hindy Najman, Jean-Sébastien Rey, and Eibert J. C. Tigchelaar. JSJSup 174. Leiden: Brill, 2016.

———. "What Does India Have to Do with Jerusalem? Ben Sira, Language, and Colonialism." Pages 136–56 in *Jewish Cultural Encounters in the Mediterranean and Near Eastern World*. Edited by Mladen Popovic, Myles Schoonover, and Marijn Vandenberghe. Leiden: Brill, 2017.

Zauzich, Karl-Heinz. "Demotische Texte römischer Zeit." Pages 77–80 in *Das römisch-byzantinische Ägypten: Akten des internationalen Symposions 26.–30. September 1978 in Trier*. Edited by Günter Grimm, Heinz Heinen, and Erich Winter. AT 2. Mainz: von Zabern, 1983.

Part 2
Sapiential and Apocalyptic Perspectives on Ancient Jewish Pedagogy

Reading Proverbs in Light of Torah: The Pedagogy of 4QBeatitudes

Elisa Uusimäki

The Jewish wisdom tradition flourished in the Second Temple period and subsequently left a mark on the history of Western civilization, especially with its impact on the formation of Christology, "gnostic" Sophia myths, and Jewish notions of the Shekhinah.[1] It may thus be surprising that wisdom became one of the core areas of biblical studies only in the late twentieth century.[2] This shift was effected by several factors: for example, scholarly interests increasingly expanded beyond historical questions; with the emergence of women's studies, special attention was paid to the female figures of Proverbs; and new textual discoveries were made at Qumran.[3]

I wish to thank Matthew Goff and Karina Martin Hogan for their valuable feedback in the preparation of this essay, which builds on my monograph *Turning Proverbs towards Torah: An Analysis of 4Q525*, STDJ 117 (Leiden: Brill, 2016).

1. See, for example, George W. MacRae, "The Jewish Background of the Gnostic Sophia Myth," *NovT* 12 (1970): 86–101; James D. G. Dunn, *Christology in the Making: A New Testament Inquiry into the Origins of the Doctrine of the Incarnation*, 2nd ed. (Grand Rapids: Eerdmans, 1989), 163–250; Peter Schäfer, *Mirror of His Beauty: Feminine Images of God from the Bible to the Early Kabbalah*, JCMAMW (Princeton: Princeton University Press, 2002), 79–135; Ismo Dunderberg, *Beyond Gnosticism: Myth, Lifestyle, and Society in the School of Valentinus* (New York: Columbia University Press, 2008), 95–118.

2. James L. Crenshaw, *Old Testament Wisdom: An Introduction*, 3rd ed. (Louisville: Westminster John Knox, 2010), 1–4.

3. For the expansion of interests beyond purely historical questions, see especially Gerhard von Rad, *Wisdom in Israel*, trans. James D. Martin (Nashville: Abingdon, 1972). On female figures in Proverbs, see especially Claudia V. Camp, *Wisdom and the Feminine in the Book of Proverbs*, BLS 11 (Decatur, GA: Almond Press, 1985); Camp, *Wise, Strange, and Holy: The Strange Woman and the Making of the Bible*, JSOTSup 320 (Sheffield: Sheffield Academic, 2000).

The Dead Sea Scrolls brought a plethora of new material to be studied along with the texts of the Hebrew Bible and the Septuagint.[4] In addition to the several copies of Instruction (1Q26, 4Q415–418, 418a, 418c, 423) and Mysteries (1Q27, 4Q299–301), parts of Wiles of the Wicked Woman (4Q184), Sapiential Admonitions B (4Q185), Ways of Righteousness[a–b] (4Q420–421), and Beatitudes (4Q525) call for closer study.[5] These texts typically reflect a mélange of traditions, such as wisdom, eschatology, prophecy, torah piety, and liturgy.[6] On basis of those texts, a more nuanced picture of early Jewish wisdom literature(s) has been reconstituted; many texts emphasize wisdom's religious and revealed aspects as well as its relevance for the acquisition of eternal life.[7]

Yet pedagogy and instruction continue to be integral components of wisdom texts. This article analyzes these themes in Beatitudes (4Q525).[8] The extant manuscript, which includes a handful of larger fragments (4Q525 2 II–III; 5; 14 II; 15; 24 II), will be shown to illustrate the development of the wisdom tradition towards a synthesis of wisdom and torah. How do these traditions meet and intersect in the pedagogy of 4Q525? For what purposes does the author make use of earlier traditions in the formation of his own pedagogical program? I argue that the text's teaching builds upon Prov 1–9, but the composition transforms this source to serve contemporary pedagogical goals, particularly the practice of torah piety. The lack of explicitly sectarian features suggests that 4Q525 illuminates

---

4. In particular, see Torleif Elgvin et al., eds., *Qumran Cave 4.XV: Sapiential Texts*, part 1, DJD 20 (Oxford: Clarendon, 1997); John Strugnell, Daniel J. Harrington, and Torleif Elgvin, eds., *Qumran Cave 4.XXIV: Sapiential Texts*, part 2, DJD 34 (Oxford: Clarendon, 1999).

5. See, for example, Matthew J. Goff, *Discerning Wisdom: The Sapiential Literature of the Dead Sea Scrolls*, VTSup 116 (Leiden: Brill, 2007); John Kampen, *Wisdom Literature*, ECDSS (Grand Rapids: Eerdmans, 2011).

6. Here and below, these terms refer to complex traditions instead of strictly defined literary genres.

7. For the redefinition of wisdom literature in the late Second Temple period, see John J. Collins, "Wisdom Reconsidered, in Light of the Scrolls," *DSD* 4 (1997): 265–81.

8. See Émile Puech, "4QBéatitudes," in *Qumrân grotte 4.XVIII: Textes hébreux (4Q521–4Q528, 4Q576–4Q579)*, ed. Puech, DJD 25 (Oxford: Clarendon, 1998), 115–78. The extant copy is from the turn of the era, while the likely date of composition is in the second century BCE; see Puech, "4QBéatitudes," 116–19; and Kampen, *Wisdom Literature*, 308.

the vitality and functions of the Jewish wisdom tradition beyond the interests of the sectarian Qumran movement.[9]

In line with the modern title Beatitudes, previous studies on the text have mostly dealt with the text's list of macarisms in 4Q525 2 II.[10] Significant remarks on 4Q525 as wisdom literature have also been made. These studies have dealt with the integration of torah piety and eschatological elements (i.e., speculation about the end times), as well as the connections between 4Q525 and Proverbs.[11] The present discussion will begin with the latter and then proceed to analyze the ways in which the pedagogy of Proverbs is shaped by torah in 4Q525.

THE EXPANSION OF PROVERBS: 4Q525 AND THE CONTINUOUS TRADITION

The corpora of Jewish literature from the late Second Temple period show that the (still open) collection of scripture had an immense influence on the textual production of that era. Traditions related to scriptural texts, as evident in Jubilees or the Temple Scroll, also constantly grew.[12] Both phenomena apply to the wisdom tradition as well: the instructions began to draw

---

9. See Jacqueline C. R. de Roo, "Is 4Q525 a Qumran Sectarian Document?," in *The Scrolls and the Scriptures: Qumran Fifty Years After*, ed. Stanley E. Porter and Craig A. Evans, JSPSup 26 (Sheffield: Sheffield Academic, 1997), 338–67. She has argued for the sectarian provenance of 4Q525, but her thesis has not received support among other scholars.

10. Several scholars have compared the macarisms of 4Q525 to the lists in Matthew (Matt 5:3–12) and Luke (Luke 6:20–26). Among numerous studies, see George J. Brooke, "The Wisdom of Matthew's Beatitudes," *ScrB* 19 (1989): 35–41; Émile Puech, "The Collections of Beatitudes in Hebrew and in Greek (4Q525 1-4 and Matt 5,3–12)," in *Early Christianity in Context: Monuments and Documents; Essays in Honour of Emmanuele Testa*, ed. Frédéric Manns and Eugenio E. Alliata, SBFCM 38 (Jerusalem: Franciscan Printing Press, 1993), 353–68.

11. See especially de Roo, "Qumran Sectarian Document?," 338–67; Goff, *Discerning Wisdom*, 198–229; Kampen, *Wisdom Literature*, 307–40. See also Elisha Qimron, "Improving the Editions of the Dead Sea Scrolls" [Hebrew], *Meghillot* 1 (2003): 135–45; Eibert J. C. Tigchelaar, "Lady Folly and Her House in Three Qumran Manuscripts: On the Relation between *4Q525 15*, *5Q16*, and *4Q184 1*," *RevQ* 23 (2008): 371–81; Elisa Uusimäki, "Use of Scripture in *4QBeatitudes*: A Torah-Adjustment to Proverbs 1–9," *DSD* 20 (2013): 71–97.

12. See, for example, the discussion on the Mosaic discourse by Hindy Najman, *Seconding Sinai: The Development of Mosaic Discourse in Second Temple Judaism*, JSJSup 77 (Leiden: Brill, 2003).

on scripture among other sources of influence, as Ben Sira and Wisdom of Solomon have long demonstrated, and the Proverbs tradition evolved and expanded along with new texts that reused (parts of) that source.

Hints about the growth of the Proverbs tradition are visible already in the book of Proverbs; chapters 1–9 were attached to the collections of sayings in the Persian or Hellenistic era.[13] The translation of the Septuagint and the composition of the Wisdom of Solomon demonstrate the Greek afterlife of Proverbs and its royal protagonist in Alexandria, while the Dead Sea Scrolls reflect the transmission of Proverbs among those who continued to write in Hebrew in Judea.[14] Only fragments of the book of Proverbs (4Q102–103, 103a) have been found, but 4Q184 and 4Q525 further testify to the precanonical expansion of the Proverbs tradition. The text of 4Q184 preserves an account of an evil woman that was inspired by Prov 1–9. The text has been discussed for decades, while the study of 4Q525 from the viewpoint of the Proverbs tradition is more recent.[15] An inspection of scriptural references demonstrates that 4Q525 draws on Prov 1–9 as well as being shaped by Psalms and Deuteronomy.

Allusions to Prov 1–9 are found in the beginning of Beatitudes, which imitates the prologue of Proverbs in 4Q525 1 2 (compare Prov 1:2). The other references to Proverbs mostly pertain to the figure and concept of wisdom, beginning with the macarisms on the search for wisdom (with 4Q525 2 II, 1–2, compare Prov 3:18; with 2 II, 2, compare Prov 7:25 (?); with 2 II, 3, compare Prov 3:13).[16] The poem that follows describes the

---

13. Michael V. Fox, *Proverbs 1–9: A New Translation with Introduction and Commentary*, AB 18A (New York: Doubleday, 2000), 48–49.

14. Note that, like Wisdom of Solomon, other Jewish texts—Song of Songs, Pss 72 and 127, and Qoheleth—were also associated with Solomon at some point of their redaction histories.

15. For a bibliography on 4Q184, see Goff, *Discerning Wisdom*, 104–5. The use of Proverbs in the text has been recently analyzed by Michael J. Lesley, "Exegetical Wiles: 4Q184 as Scriptural Interpretation," in *The Scrolls and Biblical Traditions: Proceedings of the Seventh Meeting of the IOQS in Helsinki*, ed. George J. Brooke et al., STDJ 103 (Leiden: Brill, 2012), 107–42. The editio princeps can be found in John M. Allegro, ed., *Qumran Cave 4.I: 4Q158–4Q186*, DJD 5 (Oxford: Clarendon, 1968), 82–85. For recent discussions of 4Q525 from the viewpoint of the Proverbs, see Qimron, "Improving the Editions," 135–45; Tigchelaar, "Lady Folly," 371–81; Uusimäki, "Use of Scripture," 71–97.

16. I understand an allusion here as a device which, in addition to requiring a verbal marker, contributes to the meaning of 4Q525 insofar as it suggests that the new

sage's endurance (4Q525 2 II, 5–6; compare Prov 1:26–27), while a section in the following column covers wisdom's value over material riches (4Q525 2 III, 1–3; compare Prov 3:14–15). Another parallel concerns careful speech (4Q525 14 II, 27; compare Prov 6:2). Thereafter two allusions serve as crucial interpretative keys. The reference to Proverbs in 4Q525 15 8 (see Prov 2:19) suggests that the setting of this enigmatic passage, which contains eternal curses promising fiery and serpent-filled Sheol, describes folly's underworld abode.[17] An antithesis to this motif appears in fragment 24 II, built on the theme of wisdom's house (4Q525 24 II, 4–6; compare Prov 9:1–6).[18]

The engagement of 4Q525 with Prov 1–9 is scarcely coincidental. Material reconstruction—the placement of fragments, according to damage patterns, in order to restore the original measurements of the deteriorated scroll—suggests that the references frame the composition, beginning with an allusion to Prov 1 in 4Q525 1 and ending with an allusion to Prov 9 in fragment 24 II.[19] It seems obvious that the author wished to create an instruction that—like the Wisdom of Solomon or Wiles of the Wicked Woman—turns towards Proverbs, supplementing it and providing reinterpretation. In this way, he carried on the Proverbs tradition in an era when the status of the Ketuvim was still unstable.[20] This reuse of an earlier source also directs one's attention to the importance of Proverbs for the pedagogy of wisdom teachers in the late Second Temple era.

A Pastiche of Scriptural Sources in 4Q525: Pedagogy with a Purpose

While the author of Beatitudes relies heavily upon Proverbs, there are significant differences between these two texts. What makes the pedagogy of 4Q525 different from Proverbs? One answer to the question is the influ-

---

text should be read in light of the scriptural text; see Carmela Perri, "On Alluding," *Poetics* 7 (1978): 296.

17. For further discussion on the references, see Puech, "4QBéatitudes," 121, 124, 130, 151, 153; Qimron, "Improving the Editions," 137–39; Tigchelaar, "Lady Folly," 377; Uusimäki, "Use of Scripture," 76–79.

18. For further observations on 4Q525 24 II, see Qimron, "Improving the Editions," 140–41.

19. For the placement of fragment 24 II at or towards the end of the former scroll, see Uusimäki, *Turning Proverbs Towards Torah*, 44. Discussion on 4Q525 and rewriting processes appears in Uusimäki, "Use of Scripture," 83–87.

20. Eugene Ulrich, "The Jewish Scriptures: Texts, Versions, Canons," *EDEJ* 114.

ence of other texts and traditions, since the nuances they bring clearly advance the interests of 4Q525 beyond those of Proverbs. The most significant echoes concern Psalms and Deuteronomy.[21]

Psalms 15 and 24 have left a mark on the portrayal of the wise person who does not slander and seeks "her" with pure hands and not with a deceitful heart (with 4Q525 2 II, 1, cf. Ps 15:2b–3a; with 2 II, 2–3, cf. Ps 24:4, 6). Psalm 119 is echoed in the statement that a wise person walks in God's torah (4Q525 2 II, 4; compare Ps 119:1), while the promise to tread on the high places of enemies resembles Moses's blessing (4Q525 14 II, 11; compare Deut 33:29). As for other shared imagery, the parallels to Ps 91 concern assurances of God's help, protection, and blessings (4Q525 14 II), while those to Deut 32 pertain to the underworld setting (4Q525 15 // 5Q16 1–2+5).[22]

A wealth of scriptural parallels informs the content of 4Q525, suggesting that Proverbs has been reinterpreted to show that wisdom can be found in torah and should be kept carefully (4Q525 5 7–8). An overall pedagogical purpose is clear: the prologue of Beatitudes (frag. 1) outlines an imaginary exemplar: "[which he spo]ke in wisdom given by Go[d] to him [... to kno]w wisdom and disci[pline], to comprehend [...]" (4Q525 1 1–2). The following macarisms with a flavor of liturgical poetry include this exemplary person among the fortunate. The series and the poem that follows in the composition also teach the student to seek wisdom, keep statutes, avoid the ways of injustice, bear trials and difficulties, and constantly ponder wisdom and/or torah:[23]

---

21. An echo pertains to an allusion in that a strong verbal resemblance between 4Q525 and a scriptural text can be identified. Yet it is not crucial to recognize the source in order to grasp the meaning of the new text. Therefore, an echo cannot be proved to result from a conscious authorial decision; see Tom Furniss and Michael Bath, *Reading Poetry: An Introduction* (London: Harvester Wheatsheaf, 1996), 308.

22. The major links to Ps 91 include threats such as "scourge" (נגע; 4Q525 14 II, 6; 15 7; Ps 91:10b), "evil" (רע; 4Q525 14 II, 12; Ps 91:15b), and "terror" (פחד; 4Q525 14 II, 12; 2–3 II, 5; Ps 91:5a). Both texts use the verbs "to tread" (√דרך) as referring to the victory over enemies (4Q525 14 II, 11; Ps 91:13b) and "to deliver" (√חלץ) of God's saving acts (4Q525 14 II, 12; Ps 91:15b). For links to Deut 32, see the Sheol setting (for שאול, see 4Q525 15 5; compare Deut 32:22), which is depicted as dark (for אפל, see 15 1; compare Ps 91:6a), fiery (for אש, see 15 6; compare Deut 32:22), and inhabited by venomous snakes (for פתן, חמה, רוש, and תנין, see 15 1–4; compare Deut 32:32–33; Ps 91:13).

23. The English translations of 4Q525 are my own, but they have been strongly

with a pure heart and does not slander with his tongue. *vacat* Happy are those who hold fast to her statutes and do not hold fast to the ways of injustice. *vacat* Hap[py] are those who rejoice in her and do not pour out into the ways of folly. *vacat* Happy are those who seek her with pure hands and do not search her with a deceitful heart. *vacat* Happy is the one who attains wisdom. *vacat* He walks in the Torah of the Most High: he establishes his heart in her ways. *vacat* He restrains himself with her teachings and favors her chastisements const[an]tly. He does not leave her in the face of [his] affliction[s], during the time of distress does not abandon her, does not forget her [in the day] of terror, and in the humility of his soul does not despise [her.] But he reflects on her constantly, in his distress muses [on her and in al]l his being [comprehends] her. [He sets her] in front of his eyes, lest he walk in the ways of [...]. (4Q525 2 II, 1–7)

The somewhat similar description of the people who fear and love God as well as walking in perfection in fragment 5 presents a model of wise people whom the students should emulate:

Those who fear God keep her ways and they walk in ... her statutes and her reproofs do not deny. The discerning ones attain.... Those who walk in perfection turn aside injustice and do not deny her corrections ... they are laden. The prudent recognize her ways and in her depths ... they gaze. Those who love God humble themselves in her, and in the wa[ys ...]. (4Q525 5 14–18)

Later on, the subtle and scattered traces of Ps 91 accentuate the promise of protection bestowed upon devout pupils (4Q525 14 II), while the foolish will encounter curses (4Q525 15 // 5Q16 1–2+5). The latter section is fragmentarily preserved, but folly's association with a fiery and dark underworld inhabited with poisonous snakes makes it clear that the student is exhorted to avoid the evil woman (4Q525 16–17, 21–23). The final part resumes the call to a wise life, and the instruction ends with a scene in which the student should apparently imagine himself as living in wisdom's

---

influenced by the previous English translations of the text. Particularly influential has been the translation of Michael Wise and others, published in Donald W. Parry and Emanuel Tov, eds., *Calendrical and Sapiential Texts*, vol. 4 of *The Dead Sea Scrolls Reader* (Leiden: Brill, 2004), 246–65.

house with possible eternal consequences: "my house is the house of ... my house. The one who dwells in [it ...] forever" (4Q525 24 II, 4–6).²⁴

The result is a fresh mixture of scriptural traditions and contemporary ideas: the view of the world is torah-oriented and includes eschatological beliefs in evil spirits, judgment, and punishment (4Q525 6–10, 16–23). The way in which various sources of influence intertwine to produce new meanings in 4Q525 could be characterized as the scripturalization of the wisdom tradition. In this interpretation, I rely on George Brooke, who defines scripturalization as "the use of authoritative scriptural references to adapt, expand or explain features in a received tradition."²⁵ In the case of 4Q525, the author utilizes and transforms the teaching of Proverbs with the help of other texts and contemporary beliefs. This interpretative act is undertaken to adjust Prov 1–9 to the author's own perspective and to prove its ongoing relevance by stating that religious obligation cannot be separated from the life dedicated to wisdom.

The scripturalization process is pedagogically relevant, as it illuminates the curriculum of teaching in Beatitudes. The content of 4Q525 suggests that the ideal wise person masters the ancestral writings or, at the very least, inherited texts such as Proverbs, Psalms, and Deuteronomy. In this respect, 4Q525 shares much with Ben Sira's work, although it involves only one section that offers pragmatic advice on considerate speech (4Q525 14 II, 18–28), while Ben Sira frequently discusses topics such as social interaction and duties, children's education, and financial matters. As argued by E. J. Bickerman, Ben Sira essentially portrays the ideal sage as a person who finds his education in torah, or even as a torah scholar.²⁶ Similarly to 4Q525, Proverbs provides a basis for wisdom education, but the inclusion of other scriptural texts fundamentally alters the curriculum.²⁷

---

24. Uusimäki, "Use of Scripture," 96–97.
25. George J. Brooke, "Aspects of Matthew's Use of Scripture in Light of the Dead Sea Scrolls," in *A Teacher for All Generations: Essays in Honor of James C. VanderKam*, ed. Eric F. Mason et al., 2 vols., JSJSup 153 (Leiden: Brill, 2012), 2:835.
26. E. J. Bickerman, *Jews in the Greek Age* (Cambridge: Harvard University Press, 1988), 169–71.
27. John J. Collins, *Jewish Wisdom in the Hellenistic Age* (Edinburgh: T&T Clark, 1998), 45. See also Benjamin G. Wright, "Biblical Interpretation in the Book of Ben Sira," in *A Companion to Biblical Interpretation in Early Judaism*, ed. Matthias Henze (Grand Rapids: Eerdmans, 2012), 363–88.

Divine Wisdom: The Integration of Torah into Instruction

In the Hebrew Bible, the term "wisdom" (חכמה) has countless meanings, such as mental capacity, particular skills, or a "body of knowledge."[28] While the latter sense is typical of many texts from the late Second Temple era, wisdom could cover a range of nuances, depending on the context.[29] An investigation of 4Q525's scriptural background reveals that the wisdom promoted by the author is not a human enterprise but is related to torah, although the student's commitment to the search for wisdom is no less significant (4Q525 2 II, 2–3; 4Q525 5 6–7). This is not surprising in that the majority of late wisdom texts seem to emphasize wisdom's divine and revealed sources. Note that "sources" must be written in the plural as the category is not unified; many texts refer to torah, but more esoteric sources of wisdom appear, along with invocations of other revelations directed to a specific group.[30]

The latter issue, as well as related intersections between wisdom and apocalypticism, has received much interest in Dead Sea Scrolls studies due to the prominence of the רז נהיה theme in Instruction and Mysteries.[31] Meanwhile, the torah-oriented wisdom material is only now becoming more familiar to the wider community of scholars. Even if the fusion of

---

28. R. Norman Whybray, "Slippery Words: IV; Wisdom," *ExpTim* 89 (1977–1978): 359.

29. Scholars have made use of such analytical categories as apocalyptic, mantic, prophetic, Torah-devoted, and philosophical when highlighting wisdom's connections to other patterns of thought in Jewish antiquity. For example, see George W. E. Nickelsburg, "Wisdom and Apocalypticism in Early Judaism: Some Points for Discussion," in *Conflicted Boundaries in Wisdom and Apocalypticism*, ed. Benjamin G. Wright and Lawrence M. Wills, SymS 35 (Atlanta: Society of Biblical Literature, 2005), 36–37. He stresses that wisdom, apocalyptic, eschatological, or prophetic remain "heuristic categories," as they were originally "related parts of an organic whole."

30. See, for example, Grant Macaskill, *Revealed Wisdom and Inaugurated Eschatology in Ancient Judaism and Early Christianity*, JSJSup 115 (Leiden: Brill, 2007).

31. Among numerous studies, see Armin Lange, *Weisheit und Prädestination: Weisheitliche Urordnung und Prädestination in den Textfunden von Qumran*, STDJ 18 (Leiden: Brill, 1995); Eibert J. C. Tigchelaar, *To Increase Learning for the Understanding Ones: Reading and Reconstructing the Fragmentary Early Jewish Sapiential Text 4QInstruction*, STDJ 44 (Leiden: Brill, 2001); Matthew J. Goff, *The Worldly and Heavenly Wisdom of 4QInstruction*, STDJ 50 (Leiden: Brill, 2003); Jean-Sébastien Rey, *4QInstruction: Sagesse et eschatologie*, STDJ 81 (Leiden: Brill, 2009).

wisdom and torah is not entirely new, 4Q525 can illuminate aspects of the intellectual landscape from which such claims originated.³²

In 4Q525, the wise and torah-obedient person is proclaimed to be fortunate: "Happy is the person who attains wisdom *vacat* and walks in the Torah of the Most High" (4Q525 2 II, 3–4; compare Sir 24:23). What did the author mean in his pedagogical setting with the ambiguous תורה? Whereas the wisdom texts of the Hebrew Bible typically employ the term in the etymological sense of "instruction," several teachings from the late Second Temple period employ a particularly Jewish notion of torah. Over the course of time, the concept was associated with scripture and gradually gained legal overtones also within wisdom discourse, but it simultaneously continued to cover the more general sense of instruction.³³

The exact definition of torah is specifically challenging in the case of poetic texts in which torah discourse tends to be rather abstract. The same holds true for 4Q525: wisdom is said to be embodied in torah, but the latter is never defined, nor are there any references to particular laws or figures and events of the Israelite past (nevertheless, see 4Q525 14 II, 2, 11). Yet the way in which torah is treated is typical of wisdom teachings. The aforementioned connections to scripture constitute a part of 4Q525's torah piety, but perhaps the most striking feature is the use of the feminine, third-person singular suffix ה.

Since both *wisdom* and *torah* are grammatically feminine words, the suffix ה allows for multiple interpretations. It could refer to either of them, but as the equation of wisdom with torah indicates (4Q525 2 II, 3–4), wisdom is thought to be expressed in torah. The author probably used the suffix as a literary device to point to the merging of these concepts. Such an intention is particularly visible in the macarism that speaks of those who hold fast to "her" statutes (4Q525 2 II, 1) and in the next poem, which mentions reflection on "her" (4Q525 2 II, 6). Elsewhere those who keep

---

32. See Deut 4; Ezra 7; Jer 8; Pss 1, 19, 119. The link is more explicit in the Septuagint (Sir 24; Bar 3–4). For early Judaism, see Eckhard J. Schnabel, *Law and Wisdom from Ben Sira to Paul: A Tradition-Historical Enquiry into the Relation of Law, Wisdom, and Ethics*, WUNT 2/16 (Tübingen: Mohr Siebeck, 1985).

33. For תורה in Second Temple Judaism, see the enlightening remarks of Carol A. Newsom, *The Self as Symbolic Space: Constructing Identity and Community at Qumran*, STDJ 52 (Leiden: Brill, 2004), 10–11. See also the essay in the present volume by John J. Collins.

"her" statutes, do not reject "her" punishments, and humble themselves in "her" are discussed (4Q525 5 9–13).[34]

The suggestive language refers to a broad understanding of torah; the author seems to have understood it as an equivocal concept instead of referring to an array of laws or to the Pentateuch alone. Wisdom, prudence, and torah obedience intersect in the ideal life as imagined by the author (see especially 4Q525 5). The dynamic sense of instruction made torah a particularly helpful concept for the writer, who considered the question of how to live and promulgated torah as the divine teaching of (at least some) Jews. Even so, he approached torah by the subtle means of poetry instead of focusing on details of legal observance or pentateuchal narratives.

4Q525 belongs to a stage of tradition in which the study of wisdom had come to mean the study of torah. Wisdom is thought to be embodied in this source of blessings and rich life (4Q525 14 II), and the particularity of torah is evident in the commandment not to reject one's lot and inheritance to foreigners (4Q525 5 7–8; 4Q525 13; 4Q525 14 II, 1, 14). Generally speaking, the intention of 4Q525 reminds one of the prologue to the Greek version of Sirach. The writer states that his grandfather Jesus,

> who had had devoted himself for a long time to the study of the Law, the Prophets, and the *other books of our ancestors*, was prompted to write something himself in the nature of instruction and wisdom. This he did so that those who love wisdom might, by acquainting themselves with what he too had written, make even greater progress, living in conformity with the divine law. (Sir, Prol. 3–4, emphasis added)[35]

In a similar vein, the author of 4Q525 produced literature that is not directly connected to the Mosaic torah, in contrast to texts such as Jubilees or the Temple Scroll, but that nonetheless stands in the continuum of scripture and leads the audience to wisdom and torah devotion. This pedagogical text was also written to accompany the open collection of scripture. As such, it was a means of expanding Jewish teaching, that is,

---

34. For a detailed treatment, see Elisa Uusimäki, "'Happy Is the Person to Whom She Has Been Given': The Continuum of Wisdom and Torah in *4QSapiential Admonitions B* (4Q185) and *4QBeatitudes* (4Q525)," *RevQ* 26 (2014): 345–59.

35. The English translation is from Patrick W. Skehan and Alexander A. Di Lella, *The Wisdom of Ben Sira*, AB 39 (New York: Doubleday, 1987), 131.

תורה of some kind, when the concept is understood as both instruction and Mosaic law.

Interestingly, the belief in the importance of transmitting the teaching to new generations is reflected in the portrayal of the wise pupil. In a fragmentarily preserved section that follows the lengthy passage on divine protection and blessings (4Q525 14 II, 1–14), the addressee is urged to imagine the future time of his own death, which will not bring his teaching to an end. The ones who knew him—that is, the pupil's future students once he becomes a teacher himself—will remember him: "When you are swept away to eternal rest, they shall inherit ... and in your teaching all those who know you shall walk together.... Together they shall mourn, but in your ways they shall remember you" (4Q525 14 II, 14–16). Thus his own students commit to carry on his instruction, which implies that the student is inspired to imagine himself as a great teacher-to-be.

Finally, a recognition of 4Q525's religious dimensions helps one identify the spiritual intentions that lie behind the text. The basic goal of the composition is pedagogical (i.e., the statement of purpose in frag. 1), while the mosaic of scriptural idiom and ideas, as well as the interest in torah piety, proves that the students are not prepared for wisdom merely in the sense of a good earthly life. Instead, spiritual formation is intended, as the audience is encouraged to follow torah and is made aware of the divine protection and blessings that lie behind such torah-devoted notions of wisdom.[36]

Conclusions

In spite of its fragmentary state of preservation, 4Q525 serves as an informative exemplar of Jewish pedagogy in the late Second Temple period.

---

36. This is important to acknowledge. While the content and form of late wisdom texts have been fairly widely discussed, a nuanced analysis of their purpose(s) has yet to be done; see, for example, John J. Collins, "Epilogue: Genre Analysis and the Dead Sea Scrolls," *DSD* 17 (2010): 418–30, esp. 429–30; Benjamin G. Wright, "Joining the Club: A Suggestion about Genre in Early Jewish Texts," *DSD* 17 (2010): 289–314. For the related process of identity formation in 4Q525, see Elisa Uusimäki, "Wisdom, Scripture, and Identity Formation in 4QBeatitudes," in *Social Memory and Social Identity in the Study of Early Judaism and Early Christianity*, ed. Samuel Byrskog, Raimo Hakola, and Jutta Jokiranta, NTOA, SUNT 116 (Göttingen: Vandenhoeck & Ruprecht, 2016), 175–86.

In particular, it contributes fresh Hebrew evidence for the reception and renewal of the Proverbs tradition in wisdom circles. A wise, considerate, and God-fearing attitude is promoted, as is typical of many wisdom instructions, but the impact of Prov 1–9 and other scriptural texts further suggests that the wise student and teacher-to-be was understood as being immersed in the ancestral writings of Judaism. The integration of torah piety and contemporary beliefs concerning eschatological matters supports the idea that this pedagogical material was not only intended to prepare one for a good earthly life, but it played an important role in the student's spiritual formation.

Bibliography

Allegro, John M., ed. *Qumran Cave 4.I: 4Q158–4Q186*. DJD 5. Oxford: Clarendon, 1968.
Bickerman, Elias J. *Jews in the Greek Age*. Cambridge: Harvard University Press, 1988.
Brooke, George J. "Aspects of Matthew's Use of Scripture in Light of the Dead Sea Scrolls." Pages 821–38 in vol. 2 of *A Teacher for All Generations: Essays in Honor of James C. VanderKam*. Edited by Eric F. Mason, Alison Schofield, Eugene Ulrich, Kelley Coblentz Bautch, Angela Kim Harkins, and Daniel A. Machiela. 2 vols. JSJSup 153. Leiden: Brill, 2012.
———. "The Wisdom of Matthew's Beatitudes." *ScrB* 19 (1989): 35–41.
Camp, Claudia V. *Wisdom and the Feminine in the Book of Proverbs*. BLS 11. Decatur, GA: Almond Press, 1985.
———. *Wise, Strange, and Holy: The Strange Woman and the Making of the Bible*. JSOTSup 320. Sheffield: Sheffield Academic, 2000.
Collins, John J. "Epilogue: Genre Analysis and the Dead Sea Scrolls." *DSD* 17 (2010): 418–30.
———. *Jewish Wisdom in the Hellenistic Age*. Edinburgh: T&T Clark, 1998.
———. "Wisdom Reconsidered, in Light of the Scrolls." *DSD* 4 (1997): 265–81.
Crenshaw, James L. *Old Testament Wisdom: An Introduction*. 3rd ed. Louisville: Westminster John Knox, 2010.
De Roo, Jacqueline C. R. "Is 4Q525 a Qumran Sectarian Document?" Pages 338–67 in *The Scrolls and the Scriptures: Qumran Fifty Years After*. Edited by Stanley E. Porter and Craig A. Evans. JSPSup 26. Sheffield: Sheffield Academic, 1997.

Dunderberg, Ismo. *Beyond Gnosticism: Myth, Lifestyle, and Society in the School of Valentinus*. New York: Columbia University Press, 2008.

Dunn, James D. G. *Christology in the Making: A New Testament Inquiry into the Origins of the Doctrine of the Incarnation*. 2nd ed. Grand Rapids: Eerdmans, 1989.

Elgvin, Torleif, Menachem Kister, Timothy C. Lim, Bilhah Nitzan, Stephen J. Pfann, Elisha Qimron, Lawrence H. Schiffman, and Annette Steudel, eds. *Qumran Cave 4.XV: Sapiential Texts*. Part 1. DJD 20. Oxford: Clarendon, 1997.

Fox, Michael V. *Proverbs 1–9: A New Translation with Introduction and Commentary*. AB 18A. New York: Doubleday, 2000.

Furniss, Tom, and Michael Bath. *Reading Poetry: An Introduction*. London: Harvester Wheatsheaf, 1996.

Goff, Matthew J. *Discerning Wisdom: The Sapiential Literature of the Dead Sea Scrolls*. VTSup 116. Leiden: Brill, 2007.

———. *The Worldly and Heavenly Wisdom of 4QInstruction*. STDJ 50. Leiden: Brill, 2003.

Kampen, John. *Wisdom Literature*. ECDSS. Grand Rapids: Eerdmans, 2011.

Lange, Armin. *Weisheit und Prädestination: Weisheitliche Urordnung und Prädestination in den Textfunden von Qumran*. STDJ 18. Leiden: Brill, 1995.

Lesley, Michael J. "Exegetical Wiles: 4Q184 as Scriptural Interpretation." Pages 107–42 in *The Scrolls and Biblical Traditions: Proceedings of the Seventh Meeting of the IOQS in Helsinki*. Edited by George J. Brooke, Daniel K. Falk, Eibert J. C. Tigchelaar, and Molly M. Zahn. STDJ 103. Leiden: Brill, 2012.

Macaskill, Grant. *Revealed Wisdom and Inaugurated Eschatology in Ancient Judaism and Early Christianity*. JSJSup 115. Leiden: Brill, 2007.

MacRae, George W. "The Jewish Background of the Gnostic Sophia Myth." *NovT* 12 (1970): 86–101.

Najman, Hindy. *Seconding Sinai: The Development of Mosaic Discourse in Second Temple Judaism*. JSJSup 77. Leiden: Brill, 2003.

Newsom, Carol A. *The Self as Symbolic Space: Constructing Identity and Community at Qumran*. STDJ 52. Leiden: Brill, 2004.

Nickelsburg, George W. E. "Wisdom and Apocalypticism in Early Judaism: Some Points for Discussion." Pages 17–37 in *Conflicted Boundaries in Wisdom and Apocalypticism*. Edited by Benjamin G. Wright and

Lawrence M. Wills. SymS 35. Atlanta: Society of Biblical Literature, 2005.
Parry, Donald W., and Emanuel Tov, eds. *Calendrical and Sapiential Texts*. Vol. 4 of *The Dead Sea Scrolls Reader*. Leiden: Brill, 2004.
Perri, Carmela. "On Alluding." *Poetics* 7 (1978): 289–307.
Puech, Émile. "4QBéatitudes." Pages 115–78 in *Qumrân grotte 4.XVIII: Textes hébreux (4Q521–4Q528, 4Q576–4Q579)*. Edited by Émile Puech. DJD 25. Oxford: Clarendon, 1998.
———. "The Collections of Beatitudes in Hebrew and in Greek (4Q525 1–4 and Matt 5,3–12)." Pages 353–68 in *Early Christianity in Context: Monuments and Documents; Essays in Honour of Emmanuele Testa*. Edited by Frédéric Manns and Eugenio E. Alliata. SBFCM 38. Jerusalem: Franciscan Printing Press, 1993.
Qimron, Elisha. "Improving the Editions of the Dead Sea Scrolls" [Hebrew]. *Meghillot* 1 (2003): 135–45.
Rad, Gerhard von. *Wisdom in Israel*. Translated by James D. Martin. Nashville: Abingdon, 1972.
Rey, Jean-Sébastien. *4QInstruction: Sagesse et eschatologie*. STDJ 81. Leiden: Brill, 2009.
Schäfer, Peter. *Mirror of His Beauty: Feminine Images of God from the Bible to the Early Kabbalah*. JCMAMW. Princeton: Princeton University Press, 2002.
Schnabel, Eckhard J. *Law and Wisdom from Ben Sira to Paul: A Tradition-Historical Enquiry into the Relation of Law, Wisdom, and Ethics*. WUNT 2/16. Tübingen: Mohr Siebeck, 1985.
Skehan Patrick W., and Alexander A. Di Lella. *The Wisdom of Ben Sira*. AB 39. New York: Doubleday, 1987.
Strugnell, John, Daniel J. Harrington, and Torleif Elgvin, eds. *Qumran Cave 4.XXIV: Sapiential Texts*. Part 2. DJD 34. Oxford: Clarendon, 1999.
Tigchelaar, Eibert J. C. "Lady Folly and Her House in Three Qumran Manuscripts: On the Relation between 4Q525 15, 5Q16, and 4Q184 1." *RevQ* 23 (2008): 371–81.
———. *To Increase Learning for the Understanding Ones: Reading and Reconstructing the Fragmentary Early Jewish Sapiential Text 4QInstruction*. STDJ 44. Leiden: Brill, 2001.
Ulrich, Eugene. "The Jewish Scriptures: Texts, Versions, Canons." *EDEJ* 97–119.

Uusimäki, Elisa. "'Happy Is the Person to Whom She Has Been Given': The Continuum of Wisdom and Torah in *4QSapiential Admonitions B* (4Q185) and *4QBeatitudes* (4Q525)." *RevQ* 26 (2014): 345–59.

———. "Use of Scripture in *4QBeatitudes*: A Torah-Adjustment to Proverbs 1–9." *DSD* 20 (2013): 71–97.

———. "Wisdom, Scripture, and Identity Formation in 4QBeatitudes." Pages 175–86 in *Social Memory and Social Identity in the Study of Early Judaism and Early Christianity*. Edited by Samuel Byrskog, Raimo Hakola, and Jutta Jokiranta. NTOA; SUNT 116. Göttingen: Vandenhoeck & Ruprecht, 2016.

Whybray, R. Norman. "Slippery Words: IV; Wisdom." *ExpTim* 89 (1977–1978): 359–62.

Wright, Benjamin G. "Biblical Interpretation in the Book of Ben Sira." Pages 363–88 in *A Companion to Biblical Interpretation in Early Judaism*. Edited by Matthias Henze. Grand Rapids: Eerdmans, 2012.

———. "Joining the Club: A Suggestion about Genre in Early Jewish Texts." *DSD* 17 (2010): 289–314.

Gardens of Knowledge:
Teachers in Ben Sira, 4QInstruction, and the Hodayot

Matthew Goff

The Hebrew Bible and the Dead Sea Scrolls, as documents written in the Second Temple period, constitute important evidence that some people in this era achieved a sophisticated level of education. They mastered several fields of knowledge, including the history of Israel, ritual practices, and ethics. It follows not only that there were students being trained but also teachers who themselves had gone through some sort of educational process. In this essay I would like to examine one specific aspect of the broader topic of pedagogy in ancient Judaism: how teachers legitimated their authority and the knowledge that such individuals transmitted to students. To this end I examine three early Jewish texts in which teachers are prominent: 4QInstruction, Ben Sira, and the Hodayot. How is the image of the teacher, as an authoritative and learned figure, constructed in these writings? What sort of knowledge does the teacher offer in them? How is the knowledge he conveys legitimated and understood as valuable and worthy of transmission to students? To what extent can the social setting of instruction be understood?

In my reflections on these questions, I stress three points. The first regards what teachers say in these texts about themselves. Ben Sira, with no small degree of humility, emphatically endorses himself as a teacher, praising his own wisdom and what students can learn from him. The teacher of 4QInstruction, by contrast, says virtually nothing about himself. In some hymns of the Hodayot, the speaker, not unlike Ben Sira,

---

A version of this paper was presented at a session on teachers and pedagogy in ancient Judaism organized by the Wisdom and Apocalypticism group at the 2014 Annual Meeting of the Society of Biblical Literature. I thank Kyle Roark and Christine Yoder for their feedback on this essay.

emphasizes his own importance as a source of knowledge for others. Secondly, in different ways these three texts construe as a garden the pedagogical space in which a teacher and student interact. They do this in part by drawing from the language of Gen 2–3. Lastly, these texts in different ways assert that the teacher imparts heavenly knowledge to his students. The authority of the teacher is constructed by construing him as the source of divine knowledge. I also explore at the end of this essay how the garden as an ancient Near Eastern trope may have shaped how teachers utilized this motif.

Ben Sira: A Teacher Irrigates a Garden

I begin with the book of Ben Sira. As is well known, the Jerusalem sage encourages people to acquire wisdom (e.g., Sir 4:11–19; 6:18–37; 14:20– 15:10). Wisdom in his instruction is a broad concept, signifying a way of life that encompasses being a pious and ethical person, studying the torah, and understanding the nature of the world.[1] Ben Sira encourages his students to embrace a way of living that is rigorous. Fools, he teaches, regard this way of life as too difficult to accept. Chapter 6 of the book states in the Greek that wisdom "seems very harsh to the undisciplined" (ἀπαιδεύτοις; NRSV), to those without paideia, but the Hebrew asserts that to fools she is עקובה, a word that denotes a steep or hilly path (Sir 6:20; see also 36:25; Isa 40:4).[2] According to Sir 6:22, "wisdom is like her name; she is not obvious to many" (NRSV). The NRSV translation reflects the Greek, which reads σοφία. The corresponding Hebrew, however, is not חכמה but המוסר.[3] This word derives from the root יסר, which can mean "to instruct" (*qal*) or "to rebuke" (*piel*).[4] The word המוסר in Sir 6:22, as Israel Lévi observed in 1901, likely relies on a pun with the *hophal* of the verb סור, denoting some-

---

1. John J. Collins, *Jewish Wisdom in the Hellenistic Age*, OTL (Louisville: Westminster John Knox, 1997), 46–54. See also Matthew J. Goff, "Wisdom," in *T&T Clark Companion to the Dead Sea Scrolls*, ed. George J. Brooke and Charlotte Hempel (London: T&T Clark, forthcoming); Stuart Weeks, *An Introduction to the Study of Wisdom Literature*, ApBS (London: T&T Clark, 2010), 2–3.

2. Patrick W. Skehan and Alexander A. Di Lella, *The Wisdom of Ben Sira*, AB 39 (New York: Doubleday, 1987), 193. Translations, with occasional modification, are taken from this source unless otherwise stated.

3. The Syriac here reads ܘܠܦܢܐ ("study"; compare the modern Hebrew אולפן).

4. Consult the discussion of this root in the essays by Karina Martin Hogan and Patrick Pouchelle in this volume.

thing which is removed or pushed away.[5] This fits exactly with the image of Sir 6:21, which likens the מוסר that Ben Sira advocates to a heavy stone most would push aside.

Why would a person devote himself to a way of life that many would reject? Wisdom, as the book of Proverbs stresses, is rich in rewards, including not only a successful life but also "an everlasting name," denoting that the wise person will be remembered and praised after his death (Sir 15:6). The way of life that Ben Sira advocates, the sage stresses, is worth the effort. But what way of life does he promote? While study and ethics are central to it, by themselves they are not sufficient. One must find a teacher (Sir 6:34-37; see also 8:8-9; 39:1-5).[6] One should seek him (שחריהו), and "let your foot wear out his doorstep" (Sir 6:36 NRSV). The student should spend time with his teacher, listening to his words.[7] This passage in chapter 6 then stresses constant study of the torah (Sir 6:38). The clear implication is that Ben Sira advocates study of the torah under the tutelage of a great teacher.

But where could a student ever find such a wonderful teacher? Not to worry, says Ben Sira. He offers a clear answer to this question: himself. Ultimately wisdom herself is the teacher, as in the book of Proverbs (e.g., Prov 8:4-5). Ben Sira 4:11 asserts that "wisdom teaches [למדה] her children and admonishes all who can understand her." The sage's most extensive account of wisdom is in the book's well-known twenty-fourth chapter. This text draws extensively from the description of wisdom as a woman in Prov 8. Ben Sira 24 also envisions wisdom as a verdant tree

---

5. Israel Lévi, *L'Ecclésiastique ou la Sagesse de Jésus, fils de Sira*, 2 vols. (Paris: Leroux, 1898-1901), 2:34. I thank Eric Reymond for this reference. See his review of *Weisheit aus der Begegnung: Bildung nach dem Buch Ben Sira*, by Frank Ueberschaer, *DSD* 21 (2014): 127.

6. Robert Doran, "Jewish Education in the Seleucid Period," in *Studies in Politics, Class and Material Culture*, vol. 3 of *Second Temple Studies*, ed. Philip R. Davies and John M. Halligan, JSOTSup 340 (Sheffield: Sheffield Academic, 2002), 116-32.

7. Note the parallel in chapter 6 of Abot R. Nat. [A]: "Another interpretation: 'Let your house be a meeting place for the sages' [Avot 1.4]. How so? When a scholar [תלמיד חכם] comes to your house with the request, 'Teach me,' if it is within your power to teach, teach him; otherwise let him go at once." In this passage the person coming to the house has attained a higher level of education than the visitor described in Sir 6. See Judah Goldin, *The Fathers according to Rabbi Nathan*, YJS 10 (New Haven: Yale University Press, 1983), 40; Jonathan Wyn Schofer, *The Making of a Sage: A Study in Rabbinic Ethics* (Madison: University of Wisconsin Press, 2005).

that takes root in Jerusalem (Sir 24:8–12).[8] The tree gives off beautiful fragrances, alluding to the incense of the temple. Ben Sira 24:15 likens the smell of the tree to fragrant spices such as galbanum and onycha.[9] According to Exod 30:34–35, these spices were to be used to produce the incense for the tent of meeting, a topic that Ben Sira elsewhere emphasizes (Sir 45:16).[10] One is encouraged to eat the fruit of the tree (Sir 24:17–21; see also T. Lev. 18:11). It then states that "all this is the book of the covenant of the Most High God, the law which Moses enjoined on us as a heritage for the community of Jacob" (Sir 24:23; compare Deut 33:4). This verse has been the subject of much discussion.[11] While different interpretations of it are possible, the immediate context suggests not that the torah should be identified as the entire tree but rather as its fruit.[12]

---

8. See also Sir 50:10; Prov 3:18. See Matthew J. Goff, "The Personification of Wisdom and Folly in Ancient Judaism," in *Religion and Female Body in Ancient Judaism and Its Environments*, ed. Geza Xeravits, DCLS 28 (Berlin: de Gruyter, 2015), 128–54; Collins, *Jewish Wisdom*, 49–53.

9. Skehan and Di Lella, *Wisdom of Ben Sira*, 333; Deborah A. Green, *The Aroma of Righteousness: Scent and Seduction in Rabbinic Life and Literature* (University Park: Pennsylvania State University Press, 2011), 71.

10. Gerald T. Sheppard, *Wisdom as a Hermeneutical Construct: A Study in the Sapientializing of the Old Testament*, BZAW 151 (Berlin: de Gruyter, 1980), 57–58.

11. See, for example, Benjamin G. Wright, "Torah and Sapiential Pedagogy in the Book of Ben Sira," in *Wisdom and Torah: The Reception of "Torah" in the Wisdom Literature of the Second Temple Period*, ed. Bernd U. Schipper and D. Andrew Teeter, JSJSup 163 (Leiden: Brill, 2013), 163–64; Greg Schmidt Goering, *Wisdom's Root Revealed: Ben Sira and the Election of Israel*, JSJSup 139 (Leiden: Brill, 2009), 93–96; Sheppard, *Wisdom as a Hermeneutical Construct*, 62–63; Roland E. Murphy, "The Personification of Wisdom," in *Wisdom in Ancient Israel: Essays in Honour of J. A. Emerton*, ed. John Day, R. P. Gordon, and Hugh G. M. Williamson (Cambridge: Cambridge University Press, 1995), 227.

12. This accords with Sir 24:15 and its description of wisdom with terminology that evokes the temple cult. So understood, wisdom is akin to the *kabod*, the theophanic, overpowering presence of God that resides in the temple. Following the logic of this metaphor, wisdom (the tree) represents the immanent God who gives the torah (the fruit; see 4 Ezra 9:32). Wisdom so understood constitutes a larger concept than the torah, and the two terms are not simply synonymous. Jessie Rogers argues for this position in her "'It Overflows Like the Euphrates with Understanding': Another Look at the Relationship between Law and Wisdom in Sirach," in *Ancient Versions and Traditions*, vol. 1 of *Of Scribes and Sages: Early Jewish Interpretation and Transmission of Scripture*, ed. Craig A. Evans, LSTS 50; SSEJC 9 (London: T&T Clark, 2004), 114–21. Also note that the image of eating the fruit of the tree (Sir 24:19) can be likened to

The tree in chapter 24 evokes not only Jerusalem but also Eden.[13] While the chapter mentions only one tree, it can reasonably be understood as located within a lush garden with multiple trees (Gen 2:9). Ben Sira 24:25–27 mentions six rivers, four of which are in Eden according to Gen 2:10–14: Pishon, Gihon, Tigris, and Euphrates. Ben Sira adds the Jordan and the Nile.[14] Envisioning the torah as the fruit of a tree irrigated by rivers of Eden helps convey the divine and authoritative status of the knowledge that the Pentateuch contains (see also Sir 17:8–11).[15] Ben Sira 24 is rich in riverine imagery. Ben Sira 24:25 reads: "It is full [πιμπλῶν], like the Pishon, with wisdom, and like the Tigris at the time of the new crops." Here and throughout the river verses (Sir 24:25–27) the verbs in the Greek are participles in the masculine form. The most immediately preceding noun is a feminine term, "inheritance" (κληρονομία), of Sir 24:23. The participles likely hearken back to the masculine word νόμος ("law") of this verse.[16] So understood, the torah is signified not only by the fruit of a

---

the trope of people eating scrolls, representing their acceptance of a divine text (Ezek 3:3; Rev 10:9).

13. Terje Stordalen, "Heaven on Earth—Or Not? Jerusalem as Eden in Biblical Literature," in *Beyond Eden: The Biblical Story of Paradise (Genesis 2–3) and Its Reception History*, ed. Konrad Schmid and Christof Riedweg, FAT 2/34 (Tübingen: Mohr Siebeck, 2008), 28–57; Peter T. Lanfer, *Remembering Eden: The Reception History of Genesis 3:22–24* (New York: Oxford University Press, 2012), 127–57; Jon D. Levenson, *Sinai and Zion: An Entry into the Jewish Bible* (San Francisco: HarperSanFrancisco, 1987), 128–33. For an overview of early Jewish texts that appropriate the garden of Eden, see Jacques van Ruiten, "Garden of Eden—Paradise," *EDEJ* 658–61; Eibert J. C. Tigchelaar, "Eden and Paradise: The Garden Motif in Some Early Jewish Texts," in *Paradise Interpreted: Representations of Biblical Paradise in Judaism and Christianity*, ed. Gerard P. Luttikhuizen, TBN 2 (Leiden: Brill, 1999), 37–57. Consult also Sandra R. Shimoff, "Gardens: From Eden to Jerusalem," *JSJ* 26 (1995): 144–55; Rachel Elior, "The Garden of Eden is the Holy of Holies and the Dwelling of the Lord," *StSp* 24 (2014): 63–118.

14. Nira Stone, "The Four Rivers that Flowed from Eden," in Schmid and Riedweg, *Beyond Eden*, 227–50. For Ben Sira's interpretation of Genesis, see Shane Berg, "Ben Sira, the Genesis Creation Accounts, and the Knowledge of God's Will," *JBL* 132 (2013): 139–57; Maurice Gilbert, "Ben Sira, Reader of Genesis 1–11," in *Intertextual Studies in Ben Sira and Tobit: Essays in Honor of Alexander A. Di Lella, O.F.M.*, ed. Jeremy Corley and Vincent T. M. Skemp, CBQMS 38 (Washington, DC: Catholic Biblical Association of America, 2005), 89–99.

15. Rogers, "It Overflows like the Euphrates," 116.

16. The phrase "the book of the covenant" (βίβλος διαθήκης) in Sir 24:23 is composed of feminine terms.

well-irrigated tree. It is also imagined as the water that nourishes the tree.[17] As Michael Fishbane has pointed out, early Jewish and rabbinic literature is replete with images of flowing water that evoke the torah (e.g., CD VI, 3–10; 4 Ezra 14:38–41; b. Ta'an. 7a).[18] Psalm 1, which compares those who study "the law of the Lord" to bountiful trees that grow beside streams of water (Ps 1:2–3), is important for the history of this motif.[19]

According to Sir 24, students who devote themselves to the sage can, in a sense, get back into the garden. Or perhaps it is better to say, through Ben Sira they can partake of its fruits. To understand this point, the chapter's mingling of the tree and river imagery is crucial. One does not need to enter Eden. Rather one needs access to the water that flows from it. After comparing the torah to abundant waters, Ben Sira likens himself to water: "As for me, I was like a canal from a river, like a water channel into a garden" (Sir 24:30 NRSV). Ben Sira presents himself as a tributary of the water streaming from Eden. The water no longer symbolizes only the torah but also the sage himself. It is difficult to separate the dance from the dancer, as Frank Kermode has stressed.[20] And so it is, asserts Ben Sira, with wisdom and the sage.

In Sir 24:30 the water, which clearly comes from the Edenic garden where the tree of wisdom is found, flows *into* a garden. According to Sir 24:31, the sage says: "I will water my plants, my flower bed I will drench." Ben Sira 24:30 uses the term παράδεισος (Syr. ܦܪܕܝܣܐ) to refer not to Eden but rather to the garden that Ben Sira himself irrigates. It is in this garden, if you will, that the sage teaches his students.[21] Ben Sira compares his teaching in this garden to shining light and prophecy, both images of divine revelation (Sir 24:32–33).[22] The imagery that describes the sage's

---

17. Sheppard, *Wisdom as a Hermeneutical Construct*, 69.

18. Michael A. Fishbane, "The Well of Living Water: A Biblical Motif and Its Ancient Transformations," in *Sha'arei Talmon: Studies in the Bible, Qumran, and the Ancient Near East Presented to Shemaryahu Talmon*, ed. Michael A. Fishbane and Emanuel Tov (Winona Lake, IN: Eisenbrauns, 1992), 3–16. The image is used not only for the torah but also to signify other kinds of revealed knowledge (e.g., 1 En. 48:1).

19. See also Pss 36:8–10; 92:12; Rev 22:1–2. William P. Brown, *Seeing the Psalms: A Theology of Metaphor* (Louisville: Westminster John Knox, 2002), 131–32; Fishbane, "Well of Living Water," 5.

20. Frank Kermode, *Romantic Image* (London: Routledge and Paul, 1986), 91.

21. Compare Sir 39:13: "Listen, my faithful children: open up your petals like roses planted near running waters" (see also 4Q302 2 II).

22. Alex P. Jassen, *Mediating the Divine: Prophecy and Revelation in the Dead*

utterances mingles with the language of water that flows from Eden.²³ The sage gives his teachings authority and legitimization by presenting himself as a conduit through which divine wisdom flows, from one garden (Eden) to another (Ben Sira's). The words that come from his mouth have a revelatory status.²⁴ Ben Sira makes clear that he speaks not for himself but for anyone who seeks instruction (Sir 24:34).²⁵ This emphasis suggests that he understands himself as representative of a broader class of people who offer instruction.²⁶ Ben Sira's authority and self-presentation as a sage involve an aggressive campaign of self-promotion, in which he presents himself to his students, and prospective students, as a source of divine knowledge.

4QInstruction: Students Laboring in a Garden

As its modern title expresses, 4QInstruction is an instructional text.²⁷ The composition is thoroughly pedagogical. It is addressed to a *mevin* (מבין)

Sea Scrolls and Second Temple Judaism, STDJ 68 (Leiden: Brill, 2007), 309–29; Martti Nissinen, "Transmitting Divine Mysteries: The Prophetic Role of Wisdom Teachers in the Dead Sea Scrolls," in *Scripture in Transition: Essays on Septuagint, Hebrew Bible, and Dead Sea Scrolls in Honour of Raija Sollamo*, ed. Anssi Voitila and Jutta Jokiranta, JSJSup 126 (Leiden: Brill, 2008), 513–33; Leo G. Perdue, "Ben Sira and the Prophets," in Corley and Skemp, *Intertextual Studies*, 136.

23. Ben Sira 24:27, according to the NRSV, reads: "It pours forth instruction like the Nile, like the Gihon at the time of vintage" (see also Sir 47:14). Both the Greek and the Syriac read, however, not "Nile" but rather "light" (φῶς/ܢܘܗܪܐ). This suggests that the Hebrew (which is not extant for this chapter) had יאור ("Nile"), which was understood by translators as אור ("light"). See Skehan and Di Lella, *Wisdom of Ben Sira*, 330; Moshe Segal, *The Complete Book of Ben Sira* [Hebrew] (Jerusalem: Bialik Institute, 1958), 146, 150.

24. Here again there is a parallel from chapter 6 of Avot R. Nat. [A]: "And let him [a student] not sit in your presence on the couch or stool or bench. Instead let him sit before you on the ground. And every single word which comes forth from your mouth let him take in with awe, fear, dread, and trembling—the way our fathers received (the Torah) from Mount Sinai: with awe, fear, dread, and trembling." The translation is that of Goldin, *The Fathers*, 40 (slightly modified).

25. This is also a major theme of the final poem of the book, in which a sage describes his lifelong pursuit of wisdom, urging people to follow his example by studying under him (e.g., Sir 51:23, 28).

26. Wright, "Torah and Sapiential Pedagogy," 179–80.

27. For monographs on this composition, see Matthew J. Goff, *4QInstruction*, WLAW 2 (Atlanta: Society of Biblical Literature, 2013); John Kampen, *Wisdom Lit-*

or "understanding one." The text of 4QInstruction emphasizes to him the value of learning. In 4Q418 81 17 one reads, for example, "Improve greatly in understanding and from all of your teachers get ever more learning" (cf. 4Q418 221).[28] Another fragment of the work hails angels as tireless students, who are presented as models for the *mevin* to follow (4Q418 69 II, 10–15).[29] He is often addressed in the imperative form, to encourage him to study. In 4Q417 1 I, 6–7 one reads, for example: "[… day and night meditate upon the mystery that] is to be and study (it) constantly. And then you will know truth and iniquity, wisdom [and foll]y" (compare 4Q418 43 4–5). This passage urges that the *mevin* study the *raz nihyeh*. The "mystery that is to be" could signify a written text, as Daniel Harrington has argued, or the torah itself, as Lange has stressed.[30] The nature of this *raz* is on a vast and cosmic scale (see further below). Its meaning, in my opinion, should not be restricted to a particular text.

The *raz nihyeh* stands at the center of 4QInstruction's pedagogical program.[31] Several imperatives, such as נבט ("gaze upon") and הגה ("meditate"), are employed throughout the text to encourage the addressee to study this mystery.[32] As the passage quoted above conveys, 4QInstruction makes some incredible claims with regard to what the *mevin* can learn from studying this "mystery." Through it the addressee can attain the knowledge of good and evil (a theme to which I return below), and in this way he can also know "[the path]s of all life and the manner of one's

---

erature, ECDSS (Grand Rapids: Eerdmans, 2011); Jean-Sébastien Rey, *4QInstruction: Sagesse et eschatologie*, STDJ 81 (Leiden: Brill, 2009). Its official edition is John Strugnell et al., eds., *Qumran Cave 4.XXIV: Sapiential Texts; 4QInstruction (Mûsār Lĕ Mēbîn): 4Q415ff.*, part 2, DJD 34 (Oxford: Clarendon, 1999).

28. All translations of 4QInstruction are those of Goff, *4QInstruction*.

29. Goff, *4QInstruction*, 235–38.

30. Daniel J. Harrington, *Wisdom Texts from Qumran* (London: Routledge, 1996), 49; Harrington, "The *Raz Nihyeh* in a Qumran Wisdom Text (1Q26, 4Q415–418, 423)," *RevQ* 17 (1996): 552; Armin Lange, *Weisheit und Prädestination: Weisheitliche Urordnung und Prädestination in den Textfunden von Qumran*, STDJ 18 (Leiden: Brill, 1995), 58.

31. Matthew J. Goff, "Wisdom, Apocalypticism, and the Pedagogical Ethos of 4QInstruction," in *Conflicted Boundaries in Wisdom and Apocalypticism*, ed. Lawrence M. Wills and Benjamin G. Wright, SymS 35 (Atlanta: SBL Press, 2005), 57–67.

32. For the "mystery that is to be" connected with the verb נבט ("gaze upon"), see 4Q417 1 I, 3, 18; 4Q417 2 I, 10. In 4Q416 2 III, 9, 14, it is associated with דרש ("examine"); in 4Q417 1 I, 6, with הגה ("meditate"); and in 4Q418 77 4, with לקח ("grasp").

walking that is appointed over one's deeds" (4Q417 1 I, 6–8, 19). This latter claim betrays a deterministic perspective in which history and creation unfold according to an ordained plan of God, which the addressee can understand through the mystery that is to be. The *raz* can provide exceptional knowledge about the nature of reality because, according to 4Q417 1 I, 8–9, God created the world by means of it (ברז נהיה). This mystery is also associated with a tripartite division of time: what has been, what is, and what will be (4Q417 1 I, 3–5 [2x]; 4Q418 123 II, 3–4).³³ The mystery that is to be signifies God's dominion over reality from creation to the final judgment. The comprehensive scope of the *raz* is likely expressed by the word *nihyeh*, a *niphal* participle of the verb "to be." Through the mystery that is to be, the *mevin* can learn about the nature of history and creation, and God's control over them.

How did the addressee come to possess the mystery that is be? The *mevin* is reasonably understood as a member of a community with elect status. God has placed its members, one fragment teaches, in the "lot of the holy ones," denoting that they are like the angels (4Q418 81 4–5). This same fragment describes this group with the phrase "eter[nal] planting" (מטעת עו[לם]), a botanical metaphor used elsewhere in early Jewish literature to describe an elect community (4Q418 81 13).³⁴ The *raz nihyeh* constitutes supernatural, heavenly knowledge to which the *mevin* has access, as part of his elect status.³⁵ 4QInstruction claims several times that the *raz nihyeh* has been disclosed to the *mevin*, using the verb גלה.³⁶ Unfortunately, the composition has nothing more to say on the subject. It never states how it was revealed to the addressee. There is no claim that it was disclosed to him in a vision filled with vivid and enigmatic images, in a manner akin to apocalypses such as Daniel or 4 Ezra. The *mevin* may have received the *raz nihyeh* not from his own visionary experience but from a teacher who revealed the mystery to him. The authorial voice of

---

33. Goff, *4QInstruction*, 144–47.

34. See also 1QS VIII, 5–6; 1 En. 10:16; 93:10. See Patrick A. Tiller, "The 'Eternal Planting' in the Dead Sea Scrolls," *DSD* 4 (1997): 312–35; Goff, *4QInstruction*, 256–57; Shozo Fujita, "The Metaphor of Plant in Jewish Literature of the Intertestamental Period," *JSJ* 7 (1976): 30–45.

35. The word רז signifies supernatural knowledge in the apocalypses Daniel and 1 Enoch, and in numerous other Early Jewish texts. See Samuel I. Thomas, *The "Mysteries" of Qumran: Mystery, Secrecy, and Esotericism in the Dead Sea Scrolls*, EJL 25 (Atlanta: Society of Biblical Literature, 2009), 136–86.

36. 1Q26 1 4; 4Q416 2 III, 18; 4Q418 123 II, 4; 4Q418 184 2; see also 1QH IX, 23.

4QInstruction takes great interest in the mystery that is to be and strives to ensure that the *mevin* understands its pedagogical potential. If the student has access to this mystery, his teacher does as well. But concluding that the *mevin* came to know of the *raz nihyeh* through a teacher, a position that I find plausible, is problematized by the composition's silence with regard to this figure. We can reasonably assume the authorial voice of 4QInstruction is that of a teacher since this voice gives teachings to the *mevin* throughout the work. The speaker of the composition, however, never says anything about himself. It is not clear if we should posit in 4QInstruction a single teacher or if the teacher should be understood as an office occupied over time by various individuals.

With regard to how the speaker in 4QInstruction presents himself, the contrast between this text and the book of Ben Sira could not be starker. Ben Sira, one can say, offers a teacher-focused model of pedagogy—students learn primarily because of the brilliance of their teacher and his access to privileged knowledge. The text of 4QInstruction envisages pedagogy in a more student-focused manner. This Qumran text stresses not what the teacher provides but what the student does with it. In 4QInstruction the *mevin* learns primarily not through the disclosure of supernatural revelation but through its contemplation.

A major text for understanding the *mevin*'s possession of knowledge is 4Q423 1.[37] This fragment describes a garden filled with trees that can make one wise (4Q423 1 1). The text of 4Q423 1 never suggests that the fruit of any tree in the garden is prohibited, as is also the case in Ben Sira (4Q423 1 1; compare Sir 17:7). The second line of the same fragment makes the incredible claim that the *mevin* has been given authority over this garden: "he has given you authority [המשיל] over it to till it and keep it" (4Q423 1 2). While the garden likely evokes, as in Ben Sira, the pedagogical space in which students learn from a teacher, the rhetorical strategy of 4Q423 1 is quite different from that of Ben Sira. Whereas Ben Sira and 1QH 16 (see below) stress that an authoritative teacher controls the garden and makes it available to students, the teacher figure in 4Q423 proclaims that the student is in charge of the garden. The speaker does not emphasize his control over the garden. The student receives authority over the garden not from the teacher but from God. Line 2 of 4Q423 1 states that "he"—not the speaker—gives the *mevin* this authority. The text of 4Q418 81 3 uses the

---

37. Goff, *4QInstruction*, 289–98.

same verb, המשיל, to express that God has given the student his special "inheritance," a reference to his elect status. The rhetorical strategy of the teacher in 4Q423 1 is not to stress, as one finds in Ben Sira (and in column 16 of the Hodayot), his own possession of exceptional knowledge. Rather the teacher helps make the *mevin* aware of what God has given to him.

The garden that the *mevin* possesses evokes Eden. Line 2 of 4Q423 1 asserts that the addressee is to "till" and "keep" the garden (לעבדו ולשמרו), using the same verbs that express in Gen 2:15 Adam's labor in the garden ("to till it and keep it"; לעבדה ולשמרה). Line 3 of the fragment has the phrase "thorn and thistle" (קיץ ודרדר; 4Q423 1 3). In Gen 3:18 this language (קוץ ודרדר) denotes the dry and unproductive nature of the land outside of Eden, with which Adam must contend when growing food. In 4Q423, it seems to me, the expression "thorn and thistle" is applied to the garden itself. The fragment, though admittedly fragmentary, includes no discussion of expulsion from the garden. It is up to the *mevin* to keep the garden in its verdant state through his work in the garden. If he neglects his duties, it will turn into a place of "thorn and thistle."[38]

Elsewhere 4QInstruction stresses that the addressee can learn the knowledge of good and evil from the mystery that is to be (4Q417 1 I, 6–8). The text of 4Q423 1 appropriates the theme of Adam laboring in the garden of Eden to underscore the importance of the addressee's study of the *raz nihyeh*. The book of Ben Sira likewise uses the image of agricultural work to signify the intellectual labor of a student, although never in connection with a garden (Sir 6:19). In 4QInstruction, Eden imagery helps convey an elect community's possession of divine revelation and their cultivation of knowledge through the study of this revelation. The teacher, by encouraging the *mevin* to study, helps him fulfill the special destiny that God had allotted to him through his elect status. The Eden imagery in 4Q423 1 likely gives further elaboration to the construal of the elect community as an "eternal planting."

The Hodayot: A Teacher's Garden

The last text I examine is the Hodayot.[39] First person language is prominent in this composition. There is a long history of understanding the speaker,

---

38. Contrast Ezek 36:35 and Isa 51:3, in which a dry and desolate land becomes like the garden of Eden.

39. Unless noted otherwise, translations of the Hodayot follow Hartmut Stege-

at least in some of the hymns, as their author, and that this individual is none other than the Teacher of Righteousness. Gert Jeremias in 1963, in his *Der Lehrer der Gerechtigkeit*, turned extensively to the Hodayot to write in essence a biography of this figure.[40] This maximalist view is in general not held today. More recent scholarship, by commentators such as Carol Newsom and Angela Harkins, stresses that various members of the Dead Sea sect could, when reading the Hodayot in a performative ritual context, understand themselves as the "I" mentioned in these hymns.[41] As discussed below, in some texts of the composition the "I" is reasonably understood not as a persona any member of the Dead Sea sect could identify with but more likely as an entity associated with leaders or teachers within the sect.

The idea that the "I" derives from a single leader figure is the basis of the conventional designation "Teacher Hymns" for columns X–XVII, whereas the others are typically classified as "Community Hymns."[42] It is not clear that this bifurcation should be continued. It can create the impression of an overly rigid distinction between the two blocs of material, making it difficult to appreciate points in common in both groups or to understand the diversity of material within each putative unit.[43] Nevertheless one can, without reifying the Teacher Hymns category, observe

---

mann and Eileen M. Schuller, *Qumran Cave 1.III: 1QHodayot^a, with Incorporation of 1QHodayot^b and 4QHodayot^{a-f}*, DJD 40 (Oxford: Clarendon, 2009). Note also Eileen M. Schuller and Carol A. Newsom, *The Hodayot (Thanksgiving Psalms): A Study Edition of 1QH^a*, EJL 36 (Atlanta: Society of Biblical Literature, 2012).

40. Gert Jeremias, *Der Lehrer der Gerechtigkeit*, SUNT 2 (Göttingen: Vandenhoeck & Ruprecht, 1963). See also Carol A. Newsom, *The Self as Symbolic Space: Constructing Identity and Community at Qumran*, STDJ 52 (Leiden: Brill, 2004), 289–91.

41. Newsom, *Self as Symbolic Space*, 287–346; Angela Kim Harkins, *Reading with an "I" to the Heavens: Looking at the Qumran Hodayot through the Lens of Visionary Traditions*, Ekstasis 3 (Berlin: de Gruyter, 2012). Note also Esther G. Chazon, "Lowly to Lofty: The Hodayot's Use of Liturgical Traditions to Shape Sectarian Identity and Religious Experience," *RevQ* 26 (2013): 3–19.

42. John J. Collins, "Amazing Grace: The Transformation of the Thanksgiving Hymn at Qumran," in *Psalms in Community: Jewish and Christian Textual, Liturgical, and Artistic Traditions*, ed. Harold W. Attridge and Margot E. Fassler; SymS 25 (Atlanta: Society of Biblical Literature, 2003), 75–85. See also now Trine Bjørnung Hasselbalch, *Meaning and Context in the Thanksgiving Hymns: Linguistic and Rhetorical Perspectives on a Collection of Prayers from Qumran*, EJL 42 (Atlanta: SBL Press, 2015).

43. This point is compellingly argued by Harkins, *Reading*, 20–24.

that some hymns portray the "I" as someone who possesses divine revelation that he makes available to others. For example, 1QH XII, 28–29 reads: "Through me you have illumined the faces of many.... For you have made me understand your wonderful mysteries."[44] Here the speaker, not unlike the configuration of the teacher in Ben Sira, is a teacher who transmits heavenly knowledge.

The texts of 1QH XIV and XVI contain poignant descriptions of gardens. The relevant texts are from two different hymns of the Hodayot collection.[45] Julie Hughes has observed that these hymns use imagery from Gen 2–3, including explicit references to Eden (1QH XIV, 19; XVI, 21), and that they have extensive allusions to prophetic texts of the Hebrew Bible that discuss gardens and trees, such as Isa 5 and Jer 17.[46] James Davila understands primarily 1QH XVI but also column XIV in terms of heavenly ascent traditions, suggesting that hekhalot mysticism is rooted in late Second Temple traditions evident in the Hodayot.[47] Harkins has significantly developed the perspective that the Hodayot should be understood as a catalyst for visionary activity.[48] The two poems, she argues, were generated by an author's religious experience, which a subsequent reader, by identifying himself with the "I" of the text, could reenact, engendering his own visionary experience of paradise.[49] While reading or hearing the Hodayot in antiquity could have certainly triggered some sort of ecstatic

---

44. Compare 1QH XIII, 27, in which the speaker praises God because he has shown his "gre[atness] through me."

45. The hymns at issue are, respectively, 1QH XIII, 22–XV, 8 and XVI, 5–XVII, 36. See Harkins, *Reading*, 217; Hartmut Stegemann, "The Number of Psalms in 1QHodayot[a] and Some of Their Sections," in *Liturgical Perspectives: Prayer and Poetry in Light of the Dead Sea Scrolls; Proceedings of the Fifth International Symposium of the Orion Center for the Study of the Dead Sea Scrolls and Associated Literature, 19–23 January, 2000*, ed. Esther G. Chazon, Ruth Clements, and Avital Pinnick, STDJ 48 (Leiden: Brill, 2003), 191–234.

46. Julie A. Hughes, *Scriptural Allusions and Exegesis in the Hodayot*, STDJ 59 (Leiden: Brill, 2006), 135–83. She understands 1QH XVI, 5–XVII, 36 as a description of a person's suffering and vindication that is heavily reliant on Second Isaiah. See also Harkins, *Reading*, 23; Svend Holm-Nielsen, *Hodayot: Psalms from Qumran*, ATDan 2 (Aarhus: Universitetsforlaget, 1960), 165.

47. James R. Davila, "The Hodayot Hymnist and the Four Who Entered Paradise," *RevQ* 17 (1996): 457–76. See also Davila, *Hekhalot Literature in Translation: Major Texts of Merkavah Mysticism*, JJTPSup 20 (Leiden: Brill, 2013).

48. Harkins, *Reading*, 206–66.

49. Ibid., 217, 225, 246.

experience, in neither column XIV nor XVI, nor in the composition as a whole, are there explicit accounts of people having visions or ascending to heaven. I suggest that the garden imagery of the Hodayot, much like that of Ben Sira, evokes the pedagogical space in which a teacher transmits divine knowledge to students.

The Hodayot stresses the special status of those who are with the speaker. In column XIV the phrase "eternal planting," as in 4QInstruction, describes the special allotment given to an elect community: "they become your princes in the [eternal] lo[t and] their [shoot] opens as a flower [blooms, for] everlasting fragrance, making a sprout grow into the branches of an eternal planting" (מטעת עולם; 1QH XIV, 17-18; compare Ezek 31:14).[50] Using hyperbolic, expressive language that is characteristic of the Hodayot, the tree is incredibly large, extending up to the heavens and down to *tehom* (1QH XIV, 18-19). The text, not unlike Sir 24:30-31, states not only that Eden is well irrigated but also that its water leads outward into an ocean: "All the rivers of Eden [make] its [br]an[ches m]oist, and it will (extend) to the measure[less] seas" (1QH XIV, 19-20).[51] The water is also called in line 20 a "spring of light" (מעין אור).[52] The poem's tree and water imagery is on a global scale. This may help convey the text's assertion of the comprehensive scope of the eschatological judgment (1QH XIV, 21-22; see also XI, 20-37).

The garden recounted in column XVI is not on such a vast scale. Rather the image is of the speaker tending an "actual" garden. This poem, like column XIV, uses "eternal planting" language:

> I thank [you, O Lo]rd, that you have placed me by the source of streams in a dry land, (by) a spring of water in a thirsty land, and (by) a watered garden ... a planting of juniper and elm with cedar all together for your glory, trees of life at a secret spring, hidden in the midst of all the trees by the water. And they were there so that a shoot might be made to

---

50. There are numerous other points in common between the two texts. I have elsewhere suggested that the author(s) of the Hodayot may have been familiar with 4QInstruction. See my "Reading Wisdom at Qumran: 4QInstruction and the Hodayot," *DSD* 11 (2004): 263-88.

51. The imagery of boundless waters accords with Sir 24:28-29. These verses, after mentioning the overflowing water that streams from Eden, read: "The first human never knew wisdom fully, nor will the last succeed in fathoming her. Deeper than the sea are her thoughts; her counsels, than the great abyss."

52. See the discussion above on Sir 24:27 in the Greek and the Syriac.

sprout into an eternal planting [מטעת עולם]. (1 QH XVI, 5–7; see also XV, 21–22)[53]

The poet calls this plantation of trees "a glorious Eden and [an everlasting] splen[dor]" (1QH XVI, 21). The phrase "secret spring" in XVI, 7 emphasizes the hiddenness of the pool that irrigates the grove of trees.[54] According to XVI, 13, a "whirling flame of fire" (להט אש מתחפכת) prevents people from discovering the "fountain of life" and the "eternal trees." This image utilizes language from Gen 3:24, which describes the flaming and swirling sword (להט החרב המתהפכת) that guards Eden after the expulsion of Adam and Eve.[55] This extraordinary, well-irrigated garden in which the elect are nurtured is presented as a renewal of the garden of Eden. The Hebrew for the phrase "secret spring" is מעין רז, literally a "spring of mystery," suggesting that it denotes not simply hiddenness but also divine revelation (cf. 1QH XIII, 28; XVI, 12; XVII, 23). The garden metaphor bolsters the perspective that the knowledge conveyed by the teacher has the status of revelation.

The speaker makes it unambiguously clear that the garden is under his control. He states that through his hand "you [God] opened their source" (מקורם), referring to the luxurious garden that he praises (1QH XVI, 22). He continues the hand imagery: "If I withdraw (my) hand, it becomes like a juniper [in the wilderness,] and its rootstock like nettles in salty ground. (In) its furrows thorn and thistle [קוץ ודרדר] grow up into a bramble thicket and a weed patch" (1QH XVI, 25–26).[56] The speaker's moving away of his hand likely denotes his cessation of labor in the garden. Without proper maintenance it would fall into ruin. It is in wonderful condition, but he could make that change. The Eden imagery emphasizes the authority of the teacher figure within the garden. This point becomes particularly clear when the Hodayot is compared to 4QInstruction.[57] The text of 4Q423 emphasizes that control over the garden is given to the *mevin*, as discussed above. The text of 4QInstruction affirms that the student must cultivate the garden, whereas in column XVI of the Hodayot the teacher

---

53. Fishbane, "Well of Living Water," 9.
54. Hughes, *Scriptural Allusions*, 150–52.
55. Ibid., 135.
56. Ibid., 157.
57. Goff, "Reading Wisdom," 286–87.

figure is the one who tends the garden.⁵⁸ Both texts use the "thorn and thistle" language of Gen 3:18 in reference to the garden itself, denoting its vulnerability to decay unless properly maintained; this position is explicit in 1QH XVI and implicit in 4QInstruction, as argued above. With regard to this point column XVI is closer to Ben Sira. Both texts situate the revelation of knowledge in a garden in a way that emphasizes the speaker's control of this knowledge, stressing his authoritative status.⁵⁹

The Hodayot utilizes language from Gen 2–3 to give vivid expression to the idea that an authoritative teacher possesses heavenly knowledge that he transmits to his students. This has ramifications for understanding how the hymns, especially the one that includes column XVI, functioned within the Dead Sea sect. While in general members of the group could have identified with the "I" of some hymns of the Hodayot, anyone who uttered and thus became associated with the speaker in the columns under discussion likely had an important teaching office within the sect, such as the *maskil* (1QS IX, 12–19), as Newsom has stressed.⁶⁰ The "I" may have also been understood as offering an image of the Teacher of Righteousness as an ideal figure, in whose tradition the *maskil* was to follow, bolstering the authority of the office.⁶¹

Conclusion

Harkins draws on Foucault to understand the garden in the Hodayot as a "heterotopia."⁶² A heterotopia is a site that is both a real space and outside of real space. Foucault likens such sites to a mirror, which occupies a physical space, with which a person can gaze upon him or herself, creating an image that does not exist in space that nevertheless helps the gazer reflect upon and get a better understanding of himself. As Harkins observes, Foucault's only ancient example of a heterotopia is a garden.⁶³ For her the

---

58. Contra Harkins, *Reading*, 243, who stresses that 1QH XVI is unique among Second Temple texts for envisioning a garden in which one must labor.
59. This point has been observed by Hughes, *Scriptural Allusions*, 180.
60. Newsom, *Self as Symbolic Space*, 297.
61. Ibid., 345.
62. Harkins, *Reading*, 208–15; Michel Foucault, "Of Other Spaces," trans. Jay Miskowiec, *Diacritics* 16 (1986): 22–27.
63. Foucault, "Of Other Spaces," 25–26, writes: "We must not forget that in the Orient the garden, an astonishing creation that is now a thousand years old, had very deep and seemingly superimposed meanings. The traditional garden of the Persians

ancient garden is, following Foucault, a site of simultaneity and also one of liminality. Gardens in the ancient world, particularly in Mesopotamia and Persia, were beautiful and exclusive.[64] They were sites in which a range of flora grew that did not exist together naturally, gathered together to show a ruler's power, representing the expanse of his territory in one microcosmic site. The lush and diverse garden symbolized the vitality and prosperity of the state.[65] Typically adjacent to the palace, the garden was often a liminal space in that it separated royal and common spheres of a city. There were also temple gardens that were thought to be the possession of gods, constituting a liminal space between the human and divine realms.[66]

Harkins appeals to the ancient garden as a heterotopia to put forward her understanding of garden imagery in the Hodayot.[67] By creating an idealized space in which real experiences occurred through performative reading, these texts, she suggests, generated visionary experiences of paradise. Foucault's heterotopia also offers, I think, a productive way to understand the theme of the garden I have been tracing in Ben Sira,

---

was a sacred space that was supposed to bring together inside its rectangle four parts representing the four parts of the world, with a space still more sacred than the others that were like an umbilicus, the navel of the world at its center (the basin and water fountain were there); and all the vegetation of the garden was supposed to come together in this space, in this sort of microcosm.... The garden is the smallest parcel of the world and then it is the totality of the world. The garden has been a sort of happy, universalizing heterotopia since the beginnings of antiquity."

64. Michaela Bauks, "Sacred Trees in the Garden of Eden and Their Ancient Near Eastern Precursors," *JAJ* 3 (2012): 267–301; Harkins, *Reading*, 208–9; Manfried Dietrich, "Das biblische Paradies und der babylonische Tempelgarten: Überlegungen zur Lage des Gartens Edens," in *Das biblische Weltbild und seine altorientalischen Kontexte*, ed. Bernd Janowski and Beate Ego, FAT 32 (Tübingen: Mohr Siebeck, 2001), 281–323; W. Fauth, "Der königliche Gärtner und Jäger im Paradeisos: Beobachtungen zur Rolle des Herrschers in der vorderasiatischen Hortikultur," *Persica* 8 (1979): 1–53; A. L. Oppenheim, "On Royal Gardens in Mesopotamia," *JNES* 24 (1965): 328–33.

65. This is evident for example in Berossus's description of the splendid palace of Nebuchadnezzar II, which he rebuilt with spoils from war. He claims it had terraces planted with trees and discusses the famous Hanging Gardens of Babylon (Josephus, *C. Ap.* 1.141; *Ant.* 10.226). See Gerald P. Verbrugghe and John M. Wickersham, *Berossos and Manetho, Introduced and Translated* (Ann Arbor: University of Michigan Press, 1996), 59 (frag. 9a); Julian Reade, "Alexander the Great and the Hanging Gardens of Babylon," *Iraq* 62 (2000): 199.

66. See, for example, the image of a seventh-century BCE temple garden in Nineveh, in Bauks, "Sacred Trees," 281.

67. Harkins, *Reading*, 215.

4QInstruction, and the Hodayot. None of these texts attempts to describe a garden that actually existed. They use, however, the image of the garden to describe a real phenomenon, the education of students by teachers. The garden represents the pedagogical space in which students learn from teachers who possess exceptional knowledge. It is a heterotopic site of self-formation, in which the student acquires learning and prospers. These texts, in particular 4QInstruction, turn to the metaphor of cultivation to understand the labor of study and its rewards, with the acquisition of wisdom represented as a lush garden. The emphasis on the teacher's control of the garden, a strategy that powerfully conveys his authoritative status that is clearly employed in Ben Sira and the Hodayot, may draw on the cultural trope of the garden symbolizing the dominion of the king. The three texts under discussion also betray a conception of a garden as a liminal site in which the divine and human realms overlap, through use of Eden imagery. None of the texts I have examined buttresses the authority of the teacher by presenting him as a "genius," a term that denotes the tremendous intellects of famous professors of our era, such as Stephen Hawking.[68] Rather the teacher has a garden because he has access to divine knowledge. All three texts under discussion in different ways convey the extraordinary nature of what teachers transmit to their students through creative appeals to Gen 2–3. These writings illustrate that some Jewish teachers in the late Second Temple period conceptualized the process of students acquiring special knowledge from a teacher as the formation of a luxuriant garden.

Bibliography

Bauks, Michaela. "Sacred Trees in the Garden of Eden and Their Ancient Near Eastern Precursors." *JAJ* 3 (2012): 267–301.

Berg, Shane. "Ben Sira, the Genesis Creation Accounts, and the Knowledge of God's Will." *JBL* 132 (2013): 139–57.

Brown, William P. *Seeing the Psalms: A Theology of Metaphor*. Louisville: Westminster John Knox, 2002.

---

68. Darrin M. McMahon, *Divine Fury: A History of Genius* (New York: Basic Books, 2013).

Chazon, Esther G. "Lowly to Lofty: The Hodayot's Use of Liturgical Traditions to Shape Sectarian Identity and Religious Experience." *RevQ* 26 (2013): 3-19.
Collins, John J. "Amazing Grace: The Transformation of the Thanksgiving Hymn at Qumran." Pages 75-85 in *Psalms in Community: Jewish and Christian Textual, Liturgical, and Artistic Traditions*. Edited by Harold W. Attridge and Margot E. Fassler. SymS 25. Atlanta: Society of Biblical Literature, 2003.
———. *Jewish Wisdom in the Hellenistic Age*. OTL. Louisville: Westminster John Knox, 1997.
Davila, James R. *Hekhalot Literature in Translation: Major Texts of Merkavah Mysticism*. JJTPSup 20. Leiden: Brill, 2013.
———. "The Hodayot Hymnist and the Four Who Entered Paradise." *RevQ* 17 (1996): 457-76.
Dietrich, Manfried. "Das biblische Paradies und der babylonische Tempelgarten: Überlegungen zur Lage des Gartens Edens." Pages 281-323 in *Das biblische Weltbild und seine altorientalischen Kontexte*. Edited by Bernd Janowski and Beate Ego. FAT 32. Tübingen: Mohr Siebeck, 2001.
Doran, Robert. "Jewish Education in the Seleucid Period." Pages 116-32 in *Studies in Politics, Class and Material Culture*. Vol. 3 of *Second Temple Studies*. Edited by Philip R. Davies and John M. Halligan. JSOTSup 340. Sheffield: Sheffield Academic, 2002.
Elior, Rachel. "The Garden of Eden is the Holy of Holies and the Dwelling of the Lord." *StSp* 24 (2014): 63-118.
Fauth, W. "Der königliche Gärtner und Jäger im Paradeisos: Beobachtungen zur Rolle des Herrschers in der vorderasiatischen Hortikultur." *Persica* 8 (1979): 1-53.
Fishbane, Michael A. "The Well of Living Water: A Biblical Motif and Its Ancient Transformations." Pages 3-16 in *Sha'arei Talmon: Studies in the Bible, Qumran, and the Ancient Near East Presented to Shemaryahu Talmon*. Edited by Michael A. Fishbane and Emanuel Tov. Winona Lake, IN: Eisenbrauns, 1992.
Foucault, Michel. "Of Other Spaces." Translated by Jay Miskowiec. *Diacritics* 16 (1986): 22-27.
Fujita, Shozo. "The Metaphor of Plant in Jewish Literature of the Intertestamental Period." *JSJ* 7 (1976): 30-45.
Gilbert, Maurice. "Ben Sira, Reader of Genesis 1-11." Pages 89-99 in *Intertextual Studies in Ben Sira and Tobit: Essays in Honor of Alex-*

ander A. Di Lella, O.F.M. Edited by Jeremy Corley and Vincent T. M. Skemp. CBQMS 38. Washington, DC: Catholic Biblical Association of America, 2005.

Goering, Greg Schmidt. *Wisdom's Root Revealed: Ben Sira and the Election of Israel.* JSJSup 139. Leiden: Brill, 2009.

Goff, Matthew J. *4QInstruction.* WLAW 2. Atlanta: SBL Press, 2013

———. "The Personification of Wisdom and Folly in Ancient Judaism." Pages 128–54 in *Religion and Female Body in Ancient Judaism and Its Environments.* Edited by Geza Xeravits. DCLS 28. Berlin: de Gruyter, 2015.

———. "Reading Wisdom at Qumran: 4QInstruction and the Hodayot." *DSD* 11 (2004): 263–88.

———. "Wisdom." in *T&T Clark Companion to the Dead Sea Scrolls.* Edited by George J. Brooke and Charlotte Hempel. London: T&T Clark, forthcoming.

———. "Wisdom, Apocalypticism, and the Pedagogical Ethos of 4QInstruction." Pages 57–67 in *Conflicted Boundaries in Wisdom and Apocalypticism.* Edited by Lawrence M. Wills and Benjamin G. Wright. SymS 35. Atlanta: Society of Biblical Literature, 2005.

Goldin, Judah. *The Fathers according to Rabbi Nathan.* YJS 10. New Haven: Yale University Press, 1983.

Green, Deborah A. *The Aroma of Righteousness: Scent and Seduction in Rabbinic Life and Literature.* University Park: Pennsylvania State University Press, 2011.

Harkins, Angela Kim. *Reading with an "I" to the Heavens: Looking at the Qumran Hodayot through the Lens of Visionary Traditions.* Ekstasis 3. Berlin: de Gruyter, 2012.

Harrington, Daniel J. "The *Raz Nihyeh* in a Qumran Wisdom Text (1Q26, 4Q415–418, 423)." *RevQ* 17 (1996): 549–53.

———. *Wisdom Texts from Qumran.* London: Routledge, 1996.

Hasselbalch, Trine Bjørnung. *Meaning and Context in the Thanksgiving Hymns: Linguistic and Rhetorical Perspectives on a Collection of Prayers from Qumran.* EJL 42. Atlanta: SBL Press, 2015.

Holm-Nielsen, Svend. *Hodayot: Psalms from Qumran.* ATDan 2. Aarhus: Universitetsforlaget, 1960.

Hughes, Julie A. *Scriptural Allusions and Exegesis in the Hodayot.* STDJ 59. Leiden: Brill, 2006.

Jassen, Alex P. *Mediating the Divine: Prophecy and Revelation in the Dead Sea Scrolls and Second Temple Judaism.* STDJ 68. Leiden: Brill, 2007.

Jeremias, Gert. *Der Lehrer der Gerechtigkeit.* SUNT 2. Göttingen: Vandenhoeck & Ruprecht, 1963.
Kampen, John. *Wisdom Literature.* ECDSS. Grand Rapids: Eerdmans, 2011.
Kermode, Frank. *Romantic Image.* London: Routledge and Paul, 1986.
Lanfer, Peter T. *Remembering Eden: The Reception History of Genesis 3:22–24.* New York: Oxford University Press, 2012.
Lange, Armin. *Weisheit und Prädestination: Weisheitliche Urordnung und Prädestination in den Textfunden von Qumran.* STDJ 18. Leiden: Brill, 1995.
Levenson, Jon D. *Sinai and Zion: An Entry into the Jewish Bible.* San Francisco: HarperSanFrancisco, 1987.
Lévi, Israel. *L'Ecclésiastique ou la Sagesse de Jésus, fils de Sira.* 2 vols. Paris: Leroux, 1898–1901.
McMahon, Darrin M. *Divine Fury: A History of Genius.* New York: Basic Books, 2013.
Murphy, Roland E. "The Personification of Wisdom." Pages 222–33 in *Wisdom in Ancient Israel: Essays in Honour of J. A. Emerton.* Edited by John Day, R. P. Gordon, and Hugh G. M. Williamson. Cambridge: Cambridge University Press, 1995.
Newsom, Carol A. *The Self as Symbolic Space: Constructing Identity and Community at Qumran.* STDJ 52. Leiden: Brill, 2004.
Nissinen, Martti. "Transmitting Divine Mysteries: The Prophetic Role of Wisdom Teachers in the Dead Sea Scrolls." Pages 513–33 in *Scripture in Transition: Essays on Septuagint, Hebrew Bible, and Dead Sea Scrolls in Honour of Raija Sollamo.* Edited by Anssi Voitila and Jutta Jokiranta. JSJSup 126. Leiden: Brill, 2008.
Oppenheim, A. L. "On Royal Gardens in Mesopotamia." *JNES* 24 (1965): 328–33.
Perdue, Leo G. "Ben Sira and the Prophets." Pages 132–54 in *Intertextual Studies in Ben Sira and Tobit: Essays in Honor of Alexander A. Di Lella, O.F.M.* Edited by Jeremy Corley and Vincent T. M. Skemp. CBQMS 38. Washington, DC: Catholic Biblical Association of America, 2005.
Reade, Julian. "Alexander the Great and the Hanging Gardens of Babylon." *Iraq* 62 (2000): 195–217.
Rey, Jean-Sébastien. *4QInstruction: Sagesse et eschatologie.* STDJ 81. Leiden: Brill, 2009.
Reymond, Eric. Review of *Weisheit aus der Begegnung: Bildung nach dem Buch Ben Sira*, by Frank Ueberschaer. *DSD* 21 (2014): 126–28.

Rogers, Jessie. "'It Overflows Like the Euphrates with Understanding': Another Look at the Relationship between Law and Wisdom in Sirach." Pages 114–21 in *Ancient Versions and Traditions*. Vol. 1 of *Of Scribes and Sages: Early Jewish Interpretation and Transmission of Scripture*. Edited by Craig A. Evans. LSTS 50; SSEJC 9. London: T&T Clark, 2004.

Ruiten, Jacques van. "Garden of Eden—Paradise." *EDEJ* 658–61.

Schofer, Jonathan Wyn. *The Making of a Sage: A Study in Rabbinic Ethics*. Madison: University of Wisconsin Press, 2005.

Schuller, Eileen M., and Carol A. Newsom. *The Hodayot (Thanksgiving Psalms): A Study Edition of 1QHa*. EJL 36. Atlanta: Society of Biblical Literature, 2012.

Segal, Moshe. *The Complete Book of Ben Sira* [Hebrew]. Jerusalem: Bialik Institute, 1958.

Sheppard, Gerald T. *Wisdom as a Hermeneutical Construct: A Study in the Sapientializing of the Old Testament*. BZAW 151. Berlin: de Gruyter, 1980.

Shimoff, Sandra R. "Gardens: From Eden to Jerusalem." *JSJ* 26 (1995): 144–55.

Skehan, Patrick W., and Alexander A. Di Lella. *The Wisdom of Ben Sira*. AB 39. New York: Doubleday, 1987.

Stegemann, Hartmut. "The Number of Psalms in 1QHodayot[a] and Some of Their Sections." Pages 191–234 in *Liturgical Perspectives: Prayer and Poetry in Light of the Dead Sea Scrolls; Proceedings of the Fifth International Symposium of the Orion Center for the Study of the Dead Sea Scrolls and Associated Literature, 19–23 January, 2000*. Edited by Esther G. Chazon, Ruth Clements, and Avital Pinnick. STDJ 48. Leiden: Brill, 2003.

Stegemann, Hartmut, and Eileen M. Schuller. *Qumran Cave 1.III: 1QHodayota, with Incorporation of 1QHodayotb and 4QHodayota-f*. DJD 40. Oxford: Clarendon, 2009.

Stone, Nira. "The Four Rivers that Flowed from Eden." Pages 227–50 in *Beyond Eden: The Biblical Story of Paradise (Genesis 2–3) and Its Reception History*. Edited by Konrad Schmid and Christof Riedweg. FAT 2/34. Tübingen: Mohr Siebeck, 2008.

Stordalen, Terje. "Heaven on Earth—Or Not? Jerusalem as Eden in Biblical Literature." Pages 28–57 in *Beyond Eden: The Biblical Story of Paradise (Genesis 2–3) and Its Reception History*. Edited by Konrad Schmid and Christof Riedweg. FAT 2/34. Tübingen: Mohr Siebeck, 2008.

Strugnell, John, Daniel J. Harrington, Torleif Elgvin, and Joseph A Fitzmyer, eds. *Qumran Cave 4.XXIV: Sapiential Texts; 4QInstruction (Mûsār Lĕ Mēbîn): 4Q415ff.* Part 2. DJD 34. Oxford: Clarendon, 1999.

Thomas, Samuel I. *The "Mysteries" of Qumran: Mystery, Secrecy, and Esotericism in the Dead Sea Scrolls.* EJL 25. Atlanta: Society of Biblical Literature, 2009.

Tigchelaar, Eibert J. C. "Eden and Paradise: The Garden Motif in Some Early Jewish Texts." Pages 37–57 in *Paradise Interpreted: Representations of Biblical Paradise in Judaism and Christianity.* Edited by Gerard P. Luttikhuizen. TBN 2. Leiden: Brill, 1999.

Tiller, Patrick A. "The 'Eternal Planting' in the Dead Sea Scrolls." *DSD* 4 (1997): 312–35.

Verbrugghe, Gerald P., and John M. Wickersham. *Berossos and Manetho, Introduced and Translated.* Ann Arbor: University of Michigan Press, 1996.

Weeks, Stuart. *An Introduction to the Study of Wisdom Literature.* ApBS. London: T&T Clark, 2010.

Wright, Benjamin G. "Torah and Sapiential Pedagogy in the Book of Ben Sira." Pages 158–86 in *Wisdom and Torah: The Reception of "Torah" in the Wisdom Literature of the Second Temple Period.* Edited by Bernd U. Schipper and D. Andrew Teeter. JSJSup 163. Leiden: Brill, 2013.

Paideia:
A Multifarious and Unifying Concept
in the Wisdom of Solomon

Jason M. Zurawski

In the earliest critical studies of the Wisdom of Solomon, it was the standard opinion that the text was a composite of three or more individual authors, writing at different times for different purposes.[1] However, since Carl Grimm's monumental commentary from 1860, the text's unity has no longer been seriously called into question.[2] The work of scholars such as Addison Wright, James Reese, Paolo Bizzeti, and Maurice Gilbert begun primarily in the 1960s, on the structure and genre of the text, have sufficiently confirmed the unity of the composition and its tripartite structure.[3] Yet, the purpose of the structure has remained an elusive question. The continued division of the text into three "books"—usually along the

---

I would like to thank Matthias Henze and Ben Wright for their responses at the 2013 Society of Biblical Literature Annual Meeting in Baltimore. They both pointed out several points in my paper where my arguments were neither clear nor yet fully developed. I have tried my best to address their concerns in this revised version.

1. See, e.g., Johann Gottfried Eichhorn, *Einleitung in die apokryphen Schriften des Alten Testaments* (Leipzig: Weidmann, 1795), 142–49; Karl Gottlieb Bretschneider, "De libri Sapientiae parte priore cap. I–XI e duobus libellis diversis conflata" (PhD diss., University of Wittenberg, 1804); or Johann C. C. Nachtigal, *Das Buch der Weisheit*, vol. 2 of *Die Versammlungen der Weisen* (Halle: Gebauer, 1799).

2. Carl L. W. Grimm, *Das Buch der Weisheit*, vol. 6 of *Kurzgefasstes exegetisches Handbuch zu den Apokryphen des Alten Testamentes*, ed. Otto Fridolin Fritzsche and Carl L. W. Grimm (Leipzig: Hirzel, 1860).

3. See James M. Reese, "Plan and Structure of the Book of Wisdom," *CBQ* 27 (1965): 391–99; Addison G. Wright, "The Structure of the Book of Wisdom," *Bib* 48 (1967): 165–84; Maurice Gilbert, "La structure de la prière de Salomon (Sg 9)," *Bib* 51 (1970): 301–31; Ulrich Offerhaus, *Komposition und Intention der Sapientia Salomonis*

lines of the Book of Eschatology, the Book of Wisdom, and the Book of History—which began with W. Weber in 1904, has not aided our understanding of the text but has perhaps hindered a more thorough, nuanced appreciation of the author's motivations and overall message.[4]

One consistent theme that appears throughout the text and its unique parts is the detailed understanding of God and Wisdom's paideia of humanity. This is a concept that has never been fully explored in the scholarship, with the major commentators making only passing remarks on the subject. Scholarship on the Wisdom of Solomon has, as yet, failed to notice just how important this idea was in the mind of the author and in the overall meaning of his text. While in the details the author gives us several different aspects of his understanding of paideia, viewed holistically, paideia comes to represent complete and universal education, both the content and the processes by which it is attained. It has no ethnic or particularistic significance, but instead is the determining factor of righteousness and the means by which one gains the true immortal life of the soul. It is this concept which unites the seemingly divergent sections of the text into a coherent whole.

Meanings of Paideia in the Wisdom of Solomon

Throughout this complex text, we find a number of distinct understandings of the concept of paideia, not all of them obviously related. The first hint we have of the concept comes in the author's opening address, pointing to the importance of the idea and its connection to the predominant player in his drama, the figure of Wisdom or Sophia. In Wis 1:4–5, we see that Wisdom will not be involved in deceit, transgression, or wickedness of any kind, because she is the ἅγιον πνεῦμα παιδείας, the "holy spirit of paideia."[5] The very first description of Wisdom in the text is as the source

---

(PhD diss., Friedrich-Wilhelms-Universität, 1981), 71–73; Paolo Bizzeti, *Il libro della Sapienza: Struttura e genere letterario* (Brescia: Paideia, 1984).

4. W. Weber introduced his theory in "Die Komposition der Weisheit Salomos," *ZWT* 48 (1904): 145–69.

5. For the originality of παιδείας over the minority readings of παιδίου or σοφίας, see Chrysostome Larcher, *Le livre de la Sagesse ou la Sagesse de Salomon*, 3 vols., EBib NS 1, 3, 5 (Paris: Gabalda, 1983–1985), 1:174–75; Joseph Ziegler, *Sapientia Salomonis*, VTG 12.1 (Göttingen: Vandenhoeck & Ruprecht, 1962), 96; and Ernest G. Clarke, *The Wisdom of Solomon*, CBC (Cambridge: Cambridge University Press, 1973), 16.

of paideia, humanity's educator, the one who will allow people to understand all things on earth and in heaven.⁶

Paideia as the Educational Content of the Book

While this opening highlights the importance of the concept in the author's program, it tells us little about what exactly the term παιδεία refers to in the text. The term, together with its cognate verbal form, παιδεύω, is used by the author variously to denote both the pedagogy and the educational content. We shall see later that as the means by which individuals are educated and thereby made righteous, the author's portrayal of paideia often aligns more closely with the Hebrew concept of *musar* than with the Hellenistic ideals of paideia proper. But when paideia in the Wisdom of Solomon refers to the content of education, the concept is fully compatible with Hellenistic sensibilities. In the author's second direct address to the kings and judges of the earth (Wis 6:1–21), the purpose of the first section of the text—and likely of the text in toto—is made clear, to correct the behavior of rulers before it is too late, before they are beyond repentance. In this second address, we learn that the author viewed his own teachings as paideia, as education meant to guide one on the path to wisdom and immortality.

The addressees have already gone astray: they are unjust rulers, who have neither kept the law nor lived according to God's purposes (Wis 6:4). Therefore, before God's full disciplinary wrath comes upon them, the author, in the guise of Solomon, attempts to help:

> To you, then, O rulers, my words are directed, in order that you may learn wisdom and not transgress [ἵνα μάθητε σοφίαν καὶ μὴ παραπέσητε]. For

---

6. Most modern commentators agree that the phrase in Wis 1:5, ἅγιον πνεῦμα παιδείας, should refer to Wisdom herself, not to a human spirit. As David Winston argues, Wisdom here is "the holy spirit, that divine tutor." See his *The Wisdom of Solomon*, AB 43 (New York: Doubleday, 1979), 99. According to Larcher, "L'expression *hagion pneuma paideias*, 'le saint Esprit qui éduque', glose le mot 'Sagesse' du v. précédent en introduisant la notion d'"Esprit' et *hagion* marque la transition: La Sagesse ne peut cohabiter avec la malice et la souillure, parce qu'elle est une réalité 'sainte'" (*Livre de la Sagesse*, 1:175). For Giuseppe Scarpat, "Il santo spirito della disciplina" should refer directly to Wisdom and, from that, to God. See Scarpat, *Libro della Sapienza: Testo, traduzione, introduzione e commento*, 3 vols., BibTS 1, 3, 6 (Brescia: Paideia, 1989–1999), 1:77 (see also 1:116).

whoever piously observes holy things will be made holy, and those who have been taught them will find a defense [οἱ διδαχθέντες αὐτὰ εὑρήσουσιν ἀπολογίαν]. Therefore, desire my words, long for them, and you will be educated [παιδευθήσεσθε]. (Wis 6:9–11)[7]

The entire writing then becomes a pedagogical tool, a textbook for righteous living.

The constant figure of Wisdom is the ultimate source of educational content, and devotion to her paideia is the ultimate prerequisite to acquiring Wisdom. Much like the figure of חכמה/σοφία in the book of Proverbs, Wisdom, the holy spirit of paideia, in our text is available to all who desire her; there is no hint of esotericism here (Wis 6:12–16). For those committed to her paideia, the educational and spiritual value is without end: "For she is an unfailing treasure for mortals; those who acquire it attain friendship with God, commended for the gifts that come from paideia" (διὰ τὰς ἐκ παιδείας δωρεὰς συσταθέντες; Wis 7:14). The content of Wisdom's teachings is complete, universal human knowledge:

> [15] May God grant that I speak with judgment,
> and to have thoughts worthy of his gifts,
> because he himself is both the guide of Wisdom
> and the corrector of the wise.
> [16] For both we and our words are in his hand,
> as are all understanding and skill in crafts.
> [17] For it was he who gave me unerring knowledge of existence,
> to know the structure of the universe and the operative power of the elements;
> [18] the beginning and end and middle of times,
> the alternations of the solstices and the changes of the seasons;
> [19] the cycles of the year and the positions of the stars;
> [20] the natures of animals and the tempers of beasts,
> the force of spirits and the reasonings of mortals,
> the varieties of plants and the powers of roots.
> [21] I learned both what is hidden and what is manifest;
> [22] for Wisdom, the fashioner of all things, taught me. (Wis 7:15–22)

---

7. See also Wis 6:1: ἀκούσατε οὖν, βασιλεῖς, καὶ σύνετε· μάθετε, δικασταὶ περάτων γῆς; and Wis 6:25: ὥστε παιδεύεσθε τοῖς ῥήμασίν μου, καὶ ὠφεληθήσεσθε. All translations are my own unless noted otherwise.

Those who take advantage of all Wisdom has to offer are rewarded with no less than immortality in nearness to the divine and, especially relevant to the addressees, an eternal kingdom:

> [17] The beginning of Wisdom is the truest desire for paideia,
> and concern for paideia is love for her;
> [18] love for her is the keeping of her laws,
> and attention to her laws is a guarantee of immortality,
> [19] and immortality makes one near to God;
> [20] so, the desire for Wisdom leads to a kingdom.
> [21] If, then, you delight in thrones and scepters, you rulers of the nations,
> honor Wisdom that you may rule forever. (Wis 6:17–21)

If this paideia that leads to an immortal existence can include the educational curriculum as laid out in the text itself and the "full range of human science and philosophy," as taught by Wisdom, should we associate it with other known curricula of the Jewish Hellenistic world?[8] Should we equate paideia in this text either with the encyclical educational system so well developed by this time in Alexandria, as the author's contemporary Philo often does, or with the Mosaic νόμος, with which it is identified in the Greek translation of Ben Sira and in 4 Maccabees?[9]

While it has long been observed that the author of the Wisdom of Solomon shows little overt interest in the Jewish law, especially in the particularistic aspects of it, many scholars have assumed its importance in the mind of the author.[10] Wisdom of Solomon 2:12, in which the impious are accused for sins against the law and against paideia, has been one of the decisive verses in the discussion of the author's view of the Mosaic

---

8. Winston, *Wisdom of Solomon*, 172, remarking on Wis 7:15–22.

9. Philo discusses the encyclical studies often throughout his treatises, often in the context of his allegorical understanding of the Hagar, Sarah, and Abraham narrative, where Hagar is the representative of encyclical paideia, a necessary step for Abraham in his preparation for Sarah, the representative of wisdom or virtue. See his treatise *De congressu eruditionis gratia*, as well as my article in this volume, "Mosaic Torah as Encyclical Paideia: Reading Paul's Allegory of Hagar and Sarah in Light of Philo of Alexandria's." Consult also the article in this collection by Karina Martin Hogan.

10. See, e.g., Winston, *Wisdom of Solomon*, 42–43; John J. Collins, *Jewish Wisdom in the Hellenistic Age*, OTL (Louisville: Westminster John Knox, 1997), 192; Leo G. Perdue, *Wisdom Literature: A Theological History* (Louisville: Westminster John Knox, 2007), 308; Lester Grabbe, *Wisdom of Solomon* (Sheffield: Sheffield Academic, 1997), 92.

law, the intended audience of the text, and the entire tone set forth in the book. It reads: "Let us lie in wait for the righteous man, because he is inconvenient to us and he opposes our actions; he reproaches us for sins against the law and charges us with sins against our paideia" (ἐνεδρεύσωμεν τὸν δίκαιον, ὅτι δύσχρηστος ἡμῖν ἐστιν καὶ ἐναντιοῦται τοῖς ἔργοις ἡμῶν καὶ ὀνειδίζει ἡμῖν ἁμαρτήματα νόμου καὶ ἐπιφημίζει ἡμῖν ἁμαρτήματα παιδείας ἡμῶν; Wis 2:12).[11] What exactly did the author intend by the terms νόμος and παιδεία here?

The genitive pronoun ἡμῶν in Wis 2:12d has been singled out by scholars in their understanding of these terms. As Chrysostome Larcher, following a number of earlier scholars, pointed out, the pronoun could modify either ἁμαρτήματα or παιδείας. "Sins against *our* paideia" would refer to transgressions against the education that the impious had personally received. "*Our* sins against paideia" would instead refer to transgressions "against an objective reality, a body of doctrine or standard practice."[12] Giuseppe Scarpat has argued extensively that νόμος and παιδεία here should be taken to refer exclusively to the Mosaic law, in part because the pronoun, ἡμῶν, he reasons, is inclusive of the righteous man and of the author.[13] Against those who want to see instead a reference to natural law and Greek education, Scarpat argues that the inclusive aspect of the pronoun means that the righteous man and the impious who torment him must have had the same νόμος and παιδεία, which could only have been the Mosaic torah.[14]

---

11. See Ziegler, *Sapientia Salomonis*, 100, for the variant readings for παιδείας (παιδίας, παιδιᾶς, and ἀπαιδείας).

12. Larcher, *Livre de la Sagesse*, 1:243.

13. Scarpat, *Libro della Sapienza*, 1:187.

14. Scarpat argues that νόμος and παιδεία elsewhere in the text should also refer specifically to the Jewish law. For example, with regard to Wis 6:17-19, he argues, "La stretta connessione e interdipendenza di questi termini o meglio di questa realtà religiosa è descritta nel passo di Sap. 6,17-19 costruito forse in base alle forme della logica corrente, con un sillogismo detto sorite o forse con un procedimento più semplice detto della 'catena' (vedi avanti, p. 368): la paideia è l'unico modo per essere fedeli al patto nell'osservanza delle leggi, la quale porta all'incorruttibilità, cioè alla vicinanza con Dio e fa raggiungere all'uomo l'unico regno degno di questo nome: la Sapienza" (ibid., 1:77). Georg Bertram, on the other hand, argued that the author of Wisdom accepted the pedagogical ideal of the Hellenistic world but inserted the foreign concept of divine punishment (Georg Bertram, "παιδεύω," *TDNT* 5:596-625, here 610).

The pronoun, however, should not cause any problems. First, this is a direct quote from the group of wicked men speaking to one another. This is *their* paideia (or *their* sins against paideia). There is no reason to posit that the pronoun should include the righteous man or the author and his audience. There is also no reason to assume that the righteous man is identifiably Jewish. This is never made explicit, because not only would this idea fall outside of the author's purpose, but making the righteous man specifically Jewish would actually defeat one of the text's primary goals, to show that ethnicity has no part to play in the acquisition of wisdom and immortality. This is why the composition is addressed to the gentile rulers of the earth and why, in the last section of the text, Israelite history is transformed into a universal didactic history, showing the difference between the righteous and the impious, not between Jews and gentiles. The referent of the pronoun ἡμῶν, then, makes little difference in our understanding of the verse. Only if paideia is ever associated specifically with the Mosaic torah, with a specific set of laws and/or customs, would it be significant. But this is never the case in our text. Paideia is never equated with the written law or with specific ancestral customs, and we cannot assume this was the case based on other Jewish sources like Ben Sira. The impious in Wis 2:12 are accused of sins against the paideia of all of humankind.

We have seen that the educational content of Wisdom's teachings was universal knowledge, and the language used to describe it could fit well with the various subjects taught in the gymnasium as the preliminary studies (προπαιδεύματα). But paideia clearly goes beyond these preliminary studies, including, among other things, the very lessons taught in the text itself. Therefore paideia in the text should not be identified with Greek preliminary education or with Mosaic law. It could likely include both—just as it could include the author's own book and his typological reading of Israelite history—but it could never be one or the other exclusively.

Paideia as *Musar* and Divine Testing

As the pedagogy or the means by which humanity is educated in the text, παιδεία/παιδεύω takes on a radically different meaning, the concept being stretched beyond anything found in classical Greek sources to include notions of divine retribution and physical punishment. In this, the term has taken on elements from the Hebrew יסר/מוסר foreign to the Greek concept and facilitated by the Septuagint translations of the Pentateuch and the prophetic texts.

In the Septuagint translations, the Hebrew מוסר is nearly universally translated with the Greek παιδεία, and the Hebrew verbal root יסר with the Greek παιδεύω.[15] While the Greek and Hebrew terms do often have much in common in their focus on instruction, παιδεία would not have been the most natural choice for מוסר, a term which is always connected to the process through which instruction is given, typically a form of chastisement or rebuke used on children or slaves and involving some form of physical or verbal reproof (תּוֹכַחַת).[16] The subject of מוסר is often God, who disciplines and punishes humanity, just as a parent disciplines a child.[17] This punishing, retributive aspect, often so fundamental to the concept of מוסר, is foreign to the classical Greek understanding of παιδεία, which was more naturally related to the content of instruction—for example, in music, mathematics, rhetoric, and so on—and sometimes even to the result of it, that is, the total culture of the individual (χαλοκἀγαθία). The cognate verb παιδεύω always described the means of instilling that educational content and culture. The Greek concept never originally had a punishing nuance connected to violence in any way. The connection between παιδεία and the rod would only come with the Septuagint and the assumption of those attributes inherent in the Hebrew מוסר.[18]

While in the Greek translations of the wisdom books of Proverbs and Job, the use of παιδεία/παιδεύω is fully compatible with the traditional Greek understanding of the concept, and the translations are often seen distancing the concept of paideia from overt forms of physical discipline and violence inherent in the Hebrew text,[19] the use of παιδεία/παιδεύω in

---

15. See the articles in this volume by Karina Martin Hogan and Patrick Pouchelle.

16. See, e.g., Prov 15:5 and 23:13. According to Branson, "The use of *yāsar* in the sense of 'punish,' with no suggestion of remediation, could derive from the concept of corporal punishment of students.... In this case it refers more to the act of discipline than to its result, namely instruction. The next step was the loss of any pedagogical connotations" (R. D. Branson, "יָסַר," *TDOT* 6:130).

17. E.g., Deut 8:5; Prov 3:11–12.

18. Bertram has argued that we see here the Greek terms taking on "a new and originally almost alien significance" ("παιδεύω," 5:608). Elsewhere Bertram has claimed that rendering מוסר with παιδεία led to a psychologizing of the punishing aspect inherent in מוסר. See his "Der Begriff der Erziehung in der griechischen Bibel," in *Imago Dei: Beiträge zur theologischen Anthropologie; Gustav Krüger zum siebzigsten Geburtstage am 29. June 1932 dargebracht*, ed. Heinrich Bornkamm (Giessen: Töpelmann, 1932), 33–51.

19. Prov 6:23; 10:17; 13:18; 15:10; 22:15; Job 5:17; 33:16; 36:10. For a detailed

the Pentateuch and prophetic literature is strikingly different, with the Greek terms wholly adopting the full range of meaning of the Hebrew concept of מוסר. In the Greek Pentateuch and prophetic literature, it is often impossible to read the Greek παιδεία/παιδεύω in a manner consistent with its classic semantic range. For example, in the concluding section of the Holiness Code, the Greek verb translates the Hebrew יסר:

והלכתי עמכם בחמת־קרי ויסרתי אתכם אף־אני שבע על־חטאתיכם
I will continue to be hostile to you in fury, and I myself will punish you sevenfold for your sins.

καὶ αὐτὸς πορεύσομαι μεθ᾽ ὑμῶν ἐν θυμῷ πλαγίῳ, καὶ παιδεύσω ὑμᾶς ἐγὼ ἑπτάκις κατὰ τὰς ἁμαρτίας ὑμῶν·
And I myself will walk with you with skewed wrath, and I myself will punish you sevenfold according to your sins. (Lev 26:28)[20]

Yahweh's "education" of the people here involves terror, consumption, and fear (Lev 26:16), wild animals that will kill their children and livestock (Lev 26:22), and, finally, a hunger so great that they must eat their own children (Lev 26:29). This type of pedagogy does not have a likely Greek precedent.

In the Greek translation of Isaiah, a text of which our author was well aware, paideia also takes on *musar*'s nuance of divine chastening, where God's paideia is understood as but a small affliction (θλίψει μικρᾷ) compared to the great benefit conferred (Isa 26:16).[21] This divine paideia can include exile, which at the same time expiates the guilt of the nation and forces them to remember the Lord and return to righteousness (Isa 27:7–9), and it may include even torture and death:[22]

והוא מחלל מפשענו מדכא מעונתינו מוסר שלומנו עליו ובחברתו נרפא־לנו
But he was wounded for our transgressions, crushed for our iniquities;

---

study of the phenomenon, see my "From *Musar* to *Paideia*, From *Torah* to *Nomos*: How the Translation of the Septuagint Impacted the Paideutic Ideal in Hellenistic Judaism," in *XV Congress of the International Organization for Septuagint and Cognate Studies: Munich, 2013*, ed. Wolfgang Kraus, Michaël N. van der Meer, and Martin Meiser (Atlanta: SBL Press, 2016), 531–54.

20. See also Lev 26:18, 23–24.
21. Winston, *Wisdom of Solomon*, 20–21.
22. See also Jer 46:28 LXX for a similar idea of the exile as part of God's paideia.

upon him was the מוסר that made us whole, and by his bruises we are healed.

αὐτὸς δὲ ἐτραυματίσθη διὰ τὰς ἀνομίας ἡμῶν, καὶ μεμαλάκισται διὰ τὰς ἁμαρτίας ἡμῶν· παιδεία εἰρήνης ἡμῶν ἐπ' αὐτόν, τῷ μώλωπι αὐτοῦ ἡμεῖς ἰάθημεν.
But he was wounded because of our lawless transgressions and harmed because of our sins; the paideia of our peace was upon him; by his bruises we were healed. (Isa 53:5)

In the final servant song of Second Isaiah, the righteous servant must take upon himself the paideia which makes the people whole, healthy, and at peace. Moreover, this innocent man's paideia includes being beaten to death, a pedagogical notion unthinkable in the classical Greek setting. As we shall see, the connection between the servant's paideia in the LXX version of Isaiah and the righteous man's paideia in Wis 3 is striking.[23]

This notion of paideia as מוסר or divine discipline, which the author of the Wisdom of Solomon received from the LXX translations of the Pentateuch and prophetic texts, is an idea elaborated upon throughout the composition, often portrayed as God's testing of humanity; and the author uses an amazing variety of juridical terms to describe God's (or Wisdom's) pedagogical testing of the righteous, the impious, or humanity universally: πειράζω, ἐτάζω, ἐξετάζω, καταδικάζω, νουθετέω, δοκιμάζω, κρίνω, ἐλέγχω, ἐξελέγχω, κολάζω, βασανίζω, τιμωρέω, μαστιγόω.[24] In the final third of the text, the so-called Book of History, the author transforms the unique history of the Israelites and the Exodus into a universal didactic tale, designed to highlight the differences, not among particular ethnic or cultural groups,

---

23. See George W. E. Nickelsburg, *Resurrection, Immortality, and Eternal Life in Intertestamental Judaism*, HTS 26 (Cambridge: Harvard University Press, 1972), 58-92, on the connection between Wis 2-5 and the servant song in Second Isaiah.

24. Testing of the righteous: πειράζω (Wis 2:17; 3:5; 11:9); ἐτάζω (2:19); καταδικάζω (2:20); κολάζω (3:4); παιδεύω (3:5; 11:9; 12:22); νουθετέω (11:10; 16:6); δοκιμάζω (2:19; 3:6; 11:10); κρίνω (12:21); διαφθείρω (16:5); ἀνάμνησις (ἐντολῆς νόμου σου) (16:6). Testing of the impious: ἐλέγχω/ἔλεγχος (Wis 1:3, 5, 8, 9; 2:11, 14; 4:20; 11:7; 17:7; 18:5); κολάζω (11:5, 8, 16; 16:1, 9); κρίνω (11:9; 12:10); βασανίζω (11:9; 12:23; 16:1, 4); καταδικάζω (11:10; 17:11); ἐτάζω (6:6); ἐξετάζω (11:10); τιμωρέω (12:20; 18:8); μαστιγόω (12:22). Universal testing: πειράζω (Wis 2:24); κολάζω (12:14, 15); ἐλέγχω (12:2); ὑπομιμνῄσκω (12:2); νουθετέω (12:2); κρίνω (12:13, 18); καταδικάζω (12:15); ἐξελέγχω (12:17); διοικέω (12:18).

but between the righteous and the impious or ungodly.[25] In this text we see a clear dichotomy between the righteous, who learn from God's pedagogy, and the impious, who do not, through a continuous series of divine tests that God (or Sophia) uses to instruct humankind and to give people a chance to repent for past, unwitting transgressions. David Winston has described these comparisons as the seven "antitheses," which illustrate what he argues is the author's theme, "that Egypt was punished measure for measure, whereas Israel was benefited by those very things whereby Egypt was punished."[26] But by focusing on this ethnic dichotomy, Winston and many other scholars have missed the larger issue. These "antitheses" are not meant to draw attention to some unspoken divine protection of the Israelites. Instead, they are designed to portray divine instruction through testing and the results of passing and failing the tests.

---

25. The question of the author's stance vis-à-vis Hellenistic society has been a constant focus of scholarly attention, and the final third of the text has been central in this discussion, with many commentators reading this "history" as the particularistic history of the chosen people of Israel over her enemies, despite the lack of proper names. See, e.g., Winston, *Wisdom of Solomon*, 3; Scarpat, *Libro della Sapienza*, 1:28. Gregory Schmidt Goering is one of the few scholars to take the typology of the third section seriously. In his article, "Election and Knowledge in the Wisdom of Solomon," in *Studies in the Book of Wisdom*, ed. Géza G. Xeravits and József Zsengellér, JSJSup 142 (Leiden: Brill, 2010), 163–82, Goering sets out to discover if the righteous of the text are only meant to represent Jews and the unrighteous, non-Jews. In the end, he determines that they are not and that "a more perfect wisdom is available to all who seek it, regardless of ethnic identity or religious affiliation. While the experiences of Solomon and the ancient Israelites are paradigmatic, the author's vision, like that of Philo, is nonetheless potentially universal, in that any human may seek the specialized wisdom that will permit her or him to know more sufficiently the deity and his cosmos" (Goering, "Election and Knowledge," 182). See also Michael Kolarcik, "Universalism and Justice in the Wisdom of Solomon," in *Treasures of Wisdom: Studies in Ben Sira and the Book of Wisdom; Festschrift M. Gilbert*, ed. Núria Calduch-Benages and Jacques Vermeylen, BETL 143 (Leuven: Leuven University Press, 1999), 289–301. Kolarcik notes that the problem is to reconcile the universalistic outlook found in the first two parts of the text with the particularistic outlook in the third. He claims that the author was carried away in the third section by his rhetoric, but that justice remains the guiding principle of his argumentation. "It is equally clear that the author could have recoiled from universalistic language and embraced unbridled nationalism. But this is not the case. The author maintains a universalistic spirit sympathetic to what is eminently reasonable in Hellenism" (Kolarcik, "Universalism and Justice," 301).

26. Winston, *Wisdom of Solomon*, 227.

For example, in chapter eleven, the author makes a clear reference to the story of Moses striking the rock at Horeb, providing miraculous water for the people to drink (Exod 17:6; Deut 8:15). Here it is God or Sophia who provides the righteous with water from the flinty rock (Wis 11:4).[27] The impious, however, receive a river defiled with blood (Wis 11:6). There are two intended lessons in these divine actions. First, the righteous learn both the consequences of impiety and the rewards for enduring God's trials:

⁸ δείξας διὰ τοῦ τότε δίψους
πῶς τοὺς ὑπεναντίους ἐκόλασας.
⁹ ὅτε γὰρ ἐπειράσθησαν, καίπερ ἐν ἐλέει παιδευόμενοι,
ἔγνωσαν πῶς μετ' ὀργῆς κρινόμενοι ἀσεβεῖς ἐβασανίζοντο·
¹⁰ τούτους μὲν γὰρ ὡς πατὴρ νουθετῶν ἐδοκίμασας,
ἐκείνους δὲ ὡς ἀπότομος βασιλεὺς καταδικάζων ἐξήτασας.

⁸ You revealed, by the thirst [of the righteous],
how you punished their antagonists.
⁹ For when the righteous were tested, though educated in mercy,
they came to know how the impious were tormented when judged with anger.
¹⁰ For you tested them like a reproving father,
but the others you examined like a condemning king. (Wis 11:8–10)

The righteous are those who endured God's test in the wilderness and were rewarded with miraculous water from a rock. They learned how, first, God's pedagogical discipline leads to a reward; and second, that a failure to learn leads to even greater testing.

If this were the end of the lesson, I could perhaps agree with the argument for the ethnic disparity, but we see that these two miracles were also meant to further instruct the already impious:[28]

---

27. Interestingly, Philo, in his allegorical understanding of the passage, says that the rock was divine Wisdom herself (*Leg.* 2.86). Paul, perhaps knowing the tradition, instead argues that Jesus was the rock (1 Cor 10:4).

28. Samuel Cheon, who largely follows the idea of Winston's "antitheses," notes that in Wis 11:1–14, "Pseudo-Solomon interprets this temporary thirst as God's testing of Israel and further as God's educational opportunity for the righteous people to understand how the Lord punished their enemies," without, however, making mention of the second didactic test of the impious. See Cheon, *The Exodus Story in the*

¹² διπλῆ γὰρ αὐτοὺς ἔλαβεν λύπη
καὶ στεναγμὸς μνημῶν τῶν παρελθόντων·
¹³ ὅτε γὰρ ἤκουσαν διὰ τῶν ἰδίων κολάσεων
εὐεργετημένους αὐτούς, ᾔσθοντο τοῦ κυρίου.
¹⁴ τὸν γὰρ ἐν ἐκθέσει πάλαι ῥιφέντα ἀπεῖπον χλευάζοντες,
ἐπὶ τέλει τῶν ἐκβάσεων ἐθαύμασαν
οὐχ ὅμοια δικαίοις διψήσαντες.

¹² For a twofold grief overtook [the impious]
and a groaning over the memories of what had happened.
¹³ For when they heard that through their own punishments,
the righteous had benefited, they took note of the Lord.
¹⁴ For though they had mockingly rejected the one who had formerly been cast out and exposed,
at the end of the events, they came to admire,
having thirsted in a manner unlike the righteous. (Wis 11:12–14)

The impious also come to learn the rewards for endurance and the punishments for a rejection of the divine instruction. Of course, the impious will just as soon forget their lessons and continue in their iniquity and ignorance, while the righteous will heed their teachings.[29]

This language of divine discipline and testing is imbued throughout the Wisdom of Solomon, and, even when the Greek terms παιδεία or παιδεύω are not immediately present, it is always attached to the author's idealized concept of divine, disciplinary paideia. Time and again we see that these tests, no matter how harsh, are meant to instruct and to correct behavior. In Wis 11:15, God (or Sophia) sends a multitude of irrational creatures against the impious in response to their ignorant worship of like creatures "in order that they might come to know that one will be punished through those very things by which he sins" (Wis 11:16). This is a learning opportunity designed to allow the impious to repent from their past transgressions: "Therefore, you correct little by little those who trespass, and you remind them of the things through which they sin, in order that they may be delivered from their wickedness and come to believe in

---

Wisdom of Solomon: A Study in Biblical Interpretation, JSPSup 23 (Sheffield: Sheffield Academic, 1997), 33.

29. See also Wis 12:18–27 and 16:4–9 for similar depictions of a twofold didactic test of the righteous and the impious.

you, Lord" (Wis 12:2). As in Isa 26:16 LXX, this disciplinary action is a small affliction compared to the rewards gained from the education.

Paideia as Death (Extreme *Musar*)

This notion of παιδεία as מוסר or divine discipline and testing, set together with the juridical terminology, is found not only in the final, pseudohistorical section of the text, but also in the opening chapters, where it takes on a greater, cosmic dimension and where the test can include even bodily death. The scenario outlined in the first five chapters of the Wisdom of Solomon, depicting the struggle between the anonymous righteous man and the wicked ungodly parallels that between the righteous and the impious just examined. Here we learn about a group of individuals who bring on their own destruction through their ignorance and through their rejection of paideia. The impious are those who are completely misguided about the nature of life and death. They think that this life is all that there is and that bodily death leads to extinction and nothingness (Wis 2:1–5). This worldview leads them to assume a libertine and anarchic lifestyle (Wis 2:6–11). Their views on life and death lead the impious to torment, torture, and eventually to murder the righteous man, simply because his righteousness highlights their own iniquity (Wis 2:12–20). According to the impious, the righteous man "reproaches us for sins against the law and charges us with sins against our paideia" (Wis 2:12).[30] These impious men, who have ignored or rejected their previous education, go on to test the righteous man's claims about God and about life and death by torturing and killing him (Wis 2:16–20). Yet, because of their continued ignorance, they did not know that they were not truly the ones putting the righteous man to the test. God was the one doing the testing, of both the righteous man and the impious.

At the start of chapter 3 of the Wisdom of Solomon, we see that this scenario was part of God's divine, educative test. While to the ignorant the righteous appear to die, we find out that this was not actually the case:

---

30. Wisdom of Solomon 2:12a is a near quote of Isa 3:10 LXX, which differs significantly from the Hebrew. See Michael Kolarcik, "The Book of Wisdom: Introduction, Commentary, and Reflections," in *Introduction to Wisdom Literature, the Book of Proverbs, the Book of Ecclesiastes, the Song of Songs, the Book of Wisdom, the Book of Sirach*, vol. 5 of *The New Interpreter's Bible*, ed. Richard J. Clifford et al. (Nashville: Abingdon, 1997), 463 n. 25; and Larcher, *Livre de la Sagesse*, 1:241.

> ¹ The souls of the righteous are in the hand of God,
> and no torment will ever touch them.
> ² In the eyes of the foolish they seem to have died,
> and their departure was considered a misfortune,
> ³ and their going away from us their destruction, but they are at peace.
> ⁴ For though in the sight of mortals they were punished,
> their hope is full of immortality.
> ⁵ And, having been educated a little [ὀλίγα παιδευθέντες], they will receive great good,
> because God has tested [ἐπείρασεν] them
> and found them worthy of himself.
> ⁶ Like gold in a furnace, he tried them,
> and like a sacrificial burnt offering, he accepted them. (Wis 3:1–6)

Just like the righteous who had to endure the desert and thirst before receiving their reward, the righteous here have to endure torment, torture, and even death before receiving the ultimate reward. The stakes are clearly higher this time; the righteous must have total faith in God and total faith that the life of the body is not the true life, and that the death of the body will release the soul and allow it to live the immortal life in nearness to the divine. As in Isa 53:5, if one is able to brave this brutally violent test, the reward will far outweigh the suffering.

Just as the impious in the desert received a river of gore in return for their decree to kill the innocent and a plague of irrational animals in exchange for their worship of the creatures, the impious here are punished in exact accordance with their ignorant reasoning (Wis 3:10). They believed that this life was the only life and that death meant extinction, and this is what they receive in return for their ignorant and wicked actions: the death of their souls even during their somatic existence, a fact they come to realize upon seeing the honor granted to the righteous man whom they had murdered: "So we too, as soon as we were born, ceased to be, and we had no sign of virtue to show, but were entirely consumed in our wickedness" (Wis 5:13).[31]

---

31. On the idea of psychic death during one's bodily life, see Jason M. Zurawski, "Hell on Earth: Corporeal Existence as the Ultimate Punishment of the Wicked in Philo of Alexandria and the Wisdom of Solomon," in *Heaven, Hell, and the Afterlife: Eternity in Judaism, Christianity, and Islam*, 3 vols., ed. J. Harold Ellens (Santa Barbara: Praeger, 2013), 1:193–226.

The education mentioned in Wis 3:5 above refers to both bodily life and bodily death.³² As such, it represents God's great cosmic test of humanity, where the entirety of one's corporeal existence becomes an ἀγών, a proving ground that will determine who is worthy of the immortal psychic life.³³ In chapters 3 and 4, the author draws a dichotomy between the educated righteous and the ignorant impious by bringing in examples that have, in the past, had clear Deuteronomistic or traditional sapiential implications. Problems such as childlessness (Wis 3:13–14) or dying young (Wis 4:7–15), which traditionally pointed to just punishment for sins committed, now become aspects of divine paideia. The barren woman, the eunuch, and the man who dies early are not being punished through their afflictions, but instead will be rewarded in the future for enduring them, because they know, like the righteous man, that the bodily life is not the true life. The wicked, instead, can have a brood of children and live to a long, old age, but all of this will account for nothing (Wis 3:16–17), because "those who reject wisdom and paideia are miserable [σοφίαν γὰρ καὶ παιδείαν ὁ ἐξουθενῶν ταλαίπωρος], and their hope is in vain, their labors without profit, and their works useless" (Wis 3:11).

As the wicked in the desert were educated not only through their own punishments but also through the miraculous rewards of the righteous, when they would come to see and understand God as the author of all, so here too the impious learn through their observance of the righteous man's reward of immortal life:

> ¹ Then the righteous man will stand with great confidence
> in the presence of his tormentors
> and those who had disdain for his labors.
> ² And when they see him, they will tremble with dreadful fear
> and marvel at the miracle of his salvation.
> ³ They will speak to one another in repentance,
> and, in anguish of spirit, they will groan:
> ⁴ "This is the man whom we once held in derision,
> and as a byword of reproach, fools that we are!

---

32. Larcher argues that the aorist *paideuthentes* in Wis 3:5 refers to the earthly life, but he does not make the connection with the earthly death. See Larcher, *Livre de la Sagesse*, 1:280–81.

33. See also Wis 4:2 and 10:12. On the Hellenistic *agōn* motif in the Wisdom of Solomon, see Victor C. Pfitzner, *Paul and the Agon Motif: Traditional Athletic Imagery in the Pauline Literature*, NovTSup 16 (Leiden: Brill, 1967), 54–57.

> We considered his life as madness
> and his end as being without honor.
> ⁵ How was he reckoned among the sons of God,
> and how is his lot among the holy ones?
> ⁶ But it was we who strayed from the path of truth." (Wis 5:1–6a)

But, though they have come to recognize that their views on life and death were mistaken and their actions wicked, it is too late. They have had their opportunities for learning and repentance. They have been educated, but they have rejected it and the wisdom that comes with it. The immortality and all the gifts that come with the paideia of Wisdom are forever lost to those who denounce their education.

Conclusion: Paideia as Universal Education and the Unifying Factor of the Text

In a text devoted to the divine figure of Wisdom, where the author depicts her in the loftiest possible terms, her first and primary function is as humankind's educator, the holy spirit of paideia. Though the Wisdom of Solomon exhibits differing, seemingly contrary views as to the conception of paideia, there is an overall, all-encompassing view of paideia in the text, which accounts for this plurality in meaning and the unique confluence of both educational content and pedagogy. Taken as a whole, paideia comes to represent an ideal, universal educational system which leads, ultimately, to immortality. It includes the content of education—the author's own words of paideia in the text and Wisdom's gift of complete knowledge—and it incorporates the means of distilling that education: *musar*, divine testing, even corporeal death. This paideia does not refer solely to a particular law code or ancestral tradition; it is not meant to express exclusively the curriculum of Hellenistic education. It may include both of these, but it is more. It includes the process by which God and Wisdom educate humanity, the divine test that is this world perceptible to the senses and the somatic death that is a natural part of it. It is the text of the Wisdom of Solomon itself, the author's pedagogical manual, which, he argues, comes not from apocalyptic revelation, but from the experience of this world and God's gift of divine instruction. Ethnic particularism has no place in this text, where everything is reworked into a universal drama between the righteous and the impious, where the first step on the path to gaining Wisdom is total adherence to paideia. The righteous are the beneficiaries of paideia and the ones who learn from it; the impious are those who do not, ultimately bringing on the death of their own souls. It is this broad view of paideia that becomes the unifying factor in this seemingly disparate text.

The author of the Wisdom of Solomon envisioned his work essentially as a textbook, a manual on paideia and sophia. When seen in this light, the unity of purpose becomes clear. The opening third of the text is meant to startle and shock the audience, showing the cosmic import of education and wisdom. Lack of education (ἀπαιδευσία) leads to nothing less than the death of the soul and knowledge that the righteous, those who took heed of their education, will live an immortal life in the presence of the divine. After this opening salvo, the author, in the middle section, goes on to describe the gifts that come from paideia and sophia in a much more loving, even sensual manner. Instead of the horrible fate that awaits those who do not learn, education leads to complete knowledge and immortality. Finally, in the last section of the text, the author brings in proof of this dichotomy in his universal drama, which highlights the historical results of the acceptance and disregard of God's and Wisdom's divine paideia. The structure is bold and effective, and it makes little sense until we understand the primacy of paideia in the author's purpose as the complete and universal education of all of humankind.

Bibliography

Bertram, Georg. "Der Begriff der Erziehung in der griechischen Bibel." Pages 33–51 in *Imago Dei: Beiträge zur theologischen Anthropologie; Gustav Krüger zum siebzigsten Geburtstage am 29. June 1932 dargebracht*. Edited by Heinrich Bornkamm. Giessen: Töpelmann, 1932.

———. "παιδεύω." *TDNT* 5:596–625.

Bizzeti, Paolo. *Il libro della Sapienza: Struttura e genere letterario*. Brescia: Paideia, 1984.

Branson, R. D. "יָסַר." *TDOT* 6:127–34.

Bretschneider, Karl Gottlieb. "De libri Sapientiae parte priore cap. I–XI e duobus libellis diversis conflata." PhD diss., University of Wittenberg, 1804.

Cheon, Samuel. *The Exodus Story in the Wisdom of Solomon: A Study in Biblical Interpretation*. JSPSup 23. Sheffield: Sheffield Academic, 1997.

Clarke, Ernest G. *The Wisdom of Solomon*. CBC. Cambridge: Cambridge University Press, 1973.

Collins, John J. *Jewish Wisdom in the Hellenistic Age*. OTL. Louisville: Westminster John Knox, 1997.
Eichhorn, Johann Gottfried. *Einleitung in die apokryphen Schriften des Alten Testaments*. Leipzig: Weidmann, 1795.
Gilbert, Maurice. "La structure de la prière de Salomon (Sg 9)." *Bib* 51 (1970): 301–31.
Goering, Gregory Schmidt. "Election and Knowledge in the Wisdom of Solomon." Pages 163–82 in *Studies in the Book of Wisdom*. Edited by Géza G. Xeravits and József Zsengellér. JSJSup 142. Leiden: Brill, 2010.
Grabbe, Lester. *Wisdom of Solomon*. Sheffield: Sheffield Academic, 1997.
Grimm, Carl L. W. *Das Buch der Weisheit*. Vol. 6 of *Kurzgefasstes exegetisches Handbuch zu den Apokryphen des Alten Testamentes*. Edited by Otto Fridolin Fritzsche and Carl L. W. Grimm. Leipzig: Hirzel, 1860.
Kolarcik, Michael. "The Book of Wisdom: Introduction, Commentary, and Reflections." Pages 433–600 in *Introduction to Wisdom Literature, the Book of Proverbs, the Book of Ecclesiastes, the Song of Songs, the Book of Wisdom, the Book of Sirach*. Vol. 5 of *The New Interpreter's Bible*. Edited by Richard J. Clifford, Raymond C. Van Leeuwen, W. Sibley Towner, Renita J. Weems, Michael Kolarcik, and James L. Crenshaw. Nashville: Abingdon, 1997.
———. "Universalism and Justice in the Wisdom of Solomon." Pages 289–301 in *Treasures of Wisdom: Studies in Ben Sira and the Book of Wisdom; Festschrift M. Gilbert*. Edited by Núria Calduch-Benages and Jacques Vermeylen. BETL 143. Leuven: Leuven University Press, 1999.
Larcher, Chrysostome. *Le livre de la Sagesse ou la Sagesse de Salomon*. 3 vols. EBib NS 1, 3, 5. Paris: Gabalda, 1983–1985.
Nachtigal, Johann C. C. *Das Buch der Weisheit*. Vol. 2 of *Die Versammlungen der Weisen*. Halle: Gebauer, 1799.
Nickelsburg, George W. E. *Resurrection, Immortality, and Eternal Life in Intertestamental Judaism*. HTS 26. Cambridge: Harvard University Press, 1972.
Offerhaus, Ulrich. *Komposition und Intention der Sapientia Salomonis*. PhD diss., Friedrich-Wilhelms-Universität, 1981.
Perdue, Leo G. *Wisdom Literature: A Theological History*. Louisville: Westminster John Knox, 2007.
Pfitzner, Victor C. *Paul and the Agon Motif: Traditional Athletic Imagery in the Pauline Literature*. NovTSup 16. Leiden: Brill, 1967.
Reese, James M. "Plan and Structure of the Book of Wisdom." *CBQ* 27 (1965): 391–99.

Scarpat, Giuseppe. *Libro della Sapienza: Testo, traduzione, introduzione e commento*. 3 vols. BibTS 1, 3, 6. Brescia: Paideia, 1989–1999.
Weber, W. "Die Komposition der Weisheit Salomos." *ZWT* 48 (1904): 145–69.
Winston, David. *The Wisdom of Solomon*. AB 43. New York: Doubleday, 1979.
Wright, Addison G. "The Structure of the Book of Wisdom." *Bib* 48 (1967): 165–84.
Ziegler, Joseph. *Sapientia Salomonis*. VTG 12.1. Göttingen: Vandenhoeck & Ruprecht, 1962.
Zurawski, Jason M. "From *Musar* to *Paideia*, From *Torah* to *Nomos*: How the Translation of the Septuagint Impacted the Paideutic Ideal in Hellenistic Judaism." Pages 531–54 in *XV Congress of the International Organization for Septuagint and Cognate Studies: Munich, 2013*. Edited by Wolfgang Kraus, Michaël N. van der Meer, and Martin Meiser. SCS 64. Atlanta: SBL Press, 2016.
———. "Hell on Earth: Corporeal Existence as the Ultimate Punishment of the Wicked in Philo of Alexandria and the Wisdom of Solomon." Pages 193–226 in vol. 1 of *Heaven, Hell, and the Afterlife: Eternity in Judaism, Christianity, and Islam*. 3 vols. Edited by J. Harold Ellens. Santa Barbara: Praeger, 2013.

Job and the "Mystic's Solution" to Theodicy: Philosophical Paideia and Internalized Apocalypticism in the Testament of Job

Andrew R. Guffey

The Testament of Job has sometimes been thought an anemic little book. The Testament of Job appears to flatten all the delicious ambiguity and tension of the book of Job, especially with respect to questions of theodicy.[1] In this essay I argue that, in fact, the Testament of Job attempts to resolve the tensions of the book of Job over questions of theodicy by appealing

---

This essay was first delivered at the 2012 Society of Biblical Literature Annual Meeting in Chicago, Illinois. It has been significantly revised in light of various comments and suggestions from that meeting and from subsequent iterations of the paper. My thanks are especially due to the perceptive responses by Karina Martin Hogan and Larry Wills, Matthew Goff's astute query about the category of "internalized apocalypticism," several helpful suggestions of Martien Halvorson-Taylor on an early draft, and the incisive critique of another early iteration of the paper by an anonymous reviewer.

1. In some cases, the Testament of Job merely picks up on interpretations of Job already offered in the Septuagint, though compared with the Testament of Job, Job LXX looks like a slightly cleaned up paraphrase of the Hebrew *Vorlage* (as attested by Job MT) with a few interesting additions. For Job LXX as a deliberate interpretation, not just a translation, see Natalio Fernández Marcos, "The Septuagint Reading of the Book of Job," in *The Book of Job*, ed. W. A. M. Beuken, BETL 114 (Leuven: Peeters, 1994), 251–66. Although the designation "Job LXX" may appear to imply a single translation, it ought to be pointed out that there were likely multiple Greek translations of Job, though the predominant Greek version is the one known from Origen's *Hexapla*, for which, see Markus Witte, "The Greek Book of Job," in *Das Buch Hiob und seine Interpretationen: Beitrage zum Hiob-Symposium auf dem Monte Verità vom 14.–19. August 2005*, ed. Thomas Krüger et al. (Zürich: Theologischer Verlag Zürich, 2007), 33–54.

to philosophical training in patience and culminating in contact with the divine through mystical transformation, or internalized apocalypticism.[2]

The book of Job is widely recognized as an attempt to address the question of theodicy,[3] but its "whirlwind" solution to the suffering of righteous Job seems to equivocate precisely on the matter of God's justice.[4] The book of Job (or at least the bulk of the dialogues) sets out to raise the question of the suffering of the righteous, though most scholars tend to admit the resolution of the question is partial at best.[5] Job suffers for

---

2. I have generally followed the edition and translation of Robert A. Kraft, ed., *The Testament of Job, according to the SV Text*, SBLTT 5 (Missoula, MT: Scholars Press, 1974), though I have often amended the translation and checked that edition against Sebastian Brock's (Sebastian P. Brock and Jean-Claude Picard, eds., *Testamentum Jobi; Apocalypsis Baruchi Graece* [Leiden: Brill, 1967]) and the Coptic fragments edited by Gesa Schenke and Gesine Schenke Robinson (*Das Testament des Iob*, vol. 1 of *Der Koptische Kölner Papyruskodex 3221*. PapyCol 33 [Paderborn: Schöningh, 2009]). I have followed the more conventional versification of Brock's edition, which can easily be referenced also in Kraft's.

3. The book of Job does not, however, *only* address theodicy. As Carol Newsom and others have pointed out, the book of Job also addresses questions of the motivation for piety, the character of God, and also the nature of the created order. See, e.g., Carol A. Newsom, "The Book of Job," in *The First Book of Maccabees; the Second Book of Maccabees; Introduction to Hebrew Poetry; the Book of Job; the Book of Psalms*, vol. 4 of *The New Interpreter's Bible*, ed. Robert Doran et al. (Nashville: Abingdon, 1996), 319, 334–38.

4. Marvin Pope's introduction is still excellent on this score: Marvin H. Pope, *Job: A New Translation with Introduction and Commentary*, AB 15, 3rd ed. (New York: Doubleday, 1973), lxxiii–lxxxiv. Among others, see also Joseph Blenkinsopp, *Wisdom and Law in the Old Testament* (Oxford: Oxford University Press, 1995), 60–67; Norman C. Habel, "The Verdict on/of God at the End of Job," in *Job's God*, ed. E. J. van Wolde; Concilium 4 (London: SCM, 2004), 27–38.

5. For the book of Job as a work of theodicy, see (among many others): C. L. Seow, *Job 1–21: Interpretation and Commentary*, Illuminations (Grand Rapids: Eerdmans, 2013), esp. 87–110; Leo G. Perdue, *The Sword and the Stylus: An Introduction to Wisdom in the Age of Empires* (Grand Rapids: Eerdmans, 2008), 117–18; Jack T. Sanders, "Wisdom, Theodicy, Death, and the Evolution of Intellectual Traditions," *JSJ* 36 (2005): 263–77; Edwin M. Good, "The Problem of Evil in the Book of Job," in *The Voice from the Whirlwind: Interpreting the Book of Job*, ed. Leo G. Perdue and W. Clark Gilpin (Nashville: Abingdon, 1992), 50–69; David J. A. Clines, *Job 1–20*, WBC (Waco, TX: Word, 1989), xxxvii–xxxix; Walter Bruegemann, "Theodicy in a Social Dimension," *JSOT* 33 (1985): 3–25; Ronald J. Williams, "Theodicy in the Ancient Near East," in *Theodicy in the Old Testament*, ed. James L. Crenshaw (Philadelphia: Fortress, 1983), 42–56; Pope, *Job*, lxxiii–lxxxiv; Morris Jastrow Jr., *The Book of Job: Its Origin, Growth*

a wager. He endures. He complains. He rejects charges of his guilt. He appeals to God, demanding an audience, which he gets: God shows up. Job is vindicated. But God is not justified. The complaint of incommensurate suffering is never resolved. Even though the epilogue gives Job back his possessions and a new family, the damage has been done.[6] The only convincing interpretations of Job as a response to unjust suffering—those that raise the fewest problems based on the data—read Job as a book without definite closure.[7]

Though the book of Job does not answer the question of why the righteous suffer, it does perhaps offer a model to follow for those undergoing undeserved suffering. In providing such a model—arguably a model of complaint—the book of Job makes "suffering sufferable," in the phrasing of Clifford Geertz.[8] Geertz writes, "As a religious problem, the problem of suffering is, paradoxically, not how to avoid suffering but how to suffer, how to make physical pain, personal loss, worldly defeat, or the helpless contemplation of others' agony something bearable, supportable—something,

---

and Interpretation (Philadelphia: Lippincott, 1920), esp. 25–30; Samuel R. Driver and George Buchanan Gray, *A Critical and Exegetical Commentary on the Book of Job*, ICC, 2 vols. (New York: Scribner's Sons, 1921), 1:l–lxiv.

6. And in at least one Greek version also a share in the resurrection (Job 42:17 LXX).

7. One could argue that my reading betrays a modern, Western perspective wherein wives and children are irreplaceable, and one could further argue that Job does truly enjoy a happy ending in Job 42:11–17. I would contend that the very fact that the author of the Testament of Job felt the need to substantially expand Job's story, the reasons for his suffering, and the means by which he enjoyed beatitude—not to mention the Testament of Job's concern for the final destination of his children (T. Job 39.11–40.4)—points to discontent with the ending of Job, *from the point of view of the author(s)* of the Testament of Job. Whether my construal of Job's ending betrays modern concerns or not, there is palpable anxiety over the ending of the book of Job in the Testament of Job itself. The contrast with the book of Job is admittedly, at this point, underdeveloped. I have introduced the contrast to remind interpreters that the aims of the Testament of Job cannot be assumed to have been the same as the aims of the biblical book of Job, and that the Testament of Job need not be understood as a misreading or impoverished derivative of biblical Job. Within the scope of this essay it is impossible to do justice to the complex relationship between the book of Job and the Testament of Job. The main purpose of this paper is to highlight the philosophical and mystical elements that comprise the Testament of Job's coherent theodicy.

8. On Job providing a model of complaint, see Clines, *Job 1–20*, xxxix; Newsom, "Book of Job"; James L. Crenshaw, *Old Testament Wisdom: An Introduction*, 3rd ed. (Louisville: Westminster John Knox, 2009), 116; Jastrow, *Book of Job*.

as we say, sufferable."⁹ Andrew Steinmann has likewise suggested that, because no solutions to the question of theodicy obtain in the book, theodicy must be "merely a foil for a larger issue."¹⁰ For Steinmann, the book of Job's primary purpose is to show how one should respond in a crisis—in Geertz's words, "how to suffer"—rather than to answer why the righteous suffer. Such a response to suffering includes what Steinmann calls the "mystic's solution" to theodicy.¹¹ By the end of the book, more than anything else Job just wants God to show up, to be in God's presence, because then he will understand.¹² The demand for God's presence and the critique of God's absence in the midst of suffering makes suffering sufferable.

The Testament of Job also provides a model for making suffering sufferable, but the proposed lived response of the Testament of Job finds a new idiom. Instead of complaint, the Testament of Job offers an ethical model, drawing on philosophical training. In suffering his various afflictions Job models progress in the philosophical therapy of *apatheia*. But the Testament of Job does not seek just to make suffering sufferable; it envisions the relieving of pain and affliction, even the actual cessation of suffering (T. Job 47.8). Job's *apatheia* leads to contemplation of and experience of the divine, an experience that grants the sufferer access to transcendent realities in the present and the ability to apprehend a blessed and just future. This is, I suggest, truly a "mystic's solution" to theodicy. The virtues of philosophical paideia may constitute an adequate response

---

9. Clifford Geertz, *The Interpretation of Cultures: Selected Essays* (New York: Basic Books, 1973), 104. I am indebted to Rodney Werline's fine essay on the Psalms of Solomon for drawing attention to this passage in Geertz; see Rodney A. Werline, "The Experience of God's *Paideia* in the Psalms of Solomon," in *Linking Text and Experience*, vol. 2 of *Experientia*, ed. Colleen Shantz and Rodney A. Werline, EJL 35 (Atlanta: Society of Biblical Literature, 2012), 17–44.

10. Andrew E. Steinmann, "The Structure and Message of the Book of Job," *VT* 46 (1996): 86.

11. Ibid., 100.

12. David Clines also suggests that what Job really wants is not answers to why he has suffered (although that is precisely what Job *says* he wants throughout), but rather to be in God's presence: "Viewed as an answer to the problem of suffering, then, the argument of the Book of Job is: By all means let Job the patient be your model so long as that is possible for you; but when equanimity fails, let the grief and anger of Job the impatient direct itself and yourself toward God, for only in encounter with him will the tension of suffering be resolved" (Clines, *Job 1–20*, xxxix).

to undeserved suffering in the present, but the apocalypticism of the testament answers the question of God's justice.

The Testament of Job and the Pedagogy of the Philosophical *Agōn*

In the book of Job, as David Clines puts it, complaint is the correct response "when equanimity is lost."[13] In the narrative of Job's sufferings in the Testament of Job, however, Job learns and displays the art of maintaining equanimity, a goal of Hellenistic philosophical paideia. In the Testament of Job, Job suffers because he picks a fight by destroying a shrine where Satan received worship. Job is informed by a heavenly visitor that should he destroy the shrine, Satan would attack him fiercely. "But," says the visitor, "if you endure [ἐὰν ὑπομείνῃς], I shall make your name renowned in all earthly generations until the consummation of the age.... And you will be like an athlete [ἀθλητής] who spars and endures hard labors [πόνους] and wins the crown" (στέφανον; T. Job 4.6, 10). Job's ordeals are from the beginning cast as an athletic contest.

In the Hellenistic world and in the early Roman Empire, the so-called *agōn* motif was a popular metaphor for the Cynic and Stoic way(s) of life.[14] The ancient Cynics polemicized against athletic games, claiming that the true athlete is the sage who combats his own passions (see, for example, Diogenes, *Ep.* 31). The Cynics sought happiness (εὐδαιμονία) by accommodating themselves to nature, which required training of the spirit and body, much as an athlete needs training. Just as athletes meet with many labors (πόνοι) in, for instance, the Olympian games (esp. the παγκράτιον), so also throughout their lives, sages must endure (ὑπομένειν) labors to obtain happiness (see, for example, Diogenes, *Ep.* 37). In the case of the Cynic these labors include donning the rough tunic, drinking only water and eating only bread, and sleeping on bare ground; they can include "poverty, disrepute, lowly birth, and exile" (Diogenes, *Ep.* 31.4). In short, it was not simply emotions but external disturbances as well (including other people) that provided the opportunity for the labors of the Cynics.

---

13. Clines, *Job 1–20*, xxxix.
14. A useful introduction to the tradition of the *agōn* motif is provided by Victor C. Pfitzner, *Paul and the Agon Motif: Traditional Athletic Imagery in the Pauline Literature*, NovTSup 16 (Leiden: Brill, 1967), 16–75, somewhat updated but closely followed by Martin Brändl, *Der Agon bei Paulus: Herkunft und Profil paulinischer Agonmetaphorik*, WUNT 2/222 (Tübingen: Mohr Siebeck, 2006), 32–138.

The Stoics continued the metaphor, though the goals of impassibility (ἀπάθεια) or imperturbability (ἀταραξία) receive more emphasis than achieving happiness. The Stoics also seem to have parsed the psychology or phenomenology of pain more fully than the Cynics. Pain (πάθη) was for the Stoics an improper response to an external event. It was a failure in training oneself to be led by reason (λόγος or the ἡγεμόνικον), a mistaken capitulation to sense perception.[15] Nature or the gods brought events upon people, but the proper response was to accept and, in essence, to harmonize oneself with the event, whether initially perceived as pleasant or painful.[16] The Stoic sages sought to disentangle their perceptions of the world from the world as it rightly—that is, logically—is. Reason could thus rightly respond to the occasion for pain by seeing it as part of a larger whole, and as part of the right ordering of the universe.

All of this depends on the Stoic notion of perception. Perception, for the Stoics, entailed assent to an impression. As A. A. Long puts it: "Perception is rightly treated by the Stoics as a form of judgement: in assenting to the impression we are admitting that our sense-experience corresponds to some expressible fact."[17] When the assent to the impression is understood as truth it is said to be "grasped" (κατάληψις, from καταλαμβάνω). The Stoics therefore taught that sense perceptions needed to be evaluated and discriminated, the indifferent (ἀδιάφορα) discerned from the important.

---

15. See John M. Rist, *Stoic Philosophy* (Cambridge: Cambridge University Press, 1969), 37–53.

16. "For there is a single harmony. Just as the world forms a single body comprising all bodies, so fate forms a single purpose, comprising all purposes. Even complete illiterates acknowledge it when they say that something 'brought on' this or that. Brought on, yes. Or prescribed it. And in that case, let's accept it—as we accept what the doctor prescribes. It may not always be pleasant, but we embrace it—because we want to get well. Look at the accomplishments of nature's plans in that light—the way you look at your own health—and accept what happens (even if it seems hard to accept). Accept it because of what it leads to: the good health of the world and the well-being of Zeus himself, who would not have brought this on anyone unless it brought benefit to the world as a whole. No nature would do that—bring something about that wasn't beneficial to what it governed" (Marcus Aurelius, *Med.* 5.8). Quotations from Marcus Aurelius follow the translation of Gregory Hays: Marcus Aurelius, *Meditations*, trans. Gregory Hays (New York: Modern Library, 2002).

17. A. A. Long, *Hellenistic Philosophy: Stoics, Epicureans, Sceptics* (Berkeley: University of California Press, 1986), 126; see further 123–31.

Such discernment required training, as Epictetus writes at the opening of his *Handbook* (*Enchiridion*):

> Practice, then, from the start to say to every harsh impression, "You are an impression, and not at all what you appear to be." Then examine it and test it by these rules which you have, and, first and foremost, by this: whether the impression has to do with the things which are up to us [περὶ τὰ ἐφ' ἡμῖν], or those which are not [περὶ τὰ οὐκ ἐφ' ἡμῖν]; and, if it has to do with the things that are not up to us, be ready to reply, "It is nothing to me" [οὐδὲν πρὸς ἐμέ]. (*Ench.* 1)[18]

This training was also described in terms of the athlete metaphor. As Marcus Aurelius says, "Someone like that ... is a kind of priest, a servant of the gods, in touch with what is within him and what keeps a person undefiled by pleasures, invulnerable to any pain, untouched by arrogance, unaffected by meanness, an athlete in the greatest of all contests—the struggle not to be overwhelmed by anything that happens" (*Med.* 3.4). Just as true Cynic sages accepted the labors of their ascetic way of life on the road to happiness, so Stoic sages accepted the sense impressions about pleasure and pain, good and evil, as trials of their training.

The presence of the *agōn* motif in the Testament of Job has not gone unnoticed, but following the work of Victor Pfitzner, interpreters tend to minimize the connection with philosophical athletic metaphors. Pfitzner interpreted the *agōn* of the Testament of Job as a contest between Job and Satan, not a contest of the sage against his passions or against the experience of pain. "The moralism of the Stoic picture is here completely absent," writes Pfitzner.[19] He concedes, "One could at the most see in Job a parallel to the 'athlete' in the diatribe striving to overcome the setbacks of fortune.... But the πόνοι ... are here not moral endeavours but sufferings inflicted by Satan.... The point is Job's faithfulness to God, not his fight against misfortune."[20] Pfitzner interprets the *agōn* motif in the Testament of Job, then, not as a test of morals, but as a test of faith.

But Pfitzner overlooks the fact that both the philosophical metaphor and the athletic motif in the Testament of Job center on the appropriate

---

18. My translation, following *The Discourses of Epictetus*, ed. Christopher Gill, trans. Robin Hard (London: Dent, 1995).
19. Pfitzner, *Agon Motif*, 65; see also Brändl, *Agon*, 128.
20. Pfitzner, *Agon Motif*, 65–66 n. 3.

response to suffering and pain. As we have just seen, the philosophical metaphor was not limited to the inner life of the sage, but also to those sense-impressions of pain that come from without. A closer look at the Testament of Job's narration of Job's sufferings shows that these πόνοι are indeed moral endeavors as well as sufferings inflicted by Satan.

The book of Job narrates Job's sufferings in two events—first Job loses his wealth and children (Job 1:13–22), then his health (Job 2:7–10)—but the Testament of Job narrates them in three stages. First, Job loses his livestock (T. Job 16.1–7). The Testament of Job makes a point of highlighting the direct destruction of the seven thousand sheep, three thousand camels, five hundred she-asses, and five hundred oxen by Satan, because those were the animals Job dedicated to caring for the poor, widows, and orphans (T. Job 9.3–6; 10.5–6; 16.3). The rest of Job's goods were summarily carried off by his neighbors (T. Job 16.5–6). Satan picks a particularly nasty opening attack, striking at Job's piety. He makes it impossible for Job to follow the commandments of Deut 16 and 26 to care for the widows and orphans, which, along with care of the poor, had become a standard practice of early Jewish (and Christian) piety.[21]

In the second scene of Job's afflictions, Satan incites the people to take his land and possessions and kills Job's children (T. Job 17.1–18.3). After destroying Job's life-giving wealth, Satan now destroys the fruit of his life. In order to do so, however, Satan masquerades as the Persian king. To all appearances, then, the children were struck down by a human opponent, casualties of war. Satan likes to work in disguise in the Testament of Job, receiving worship incognito at a pagan shrine (T. Job 3.3), humiliating Job's wife, Sitidos, by persuading her to sell her hair for bread while he is disguised as a baker (T. Job 23.1–11), and apparently goading on Sitidos's rebuke of Job (T. Job 26.6). This is the Testament of Job's mechanism for discerning demonic forces behind the situations of life. Why does Job's wife sell her hair and speak as "one of the foolish women"? Why do people worship false gods? Why are the righteous subjected to the loss and insecurity of foreign domination? Satan, Job's antagonist—that is, his sparring partner—is behind them all.

Finally, in the third affliction scene, Satan overthrows Job's throne (Job is equated, as in the Septuagint, with Jobab, and supposed to be the

---

21. See, for example, 2 Macc 3:10, 8:28–30; Tob 1:8; Sir 4; 2 En. 42:7; Jas 1:27; Mark 10:21 parr.

king of Egypt) and afflicts Job with disease. Job therefore removes himself from the city and sits upon the dunghill. As Job observes the maltreatment of his wife, he becomes indignant, apparently moved for a moment by the injustice of the situation (T. Job 21.3). The next line, however, is telling. After his brief indignation he says, "After this I regained my senses" (ἀπελάμβανον λογισμὸν [μακρόθυμον]; T. Job 21.4). Job's response showed that he was still attached to earthly concerns (his wife!) for a moment, which caused him to suffer, but he came to his logical senses again, freeing himself from this "harsh impression." Otherwise Job sits atop the dunghill oblivious to his own state and to the suffering of his wife. In the end, she must upbraid him to get a response, once she has reached a point of desperation, culminating in her famous phrase: "Say a word against the Lord and die" (T. Job 24.1-10; 25.9-10; compare Job 2:9).[22] Some scholars have taken this scene as a positive sign of Sitidos's devotion to Job.[23] But Job does not see it that way. "Behold," he says, "I have existed for seventeen years with diseases, submitting to the worms in my body, and have not been as depressed in my soul by the pains [πόνους] as by the word you spoke" (T. Job 26.1-2). Job protests that he bears the evils (κακά) of the loss of wealth and children as much as she, but he reminds her that alienating himself from God would only alienate him from his greatest treasure (T. Job 26.4). Moreover, Job reminds Sitidos of their previous

---

22. Καὶ εἰπὸν τι ῥῆμα πρὸς κύριον καὶ τελεύτα (T. Job 25.10). In these scenes a number of lines come directly from, or are paraphrases of, verses or lines in the book of Job, but they have been set in new context by an expanded narrative frame. Here, for instance, the Testament of Job preserves the same rendering of the Hebrew as the Septuagint, but with the variant πρός ("against") instead of εἰς ("to"/"toward"). Granted, this variant is supported by a great cloud of witnesses for the Septuagint, such that the reading of εἰς here must be attributed to the logic of the *lectio difficilior* (see the impressive manuscript support for πρός in Joseph Ziegler, ed., *Iob*, SVTG 11.4 [Göttingen: Vandenhoeck & Ruprecht, 1982], 219). Even so, the context of the saying is quite different, following on the heels of Satan's humiliation of Sitidos (making her sell her hair for bread). In Job LXX the logic for the line follows Hebrew Job: Job's wife points to the utter loss and devastation that has befallen Job and thus asks for Job to say a word to God and die, possibly as an act of compassion toward Job. In the Testament of Job, however, it is Sitidos's disgrace that causes her to counsel Job thus, presumably out of her own perturbation and bitterness, which is why the scene pains him so (T. Job 26.1-2).

23. E.g., Pieter Willem van der Horst, "Images of Women in the *Testament of Job*," in *Studies on the Testament of Job*, ed. Michael A. Knibb and Pieter Willem van der Horst, SNTSMS 66 (Cambridge: Cambridge University Press, 1989), 93-116.

wealth, concluding, "If then we have received the good things from the hand of the Lord, shall we not in turn endure [ὑπομένομεν] the bad things? But let us be patient [μακροθυμήσωμεν] in everything until the Lord in compassion shows us mercy" (T. Job 26.5).

Job's perspective, unlike that of Sitidos, is one of renunciation. Just as the Cynics gave up the luxuries of life, Job interprets his misfortunes as training in patience. No doubt Pfitzner would object at this point that Job's patience is directed by his fidelity toward God and his faith in God's own fidelity and justice. But the theme of God's will overlaps with the counsel to renounce one's desires among the Hellenistic philosophers. Epictetus describes the utter failure of Medea to bracket her desires for her situation to be other than it was and the consequences of that failure: she murdered her children. Medea perceived rightly that her desires had been frustrated, but she did not endure (οὐχ ὑπομείνασα; *Diatr.* 2.17.19) such thwarted desire and did not understand that the remedy was to be found not in obtaining externally what she desired, but in internally releasing such desires. In his imaginative counsel to Medea, Epictetus folds in the notion of God's will:

> Do not desire to remain in Corinth, and, in a word, want nothing but what God wants. And who shall hinder you, who shall compel you? Nobody could do so, any more than he could for Zeus. When you have such a leader [as Zeus] and you desire and wish in accordance with such a one, why are you still afraid that you will fail? Give your aversion and your desire to Zeus and the other gods. Hand them over to them, let them navigate, let your desire and your aversion be ranged on their side; and how thenceforth can you be unhappy? (*Diatr.* 2.17.22–26)[24]

The language is not very different from that of Job's renunciation, which had begun even before his health had been affected. Says Job:

> I became as one wishing to enter a certain city to discover its wealth and gain a portion of its splendor, and as one embarked with cargo in a seagoing ship. Seeing at mid-ocean the third wave and the opposition of the wind, he threw the cargo into the sea, saying, "I am willing to lose everything in order to enter this city so that I might gain both the ship and things better than the payload." Thus I also considered my goods as nothing compared to the city about which the angel spoke to me. (T. Job 18.6–8)

---

24. My translation, following Hard; see n. 18 above.

Job had begun to renounce his goods and even his children for a deferred, heavenly prize and in conformity with God's (apparent) will.[25] Sitidos was still attached to them, and Job finishes his speech as an athlete swings his decisive blow: "Do you not see the devil standing behind you and troubling your reasoning [ταράσσοντα τοὺς διαλογισμούς σου] so that he might deceive even me? For he seeks to display you as one of the senseless women who deceive their husbands' integrity" (ἁπλότητα; T. Job 25.6; compare Job 2:10).

When Job calls Satan out from behind his wife, Satan yields the contest. He had thrown every move he had at Job, but Job endured them all and bested Satan. The superiority of the winning athlete in Greek was often acclaimed with the superlative adjective, κρείσσων. When Job finishes this part of his story he concludes with a moral, which most scholars have taken as the moral for the entire testament: "Now then, my children, you also must carry yourselves with patience [μακροθυμήσατε] in everything that encounters you, for *patience* [μακροθυμία] is greater than [κρείττων/κρείσσων] everything" (T. Job 27.7, emphasis added).

Job's Cynic- and Stoic-inflected philosophy of patient detachment represents the appropriate response of a righteous sufferer. Suffering is pedagogical; it teaches virtue. Suffering, in short, teaches one how to endure. But Job is not simply a model Stoic sage, nor is Job's hope entirely left for the future. The dialogues and testamentary frame of the Testament of Job point toward a further resolution for the question of righteous suffering. Not only can the wise train themselves to endure suffering, but indeed, they are even able to access divine blessedness in the present. The philosophical paideia in the Testament of Job culminates in mystical transformation.

The Testament of Job and Internalized Apocalypticism

In the Testament of Job, the cause of Job's suffering is not a wager between the satan (an accuser in God's heavenly court) and God, but rather Satan's

---

25. The most interesting parallels come from Matt 6:19–21 (storing up treasures in heaven: "For where your treasure is there your heart will be also" [NRSV]) and Matt 13:44–46 (the parables of the treasure in the field and the pearl of great price). But see also Mark 10:28 parr., where Peter claims the disciples have given up everything and followed Jesus; and Phil 3:8, where Paul considers his gain as loss compared to knowing Jesus.

wrath from his loss of honor (τιμία), precipitated by Job's righteous zeal in destroying a pagan shrine where Satan received worship as a pagan idol. God may not be as culpable for Job's afflictions as in the book of Job (though one should not overlook T. Job 37.3–4), but what, if anything, does God do to redress the suffering of Job? In fact, God does very little. The supreme God (ὁ θεός) does not intervene, but Job does receive messengers who guide him and present him with the means of his eventual cure and, moreover, the means of accessing divine power and beatitude in his earthly life. The final message of the Testament of Job, in other words, is actually (*pace* Steinmann) a mystic's solution to theodicy.

The mystical elements of the Testament of Job have often been noted, especially in connection with Job's daughters and the heavenly cords he bequeaths to them.[26] The term *mysticism* and its cognates are, of course, generally suspect among scholars at present because they have often been used in imprecise ways. The legitimacy of describing "Jewish mysticism" remains a fraught enterprise as well.[27] Still, such terms have their uses. John Collins understands Jewish mysticism in terms of "appealing to a higher revelation of a transcendent world," a definition that sounds very much like the definitions of apocalyptic/apocalypticism proffered by Michael Stone and Christopher Rowland.[28] Gershom Scholem highlighted the "experience of the inner self which enters into immediate contact with God or the metaphysical Reality" as the center of "mysticism."[29] Follow-

---

26. See esp. Howard C. Kee, "Satan, Magic, and Salvation in the *Testament of Job*," in *Society of Biblical Literature 1974 Seminar Papers*, 2 vols., SBLSP 13 (Cambridge, MA: Society of Biblical Literature, 1975), 1:53–76; Rebecca Lesses, "Amulets and Angels: Visionary Experience in the *Testament of Job* and the Hekhalot Literature," in *Heavenly Tablets: Interpretation, Identity and Tradition in Ancient Judaism*, ed. Lynn R. LiDonnici and Andrea Lieber, JSJSup 119 (Boston: Brill, 2007), 49–74; and Horst, "Images of Women."

27. A fine discussion can be found in Peter Schäfer, *The Origins of Jewish Mysticism* (Tübingen: Mohr Siebeck, 2009), 1–20.

28. John J. Collins, *Between Athens and Jerusalem: Jewish Identity in the Hellenistic Diaspora*, 2nd ed., BRS (Grand Rapids: Eerdmans, 2000), 210; see also Michael E. Stone, "Lists of Revealed Things in the Apocalyptic Literature," in *Magnalia Dei: The Mighty Acts of God; Essays on the Bible and Archaeology in Memory of G. Ernest Wright*, ed. Frank Moore Cross, Werner E. Lemke, and Patrick D. Miller (Garden City, NY: Doubleday, 1976), 414–52; Christopher Rowland, *The Open Heaven: A Study of Apocalyptic in Judaism and Early Christianity* (New York: Crossroad, 1982).

29. Gershom Scholem, *Major Trends in Jewish Mysticism* (New York: Schocken Books, 1974), 4.

ing Scholem (to an extent), Elliot Wolfson has more recently highlighted the experience of the "'angelification' of the human being who crosses the boundary of space and time and becomes part of the heavenly realm" as the heart of early Jewish mysticism.[30]

April DeConick has offered a similar understanding of early Jewish mysticism, which centers "on the belief that a person directly, immediately and before death can experience the divine, either as a rapture experience or one solicited by a particular praxis."[31] But she adds a hermeneutical element: the early Jews and Christians retold stories of their heroes according to their belief in (the possibility of) an immediate encounter with the divine in the present life. As DeConick argues, "they were providing in these works counter-readings of the old scriptures, recomposing the stories through a new hermeneutic for a contemporary audience." Thus, the "mysticism" of early Jewish and Christian texts lies at the "intersection of hermeneutics and experience."[32] The patriarchs and heroes of the faith became models of such mystical experience, especially in the ascent literature of early Judaism (e.g., Songs of the Sabbath Sacrifice; 1 En. 1–36; 1 En. 37–71; the Testament of Levi; the Apocalypse of Abraham; the Ascension of Isaiah; the Apocalypse of Zephaniah).[33] DeConick describes this perspective as "internalized apocalypse": the eschatological hopes for the renewal of the divine image in humanity could be a reality before death or the eschaton, through mystical experience.[34]

The apocalyptic mysticism of the Testament of Job shows up mainly in second half of the work—the dialogues of Job with his friends and the

---

30. Elliot R. Wolfson, "Mysticism and the Poetic-Liturgical Compositions from Qumran: A Response to Bilhah Nitzan," *JQR* 85 (1994): 186.

31. April D. DeConick, "What Is Early Jewish and Christian Mysticism?," in *Paradise Now: Essays on Early Jewish and Christian Mysticism*, ed. April D. DeConick, SymS 11 (Atlanta: Society of Biblical Literature, 2006), 1.

32. Ibid., 7.

33. I cannot in this essay situate the Testament of Job precisely in the historical span and potential development of these works. The Testament of Job was apparently composed sometime between about the first century BCE and the second century CE. A more precise date is not necessary for the purposes of this paper, as the works listed above span from roughly the third or second century BCE to the first or second century CE. We need not posit an unduly early date for the Enochic literature nor anachronistically invoke the *hekhalot* literature to find hints of mystical ascent practices and ideas at the time in which the Testament of Job is supposed to have been written.

34. DeConick, "Early Jewish and Christian Mysticism," 18–22.

scene of his death. The dialogues are remarkably condensed in the Testament of Job, and their subject matter is very different from the book of Job. Elious (Elihu) begins (!) the dialogues with a lament. The lament (T. Job 32.1–11) and Job's response (T. Job 33.1–4) reveal not only that Job has learned patience but that he has also acquired the ability to perceive supramundane realities.[35] The refrain of the lament, "Where now is the splendor of your throne?" refers to Job's earthly wealth and status (as king of Egypt). But as Elious finishes the lament, Job responds by pointing to the splendor of his real throne—among the holy ones, in the supraterrestrial realm, the splendor of which is from the right hand of the Father (T. Job 33.2); it is eternal and part of his eternal kingdom (T. Job 33.3–4).[36] Job has grasped the heavenly reality of his blessed royalty, and not the apparent reality of his despoiled, earthly royalty, as true reality.

Because the friends suppose Job may be out of his mind with grief, the debate over God's justice is folded into a dialogue about Job's sanity. Baldas (Bildad) asks Job in whom he hopes and who it is that afflicts him (T. Job 37.1–4). Job responds by indicating that God is the answer to both queries. When Baldas presses Job further, pointing out that this is contradictory (just as it is in the book of Job), Job demonstrates his sanity by responding with an insoluble riddle akin to the book of Job's whirlwind speech (T. Job 38.3–5): If food and drink go through the same stomach, who separates them out again when they leave the body? Since Baldas admits ignorance, Job makes his point, "If you do not understand the function of the body, how will you grasp [καταλάβῃ] the heavenly [τὰ ἐπουράνια] matters?" Job's heart "is not involved with earthly things, since the earth and those who dwell in it are unstable. But [his] heart is involved in heavenly things, for there is no upheaval in heaven" (διότι οὐχ ὑπάρχει ἐν οὐρανῷ ταραχή; T. Job 36.3).

The perception of heavenly realities is characteristic of apocalyptic literature, especially otherworldly journeys or ascents, but we should not fail to notice how the philosophical has been stitched into the apocalyptic perspective here. Job uses the verb καταλαμβάνω to talk about grasping or understanding heavenly matters, which as we have seen was a technical Stoic term for an act of true perception. Again, Job's mind is on the heavenly things precisely because there is no "upheaval" in heaven. This

---

35. See also Collins, *Between Athens and Jerusalem*, 242–43.

36. This is Job's eternal kingdom. Compare Jesus's words about his kingdom before Pilate (John 18:36).

word for upheaval (ταραχή) comes from the same root (ταράσσω) as philosophical language for imperturbability (ἀταραξία).³⁷ This theme has been folded into an apocalyptic construction of reality, where devils and other maleficent intangibles can cause disturbance on the earth. In other words, Job responds now to the question of theodicy through his investment in the heavenly realms and his heavenly throne.

Job refers to his eternal throne. The viceregal enthronement of exceptional humans is well attested in early Jewish mystical and apocalyptic texts. As Collins has argued, a War Scroll fragment from Cave 4 of Qumran (4QM 11) offers evidence for a teacher who apprehended himself as enthroned in heaven, and so able to declaim divine doctrine.³⁸ Enoch is, however, the most obvious and popular example of an enthroned patriarch, especially in his role as Metatron (3 En. 15).³⁹ Adam and Abel sit enthroned as judges in the Testament of Abraham (T. Ab., rec. A, 11.4–12; 13.2–6) with Enoch as Abel's assistant in one recension (T. Ab., rec. B, 11.1–4). Moses accedes to a (if not the) heavenly throne in Ezekiel's *Exagōgē* (Ezek. Trag. 68–76), wherein he receives a crown and scepter, tokens of a heavenly kingship. According to the Testament of Job, the same reward awaits Job.

Like other enthroned figures in early Jewish literature, Job's expected enthronement in the heavens entails a transformation on Job's part.⁴⁰ The

---

37. For a lively exposition of the Skeptic version, see Martha C. Nussbaum, *The Therapy of Desire: Theory and Practice in Hellenistic Ethics* (Princeton: Princeton University Press, 1994), 280–315. Epicurus includes the theme in his *Kyriai Doxai* 17 (see also Diogenes Laertius, *Vit. phil.* 10.144): Ὁ δίκαιος ἀταρακτότατος ὁ δ'ἄδικος πλείστης ταραχῆς γέμων ("The just person is most undisturbed, but the unjust person is full of the most disturbance").

38. John J. Collins, "A Throne in the Heavens: Apotheosis in Pre-Christian Judaism," in *Death, Ecstasy, and Otherworldly Journeys*, ed. John J. Collins and Michael Fishbane (Albany: State University of New York Press, 1995), 43–58.

39. For the Enoch–Metatron tradition, see Andrei A. Orlov, *The Enoch-Metatron Tradition*, TSAJ 107 (Tübingen: Mohr Siebeck, 2005).

40. See also 1 En. 71; 2 En. 22.8–10. See C. R. A. Morray-Jones, "Transformational Mysticism in the Apocalyptic-Merkabah Tradition," *JJS* 43 (1992): 1–31; Crispin H. T. Fletcher-Louis, "Angelomorphic Humanity among the Dead Sea Scrolls," *DSD* 7 (2000): 292–312; Gilles Quispel, "Transformation through Vision in Jewish Gnosticism and the Cologne Mani Codex," *VC* 49 (1995): 189–91; George J. Brooke, "Men and Women as Angels in *Joseph and Aseneth*," *JSP* 14 (2005): 159–77; Charles A. Gieschen, *Angelomorphic Christology: Antecedents and Early Evidence*, AGJU 42 (Leiden: Brill, 1998), esp. 152–83; Larry W. Hurtado, *One God, One Lord: Early Christian Devotion and Ancient Jewish Monotheism*, 2nd ed. (New York: T&T Clark, 1998), 51–70.

transformation becomes available when Job receives three cords from heaven that heal him of his disease.[41] These are the inheritance Job has in mind for his daughters. As Job describes them, the cords keep the wearer from suffering (T. Job 52.1–2). They take away all bodily pain, and even pain in the heart (i.e., painful memories; T. Job 47.8), but even more, Job says, "these bands will lead you into the better world, to live in the heavens" (T. Job 47.3). In other words, they are even more effective than Job's philosophical detachment, effecting a transformation into an angelic existence of bliss, regardless of the chaos in the world around. When the daughters put on the cords they each speak—or rather, sing—in angelic dialects, and their hearts are no longer set on earthly matters (T. Job 48.1; 49.1; 50.1). The cords perform exactly as they were described.

Howard Clark Kee argues that the original context for the Testament of Job was indebted to the early stages of *merkabah* mysticism.[42] In the later stages of the *merkabah* traditions, and in the *hekhalot* literature in particular (but also already in the Ascension of Isaiah), the "descender" to the chariot or practitioner of the ritual ascent required certain seals to pass the various levels of the ascent/descent (e.g., Hekh. Rabb. 4–6). Rebecca Lesses is probably correct to see the cords of the Testament of Job as analogs to such seals or amulets, though in my view she overemphasizes the apotropaic aspect of the cords (as phylacteries), neglecting their apparent instrumentality in angelomorphic transformation, clearly another way of gaining power.[43] James Davila connects these seals to ritual practices and possibly to ritual implements like *tefillin*.[44] The *hekhalot* texts are, of course, quite a bit later than the Testament of Job, though there is clear resonance between the *hekhalot* traditions and earlier apocalyptic traditions.[45] Whether or not mystical implements were employed by the author

---

41. Various Greek terms are used to describe these items, and they have been variously translated as "cords," "sashes," "girdles," or "phylacteries." "Cords" ($\chi o \rho \delta a i$) is the most frequently attested term in the testament (though none predominates) and it is perhaps the most neutral of the terms, so I have chosen to call them cords throughout.

42. Kee, "Satan, Magic, and Salvation."

43. Lesses, "Amulets and Angels"; see also Rebecca Lesses, *Ritual Practices to Gain Power: Adjurations in the Hekhalot Literature, Jewish Amulets, and Greek Revelatory Adjurations* (Harrisburg, PA: Trinity International, 1997).

44. James R. Davila, *Descenders to the Chariot: The People behind the Hekhalot Literature*, JSJSup 70 (Leiden: Brill, 2001), e.g., 109, 116, 191, and esp. 214–56.

45. The *hekhalot* texts are not earlier than the early medieval period (Cairo Geniza fragments), and most scholars date the *hekhalot* traditions to not earlier than

of the Testament of Job and his religious community, the analogy with the *hekhalot* literature, incantation bowls, and Greek amulets suggests that such a context is at least possible and perhaps even probable. The cords of the Testament of Job may reflect implements used in rituals of mystical transformation by the author and his coreligionists. While such an interpretation cannot be adequately demonstrated here (or perhaps at all), it is suggestive of the further interpretation of Job as a model mystic to be emulated in the Testament of Job.

Kee identifies the mystical element in the Testament of Job as the "highest aspiration" for mortals in the perspective of the author: "the vision of God, mystically in the present age, and ultimately before the Throne itself in heaven."[46] But it is more than vision; it is also transformation. If the effects of the cords do not reflect the kind of "angelification" Wolfson posited as distinctive of Jewish mysticism, I am at a loss to think of any text that does. Job's transcendent throne and kingdom may be the final consummation of Job's renewal after his soul's translation to heaven, but he is able to experience that transcendence through the divine gift of cords in his earthly sojourn. Even on his deathbed, he lay without suffering (πόνος) or pains because of the cord around him. This gift of God does more to redress Job's suffering than any philosophical act of perception and assent. The cords are gifts from God, and they redress Job's pain in the present and even remove those of the past. The gift of mystical perception of and participation in the divine ultimately demonstrates the justice of God.

What, then, is the relationship between the philosophical themes of the first half of the Testament of Job and the mystical themes of the latter half? Does the apocalypticism of the Testament of Job fulfill the philosophical asceticism or does it call it into question? When Job proclaims in the middle of the testament that patience is greater than anything, does he mean it is even greater than a heavenly throne?[47] The problem is

---

the fourth century CE, whereas the Testament of Job was composed not later than the second century CE. A fine introduction to the *hekhalot* texts and their date and provenance can be found in James R. Davila, *Hekhalot Literature in Translation: Major Texts of Merkavah Mysticism*, JJTPSup 20 (Leiden: Brill, 2013), 1–36. On the connection between apocalyptic texts and the *merkabah* traditions preserved in the *hekhalot* texts, Ithamar Gruenwald's work remains the clearest exposition; see his *Apocalyptic and Merkavah Mysticism*, 2nd ed., JJTPSup 20 (Leiden: Brill, 2014).

46. Kee, "Satan, Magic and Salvation," 70.

47. My thanks to Karina Martin Hogan's comments on an earlier draft for raising these questions.

worth considering, but it is not an insoluble riddle. The interpretation of early Jewish mysticism as internalized (or interiorized) apocalypse opens up the possibility of dialogue with Hellenistic moral philosophy, because once apocalypse has been internalized, both discourses (philosophical and mystical) partake of the same care and government of the self about which Foucault thought a great deal in his late work.[48] The revelation of the heavenly world and of the future, which is characteristic of literary apocalypses, takes place in the site of Job's body. Job does not experience the actual end of the age, but a revelation of the divine—we might even say, of God's final purpose or meaning—in his own body. Perhaps philosophical *apatheia* prepares one to receive angelic transformation, or perhaps such transformation only occurs through certain ritual implements (cords) or practices. Both Hellenistic moral training and early Jewish mysticism have their techniques or technologies of the self.[49] Raising the question of the connection between the two is important, though, for pointing out that the final word of the Testament of Job is not patience, but rather beatitude. Hellenistic philosophy only prepares one to tolerate the dung-heap and to command the worms, but angelomorphic transformation and accession to a divine throne actually take away the pain. Philosophical *apatheia* is only half the story in the Testament of Job; the rest is angelomorphic transformation, or internalized apocalypse.

---

48. Michel Foucault, *The Care of the Self*, vol. 3 of *The History of Sexuality* (New York: Vintage Books, 1988); Foucault, *Technologies of the Self: A Seminar with Michel Foucault*, ed. Luther H. Martin, Huck Gutman, and Patrick H. Hutton (Amherst: University of Massachusetts Press, 1988); Foucault, *Hermeneutics of the Subject: Lectures at the Collège de France, 1981–1982* (New York: Picador, 2005); Foucault, *The Government of the Self and Others: Lectures at the Collège de France, 1982–1983* (New York: Picador, 2011); Foucault, *The Courage of Truth: The Government of the Self and Others II; Lectures at the Collège de France, 1983–1984* (New York: Picador, 2012).

49. An interesting connection between Foucault and the Testament of Job is the Therapeutae, described in Philo's *On the Contemplative Life*. Foucault finds in the Therapeutae an example of "concern for the self which gave rise to technologies of the self" (i.e., ascetic practices); see Foucault, *Hermeneutics*, 166–170; Foucault, *Technologies*, 21. The Therapeutae have sometimes also been conjectured as the immediate context out of which the Testament of Job was composed (see R. P. Spittler, "Testament of Job," in *Apocalyptic Literature and Testaments*, vol. 1 of *The Old Testament Pseudepigrapha*, ed. James H. Charlesworth [New York: Doubleday, 1983], 833–34). Clearly, this is a provocative suggestion that cannot be taken up here.

Conclusion

The deployment of Greek philosophical themes and the emphasis on mystical transformation set the message of the Testament of Job apart from the dialogical theology of the book of Job.[50] Because the first half of this claim is more novel than the second, I have focused the argument of this paper more on demonstrating the resonance of the Testament of Job with philosophical paideia. Yet, the philosophical elements of the Testament of Job are taken up into what is finally a mystical model for overcoming suffering, a divergence from the book of Job that is no less striking than the Testament of Job's reliance on philosophical tropes. In the book of Job the relationship between Job and God, as Leo Perdue has adequately demonstrated, has a pronounced mythical quality.[51] Job does not engage in visionary practices or angelomorphic transformation in order to apprehend his vision of God; he complains and he sees. When God shows up, God condescends to appear on the earth, in a whirlwind, not in a vision or a dream, and not in the heavens. There is no mystical union or apprehension of a supramundane, nonobvious world by Job in the biblical book; there is instead a very obvious and unmistakable deity from whom Job remains all too separate. While both the book of Job and the Testament of Job might be said to emphasize divine presence, we must distinguish these modes of divine presence. To put the matter a bit crudely, in the mythical pattern (book of Job) God descends to earth and is described in anthropomorphic terms, but in the mystical pattern (Testament of Job) the one who apprehends God ascends to the heavens and is described in angelomorphic terms. The mythical pattern is concerned with the presence of God in this world; the mystical pattern with the presence of the human in the divine world. In the mythical pattern God comes down among mortals; in the mystical pattern mortals ascend toward God.

The distinction between mythical and mystical makes sense also of the necessary addition of the qualifier "internalized" to apocalypse to describe the mysticism of the testament. As a literary genre and as eschatological discourse, apocalypse is a mythic event. As mystical praxis, on the other

---

50. On the theology of the book of Job as dialogical in character, see Carol Newsom, *The Book of Job: A Contest of Moral Imaginations* (New York: Oxford University Press, 2003).

51. Leo G. Perdue, *Wisdom in Revolt: Metaphorical Theology in the Book of Job* (Sheffield: JSOT Press, 1991), esp. 61–73, 267–69.

hand, apocalypse locates the revelation of the future and of supramundane realities in the mind or body of the practitioner.[52] This is also not to say that apocalypticism has taken a "noetic turn."[53] Apocalypse has not been noeticized through allegorical appropriation, but rather internalized (the narrative form remains). The biblical book of Job has been interpreted as an apocalyptic work, in part on account of the theophany at the end of Job (Job 38–41).[54] But Job is not a mystical book. In the Testament of Job, the agonisitic theophany from Job 38–41 has not been interiorized, but the same epiphanic revelation does occur in the angelomorphic transformation of Job (and his daughters).

The relationship between Job and God in the biblical book is one of (mythical) confrontation, while in the Testament of Job the narrative is entirely about Job's transformation, that is, his techniques or technology of the self.[55] Lawrence Wills reads the Testament of Job similarly, arguing that the composition represents an ascetic discourse, which (along with other works) anticipated the rise of Christian monastic ascetical theology.[56] In the course of his argument Wills also draws on Foucault's notion of "technologies of the self" (and Elizabeth Castelli's modification of Foucault, "transformative work on the self") as a rich explication of the analytic term *asceticism*. In this sense, what I am calling the "mystic's solution" to theodicy could also be called the "ascetic's solution," though such a description does not, perhaps, incorporate also the internalized apocalypticism of the work.

---

52. These observations also reflect Moshe Idel's distinction between theosophical-theurgic and ecstatic types of Jewish mysticism; see Moshe Idel, *Kabbalah: New Perspectives* (New Haven: Yale University Press, 1988), xi.

53. Dragoş A. Giulea, "The Noetic Turn in Jewish Thought," *JSJ* 42 (2011): 23–57.

54. Timothy Jay Johnson, *Now My Eye Sees You: Unveiling an Apocalyptic Job*, HBM 24 (Sheffield: Sheffield Phoenix, 2013).

55. I am not yet persuaded that decentering of the self is the right language for what Foucault has in mind or for what is going on in these texts. Foucault argued that technologies of the self flowed directly from "care for the self," not from a kind of abandonment of the self (see Foucault, "Technologies," 19–22; Foucault, *Hermeneutics*). The Testament of Job is also trying to recenter the self, then, but in a divine existence that is transcendent. In the book of Job, I think it is more accurate to say that Job is actually trying to recenter the world according to the self, precisely backward from a Stoic ethical viewpoint.

56. Lawrence M. Wills, "Ascetic Theology before Asceticism? Jewish Narratives and the Decentering of the Self," *JAAR* 74 (2006): 902–25.

Morris Jastrow once argued that the book of Job was the work of a group of postexilic Jewish freethinkers. It is "a skeptical composition—skeptical in the sense of putting a question mark after the fundamental axiom ... that the government of the universe rests on justice."[57] But Jastrow further mused:

> One wonders if the original Book of Job had been written several centuries later, say about 100 B.C., what the attitude of the circle of free inquiry would have been towards the new doctrine of life after death which by that time had taken a firm hold on pious minds ... and according to which there was a distinction between the ultimate fate of the virtuous and the wicked.... It must be admitted that the philosophy of the Book of Job would have been considerably strengthened by either [the doctrine's] acceptance or by its rejection on good grounds.[58]

If Jastrow had read the Testament of Job, he would not have had to wonder. The author(s) of the Testament of Job did in fact accept the notion of eschatological justice, and reshaped the Job story accordingly. The death and loss that the righteous suffer comes from Satan. God allows the righteous to suffer in order to purify them and to assure them of a greater reward at the "consummation of the age." Enduring hardship will build up the righteous and their future reward, but it can also lead them to perceive and even partake of the heavenly life in the present. In the face of that reality, questions of theodicy fall away. Unlike the book of Job, however, this encounter with God is not a whirlwind that batters, but an angelic life of song and bliss.

Bibliography

Blenkinsopp, Joseph. *Wisdom and Law in the Old Testament*. Oxford: Oxford University Press, 1995.

Brändl, Martin. *Der Agon bei Paulus: Herkunft und Profil paulinischer Agonmetaphorik*. WUNT 2/222. Tübingen: Mohr Siebeck, 2006.

Brock, Sebastian P., and Jean-Claude Picard, eds. *Testamentum Jobi; Apocalypsis Baruchi Graece*. PVTG 2. Leiden: Brill, 1967.

---

57. Jastrow, *Book of Job*, 26.
58. Ibid., 171–72, 174.

Brooke, George J. "Men and Women as Angels in *Joseph and Aseneth*." *JSP* 14 (2005): 159–77.
Bruegemann, Walter. "Theodicy in a Social Dimension." *JSOT* 33 (1985): 3–25.
Clines, David J. A. *Job 1–20*. WBC. Waco, TX: Word, 1989.
Collins, John J. *Between Athens and Jerusalem: Jewish Identity in the Hellenistic Diaspora*. 2nd ed. BRS. Grand Rapids: Eerdmans, 2000.
———. "A Throne in the Heavens: Apotheosis in Pre-Christian Judaism." Pages 43–58 in *Death, Ecstasy, and Otherworldly Journeys*. Edited by John J. Collins and Michael Fishbane. Albany: State University of New York Press, 1995.
Crenshaw, James L. *Old Testament Wisdom: An Introduction*. 3rd ed. Louisville: Westminster John Knox, 2010.
Davila, James R. *Descenders to the Chariot: The People behind the Hekhalot Literature*. JSJSup 70. Leiden: Brill, 2001.
———. *Hekhalot Literature in Translation: Major Texts of Merkavah Mysticism*. JJTPSup 20. Leiden: Brill, 2013.
DeConick, April D. "What Is Early Jewish and Christian Mysticism?" Pages 1–24 in *Paradise Now: Essays on Early Jewish and Christian Mysticism*. Edited by April D. DeConick. SymS 11. Atlanta: Society of Biblical Literature, 2006.
Driver, Samuel R., and George Buchanan Gray. *A Critical and Exegetical Commentary on the Book of Job*. ICC. 2 vols. New York: Scribner's Sons, 1921.
Epictetus. *The Discourses of Epictetus*. Edited by Christopher Gill. Translated by Robin Hard. London: Dent, 1995.
Fernández Marcos, Natalio. "The Septuagint Reading of the Book of Job." Pages 251–66 in *The Book of Job*. Edited by W. A. M. Beuken. BETL 114. Leuven: Peeters, 1994.
Fletcher-Louis, Crispin H. T. "Angelomorphic Humanity among the Dead Sea Scrolls." *DSD* 7 (2000): 292–312.
Foucault, Michel. *The Care of the Self*. Vol. 3 of *The History of Sexuality*. New York: Vintage Books, 1988.
———. *The Courage of Truth: The Government of the Self and Others II; Lectures at the Collège de France, 1983–1984*. New York: Picador, 2012.
———. *The Government of the Self and Others: Lectures at the Collège de France, 1982–1983*. New York: Picador, 2011.
———. *Hermeneutics of the Subject: Lectures at the Collège de France, 1981–1982*. New York: Picador, 2005.

———. *Technologies of the Self: A Seminar with Michel Foucault.* Edited by Luther H. Martin, Huck Gutman, and Patrick H. Hutton. Amherst: University of Massachusetts Press, 1988.

Geertz, Clifford. *The Interpretation of Cultures: Selected Essays.* New York: Basic Books, 1973.

Gieschen, Charles A. *Angelomorphic Christology: Antecedents and Early Evidence.* AGJU 42. Leiden: Brill, 1998.

Giulea, Dragoş A. "The Noetic Turn in Jewish Thought." *JSJ* 42 (2011): 23–57.

Good, Edwin M. "The Problem of Evil in the Book of Job." Pages 50–69 in *The Voice from the Whirlwind: Interpreting the Book of Job.* Edited by Leo G. Perdue and W. Clark Gilpin. Nashville: Abingdon, 1992.

Gruenwald, Ithamar. *Apocalyptic and Merkavah Mysticism.* 2nd ed. JJTP-Sup 20. Leiden: Brill, 2014.

Habel, Norman C. "The Verdict on/of God at the End of Job." Pages 27–38 in *Job's God.* Edited by E. J. van Wolde. Concilium 4. London: SCM, 2004.

Horst, Pieter Willem van der. "Images of Women in the *Testament of Job.*" Pages 93–116 in *Studies on the Testament of Job.* Edited by Michael A. Knibb and Pieter Willem van der Horst. SNTSMS 66. Cambridge: Cambridge University Press, 1989.

Hurtado, Larry W. *One God, One Lord: Early Christian Devotion and Ancient Jewish Monotheism.* 2nd ed. New York: T&T Clark, 1998.

Idel, Moshe. *Kabbalah: New Perspectives.* New Haven: Yale University Press, 1988.

Jastrow, Morris, Jr. *The Book of Job: Its Origin, Growth and Interpretation.* Philadelphia: Lippincott, 1920.

Johnson, Timothy Jay. *Now My Eye Sees You: Unveiling an Apocalyptic Job.* HBM 24. Sheffield: Sheffield Phoenix, 2013.

Kee, Howard Clark. "Satan, Magic, and Salvation in the *Testament of Job.*" Pages 53–76 in vol. 1 of *Society of Biblical Literature 1974 Seminar Papers.* 2 vols. SBLSP 13. Cambridge, MA: Society of Biblical Literature, 1975.

Kraft, Robert A., ed. *The Testament of Job, according to the SV Text.* SBLTT 5. Missoula, MT: Scholars Press, 1974.

Lesses, Rebecca. "Amulets and Angels: Visionary Experience in the *Testament of Job* and the Hekhalot Literature." Pages 49–74 in *Heavenly Tablets: Interpretation, Identity and Tradition in Ancient Judaism.*

Edited by Lynn R. LiDonnici and Andrea Lieber. JSJSup 119. Boston: Brill, 2007.

———. *Ritual Practices to Gain Power: Adjurations in the Hekhalot Literature, Jewish Amulets, and Greek Revelatory Adjurations*. Harrisburg, PA: Trinity International, 1997.

Long, A. A. *Hellenistic Philosophy: Stoics, Epicureans, Skeptics*. Berkeley: University of California Press, 1986.

Marcus Aurelius. *Meditations*. Translated by Gregory Hays. New York: Modern Library, 2002.

Morray-Jones, C. R. A. "Transformational Mysticism in the Apocalyptic-Merkabah Tradition." *JJS* 43 (1992): 1–31.

Newsom, Carol A. "The Book of Job." Pages 317–637 in *The First Book of Maccabees; the Second Book of Maccabees; Introduction to Hebrew Poetry; the Book of Job; the Book of Psalms*. Vol. 4 of *The New Interpreter's Bible*. Edited by Robert Doran, Adele Berlin, Carol A. Newsom, and J. Clinton McCann. Nashville: Abingdon, 1996.

———. *The Book of Job: A Contest of Moral Imaginations*. New York: Oxford University Press, 2003.

Nussbaum, Martha C. *The Therapy of Desire: Theory and Practice in Hellenistic Ethics*. Princeton: Princeton University Press, 1994.

Orlov, Andrei A. *The Enoch-Metatron Tradition*. TSAJ 107. Tübingen: Mohr Siebeck, 2005.

Perdue, Leo G. *The Sword and the Stylus: An Introduction to Wisdom in the Age of Empires*. Grand Rapids: Eerdmans, 2008.

———. *Wisdom in Revolt: Metaphorical Theology in the Book of Job*. Sheffield: JSOT Press, 1991.

Pfitzner, Victor C. *Paul and the Agon Motif: Traditional Athletic Imagery in the Pauline Literature*. NovTSup 16. Leiden: Brill, 1967.

Pope, Marvin H. *Job: A New Translation with Introduction and Commentary*. AB 15. 3rd ed. New York: Doubleday, 1973.

Quispel, Gilles. "Transformation through Vision in Jewish Gnosticism and the Cologne Mani Codex." *VC* 49 (1995): 189–91.

Rist, John M. *Stoic Philosophy*. Cambridge: Cambridge University Press, 1969.

Rowland, Christopher. *The Open Heaven: A Study of Apocalyptic in Judaism and Early Christianity*. New York: Crossroad, 1982.

Sanders, Jack T. "Wisdom, Theodicy, Death, and the Evolution of Intellectual Traditions." *JSJ* 36 (2005): 263–77.

Schäfer, Peter. *The Origins of Jewish Mysticism*. Tübingen: Mohr Siebeck, 2009.

Schenke, Gesa, and Gesine Schenke Robinson. *Das Testament des Iob*. Vol. 1 of *Der Koptische Kölner Papyruskodex 3221*. PapyCol 33. Paderborn: Schöningh, 2009.

Scholem, Gershom. *Major Trends in Jewish Mysticism*. New York: Schocken Books, 1974.

Seow, C. L. *Job 1–21: Interpretation and Commentary*. Illuminations. Grand Rapids: Eerdmans, 2013.

Spittler, R. P. "Testament of Job." Pages 829–868 in *Apocalyptic Literature and Testaments*. Vol. 1 of *The Old Testament Pseudepigrapha*. Edited by James H. Charlesworth. New York: Doubleday, 1983.

Steinmann, Andrew E. "The Structure and Message of the Book of Job." *VT* 46 (1996): 85–100.

Stone, Michael E. "Lists of Revealed Things in the Apocalyptic Literature." Pages 414–52 in *Magnalia Dei: The Mighty Acts of God; Essays on the Bible and Archaeology in Memory of G. Ernest Wright*. Edited by Frank Moore Cross, Werner E. Lemke, and Patrick D. Miller. Garden City, NY: Doubleday, 1976.

Werline, Rodney A. "The Experience of God's *Paideia* in the Psalms of Solomon." Pages 17–44 in *Linking Text and Experience*. Vol. 2 of *Experientia*. Edited by Colleen Shantz and Rodney A. Werline. EJL 35. Atlanta: Society of Biblical Literature, 2012.

Williams, Ronald J. "Theodicy in the Ancient Near East." Pages 42–56 in *Theodicy in the Old Testament*. Edited by James L. Crenshaw. Philadelphia: Fortress, 1983.

Wills, Lawrence M. "Ascetic Theology before Asceticism? Jewish Narratives and the Decentering of the Self." *JAAR* 74 (2006): 902–25.

Witte, Markus. "The Greek Book of Job." Pages 33–54 in *Das Buch Hiob und seine Interpretationen: Beitrage zum Hiob-Symposium auf dem Monte Verità vom 14.–19. August 2005*. Edited by Thomas Krüger, Manfred Oeming, Konrad Schmid, and Christof Uehlinger. ATANT 88. Zürich: Theologischer Verlag Zürich, 2007.

Wolfson, Elliot R. "Mysticism and the Poetic-Liturgical Compositions from Qumran: A Response to Bilhah Nitzan." *JQR* 85 (1994): 185–202.

Ziegler, Joseph, ed. *Iob*. SVTG 11.4. Göttingen: Vandenhoeck & Ruprecht, 1982.

Part 3
Hellenism and Paideia in Early Christianity

The Mysteries of Paideia: "Mystery" and Education in Plato's *Symposium*, 4QInstruction, and 1 Corinthians

C. Andrew Ballard

Three texts from antiquity demonstrate the various ways that ancient authors could employ particular conceptions of "mystery" as a tool for establishing their own esoteric forms of paideia: Plato's *Symposium*, 4QInstruction, and 1 Corinthians. These texts utilize the language of mystery in order to set apart their pedagogical systems from other dominant forms of education. To be sure, these texts have varying definitions of "mystery" and disparate ends to which their mysteries point. Plato's *Symposium* used the concept of "mystery" to describe an ascent into the heights of philosophical contemplation in which the goal was an ultimate vision of the Platonic world of Forms. For 4QInstruction, "the mystery that is to be" refers to the cosmic plan of God, which had both immediate and eschatological implications for the addressees. Paul used "mystery" to explain how the crucifixion of Christ should shape the lives and attitudes of the Corinthian assembly. While the meanings of "mystery" differ for each text, the usage of "mystery" language has three similar functions in these texts: to establish authority and legitimacy for the instructor, to point the pupil toward a path for understanding esoteric teaching, and to direct the pupil to an extraordinary, transformative vision. Through the juxtaposition of these disparate texts we will garner a clearer understanding of the role that conceptions of "mystery" played in ancient, alternative forms of paideia.

This essay is a revised and expanded version of a paper I presented in the Wisdom and Apocalypticism section at the 2013 Society of Biblical Literature Annual Meeting in Baltimore. I would like to thank Troy Martin for his insightful response to my paper during that conference session, which has prompted numerous revisions throughout.

Paideia as Initiation into Mysteries

In ancient Greek literature, paideia was often compared to the act of initiation into the mystery of a god or goddess. The process of education necessarily involves those who know and those who do not know: the ignorant and the knowledgeable, the insiders and the outsiders. The nature and extent of the material gained during the pedagogical process is often unknown to those outside of the relationship between master and pupil. In that sense, the outsiders are "uninitiated" into the realm of knowledge found within a particular educational setting. It is easy to see, then, how the language of mystery initiation would have become useful to ancient Greeks who wanted to describe the secrecy and value of specialized knowledge.

In the early fourth century BCE, the Greek physician Hippocrates compared the act of learning to a mystery initiation.[1] In *Law*, in which Hippocrates sets forth an admonition to all physicians that they pursue proper training, he states, "There are in fact two things, science and opinion; the former begets knowledge, the latter ignorance. Things however that are holy [τὰ ἱερά] are revealed [δείκνυμι] only to men who are holy. The profane may not learn them until they have been initiated [τελέω] into the mysteries [ὄργια] of science" (*Lex* 4–5). The Greek terms used here are explicit references to initiation into ancient mystery cults.[2] For

---

1. On the dating of the Hippocratic corpus, see Elizabeth M. Craik, *The "Hippocratic" Corpus: Context and Content* (New York: Routledge, 2015), 155.

2. The ἱερά (sacred objects) were revealed at the climax of the Eleusinian mysteries by the highest official, known as the hierophant ("one who reveals the sacred objects"). See Jan N. Bremmer, *Initiation into the Mysteries of the Ancient World*, MVAW 1 (Berlin: de Gruyter, 2014), 14; Kevin Clinton, *Myth and Cult: The Iconography of the Eleusinian Mysteries* (Athens: Svenska Institutet, 1992), 90–95. Plutarch mentions three components of ancient mystery initiation: *legomena* (things said), *drōmena* (things done), and *deiknymena* (things shown). For the *legomena* and *drōmena*, see Plutarch, *Is. Os.* 378B: "It is especially necessary that we adopt, as our guide in the mysteries, the reasoning that comes from philosophy, and consider reverently each one of the things that are said and done" (λεγόμενα καὶ δρώμενα). On the *deiknymena*, see Plutarch, *Alc.* 22.3: "[Alcibiades was] mimicking the mysteries and showing them forth [δείκνυμι] to his companions in his own house, wearing a robe such as the High Priest wears when he shows forth [δείκνυμι] the sacred secrets to the initiates." See further George E. Mylonas, *Eleusis and the Eleusinian Mysteries* (Princeton: Princeton University Press, 1961), 261–74. On the use of τελέω and ὄργια in descriptions of ancient mystery cults, see Feyo L. Schuddeboom, *Greek Religious Terminology: Telete and Orgia; A Revised*

Hippocrates, the secrecy of the rituals and knowledge one would gain in a mystery cult initiation was analogous to the esoteric knowledge one acquires when specializing in medicine. Werner Jaeger commented, "Here we have mankind divided, as if by a religious rite, into two classes, one of which is severely debarred from an arcane knowledge. This line of thought raises the doctor's importance above that of a mere artisan."[3] Only the initiated are privy to the mysteries, which are hidden from the general public. Additionally, in order to be a competent physician, one must be guided and initiated into the mysteries of science by a knowledgeable mystagogue: "The teaching of the art ... must be acquired intelligently by one who from a child has been instructed in a place naturally suitable for learning" (*Lex* 2). The mystagogues themselves must have proper training. Those who find the proper mystagogue are able, with diligence, to pass through the initiation process and attain the goal of knowledge. Those whose mystagogues are inept, and whose work ethic is lacking, fool themselves and others into thinking they are initiates; however, they remain in ignorance and folly.

The mysteries of education were also subjects of interest for Plutarch in the first century CE. In *On the Education of Children,* Plutarch compared instructors of children to hierophants (high priests and "revealers of sacred objects") and *dadychoi* ("torch-bearers" and second-highest-ranking officials) of the mystery cults.[4] While explaining how it is dishonorable to punish a pupil during a fit of anger, Plutarch lists examples of men like Plato who were able to control their fiery tempers. Following these exemplars, Plutarch states, "Yet we, no less than they, feeling ourselves to be the high priests [ἱεροφάνται] of God's mysteries and torch-bearers [δαδοῦχοι] of wisdom, do attempt, so far as lies in our power, to imitate and to get a little taste of such conduct for ourselves" (*Lib. ed.* 10E). Just as the officials of the mystery cults reveal holy objects and provide sacred light, Plutarch thought that educators should be ones who initiate and enlighten pupils in their search for wisdom. Additionally, he stated that his position as an

---

and Expanded English Edition of the Studies by Zijderveld and Van der Burg, RGRW 169 (Leiden: Brill, 2009).

3. Werner Jaeger, *Paideia: The Ideals of Greek Culture,* 3 vols., trans. Gilbert Highet (Oxford: Oxford University Press, 1986), 3:11.

4. On the duties of these two figures and the honors afforded to them, see Kevin Clinton, *The Sacred Officials of the Eleusinian Mysteries* (Philadelphia: American Philosophical Society, 1974), 10–68; Mylonas, *Eleusis,* 208–318.

instructor involved "transferring the fear which we learned from the divine secrets [i.e., in the mysteries] to the safe keeping of the secrets of men" (*Lib. ed.* 10F). As he taught his students how to be disciplined and reverent, Plutarch served the mystagogic function of passing on divine secrets to trusted pupils. Furthermore, the mystery cult metaphors that Plutarch used to describe his pedagogy suggest that he believed his students to be part of a privileged community that was separated from the "uninitiated" whole of humanity. Richard Hunter argues, "The kind of paideia which Plutarch has in mind is not, of course, for everyone. Plutarch is aiming to reproduce his own kind, an elite class whose cultural power depends on shared values."[5] Plutarch saw himself as a mystagogue of an esoteric paideia for an initiated circle of students.

As part of the educational context, ancient authors also used mystery terminology to describe the process of being trained in rhetoric. Plato seems to have popularized the idea that rhetorical education was a type of mystery initiation, as we will see shortly.[6] Later Hellenistic authors followed this usage of mystery terminology to describe their own views on rhetorical training. In the first century BCE, Dionysius of Halicarnassus used a mystery metaphor to teach the importance of "meter" in "spoken verse":

> Now I must try, here as before, to state my views. But this new subject is like the mysteries: it cannot be divulged to people in large numbers. I should not, therefore, be guilty of rudeness, if I invited only "those with a sacred right" to approach the initiation rituals of style, while telling the "profane" to "close the gates of their ears." Some people reduce the most serious subject to ridicule through their own callowness, and no doubt there is nothing unnatural in their attitude. Well, my views are as follows. Any passage that is composed without meter is incapable of acquiring the music of spoken verse or the grace of lyric, at least through mere word-arrangement. (*Comp.* 25)

Dionysius viewed the act of rhetorical training as a sacred mystery ceremony available only to initiates who had been invited by their instructors

---

5. Richard Hunter, *Critical Moments in Classical Literature: Studies in the Ancient View of Literature and Its Uses* (Cambridge: Cambridge University Press, 2009), 171.

6. Christina Schefer, "Rhetoric as Part of an Initiation into the Mysteries: A New Interpretation of the Platonic *Phaedrus*," in *Plato as Author: The Rhetoric of Philosophy*, ed. Ann N. Michelini (Leiden: Brill, 2003), 175–96.

to witness the holy rites.[7] The uninitiated ones must close their ears to the "initiation rituals of style," lest they be guilty of hearing the mysteries in an unprepared and profane state. Dionysius thus viewed himself as a mystagogue of rhetoric.

Similarly, Quintilian thought the act of instructing pupils in rhetorical training was analogous to mystery initiation. In *Inst.* 5, after discussing effective techniques for orators, Quintilian states, "I seem to have finished playing the part of initiator into these mysteries; next comes the place for practical advice" (*Inst.* 5.14.27).[8] His rhetorical instruction was a mystery initiation for the neophytes under his tutelage. Additionally, Quintilian refers to the rules of rhetoric as mystagogic instruction: "For almost all those who have laid down the law of speaking as though it was some sort of mystery have tied us down, not only to specific topics for discovering arguments, but to specific rules for validating them" (*Inst.* 5.13.60). Donald A. Russell rightly commented that Quintilian viewed rhetorical instruction as "a secret religious rite into which one has to be initiated."[9] Moreover, Quintilian described the relationship that his students had with one another as comparable to the bonds formed between initiates in mystery celebrations. He derided the person who undertook rhetorical training apart from a community of students because that one, he writes,

> has learned as a solitary something which can only be practiced among many. I say nothing of the friendships which endure firm and unbroken to old age, imbued with almost religious feelings of attachment. Initiation in the same studies is no less binding than initiation in the same mysteries. And where will he learn what we call common feeling if he shuts himself off from society, which is natural not only to humans but to the dumb animals? (*Inst.* 1.2.18–20)

Quintilian's students became bound together in friendship because of their shared experience in the educational setting. They were co-initiates in Quintilian's cult of rhetorical mysteries. He, in turn, was their mysta-

---

7. On Dionysius and mystery cult terminology, see Casper Constantijn de Jonge, "The Initiation Rites of Style: Dionysius on Prose, Poetry, and Poetic Prose," in Jonge, *Between Grammar and Rhetoric: Dionysius of Halicarnassus on Language, Linguistics, and Literature*, MnemosyneSup 301 (Leiden: Brill, 2008), 329–66.

8. *Peregisse mihi videor sacra tradentium partes, sed consilio locus superest.*

9. Donald A. Russell, *Quintilian: The Orator's Education*, 5 vols., LCL (Cambridge: Harvard University Press, 2002–2014), 1:499 n. 47.

gogue who led them on to the glories of rhetorical perfection. It is evident, then, that education in the ancient world was often thought of as an initiation into mysterious, esoteric knowledge.

Paideia and Mystery in the *Symposium*

Plato's *Symposium* relates the story of a group of friends who meet for a dinner party at the house of Agathon, a wealthy Athenian tragedian. During the party, the guests, in turn, agree to proffer encomiastic speeches to Eros, the god of desire and love. After Agathon ends his speech, gaining roaring applause in the process, Socrates reluctantly agrees to give his own panegyric in praise of Eros. However, instead of launching directly into the speech, as all the other dinner guests had done, Socrates begins by asking questions to Agathon—questions that challenge the very basis of his knowledge of the god Eros. Socrates's questions effectively nullify Agathon's encomium and destroy his confidence in his own ability as a rhetorician.[10] Agathon replies to Socrates's questioning, "It turns out, Socrates, I didn't know what I was talking about in that speech" (*Symp.* 201c). By guiding Agathon along the dialectical path of self-examination, Socrates is able to begin teaching him the true path to understanding Eros. The fact that Socrates uses such a different method than the other speakers is a signal that the sacred path to Truth and Beauty is not found through conventional wisdom, rhetoric, or sophistry.[11] This sets apart Socrates as a guide into what he will call "the mysteries" of Love/Eros.

It is imperative for Plato to differentiate Socrates from the other speakers at the dinner party, because, as Jaeger has pointed out, "men representing every type of Greek culture are gathered at the table of Agathon."[12] The fact that Socrates "wins" the contest shows that Plato desires to set up his own paideia over against the dominant Athenian one.[13] Socrates refused to praise Eros with vain, rhetorical platitudes as the others had

---

10. See the discussion in Elizabeth S. Belfiore, *Socrates' Daimonic Art: Love for Wisdom in Four Platonic Dialogues* (Cambridge: Cambridge University Press, 2012), 161–97.

11. Daniel Boyarin, *Socrates and the Fat Rabbis* (Chicago: University of Chicago Press, 2009), 50.

12. Jaeger, *Paideia*, 2:176.

13. On Socrates's pedagogical goals, see Gary Alan Scott, *Plato's Socrates as Educator* (Albany: State University of New York Press, 2000), 1–50.

done, and instead opted for an entirely different method of encomium: the dialogue with Diotima. The reason for this is clear. In Plato's other writings, especially the *Republic*, he seeks to establish his own "ethicopolitical program" that threatens to displace the established paideia of the Athenian elite.[14] So Josiah Ober writes, "Plato had argued in the *Republic* for a new form of moral and political education that sought to invalidate and obviate the rhetorical paideia" on which Athenian society was built.[15] Furthermore, according to Jaeger, "contemporary education and pedagogy [was] for Plato a caricature of real paideia."[16] Socrates, then, becomes the herald of Plato's alternative pedagogical system for educating citizens in the ways of philosophy and virtue.

Socrates, as the masterful instructor, relates to the guests the means by which he himself was educated into the knowledge of truth and virtue, which Plato describes as "mysteries" (*Symp.* 201d).[17] Socrates had come to know the mysteries of Love by means of a guide, a woman named Diotima. She is a mysterious figure, the details about whom remain ambiguous.[18] Her name means "Honor to Zeus" or "Honored by Zeus,"[19] and she comes from a town called Mantinea, whose name is a cognate of μάντις, or "prophet." Daniel Boyarin has commented that Diotima is "the prophetess from Prophetville."[20] It is not clear how Socrates is supposed to have

---

14. Josiah Ober, "I, Socrates... The Performative Audacity of Isocrates' *Antidosis*," in *Isocrates and Civic Education*, ed. Takis Poulakos and David J. Depew (Austin: University of Texas Press, 2004), 27.

15. Ibid.

16. Jaeger, *Paideia*, 2:270.

17. Some have suggested that the speech of Diotima is directed at Agathon in particular. Diotima may be an "alter ego" of Socrates, while Socrates, as the interlocutor of Diotima, may be a representation of Agathon. See James Rhodes, *Eros, Wisdom, and Silence* (Columbia: University of Missouri Press, 2003), 302–17.

18. On Diotima, see David M. Halperin, "Why Is Diotima a Woman? Platonic *Erōs* and the Figuration of Gender," in *Before Sexuality: The Construction of Erotic Experience in the Ancient Greek World*, ed. Froma I. Zeitlin, John J. Winkler, and David M. Halperin (Princeton: Princeton University Press, 1990), 257–308; repr. in Halperin, *One Hundred Years of Homosexuality: And Other Essays on Greek Love* (New York: Routledge, 2012), 113–52. See also Hilda L. Smith and Bernice A. Carroll, eds., *Women's Political and Social Thought: An Anthology* (Bloomington: Indiana University Press, 2000), 13–19.

19. Rhodes, *Eros, Wisdom, and Silence*, 302.

20. Daniel Boyarin, "What Do We Talk about When We Talk about Platonic Love?," in *Toward a Theology of Eros: Transfiguring Passion at the Limits of Discipline*,

met her or how he knows her. The only thing he says of their general relationship is that she was "an expert on many subjects ... it was she who taught me the whole subject of love" (*Symp.* 201d). Socrates's speech, then, is essentially his rehearsing of the speech (or dialectical questioning) that Diotima presented to him. So how does Socrates enter into the mysteries of Eros?

Diotima's argument consists of many intricate steps, and we will not rehearse all of them here. There comes a turning point in the argument, however, when Diotima explains that every person is pregnant both in body and soul, and when one reaches a certain age in life one wishes to "give birth in beauty" (*Symp.* 206c).[21] The meaning of this obscure phrase is not only lost on the reader, it is lost on Socrates himself: "It would take divination [μαντεία] to tell me what you mean. I don't understand" (*Symp.* 206c). Thankfully, Diotima, who hails from Μαντινέη, can provide such μαντεία. Those who are pregnant in body are drawn to beautiful bodies and choose to remain in the lower mysteries of loving beautiful bodies, but those who are pregnant in soul are drawn to beautiful souls and are able to move up to the higher mysteries of loving beautiful souls (*Symp.* 209a).[22] This pathway toward understanding the mysteries of Eros is called "pedagogy" by Diotima (*Symp.* 210e). Yet Diotima doubts that Socrates would be able to attain the final and highest (τέλεα καὶ ἐποπτικά) mystery of Love—a reference to the climactic initiation rites of the Eleusinian mysteries.[23] She tells him, "I'm not sure if you have the capability ... you must try to follow if you can" (*Symp.* 210a).

In order to ascend the "ladder" of the mysteries of Eros, one must first love beautiful bodies and beget beautiful ideas there (*Symp.* 211c).[24] At this point Socrates can begin to understand what Diotima means by "giving

---

ed. Virginia Burrus and Catherine Keller (New York: Fordham University Press, 2006), 7. See also Halperin, *One Hundred Years*, 121.

21. On this phrase, see Frisbee C. C. Sheffield, *Plato's Symposium: The Ethics of Desire* (Oxford: Oxford University Press, 2009), 86–94.

22. See also the discussion in Belfiore, *Socrates' Daimonic Art*, 137–60.

23. On the various stages of initiation in the Eleusinian mysteries, including the Greater and Lesser Mysteries, see Kevin Clinton, "Stages of Initiation in the Eleusinian and Samothracian Mysteries," in *Greek Mysteries: The Archaeology of Ancient Greek Secret Cults*, ed. Michael B. Cosmopoulos (New York: Routledge, 2002), 50–78.

24. On Diotima's ladder and the ascent toward Beauty, see Kevin Corrigan and Elena Glazov-Corrigan, *Plato's Dialectic at Play: Argument, Structure, and Myth in the Symposium* (University Park: Pennsylvania State University Press, 2010), 107–235.

birth in beauty"—namely, begetting beautiful ideas into another beautiful body. Afterward, one must learn to love beautiful souls more than bodies to the point that bodily beauty no longer matters. Furthermore, one must learn to love the beauty of knowledge and wisdom. The final step comes when one is able to look past all the former, ultimately experiencing a great *epoptic* vision of Beauty itself, that is, the Form of Beauty.[25] When one gains access to the *epoptic* vision of Beauty, that transformative view of reality allows one to cultivate true virtue in the way one cares for oneself and for others, which Socrates so aptly embodies in the speech of Alcibiades (*Symp.* 219c).

To pass through these stages, however, one must have a guide into the mysteries—a mystagogue. "The correct way for him to go, or be led by another, to the things of love, is to begin from the beautiful things in this world, and using these as steps, to climb ever upwards for the sake of that other beauty" (*Symp.* 210a–211e). In this speech, Diotima has served as Socrates's leader and mystery initiator.[26] Moreover, by rehearsing the speech of Diotima to the dinner guests, Socrates himself has become a mystagogue for the dinner guests. Socrates has begun the process of birthing beautiful ideas into beautiful bodies, especially Agathon, who is represented as young and beautiful.[27] He has directed the uninitiated into the mysteries of Eros. At the climax of the Eleusinian mysteries, light would flood into the dark sanctuary and a mysterious object would be exalted for all initiates to behold.[28] In the mystery initiation of Socrates's pupils, the speech of Alcibiades provides the climax. However, in this final speech, the encomium is no longer offered in praise of Eros, but in praise of the mystagogue of Eros, Socrates himself. Alcibiades states at the introduction and at the conclusion of his speech that he is giving a "praise of Socrates" (*Symp.* 215B; 222B). As he draws his speech to a close,

---

25. On ancient Greek philosophy as an *epoptic* experience, see Barbara Sattler, "The Eleusinian Mysteries in Pre-Platonic Thought: Metaphor, Practice and Imagery for Plato's Symposium," in *Philosophy and Greek Religion*, ed. Vishwa Adluri (Berlin: de Gruyter, 2013), 151–90.

26. On Diotima as mystagogue, see Nancy Evans, "Diotima and Demeter as Mystagogues in Plato's *Symposium*," *Hypatia* 21 (2006): 1–27; Schefer, "Rhetoric," 175–96.

27. Rhodes, *Eros, Wisdom, and Silence*, 317.

28. See also Plutarch, *Them.* 15; *De Perfectu in Virtute* 81d–e. See Mylonas, *Eleusis*, 243–85; N. J. Richardson, *The Homeric Hymn to Demeter* (Oxford: Clarendon, 1974), 26; Bremmer, *Initiation*, 33.

Alcibiades remarks that Socrates's philosophical arguments are "godlike" and are essential for anyone who wishes to become good (*Symp.* 222a).

In contrast to the paideia of Athens, Platonic paideia, as embodied by Socrates, is the true path to virtue and goodness.[29] Socrates is set apart from the other "teachers" at the party through the use of "mystery" language and imagery. Socrates, as mystagogue, guides the guests and the reader along the mysterious, esoteric path toward the *epoptic* vision of Beauty. He is, as Diotima taught him, implanting his mystic knowledge into beautiful souls. Thus, the concept of "mystery" is employed by Plato for several reasons: (1) it helps to establish Plato's alternative vision of paideia, which is inaccessible to outsiders; (2) it distinguishes Socrates as a mystagogue, one through whom initiates must pass in order to reach the completion of paideia; and (3) it illustrates the fact that paideia is a slow, step-by-step process that cannot be achieved quickly or easily. Plato's paideia is "godlike" and illuminating, as is the mystagogue Socrates. When the dinner party reaches its end and all the guests drift off to sleep, Socrates alone avoids the allurement of sleep. As the fully initiated mystagogue, Socrates is the only one who is truly awake.

Paideia and Mystery in 4QInstruction

The impartation of mysterious knowledge is a key theme in several texts from Qumran, especially 4QInstruction.[30] The author of 4QInstruction attempts to guide the readers to a greater comprehension of the secret knowledge of God by instructing them to both behold and ponder what has been given through special revelation. He writes, "You, under[stan]

---

29. John J. Cleary, "Erotic Paideia in Plato's *Symposium*," in *Studies on Plato, Aristotle and Proclus: The Collected Essays on Ancient Philosophy of John Cleary*, ed. John Dillon, Brendan O'Byrne, and Fran O'Rourke (Leiden: Brill, 2013), 53–72.

30. Although 4QInstruction appears to have been quite popular among members of the Qumran sect given the number of manuscripts of this text found there, it was most likely not written by the Qumran community, but was written at an earlier date. The authors of both the Community Rule and the Hodayot used 4QInstruction as a source for their compositions. Additionally, 4QInstruction presupposes a different *Sitz im Leben* and lacks many of the sectarian themes that are prominent in texts written at Qumran. See Matthew J. Goff, *The Worldly and Heavenly Wisdom of 4QInstruction*, STDJ 50 (Leiden: Brill, 2003), 228–32. Conceptions of "mystery" also loom large in other Qumran documents such as Mysteries and the Treatise on the Two Spirits (1QS III, 13–IV, 26).

ding one ... the wond[ro]us mysteries [of the God of awesome deeds you shall understand] ... and gaze [upon the mystery that is to be and the deeds of] old, at what exists and what [has existed, upon what will be]" (4Q417 1 I, 1–4).³¹ The phrase "wondrous mysteries" (רזי פלא) seems to refer to revealed knowledge of God's power and glory demonstrated through his mighty deeds.³² Elsewhere in the Qumran texts the "wondrous mysteries" are said to be revealed to the leaders of the community so that they can teach them to the other members of the group.³³ For example, in the Hodayot the speaker proclaims, "You have set me like a banner for the elect of justice, like a knowledgeable mediator of wondrous mysteries" (רזי פלא; 1QH V, 8). These "mediators of mysteries" guide other members of the community into a deeper understanding of God's hidden teachings. The addressee is called "understanding one" (*mevin*) because he is one of the elect of God and has been a recipient of God's supernatural revelation; he is on the inside. The esoteric knowledge of the mysteries of God has also been taught to the community of "understanding ones," and they are expected to have the ability to discern the meaning of such mysteries.³⁴ The leaders of the community, then, were meant to serve as guides into the mysteries of God's awesome deeds. Likewise, the author of 4QInstruction situated himself as an authoritative teacher of mysteries for the *mevin*.

Not only is the *mevin* guided into the revealed knowledge of God's previous actions, but he is exhorted to gaze upon the רז נהיה (*raz nihyeh*), "the mystery that is to be." This phrase has been notoriously difficult to translate, and there are a variety of renderings from which to choose.³⁵

---

31. Translation from Matthew J. Goff, *4QInstruction*, WLAW 2 (Atlanta: Society of Biblical Literature, 2013), 138; all subsequent references to 4QInstruction are taken from Goff's translation.

32. Eibert J. C. Tigchelaar, *To Increase Learning for the Understanding Ones: Reading and Reconstructing the Fragmentary Early Jewish Sapiential Text 4QInstruction*, STDJ 44 (Leiden: Brill, 2001), 204; Matthew J. Goff, *Discerning Wisdom: The Sapiential Literature of the Dead Sea Scrolls*, VTSup 116 (Leiden: Brill, 2007), 142.

33. Goff, *Worldly and Heavenly Wisdom*, 36.

34. Goff, *4QInstruction*, 10.

35. See the discussion in Samuel Thomas, *The "Mysteries" of Qumran: Mystery, Secrecy, and Esotericism in the Dead Sea Scrolls*, EJL 25 (Atlanta: Society of Biblical Literature, 2009), 150–60. A small sample of the various translations include "the mystery that is to come," "the mystery of existence," and "the approaching mystery." See John Strugnell et al., eds., *Qumran Cave 4.XXIV: Sapiential Texts; 4QInstruction (Mûsār Lĕ Mēbîn): 4Q415ff.*, part 2, DJD 34 (Oxford: Clarendon, 1999); Florentino

Karina Martin Hogan advises, "The ambiguous part of the phrase is נהיה (*nihyeh*), a Niphal participle of the verb 'to be,' which often has a future sense in the Qumran scrolls and other texts of the Second Temple period, although it can also refer to 'the totality of the temporal order.' In 4QInstruction, not all of the uses of *raz nihyeh* refer to the future."[36] Therefore, the translation of John Collins, Matthew Goff, Karina Martin Hogan, and Samuel Thomas ("the mystery that is to be") is preferable since it captures both the present and future sense of the phrase.[37] From the immediate context, the mystery that is to be includes an understanding of the entire time span of history. The reader is told to consider "what exists and what [has existed, upon what *will be*]" (4Q417 1 I, 1–4, emphasis added). His ponderings are to include what happened in the past, what is happening in the present (his present), and what will come in the future. By contemplating the history of existence—past, present, and future—the reader should be able to decipher its meaning and apply it to his own life. The *raz nihyeh*, then, refers to the totality of God's predetermined purposes for creation and humanity. Collins argues that the *raz nihyeh* "seems to encompass the entire divine plan, from creation to eschatological judgment."[38] Through the powerful wisdom of the mystery that is to be, the reader is expected to understand his place within God's plan for the world.

One comes to recognize the *raz nihyeh* not only by supernatural revelation and by the guidance of a teacher of mysteries, but also by constant study, meditation, and visual perception. Goff notes that the mystery that is to be "signifies a comprehensive divine scheme that orchestrates the cosmos."[39] He also observes that knowledge of this extraordinary plan of God "can be ascertained through the study of supernatural revelation." The *mevin* is told to "gaze [נבט] upon the mystery that is to be" (4Q417 1 I, 3). Goff writes, "In rabbinic Hebrew נבט can refer to having a vision. This suggests that gazing upon the mystery that is to be might have been

---

García Martínez and Eibert J. C. Tigchelaar, *The Dead Sea Scrolls Study Edition*, 2 vols. (Leiden: Brill; Grand Rapids: Eerdmans, 1997–1998), 2:858; Geza Vermes, *The Complete Dead Sea Scrolls in English* (London: Penguin Books, 2004), 432.

36. Karina Martin Hogan, *Theologies in Conflict in 4 Ezra: Wisdom, Debate, and Apocalyptic Solution*, JSJSup 130 (Leiden: Brill, 2008), 49.

37. Ibid., 49; Goff, *Worldly and Heavenly Wisdom*, 34; John J. Collins, *Jewish Wisdom in the Hellenistic Age*, OTL (Louisville: Westminster John Knox, 1997), 122.

38. Collins, *Jewish Wisdom*, 122.

39. Goff, *4QInstruction*, 15.

a type of visionary experience."⁴⁰ Collins proposes that both the "vision of meditation" (חזון ההגו)⁴¹ in 4Q417 1 I, 16 and the repeated exhortations to "gaze upon the mystery that is to be" suggest "an absorption of a prophetic form, the vision, in the genre of wisdom instruction."⁴² Unfortunately there are no descriptions in the text explaining how such a vision might have taken place, whether by dreams, or angelic messengers, or heavenly journeys. Indeed, it seems that the revelation of the mystery that is to be has already happened sometime in the past.⁴³ For example, in this same passage the writer says that in the past God fashioned the world by means of the mystery that is to be (4Q417 1 I, 9). In the past, God laid out for "their" understanding every deed so that a person may walk in the inclination of intelligence (4Q417 1 I, 11). In the past, God "spread out" some type of revelation for Adam, though a lacuna in the text prevents us from knowing precisely what that was. In the past, God made known the secrets of his plan with a precision of intelligence. The *mevin* has already experienced the unveiling of God's hidden, divine knowledge. However, by continually gazing upon the supernatural revelation of the mystery that is to be he can, in the present, comprehend the secrets of God's plans, including the eschatological judgment of the wicked and the vindication of the righteous.⁴⁴

The disclosure of the *raz nihyeh* to the community of *mevinim* effectively sets them apart from the rest of humanity, and forms the basis for a type of esoteric paideia. The esoteric nature of the instruction for the

---

40. Goff, *Worldly and Heavenly Wisdom*, 38.

41. This represents Goff's reconstruction of the phrase. Others have reconstructed it as (חזון ההגי). See Florentino García Martínez and Eibert J. C. Tigchelaar, eds., *The Dead Sea Scrolls Study Edition*, 2 vols. (Leiden: Brill; Grand Rapids: Eerdmans, 1997–1998), 2:858. On the "vision of meditation," see Goff, *Worldly and Heavenly Wisdom*, 83–120; Cana Werman, "What Is the *Book of Hagu*?," in *Sapiential Perspectives: Wisdom Literature in Light of the Dead Sea Scrolls; Proceedings of the Sixth International Symposium of the Orion Center for the Study of the Dead Sea Scrolls and Associated Literature, 20–22 May, 2001*, ed. John J. Collins, Gregory Sterling, and Ruth Clements, STDJ 51 (Leiden: Brill, 2004), 125–40.

42. Collins, *Jewish Wisdom*, 125.

43. Matthew J. Goff, "Wisdom, Apocalypticism, and the Pedagogical Ethos of 4QInstruction," in *Conflicted Boundaries in Wisdom and Apocalypticism*, ed. Lawrence M. Wills and Benjamin G. Wright, SymS 35 (Atlanta: Society of Biblical Literature, 2005), 64.

44. John Kampen, *Wisdom Literature*, ECDSS (Grand Rapids: Eerdmans, 2011), 50.

mevinim has been noticed already by Goff: 4QInstruction "diverges from Ben Sira in its assertion that esoteric, supernatural revelation should be studied."[45] Moreover, Collins argues that 4QInstruction is meant for a specialized, "initiated" audience: "The importance attached to this education is entailed by the importance of 'the mystery that is to be.' It also suggests that this document is not addressed to Jewish society at large, but to those who share an understanding of this mystery and therefore have been initiated into some kind of movement, whatever its relationship to the settlement at Qumran."[46]

That instruction in Jewish wisdom could be thought of as paideia should be clear from the LXX, where the term παιδεία occurs one hundred ten times.[47] The term figures prominently in the LXX version of Proverbs, where it often occurs in the context of receiving instruction and discipline (e.g., Prov 24:32). Duane Garret has argued that Proverbs is "a book of education. It is the textbook of Israelite paideia."[48] Similarly, Leo Perdue defines paideia in Proverbs as "education that includes both a course of study embodied in 'teachings' or 'instructions' and the moral formation of character."[49] Both of these elements—instruction and character formation—are present in 4QInstruction.[50] Furthermore, it appears that the teacher in 4QInstruction wishes to set up his own form of esoteric paideia as an alternative to the wisdom of other competing pedagogical systems—namely, those of the wicked. Throughout the work, the "spiritual" people of the elect are contrasted with the "fleshly spirit" of the wicked.[51] The

---

45. Goff, *4QInstruction*, 279.
46. Collins, *Jewish Wisdom*, 120.
47. See also the essay by Karina Martin Hogan in this volume.
48. Duane Garrett, *Proverbs, Ecclesiastes, Song of Solomon* (Nashville: Broadman, 1993), 57. On ancient Israelite education, see James L. Crenshaw, "Education in Ancient Israel," *JBL* 104 (1985): 601–15; André Lemaire, "Education," *ABD* 2:301–12. See also James L. Crenshaw, *Education in Ancient Israel: Across the Deadening Silence*, ABRL (New York: Doubleday, 1998); Wendy L. Widder, *"To Teach" in Ancient Israel: A Cognitive Linguistic Study of a Biblical Hebrew Lexical Set*, BZAW 456 (Berlin: de Gruyter, 2014).
49. Leo G. Perdue, *Proverbs*, IBC (Louisville: Westminster John Knox, 2000), 9.
50. Goff, *4QInstruction*, 10, 152.
51. E.g., 4Q418 81 1–5. See also Matthew J. Goff, "Being Fleshly or Spiritual: Anthropological Reflection and Exegesis of Genesis 1–3 in 4QInstruction and First Corinthians," in *Christian Body, Christian Self: Concepts of Early Christian Personhood*, ed. Clare K. Rothschild and Trevor W. Thompson, WUNT 284 (Tübingen: Mohr

mevin is to "separate" himself from the actions and teachings of the fleshly spirit in order to withstand the final judgment of God and gain the inheritance of the angels (4Q418 81 1–2). In order to do this, he must study the *raz nihyeh* and "improve greatly in understanding and from all your teachers get ever more learning" (4Q418 81 17). The teachers of the elect community, as opposed to the teachers of the non-elect, provide instruction in the mysteries of God's plan for the righteous and the unrighteous. The community of the *mevinim*, then, has access to both supernatural revelation and to instructors of alternative paideia, which distinguishes them from the society in which they live.

The pedagogical nature of the *raz nihyeh* also aids the community in understanding the mundane aspects of life and in living a virtuous life. When a person studies the mystery that is to be, he can develop the ability to "examine closely all the ways of truth and discern all the roots of injustice" in the world (4Q416 2 III, 14). With this knowledge one can then learn to treat others with respect: "then you will know what is bitter to a man and what is sweet for a person" (4Q416 2 III, 15). The *raz nihyeh* teaches a person how to honor their parents, as well as how to live in harmony with one's wife: "Honor your father in your poverty and your mother in your lowly state.... When you marry, walk together with the help of your flesh" (4Q416 2 III, 15–16, 21). The mystery that is to be illuminates the quotidian affairs of the *mevin*, thereby allowing him to cultivate correct action toward other people and toward God. Thus Goff comments, "The 'mystery' has pedagogical potential because of its association with the created order."[52] Concerning 4QInstruction and the created order, John Kampen writes, "within *Instruction* the reader or adherent can only expect to understand the future as one understands the creation and its purposes as well as the development of history and direction."[53] Similarly, Lawrence Schiffman remarks, "*raz* refers to the mysteries of creation, that is, the natural order of things, and to the mysteries of the divine role in the historical processes."[54] Meditating upon the *raz nihyeh* allows one, with

---

Siebeck, 2011), 41–60; Eibert J. C. Tigchelaar, "'Spiritual People,' 'Fleshly Spirit,' and 'Vision of Meditation': Reflections on *4QInstruction* and 1 Corinthians," in *Echoes from the Caves: Qumran and the New Testament*, ed. Florentino García Martínez, STDJ 85 (Leiden: Brill, 2009), 103–18.

52. Goff, *4QInstruction*, 15.
53. Kampen, *Wisdom Literature*, 47.
54. Lawrence H. Schiffman, *Reclaiming the Dead Sea Scrolls: The History of Juda-*

proper training, to interpret correctly the visible creation, which leads to a greater understanding of God's eschatological intentions: "The future unfolds as one begins to understand the natural world and the course of human history, which itself is developing in light of an inevitable future."[55] On the other hand, the author of 4QInstruction wants to make clear that gazing upon the supernatural revelation of the *raz nihyeh* is to be preferred over meditation on the patterns of normal human life. For example, 4Q417 1 I, 27 asserts that a person should not rely on his own heart and eyes in order to gain wisdom, but should seek after the *raz nihyeh*.[56] This stands in contrast to the sapiential trajectory of Proverbs and Ben Sira, in which wisdom is not a mysterious, revealed knowledge, but is garnered through study of the natural, created order. "The role of revelation in obtaining knowledge is a trope alien to the traditional wisdom of Proverbs but consistent with the apocalyptic tradition."[57] Thus, for 4QInstruction, the impartation of the mysteries of God comes through special revelation, through the mature teachers within the community, and through gazing upon and studying the marvelous *raz nihyeh*. The "mystery" in this text functions to set apart the community from the "fleshly spirit" of the non-elect, and to distinguish the teachers within the community as those who understand the "mystery" of God's operation in the world.

Paideia and Mystery in 1 Corinthians

The source(s) of Paul's "mystery terminology"[58] have been both widely recognized and widely debated among Pauline scholars. Positions range from a complete denial that Paul's language had anything to do with Greek mysteries to an attempt to argue that Paul's religion was itself a full-blown

---

ism, the Background of Christianity, the Lost Library of Qumran (New York: Doubleday, 1995), 206.

55. Kampen, *Wisdom*, 48.
56. See Goff, *4QInstruction*, 27.
57. Goff, "Wisdom, Apocalypticism, and the Pedagogical Ethos," 65.
58. On the terminology associated with mystery cults see, Christoph Riedweg, *Mysterienterminologie bei Platon, Philo, und Klemens von Alexandria*, UALG 26 (Berlin: de Gruyter, 1987). On the uses of the term "mystery" in Semitic texts, see Raymond E. Brown, *The Semitic Background of the Term "Mystery" in the New Testament* (Philadelphia: Fortress, 1968); Thomas, *"Mysteries" of Qumran*; Benjamin L. Gladd, *Revealing the* Mysterion: *The Use of Mystery in Daniel and Second Temple Judaism with Its Bearing on First Corinthians*, BZAW 160 (Berlin: de Gruyter, 2008).

Greco-Roman mystery cult. Additionally, there are numerous mediating positions between the two extremes.[59] The purpose of this paper is not to endeavor to solve this problem, but to discover how Paul's use of "mystery" aids him as a teacher of the Corinthian assembly.

The context of 1 Cor 1–4 indicates that after Paul left Corinth, a number of factions arose within the community of believers, in which disparate groups allied themselves with various leaders who had been teachers of the Corinthians.[60] Paul describes the situation: "It has been reported to me by Chloe's people that there are quarrels among you, my brothers and sisters. What I mean is that each of you says, 'I belong to Paul,' or 'I belong to Apollos,' or 'I belong to Cephas,' or 'I belong to Christ'" (1 Cor 1:11–12).[61] Paul is dismayed, "Has Christ been divided? Was Paul crucified for you? Or were you baptized in the name of Paul?" (1 Cor 1:13). Paul thus wrote to the Corinthians to attempt to bring about concord among the factions, using several techniques from the genre of *homonoia* speeches.[62] Scholars have often speculated concerning the exact nature of the four factions of 1 Cor 1:12 and have assumed that since Paul lists four names, there

---

59. The two ends of the spectrum regarding the issue of the influence of mystery cults on the earliest Christians are found in Alfred Loisy, *Les mystères païens et le mystère chrétien* (Paris: Nourry, 1930), who argues for mystery cult influence; and Carl Clemen, *Die Einfluss der Mysterienreligionen auf das älteste Christentum*, RVV 13.1 (Giessen: Töpelmann, 1913), who argues against mystery cult influence. Clemen quotes C. F. Georg Heinrici as saying "Christianity was more of an anti-mystery religion than a mystery religion." See also Samuel Angus, *The Religious Quests of the Greco-Roman World* (New York: Scribner's Sons, 1929), 84. On the debates over mystery cult influence on Christianity, see Richard Reitzenstein, *Die hellenistischen Mysterienreligionen* (Leipzig: Teubner, 1920); Jonathan Z. Smith, *Drudgery Divine: On the Comparison of Early Christianities and the Religions of Late Antiquity* (Chicago: University of Chicago Press, 1994), 62–84; A. D. Nock, *Early Gentile Christianity and Its Hellenistic Background* (New York: Harper and Row, 1964); A. J. M. Wedderburn, *Baptism and Resurrection: Studies in Pauline Theology against Its Graeco-Roman Background*, WUNT 44 (Tübingen: Mohr Siebeck, 1987).

60. L. L. Welborn, *Politics and Rhetoric in the Corinthian Epistles* (Macon, GA: Mercer University Press, 1997), 1–42.

61. All biblical quotations are taken from the NRSV.

62. Margaret M. Mitchell, *Paul and the Rhetoric of Reconciliation: An Exegetical Investigation of the Language and Composition of 1 Corinthians* (Louisville: Westminster John Knox, 1991), 20–64; Dale B. Martin, *The Corinthian Body* (New Haven: Yale University Press, 1999), 38–58.

must be four literal "parties" within the Corinthian assembly.[63] However, as Johannes Weiss and many others have noted, it is a mistake to insist on four factions at Corinth.[64] In fact, when Paul mentions the "slogans" of the factions again in 1 Cor 3:4, there are only two groups: "For when one says, 'I belong to Paul,' and another, 'I belong to Apollos,' are you not merely human? What then is Apollos? What is Paul?" Moreover, the real issue that defines the conflicting groups at Corinth is one of status—the strong versus the weak, the higher status members versus the lower status members—as Gerd Theissen, L. L. Welborn, and Dale Martin have aptly argued.[65] It is in this context that Paul employs the language of "mystery" as an educational tool to bring about unity between the "strong" and the "weak" at Corinth.

As a teacher of mysteries, Paul first establishes himself as an authoritative instructor. Following the greeting and acknowledgment of the divisions within the assembly (1 Cor 1:1–17), Paul immediately sets out to disarm those who seek after the values and norms of traditional Greco-Roman society—"worldly" wisdom, power, prestige, nobility, status. He states that God has destroyed the wisdom of the wise and has brought to nothing the discernment of the discerning (1 Cor 1:19). God has utterly confounded the Jews who seek after a sign and the Greeks who seek after wisdom (1 Cor 1:22). "Paul first cuts everyone down to size, perhaps even some of those 'of Paul,' by reminding them that the wisdom which really counts, God's wisdom, Christ-crucified, is the exact opposite of that praised in this world, and is, in fact, 'foolishness,' when measured by those standards."[66] The dichotomies that Paul sets up in this section of the letter are striking: power versus foolishness (1 Cor 1:18), perishing versus being saved (1 Cor 1:18), wisdom of the world versus wisdom of God (1 Cor 1:20–21), this age versus the (implied) age to come (1 Cor 1:20), human wisdom and power versus God's wisdom and power (1 Cor 1:25), wise versus foolish (1 Cor 1:27), strong versus weak (1 Cor 1:27), noble versus lowly and despised (1 Cor 1:28). In this way, Paul envisions "two opposing realms of

---

63. See the discussion in James D. G. Dunn, *1 Corinthians* (Sheffield: Sheffield Academic, 1997), 27–45.

64. Johannes Weiss, *Earliest Christianity*, 2 vols. (New York: Harper, 1959), 1:340.

65. Gerd Theissen, *The Social Setting of Pauline Christianity* (Philadelphia: Fortress, 1982); Welborn, *Politics and Rhetoric*, 1–42; Martin, *The Corinthian Body*, 37–68.

66. Mark D. Given, *Paul's True Rhetoric: Ambiguity, Cunning, and Deception in Greece and Rome* (Harrisburg: Trinity Press International, 2001), 95.

reality," each with their own values and status systems.[67] The conceptual framework of this worldview draws heavily on language and themes that are widespread within Jewish apocalyptic literature, especially the notion of role reversal within God's eschatological economy.[68] By arguing for the superiority of the foolish message of the cross, Paul effects a role reversal of his own—one who is an amateur (ἰδιώτης) in rhetoric (2 Cor 11:6) stands toe to toe with the "debater of this age" and overpowers him.[69] Paul, who is "called" to be an apostle of Christ Jesus (1 Cor 1:1) identifies himself with those who are "called" (1 Cor 1:24) to proclaim the power and wisdom of God in Christ crucified. Paul, therefore, presents himself as an authoritative teacher of the powerful wisdom he finds in the message of the cross.

Stanley Stowers finds Pierre Bourdieu's sociological theory helpful in explaining how the Corinthians came to see Paul as an authority figure. Stowers argues, using the language of Bourdieu, that the social matrix in which Paul and the Corinthians operated can be viewed as a "field" in which religious specialists competed with one another and with the dominant legitimized tradition of Greek paideia.[70] In this setting, one may view Paul as a "producer and distributor of an alternative esoteric paideia different from the dominant sophistic or philosophical kinds, yet still recognizable as a form of the same broader genre of specialized literate learning."[71] Paul's esoteric paideia, which would include a disclosure of the mysteries of God, may have found favor with many in the Corinthian *ekklēsia* who felt alienated from the dominant form of traditional Greek paideia present in their culture.[72] Given the fact that Paul writes "not many of you were wise by human standards, not many were powerful, not many were of noble birth" (1 Cor 1:26), it is reasonable to assume that the majority of the Corinthians belong to the lower status ranks of society.[73] Thus, Paul's message of an apocalyptic role reversal in which the

---

67. Martin, *Corinthian Body*, 59.

68. John J. Collins, *The Apocalyptic Imagination: An Introduction to Jewish Apocalyptic Literature* (Grand Rapids: Eerdmans, 1998), 1–42.

69. See the discussion in Frank J. Matera, *II Corinthians: A Commentary* (Louisville: Westminster John Knox, 2003), 247–50.

70. Stanley K. Stowers, "Kinds of Myth, Meals, and Power: Paul and the Corinthians," in *Redescribing Paul and the Corinthians*, ed. Ron Cameron and Merrill P. Miller, ECL 5 (Atlanta: Society of Biblical Literature, 2011), 105–50, here 114.

71. Ibid., 117.

72. Ibid., 116.

73. We should assume, however, that at least a few *did* belong to higher status

weak are exalted over the powerful would have resonated with many of the Corinthians. Indeed, many would have welcomed Paul's alternative model of paideia, which proclaimed that the mysteries of the cosmos have been hidden from the "rulers of this age" and revealed to the "nothings and nobodies" (1 Cor 1:28).

When Paul announced the logos of the cross in Corinth, he did not come "proclaiming the mystery of God to you in lofty words or wisdom" (1 Cor 2:1).[74] In 1 Cor 1:22, Paul insists that he intends to correct the misguided expectations of both "Jews who ask for signs, and Greeks who seek wisdom." Thus, in 1 Cor 2:1 and 2:7, he employs the term μυστήριον ("mystery"), which had a rich history in the literature of both Jews and Greeks.[75] For Greeks, Paul's use of μυστήριον would have called to mind the mystery cults, which were prevalent in the Greco-Roman world of the first century.[76] For example, the mysteries of Cybele, the Great Mother goddess of Anatolia, were formally accepted into the state religion of

---

ranks. On this point see Theissen, *The Social Setting of Pauline Christianity*, 72; Wayne A. Meeks, *The First Urban Christians: The Social World of the Apostle Paul* (New Haven: Yale University Press, 1983), 52–53.

74. μυστήριον is a variant reading in 1 Cor 2:1. An alternate reading μαρτύριον is also extant. Hans Conzelmann comments that it is "impossible to decide" which is the correct reading, but notes that μυστήριον is supported by Lietzmann and Bornkamm for reasons of content. See Hans Conzelmann, *1 Corinthians: A Commentary on the First Epistle to the Corinthians*, Hermeneia (Philadelphia: Fortress, 1975), 53. The reading μυστήριον is chosen by NA[28]. Both the external and internal evidence point toward the more difficult reading of μυστήριον. See the discussion in Gladd, *Revealing the Mysterion*, 123–26. See also Bruce M. Metzger, *A Textual Commentary on the Greek New Testament* (New York: United Bible Societies, 1971), 545.

75. Paul uses μυστήριον eight times in the undisputed letters: Rom 11:25; 16:25; 1 Cor 2:1; 2:7; 4:1; 13:2; 14:2; 15:51. On the history of the term and its various uses, see the discussion in Günther Bornkamm, "μυστήριον," *TDNT* 4:802–28.

76. For a general overview of the mystery cults, see Walter Burkert, *Ancient Mystery Cults* (Cambridge: Harvard University Press, 1987); Hans-Josef Klauck, *The Religious Context of Early Christianity: A Guide to Graeco-Roman Religions* (Edinburgh: T&T Clark, 2000); Hugh Bowden, *Mystery Cults of the Ancient World* (Princeton: Princeton University Press, 2010); Marvin Meyer, *The Ancient Mysteries: A Sourcebook* (Philadelphia: University of Pennsylvania Press, 1999); Richard Reitzenstein, *Hellenistic Mystery-Religions: Their Basic Ideas and Significance* (Eugene: Pickwick, 1978); Fritz Graf, "Mysteries," *BNP* 9:443–44; Richard L. Gordon, "Mysteries," *OCD*, 1017. For an extensive bibliography on the mystery cults, see Bruce M. Metzger, *A Classified Bibliography of the Graeco-Roman Mystery Religions 1924–1973: With a Supplement 1974–1977* (Berlin: de Gruyter, 1984).

Rome in 204 BCE and quickly found popularity among the Romans (Livy, *Ab urbe cond.* 29.10–14).⁷⁷ In the first century CE, "the Roman emperors increasingly favored her worship, beginning with Claudius, who opened the way for increased attention to be paid to the *Magna Mater* and now to [her consort] Attis also."⁷⁸ Similarly, the mysteries of the Egyptian goddess Isis were ubiquitous throughout Greece and Rome during the Hellenistic period. Diodorus, writing in the first century BCE, states, "The whole inhabited world bears testimony to her [Isis] and offers her honors because of her self-disclosures through healing" (*Bib. hist.* 1.25.4). Likewise, Plutarch, in his *Isis and Osiris*, writes, "As for Isis, and the gods associated with her, all peoples own them and are familiar with them" (*Is. Os.* 377D). These mystery cults, then, had a wide-ranging appeal. There are a multitude of reasons that a person might wish to be initiated into a mystery cult: to experience an extraordinary and personal encounter with the divine, to gain social prestige, to transcend the mundane aspects of daily life, to experience healing, to garner the aid and protection of the god/goddess, to gain prosperity in this life, and (for some mysteries) to receive a promise of blessing in the afterlife.⁷⁹ In light of their widespread acceptance and influence in antiquity, Dale Martin argues, "Paul's reference to the 'mystery' of Christ would have had a certain kind of resonance for any Greek speaker, evoking the mystery cults that were so important in Greek culture and were simply taken for granted as an ancient and important element in the Mediterranean city."⁸⁰

Yet, the pagans were not the only ones interested in μυστήριον. The literature of Jews in the Second Temple period was also full of references to "mystery." Raymond Brown has outlined three different ways "mystery" was used in Jewish apocalyptic texts like 1 Enoch, much of which dates to the second and third centuries BCE.⁸¹ Brown recognizes three distinct uses: (1) evil mysteries of sorcery, idolatry, war, and seduction, which were

---

77. See also Meyer, *Ancient Mysteries*, 120; Burkert, *Ancient Mystery Cults*, 6.
78. Meyer, *Ancient Mysteries*, 114.
79. Klauck, *Religious Context*, 103–17; Burkert, *Ancient Mystery Cults*, 12–29.
80. Martin, *Corinthian Body*, 57.
81. Brown, *Semitic Background*, 12–19. The Ethiopic text uses the words *meštir* and *xabu'* to translate the Greek μυστήριον. See George W. E. Nickelsburg, *1 Enoch 1: A Commentary on the Book of 1 Enoch*, Hermeneia (Minneapolis: Fortress, 2001), 170, 533; Chrys C. Caragounis, *The Son of Man: Vision and Interpretation*, WUNT 38 (Tübingen: Mohr Siebeck, 1986), 106.

taught to humans by the rebellious angels; (2) cosmic mysteries pertaining to heavenly luminaries and storms; and (3) mysteries of God's will for humans and angels, especially regarding the eschatological judgment. In the Septuagint, μυστήριον is used in Judith, Tobit, 2 Maccabees, Wisdom of Solomon, Sirach, and Daniel.[82] The word is used in the sense of "keeping a secret" (for a king or a friend) in Judith, Tobit, 2 Maccabees, and Sirach.[83] The Wisdom of Solomon uses μυστήριον to describe ungodly idolaters who participate in "secret rites" (μυστήρια) and "initiations" (τελετάς; Wis 14:15, 23),[84] and makes reference to the "mysteries of God" (μυστήρια θεοῦ) concerning God's plans for the exaltation of the righteous and the destruction of the wicked (Wis 2:22). The text of Daniel in the Septuagint employs μυστήριον to translate the Aramaic raz, which in Daniel refers to the mystery of a dream and the mystery of its interpretation (Dan 2:18–47).[85] Daniel tells the king "there is a God in heaven who reveals mysteries (μυστήρια), and he has disclosed to King Nebuchadnezzar what will happen at the end of days" (ἐσχάτων τῶν ἡμερῶν; Dan 2:28). Daniel's interpretation of the dream outlines a series of earthly kingdoms that will eventually fall. Then, in the "final days," God will establish an everlasting kingdom that will crush all other earthly kingdoms (Dan 2:44–45). Thus, in Daniel μυστήριον can describe the eschatological plans of God to destroy the rulers of the kingdoms of earth, thereby establishing God's eternal rule and reign.[86] Both Philo and the Qumran texts utilize various conceptions of "mystery," some of which we have seen in our previous discussion of 4QInstruction.[87]

---

82. Jdt 2:2; Tob 12:7–11; 2 Macc 13:21; Wis 2:22; 6:22; 14:15–23; Sir 22:22; 27:16–21; Dan 2:18–47.

83. Brown, *Semitic Background*, 6–12; Bornkamm, "μυστήριον," 4:813–17.

84. This is almost certainly a reference to the mystery cults. See Bornkamm, "μυστήριον," 4:814; Klauck, *Religious Context*, 84.

85. Brown, *Semitic Background*, 7.

86. John J. Collins, *Daniel: A Commentary on the Book of Daniel*, Hermeneia (Minneapolis: Fortress, 1993), 175; Bornkamm, "μυστήριον," 4:814; Brown, *Semitic Background*, 8.

87. Marcus N. A. Bockmuehl, *Revelation and Mystery in Ancient Judaism and Pauline Christianity*, WUNT 2/36 (Tübingen: Mohr Siebeck, 1990); Gladd, *Revealing the* Mysterion, 51–84; Brown, *Semitic Background*, 22–30; Goff, *Discerning Wisdom*, 1–103. On Philo's use of μυστήριον and related terms, see Peter Schäfer, *The Origins of Jewish Mysticism* (Princeton: Princeton University Press, 2011), 154–74; Gladd, *Revealing the* Mysterion, 99–101; John J. Collins, *Between Athens and Jerusalem:*

Paul's use of μυστήριον, then, would have a multiplicity of connotations for both Jews and Greeks. Dale Martin argues, "for Paul the apocalypticist, 'mystery' refers to the apocalyptic narrative in which the expected revelation of the heavenly Christ will overturn the structures of the world."[88] In fact, Paul praises the Corinthians for "waiting for the revealing [ἀποκάλυψις] of our Lord Jesus Christ" (1 Cor 1:7). At the time of the future apocalypse of Jesus, Paul insists that the rulers of this age will be "doomed to perish" (1 Cor 2:6). Some of the Corinthians would have understood Paul's proclamation of the "mysteries of God" to include apocalyptic themes such as the judgment of the ungodly and the exaltation of the righteous. Yet Paul also denigrates the "worldly" wisdom and rhetorical sophistication of the Greek tradition.[89] Paul's use of μυστήριον in the context of criticizing certain aspects of Greek rhetorical training would have been immediately recognized by those who were familiar with the literature of classical rhetoric. For example, in Plato's *Phaedrus*, Socrates and Phaedrus discuss, among other topics, the "art of rhetoric" (*Phaedr.* 261b). In this dialogue, the man who comes to the most complete understanding of rhetoric and philosophy is like one who has been initiated into the great mysteries.[90] Additionally, as has been noted above, in *Symposium* the ultimate goal of Socrates's rhetoric is to lead his pupils toward a magnificent *epoptic* vision, likened to the climax of the Eleusinian mystery initiation ritual (*Symp.* 210a).[91] Socrates's instructor Diotima is not simply a mystagogue, however. When Diotima explains the nature of Eros to Socrates, he comments, "in the manner of a perfect sophist she spoke [to me]" (*Symp.* 206c). Diotima is compared to a sophist, a professional rhetorician. Thus, Plato believed that philosophical and rhetorical training were analogous to initiation into the mysteries. Paul's use of μυστήριον, then, "has currency in both realms," that is, the realms of Jewish apocalypticism and of Greco-Roman rhetorical education, and it "functions as

---

Jewish Identity in the Hellenistic Diaspora, 2nd ed. (Grand Rapids: Eerdmans, 2000), 214–16; Riedweg, *Mysterienterminologie*, 70–115.

88. Martin, *Corinthian Body*, 57.

89. On this point, see Bruce W. Winter, *Philo and Paul among the Sophists*, SNTSMS 96 (Cambridge: University of Cambridge Press, 1997), 145–202.

90. Schefer, "Rhetoric," 189–90.

91. On Diotima as a sophist, see Gary Alan Scott, *Erotic Wisdom: Philosophy and Intermediacy in Plato's Symposium* (Albany: State University of New York Press, 2008), 125.

a bridge between the two discourses."[92] It is a mistake to insist that the "background" to Paul's μυστήριον is *only* Semitic literature or *only* pagan Hellenistic literature.[93] Rather, Paul draws from a variety of sources and contexts to communicate his message to a diverse audience. By employing this multivalent term, Paul was able to legitimize himself as a proclaimer of esoteric paideia and as a teacher of mysteries to those in Corinth who questioned both his adequacy to provide eschatological wisdom and his ability to speak in a rhetorically sophisticated manner.

Functions of "Mystery"

The three texts we have been discussing present varying definitions and conceptions of "mystery." In juxtaposing these texts, I am not proposing a genealogical lineage or direct line of influence. Rather these three texts demonstrate the various ways that an ancient author's conception of "mystery" could aid in the production of an esoteric, alternative paideia. A comparison of these texts will reveal at least three ways that "mystery" functioned to support each text's model of esoteric paideia.

First, "mystery" is used to provide authority for the expert and to establish the expert as an indispensable guide. This is evident in several places in the *Symposium*, but especially when Diotima asks Socrates how he expects to master the art of love if he cannot understand the most basic principles. Socrates replies, "But Diotima, as I said just now, it is precisely because I recognize that I need teachers that I have come to you" (*Symp.* 207c; see also 210a–211e). Socrates is led into the mystery of Love by his guide, Diotima. As she leads him through the process, Diotima highlights Socrates's need for guidance, "These are aspects of the mystery of love that perhaps you too, Socrates, might be initiated into…. But for the final initiation and revelation, I am not sure if you have the capability" (*Symp.*

---

92. Martin, *Corinthian Body*, 57.

93. On the problematic dichotomy of Judaism versus Hellenism, see the essays in Troels Engberg-Pedersen, ed., *Paul Beyond the Judaism/Hellenism Divide* (Louisville: Westminster John Knox, 2001); Shaye J. D. Cohen, *From the Maccabees to the Mishnah*, 2nd ed. (Louisville: Westminster John Knox, 2006), 26–36; John J. Collins, *Jewish Cult and Hellenistic Culture: Essays on the Jewish Encounter with Hellenism and Roman Rule*, JSJSup 100 (Leiden: Brill, 2005), 1–20; Erich S. Gruen, *Heritage and Hellenism: The Reinvention of Jewish Tradition* (Berkeley: University of California Press, 1998); Lee I. Levine, *Judaism and Hellenism in Antiquity: Conflict or Confluence?* (Seattle: University of Washington Press, 1998).

209e–210a). By leading Socrates into the unknown, "Diotima adopts the authoritative tone of the mystagogue."[94]

In 4QInstruction as well, the speaker intends to guide the pupil into a greater understanding of the mysteries of God, specifically the mystery that is to be. Goff argues that 4QInstruction was probably not written to a general audience but to a distinct group: "The addressees have elect status. The mystery that is to be is revealed to them and they are taught that they are in the lot of the angels.... The text seems to be designed to provide instruction for a specific group."[95] Moreover, "it seems clear that the authorial voice of 4QInstruction is that of a teacher."[96] The teacher, then, directs the *mevin* in the study of the mysterious *raz nihyeh* and functions as his authoritative instructor.

Likewise, Paul presents himself as a guide to the Corinthians. He speaks of God's wisdom as a mystery among the perfected ones (1 Cor 2:6).[97] Paul is like a nurse, who must feed the Corinthians with milk because they are unable to digest solid food (1 Cor 3:2).[98] Ultimately, Paul claims that he is their father, and has the right to discipline them in order to keep them on the right path (1 Cor 4:15–21). By presenting himself as a mystery teacher, a nurse, and a father, Paul demonstrates that the Corinthians need him to be their guide, lest they fail to understand the mysteries of God's plan.

Secondly, the pursuit of "mystery," variously conceived, necessitates a path that the pupil must follow in order to reach the goal of full comprehension. This, in turn, serves to reinforce the necessity of a proper instructor who can guide one along the mysterious path. For Socrates, the path is the "ladder of love," outlined by Diotima. The ascent up the ladder involves passing through the lower mysteries of loving beautiful bodies, then beautiful souls, and then beautiful knowledge. Finally one may reach the highest mysteries of loving the Form of Beauty. The

---

94. L. L. Welborn, *Paul, the Fool of Christ: A Study of 1 Corinthians 1–4 in the Comic-Philosophic Tradition* (New York: T&T Clark, 2005), 196.

95. Goff, *Worldly and Heavenly Wisdom*, 18.

96. The voice of the instructor in 4QInstruction should not be confused with the "Teacher of Righteousness" mentioned elsewhere in the Qumran texts. See Goff, *4QInstruction*, 27–28.

97. The word τέλειος can be translated as "perfect," "mature," or "initiated"; see BDAG, s.v. "τέλειος." On the rendering "initiated," see Conzelmann, *1 Corinthians*, 60.

98. On Paul as a nurse, see Abraham J. Malherbe, "'Gentle as a Nurse': The Cynic Background to 1 Thessalonians 2," in *Paul and the Popular Philosophers* (Minneapolis: Fortress, 1989), 35–48.

key to making progress along this path is Socrates's method of dialogical questioning, which leads one to philosophical contemplation.[99] Plato's philosophical path begins with "an eros only of eyes and ideas and ends with the contemplation of Beauty itself (the greater mysteries)."[100] Both the journey motif and one's progression through stages of initiation on the path to enlightenment are well-documented aspects of the Eleusinian mysteries.[101] By invoking the language of these mysteries, whose ceremonies took place outside of the city of Athens, and by making Diotima (a foreigner) the mystagogue of the highest mysteries, Plato reinforced the idea that the way to goodness, truth, and beauty would not be found in the dominant system of Athenian paideia, but in his alternate paideia of philosophical mysteries.[102]

In 4QInstruction, the author prods the *mevin* to take the pathway illuminated by the mystery that is to be: "And you, understanding son, gaze upon the mystery that is to be and know [the path]s of all life and the manner of one's walking that is appointed over [his] deed[s]… [under]stand the difference between great and small" (4Q417 1 I, 18–20). Goff remarks, "4QInstruction sets before the addressee a right path and a wrong path. The addressee should be devoted to righteous conduct and the acquisition of wisdom through the mystery that is to be."[103] Studying the "mystery" is essential to understanding how one should live and which path one should take. The mystery that is to be functions to highlight the pathway that is available to the *mevin*. Moreover, he is "inclined toward righteousness, being in the lot of the angels."[104] Thus, the mystery that is to be helps to enlighten the *mevin* as to his true nature—a nature that is inclined toward the good and away from the mass of "fleshly" humanity. The goal of the *mevin*'s pursuit will be "eternal joy" for those who gaze upon the mystery that is to be and for those who "seize the birth times of their salvation" (4Q417 2 I, 11–12). As Goff writes, "'Eternal joy' is reasonably understood as a reference to the eternal life [the *mevin*] can obtain

---

99. On this point, see Charles H. Kahn, *Plato and the Socratic Dialogue: The Philosophical Use of a Literary Form* (Cambridge: Cambridge University Press, 1998).
100. Boyarin, *Socrates and the Fat Rabbis*, 298.
101. Burkert, *Ancient Mystery Cults*, 20–21; Clinton, "Stages of Initiation," 50–78.
102. Boyarin, *Socrates and the Fat Rabbis*, 297–308; Halperin, "Why Is Diotima a Woman?," in Zeitlin, Winkler, and Halperin, *Before Sexuality*, 288–98.
103. Goff, *Worldly and Heavenly Wisdom*, 123.
104. Ibid.

after death ... [and] given the composition's emphasis on his affinity with the angels, one can plausibly assert that he will join them after death."[105] Following the path that is elucidated by the mystery that is to be will ultimately lead the *mevinim* to a final, glorious state in which they will be exalted. The "fleshly" will be destroyed, along with their false wisdom.

The mystery that Paul proclaims in 1 Cor 1–4 demonstrates that there is a path that the Corinthians must follow if they are to reach completion in the ways of Christ. At the time that Paul writes the letter, he views the Corinthians as infants who still need milk to help them mature.[106] Their jealousy and quarreling has revealed the fact that they are living according to the σάρξ ("flesh") and not according to the divine πνεῦμα ("spirit").[107] To lead them in the right direction, Paul proclaims that he has a mystery that only the *pneumatic* people (those empowered with divine πνεῦμα) can understand.[108] In order for the Corinthians to become *pneumatics* themselves they must follow the way of humbleness established by the life of Paul himself, and ultimately the life of Paul's exemplar, Christ. Paul demonstrates this to the Corinthians by reminding them that although he was the first to "plant" the assembly at Corinth and although he was their "skilled master builder," he considers himself a servant (διάκονος; 1 Cor 3:5).[109] In

---

105. Goff, *4QInstruction*, 18.

106. On the Corinthians as "infants," see W. Grundmann, "Die ΝΗΠΙΟΙ in der urchristlichen Paränese," *NTS* 5 (1958/1959): 188–205; Raymond F. Collins, *First Corinthians* (Collegeville, MN: Liturgical Press, 1999), 139–41; Conzelmann, *1 Corinthians*, 71; Winter, *Philo and Paul*, 174–75; L. L. Welborn, *An End to Enmity: Paul and the "Wrongdoer" of Second Corinthians*, BZNW 185 (Berlin: de Gruyter, 2011), 83.

107. On spirit versus flesh in the Corinthian correspondence, see Birger A. Pearson, *The Pneumatikos-Psychikos Terminology in 1 Corinthians: A Study in the Theology of the Corinthian Opponents of Paul and Its Relation to Gnosticism*, SBLDS 12 (Missoula, MT: Scholars Press, 1973); Richard Horsley, "Pneumatikos vs. Psychichos: Distinctions of Spiritual Status among the Corinthians," *HTR* 69 (1976): 269–88; John R. Levison, *Filled with the Spirit* (Grand Rapids: Eerdmans 2009), 282–83; Goff, "Being Fleshly or Spiritual," 41–60; Tigchelaar, "'Spiritual People,' 'Fleshly Spirit,'" 103–18; Conzelmann, *1 Corinthians*, 72.

108. On Paul and pneuma, see Clint Tibbs, *Religious Experience of the Pneuma: Communication with the Spirit World in 1 Corinthians 12 and 14*, WUNT 2/230 (Tübingen: Mohr Siebeck, 2007); Martin, *Corinthian Body*; Troels Engberg-Pedersen, *Cosmology and the Self in the Apostle Paul: The Material Spirit* (Oxford: Oxford University Press, 2010).

109. On these metaphors in 1 Corinthians, see Collins, *First Corinthians*, 148–50; Welborn, *Paul, the Fool of Christ*, 108, 240.

1 Cor 4:1 he writes, "Think of us in this way, as servants [ὑπηρέτας] of Christ and stewards [οἰκονόμους] of God's mysteries."[110] The terms Paul uses to describe himself highlight the fact that he lives a life of service and submission to God. The word διάκονος was used to describe a courier, an assistant, or a table attendant; a ὑπηρέτης was a subordinate, a helper, or an assistant; an οἰκονόμος was a household manager, a steward, a city treasurer, or an administrator, and was often a slave.[111] The οἰκονόμος, while serving as a slave to the head of the household, could also be in a position of authority over other slaves under him.[112] Thus Paul is suggesting that he is both a servant and a leader for the Corinthians. Lastly, Paul appeals to the Corinthians as their father and instructs them to "be imitators of me" (1 Cor 4:15–16).[113] The mysterious path that Paul proclaims to them is the way of suffering and humbleness, exemplified by Paul himself and by the foolishness of Christ crucified.

Thirdly, the use of "mystery" points the pupils toward an ultimate goal involving a transformative vision, unlocking the true meaning of the mystery. To understand the mystery, one must look past the mundane aspects of the world to see the truth behind the veil. Diotima tells Socrates she is skeptical that he will be able to grasp the final and highest (τέλεα καὶ ἐποπτικά) mystery of Love. Socrates must see beyond the beauty of physical bodies and realize the beauty of souls; only then can he make his ascent into the mystery of Eros that will culminate with an *epoptic* vision of Beauty. The dinner guests are fortunate enough to behold the transformation of Socrates over the course of the night. When Diotima attempts to explain the mystery of Eros to Socrates, he is baffled at every turn, like an uneducated schoolboy who cannot grasp the subject being taught (*Symp.* 204b). However, by the conclusion of Socrates's speech, he has become the educator of all in attendance. Socrates's purification and initiation is on

---

110. On the debate over what Paul means by "stewards of the mysteries," see Brown, *Semitic Background*, 44–45; Gladd, *Revealing the* Mysterion, 165–90; Conzelmann, *1 Corinthians*, 82.

111. For these three terms, see, respectively, BDAG, s.vv. "διάκονος," "ὑπηρέτης," and "οἰκονόμος." Consult also Martin, *Corinthian Body*, 65; Martin, *Slavery as Salvation: The Metaphor of Slavery in Pauline Christianity* (New Haven: Yale University Press, 1990), 15–17, 80.

112. Otto Michel, "οἰκονόμος," *TDNT* 5:149.

113. On this point, see Hans Dieter Betz, *Nachfolge und Nachahmung Jesu Christi im Neuen Testament*, BHT 37 (Tübingen: Mohr Siebeck, 1967); Elizabeth A. Castelli, *Imitating Paul: A Discourse of Power* (Louisville: Westminster John Knox, 1991).

display for all. As Mark J. Lutz writes, "As in traditional mystery rites, this ascent to philosophy is a process of purification. At each stage the initiate becomes purer and more beautiful by loving purer and more beautiful things. Finally, one gives birth to true virtue when one casts off all concern with 'worldly' things and devotes oneself to the universal, non-material, 'non-practical,' immortal and 'suprahuman.'"[114] The speech of Alcibiades is the conclusive proof of Socrates's ascent into the mysteries of Eros: Socrates transcends the erotic desire for bodily pleasure and yearns for the joys of conversation and philosophical dialogue (*Symp.* 219c). Socrates has been transformed by his divine vision of true Beauty.

In 4QInstruction, we have seen that the reader is often told to "gaze" upon the mystery that is to be, an activity that could have involved an extraordinary visionary experience (4Q417 1 I, 3). By constant "gazing" and study of the mystery, the *mevin* comes to realize his true nature as one made in "the likeness of the holy ones" (i.e., the angels; 4Q417 1 I, 17). He has been separated from the "fleshly spirit" and is joined with the "spiritual people" who have access to the "vision of meditation" (4Q417 1 I, 16).[115] Through the power of the mystery that is to be, he will discern his path and his potential for glory. The teacher proclaims that God has "established you as most holy [of all the people of the] world. And among all the [a]n[gels] he has cast your lot and your glory he has greatly magnified" (4Q418 81 4-5). By following the supernatural revelation of the mystery that is to be and by heeding the guidance of the teacher, the *mevin* embarks on a journey "that will help him attain the full realization of his elect status so that he can join the angels in eternal fellowship after death."[116]

When Paul presents himself as a mystery teacher in 1 Corinthians, he also intends for the Corinthians to gaze upon a mysterious spectacle. Paul says that the wisdom contained in God's hidden mystery is one "which none of the rulers of this age has understood; for if they had understood it they would not have crucified the lord of glory" (1 Cor 2:8). When he claims that Jews are demanding "signs," he says that he "proclaims Christ crucified" (1 Cor 1:23). When Paul came announcing the mystery of God to the Corinthians, he "decided to know nothing among you except Jesus Christ, and him crucified" (1 Cor 2:2). Paul's

---

114. Mark J. Lutz, *Socrates' Education to Virtue: Learning the Love of the Noble* (Albany: State University of New York Press, 1998), 98.

115. Goff, "Being Fleshly or Spiritual," 41-60.

116. Goff, *4QInstruction*, 245.

mystery-speech was also accompanied by a "demonstration of the spirit and of power" (1 Cor 2:4). The transformative vision that Paul wants them to comprehend fully is the body of the crucified Christ. How might Paul have demonstrated this vision to them? Elsewhere, in Gal 3, Paul tells the Galatians that Jesus Christ was "publicly exhibited as crucified"[117] before their very eyes (Gal 3:1). Hans Dieter Betz comments: "One of the goals of the ancient orator was to deliver his speech so vividly and impressively that the listeners imagined the matter to have happened right before their very eyes. All kinds of techniques were recommended to achieve this effect, including impersonations and even holding up painted pictures."[118] Paul's message of the crucified Lord was so detailed and realistic that he considers the Galatians to have witnessed the gruesome death firsthand.[119] Given Paul's emphasis on the "word of the cross" in 1 Corinthians, it is reasonable to think that Paul's proclamation in Corinth involved a similar vividness.

A second way that the cross was demonstrated to the Corinthians was through the life of Paul himself. Paul was among them with "weakness and in fear and in much trembling" (1 Cor 2:3). Paul has already linked "weakness" with the foolish message of the cross in 1 Cor 1:22–25. He furthers his identification with the death of Jesus in 1 Cor 4:8–13. God has exhibited him as an apostle "last of all, as though sentenced to death"; he has become a "spectacle to the world, to angels and to mortals" (1 Cor 4:9). He is a "fool for the sake of Christ" (1 Cor 4:10). His life is characterized by hunger, thirst, lack of clothing, homelessness, physical abuse by others,

---

117. Hans Dieter Betz notes that προγράφω can mean here "portray publicly" or "proclaim publicly," and that although modern commentators prefer the latter, the rhetorical material lends support to the former. See his *Galatians: A Commentary on Paul's Letter to the Churches in Galatia*, Hermeneia (Minneapolis: Fortress, 1979), 131 n. 39.

118. Betz (ibid., 131) quotes Quintilian as describing orators who would "bring into court a picture of a crime painted on wood or canvas, that the judge might be stirred to fury by the horror of the sight."

119. It is possible, though speculative, that Paul may have performed or presented some type of physical reenactment of the crucifixion for the Galatians. On suggestions that come close to this one, see David L. Balch, "The Suffering of Isis/Io and Paul's Portrait of Christ Crucified (Gal. 3:1): Frescoes in Pompeian and Roman Houses and in the Temple of Isis in Pompeii," *JR* 83 (2003): 24–55; Jennifer A. Glancy, "Boasting of Beatings (2 Corinthians 11:23–25)," *JBL* 123 (2004): 99–135.

weariness, insults, and disrepute.[120] All of these descriptions of Paul's life would appear later in the depictions of the death of Jesus found in the four gospels. The manner of Paul's life, then, publicly exhibits Christ crucified to the Corinthians.

A third way that Paul publicly portrayed the crucifixion to the Corinthians was through the Lord's Supper. Paul states that he has already proclaimed (καταγγέλλων) the mystery of God to the Corinthians (1 Cor 2:1), and now, when they properly partake of the body and blood of the Lord, they "proclaim [καταγγέλλετε] the Lord's death until he comes" (1 Cor 11:26). The mystery of the suffering Lord is proclaimed in the sacred meal. The higher-status Corinthians, however, had not properly discerned the mystery of the crucified body of Christ, which should have produced unity among the members.[121] Instead they practiced gluttony and drunkenness, and, refusing to be unified with lower status members, they humiliated those who had nothing. Paul desired that the Corinthians would come to understand properly the mysterious, transforming vision of the cross—a vision that would unite them all under the foolish message of Christ crucified. Paul's insistence that upper and lower status individuals be united in a community based on equality (2 Cor 8:13–15) was a "paradigm shift" that "promoted an alternative to the [Roman cultural system of] patronage."[122] Paul thus used his understanding of "mystery" to support his alternative, esoteric paideia based on the λόγος of the cross.

Conclusion

In this essay I have examined three models of alternative paideia in which the instructor employs a conception of "mystery" to aid in the training of pupils. For the *Symposium*, the mystery is explained as the journey from loving beautiful bodies to loving beautiful souls, and ultimately of

---

120. These descriptions represent stock traits of the trope of "the fool" in ancient literature. See Welborn, *Paul, the Fool of Christ*, 49–101.

121. On the role that social status played in the divisions at the Lord's Supper, see Theissen, *Social Setting*, 96–106; Martin, *Corinthian Body*, 73–76, 190–97; Stowers, "Kinds of Myth," 127–49.

122. John T. Fitzgerald, "Paul and Paradigm Shifts: Reconciliation and Its Linkage Group," in Engberg-Pedersen, *Paul Beyond the Judaism/Hellenism Divide*, 241–62; L. L. Welborn, "'That There May Be Equality': The Contexts and Consequences of a Pauline Ideal," *NTS* 59 (2013): 89.

having an *epoptic* vision of Beauty itself. This process purifies the initiate and allows for true philosophical contemplation, thus reaching the heights of the divine. By associating the progress of the philosopher with that of the mystery initiate, Plato is able to introduce his theory of Forms as ultimate reality. In 4QInstruction the addressee is told to gaze upon the supernatural revelation of the mystery that is to be. By doing so, the *mevin* will be able to discern the ways of holiness and join the lot of the angels after death. For Paul, the mystery of God includes the revelation that God has put the wisdom of the world to shame through the foolishness of the crucified messiah. This speech concerning mystery is intended to bring about humility and unity among the members of the assembly who have been divided into factions based on wealth, status, knowledge, and spiritual gifts. "Mystery," variously conceived, has three particular functions in these texts: to establish authority and legitimacy for the instructor, to point the pupil toward a path he or she must take, and to direct the pupil toward an extraordinary vision that will change them indefinitely. Though these texts vary widely in their understanding of the content of "mystery," the functions of "mystery" for each author serve to establish an esoteric paideia for the enlightened community.

Bibliography

Angus, Samuel. *The Religious Quests of the Greco-Roman World*. New York: Scribner's Sons, 1929.

Balch, David L. "The Suffering of Isis/Io and Paul's Portrait of Christ Crucified (Gal. 3:1): Frescoes in Pompeian and Roman Houses and in the Temple of Isis in Pompeii." *JR* 83 (2003): 24–55.

Belfiore, Elizabeth S. *Socrates' Daimonic Art: Love for Wisdom in Four Platonic Dialogues*. Cambridge: Cambridge University Press, 2012.

Betz, Hans Dieter. *Galatians: A Commentary on Paul's Letter to the Churches in Galatia*. Hermeneia. Minneapolis: Fortress, 1979.

———. *Nachfolge und Nachahmung Jesu Christi im Neuen Testament*. BHT 37. Tübingen: Mohr Siebeck, 1967.

Bockmuehl, Marcus N. A. *Revelation and Mystery in Ancient Judaism and Pauline Christianity*. WUNT 2/36. Tübingen: Mohr Siebeck, 1990.

Bornkamm, Günther. "μυστήριον." *TDNT* 4:802–28.

Bowden, Hugh. *Mystery Cults of the Ancient World*. Princeton: Princeton University Press, 2010.

Boyarin, Daniel. *Socrates and the Fat Rabbis*. Chicago: University of Chicago Press, 2009.

———. "What Do We Talk about When We Talk about Platonic Love?" Pages 3–22 in *Toward a Theology of Eros: Transfiguring Passion at the Limits of Discipline*. Edited by Virginia Burrus and Catherine Keller. New York: Fordham University Press, 2006.

Bremmer, Jan N. *Initiation into the Mysteries of the Ancient World*. MVAW 1. Berlin: de Gruyter, 2014.

Brown, Raymond E. *The Semitic Background of the Term "Mystery" in the New Testament*. Philadelphia: Fortress, 1968.

Burkert, Walter. *Ancient Mystery Cults*. Cambridge: Harvard University Press, 1987.

Caragounis, Chrys C. *The Son of Man: Vision and Interpretation*. WUNT 38. Tübingen: Mohr Siebeck, 1986.

Castelli, Elizabeth A. *Imitating Paul: A Discourse of Power*. Louisville: Westminster John Knox, 1991.

Cleary, John J. "Erotic Paideia in Plato's *Symposium*." Pages 53–72 in *Studies on Plato, Aristotle and Proclus: The Collected Essays on Ancient Philosophy of John Cleary*. Edited by John Dillon, Brendan O'Byrne, and Fran O'Rourke. Leiden: Brill, 2013.

Clemen, Carl. *Die Einfluss der Mysterienreligionen auf das älteste Christentum*. RVV 13.1. Giessen: Töpelmann, 1913.

Clinton, Kevin. *Myth and Cult: The Iconography of the Eleusinian Mysteries*. Athens: Svenska Institutet, 1992.

———. *The Sacred Officials of the Eleusinian Mysteries*. Philadelphia: American Philosophical Society, 1974.

———. "Stages of Initiation in the Eleusinian and Samothracian Mysteries." Pages 50–78 in *Greek Mysteries: The Archaeology of Ancient Greek Secret Cults*. Edited by Michael B. Cosmopoulos. New York: Routledge, 2002.

Cohen, Shaye J. D. *From the Maccabees to the Mishnah*. 2nd ed. Louisville: Westminster John Knox, 2006.

Collins, John J. *The Apocalyptic Imagination: An Introduction to Jewish Apocalyptic Literature*. Grand Rapids: Eerdmans, 1998.

———. *Between Athens and Jerusalem: Jewish Identity in the Hellenistic Diaspora*. 2nd ed. Grand Rapids: Eerdmans, 2000.

———. *Daniel: A Commentary on the Book of Daniel*. Hermeneia. Minneapolis: Fortress, 1993.

———. *Jewish Cult and Hellenistic Culture: Essays on the Jewish Encounter with Hellenism and Roman Rule*. JSJSup 100. Leiden: Brill, 2005.

———. *Jewish Wisdom in the Hellenistic Age*. OTL. Louisville: Westminster John Knox, 1997.

Collins, Raymond F. *First Corinthians*. Collegeville, MN: Liturgical Press, 1999.

Conzelmann, Hans. *1 Corinthians: A Commentary on the First Epistle to the Corinthians*. Hermeneia. Philadelphia: Fortress, 1975.

Corrigan, Kevin, and Elena Glazov-Corrigan. *Plato's Dialectic at Play: Argument, Structure, and Myth in the Symposium*. University Park: Pennsylvania State University Press, 2010.

Craik, Elizabeth M. *The "Hippocratic" Corpus: Context and Content*. New York: Routledge, 2015.

Crenshaw, James L. "Education in Ancient Israel." *JBL* 104 (1985): 601–15.

———. *Education in Ancient Israel: Across the Deadening Silence*. ABRL. New York: Doubleday, 1998.

Dunn, James D. G. *1 Corinthians*. Sheffield: Sheffield Academic, 1997.

Engberg-Pedersen, Troels. *Cosmology and the Self in the Apostle Paul: The Material Spirit*. Oxford: Oxford University Press, 2010.

———, ed. *Paul Beyond the Judaism/Hellenism Divide*. Louisville: Westminster John Knox, 2001.

Evans, Nancy. "Diotima and Demeter as Mystagogues in Plato's *Symposium*." *Hypatia* 21 (2006): 1–27.

Fitzgerald, John T. "Paul and Paradigm Shifts: Reconciliation and Its Linkage Group." Pages 241–62 in *Paul Beyond the Judaism/Hellenism Divide*. Edited by Troels Engberg-Pedersen. Louisville: Westminster John Knox, 2001

García Martínez, Florentino, and Eibert J. C. Tigchelaar. *The Dead Sea Scrolls Study Edition*. 2 vols. Leiden: Brill; Grand Rapids: Eerdmans, 1997–1998.

Garrett, Duane. *Proverbs, Ecclesiastes, Song of Solomon*. Nashville: Broadman, 1993.

Given, Mark D. *Paul's True Rhetoric: Ambiguity, Cunning, and Deception in Greece and Rome*. Harrisburg: Trinity Press International, 2001.

Gladd, Benjamin L. *Revealing the* Mysterion: *The Use of Mystery in Daniel and Second Temple Judaism with Its Bearing on First Corinthians*. BZAW 160. Berlin: de Gruyter, 2008.

Glancy, Jennifer A. "Boasting of Beatings (2 Corinthians 11:23–25)." *JBL* 123 (2004): 99–135.

Goff, Matthew J. "Being Fleshly or Spiritual: Anthropological Reflection and Exegesis of Genesis 1–3 in 4QInstruction and First Corinthians." Pages 41–60 in *Christian Body, Christian Self: Concepts of Early Christian Personhood*. Edited by Clare K. Rothschild and Trevor W. Thompson. WUNT 284. Tübingen: Mohr Siebeck, 2011.

———. *Discerning Wisdom: The Sapiential Literature of the Dead Sea Scrolls*. VTSup 116. Leiden: Brill, 2007.

———. *4QInstruction*. WLAW 2. Atlanta: Society of Biblical Literature, 2013.

———. "Wisdom, Apocalypticism, and the Pedagogical Ethos of 4QInstruction." Pages 57–67 in *Conflicted Boundaries in Wisdom and Apocalypticism*. Edited by Lawrence M. Wills and Benjamin G. Wright. SymS 35. Atlanta: Society of Biblical Literature, 2005.

———. *The Worldly and Heavenly Wisdom of 4QInstruction*. STDJ 50. Leiden: Brill, 2003.

Gordon, Richard L. "Mysteries." *OCD*, 1017–18.

Graf, Fritz. "Mysteries." *BNP* 9:443–44.

Gruen, Erich S. *Heritage and Hellenism: The Reinvention of Jewish Tradition*. Berkeley: University of California Press, 1998.

Grundmann, W. "Die ΝΗΠΙΟΙ in der urchristlichen Paränese." *NTS* 5 (1958/1959): 188–205.

Halperin, David M. *One Hundred Years of Homosexuality: And Other Essays on Greek Love*. New York: Routledge, 2012.

———. "Why is Diotima a Woman? Platonic *Erōs* and the Figuration of Gender." Pages 257–308 in *Before Sexuality: The Construction of Erotic Experience in the Ancient Greek World*. Edited by Froma I. Zeitlin, John J. Winkler, and David M. Halperin. Princeton: Princeton University Press, 1990.

Hogan, Karina Martin. *Theologies in Conflict in 4 Ezra: Wisdom, Debate, and Apocalyptic Solution*. JSJSup 130. Leiden: Brill, 2008.

Horsley, Richard A. "Pneumatikos vs. Psychichos: Distinctions of Spiritual Status among the Corinthians." *HTR* 69 (1976): 269–88.

Hunter, Richard. *Critical Moments in Classical Literature: Studies in the Ancient View of Literature and Its Uses*. Cambridge: Cambridge University Press, 2009.

Jaeger, Werner. *Paideia: The Ideals of Greek Culture*. 3 vols. Translated by Gilbert Highet. Oxford: Oxford University Press, 1986.

Jonge, Casper Constantijn de. *Between Grammar and Rhetoric: Dionysius of Halicarnassus on Language, Linguistics, and Literature.* MnemosyneSup 301. Leiden: Brill, 2008.

Kahn, Charles H. *Plato and the Socratic Dialogue: The Philosophical Use of a Literary Form.* Cambridge: Cambridge University Press, 1998.

Kampen, John. *Wisdom Literature.* ECDSS. Grand Rapids: Eerdmans, 2011.

Klauck, Hans-Josef. *The Religious Context of Early Christianity: A Guide to Graeco-Roman Religions.* Edinburgh: T&T Clark, 2000.

Lemaire, André. "Education." *ABD* 2:301–12.

Levine, Lee I. *Judaism and Hellenism in Antiquity: Conflict or Confluence?* Seattle: University of Washington Press, 1998.

Levison, John R. *Filled with the Spirit.* Grand Rapids: Eerdmans 2009.

Loisy, Alfred. *Les mystères païens et le mystère chrétien.* Paris: Nourry, 1930.

Lutz, Mark J. *Socrates' Education to Virtue: Learning the Love of the Noble.* Albany: State University of New York Press, 1998.

Malherbe, Abraham J. "'Gentle as a Nurse': The Cynic Background to 1 Thessalonians 2." Pages 35–48 in *Paul and the Popular Philosophers.* Minneapolis: Fortress, 1989.

Martin, Dale B. *The Corinthian Body.* New Haven: Yale University Press, 1999.

———. *Slavery as Salvation: The Metaphor of Slavery in Pauline Christianity.* New Haven: Yale University Press, 1990.

Matera, Frank J. *II Corinthians: A Commentary.* Louisville: Westminster John Knox, 2003.

Meeks, Wayne A. *The First Urban Christians: The Social World of the Apostle Paul.* New Haven: Yale University Press, 1983.

Metzger, Bruce M. *A Classified Bibliography of the Graeco-Roman Mystery Religions 1924–1973: With a Supplement 1974–1977.* Berlin: de Gruyter, 1984.

———. *A Textual Commentary on the Greek New Testament.* New York: United Bible Societies, 1971.

Meyer, Marvin. *The Ancient Mysteries: A Sourcebook.* Philadelphia: University of Pennsylvania Press, 1999.

Michel, Otto. "οἰκονόμος." *TDNT* 5:149–51.

Mitchell, Margaret M. *Paul and the Rhetoric of Reconciliation: An Exegetical Investigation of the Language and Composition of 1 Corinthians.* Louisville: Westminster John Knox, 1991.

Mylonas, George E. *Eleusis and the Eleusinian Mysteries.* Princeton: Princeton University Press, 1961.

Nickelsburg, George W. E. *1 Enoch 1: A Commentary on the Book of 1 Enoch*. Hermeneia. Minneapolis: Fortress, 2001.
Nock, A. D. *Early Gentile Christianity and Its Hellenistic Background*. New York: Harper & Row, 1964.
Ober, Josiah. "I, Socrates... The Performative Audacity of Isocrates' *Antidosis*." Pages 21–43 in *Isocrates and Civic Education*. Edited by Takis Poulakos and David J. Depew. Austin: University of Texas Press, 2004.
Pearson, Birger A. *The Pneumatikos-Psychikos Terminology in 1 Corinthians: A Study in the Theology of the Corinthian Opponents of Paul and Its Relation to Gnosticism*. SBLDS 12. Missoula, MT: Scholars Press, 1973.
Perdue, Leo G. *Proverbs*. IBC. Louisville: Westminster John Knox, 2000.
Reitzenstein, Richard. *Hellenistic Mystery-Religions: Their Basic Ideas and Significance*. Eugene: Pickwick, 1978.
———. *Die hellenistischen Mysterienreligionen*. Leipzig: Teubner, 1920.
Rhodes, James. *Eros, Wisdom, and Silence*. Columbia: University of Missouri Press, 2003.
Richardson, N. J. *The Homeric Hymn to Demeter*. Oxford: Clarendon, 1974.
Riedweg, Christoph. *Mysterienterminologie bei Platon, Philo, und Klemens von Alexandria*. UALG 26. Berlin: de Gruyter, 1987.
Russell, Donald A. *Quintilian: The Orator's Education*. 5 vols. LCL. Cambridge: Harvard University Press, 2002–2014.
Sattler, Barbara. "The Eleusinian Mysteries in Pre-Platonic Thought: Metaphor, Practice and Imagery for Plato's Symposium." Pages 151–90 in *Philosophy and Greek Religion*. Edited by Vishwa Adluri. Berlin: de Gruyter, 2013.
Schäfer, Peter. *The Origins of Jewish Mysticism*. Princeton: Princeton University Press, 2011.
Schefer, Christina. "Rhetoric as Part of an Initiation into the Mysteries: A New Interpretation of the Platonic *Phaedrus*." Pages 175–96 in *Plato as Author: The Rhetoric of Philosophy*. Edited by Ann N. Michelini. Leiden: Brill, 2003.
Schiffman, Lawrence H. *Reclaiming the Dead Sea Scrolls: The History of Judaism, the Background of Christianity, the Lost Library of Qumran*. New York: Doubleday, 1995.
Schuddeboom, Feyo L. *Greek Religious Terminology: Telete and Orgia; A Revised and Expanded English Edition of the Studies by Zijderveld and Van der Burg*. RGRW 169. Leiden: Brill, 2009.
Scott, Gary Alan. *Erotic Wisdom: Philosophy and Intermediacy in Plato's Symposium*. Albany: State University of New York Press, 2008.

———. *Plato's Socrates as Educator*. Albany: State University of New York Press, 2000.

Sheffield, Frisbee C. C. *Plato's Symposium: The Ethics of Desire*. Oxford: Oxford University Press, 2009.

Smith, Hilda L., and Bernice A. Carroll, eds. *Women's Political and Social Thought: An Anthology*. Bloomington: Indiana University Press, 2000.

Smith, Jonathan Z. *Drudgery Divine: On the Comparison of Early Christianities and the Religions of Late Antiquity*. Chicago: University of Chicago Press, 1994.

Stowers, Stanley K. "Kinds of Myth, Meals, and Power: Paul and the Corinthians." Page 105–50 in *Redescribing Paul and the Corinthians*. Edited by Ron Cameron and Merrill P. Miller. ECL 5. Atlanta: Society of Biblical Literature, 2011.

Strugnell, John, Daniel J. Harrington, Torleif Elgvin, and Joseph A Fitzmyer, eds. *Qumran Cave 4.XXIV: Sapiential Texts; 4QInstruction (Mûsār Lĕ Mēbîn): 4Q415ff.* Part 2. DJD 34. Oxford: Clarendon, 1999.

Theissen, Gerd. *The Social Setting of Pauline Christianity*. Philadelphia: Fortress, 1982.

Thomas, Samuel. *The "Mysteries" of Qumran: Mystery, Secrecy, and Esotericism in the Dead Sea Scrolls*. EJL 25. Atlanta: Society of Biblical Literature, 2009.

Tibbs, Clint. *Religious Experience of the Pneuma: Communication with the Spirit World in 1 Corinthians 12 and 14*. WUNT 2/230. Tübingen: Mohr Siebeck, 2007.

Tigchelaar, Eibert J. C. "'Spiritual People,' 'Fleshly Spirit,' and 'Vision of Meditation': Reflections on *4QInstruction* and 1 Corinthians." Pages 103–18 in *Echoes from the Caves: Qumran and the New Testament*. Edited by Florentino García Martínez. STDJ 85. Leiden: Brill, 2009.

———. *To Increase Learning for the Understanding Ones: Reading and Reconstructing the Fragmentary Early Jewish Sapiential Text 4QInstruction*. STDJ 44. Leiden: Brill, 2001.

Vermes, Geza. *The Complete Dead Sea Scrolls in English*. London: Penguin Books, 2004.

Wedderburn, A. J. M. *Baptism and Resurrection: Studies in Pauline Theology against Its Graeco-Roman Background*. WUNT 44. Tübingen: Mohr Siebeck, 1987.

Weiss, Johannes. *Earliest Christianity*. 2 vols. New York: Harper, 1959.

Welborn, L. L. *An End to Enmity: Paul and the "Wrongdoer" of Second Corinthians*. BZNW 185. Berlin: de Gruyter, 2011.

———. *Paul, the Fool of Christ: A Study of 1 Corinthians 1–4 in the Comic-Philosophic Tradition*. New York: T&T Clark, 2005.

———. *Politics and Rhetoric in the Corinthian Epistles*. Macon, GA: Mercer University Press, 1997.

———. "'That There May Be Equality': The Contexts and Consequences of a Pauline Ideal." *NTS* 59 (2013): 73–90.

Werman, Cana. "What is the *Book of Hagu*?" Page 125–40 in *Sapiential Perspectives: Wisdom Literature in Light of the Dead Sea Scrolls; Proceedings of the Sixth International Symposium of the Orion Center for the Study of the Dead Sea Scrolls and Associated Literature, 20–22 May, 2001*. Edited by John J. Collins, Gregory Sterling, and Ruth Clements. STDJ 51. Leiden: Brill, 2004.

Widder, Wendy L. *"To Teach" in Ancient Israel: A Cognitive Linguistic Study of a Biblical Hebrew Lexical Set*. BZAW 456. Berlin: de Gruyter, 2014.

Winter, Bruce W. *Philo and Paul among the Sophists*. SNTSMS 96. Cambridge: University of Cambridge Press, 1997.

Mosaic Torah as Encyclical Paideia: Reading Paul's Allegory of Hagar and Sarah in Light of Philo of Alexandria's

Jason M. Zurawski

For many Jews in the Hellenistic Diaspora of the Second Temple period, the Mosaic torah was a means to an end. In the torah, the Jews had possession of the most perfect form of paideia possible, which led the follower of the individual enactments on the road to attaining that most sought-after goal of Greek philosophy, wisdom. This does not mean that the Mosaic law was superfluous. On the contrary, the torah was a gift, given graciously by God in order that the Jews, by adhering to its precepts, could live according to the universal law of nature. For the Letter to Aristeas, for example, the dietary laws were not set forth because some animals are inherently unclean, but because the laws had pedagogical value and taught their followers to live according to nature: "For the law was not drawn up without reason or according to whatever may have occurred to the soul but with a view to truth and an indication of right reason" (ὀρθοῦ λόγου; Let. Aris. 161).[1]

I would like to thank Karina Martin Hogan and Larry Wills for their thoughtful and helpful responses to my paper at the Wisdom and Apocalypticism in Early Judaism and Christianity session at the 2012 Society of Biblical Literature Annual Meeting in Chicago.

1. The translation is my own. *Orthos logos* is one of the principal phrases used for describing the universal natural law, as found in both the early Stoa and in Philo. See, e.g., Diogenes Laertius, *Vit. Phil.* 7.87–88 for the Stoic notion, and *Opif.* 143 for Philo's view. Several scholars have written on the understanding of natural law in both Second Temple Judaism in general and in Philo in particular. See Helmut Koester, "ΝΟΜΟΣ ΦΥΣΕΩΣ: The Concept of Natural Law in Greek Thought," in *Religions in Antiquity: Essays in Memory of Erwin Ramsdell Goodenough*, ed. Jacob Neusner (Leiden: Brill,

Similarly, 4 Maccabees succinctly describes how the Mosaic law is a form of paideia that leads to wisdom: "Now, reasoning is the mind that, with right reason [ὀρθοῦ λόγου], prefers the life of wisdom. Wisdom, next, is the knowledge of divine and human matters and their causes. This, in turn, is the education of the law [ἡ τοῦ νόμου παιδεία], by which we learn divine matters reverently and human matters to our advantage" (4 Macc. 1:15–17 my translation). Ben Sira's grandson, in the prologue to his translation, understood the Mosaic torah as a means to attaining wisdom, like his grandfather: "Many great teachings have been given to us through the Law and the Prophets and the others that followed them, and for these we should praise Israel for education and wisdom" (παιδείας καὶ σοφίας; Sir, Prol. 1–3 my translation).

Finally, for Philo, the Mosaic law was the most perfect copy of the universal natural law possible in a written law code: "if anyone were inclined to examine with accuracy the powers of each individual and particular law, he will find them all aiming at the harmony of the universe, and corresponding to the logos of eternal nature" (*Mos.* 2.52).[2] Therefore, "the man who adhered to these laws, and clung closely to a connection with and obedience to nature would live in a manner corresponding to the arrangement of the universe with a perfect harmony and union between his words and his actions and between his actions and his words" (*Mos.* 2.48). For Philo, following the Mosaic law was a means to the true goal of following the natural law, the perfect order of the universe.

While the Mosaic law was, for many Jews, unquestionably the ultimate form of paideia, there was the immediately pragmatic question as to whether or not non-Jewish education could also be a means of attaining loftier virtue and wisdom. This was not simply a theoretical, philosophical inquiry. The answer to the question had practical implications for those

---

1968), 521–41; Valentin Nikiprowetzky, "Loi de Moïse, Loi de Nature, Sagesse," in *Le commentaire de L'Ecriture chez Philon d'Alexandrie: Son caractère et sa portée, observations philologiques* (Leiden: Brill, 1977), 116–54; Richard A. Horsley, "The Law of Nature in Philo and Cicero" *HTR* 71 (1978): 35–59; Markus Bockmuehl, "Natural Law in Second Temple Judaism," *VT* 45 (1995): 17–44; Hindy Najman, "The Law of Nature and the Authority of Mosaic Law," *SPhiloA* 11 (1999): 55–73; and Najman, "A Written Copy of the Law of Nature: An Unthinkable Paradox?," *SPhiloA* 15 (2003): 54–63. All translations of the Letter of Aristeas are those of R. H. Charles, ed., *The Apocrypha and Pseudepigrapha of the Old Testament in English* (Oxford: Clarendon, 1913). All other translations are my own unless noted otherwise.

2. All translations of Philo of Alexandria are my own.

Jews living in major Hellenistic cities like Alexandria, such as whether or not parents should send their children to the Greek gymnasium for their education. It is precisely this type of question that Philo addresses in his allegorical reading of the Hagar, Sarah, and Abraham narrative, namely, the advantages, and possible disadvantages, of a Greek education. On Philo's reading, Hagar represents encyclical (ἐγκύκλιος) or preliminary paideia—what would later come to be known as the *artes liberales*—which included subjects such as grammar, mathematics, music, and other subjects pertaining to a specifically Greek education. This type of education was an essential step for Abraham in his desire to attain Sarah, the representative of virtue or wisdom. Only by first preparing himself with Hagar/encyclical paideia could he then move on to the loftier form of knowledge, Sarah/wisdom. So, for Philo, Greek paideia was an often necessary means to attaining wisdom.[3] But, there were dangers involved in this process—namely, becoming too devoted to the handmaiden to the detriment of the mistress—and so, once the goal of wisdom was achieved, the preliminary studies were to be abandoned.

Although Paul's allegorical reading of the Genesis narrative seems, on the surface, to be quite different from Philo's, there is good reason for attempting to read Paul's exegesis in light of Philo's. This is not to suggest that Paul was reading Philo (although I do not roundly dismiss the possibility), but simply that he may have been aware of this, perhaps popular, way of reading the Genesis account in the diaspora, as Paul and Philo were both part of the same universe of discourse.[4] Given his activities in

---

3. Note that Philo never explicitly identifies the preliminary studies as "Greek." He does not draw a dichotomy between Jewish and Greek paideia in such a facile manner. Instead the *encyclia* are simply one form of paideia, necessary for most people who hope to gain a higher form of wisdom.

4. See Gregory E. Sterling's excellent article, "'Philo Has Not Been Used Half Enough': The Significance of Philo of Alexandria for the Study of the New Testament," *PRSt* 30 (2003): 251–69. Sterling notes, "I think that the Philonic corpus is the single most important body of material from Second Temple Judaism for our understanding of the development of Christianity in the first and second centuries. Perhaps this will strike you as an extravagant claim in light of the Dead Sea Scrolls and the Josephan corpus. I would not deny the importance of either of those corpuses for the study of the New Testament and Christian origins. I am convinced, however, that the Philonic corpus helps us to understand the dynamics of early Christianity more adequately than any other corpus. I do not want to suggest that Philo or his corpus was directly responsible for the development of Christian thought, but that his corpus is a window

major Hellenistic cities, it is plausible that Paul would have been conscious of these two popular topics of conversation: the Mosaic law as paideia, as a means of attaining wisdom, and Greek paideia as a more cautious means of attaining wisdom. Paul's reading in Galatians becomes part of these same conversations, though not without some fairly drastic innovation. In his allegory, Paul conflates the two paths to wisdom, Mosaic law and preliminary studies (προπαιδεύματα), the torah itself becoming Philo's encyclical paideia or Hagar, something which has a purpose but is no longer needed once the end goal, wisdom, has been attained. This is an argument with which most of Paul's fellow Jews would not have agreed,[5] but it is a move that Paul makes due to his conviction that Christ—and therefore, wisdom—is freely given to those who believe. Just as Philo sternly warns his readers of the dangers of going back to encyclical paideia once having attained true wisdom, Paul warns the Galatians of the dangers of turning back to the Mosaic law, as paideia, once having attained true wisdom via Christ. The allegory is a continuation or expansion of Paul's argument about the law as pedagogue, a tool which served an educational purpose at one time but is no longer needed. The concept of the Mosaic law as pedagogue or as preliminary paideia is not only confined to these few verses (Gal 3:24–25; 4:21–5:1), but forms the core of Paul's main argument in Galatians, which begins at Gal 3:1. This reading of the allegory, then, brings out a consistency in Paul's argumentation throughout this central section of the letter, a consistency that has often been overlooked due to other interpretations of the allegory.

Philo's Allegory

Philo discusses his allegorical understanding of the Abraham, Hagar, and Sarah narratives in a surprisingly consistent, coherent manner in several of his treatises, a fact that speaks to the place this reading held for him throughout his career. Whether Philo was following the lead of other

---

into the world of Second Temple Judaism in the Diaspora that formed the matrix for Christian theology" (252).

5. See Philo's arguments against the "extreme allegorizers," who thought that they could dismiss the literal precepts of the law because they had learned the true, allegorical interpretations of the law (*Migr.* 89–94). Although, it must be noted, the fact that Philo is arguing against these Jews testifies to the fact that Paul was not the first, or the only Jew to make this move.

Jewish exegetes before him in this novel reading of the Genesis story or was the innovator of the interpretation can only be guessed,[6] but what is certain is that the relationship between paideia and wisdom or philosophy was a topic much discussed by Greek philosophers. The Stoic Ariston of Chios argued that "those who labor with the preliminary studies but neglect philosophy are like the suitors of Penelope, who, when they failed to win her over, took up with her maid servants instead."[7] Philo, having no desire to read Homer allegorically, applies similar principles to his reading of the Genesis narrative. In book three of his *Allegorical Laws*, Philo gives us a succinct overview of his allegorical interpretation:

> But it is necessary to consider another woman, of what sort Sarah happened to be, the governing virtue [τὴν ἄρχουσαν ἀρετήν]; and the wise Abraham was guided by her, when she recommended him such actions as were good. For before this time, when he was not yet perfect, but even before his name was changed, he gave his attention to subjects of lofty philosophical speculation; and she, knowing that he could not produce anything out of perfect virtue [ἐπισταμένη ὅτι οὐκ ἂν δύναιτο γεννᾶν ἐξ ἀρετῆς τελείας], counseled him to raise children out of her handmaid, that is to say out of encyclical education [ἐκ τῆς παιδίσκης τουτέστι παιδείας τῆς ἐγκυκλίου], out of Agar, which name being interpreted means a dwelling

---

6. See, for example, Niehoff's discussion of the allegorization of Sarah in Maren R. Niehoff, "Mother and Maiden, Sister and Spouse: Sarah in Philonic Midrash," *HTR* 97 (2004): 413–44. Niehoff asserts: "In the realm of allegory, Philo is conversant with an existing exegetical tradition on which he freely draws. Yet he also makes his own contributions to that tradition" (ibid., 433).

7. Ἀρίστων ὁ Χῖος τοὺς περὶ τὰ ἐγκύκλια μαθήματα πονουμένους, ἀμελοῦντας δὲ φιλοσοφίας, ἔλεγεν ὁμοίους εἶναι τοῖς μνηστῆρσι τῆς Πηνελόπης, οἳ ἀποτυγχάνοντες ἐκείνης περὶ τὰς θεραπαίνας ἐγίνοντο (*SVF* 1:350). Stobaeus preserves the fragment. Elsewhere the comment is credited to Gorgias (*GV* 166). See Albert Henrichs, "Philosophy, the Handmaiden of Theology," *GRBS* 9 (1968): 444; and Kathleen Freeman, *Ancilla to the Pre-Socratic Philosophers: A Complete Translation of the Fragments in Diels* Fragmente der Vorsokratiker (Cambridge: Harvard University Press, 1957), 139. According to Pseudo-Plutarch, the statement is the philosopher Bion's: ἀστείως δὲ καὶ Βίων ἔλεγεν ὁ φιλόσοφος ὅτι ὥσπερ οἱ μνηστῆρες τῇ Πηνελόπῃ πλησιάζειν μὴ δυνάμενοι ταῖς ταύτης ἐμίγνυντο θεραπαίναις, οὕτω καὶ οἱ φιλοσοφίας μὴ δυνάμενοι κατατυχεῖν ἐν τοῖς ἄλλοις παιδεύμασι τοῖς οὐδενὸς ἀξίοις ἑαυτοὺς κατασκελετεύουσι (*Lib. ed.* 7d). See also Yehoshua Amir, "The Transference of Greek Allegories to Biblical Motifs in Philo," in *Nourished with Peace: Studies in Hellenistic Judaism in Memory of Samuel Sandmel*, ed. Frederick E. Greenspahn, Earle Hilgert, and Burton L. Mack (Chico, CA: Scholars Press, 1984), 15–25.

near; for he who meditates dwelling in perfect virtue, before his name is enrolled among the citizens of that state, dwells among the encyclical studies [τοῖς ἐγκυκλίοις μαθήμασι], in order that through their instrumentality he may make his approaches at liberty towards perfect virtue. After that, when he saw that he had become perfect, and was now able to become a father, although he himself was full of gratitude towards those studies [τὰ παιδεύματα], by means of which he had been recommended to virtue, and thought it hard to renounce them; he was well inclined to be appeased by an oracle from God which laid this command on him. "In everything which Sarah says, obey her voice." (*Leg.* 3.244–245)

Here we see the necessary role the encyclical studies play for the virtue-desiring Abraham. This paideia (Hagar) was given to Abraham by his wife Sarah because he was not yet ready for her, that is, for virtue or wisdom. By means of this paideia Abraham was educated and prepared to finally attain the loftier knowledge that he sought, but in so doing, he had to give up this instruction, even though he cared a great deal for these studies.

Thankfully for us, Philo devotes an entire treatise to the encyclical studies, *On Mating with the Preliminary Studies*; so we know, in some detail, how he viewed this paideia, both its benefits and its dangers.[8] Philo saw this paideia as necessary for most people who desire true wisdom: "For we are not as yet capable of becoming the fathers of the offspring of virtue, unless we first of all have a connection with her handmaiden; and the handmaiden of wisdom is the encyclical knowledge of music and logic, arrived at by previous instruction.... So the encyclical branches of instruc-

---

8. Most studies related to Philo and paideia have focused exclusively on his relationship to the encyclical or preliminary paideia. See Paul Wendland, *Die hellenistisch-römische Kultur in ihren Beziehungen zu Judentum und Christentum*, HNT 1.2 (Tübingen: Mohr Siebeck, 1907), 114–20; F. H. Colson, "Philo on Education," *JTS* 18 (1917): 151–62; Isaak Heinemann, *Philons griechische und jüdische Bildung: Kulturvergleichende Untersuchungen zu Philons Darstellung der jüdischen Gesetze* (Hildesheim: Olms, 1962); Monique Alexandre, *De congressu eruditionis gratia*, OPA 16 (Paris: Cerf, 1967); Thomas Conley, *"General Education" in Philo of Alexandria*, PSC 15 (Berkeley: Center for Hermeneutical Studies in Hellenistic and Modern Culture, 1975); and Alan Mendelson, *Secular Education in Philo of Alexandria*, HUCM 7 (Cincinnati: Hebrew Union College Press, 1982). One of the rare exceptions is W. H. Wagner, "Philo and Paideia," *Cithara* 10 (1971): 53–64, a brief but nevertheless thorough discussion of Philo's complex views on paideia. See also Tae Won Kang, "Wisdom Mythology and Hellenistic Paideia in Philo: A Case Study of *De Congressu Quaerendae Eruditionis Gratia*" (PhD diss., The Claremont Graduate School, 1999).

tion are placed in front of virtue, for they are the road which conducts to her" (*Congr.* 9–10). While Philo continually points out the importance of this encyclical paideia for most people, the exemplar being Abraham, who is the type of one who acquires wisdom through instruction,[9] there are some who do not need this paideia in their attainment of virtue, such as Isaac: "But the self-taught race [αὐτομαθὲς γένος], of which Isaac was a partaker, the greatest joy of good things, has received as its share a nature simple, unmixed, and pure, standing in need of neither training nor instruction, in which there is need of the concubine sciences and not only of the citizen wives" (*Congr.* 36).

The benefits of the preliminary studies are, then, for the majority of people, clear and profound. But, this is not the end of the narrative. Philo must explain why Sarah banishes Hagar and forces Abraham to abandon this paideia, of which he was so fond. Could they not coexist? In beginning to understand Philo's reading of this important piece of the Genesis narrative, we must be aware that Philo, often forcefully, makes clear that the handmaiden, paideia, is in no way to be confused with the true mistress, wisdom. First of all, as opposed to one's connection with wisdom, which is noetic (i.e., via the mind or νοῦς), the connection to encyclical paideia is somatic and sensory (i.e., via the body or σῶμα and the senses, or αἰσθήσεις):

> For it follows of necessity that the man who delights in the encyclical contemplations, and who joins himself as a companion to varied learning, is as such enrolled under the banners of the earthly and Egyptian body [ἀνάγκη γὰρ τὸν ἐγχορεύοντα ταῖς ἐγκυκλίοις θεωρίαις καὶ πολυμαθείας ἑταῖρον ὄντα τῷ γεώδει καὶ Αἰγυπτίῳ προσκεκληρῶσθαι σώματι]; and that he stands in need of eyes in order to see and to read, and of ears in order to attend and to hear, and of his other external senses, in such a manner as to be able to unfold each of the objects of the external sense [τῶν αἰσθητῶν]. (*Congr.* 20)

Because of this bodily connection, the sarkic desires tend to weigh down and oppress the soul. Herein lies the potential danger of Greek paideia, becoming too infatuated with the handmaiden to the detriment

---

9. See *Migr.* 88, where Abraham is the exemplar of one who acquires virtue through instruction (διδακτική), Jacob through practice (ἀσκητική), while Isaac is a rare member of the self-taught race (αὐτομαθὲς γένος).

of the mistress: "For some men, being attracted by the charms of handmaidens, have neglected their true mistress, philosophy, and have grown old, some in poetry, and others in the study of painting, and others in the mixture of colors, and others in ten thousand other pursuits, without ever being able to return to the proper mistress" (*Congr.* 77). The neglected mistress will not just sit idly by, but will convict the guilty party to his face:

> I am treated unjustly, and in utter violation of our agreement, as far as depends on you who transgress the covenants entered into between us; for from the time that you first took to your bosom the elementary branches of education, you have honored above measure the offspring of my handmaiden, and have respected her as your wife, and you have so completely repudiated me that you never by any chance came to the same place with me. (*Congr.* 151–152; see also 158–159)

Because of this danger, this pull to infatuation with the preliminary studies, they must be given up entirely if one is to fully embrace the true "wife" of virtue or wisdom.

Another area where we see the marked difference, in other treatises, between paideia and wisdom is in Philo's depictions of Ishmael and Isaac. While Isaac, the child of Sarah, represents a σοφός, a wise man, Ishmael, Hagar's son, represents a sophist:

> For Isaac received wisdom for his inheritance, and Ishmael sophistry [σοφίαν μὲν γὰρ Ἰσαάκ, σοφιστείαν δὲ Ἰσμαὴλ κεκλήρωται].... For the same relation which a completely infant child bears to a full-grown man, the same does a sophist bear to a wise man, and the encyclical branches of education to real knowledge in virtue." (*Sobr.* 9)

With this strong dichotomy between encyclical paideia and wisdom explicitly made, we now can understand why Sarah had to banish Hagar and why Abraham had to give up his precious studies. As Philo explains elsewhere:

> But when Abram, instead of an inquirer into natural philosophy, became a wise man and a lover of God ... then too those elementary branches of instruction which bear the name of Agar, will be cast out, and their sophistical child will also be cast out, who is named Ishmael. And they shall undergo eternal banishment, God himself confirming their expulsion,

when he bids the wise man obey the word spoken by Sarah, and she urges him expressly to cast out the serving woman and her son; and it is good to be guided by virtue, and especially so when it teaches such lessons as this, that the most perfect natures are very greatly different from the mediocre habits, and that wisdom is a wholly different thing from sophistry [σοφία σοφιστείας ἀλλότριον]; for the one labors to devise what is persuasive for the establishment of a false opinion, which is pernicious to the soul, but wisdom, with long meditation on the truth by the knowledge of right reason [ὀρθοῦ λόγου], brings real advantage to the intellect. (*Cher.* 7–9)

Sarah's banishing of Hagar and Ishmael is meant to demonstrate to the reader the vast difference between paideia and wisdom and the need to dispose of preliminary education, once having attained virtue, lest one is tempted by her (bodily) charms and begins to mistake the handmaiden for the mistress.

Philo's allegorical interpretation of the Hagar/Sarah narrative is extremely well developed and consistently applied throughout several treatises of his corpus. The topic was obviously an extremely important one for Philo, living in the most Hellenistic of cities, and his allegorical understanding of the Genesis story is an attempt to reconcile the obvious benefits he perceives in a traditional Greek education with the possibly disastrous influences it could play in the Jewish community if not undertaken with proper care. For Philo, this paideia was a means to an end, like the torah itself. In contrast to the Mosaic law, however, Philo insists that once the end is achieved—the attainment of wisdom or virtue—this paideia must be set aside. The temptations of the handmaiden are just too great to allow her to live in the same house as the mistress.

Paul's Allegory

Paul's allegorical understanding of Sarah and Hagar in Galatians has been widely studied, as it speaks to many of the themes continuously at the forefront of Pauline studies, such as Paul's relationship with and understanding of the Jewish law and his overall conception of the Christian community. Recent studies, beginning with Barrett's 1976 article,[10] have largely moved

---

10. C. K. Barrett, "The Allegory of Abraham, Sarah, and Hagar in the Argument of Galatians," in *Rechtfertigung: Festschrift für Ernst Käsemann zum 70. Geburtstag*, ed. Johannes Friedrich, Wolfgang Pöhlmann, and Peter Stuhlmacher (Tübingen: Mohr Siebeck, 1976), 1–16. Barrett notes the two main problems with which commentators

away from the traditional understanding of the allegory as anti-Jewish rhetoric and have, instead, given a more nuanced reading, often in light of recent depictions of Paul associated with the "new perspective" or with the "radical new perspective."[11] Despite the great strides made in recent years,

---

have struggled in dealing with the allegory: the interpretation of its details and the reason Paul included it in his letter. With a few exceptions, Barrett dismisses most previous scholarship on the topic due to the fact that most scholars had either ignored the allegory altogether, or they simply dismissed its importance and place within the letter, relegating it to a minor (and not very convincing) support to Paul's larger argument. Barrett attempts to rectify this situation and, in so doing, begins a new history of interpretation followed by many modern Pauline scholars. He argues that Paul's use of scripture in Gal 3 and 4 is directly due to the fact that his opponents in Galatia used those same passages to their own ends, and Paul, then, tries to turn the tables on them. In the case of the allegory, Paul's opponents used the Sarah/Hagar story, interpreting the Genesis passages literally, in support of their own argument: they are the true descendants of Abraham through the covenant made with God through circumcision; the gentiles are descendants of Hagar; if they want to be a part of Abraham's seed, they must be circumcised; if not, they must be cast out like Hagar and Ishmael. This move by his opponents gives Paul the impetus to take up these passages from Genesis, passages which he would not have used otherwise (due to this literal interpretation). While his opponents interpret literally, Paul asserts that the matters are to be spoken of or interpreted allegorically. When they are, the opponents' position is reversed: the physical descendants of Sarah become the spiritual descendants of Hagar, whereas the physical descendants of Hagar (i.e., gentiles) become the spiritual descendants of Sarah, the inheritors of the promise.

11. Representing the "new perspective," James D. G. Dunn (*Galatians*, BNTC [London: Black, 1993], 256–57) does not see in the allegory a contrast between the Jews and the Christians, but instead between those of the spirit versus those who rely on circumcision as a marker of covenant: "The child of Hagar is the child 'born according to the flesh'; but that corresponds, *not* to the descendants of Ishmael, but to the Jews, or at least those of them who relied on their physical ('according to the flesh') descent from Abraham" (emphasis Dunn's). So, for example, in Gal 4:28, "But you, brothers, are children of the promise like Isaac," Dunn emphasizes that Paul is saying, "not 'you' gentiles over against or excluding Jews in whole or part, but 'you' gentile believers in particular, 'you too.'" Dunn does not see Paul conceiving of two separate covenants here, but only one, with Hagar and her offspring representing the covenant wrongly perceived. Representing the "radical new perspective" is Mark D. Nanos, "What Does 'Present Jerusalem' (Gal 4:25) in Paul's Allegory Have to Do with the Jerusalem of Paul's Time, or the Concerns of the Galatians?" (paper presented at the Annual Meeting of the Central States Region of the Society of Biblical Literature, Saint Louis, MO, 28–29 March 2004). Nanos does not see a dichotomy between Jew and Christian or between gentile Christian and Jewish Christian in Paul's allegory.

nearly all scholars continue to overlook the possible connection between Paul's allegory and Philo's and, therefore, to miss a potentially illuminating comparison.[12]

Moving from Philo's allegorical reading of the Genesis narrative to Paul's, we find that Paul's interpretation has at its foundation a tradition akin to Philo's, but with two significant modifications: the Mosaic law itself has become a type of Philo's encyclical or preliminary paideia; and the loftier goal of wisdom has been freely given to the community of believers. This first alteration, torah as paideia, seems to be one of the overarching themes of Paul's central argument in his letter to Galatia.[13] In Gal 3:1–18, Paul explains to the Galatians that the law was never intended to provide justification of sins, and that belief and faith are the keys to becoming inheritors of the promise given to Abraham and his seed. So he writes: "Did you receive the spirit through works of the law or through the hearing of faith?" (Gal 3:2); "Therefore, does he supply you with the spirit and work powers among you because of works of the law or because of the

---

Paul instead uses the allegory in support of his argument against proselyte conversion for gentiles. The Sarah covenant represents the birth of free sons, "Israelites and those from the nations who join them through faith in Christ," while Hagar represents the birth of slave sons, or Jewish proselytes (Nanos, "Present Jerusalem," 4). Gentiles have no need to become full proselytes; in fact, they must not, as it directly opposes Paul's view of monotheism. Jews must remain Jews and gentiles must remain gentiles.

12. Peder Borgen ("Some Hebrew and Pagan Features in Philo's and Paul's Interpretation of Hagar and Ishmael," in *The New Testament and Hellenistic Judaism*, ed. Peder Borgen and Søren Giversen [Aarhus: Aarhus University Press, 1995], 151–64) is the only recent scholar who has attempted to read the allegory of Paul in light of Philo of Alexandria's in order to see what light may be thrown upon Paul's interpretation of the Genesis passage. Although he discusses Philo's allegorical interpretation briefly, it is chiefly in his more literal exegesis of the Genesis narrative that Borgen finds a possible background for Paul's allegory. In *Abr.* 247–251, Philo portrays Hagar as a sort of "borderline" figure. She is "an Egyptian by birth, but a Hebrew by choice" (*Abr.* 251), and so, for Borgen, a Jewish proselyte. It is against this type of exegetical background that Paul, then, makes his chief argument in the allegory: Hagar and Ishmael represent the model for Jewish proselytes and those Judaizers in Galatia who want to make slaves out of the Christian gentiles.

13. Most commentators view Gal 3–4 as containing the crux of Paul's message to the Galatians. See, for example, Hans Dieter Betz, *Galatians: A Commentary on Paul's Letter to the Churches in Galatia*, Hermeneia (Philadelphia: Fortress, 1979), 128, who views the allegory as the concluding argument in the *probatio* section of the letter, the most decisive section of the text where Paul presents his proofs, which begins at Gal 3:1.

hearing of faith?" (Gal 3:5); "You know that it is those of faith who are the sons of Abraham" (Gal 3:7); "So, those of faith are blessed with the faithful Abraham" (Gal 3:9); "For it is clear that no one is justified before God by the law; for 'The righteous one will live by faith'" (Gal 3:11); and finally, "For if the inheritance is from the law, it is no longer from the promise; but God freely gave it to Abraham through a promise" (Gal 3:18).

If justification of sins was not the purpose of the law, why then the law? Paul tells us exactly why in Gal 3:19–4:2. The law "was given for the sake of transgressions, until the seed to whom it was promised should come" (Gal 3:19). Despite what some commentators suggest, this verse does not have any negative connotation with regard to the law.[14] If we follow Paul's logic, what he suggests is that the promise was given to Abraham because of his faith, and to those after him through faith, but transgressions continued to increase. Therefore, the law was given in order to educate the Jews and to inform them of their sins. As opposed to those not under the law, who may transgress without knowing it, the Jews have been given a great gift and a great help.

Galatians 3:23 is another verse which many scholars view as key to Paul's negative portrait of the law: "Before the faith came, we were protected under the law, contained until the faith would be revealed."[15] Again, Paul seems to be suggesting that the law has a preparatory, custodial purpose, a point made most explicit in his depiction of the law as a child's pedagogue: "So then the law was our pedagogue until Christ, in order that we might be justified by faith. But now that the faith has come, we are no longer under a pedagogue" (ὑπὸ παιδαγωγόν; Gal 3:24–25). While there is no room here for a full study of Paul's use of the term παιδαγωγός, it is clear that the figure of the pedagogue is often given an

---

14. Traditional interpretation of Gal 3:19a has long understood this (and see also Rom 5:20) as Paul arguing that the law was given to actually produce sin and increase wickedness, with Gal 3:19b referring to the inferiority of the law due to angelic or even demonic mediation. See the discussion and bibliography, as well as Dunn's refutation of this line of interpretation, in James D. G. Dunn, *The Theology of Paul the Apostle* (Grand Rapids: Eerdmans, 1998), 139–40. For a more recent understanding of Gal 3:19 along traditional lines, see Chris VanLandingham, *Judgment and Justification in Early Judaism and the Apostle Paul* (Peabody, MA: Hendrickson, 2006), 207.

15. Πρὸ τοῦ δὲ ἐλθεῖν τὴν πίστιν ὑπὸ νόμον ἐφρουρούμεθα συγκλειόμενοι εἰς τὴν μέλλουσαν πίστιν ἀποκαλυφθῆναι. Most modern English translations assign the law here the role of jailor as opposed to guard or protector, as my translation attempts to make clear.

all too negative portrayal in traditional scholarship.[16] It is true that the ancient pedagogue was often a rather strict disciplinarian, but he served a necessary purpose in a child's upbringing. The pedagogue was responsible for protecting the children under his care on their way to and from school, and, depending on the slave's own literate education, he would tutor the children in their lessons and sometimes even give primary instruction himself.[17] Therefore, in making this comparison, Paul asserts that the law had a necessary pedagogical and protective purpose at one time for the Jews, as preparation for the time when the Jewish messiah would come and the promise of Abraham's inheritance would be given to those who have faith in that messiah.

Paul continues this preparatory imagery in Gal 4:1–2: "What I am saying is that for a certain period of time the heir is an infant, no better than a slave, though he may be the lord of the whole estate; but he is under guardians and administrators [ὑπὸ ἐπιτρόπους ... καὶ οἰκονόμους] until the time set by his father." Despite the depiction of the helpless child, an heir though a slave, these administrators cannot have a negative connotation. Of course the child needs them; a child heir without professional adults to aid him would no doubt lose his inheritance rather quickly.

Paul's message has been consistent throughout his argument: the law did have its purpose for those under it, just as Philo's encyclical paideia has a purpose for those who desire the greater goal of wisdom. Both Paul and Philo use imagery related to children. Philo's προπαιδεύματα consisted of those subjects typically taught to children; as an infant relates to an adult, so the preliminary studies relate to wisdom (*Sobr.* 9). Paul depicts

---

16. See for example, Richard N. Longenecker, "The Pedagogical Nature of the Law in Galatians 3:19–4:7," *JETS* 25 (1982): 53–61. Longenecker, based on his examination of the pedagogue in Greek and Hebrew sources, asserts that "It is not possible to interpret Gal 3:24–25 as assigning a positive preliminary or preparatory role to the Law. The point of the analogy for Paul is not that the Law was a preparation for Christ. Rather, the focus is on the inferior status of one who is under a pedagogue and the temporary nature of such a situation" (ibid., 55–56). Unfortunately, Longenecker's investigation does not include Philo's usage of *paidagōgos*, who often pairs the pedagogue with *didaskoloi*. Often Philo does depict the pedagogue as rather harsh, but he is nevertheless necessary for children. For fairer treatments see Norman H. Young, "*Paidagogos*: The Social Setting of a Pauline Metaphor," *NovT* 29 (1987): 150–76; and Philip F. Esler, *Galatians*, NTR (London: Routledge, 1998), 200–202.

17. See Stanley F. Bonner, *Education in Ancient Rome: From the Elder Cato to the Younger Pliny* (Berkeley: University of California Press, 1977), 34–46.

the law as serving as a child's pedagogue or as an infant heir's trustees. His imagery may at times be a bit harsher than Philo's, but the purpose for both Philo and Paul is largely the same: preparatory. Just as Philo's paideia prepares the student for true wisdom, Paul's torah prepares the ward for his true inheritance. The glaring difference, of course, is that Philo gives the clearly subordinate position to Greek paideia, which must, at some point, be abandoned, whereas Paul gives the same place to Jewish paideia.

Like Philo, Paul uses language that suggests the inherent dangers of the preliminary studies. In Gal 4:3, Paul completes the analogy begun in Gal 3:24–25 and 4:1–2. Just as children are under the control of their pedagogue or their trustees until maturity, "So too with us; when we were infants, we were enslaved under the elements of the cosmos" (ὑπὸ τὰ στοιχεῖα τοῦ κόσμου). This passage and the precise reference of these στοιχεῖα τοῦ κόσμου has long been the topic of extensive scholarly discussion.[18] The Greek term στοιχεῖον has the basic meaning of a part of a larger whole or series and, in classical Greek literature, commonly refers to an element of language or music—for example, a syllable, the initial sound of a word, a letter, a part of speech, a note, and so on—an elementary or foundational principle, or one of the four basic elements which make up the universe and everything in it: earth, water, air, and fire. In attempting to understand Paul's aim in Gal 4:3 (and 4:9), scholars have posited all extant meanings of the term and some not explicitly occurring in classical Greek sources, most popularly that the στοιχεῖα τοῦ κόσμου are pagan elemental or astrological spirits or deities.[19] The phrase in Gal 4 occurs at a crucial point in Paul's argument concerning the (once) pedagogical nature of the Mosaic law, as he is transitioning from discussing solely the Jewish people to a broader consideration of the Jews and the gentiles together. Most understandings of the στοιχεῖα τοῦ κόσμου, however, have relegated them to the sole provenance of the gentiles—for example, astral deities—which

---

18. For reviews of the pertinent secondary literature, see Gerhard Delling, "στοιχεῖον," *TDNT* 7:670–87; David R. Bundrick, "Ta stoicheia tou kosmou (Gal 4:3)," *JETS* 34 (1991): 353–64; and Martinus C. de Boer, "The Meaning of the Phrase τὰ στοιχεῖα τοῦ κόσμου in Galatians," *NTS* 53 (2007): 204–224.

19. See, e.g., Betz, *Galatians*, 205. Note that though we do not have clear evidence for this meaning of *stoicheia* in classical Greek literature, we do find that both Philo (*Contempl.* 3–5) and the author of the Wisdom of Solomon (Wis 7:17–19; 13:1–3) alluded to worship or deification of the cosmic elements. This has been a favored understanding of the phrase in Gal 4 since the early patristic period.

disrupts Paul's rhetorical point throughout his larger argument concerning the efficacy and necessity of the law. Martinus de Boer's recent article has come the closest to reconciling this apparent dilemma.

Following the work of Josef Blinzler, Eduard Schweizer, and Dietrich Rusam, Boer confidently begins from the assumption that "the phrase τὰ στοιχεῖα τοῦ κόσμου is a technical expression referring in the first instance to the four elements of the physical universe: earth, water, air, fire," and that the Galatians would have understood the phrase immediately in this sense.[20] These στοιχεῖα were, additionally, the weak, impotent things, which are not gods by nature (Gal 4:8–9), but which the Galatians had at one point apparently worshiped as such. Using texts from Philo and the Wisdom of Solomon as support for the idea that at least some Jews conceived of gentiles worshiping the elements of the universe, Boer takes Paul's use of the phrase τὰ στοιχεῖα τοῦ κόσμου as a metonym for a wider complex of Galatian religious beliefs and practices centered on the four constituent elements.[21]

Despite this clear referent, Boer is not convinced that this meaning is adequate to Paul's argument at this point in the text and argued that the phrase must have had some additional intended meaning. Pointing out that the phrase ὑπὸ νόμον in Gal 4:4–5 serves as an "apparent synonym" for the phrase ὑπὸ τὰ στοιχεῖα τοῦ κόσμου and is meant to echo Gal 3:25, where Paul argues that, with the arrival of Christ, the people are no longer ὑπὸ παιδαγωγόν, Boer understands Paul to be establishing a parallel between existence ὑπὸ στοιχεῖα and that ὑπὸ νόμον, where a return to observance of the Jewish law is equivalent to a return to the worship of the στοιχεῖα.[22] This is the reason Paul decided to bring the στοιχεῖα τοῦ κόσμου into the discussion at this point in his argument: "In Paul's mind the observance of the Law and the veneration of the στοιχεῖα were in some sense functionally and thus also conceptually equivalent."[23] Paul, then, reinforces this equivalence in his deprecation of calendrical observances, using terminology that would apply to both Jewish and pagan festivals (Gal 4:10). In the end, according to Boer, Paul argues that, with the coming of Christ and the gift of redemption through faith, enslavement to the στοιχεῖα τοῦ κόσμου is no different from enslavement to the Jewish law, and that to turn to the

---

20. Boer, "Meaning of the Phrase," 207–8.
21. Ibid., 220.
22. Ibid., 213–16.
23. Ibid., 215.

Jewish law now would, in effect, return the Galatians to a time when they still worshipped the στοιχεῖα.

In his article from a year later, Johannes Woyke takes up Boer's work, attempting to better understand how Paul could conceptually equate observance of the Jewish law with pagan worship of the στοιχεῖα.[24] In this, Woyke sees the depiction of the στοιχεῖα in Gal 4:9 as "weak and impotent" as particularly enlightening, and comes to understand this impotence as the inability of the στοιχεῖα to overcome the passions and desires of the flesh. Woyke finds help in Philo's allegorical reading of Gen 15, found primarily in his treatise *Quis rerum divinarum heres sit*, where Philo asks whether an individual who is dependent on the body and the sense-perceptible world is capable of inheriting incorporeal and divine things (*Her.* 63). In order to become heir of the spiritual, Abraham had to abandon his ties to the earthly and to the flesh, symbolized by his former Chaldean home and his former gods, and instead focus on the noetic and incorporeal. While in *Her.* 274, Philo makes clear that the mind, which must reside in the body, requires encyclical education in order to return back to its original, desired state as pure soul or mind, Woyke here assumes that this "Tugendbildung" is exemplified in the Mosaic law,[25] setting up a clear distinction between Philo's dichotomy between the στοιχεῖα of Abraham's Chaldean past and the νόμος that allows Abraham to become the true heir, and Paul's equivalence between the Jewish νόμος and the pagan στοιχεῖα. Paul, for Woyke, understands both the νόμος and the στοιχεῖα as relegated to the earthly and fleshly domains and imbued, therefore, with sin. Woyke finds Philo's reading of Gen 15:15 in *Her.* 277–279 so analogous to Paul's argument of returning to the στοιχεῖα that he allows for the possibility that Paul was facing opponents in Galatia with knowledge of this Jewish-Hellenistic interpretation.[26]

Both Boer's and Woyke's works have much to offer for understanding Paul's use of the phrase τὰ στοιχεῖα τοῦ κόσμου at this particular point in his argument, and they give us a solid starting point from which to begin, though their arguments are not without problems. First, Boer insists that the Mosaic law as pedagogue cannot be interpreted in a positive light, that is, as protective or pedagogical, but only in a restrictive and oppressive

---

24. Johannes Woyke, "Nochmals zu den 'schwachen und unfähigen Elementen' (Gal 4.9): Paulus, Philo und die στοιχεῖα τοῦ κόσμου," *NTS* 54 (2008): 221–34.

25. Ibid., 229.

26. Ibid., 233.

sense. The law is the jailor, depriving humans of freedom and keeping them from righteousness, like the child heir under his guardians and household managers.[27] Second, and more problematic, neither Boer nor Woyke consider what light might be shed from Philo's allegorical reading of the Hagar, Sarah, and Abraham narrative. This is particularly surprising in Woyke's article, as he uses other aspects of Philo's allegorical interpretation of the Abraham story to help in explaining the connection between the στοιχεῖα and the law. It is, in fact, Philo's explanation of the Sarah/Hagar narrative that helps to best explain the dual referent of the στοιχεῖα τοῦ κόσμου as both pagan religiosity and the precepts of the Mosaic law.

While Boer makes the case that only with the calendrical observances does Paul's reference to the veneration of the στοιχεῖα serve fully as an actual equivalent to the observance of the law,[28] I argue that Paul's reference to the στοιχεῖα was intended to be simultaneously understood as both the elements which comprise the universe and the elements which comprise the torah. Paul is purposefully drawing on the ambiguity of the Greek term στοιχεῖον, which, as we saw, could regularly refer to either an element of the cosmos or to an element of language, most telling in the case of Paul, to a letter, or γράμμα. While technically the στοιχεῖα were to be distinguished from the γράμματα, in many classical authors they appear as virtual synonyms.[29] It is this common usage of στοιχεῖα as γράμματα that Paul expects his readers to understand as the second referent in Gal 4:3 and 4:9, and, in this way, we are reminded of Paul's typical antithesis between the letter of the law and the spirit, particularly after the death of Christ: "For, while we were in the flesh, the sinful desires, which come via the law, were at work in our limbs to bear fruit for death. But now we have been released from the law, having died to that by which we were bound, so that we are slaves [δουλεύειν ἡμᾶς] in the newness of the spirit, not in the oldness of the letter" (γράμματος; Rom 7:5–6; see also Rom 2:27–29;

---

27. Boer, "Meaning of the Phrase," 211–13. Woyke seems to back off a bit from this thoroughly negative view of the law: "Gal 4.3, 9 als Gleichsetzung jüdischer und paganer Religiosität zu verstehen, wäre indes eine Fehlinterpretation. Vielmehr weist Paulus dem jüdischen νόμος eine wichtige, aber heilsgeschichtlich letztlich episodenhafte Funktion zu, welche ihren Telos in der Neuschöpfung durch den Glauben an Christus findet" ("Schwachen und unfähigen Elementen," 233).

28. Boer, "Meaning of the Phrase," 222–23.

29. See, e.g., Plato, *Theaet.* 202E–203A. Philo often uses the term to refer either to individual vowels or to letters in general (*Opif.* 126; *Sacr.* 74; *Agr.* 136; *Her.* 282; *Congr.* 150; *Leg.* 1.14; 3.121). See the discussion in LSJ, s.v. στοιχεῖον, II.1.

2 Cor 3:5–8). Just as the people were enslaved to the στοιχεῖα τοῦ κόσμου prior to Christ, so too were they enslaved to the letter of the law. In Gal 4:3, Paul chose the term στοιχεῖα over the near equivalent γράμματα, so that he could make the passage relevant to the gentiles as well as the Jews: as the gentiles were enslaved to their elemental deities, the Jews were enslaved to the precepts of the torah. The conceptual equivalence, as argued by Boer and then Woyke, between the pagan religiosity and Jewish torah practice becomes even clearer if we read the στοιχεῖα as referring to religious and/or cultural foundations fundamental to both gentiles and Jews, especially after the arrival of Christ.

Paul continues with the imagery of slavery to the στοιχεῖα in Gal 4:8–9: "But then, when you did not know God, you served those things which by nature are not gods. But now that you have come to know God, or rather to be known by God, how can you turn back again to the weak and beggarly elements [τὰ ἀσθενῆ καὶ πτωχὰ στοιχεῖα], to which you again wish to be enslaved?" While this language may seem excessive as a description of the Mosaic law, it makes sense if Paul understands the law as paideia preliminary to wisdom and as unnecessary or even dangerous once wisdom is achieved. Just as the gentiles served the elements as if they were actually deities, the Jews served the elements of the law as if they were themselves gods, and now that Christ has come, and with him, free access to the desired goal of wisdom, the elements of the law are just as weak and ineffectual as the cosmic elements.

Paul is adamant in his warning about the dangers of becoming too devoted to the Mosaic pedagogue, particularly because of the second major modification he makes to the Philonic interpretation of the Hagar/Sarah allegory: Christ has come and thereby provided the goal to which the Mosaic law served as preparation. The law did have its purpose at one time, but that time has since passed. Those of faith are no longer infants, but full-grown adults, and to go backwards is not an option. This is a move that Paul makes repeatedly throughout his letters (e.g., Rom 7:4; 10:4), and it is explicitly made in the argument leading up to the allegory. A key passage is Gal 3:13–14: "Christ redeemed us from the curse of the law, becoming a curse for us … in order that the blessing of Abraham might come to the gentiles, in order that we might receive the promise of the spirit through our faith." Christ has released humanity from the need for preliminary education through the torah. The goal to which the torah was preparatory has now been freely given: "But when the fullness of time had come, God sent forth his son, born from a woman, born under the law, in order that he might redeem those under the law, in order that we might receive adoption as sons. And because you are sons, God sent forth the spirit of his son into your hearts, crying out, 'Abba! Father!' so that you are no longer a slave but a son, and an heir through God" (Gal 4:4–7). The language of adoption provides further confirmation that Paul had intended the στοιχεῖα to have a dual referent. Christ came to first redeem those ὑπὸ νόμον—that is, the Jews—and then those who would be adopted into the family—that is, the gentiles.

Paul's argument leading up to the allegory, then, is that the Mosaic law had a specific and necessary function at one time. It was designed to manage sin and to prepare one for the time of faith when Abraham's inheritance would be made available, but now that Christ has come and died, the inheritance is possible for those who are of faith, both Jews and gentiles. Therefore, the preparatory role of the Mosaic law is no longer necessary for the believer. Because of this, Paul warns his audience, with sometimes quite harsh language, of the dangers of being too enticed by the law and admonishes them for wishing to return to it. After a passionate, personal plea with the Galatians (Gal 4:11–20), Paul moves on to the final, closing piece of his argument, the allegory of Hagar and Sarah.

We may best understand the crisis in the Galatian communities by assessing Paul's motivations, not only for using the allegory at this point in his argument, but also for explicitly stating that these passages from Genesis are spoken of allegorically (Gal 4:24).[30] Nowhere else does Paul make such an unequivocal reference to his allegorical interpretation of scripture, and, in so doing, he attempts to alert his audience to the allegorical understanding of the narrative of which they were already aware, namely, an exegetical tradition similar to Philo's, the only allegorical interpretation of Hagar and Sarah we know of at this time.[31]

---

30. I prefer to understand Paul's phrase ἅτινά ἐστιν ἀλληγορούμενα as meaning "these things are *spoken of* allegorically," as opposed to "*interpreted* allegorically," as many commentators have it. While the difference may seem slight—for if something is spoken of allegorically then it must, out of necessity, be interpreted that way—there is a crucial nuance missed if this participle is not properly understood. Paul is not simply saying that he plans on giving his own, allegorical, interpretation of the Genesis passages. He is affirming that when Moses wrote these passages, he specifically wrote them allegorically, with the intended meaning which Paul wants to explain. The difference lies in the authority given to the interpretation. One is Paul's own; the other is Moses's original meaning that Paul is bringing to light.

31. Elizabeth Castelli points out the importance of a common base between author

Following the lead of Barrett, we could imagine a plausible scenario in which Paul's opponents in Galatia did use these passages from Genesis in support of their own agenda.[32] They hoped to convince the Christ believers that it was necessary to hold to the Mosaic law in its entirety. They used, therefore, a more literal exegesis of the narrative to support their argument: they are the ethnic heirs to the covenant made with Abraham by means of circumcision; if anyone hopes to be heirs as well, they must be circumcised and follow the precepts of the torah. Given Paul's vehement stance in the letter, this argument was obviously quite persuasive to some of the Galatians. Paul, then, responds by telling his audience that the text is not meant to be read literally, but allegorically, as Moses intended. Hagar does not represent the uncircumcised, but preliminary paideia; Sarah does not represent followers of the Mosaic law, but wisdom and virtue. Paul had already modified this allegorical tradition by claiming that the Mosaic law is part of this preliminary paideia, the preparatory study of which is no longer needed now that the promise and wisdom through Christ has been given to those of faith. He reinforces his new understanding of the tradition in the allegory by drawing the contrast between the "slave woman" and the "free woman," a contrast lacking in Philo's exegesis. Hagar's connection to slavery is emphasized in order to demonstrate to the Galatians the mistake of becoming again enslaved to the elements of the Jewish paideia now that the goal of Sarah, the free woman, has been attained. We are free, because "Christ has

---

and reader when dealing with allegory: "It is crucial that the interpreter and the reader share some common understanding about the elements of the allegory. In other words, allegory presumes a kind of pre-existing, if not absolute, consensus between writer and reader." See Elizabeth A. Castelli, "Allegories of Hagar: Reading Galatians 4:21–31 with Postmodern Feminist Eyes," in *The New Literary Criticism and the New Testament*, ed. Elizabeth Struthers Malbon and Edgar V. McKnight, JSNTSup 109 (Sheffield: Sheffield Academic, 1994), 231). See also Charles H. Cosgrove, "The Law Has Given Sarah No Children (Gal. 4:21–30)" *NT* 29 (1987): 220, who asserts that the allegorical interpreter "would make points via allegorical exegesis with which his audience was already in sympathy." A very different view is taken by Jeremy Punt, who sees allegory as often having a "counter-conventional force, which Paul applied with great effect in Gal 4"; see Jeremy Punt, "Revealing Rereading. Part 1: Pauline Allegory in Galatians 4:21–5:1," *Neot* 40 (2006): 87; and Punt, "Revealing Rereading. Part 2: Paul and the Wives of the Father of Faith in Galatians 4:21–5:1," *Neot* 40 (2006): 101–118. In this view of allegory, Punt is following David Dawson, *Allegorical Readers and Cultural Revision in Ancient Alexandria* (Berkeley: University of California Press, 1992).

32. See above, n. 10.

freed us for freedom [like Sarah]; therefore stand fast, and do not *again* be held to the yoke of slavery [like Hagar]" (Gal 5:1, emphasis added).

This dichotomy is also seen in Paul's contrast between Ishmael and Isaac. For Philo, Ishmael, as the offspring of the somatic connection between Abraham and Hagar, was the heir and representative of sophistry, while Isaac, the offspring of the noetic union between Abraham and Sarah, was heir to wisdom. Paul draws a similar contrast, using his typical language of flesh and spirit, which may be compared to Philo's typical opposition between body and soul/mind. Ishmael, "born according to flesh" (Gal 4:23), was born into slavery to the Mosaic paideia, being, in essence, a sophist, slavishly devoted to the letter of the law. Isaac was born "through a promise" (Gal 4:23), that is, through Sarah, and therefore born into freedom, being a σοφός and Abraham's true heir. As we saw, God did not give the inheritance through the law (i.e., Hagar), "but God freely gave it to Abraham *through a promise*" (Gal 3:18; emphasis added). Philo tells us that one reason Ishmael was banished with his mother was "because he, being illegitimate, was mocking the legitimate son, as though he were on terms of equality with him" (*Sobr.* 8).

For Paul, Ishmael was banished because "the one born according to the flesh persecuted the one born according to the spirit" (Gal 4:29). In contrast to his opponents in Galatia, Paul makes clear to his audience that, "You, brothers, are children of the promise like Isaac" (Gal 4:28). They are children "like Isaac" for several reasons. First, and most obviously, Isaac was Sarah's son and Abraham's heir. Next, Isaac is a representative of the pneumatic union between Abraham and Sarah, while Ishmael represents the dangers associated with the sarkic desires of preliminary paideia. Finally, Paul may have known of the interpretation found in Philo, where Isaac is the representative of the "self-taught race" (αὐτομαθὲς γένος), those who have no need of outside instruction in order to attain wisdom:

> But these men were husbands of many wives and concubines, not only those who were citizens, as the sacred scriptures tell us. But Isaac had neither many wives nor any concubine at all, but only his first and wedded wife, who lived with him all his life. Why was this? Because the virtue which is acquired by teaching [ἡ διδακτικὴ ἀρετή], which Abraham pursues, requires many things, both contemplations legitimate according to prudence and those which are illegitimate according to the encyclical, preliminary studies [τὰ ἐγκύκλια προπαιδεύματα].... But the self-taught race [αὐτομαθὲς γένος], of which Isaac was a partaker, the greatest joy of good things, has received as its share a nature simple, unmixed, and

pure, standing in need of neither training nor instruction, in which there is need of the concubine sciences and not only of the citizen wives. For, when God had showered down from above the noble self-learned and self-taught race, it would have been impossible to continue to live with the slavish and concubine arts, desiring illegitimate doctrines as if children. (*Congr.* 34–36)

Here we find a twofold connection to Paul's allegory: Abraham as an example of one who needed paideia to attain loftier wisdom, and Isaac as one who is freely given wisdom, with no need for external instruction or training. Paul is, in essence, telling the community that they are like Isaac because they no longer need preparatory instruction in order to attain the promise. They have already received it because of their faith.

Paul begins the central argument of his letter on the same premises with which he ends it in his allegory: "Are you so foolish that, having begun in the spirit, will you now finish in the flesh?" (Gal 3:3); or in other words, "Are you so foolish that, having begun as Isaac (being an inheritor of the promise) you will now finish like Ishmael (enslaved to the elements of the Mosaic paideia)?" Philo would make the same argument with respect to Greek paideia. For the self-taught Isaac, who begins with wisdom, to become enamored of the encyclical studies is an absurd and contrary notion.

Conclusion

By viewing Paul's chief argument in his letter as a whole, of which the allegory is an essential part, and not looking at Gal 4:21–31 in isolation from what surrounds it, we see that Paul is consistent and coherent in his message. Similar metaphorical imagery is used throughout. Just as the pedagogue serves a preparatory purpose for his student, and just as managers serve a child heir until he reaches maturity, so Hagar served as a means of preparing Abraham for Sarah. Philo makes the connection between Hagar and Greek paideia in order both to encourage his audience to take up the encyclical studies and to warn them of their dangers. Paul makes the connection between Hagar and Jewish paideia in order to explain the role the torah had played for the Jews and to warn his audience of its potential dangers. Unlike Philo, Paul does not encourage those in the community to take up the Mosaic law as paideia, because a new means of attaining Abraham's inheritance has been found in the messiah's justifying death and the believer's faith in the messiah. While Paul does make the rather drastic move of equating the Mosaic law with Philo's preliminary paideia, something which should be discarded once the goal of wisdom is attained, this does not mean that Paul thought of the law in essentially negative terms. Paul never, here or elsewhere, tells us that the law itself is bad or opposed to the will of God. It is one's overzealous devotion to the letter of the law, mistaking the created for the creator, which becomes problematic, especially given Paul's addition of Christ into the equation. For Paul, as for Philo, as for the author of the Letter of Aristeas, the Mosaic torah was a means to an end. Paul diverges from these authors by insisting that the means are no longer needed once the end is achieved.

Bibliography

Alexandre, Monique. *De congressu eruditionis gratia*. OPA 16. Paris: Cerf, 1967.

Amir, Yehoshua. "The Transference of Greek Allegories to Biblical Motifs in Philo." Pages 15–25 in *Nourished with Peace: Studies in Hellenistic Judaism in Memory of Samuel Sandmel*. Edited by Frederick E. Greenspahn, Earle Hilgert, and Burton L. Mack. Chico, CA: Scholars Press, 1984.

Barrett, C. K. "The Allegory of Abraham, Sarah, and Hagar in the Argument of Galatians." Pages 1–16 in *Rechtfertigung: Festschrift für Ernst Käsemann zum 70. Geburtstag*. Edited by Johannes Friedrich, Wolfgang Pöhlmann, and Peter Stuhlmacher. Tübingen: Mohr Siebeck, 1976.

Betz, Hans Dieter. *Galatians: A Commentary on Paul's Letter to the Churches in Galatia*. Hermeneia. Philadelphia: Fortress, 1979.

Bockmuehl, Markus. "Natural Law in Second Temple Judaism." *VT* 45 (1995): 17–44.

Boer, Martinus C. de. "The Meaning of the Phrase τὰ στοιχεῖα τοῦ κόσμου in Galatians." *NTS* 53 (2007): 204–24.

Bonner, Stanley F. *Education in Ancient Rome: From the Elder Cato to the Younger Pliny*. Berkeley: University of California Press, 1977.

Borgen, Peder. "Some Hebrew and Pagan Features in Philo's and Paul's Interpretation of Hagar and Ishmael." Pages 151–64 in *The New Testament and Hellenistic Judaism*. Edited by Peder Borgen and Søren Giversen. Aarhus: Aarhus University Press, 1995.

Bundrick, David R. "*Ta stoicheia tou kosmou* (Gal 4:3)." *JETS* 34 (1991): 353–64.
Castelli, Elizabeth A. "Allegories of Hagar: Reading Galatians 4:21–31 with Postmodern Feminist Eyes." Pages 228–50 in *The New Literary Criticism and the New Testament*. Edited by Elizabeth Struthers Malbon and Edgar V. McKnight. JSNTSup 109. Sheffield: Sheffield Academic, 1994.
Charles, R. H., ed. *The Apocrypha and Pseudepigrapha of the Old Testament in English*. Oxford: Clarendon, 1913.
Colson, F. H. "Philo on Education." *JTS* 18 (1917): 151–62.
Conley, Thomas. *"General Education" in Philo of Alexandria*. PSC 15. Berkeley: Center for Hermeneutical Studies in Hellenistic and Modern Culture, 1975.
Cosgrove, Charles H. "The Law Has Given Sarah No Children (Gal. 4:21–30)." *NT* 29 (1987): 219–35.
Dawson, David. *Allegorical Readers and Cultural Revision in Ancient Alexandria*. Berkeley: University of California Press, 1992.
Delling, Gerhard. "στοιχεῖον." *TDNT* 7:670–87.
Dunn, James D. G. *Galatians*. BNTC. London: Black, 1993.
———. *The Theology of Paul the Apostle*. Grand Rapids: Eerdmans, 1998.
Esler, Philip F. *Galatians*. NTR. London: Routledge, 1998.
Freeman, Kathleen. *Ancilla to the Pre-Socratic Philosophers: A Complete Translation of the Fragments in Diels* Fragmente der Vorsokratiker. Cambridge: Harvard University Press, 1957.
Heinemann, Isaak. *Philons griechische und jüdische Bildung: Kulturvergleichende Untersuchungen zu Philons Darstellung der jüdischen Gesetze*. Hildesheim: Olms, 1962.
Henrichs, Albert. "Philosophy, the Handmaiden of Theology." *GRBS* 9 (1968): 437–450.
Horsley, Richard A. "The Law of Nature in Philo and Cicero." *HTR* 71 (1978): 35–59.
Kang, Tae Won. "Wisdom Mythology and Hellenistic Paideia in Philo: A Case Study of *De Congressu Quaerendae Eruditionis Gratia*." PhD diss., The Claremont Graduate School, 1999.
Koester, Helmut. "ΝΟΜΟΣ ΦΥΣΕΩΣ: The Concept of Natural Law in Greek Thought." Pages 521–41 in *Religions in Antiquity: Essays in Memory of Erwin Ramsdell Goodenough*. Edited by Jacob Neusner. Leiden: Brill, 1968.

Longenecker, Richard N. "The Pedagogical Nature of the Law in Galatians 3:19–4:7." *JETS* 25 (1982): 53–61.
Mendelson, Alan. *Secular Education in Philo of Alexandria.* HUCM 7. Cincinnati: Hebrew Union College Press, 1982.
Najman, Hindy. "The Law of Nature and the Authority of Mosaic Law." *SPhiloA* 11 (1999): 55–73.
———. "A Written Copy of the Law of Nature: An Unthinkable Paradox?" *SPhiloA* 15 (2003): 54–63.
Nanos, Mark D. "What Does 'Present Jerusalem' (Gal 4:25) in Paul's Allegory Have to Do with the Jerusalem of Paul's Time, or the Concerns of the Galatians?" Paper presented at the Annual Meeting of the Central States Region of the Society of Biblical Literature. Saint Louis, MO, 28–29 March 2004.
Niehoff, Maren R. "Mother and Maiden, Sister and Spouse: Sarah in Philonic Midrash." *HTR* 97 (2004): 413–44.
Nikiprowetzky, Valentin. "Loi de Moïse, Loi de Nature, Sagesse." Pages 116–54 in *Le commentaire de L'Ecriture chez Philon d'Alexandrie: Son caractère et sa portée, observations philologiques.* Leiden: Brill, 1977.
Punt, Jeremy. "Revealing Rereading. Part 1: Pauline Allegory in Galatians 4:21–5:1." *Neot* 40 (2006): 87–100.
———. "Revealing Rereading. Part 2: Paul and the Wives of the Father of Faith in Galatians 4:21–5:1." *Neot* 40 (2006): 101–18.
Sterling, Gregory E. "'Philo Has Not Been Used Half Enough': The Significance of Philo of Alexandria for the Study of the New Testament." *PRSt* 30 (2003): 251–69.
VanLandingham, Chris. *Judgment and Justification in Early Judaism and the Apostle Paul.* Peabody, MA: Hendrickson, 2006.
Wagner, W. H. "Philo and Paideia." *Cithara* 10 (1971): 53–64.
Wendland, Paul. *Die hellenistisch-römische Kultur in ihren Beziehungen zu Judentum und Christentum.* HNT 1.2. Tübingen: Mohr Siebeck, 1907.
Woyke, Johannes. "Nochmals zu den 'schwachen und unfähigen Elementen' (Gal 4.9): Paulus, Philo und die στοιχεῖα τοῦ κόσμου." *NTS* 54 (2008): 221–34.
Yonge, C. D. *The Works of Philo: Complete and Unabridged.* Peabody, MA: Hendrickson, 2008.
Young, Norman H. "*Paidagogos*: The Social Setting of a Pauline Metaphor." *NovT* 29 (1987): 150–76.

Wily, Wise, and Worldly: Instruction and the Formation of Character in the Epistle to the Hebrews

Ellen Bradshaw Aitken

The Epistle to the Hebrews constructs a world of meaning, identity, and relationship for its audience. In order to understand how this discourse does so, it is appropriate to investigate both what the text says and what the text does. This approach locates the text as a subject capable of acting upon an audience. It also recognizes that the discourse can be self-reflexive and contain indications of its own practices inscribed variously within its discussion of other topics. "Instruction," broadly understood in relation to the formation of character, provides a useful site for exploring the interrelation of the practices of Hebrews with its arguments about such matters as the character and work of Christ, the goal of a godly life, and the ethos of the community. This essay is part of a larger project that considers how Hebrews responds to the cultural, religious, and political environment of first-century Rome, including how Hebrews's interest in instruction participates in a range of existing philosophical practices. Looking at the practices of instruction in Hebrews also illumines a subsidiary issue, namely, how sapiential and apocalyptic motifs are intertwined in a single text and function to form the character of the audience. The coexistence of sapiential and apocalyptic motifs in a single text suggests that these registers of communication belong not to separate and distinct groups of religious practitioners, but rather that they can be drawn upon together in

---

This chapter was originally published in Ian H. Henderson and Gebern S. Oegema, eds., *The Changing Face of Judaism, Christianity, and Other Greco-Roman Religions in Antiquity*, JSHRZ 2 (Gütersloh: Gütersloher Verlagshaus, 2006), 296–307. It is reprinted with permission of the publisher.

the context of a specific attempt to shape a community's life in relation to the divine.[1]

In seeking to understand how instruction is "performed" or practiced in Hebrews, this essay examines the matrix of instruction, character formation, and community formation as these take place in Hebrews through scripture and its interpretation. It attends to how Hebrews instructs its inscribed audience in the ways to engage the scriptures of Israel and to locate their own identity through scripture.[2] Although this scriptural matrix is informed primarily by the Sinai covenant (together with traditions of its renewal) and the wilderness journey (see especially Heb 3:7–4:11; 8:8–9:5), it also draws significantly upon material and strategies from wisdom literature. It utilizes, furthermore, some dimensions of an apocalyptic view of the cosmos to depict the contrasting ends of the faithful and of those who "fall away" (Heb 10:26–31).[3] Through this scriptural

---

1. An earlier version of this essay was presented as part of the ongoing work of the Wisdom and Apocalypticism in Early Judaism and Early Christianity Group of the Society of Biblical Literature, meeting in Toronto, 23 November 2002. I am grateful to the members of the group, and especially to my respondents, Christine Thomas and Jonathan Draper, for their comments. The work of this research group has focused on the interrelation of sapiential and apocalyptic modes of communication and their practitioners; it interrogates the scholarly paradigm that assigns wisdom and apocalyptic, respectively, to separate groups with distinct religious and social interests in antiquity, attributing, for example, wisdom to world-affirming scribal circles and apocalypticism to world-subverting disaffected sectarian groups. See George W. E. Nickelsburg, "Wisdom and Apocalypticism in Early Judaism: Some Points for Discussion," in *Society of Biblical Literature 1994 Seminar Papers*, SBLSP 33 (Atlanta: Society of Biblical Literature, 1994), 715–32.

2. By "inscribed audience" I mean those whom the text rhetorically constructs as its addressees principally by means of the use of second-person and first-person plural pronouns. The use of the term "inscribed audience" distinguishes these rhetorically constructed addressees from the actual historical audiences of the discourse in its ancient settings or in any subsequent period. See Elisabeth Schüssler Fiorenza, *Rhetoric and Ethic: The Politics of Biblical Interpretation* (Minneapolis: Fortress, 1999), 123–28. In the space of this essay I do not attempt to develop a full profile of this inscribed audience.

3. It is not my purpose in this paper to examine which aspects of Hebrews belong to sapiential tradition and which to apocalyptic, although I shall note these in connection with other observations. I would simply flag here some of the instances of each, as summarized in Harold W. Attridge, *The Epistle to the Hebrews: A Commentary on the Epistle to the Hebrews*, Hermeneia (Philadelphia: Fortress, 1989). Apocalyptic motifs include the notion of a final consummation, "the approaching day" (Heb

matrix and the techniques of scriptural interpretation in which the audience is trained, Hebrews endeavors to shape community and character in terms of mutual solidarity.

Juxtaposed to the strategies of deploying scripture that Hebrews demonstrates to its inscribed audience are explicit statements about instruction. These focus on the necessity of learning through suffering and hardship more than on the social structures or institutions of learning, as we shall see below. The emphasis is on character formation, to which participation in the community is seen as integral. The contrast exists, therefore, between the explicit statements about instruction or learning, on the one hand, and the practices utilized by the text itself, on the other. This contrast prompts the question about the relation between learning through suffering and being skilled in the interpretation of scripture, skilled, that is, in locating one's identity through the medium of scripture. I would propose that one way in which to resolve this contrast is to understand the skills in the arts of scriptural interpretation as comprising part of the capacity that the audience needs in order successfully to endure suffering and to maintain solidarity with the community. Moreover, the particular art of interpreting scripture demonstrated by Hebrews is one appropriate to the versatility of character necessary to the endurance of suffering. I suggest

---

10:25), the "coming world" (Heb 2:5), and the use, to undergird various warnings, of language that recalls apocalyptic judgment (Heb 6:8; 10:29–31; 12:29). Attridge also mentions positive images rooted in apocalyptic tradition: the promised "rest" (Heb 4:1–11), the resurrection of the dead (Heb 6:2; 11:19), a heavenly home or the heavenly Jerusalem (Heb 11:10, 16; 12:22–28); and the motif of a reward (Heb 11:6, 26); see Attridge, *Hebrews*, 27–28. It is striking that many of these motifs are found in the catalogue of faithful heroes in Heb 11, a catalogue which in many ways is similar to the lists of exemplary figures in sapiential literature, as, for example, in Sir 44–50. Wisdom material in Hebrews includes the formulation of the journey into the heavenly realm in terms of the exodus and wilderness story, as in Wis 10:15–21 as well as the "sapientially inspired mythical pattern of the exordium" (Attridge, *Hebrews*, 80). It is widely agreed that depiction of the Son in the exordium, relying most likely on an early Christian hymn, tropes the portrayal of divine Wisdom in Wis 7:25–26. The portrayal of the word of God in Heb 4:12–13 may also draw upon the depiction of Wisdom in Wis 7:23–24. In addition, the compositional technique of using catchwords (see Albert Vanhoye, *La structure littéraire de l'Épître aux Hébreux*, StudNeot 1 [Paris: Desclée de Brouwer, 1963]) to link one thought to the next may also point to a sapientially informed didactic context. The intertwining of sapiential and apocalyptic strands is evident in the exordium itself, which presents the "Son" within a wisdom Christology as the means of God's speech "in the end of these days" (Heb 1:2).

therefore that in these ways Hebrews aims at forming a community skilled in what James C. Scott has termed "the arts of resistance."[4]

I turn now to a detailed examination of what Hebrews says overtly about instruction and learning, with an eye to seeing the place of instruction and learning within Hebrews's overall scheme of the journey toward perfection. We may think of Hebrews as containing two intersecting narratives: one of Jesus's descent from the heavenly realm, earthly residence, and return to the celestial temple and the other, modeled on the exodus and wilderness journey of the people of God, concerned with the progress of the audience, who are enabled through Jesus's death to be perfected (Heb 2:10) and to enter into the promised heavenly place of "rest" (Heb 4:9) and into the celestial temple (Heb 10:19).[5] A useful question then is to ask where in these narratives Hebrews locates "instruction." Another, complementary way of thinking about this question is to focus on Hebrews as a paraenetic text, built out of homiletic material, and to examine the role that statements about instruction or references to it play as strategies to motivate the audience.[6]

We may note first that those "instructed" in and through this text are addressed neither as students or disciples, nor in subordinating familial language such as "my son" or "children." Rather, the inscribed audience is addressed as "brothers" (ἀδελφοί; Heb 3:12; 10:19; 13:22) or "holy brothers" (ἀδελφοὶ ἅγιοι; Heb 3:1). This form of address is consonant with the

---

4. James C. Scott, *Domination and the Arts of Resistance: Hidden Transcripts* (New Haven: Yale University Press, 1990). My thinking about Hebrews is informed by Scott's work, although I am not working fully with his notion of a hidden transcript. Scott develops his analysis of resistance with reference to class difference, particularly the conflict between peasants and elites, a social framework that is not appropriate to Hebrews. I use the term to denote the variety of ways in which a subordinate or subject community cultivates and maintains its identity and values in the midst of a dominant culture that it perceives as exerting various sorts and degrees of pressure to change the values, behaviors, and affiliations of the subject group.

5. George W. MacRae, "Heavenly Temple and Eschatology in the Letter to the Hebrews," *Semeia* 12 (1978): 190. See also Aelred Cody, *Heavenly Sanctuary and Liturgy in the Epistle to the Hebrews* (St. Meinrad, IL: Grail, 1960), 1–2.

6. See Lawrence M. Wills, "The Form of the Sermon in Hellenistic Judaism and Early Christianity," *HTR* 77 (1984): 277–99; C. Clifton Black, "The Rhetorical Form of the Hellenistic Jewish and Early Christian Sermon: A Response to Lawrence Wills, *HTR* 81 (1988): 1–18; Harold W. Attridge, "Paraenesis in a Homily (λόγος παρακλήσεως)" *Semeia* 50 (1990): 211–26.

soteriological construction of the audience as those whom Jesus presents to God as his siblings (Heb 2:11–13). Here the solidarity of Jesus with the community is central to his work of bringing them to perfection. In this same context, Jesus's being perfected through suffering, being tested as his siblings are, and becoming like them in every respect (Heb 2:10–18) all underscore the cohesion of the group. Although the inscribed author occasionally speaks to the audience in the second person plural (Heb 3:12; 5:11–12; 12:12–13; 13:1–19), much of the time the exhortations and addresses are in the first person plural, wrapping the author and audience into the same group and further emphasizing the solidarity. There are no offices mentioned, only the command to remember "those who lead you" (τῶν ἡγουμένων; Heb 13:7).[7] Thus the audience is not addressed in ways that draw attention to the practices of instruction.

A critical text for understanding the place of instruction in Hebrews is the lengthy quotation of Jer 31:31–34 in Heb 8:8–12. This quotation functions to introduce the contrast developed in Heb 9–10 between the "first" covenant and a "new" covenant (Heb 8:13–9:1) established through Jesus's death. Along with the new covenant, according to Jeremiah, comes knowledge of God throughout the community, along with the end of instruction.

> This is the covenant that I will make with the house of Israel after those days, says the Lord: I will put my laws in their minds, and write them on their hearts, and I will be their God, and they shall be my people. And they shall not teach one another or say to each other, "Know the Lord," for they shall all know me, from the least of them to the greatest. (Heb 8:10–11)[8]

Although the end of instruction and the unlimited availability of knowledge of God are not facets of the quotation that Hebrews explicitly draws upon in the subsequent chapters, I would suggest that the quotation indicates indirectly that instruction, teaching, and insufficient knowledge all belong to the time of journeying into perfection and "rest." That is, when the community experiences the full rewards of covenant faithfulness and

---

7. Rather than indicating fixed offices, the participial form ("those leading you"), in my view, draws attention here to the motif of the wilderness journey under the leadership of Moses and Joshua, as a typology for the life of the community.

8. All translations of Hebrews are those of the NRSV unless noted otherwise.

shares with Jesus in heavenly glory, then instruction will no longer be necessary, because of the complete internalization of the covenant ("I will put my laws in their minds and write them on their hearts"). Hebrews 10:12–18, in again citing Jer 31:33, makes this internal inscribing of the covenant the result of Jesus's work of perfecting and sanctifying the community. Instruction therefore belongs not to heavenly life, but to the present situation of the audience, in which the text exhorts them to "hold fast" and "not to fall away" (e.g., Heb 2:1; 6:6).[9]

Hebrews 5:11–6:3 contains explicit discussion of levels of instruction and of what is expected of the inscribed audience. Here the author reproaches the audience for not being where they ought in the process of learning, "for though by this time you ought to be teachers, you need someone to teach you again the basic elements of the oracles of God" (Heb 5:12). They need "milk," rather than "solid food." This common Hellenistic metaphor for levels of instruction would appear here to distinguish elementary learners from advanced ones, "neophyte Christians" from "mature Christians," and the basics of Christian teaching from the more complex teaching taking place in Hebrews itself.[10] What follows in Heb 6:1–3 supports this dichotomy in that it separates "going on toward perfection" from the "foundation" or "the basic teaching about Christ," which is spelled out as a "repentance from dead works and faith toward God, instruction about baptisms, laying on of hands, resurrection of the dead, and eternal judgment" (Heb 6:1–2). We should note, however, that Hebrews speaks of "solid food" as what is proper for the τέλειοι ("mature," Heb 5:14) rather than for the νήπιοι ("infants," Heb 5:13). Although this diction is found in other instances of reflection upon the educational process (e.g., Philo, *Agr.* 9), it may well be an example of Hebrews's tendency to employ the techniques of double entendre. That is, within the larger conceptual scheme of Hebrews, being τέλειοι is something more than pos-

---

9. Hebrews speaks in a variety of ways of the contrast between faithfulness and rebellion; the various exhortations to remain faithful or to hold fast (to the confession, the confidence, the hope, etc.) underscore the theme of staying with the community (Heb 10:25), whereas the exhortations not to rebel or to fall away from the community are grounded in the story of the disobedience of the wilderness generation. The paraenetic contrast is developed most fully in the quotation of Ps 95 and its interpretation in Heb 3–4.

10. For different levels of instruction, see Attridge, *Hebrews*, 159, who cites Philo, *Agr.* 9; *Congr.* 19; *Migr.* 29; *Somn.* 2.9; *Prob.* 160; Epictetus *Diatr.* 2.16.39; 3.24.9; and 1 Cor 3:1–3. For the more complex teaching in Hebrews itself, see Attridge, *Hebrews*, 162.

sessing maturity; it designates being perfected or sanctified, entering into the heavenly sanctuary, and completing the journey with Jesus and the community into the promise.[11] The term may be employed here in a proleptic manner to designate those who are on their way toward perfection, that is, those who maintain solidarity with Jesus and the community.

Those who are τέλειοι are further described as "those whose senses [αἰσθητήρια] have been trained [γεγυμνασμένα] through habit [ἕξις] to distinguish good and evil" (Heb 5:14 NRSV, modified). This statement also utilizes vocabulary of Hellenistic instructional practices, particularly around the development of ethical discernment.[12] With the athletic imagery of the gymnasium, it points to an instructional mode that is concerned with the formation of the whole person through the cultivation of one's habits. Here recent discussions of asceticism provide a useful framework, following Richard Valantasis, who defines "asceticism" as "performances designed to inaugurate an alternative culture, to enable different social relations, and to create a new identity," thus permitting the practitioner "to function within the re-envisioned or re-created world."[13] By employing the term "asceticism" here, I do not intend it in a narrow sense of certain practices of bodily deprivation, but to indicate "character formation" in the broadest sense, pertaining to the ethos of a person within a community. Elsewhere in Hebrews, agonistic vocabulary and metaphors are employed to speak of the work in which the community is engaged, as, for example, at Heb 12:1–2, with the image of "running the race" (ἀγών). The situation of the audience is envisioned in the text as a time of ἀγών, in which

---

11. Compare the use of τελειότης ("perfection") at Heb 6:1; τελειόω at Heb 10:14; 11:40; and 12:23; and τελειωτής at Heb 12:2.

12. Attridge, *Hebrews*, 161.

13. Richard Valantasis, "A Theory of the Social Function of Asceticism," in *Asceticism*, ed. Vincent L. Wimbush and Richard Valantasis (New York: Oxford University Press, 1995), 548, 550. This definition seeks to avoid conceiving of the ascetic as exotic, but draws instead upon the classical and Hellenistic Greek notion of ἄσκησις as exercise, practice, or training in a profession, set of skills (for example, in poetry, the gymnasium, or the military), or a mode of living. The asceticism of the Hellenistic gymnasium aims at cultivating in the ephebes of the city the practices, relationships, and character appropriate to civic culture. For a more extended discussion of Hebrews in relation to asceticism thus understood, see Ellen Bradshaw Aitken, "The Hero in the Epistle to the Hebrews: Jesus as an Ascetic Model," in *Early Christian Voices: In Texts, Traditions, and Symbols; Essays in Honor of François Bovon*, ed. David Warren, Ann Graham Brock, and David Pao; BibInt 66 (Leiden: Brill, 2003), 179–88.

they are both learning the practices necessary for reaching the goal and developing the orientations (covenant faithfulness, obedience, solidarity) proper to their heavenly identity as the brothers and sisters of Jesus.

Athletic imagery is also employed in a third passage where Hebrews reflects on instruction itself, Heb 12:3–12, which follows immediately upon and draws upon the metaphor of "running the race," looking toward Jesus as the ἀρχηγός ("forerunner"). Here again the ethical dimension is foregrounded, since the audience is reminded of their "struggling against [ἀνταγωνιζόμενοι] sin" (Heb 12:4), which is linked to Jesus's endurance of "hostility from sinners" (Heb 12:3). The discussion moves to the topic of παιδεία ("instruction"),[14] drawing upon the quotation of Prov 3:11–12, in which παιδεία comes from "the Lord" and is connected to being disgraced or shamed (ἐλεγχόμενος) and scourged (μαστιγοῖ), as well as seen as part of God's love and acceptance. This complex quotation, as it is utilized here, does important work for the argument of Hebrews. First, it connects whatever suffering is endured by the community not only to Jesus's endurance, but also to the process of παιδεία. That is, it interprets suffering and hardship within an instructional framework, suggesting that the social experience of instruction is a meaningful organizing principle for this community. Second, the experience of such παιδεία is used here as a criterion of legitimacy for belonging to God's family: "If you do not have that παιδεία in which all sons share, then you are illegitimate and not sons" (Heb 12:8 NRSV, modified). Within the larger context of Hebrews, experiencing παιδεία thus supports the theological claim that the community participates with Jesus in God's household as legitimate children (see Heb 2:10–18). It is thus tied to the notion of family solidarity for the community as they journey together, in Jesus's wake, toward their promised goal, as long as they remain faithful. Interpreting as παιδεία experiences of hardship that might cause the community to lose heart and fall away (e.g., Heb 10:32–39) situates those experiences as proof of God's faithfulness to the covenant and functions rhetorically to encourage the community. The conclusion of the section (Heb 12:12–13) expresses this encouragement clearly with further scriptural and agonistic imagery ("therefore lift your drooping hands and strengthen your weak knees," alluding to Isa 35:3).

---

14. On παιδεία generally, see the classic work of Werner Jaeger, *Paideia: The Ideals of Greek Culture*, trans. Gilbert Highet, 3 vols. (Oxford: Blackwell, 1939–1945).

In this context, moreover, we may note that the goal of the ἀγών, the result of successfully experiencing παιδεία, is envisioned in apocalyptic terms in Heb 12:18-29. Here the ends of faithfulness and rebellion are contrasted through the opposition of the heavenly Jerusalem, the unshakeable kingdom, with the shaking and removal of created things on earth. Here the shaking of the earth functions as a threat against those who would "reject the one who warns from heaven," from whom they "will not escape" (Heb 12:25). Thus the ultimate outcome of successful instruction in the fullest sense is participating in the realm that remains unshakeable in the last days. Apocalyptic imagery here functions as a sanction on covenant faithfulness, which is cultivated through the practices of παιδεία.

The instructional ἀγών of the community is seen in Hebrews as undertaken in solidarity with Jesus and by following Jesus's leadership (e.g., Heb 12:1-3). It is striking, however, that Hebrews does not speak of Jesus as a teacher but as one who learns. Hebrews 5:7-10, utilizing traditions of Jesus's passion,[15] portrays Jesus as one who "although he was a son, learned obedience through what he suffered" (Heb 5:8). Here the wordplay between ἔμαθεν ("he learned") and ἔπαθεν ("he experienced" or "he suffered") engages a common instructional proverb about learning through experience but is here particularized in terms of Jesus's passion.[16] It thus focuses the instructional experience on the engagement of suffering with endurance and faithfulness. Suffering, for Jesus, becomes the instructional means for the formation of character here both as "son" and as "high priest." As in Heb 12:3-12, instruction is presented as the interpretive framework for suffering, suggesting that the practices of instruction were significant to the community's identity and self-understanding.

Moreover, since Jesus is a pattern of faithfulness for the community, this passage implicitly encourages the community in the embrace of suffering as part of their instructional practices. At other points Hebrews exhorts the community to enter into the situation of suffering of others in the community (e.g., Heb 13:1-3; see also 10:33) as part of the ethic of solidarity; thus one of the results of Hebrews's argument is the redefinition of existing instructional practices to include embracing the suffering of

---

15. See Ellen Bradshaw Aitken, *Jesus' Death in Early Christian Memory: The Poetics of the Passion*, NTOA; SUNT 53 (Göttingen: Vandenhoeck & Ruprecht, 2004), 143-58.

16. See, for example, Aeschylus, *Ag.* 177; Herodotus, *Hist.* 1.207; and the discussion in Attridge, *Hebrews*, 152-53.

others in the community. In other words, this is a community with existing instructional practices, one in which instruction appears to have been central to the practices that defined and constituted the community. The author can therefore draw upon these practices not only as an organizing principle for the experience of suffering but also as a rhetorical strategy for cultivating an ethic of solidarity in suffering within the community.

I would turn now to the question of how the text performs instruction for its audience. Here the skills that the text demonstrates and calls upon in relation to the interpretation of scripture are at the forefront. Hebrews is a text that summons the resourcefulness and versatility of its audience and challenges them consistently to "get," that is, to understand and appropriate, the right message. The rich texture of the discourse challenges the audience's interpretive skills in a variety of ways, requiring—to list a few examples—not only the ability to following a complex treatment of a quotation from the scriptures of Israel (as with the exposition of Ps 95 in Heb 3–4) or the allegorization of Israelite cult practice (Heb 9:1–10:18), but also familiarity with a scriptural context and tradition around and beyond what is specifically quoted (as in the portrayal of Jesus's agonized prayer in Heb 5:7–10).[17] The rhetorical and homiletical strategies of Hebrews also draw upon the audience's ability to understand puns and double entendres and above all to follow the twists and turns of a complex, wide-ranging, yet highly cohesive argument in such a way as to obtain its theological and ethical import. In other words, inasmuch as successful rhetoric relies upon an audience's ability to "get" and to act upon the values that it promotes, Hebrews's ideal audience needs expertise in the art of interpretation, as well as certain orientations in the ethical and affiliative aspects of living.[18]

---

17. This portrayal of Jesus's suffering and prayer draws upon a wider psalmic tradition of suffering and vindication (Strobel), as well as the ways in which the prayer of the righteous person is typically depicted (Attridge). See August Strobel, "Die Psalmengrundlage der Gethsemane-Parallele: Hebr 5:7ff.," *ZNW* 45 (1954): 252–66; Attridge, *Hebrews*, 147–48; and Harold W. Attridge, "'Heard because of His Reverence' (Heb 5:7)," *JBL* 98 (1979): 90–93. I would also argue that this passage shows familiarity with ways of narrating Jesus's suffering and death, in existence prior to and contributing to the written passion narratives; see further Aitken, *Jesus' Death*, 143–48.

18. This is reflected in the judgment of many modern commentators on Hebrews when they remark that Hebrews aims at an audience with esoteric knowledge and an advanced experience and expertise in Christian tradition and practice; see for example Helmut Koester, *History and Literature of Early Christianity*, vol. 2 of *Introduction to the New Testament*, 2nd ed. (Berlin: de Gruyter, 2000), 277–78.

I have argued elsewhere that by the opening adverb πολυτρόπως ("with versatility," or "with many forms") in Heb 1:1 the discourse marks its strategies as requiring resourcefulness and versatility.[19] This textual strategy is of a piece with the portrayal of Jesus along the model of the protean shape-shifting hero (like Odysseus) and with the character of audience as Hebrews seeks to form it as capable of shifting place into solidarity with the suffering of others (Heb 13:1–3). These strategies contribute to the instructional work of developing character capable of resisting suffering imposed by the hostility of others outside the community. Hebrews can thus be understood as developing a culture and community character skilled in the arts of resistance. Within this framework, the various methods of scriptural interpretation and the appropriation of other cultural material[20] contribute to the development of ethical, noetic, and rhetorical resourcefulness, as strategies of resistance, within the ideal community.

The performance of scripture in Hebrews allows us to see how this method of instruction works. A notable feature of the quotation of scripture in Hebrews is that it is consistently placed in the mouth of a divine figure: God, Jesus, or the Spirit. Attridge has described this technique as "ventriloquism."[21] The result is that Hebrews portrays God, Jesus, or the Spirit speaking enigmatic utterances that require interpretation. The divine speaker is thus one who possesses expertise in a modality of discourse wherein multiple meanings are possible, but those "in the know" are capable of "getting" the proper and singular meaning. Thus the speaker, through the medium of the enigmatic utterance, tests the mettle of the audience. This is consistent with the function of scripture in Hebrews, particularly the use of Ps 95 and the story of the Israelites in the wilderness. The audience is put to the test to see if they "get" the true meaning for themselves, namely, that by not falling away from the community and thus not being like the ancestors who perish, but rather by holding fast to Jesus the ἀρχηγός, they

---

19. Ellen Bradshaw Aitken, "Hebrews and the Arts of Resistance" (paper presented at the International Meeting of the Society of Biblical Literature, Berlin, 21 July 2002); see also Aitken, "Hero in the Epistle," 186–88.

20. For example, the imagery and motifs of the Roman triumph as it was celebrated and monumentalized in the city of Rome after the First Jewish War; see Ellen B. Aitken, "Portraying the Temple in Stone and Text: The Arch of Titus and the Epistle to the Hebrews," in *Religious Texts and Material Contexts*, ed. James R. Strange (Buffalo: State University of New York Press, 2001), 73–88.

21. Harold W. Attridge, "Divine Dialogue in Hebrews" (paper presented at the International Meeting of the Society of Biblical Literature, Rome, 11 July 2001).

are able to reach the goal of the journey and enter God's rest. Hebrews works with scripture in this way, demonstrating its need for interpretation and instructing its audience in the means of finding the true meaning, namely, by looking to Jesus (Heb 12:2). In particular, Hebrews emphasizes that when the audience "looks to Jesus" they are to see not only his humiliation and shame (Heb 5:7–10), but also his being crowned with glory and honor (Heb 2:9). It is this capacity to recognize Jesus that functions as the guarantee of hope for the audience, hope, that is, for their own entrance into the heavenly realm. Paideia accordingly functions as training in getting the meaning hidden in the midst of suffering and using that meaning as the groundwork for an ethic of solidarity with those who are suffering.

The way in which instruction is performed in Hebrews works thus toward the development of a modality of discourse and a modality of ethical action in the audience. The modality of discourse is demonstrated through the versatility of divine speech as testing the mettle of the audience and in training them in similar ways of reading scripture, through the lens of Jesus's suffering and glory. I suggest that this modality is employed in Hebrews not only as part of the persuasive strategies of this text but also to educate the audience in similar arts of speaking with multiple meaning. The modality of action is cultivated through instruction in the embrace of suffering and the maintenance of solidarity within the community. This embrace of suffering relates to the modality of discourse in that it provides the interpretive key for the community and renders them expert in getting the right meaning from scripture. The community is in this sense to be wily and wise, but also worldly in their canniness in enduring suffering and maintaining the character of the community in the face of hostility.

In sum, Hebrews both reflects upon the process of instruction and performs instruction in ways significant for the formation of character and community. Hebrews also relies on a framework of instructional practices in order to organize its theological and ethical points and as a basis for its persuasive strategies. In portraying the divine voice with the authority of one who trains students in the interpretation of enigmatic utterances, Hebrews further inscribes instructional practices in its theological structure. In other words, the authority of the teacher is deeply encoded in the text, both in the voice of the inscribed author and in the depiction of God. It may be useful to think of Hebrews as a "teacherly text,"[22] in that it

---

22. This phrase draws upon Roland Barthes's distinction between "readerly texts"

deploys many types of materials, including wisdom and apocalyptic, in the service of training a community and equipping them to be teachers of one another, until the "coming day" when they shall need teachers no more. It is thus a text that belongs for its audience in the midst of the ἀγών of life as a manual of instruction as much as word of exhortation.

Bibliography

Aitken, Ellen Bradshaw. "Hebrews and the Arts of Resistance." Paper presented at the International Meeting of the Society of Biblical Literature. Berlin, 21 July 2002.

———. "The Hero in the Epistle to the Hebrews: Jesus as an Ascetic Model." Pages 179–88 in *Early Christian Voices: In Texts, Traditions, and Symbols; Essays in Honor of François Bovon*. Edited by David Warren, Ann Graham Brock, and David Pao. BibInt 66. Leiden: Brill, 2003.

———. *Jesus' Death in Early Christian Memory: The Poetics of the Passion*. NTOA; SUNT 53. Göttingen: Vandenhoeck & Ruprecht, 2004.

———. "Portraying the Temple in Stone and Text: The Arch of Titus and the Epistle to the Hebrews." Pages 73–88 in *Religious Texts and Material Contexts*. Edited by James R. Strange. Buffalo: State University of New York Press, 2001.

Attridge, Harold W. "Divine Dialogue in Hebrews." Paper presented at the International Meeting of the Society of Biblical Literature. Rome, 11 July 2001.

———. *The Epistle to the Hebrews: A Commentary on the Epistle to the Hebrews*. Hermeneia. Philadelphia: Fortress, 1989.

———. "'Heard because of His Reverence' (Heb 5:7)." *JBL* 98 (1979): 90–93.

———. "Paraenesis in a Homily (λόγος παρακλήσεως)." *Semeia* 50 (1990): 211–26.

Barthes, Roland. *S/Z: An Essay*. Translated by Richard Miller. New York: Hill & Wang, 1971.

Black, C. Clifton. "The Rhetorical Form of the Hellenistic Jewish and Early Christian Sermon: A Response to Lawrence Wills." *HTR* 81 (1988): 1–18.

---

and "writerly texts"; see Roland Barthes, *S/Z: An Essay*, trans. Richard Miller (New York: Hill & Wang, 1971), 4–6. I am grateful to Karen King and the Advanced New Testament Seminar at Harvard Divinity School in the fall of 2002 for coining this phrase in the context of a discussion of the Gospel of Truth.

Cody, Aelred. *Heavenly Sanctuary and Liturgy in the Epistle to the Hebrews.* St. Meinrad, IL: Grail, 1960.

Jaeger, Werner. *Paideia: The Ideals of Greek Culture.* Translated by Gilbert Highet. 3 vols. Oxford: Blackwell, 1939–1945.

Koester, Helmut. *History and Literature of Early Christianity.* Vol. 2 of *Introduction to the New Testament.* 2nd ed. Berlin: de Gruyter, 2000.

MacRae, George W. "Heavenly Temple and Eschatology in the Letter to the Hebrews." *Semeia* 12 (1978): 177–99.

Nickelsburg, George W. E. "Wisdom and Apocalypticism in Early Judaism: Some Points for Discussion," Pages 715–32 in *Society of Biblical Literature 1994 Seminar Papers.* SBLSP 33. Atlanta: Society of Biblical Literature, 1994.

Schüssler Fiorenza, Elisabeth. *Rhetoric and Ethic: The Politics of Biblical Interpretation.* Minneapolis: Fortress, 1999.

Scott, James C. *Domination and the Arts of Resistance: Hidden Transcripts.* New Haven: Yale University Press, 1990.

Strobel, August. "Die Psalmengrundlage der Gethsemane-Parallele: Hebr 5:7ff." *ZNW* 45 (1954): 252–66.

Valantasis, Richard. "A Theory of the Social Function of Asceticism." Pages 544–52 in *Asceticism.* Edited by Vincent L. Wimbush and Richard Valantasis. New York: Oxford University Press, 1995.

Vanhoye, Albert. *La structure littéraire de l'Épître aux Hébreux.* StudNeot 1. Paris: Desclée de Brouwer, 1963.

Wills, Lawrence M. "The Form of the Sermon in Hellenistic Judaism and Early Christianity." *HTR* 77 (1984): 277–99.

Paideia and Polemic in Second-Century Lyons: Irenaeus on Education

D. Jeffrey Bingham

In 1949, Robert Grant wrote his article "Irenaeus and Hellenistic Culture" for the *Harvard Theological Review*.[1] Grant's analysis of Irenaeus's philosophical acumen, in the end, led him to two conclusions. First, philosophically, Irenaeus is eclectic and so cannot be "classified among philosophical schools," though he "inclines toward skepticism."[2] Second, for Grant, Irenaeus is "more rhetorical than philosophical."[3] Although Irenaeus is not very sophisticated philosophically, he does show substantial training in rhetoric. Grant's analysis is an important starting point for understanding Irenaeus's interaction with traditional Greco-Roman education.

Neither Grant nor his successors, however, have offered a developed treatment of Irenaeus's theory of education. A number of studies have clarified the extent of his training, but here we shall focus on how the bishop employed this education in confronting those he considered heretical. Thus, we shall ask: What was the relationship between polemic and paideia? The question is especially relevant because Irenaeus is an educated author, and he offers the first fully developed polemical theology. This theology presents the history of redemption as humanity's sphere of education, a process by which humankind is trained by God for perfection.

For Jill Peláez Baumgaertner in celebration of her excellence as Dean of Humanities and Theological Studies at Wheaton College, Illinois.

1. Robert M. Grant, "Irenaeus and Hellenistic Culture," *HTR* 42 (1949): 41–51. See also D. B. Reynders, "La polemique de S. Irénée," *RTAM* 7 (1935): 5–27; T. A. Audet, "Orientations théologiques chez S. Irénée," *Traditio* 1 (1943): 15–54; M. S. Enslin, "Irenaeus: Mostly Prolegomena," *HTR* 40 (1947): 137–65.
2. Grant, "Irenaeus and Hellenistic Culture," 46–47.
3. Ibid., 47.

The breadth of his education is evident both in his elegant polemic and in his overarching theological views about the education of humanity.

My argument is that Irenaeus developed and Christianized Greco-Roman educational concepts and curriculum in constructing his polemical theology. On this approach, he represents an early, if not the earliest, Christian thinker who appropriates classical education in substantial ways. To this end, I first investigate Irenaeus's notion of education as the foundation of the redemptive economy and then treat his explicit statements about the importance of classical education for artful theological construction. Finally, I will consider questions about the extent of his training in the classical curriculum, especially as evident in certain of his polemics and exhortations to virtue.

The Redemptive Economy as Education

F. R. Montgomery Hitchcock's monograph on Irenaeus contains a very dated chapter entitled "The Education of Man," which nevertheless provides a helpful introduction to the topic.[4] As he explains, one essential difference between humanity and God for Irenaeus is that humanity is always under construction, always being developed, always in the process of being educated by God (*Haer.* 4.11.2).[5] Parallel theological notions propel this overarching construct. God is Creator, Maker, and always the same; this identity as Creator entails that he is always the same, never changing, immutable. By contrast, humanity is a creature, something that is made, and so is always in need of change, progress, and improvement. Humanity needs to advance and needs to be trained, educated, and molded so that there will be perpetual growth towards God. So, "God should forever teach [*doceo*] and humanity should forever learn [*disco*] from God" (*Haer.* 2.28.3).[6] As Irenaeus explains:

> The faith concerning our Master endures unchangeably, assuring us that there is only one true God, and that we should truly love him forever, because he is the only Father, and we hope to receive and learn [*disco*; διδάσκω] from God forever because he is good, and possesses boundless

---

4. F. R. M. Hitchcock, *Irenaeus of Lugdunum* (Cambridge: Cambridge University Press, 1914), 52–64.

5. See also *Haer.* 2.25.3; 4.5.5; 4.13.2; 4.15.2; 4.18.6; 5.1.1.

6. Translations are my own except where noted otherwise.

riches, a kingdom without end, and knowledge without measure. (*Haer.* 2.28.3)

The church's rule of truth, the faith received at baptism, is unchanging, but humanity is to continually learn about the immensity of God because lessons about the divine nature are inexhaustible.

Repeatedly in the *Adversus haereses*, Irenaeus describes history as a schoolroom in which God intends to gradually educate humanity, by his Word and Spirit. Although God could have created humanity perfect from the beginning, he elected not to do so. Humanity, in its weakness, was unable to bear perfection at first and so had to grow into it. Humankind was "necessarily imperfect, infantile, and untrained in the perfect discipline" (*Haer.* 4.38.1). Informed by the words of Paul to the Corinthians (1 Cor 3:2) about infants who feed only on milk, the bishop insists that humanity was at first incapable of stomaching perfection. In this infantile state, humankind needs to be trained, taught, and perfected by its Creator-Father so that it can appropriately mature. To this end, God providentially arranges all periods of redemptive history and puts even humanity's failures to good use. It is ultimately in the church that humanity reaches maturity and can be blessed with a vision and understanding of God. He writes:

> On our behalf God permitted all these things, so that, having been taught [*erudio*] in all ways by them, we might be attentive in all things, and that, having been taught [*edoceo*] reasonably [*rationabiliter*] to love God, we may persevere in his love, for God has displayed long-suffering in the case of humanity's apostasy, and humanity has been instructed by means of it, as the prophet says, "Your apostasy will heal you" (Jer 2:19). Thus God predetermined all things in order to bring humanity to perfection and to realize and manifest the economies so that goodness might be exhibited, righteousness perfected, the church fashioned after the image of his Son, and so that finally humanity might be brought to maturity, becoming ripe through such privileges to see and comprehend God. (*Haer.* 4.37.7)

God employs the patriarchs, law, prophets, gospel, apostles, and the twists and turns of history, in proper sequence, to educate and perfect humanity. Beginning with the patriarchs, Irenaeus says, God "formed the people in advance, teaching [*doceo*] the ignorant ones to follow him" (*Haer.* 4.14.2), teaching (*doceo*) them his will through the prophets. By means of the patriarchs and the prophets (as well as the apostles), and within each period of history, God formed humanity.

For Irenaeus, institutions like the temple, the Levitical priesthood, sacrifices, oblations, and circumcision were educative signs, but they are not perfect or consummative (*Haer.* 4.14.3–4.16.4). The gospel cancels these signs, those laws appropriate to a younger phase of human history, but it also enlarges the scope of the natural, universal laws found in the Decalogue. This expansion is consonant with the new and more liberal relationship between God the Father and faithful humanity, those who are not slaves but sons and daughters. This more mature relationship is characterized not by the obedience a slave might pay to a master but by the love and reverence a child would have for a father. Thus, it is as a father, through the gospel, that God educates his children. All of history, all prior educational arrangements, have been moving toward the period of the new covenant, the age of freedom, the day of adoption through Christ when God would instruct the faithful as Father.

Irenaeus frequently employs Paul's language in Gal 4:1–7 and Rom 8:14–17. Christians are those "sons" who are no longer slaves, for they have experienced the grace of adoption by the gift of the Spirit who calls out "Abba, Father" (Rom 8:15) and hence are able to make the same cry.[7] Although these Pauline texts are important for his thought, he also draws on Isaiah to announce that God has built a community of children: "I will bring your seed from the east and I will gather you from the west. To the north I will say, 'Give them up!' And to the south, 'Do not hold them back! Bring my sons from far away, and my daughters from the ends of the earth'" (Isa 43:5–6, quoted in *Haer.* 4.14.1). Irenaeus's use of Isaiah indicates that, to some extent, the prophet's eschatological expectations have come to pass in the new covenant blessings that are experienced by the disciples and their descendants. Both Isaiah and Paul thus help Irenaeus to explain the enduring plan of God to relate to faithful humanity as a father to a child. For Irenaeus, however, God does not relate to all as Father. To the Jews, the relationship is more forensic, but to the Gentiles it is one of potency; only to the adopted faithful is he Father. Irenaeus sets this forth in his summary of the body of truth found in the *Demonstration*:

---

7. *Haer.* 3.6.1 (citing Rom 8:15); 3.18.7; 3.19.1; 4.9.1; 4.9.2 (citing Gal 4:6); 4.16.5. See language about "slaves" and "sons" in *Haer.* 4.9.1; 4.16.5.

However, to the faithful he is as Father, since "in the last times" he opened the testament of the adoption as sons; while to the Jews he is as Lord and Lawgiver, since in the intervening period, when mankind had forgotten, abandoned and rebelled against God, he brought them into slavery by means of the law, that they might learn that they have [as] Lord the Maker and Fashioner, who also bestows the breath of life, and to him we must offer worship by day and by night; and to the Gentiles he is as Creator and Almighty. (*Epid.* 8)[8]

God's activity in history, though progressive, coordinates the prophets with his Son. As the teaching Father, he assures that all those who reveal his will speak with one voice to matters of both ethics and doctrine, and he creates a Christian community that interprets that revelation with one mind. Revelation in history, whether through words, the ministry of the prophets, Israel's travails, or the person of the Son, is in agreement because God oversees all things. Likewise, God assures that all ecclesiological interpretation is without contradiction. To this effect Irenaeus writes:

> We follow as our teacher [*doctor*] the one and only true God, and we take his words as the rule of truth. We always understand the same texts in the same manner, knowing only one God, the Creator of the universe, who sent the prophets, who led forth the people from the land of Egypt, and who in these last times manifested his own Son, so that he might confuse the unbelievers and bring forth the fruit of righteousness. (*Haer.* 4.35.4)

Here God oversees and reveals himself in history, in accord with his pedagogical purposes. Furthermore, the church's hermeneutics are overseen by God so that all ecclesiological interpretation is without contradiction. God's teaching activity guarantees the coherence of the content as well as the comprehension of the student.

Irenaeus's idea of history as a schoolroom within which God the Father educates his children departs a bit from typical Greco-Roman models of education. As is well known among scholars of Greco-Roman education, the common arrangement within households was for the father to hire a freeman as tutor, a pedagogue, or to purchase a household slave for the

---

8. John Behr, ed. and trans., *St. Irenaeus of Lyons: On the Apostolic Preaching* (Crestwood, NY: St. Vladimir's Seminary Press, 1997).

purpose.⁹ The quality of such education, of course, varied in accordance with the quality of pedagogue that the head of the family could afford. It was generally the elite families that could provide the best education. Despite the common use of pedagogues, Irenaeus prefers to highlight the important role the father is understood to play in education.

Although it does not reflect the norms of traditional education, Irenaeus's emphasis on the role of the father is not completely foreign to Greco-Roman thought. For instance, Plato has Protagoras easily listing the father alongside the tutor or pedagogue as one who instructs the child from the earliest age as to just, noble, and holy behavior and speech (*Prot.* 325c–d), and Plutarch makes similar statements (*Quo. adol.* 14 [36e]). Philo clarifies that even the mere presence of a tutor or father is influential, since parents monitor behavior (*Mut.* 217).

Aristotle goes a step further than Plato, Philo, and Plutarch. In the final book of the *Nicomachean Ethics*, he explains the unique character and benefits of paternal instruction (*Eth. nic.* 10.9.14–16; 1180a29–1180b23).[10] Here he calls for public, legislated education but also pauses to explain the advantages of home schooling as well. On his theory, a father's teaching should prevail just as much as, if not more than, the public, citywide institution for which he argues. Familial ties and a child's sense of obligation to the head of the household guarantee that they receive superior learning, for nature assures that obedience and affection are paired within a family. Furthermore, a father is able to mentor his child in a way that fits the child's individual needs. Such personal, private instruction suits individual strengths and weaknesses in a way that his ideal of public education cannot.

In the later writings of the Stoic Epictetus, the idea of the father as teacher serves as a model for the ideal philosopher who serves Zeus by imitating him.[11] Here Epictetus describes the Cynic Diogenes in Stoic terms as one who cares for others in the spirit of a father seeking to impart

---

9. For an excellent textual orientation to the pedagogue in Greco-Roman society, see Norman H. Young, "*Paidagogos*: The Social Setting of a Pauline Metaphor," *NovT* 29 (1987): 150–76.

10. See R. E. Curren, *Aristotle on the Necessity of Public Education* (Lanham, MD: Rowman & Littlefield, 2000), 81–82.

11. Egyptian papyri from the Hellenistic period mention the father's responsibility for education; see Raffaella Cribiore, *Writing, Teachers, and Students in Graeco-Roman Egypt*, ASP 36 (Atlanta: Scholars Press, 1996), 15.

wisdom to all. Moreover, in doing so, Diogenes has the fatherhood of Zeus as an example. For Epictetus,

> [Diogenes has] made all mankind his children; the men among them he has as sons, the women as daughters; in that spirit he approaches them all and cares for them all. Or do you fancy that it is in the spirit of idle impertinence he reviles those he meets? It is as a father he does it, as a brother, and as a servant of Zeus, who is Father of us all. (*Diatr.* 3.22.81–82)[12]

In his biographical writings on Cato the Elder, Plutarch also emphasizes the importance of the father as educator. He describes Cato the Elder as eager to teach his son: he rushes home from the Senate house to be with his son before bedtime, and only pressing state business would force him to sacrifice this joyous meeting. Although public business makes constant demands upon his time and he has a competent tutor in his slave, he prefers to teach his own son to read and write. Plutarch writes:

> As soon as the boy showed signs of understanding, his father took him under his own charge and taught him to read, although he had an accomplished slave, Chilo by name, who was a school-teacher, and taught many boys. Still, Cato thought it not right, as he tells us himself, that his son should be scolded by a slave, or have his ears tweaked when he was slow to learn, still less that he should be indebted to his slave for such a priceless thing as education. He was therefore himself not only the boy's reading-teacher, but his tutor in law, and his athletic trainer, and he taught his son not merely to hurl the javelin and fight in armour and ride the horse, but also to box, to endure heat and cold, and to swim lustily through the eddies and billows of the Tiber. (*Cat. Maj.* 20.4–5)[13]

Along the same lines, we hear from Pliny the Younger that in ancient times boys learned by watching their elders and heeding their advice. "Everyone,"

---

12. *Epictetus: The Discourses, Books III–IV; Fragments; Encheiridion*, trans. W. A. Oldfather, LCL (Cambridge: Harvard University Press, 1928). Epictetus's ideal Cynic fits the model of the Stoic sage; see, e.g., Seneca's representation of the philosopher as pedagogue of the human race in *Ep.* 89.13.

13. Plutarch, *Lives: Themistocles and Camillus, Aristides and Cato Major, Cimon and Lucullus*, trans. Bernadotte Perrin, LCL (Cambridge: Harvard University Press, 1914); See also Stanley Bonner, *Education in Ancient Rome: From the Elder Cato to the Younger Pliny* (London: Routledge, 1977), 10.

he notes, "had a teacher [*magister*] in his own father, or, if he was fatherless, in some older man of distinction who took his father's place" (*Ep.* 8.14.6).[14] We must also imagine that fathers were not solely responsible for education at the level of the family. Mothers were sometimes viewed as indispensable, and we are fortunate to have moving accounts of highly educated women.[15]

Irenaeus's notion of God as father-teacher thus takes a relatively peripheral idea about the role of fathers in Greco-Roman education and moves it to the very center of a distinctive educational program. God as Father orchestrates the education of his people in history, even if he sometimes uses mediators such as the patriarchs, prophets, apostles, his Son, or his Spirit. Though typically secondary to that of a hired pedagogue in other literature, the role of the father becomes primary in Irenaeus's thought. Here we observe his appropriation and Christianization of common educational norms and practices. He does not simply present God the Father as the one with the power and responsibility to provide for his child's education, the one who exercised *patria potestas* as *paterfamilias*. Instead, Irenaeus portrays God as the *paterfamilias*, who acts directly as *doctor* (teacher, instructor) and *magister* (tutor, educator) for his children.[16]

Human history, for Irenaeus, is not probationary, as if humanity is being tested to determine its fitness to be in an appropriate relationship with God. Instead, the Creator uses various means to educate his human creatures, both morally and spiritually. God thus moves along humanity from alienation to redemption, from corruptibility to incorruptibility, from death to resurrection, from infancy to maturity.[17] In the process, human beings learn that they are frail, mortal, and doomed to die, but that God is immortal and omnipotent. Irenaeus's theology of God's training and transformation of humanity has a category for both the individual person

---

14. Pliny, *Letters, Books VIII–X, and Panegyricus*, trans. Betty Radice, LCL (Cambridge: Harvard University Press, 1969).

15. E.g., Cornelia in Plutarch (*Ti. C. Gracch.* 19) and Sempronia in Sallust (*Bell. Cat.* 25.2). See also Tacitus, *Dial.* 28; Johannes Christes, "Education," *BNP* 4:821; Bonner, *Education in Ancient Rome*, 32–33.

16. It should also be noted that Irenaeus's emphasis on the father as teacher is in keeping with notions of the father as teacher of the torah, *miqra*, and wisdom in Jewish traditions. Both Josephus and Philo, for instance, note that it is the chief responsibility of Jewish parents to educate their children well (Josephus, *C. Ap.* 1.12.2; Philo, *Legat.* 16.31). Evidence for this tradition is also found in both legal materials and in wisdom literature (e.g., Deut 6:4–9; 11:13–21; Prov 1:8; 4:1; 6:20; 13:1).

17. *Haer.* 5.1.1; 3.20.1, 2; 5.3.1; 4.38.4; 4.39.1, 2; 5.2.3.

and for humanity as a whole. Individual human beings are responsible for choosing faith and obedience in order to be transformed and to attain an incorruptible nature. The infantile type of human being was created in the first Adam, but after Adam's disobedience humankind experienced sin and death. In the current phase of God's educational program, the individual can now participate in God's transformation of humankind by faith. As M. C. Steenberg notes, for Irenaeus, "Humanity is multiple, complex and divided, but also intrinsically unitary, simple, and whole."[18] On this view, God created on all the earth "one human race" (*unum genus humanum*) from "one blood" (*uno sanguine*) and of this one, same substance (*substantia*), Christ took the human flesh that had originally been made for Adam from dirt.[19] There is, therefore, one human nature in which all human beings participate. In each of the economies that make up the one economy of redemptive history, God perfects faithful individuals through his Son and Spirit. These faithful will one day make up the kingdom.

Irenaeus's theology of redemptive history gives a central role to the idea of God as educator. In developing this view of history, Irenaeus places a high value on the created order. In this way, he argues implicitly and explicitly against the dualism of his "heretical" rivals. Because God builds education into his creation and into its history, the mundane, the earthly, and the temporal are all construed as holy; they contribute to the perfection of the human race. Learning, too, is holy, and it sanctifies and purifies humanity. Furthermore, mind, soul, reason, rationality, and the body are all in harmony. Thus construed, the mundane, intellectual, and spiritual are all joined. Knowledge (γνῶσις) is gained from experiences within history, from within the material world that is created and ordered by the Creator-Father. Sanctified and edifying knowledge comes through various instructive means, but God superintends them all. As a result, human beings are taught (in continuity with reason) to love God and to persevere in this love for him (*Haer.* 4.37.7).

So far we have looked at Irenaeus's teaching from *Haer.* 4.37.7 in considerable detail. What we have not yet considered, however, is how he develops the crucial idea of persevering in God's love from John 15:10.

---

18. M. C. Steenberg, *Of God and Man: Theology as Anthropology from Irenaeus to Athanasius* (London: T&T Clark, 2009), 46.

19. *Haer.* 3.12.9; 5.14.2; 1.9.3. Here Irenaeus draws on Acts 17:26 and John 1:3. See also Adelin Rousseau, ed., *Irénée de Lyon: Contre les hérésies, livre 5*, SC 152 (Paris: Cerf, 1969), 266.

It will benefit us to pause and examine Irenaues's concept of the end of knowledge as a love for God that perseveres.

For Irenaeus, love for God is a key doctrine. For example, when he employs the apostle's words in 2 Thess 2:10 that speak of the judgment against those who "did not receive the love of the truth," he reads Paul's text in a manner that makes God the ultimate object of love. Citing Paul, he writes of "love of the truth" (*dilectionem veritatis*) in *Haer.* 5.25.3, but this soon becomes "love towards God" (*dilectionem Dei*) when he next cites it in 5.28.2, and again when he refers back to it in 5.32.1.[20] Furthermore, we find in the rule of faith (*Haer.* 1.10.1) a partial citation of John 15:10, as Irenaeus states that the gift of incorruptibility and everlasting glory is promised to those "who kept his commandments and who persevered in his love." A brief survey of his use of John 15:10 will aid our understanding of this notion of an enduring love for God.[21]

For Irenaeus, love for God first of all means humble assent to the first two articles of the church's rule: God's unity and the unity of Jesus Christ incarnate and crucified. To love God is to confess this faith. This love for God is envisioned as an alternative to the arrogant speculations of his opponents that imagine a god other than the one Creator. The Valentinians hold that a distinction between their primordial Father and the Demiurge of the created order solves various problems in cosmology. Irenaeus, however, argues that ignorance is better than certain pseudosolutions. One should instead "believe in God and abide in his love" (*Haer.* 2.26.1).[22] In addition to faith in God's unity, he later adds the crucified Son, Jesus Christ, so that to refuse to love God is to fall away "from that love which vivifies humankind" (*Haer.* 2.26.1). Second, one who loves God denies that human beings are naturally incorruptible, as Irenaeus's opponents teach (see *Haer.* 1.6.2). Salvation is a gift that comes through conversion and participation in the

---

20. *Haer.* 5.25.3; 5.28.2; 5.32.1; see also *Haer.* 5.27.2.

21. See D. Jeffrey Bingham, "Knowledge and Love in Irenaeus of Lyons," in *Papers Presented at the Thirteenth International Conference on Patristic Studies, Held in Oxford 1999*, ed. Maurice F. Wiles, Edward J. Yarnold, and Paul M. Parvis, StPatr 36 (Leuven: Peeters, 2001), 184–99.

22. This translation reflects the emendations of Adelin Rousseau and Louis Doutreleau, *Irénée de Lyon: Contre les hérésies, livre 2*, SC 293 (Paris: Cerf, 1982), 305–6. Rousseau and Doutreleau follow the Syriac reading of *perseverare in eius dilectione* rather than the major Latin reading of *perseverare eos in dilectione* on the grounds that the other occurrences of the phrase in *Adversus haereses* (*Haer.* 1.10.1; 3.20.2; 4.37.7) also have *eius*.

divine nature. This constitutes a gift that is received through love for God rather than pride.[23] Again he cites John 15:10 and claims that "abiding in God's love" means to follow the lesson of Luke 7:42–43 on love and forgiveness: "the one to whom more is forgiven loves more" (*Haer.* 3.20.2). Love is received from the Holy Spirit and offers thanks to God for the gift of incorruptibility (*Haer.* 4.33.9).[24] Finally, a persevering love for God rejects the determinism of Irenaeus's adversaries and instead confesses that free human will has a role in redemption. In line with his reading of Matt 11:12 and 1 Cor 9:24–27, Irenaeus argues that incorruptibility is something received through an abiding love that freely wrestles and struggles (*Haer.* 4.37.7).[25] He develops this principle in connection with the notion that love for God should increase, be preserved, and grow.[26] A love that leads to salvation survives the arduous struggle that is characteristic of humanity's progressive education. Salvation does not occur spontaneously, as though one is naturally destined for the *plērōma*. John 15:10, often linked together with other biblical texts, provides a catholic soteriological perimeter for Irenaeus's thought. Similarly, John 15:10 is also central to a strategic formulation of the church's faith in *Haer.* 1.10.1.

Irenaeus insists that love brings humanity to perfection and to a vision of God, not the "perfect" pseudoknowledge of his opponents (*Haer.* 4.12.2; 4.26.1).[27] Love for the Father-Creator, the one who providentially cares for humanity, constitutes true knowledge and authentic faith. As Paul writes in 1 Cor 13:2, 13 and Rom 13:10, faith and knowledge do not avail without love (*Haer.* 4.12.2). Ultimately, then, love is "more precious than knowledge" (*Haer.* 4.33.8).

In spite of the preeminence of love, knowledge also plays a pivotal role in redemptive history and in salvation.[28] Irenaeus understands love as something that works to define and delimit the scope of true knowledge.

---

23. Ysabel de Andia, *Homo Vivens: Incorruptibilité et divinisation de l'homme selon Irénée de Lyons* (Paris: Etudes Augustiniennes, 1986), 106.

24. See R. Tremblay's argument ("Le martyre selon saint Irénée de Lyon," *StudMor* 16 [1978]: 183 n. 68) that the gift of love is the person of the Holy Spirit.

25. On John 15:10, see Adelin Rousseau et al., eds., *Irénée de Lyon: Contre les hérésies, livre 4*, SC 100.2 (Paris: Cerf, 1965), 942 (line 168).

26. *Haer.* 2.28.1 (*augeo*); 4.9.2 (*proficio*); 4.28.3 (*custodio*); 4.37.7 (*persevero*).

27. See also *Haer.* 1.6.1 (*scientia, agnitio*); 1.21.2 (*scientia*); 1.29.3 (*agnitio*); 1.31.2 (*scientia*).

28. See, for instance, the language of *agnitio* in *Haer.* 3.9.1; 3.10.2; 3.12.3; 3.12.5; 3.16.4; 4.36.7; 5.25.5; *scientia* in 2.20.3; 5.12.4.

That is, love for God provides knowledge with a safety margin; it institutes order and limits.[29] Love establishes boundaries for knowledge, and this is particularly important because the church competes with "heretical" opponents who lay claim to "knowledge" falsely so called.[30] Irenaeus explains this clearly in his exposition of 1 Cor 8:1: "knowledge puffs up, but love builds up" (*Haer.* 2.26). To possess pseudoknowledge is to think oneself as perfect in knowledge and to conceive of and disparage an imperfect creator (Demiurge), instead of acknowledging the truly perfect Father. Thus construed, the one who divides Creator and Father does not love. Furthermore, such pseudoknowledge does not "puff up" in the sense that it can "cause ascent" into the *plērōma*; rather, it causes a descent, a fall from true life and piety. It is only the persevering love for the one God that gives life and builds up to immortality.[31]

Irenaeus understands the ultimate goal of this divine educational process as the attainment of moral virtue. According to his definition, this means that humanity as pupil is to be converted from a prideful love of self to a humble, pious love of God. Although developed in conversation with Johannine theology, Irenaeus's thought is also influenced by notions of moral virtue familiar from Greco-Roman culture. In his treatise *On the Education of Children*, Plutarch writes of philosophy (perhaps in the stricter sense of moral philosophy) as the chief subject through which a boy should learn moral virtues, particularly those of piety, regard for others, self-control, and moderation. He writes:

> Wherefore it is necessary to make philosophy as it were the head and front of all education. For as regards the care of the body men have discovered two sciences, the medical and the gymnastic, of which the one implants health, the other sturdiness, in the body; but for the illnesses and affections of the mind philosophy alone is the remedy. For through philosophy and in company with philosophy it is possible to attain knowledge ... that one ought to reverence the gods, to honor one's parents, to respect one's elders, to be obedient to the laws, to yield to those in authority, to love one's friends, to be chaste with women, to be affectionate with children, and not to be overbearing with slaves; and, most important of all, not to be over joyful at success or overly distressed at misfortune, nor to be dissolute in pleasures, nor impulsive and brutish in

---

29. *Haer.* 2.25.4 uses the language of *ordo*.
30. *Haer.* 1, Pref. 1; 1.23.4; 2, Pref. 1; 2.14.7; 3.11.1; 3.12.12; 3.16.8; 4.39.4; 5, Pref.
31. *Haer.* 2.26, with allusion to John 15:10.

temper. These things I regard as pre-eminent among all the advantages which accrue from philosophy. (*Lib. ed.* 7d–f)[32]

Other examples of the relationship of moral virtue to education may be observed within Greco-Roman discourse about literary education. For many writers, literary education is a sign of moral strength and prestige; it indicates that one is a just citizen who operates with integrity and is capable of honorable public service. Members of the literate elite culture, those who had read both grammar and rhetoric, are marked as virtuous. According to many writers, such persons were eloquent, disciplined, and diligent, and they possessed the fortitude to persevere in adversity. These and other qualities marked them as fit to shoulder the burden of state affairs.[33]

Successful training in letters required self-control, and, as Peter Brown notes, "formalized speech was held to be, in itself, a form of self-control."[34] A cultivated rhetorician was supposed to have tamed the unruly forces of grammar, logic, and speech. If he could master such difficult skills, this was also assumed to be evidence of a high degree of self-control.[35] The road to letters was arduous and demanded the virtue of temperance. As Kaster writes:

> It was gradual, painstaking—and painful. Like the athlete trained in the old gymnasium, the student of literature slowly acquired his knowledge and skills by replacing unrefined habits with good habits until they (ideally) became second nature; lapses into the bad, old habits were repaid with a beating. Unlike the initiate, the gymnast was not separated decisively from his past but had to struggle constantly against it, using constantly his virtues—memory, diligence, discipline—to fight free of the old ways and so rise above himself.[36]

---

32. Translation slightly modified from *Plutarch: Moralia*, vol. 1, trans. Frank Cole Babbit, LCL (London: Heinemann; New York: Putnam, 1927). See Quintilian, *Inst.* 12.2.15–17, for philosophy as "moral" philosophy. Edmund G. Berry ("The *De liberis educandis* of Pseudo-Plutarch," *HSCP* 63 [1958]: 389), characterizes Plutarch's work as a "synthesis of the classical tradition."

33. See Robert A. Kaster, *Guardians of Language: The Grammarian and Society in Late Antiquity* (Berkeley: University of California Press, 1997), 27.

34. Peter Brown, *Power and Persuasion in Late Antiquity: Towards a Christian Empire* (Madison: University of Wisconsin Press, 1992), 48.

35. Brown, *Power and Persuasion*, 48; Kaster, *Guardians of Language*, 18.

36. Kaster, *Guardians of Language*, 17.

This emphasis on the need for self-control is also in keeping with discussions of ancient ethical theory and practice. For instance, when Aristotle divides virtues into intellectual and moral categories, he also defines temperance as the basis for moral virtue (*Eth. nic.* 1103a20). Similarly, self-control is one of Plato's four cardinal virtues and occurs in the main Stoic lists.[37]

According to much ancient thought about education, training both in moral philosophy and in letters is important for moral formation, but so too is education in other subjects. We are unable to touch on all of them here, but examples drawn from music will enrich the analysis.[38] For Plato, music was a worthy course of study because it embeds harmony and rhythm and so helps to make souls graceful. Those who have mastered musical skills will have developed habits of taste, discretion, and perception that can be applied in other areas. The appropriate kind of musical education promises to build one's intuitive capacity to discern and appreciate good musical harmony and rhythm. With mastery, the student will also be capable of discerning harmony from discord in other areas, such as good from bad or order from chaos. Maturity and mastery in music thus encourages a more reasoned discernment. Addressing Glaucon, Socrates describes musical training as:

> a more potent instrument than any other, because rhythm and harmony find their way into the inward places of the soul, onto which they firmly fasten, imparting grace, and making the soul of the pupil who is rightly educated graceful, or making the soul of the one who is not well-educated ungraceful. Such musical training is also potent because the one who has received this true education of the inner being will most shrewdly perceive omissions or faults in art and nature, and with a true taste, while praising, rejoicing over and receiving into his soul the good, becomes noble and good, will justly blame and hate the bad, now in the days of his youth, even before he is able to know the reason why, and then later when reason comes he will recognize and welcome

---

37. Plato, *Resp.* 4.427E, 430D–432B; Alcinous, *Epit.* 29.2; Diogenes Laertius, *Vit. Phil.* 7.92.

38. We could also mention, for example, physics, mathematics, medicine, metaphysics, and cosmology. See G. E. R. Lloyd, "Science and Morality in Greco-Roman Antiquity," in *Methods and Problems in Greek Science: Selected Papers* (Cambridge: Cambridge University Press, 1991), 370.

the friend with whom his education had made him long familiar. (*Resp.* 3.401d–e)[39]

Elsewhere Plato insists: "The whole of one's life necessitates rhythm and harmony" (*Prot.* 326B), and describes the master of music as one who, through musical lessons, helps to impart these graces. Ideally, the master acquaints the students with scales and rhythm and thereby helps them to become gentle, balanced, and efficient in their speech and conduct.

Robert Kaster characterizes Greco-Roman education as follows: "*Doctrina* presumed *mores*; to be a scholar presumed that one was the right sort of person, a gentleman.... Letters validated claims to status, both moral status and social, although the two were hardly separate in the eyes of the traditionally cultured man."[40] Put simply, the learned were *boni* (the good) while the uneducated were *invertes*, the "crude" and "slothful" (Aurelius Victor, *Caes.* 9.12).[41] This perspective is not limited to the study of grammar and rhetoric, but is also evident in musical education. Aristotle, for instance, takes a similar view in his writing on the aesthetics of music. For him, the unlearned have never been morally formed, and this prevents them from feeling pleasure or pain in accord with virtue. They are only able to enjoy a type of music that appeals to their base, uneducated, and warped nature. The reverse is true for the learned; their more virtuous nature allows them to appreciate more complex, sophisticated, and elegant forms of music (Aristotle, *Pol.* 1342a23–26).[42]

Irenaeus's emphasis on moral virtue has much in common with elite discourse about paideia and learning, though he defines these virtues in distinctive ways. The bishop emphasizes piety and a humble, doctrinally faithful love for God as the ultimate virtue, while the philosophical and literary culture of his time tended rather to prize self-control and moderation, though this often included piety in some form.

---

39. Translation revised from Benjamin Jowett, trans., *Plato: The Republic* (New York: Vintage, 1991).

40. Kaster, *Guardians of Language*, 27; see also ibid., 15–19.

41. Ibid., 27 n. 66.

42. See Elizabeth M. Jones, "Allocating Musical Pleasure: Performance, Pleasure, and Value in Aristotle's *Politics*," in *Aesthetic Value in Classical Antiquity*, ed. Ineke Sluiter and Ralph M. Rosen, MnemosyneSup 350 (Leiden: Brill, 2012), 179–80.

The Necessity of the Classical Curriculum

Not only is education and training woven into the warp and woof of Irenaeus's notion of a human history ordered by God, but his polemics also make use of tropes drawn from classical education. This makes sense because both Irenaeus and other educated elites held that virtue is gained through education. Thus, it is not surprising to find him investigating, identifying, and exploiting alleged weaknesses in the education of his opponents and employing the fruits of his own education to do so. For example, he characterizes Marcion, the Valentinians, and others who would destroy the church's quadriform gospel as "vain, unlearned [*indoctus*], and also audacious" (*Haer.* 3.11.9). Elsewhere, those who do not affirm one God of both old and new covenants are "unlearned [*indoctus*] and presumptuous, even lacking common sense" (*Haer.* 4.27.4). In another context, Irenaeus characterizes all his opponents as "unlearned" (*indoctus*; *Haer.* 5.19.2).

The strategy of disparaging the learnedness of one's opponent is common in other interreligious polemics of the second century. We see it in Celsus, who ridicules the Christians:

> "Let no one educated, no one wise, no one sensible draw near to us Christians, for we think these abilities are evil. But if any are ignorant, or stupid, or uneducated, or foolish, they should come with confidence." Christians themselves acknowledge that such people are worthy of their God, and they confirm that they desire and are able to convince only the foolish, the dishonorable, the stupid, along with slaves, women and children. (*Cels.* 3.44; cf. 3.50, 55)[43]

According to Origen, Celsus claims that Christians prioritize faith over reason. Comparing Christianity to other religions that attract the unreasonable, the wicked, the ignorant, and easily deceived, he insists that the Christian community is comprised of people who "do not wish either to give or receive a reason for their faith, but keep repeating such mottos as, 'Do not examine, but believe!' and 'Your faith will save you!'" (*Cels.* 1.9).[44]

---

43. See T. R. Glover, *The Conflict of Religions in the Early Roman Empire* (Boston: Beacon, 1909), 241–42.

44. R. L. Wilken recognizes that this type of fideism may have been common, but he also insists that Christianity was developing a learned core group of thinkers. See his *The Christians as the Romans Saw Them*, 2nd ed. (New Haven: Yale University Press, 2003), 77–78.

As observed already, the polemics of Irenaeus include criticism of his adversaries as "unlearned." In these cases, Irenaeus does not only mean that they are poorly catechized or ignorant of proper biblical and theological teachings. Although such issues might very well be implied, he also develops these concerns in ways that draw on the classical curriculum. When Irenaeus addresses the weakness of the Carpocratians, for instance, he indicts them for failing to master the subjects of a classical education. On this presentation, the Carpocratians seek to achieve perfection, but they fail to pursue the artistic disciplines that would make them truly virtuous. He writes:[45]

> For if they wish to experience every work and activity, first they ought to learn all the arts, whether the theoretical arts, or practical arts, or those arts learned through work, meditation, and perseverance. For example, I mean every form of music, arithmetic, geometry, astronomy, and all the other theoretical disciplines. They should study the whole of medicine and the science of pharmacy and all the disciplines related to human health, as well as painting, sculpture, working in bronze and marble, and other arts like these. Furthermore, they should study every form of agriculture and the care of horses and of flocks and herds, and the technical arts, which are said to involve all the other techniques. Finally, they should learn navigation, gymnastics, hunting, the art of war, and the art of government without counting the many other arts that exist.... Of all these disciplines, however, they do not learn even one. (*Haer.* 2.32.2)

Here Irenaeus catalogues the subjects that a student would be likely to study after grammar, rhetoric, and dialectic. This list of subjects also moves from literature to more theoretical and practical material.[46] The theoretical pursuits involve music, arithmetic, geometry, and astronomy, which would treat harmony, numbers, abstract principles, and divine things, respectively. Aristotle had already distinguished between the theoretical (e.g., physics) and practical arts (e.g., ethics), a distinction that was common in

---

45. Robert M. Grant, trans., *Irenaeus of Lyons*, ECF (London: Routledge, 1997).
46. Robert M. Grant, "Carpocratians and Curriculum: Irenaeus' Reply," *HTR* 79 (1986): 129. Grant's essay informs my discussion of the concepts related to ancient education in this Irenaean passage.

Irenaeus's time.[47] In this case, however, Irenaeus seems to liken the practical arts to more technical crafts like agriculture, hunting, and navigation.

Some second and third-century writers present lists of subjects that are similar to Irenaeus's in *Haer.* 2.32.2. In this case, Irenaeus does not explicitly rate these disciplines in terms of his perception of their value, but others do.[48] Galen provides a catalogue of what he considers to be the preferred subjects of study, namely those pursued by devotees of Mercury (Hermes). Those who pursue such studies are blessed by Mercury and considered to be worthy of respect, unlike those who pursue Fortune. Those closest to Mercury are "the geometricians, mathematicians, philosophers, physicians, astronomers, and philologists. In second place are the painters, sculptors, teachers of grammar, carpenters, architects, and lapidaries. In third rank are the other artists" (Galen, *Protr.* 5).[49] Later in the *Protrepticus*, with some duplication, Galen discusses those arts that require more than mere physical strength, and describes these as the honorable or liberal arts. For Galen, these are medicine, rhetoric, music, geometry, arithmetic, philosophy, astronomy, literature, jurisprudence, sculpture, and painting (*Protr.* 14). Similarly, Philostratus provides both a two- and a three-tiered catalog (*Gymn.* 1; *Vit. Apoll.* 8.7.9). In the *Life of Apollonius*, he characterizes poetry, music, astronomy, and rhetoric (except forensic speaking) as the most venerable arts, and in the *Gymnasticus* he adds philosophy and geometry. In the *Gymnasticus*, Philostratus also adds painting, sculpture, navigation, and farming, but views these as less valuable, with navigation and gymnastics as the least valuable of all. In the *Life of Apollonius*, military science, medicine, painting, sculpture, gem-cutting, and the metal arts are second in rank after theoretical subjects.

These examples suggest at least two important points about Irenaeus's critique of the Carpocratians. On the one hand, we see that Irenaeus criticizes his opponents for not having been educated in the classical curriculum. This fits well with other aspects of Irenaeus's polemic, which seems to expect that the dualism of his "gnostic" opponents renders them unenthusiastic about "mundane and ordinary studies," especially their strong oppositions between earthly and heavenly, the historical and the

---

47. Aristotle, *Metaph.* 2.1.5 (A 993b21); 6.1.4 (E 1025b20–21); 6.1.5 (E 1025b23–25): Philo, *Leg.* 1.57; Quintilian, *Inst.* 2.18.

48. See Grant, "Carpocratians and Curriculum," 130.

49. I follow the English translation of Joseph Walsh, "Galen's Exhortation to the Study of the Arts, Especially Medicine," *ML* 37 (1930): 507–529.

celestial.⁵⁰ Other sources suggest that Irenaeus's view of his opponents is relatively accurate, at least for some of the Carpocratians and Valentinians.⁵¹ For instance, the Valentinian treatise known as the Tripartite Tractate argues that the curriculum and arts associated with ancient paideia are vain, illusory, and foolish. In fact, the writer charges that the educated have been drawn into a conspiracy orchestrated by the Demiurge and his fallen agents against their primordial Father. The classical arts do not provide true knowledge; they only offer conflicting theories. By contrast, true knowledge is ineffable:

> Those who were wise among the Greeks and the barbarians have advanced to the powers which have come into being by way of imagination and vain thought. Those who have come from these ... also spoke in a likely, arrogant, and imaginary way concerning the things which they thought of as wisdom, although the likeness deceived them, since they thought that they had attained the truth, when they had [only] attained error. (They did so) not simply in minor appellations, but the powers themselves seem to hinder them, as if they were the Totality. Therefore, the order was caught up in fighting itself alone, because of the arrogant hostility of one of the offspring of the archon who is superior, who exists before him. Therefore, nothing was in agreement with its fellows, nothing, neither philosophy nor types of medicine nor types of rhetoric nor types of music nor types of logic, but they are opinions and theories. Ineffability held sway in confusion, because of the indescribable quality of those who hold sway, who give them thoughts. (Tri. Trac. 109.24–110.24)⁵²

---

50. Grant, "Carpocratians and Curriculum," 135.

51. Clement of Alexandria tells us that Carpocrates educated his son, Epiphanes, in the classical curriculum and in Platonic philosophy (*Strom.* 3.5.3). Even if this is accurate, the Carpocratians known by Irenaeus, or even the Carpocratians in general, need not have embraced a positive view of education. After all, Irenaeus's account of their teachings in *Haer.* 1.25.1–5 is based on his reading of their own texts (*Haer.* 1.25.5) and he claims knowledge of Valentinian commentaries in *Haer.* 1, Pref. 2. Furthermore, Irenaeus notes that their failure to learn the arts is related to their imitation of Epicurus's philosophy and what he labels as the "indifference" of the Cynics (*Haer.* 2.32.2). If they have learned some philosophy, he concludes, they have applied it against learning the arts; *contra* Grant, "Carpocratians and Curriculum," 131.

52. Trans. Harold W. Attridge and Dieter Mueller in James M. Robinson, ed., *The Nag Hammadi Library in English*, rev. ed. (New York: HarperCollins, 1988). See also Grant, "Carpocratians and Curriculum," 135–36. We should note also that this treatise itself reflects sophisticated learning and requires a community that, in some way, promoted such learning, even if it derides paideia.

From this perspective, paideia is a product of the Demiurge, the archon responsible for the mundane world that is disparaged by those who yearn for true knowledge and a return to the *plērōma*. For the Valentinian writers of this tractate, paideia offers only pseudoknowledge that is ultimately as empty and misguided as the material world itself. Here we see some similarities between Irenaeus's portrayal of the Carpocratians and the Valentinian views found in the Tripartite Tractate. This suggests that for some second-century "gnostic" communities, paideia could at best yield only misleading, pseudoknowledge that blocks salvation.

In his critique of the Carpocratians, Irenaeus portrays catholic theology as a virtuous faith that leads to moral improvement. This tradition is also so consonant with classical learning that its intellectuals must be well educated. Though this education is not required of all Christians, some elites within the community (such as himself) must pursue this education in order to protect and redeem the simple. In addition to attaining the requisite education, these elites are also responsible for reading the texts of the Valentinians and engaging them in conversation (*Haer.* 1, Pref. 1–3).

In numerous other cases, Irenaeus demonstrates knowledge of the arts associated with classical paideia. Alluding to well-known tropes about music, he places a high value on harmony (*Haer.* 2.25.2), and elsewhere demonstrates knowledge of arithmetic (*Haer.* 2.16.4) and of the geometric forms (*Haer.* 2.13.6). He also frequently uses examples drawn from the medical world (*Haer.* 1.16.3; 3.5.2; 3.25.7). In one instance he uses the metaphor of a mosaic to critique Valentinian theologians, and elsewhere demonstrates a basic knowledge of sculpture (*Haer.* 1.8.1; 2.15.3; 2.19.8). In the same vein, he also compares the duplicity of his adversaries with the arts relating to gems and metals (*Haer.* 1, Pref. 2). In other cases, he uses metaphors drawn from wrestling and hunting (*Haer.* 5.13.2; 1.31.4), and as we will see below, his writings demonstrate knowledge of physics, cosmology, and literature as well.

As Grant argues, Irenaeus shows a familiarity with subjects that parallel "much of the Greco-Roman curriculum."[53] An appreciation for the breadth and depth of this learning provides an important corrective to our understanding of second-century Christian intellectuals. Scholars of the Christian tradition typically focus on figures such as Justin and Athe-

---

53. Grant, "Carpocratians and Curriculum," 135.

nagoras, or certain contemporaries of Galen and Celsus.⁵⁴ Because earlier scholarship is critical of Irenaeus's level of education, however, they tend to sideline his contributions. Hugo Koch, for example, criticizes his traditionalism and brands him as a writer lacking in intellectual ability and sophistication.⁵⁵ In Koch's view, Irenaeus is not a systematic thinker, and his writings show little interest in well-reasoned, carefully developed argument. Other interpreters hold that his traditionalism limits his intellectual productivity, his originality, the unity of *Adversus haereses*, and the coherence of his thought.⁵⁶ For instance, Hans Hinrich Wendt claims that Irenaeus's anthropology is contradictory, and Adolf von Harnack finds contradiction in both his anthropology and soteriology.⁵⁷ Likewise, Friedrich Loofs offers disparaging comments about Irenaeus as a theologian;⁵⁸ Johannes Quasten holds that his work lacks organization and unity;⁵⁹ and Frederik Wisse expresses skepticism that the bishop had first-hand knowledge of his opponents' literature, casting doubt on the accuracy of his representations of their beliefs. Wisse even goes so far as to argue that Irenaeus knows only Ptolamaean and Marcosian propaganda.⁶⁰ Such scholarship has slowed the appreciation of Irenaeus's level of education.⁶¹

---

54. See, e.g., Wilken, *Christians as the Romans Saw Them*, 77–78.

55. Hugo Koch, "Zur Lehre vom Urstand und von der Erlösung bei Irenäus," *TSK* 96–97 (1925): 183–214.

56. For a helpful overview of the earlier scholarship, see Philippe Bacq, *De l'ancienne a la nouvelle alliance selon S. Irénée: Unité du livre IV de l'Adversus haereses*, SSH (Paris: Lethielleux, 1978), 364–69.

57. Hans Hinrich Wendt, *Die christliche Lehre von der menschlichen Vollkommenheit* (Göttingen: Vandenhoeck & Ruprecht, 1882), 20–30; Adolf von Harnack, *History of Dogma*, trans. Neil Buchanan, 7 vols. (Boston: Little, Brown, 1899–1907), 2:267–75, esp. 267, 272–73.

58. Friedrich Loofs, *Theophilus von Antiochien Adversus Marcionem und die anderen theologischen Quellen bei Irenaeus*, TU 46.2 (Leipzig: Hinrichs, 1930), 432.

59. Johannes Quasten, *The Beginnings of Patristic Literature from the Apostles Creed to Irenaeus*, vol. 1 of *Patrology* (Utrecht: Spectrum, 1950), 289.

60. Frederik Wisse, "The Nag Hammadi Library and the Heresiologists," *VC* 25 (1971): 216.

61. More recently, see Denis Minns, *Irenaeus: An Introduction* (London: T&T Clark, 2010), who depends on the older source-critical theories.

Catholic Exploitation of the Classical Curriculum

As argued above, Irenaeus closely associates legitimate Christian intellectuals with a trustworthy account of the faith and with classical education. Further evidence of his appropriation of Greco-Roman paideia appears in his constructive theology, particularly his view that the classical curriculum protects Christian thinkers from heresy. Though some scholars argue that Irenaeus probably did have "more than rudimentary education,"[62] many prefer the view articulated by William Schoedel that "Irenaeus had at some time been exposed to the fundamentals of Hellenistic education, grammar and rhetoric, but that his acquaintance with the higher discipline of philosophy had remained somewhat elementary in character."[63] On this approach, he certainly knew at least the doxographies and some of the philosophical handbooks, but little more.[64] Largely in keeping with this view, Eric Osborn's more recent work argues that Irenaeus demonstrates more knowledge of literature than of philosophy.[65] For Osborn, Irenaeus shows some familiarity with the works of Homer, Hesiod, and Pindar. But although he uses Xenophanes without attribution and knows a bit of Plato, Middle Platonism, and Stoicism, he lacks a sophisticated knowledge of philosophy. There is much to commend these views, but the scholarly discussion of Irenaeus's level of education can be helpfully expanded by considering his knowledge of music, physics, and literature. Though Irenaeus may have gone to Rome to learn rhetoric, it is also noteworthy that his home town of Smyrna was a hub of the Second Sophistic movement.[66]

Music Theory

In his treatment of the problem of the one and the many (or the unity of God and the diversity of creation), Irenaeus eloquently joins together musicology and theology. He writes:

---

62. Minns, *Irenaeus*, 1.

63. William Schoedel, "Philosophy and Rhetoric in the *Adversus Haereses* of Irenaeus," *VC* 13 (1959): 31.

64. Schoedel, "Philosophy and Rhetoric," 22–26; Grant, "Irenaeus and Hellenistic Culture," 42.

65. Eric Osborn, *Irenaeus of Lyons* (Cambridge: Cambridge University Press, 2001), 3, 7–8, 32. See also Schoedel, "Philosophy and Rhetoric," 26, on Xenophanes.

66. See Pierre Nautin, *Lettres et écrivains chrétiens des IIe et IIIe siècles* (Paris: Cerf, 1953), 93, on Irenaeus's possible journey to Rome for his education.

But since created things are various and numerous, they are well fitted and adapted to the whole creation; yet, when they are viewed individually, they appear mutually opposite and inharmonious. It is just as when the sound of the lyre, which consists of many and opposite notes, gives rise to one unbroken melody. The lover of truth therefore should not to be deceived by the interval between each note, nor should that person imagine that one note was due to one artist and composer, and a different note to another; nor should the lover of truth imagine that one musician fitted the treble, another the bass, and yet another the tenor strings; but the lover of truth should hold that one and the same musician formed the whole. Those, too, who listen to the melody, ought to praise and extol the single artist ... neither giving up the artist, nor casting off faith in the one God who formed all things, nor blaspheming our Creator. (*Haer.* 2.25.2)

Informed by music theory, Irenaeus explains how diversity in artistic design indicates that there is only one God rather than many.[67] As noted earlier, he elsewhere scolds his opponents for their lack of education and specifically refers to musical knowledge in this context. As is well known, the education of the Greek and the Roman children differed only moderately, and typically included instruction in music along with grammar, mathematics, and gymnastics.[68] In his *Protagoras*, Plato argues that the study of music teaches harmonies and rhythms "familiar to the children's souls, in order that they may learn to be more gentle, and harmonious, and rhythmical, and thereby more fitted for speech and action; for every part of life has need of harmony and rhythm" (*Prot.* 325d–326b).[69] Irenaeus

---

67. Irenaeus is responding to the Valentinians, who, in making note of the great diversity among the names of people, events, places, and things found throughout the creation and within the scriptures, apply typology and numerology to them, and arrive at the conclusion that there are many divine beings. See *Haer.* 2.20.1–2.25.2.

68. Bonner, *Education in Ancient Rome*, 44, 77; M. L. Clarke, *Higher Education in the Ancient World* (Albuquerque: University of New Mexico Press, 1971), 45–54; F. Kühnert, *Allgemeinbildung und Fachbildung in der Antike* (Berlin: Akademie, 1961); James Mountford, "Music and the Romans," *BJRL* 47 (1964): 198–211; G. Wille, *Musica Romana: Die Bedeutung der Musik im Leben der Römer* (Amsterdam: Schippers, 1967). See Cicero, *De or.* 3.23.87; Propertius, *El.* 1.2, 27–8; 2.1.9–10; Statius, *Silv.* 3.5.64; Juvenal, *Sat.* 7.175–7; Horace, *Sat.* 1.10.90–91; Columella, *Rust.* 1, Pref. 3, 5; Seneca, *Ep.* 90.19.

69. Translation revised from Benjamin Jowett, trans., *Plato: Protagoras, Philebus, and Gorgias* (Amherst, NY: Prometheus, 1996).

takes these ideas further and argues that music provides a model for the harmony and unity of the divine nature.

Physics and Cosmology

In his famous article on Irenaeus, Grant discusses doxographical collections and shows how early Christian writers used them for their quotations of Greek philosophical ideas. He shows that early Christian thinkers are dependent on Aetius's original compilation. This collection dates to the reign of Augustus, but is reconstructed by Hermann Diels from two later parallel sources: Pseudo-Plutarch, *Placita Philosophorum* (*Opinions of the Philosophers*), dated around 150 CE, and John Stobaeus, *Eclogae Physicae* (*Physical Passages*), from the fifth century. Following Diels, Grant shows that Irenaeus follows Pseudo-Plutarch, and identifies two instances where Irenaeus's characterization of philosophers and poets imitates that of Pseudo-Plutarch (*Haer.* 2.14.1–6).[70] Grant also draws attention to another case in *Adversus haereses* (*Haer.* 2.28.1–2.) that was apparently unnoticed by Diels. In this case, Irenaeus discusses scientific problems that, as Grant explains, "are almost entirely taken from the headings of Pseudo-Plutarch: why the Nile rises, where birds winter, what causes tides, what lies beyond the ocean, what causes various weather phenomena, what causes the moon's phases, what is responsible for the difference between fresh and salt water, what accounts for differences between metals and minerals?"[71]

Irenaeus's treatment of what Grant typifies as the "insoluble difficulties in science," also discusses multiple explanations of such problems without arriving at specific resolutions. Grant argues that this may derive from Skeptic thought, for as Sextus Empiricus indicates, the Skeptics also avoid firm conclusions about physical theories (*Pyr.* 1.18).[72] Ultimately, Grant characterizes Irenaeus as eclectic, but Irenaeus's treatment of these problems suggests several possible sources. For instance, Irenaeus's writings may also show the influence of Epicureanism.[73] Epicurus argues that, in

---

70. See Hermann Diels, *Doxographi graeci* (Berlin: Reimer, 1879), 171–72.

71. Grant, "Irenaeus and Hellenistic Culture," 43–44; Schoedel, "Philosophy and Rhetoric," 23–24.

72. See Grant, "Irenaeus and Hellenistic Culture," 46.

73. J. R. Milton, "The Limitations of Ancient Atomism," in *Science and Mathematics in Ancient Greek Culture*, ed. C. J. Tuplin and T. E. Rehill (Oxford: Oxford University Press, 2002), 180–85.

cases where the objects of inquiry could not be investigated directly, such as atoms and the waxing and waning of the moon, one should aim for explanations that could not be refuted by contrary evidence. With this criterion, there could be many explanations rather than a single one. In these cases, Epicurus seems to prefer rival but plausible explanations rather than singular ones (*Ep. Pyth.* 94).[74]

Other aspects of Irenaeus's writings suggest training in classical paideia. For instance, Irenaeus's view on the relationship between cosmological or metaphysical speculation and theology does not seem far from the views of Socrates, at least as presented by Xenophon and Cicero (Xenophon, *Mem.* 1.4.1–20; 4.3.3–14).[75] Further, Irenaeus presents a list of problems in physics and cosmology as a setup to a discussion about the divine attributes of omniscience and truthfulness. Many of the issues Irenaeus catalogues had received proposed solutions, but he elects to ignore them.[76] Another precedent for these views may be found in the writings of Strabo, where he dismisses the Stoic Posidonius's enthusiastic "Aristotelian" theorizing

---

74. As J. R. Milton explains, for Epicurus "the purpose of multiple explanations was not to gain a deeper understanding of nature, but rather to promote peace of mind" (Milton, "Limitations of Ancient Atomism," 182). According to Elizabeth Asmis, given the widespread popularity of Epicureanism in Asia Minor and Italy, it is not hard to imagine that Irenaeus's education included Epicurean teachings (see Elizabeth Asmis, "Basic Education in Epicureanism," in *Education in Greek and Roman Antiquity*, ed. Y. L. Too [Leiden: Brill, 2001], 212–16). It is helpful to note that for Eleatics, as well, physical science was a "doctrine of opinions," not true knowledge. See J. Drever, *Greek Education: Its Practice and Principles* (Cambridge: Cambridge University Press, 1912), 49.

75. See Mark L. McPherran, *The Religion of Socrates* (University Park: Pennsylvania State University Press, 1996), 273–91; T. K. Johansen, *Plato's Natural Philosophy: A Study of the Timaeus-Critias* (Cambridge: Cambridge University Press, 2004), 3–5, and 3 n. 9; David Sedley, *Creationism and Its Critics in Antiquity* (Berkeley: University of California Press, 2007), 91. Xenophon distinguishes Socrates from those scholars (i.e., certain of the pre-Socratics) whose investigations end only in theories about the mechanistic, physical causes behind natural phenomena. In Socrates's view such study of cosmology and physics is impious because it ignores or subordinates the primary purpose of theorizing about the cosmos, which should be teleological. Investigation of the cosmos should point to god, the designer-creator, not to the theorists or physical theories. Cicero discusses similar mysteries in an argument for divine providence (*Nat. d.* 2.130–136). See Grant, "Irenaeus and Hellenistic Culture," 44. It might be that Irenaeus, informed by Cicero, understands natural mysteries as ultimately pointing to some aspect of the perfect divine nature.

76. Grant, "Irenaeus and Hellenistic Culture," 44–46.

about etiology. Strabo writes: "For in Posidonius there is much inquiry into causes and much imitating of Aristotle—precisely what our people [i.e., school] avoid, on account of the obscurity of the causes" (*Geogr.* 2.3.8 [C 104]).[77] For Strabo and other critics—possibly including Irenaeus—the ultimate causes of these natural phenomena remain hidden.[78] As Irenaeus develops this critique, he argues that only God understands these causes; the lack of ultimate knowledge on cosmological or metaphysical matters thus points to divine omniscience.

Irenaeus also emphasizes the uncertainty of human inquiry when he discusses the process by which one may arrive at legitimate theological conclusions. On this view, the heretics commit blasphemy precisely because they claim to derive certain knowledge about difficult biblical passages. In fact, their misguided desire for sure conclusions drives them to construct an erroneous myth. Irenaeus, in contrast, argues for simplicity and humility when approaching the biblical texts, insisting that ignorance must be embraced as part of the creature's condition, and that humanity should be content with applying the church's rule of truth. If no obviously "catholic" interpretation is forthcoming, the faithful are to humbly confess the church's faith. On this approach, the catholic interpreter is to accept the faith and unique omniscience of God. In these discussions, Irenaeus's education in physical theories comes to the fore. In fact, they ground his confidence in these hermeneutic principles. The dizzying variety of competing theories among philosophers and scientists has the effect of reorienting him to the one faith. Emphasizing the diversity of views, he writes:

> For what can we say if we try to explain the cause of the flooding of the Nile? We may say a great deal, plausible or otherwise, on the subject. However, the true, sure, and incontrovertible explanation regarding it belongs only to God. Also, what explanation can we give for the flow and ebb of the ocean, although everyone admits there must be a certain cause? What, furthermore, can we say as to the formation of rain,

---

77. See Daniela Dueck, *Strabo of Amasia: A Greek Man of Letters in Augustan Rome* (London: Routledge, 2000), 62. Diogenes Laertius comments on Aristotle: "In the sphere of natural science he surpassed all other philosophers in the investigation of causes, so that even the most insignificant phenomena were explained by him. Hence, he compiled an unusual number of scientific notebooks" (*Vit. Phil.* 5.32).

78. Michael Frede, *Essays in Ancient Philosophy* (Minneapolis: University of Minnesota Press, 1987), 130.

lightning, thunder, gatherings of clouds, vapors, the bursting forth of winds, and the like; or what can we say as to the storehouses of snow, hail, and other similar things? What do we know about the conditions necessary for the formation of clouds, or how to account for the vapors in the sky? What about the reason for why the moon waxes and wanes, or what the cause is for the difference between various types of waters, metals, stones, and such things? On all these points we may indeed say a great many things while we search into their causes, but only God who made them can declare the truth regarding them. (*Haer.* 2.28.2)

Once again, Irenaeus seems to take lessons learned in school and exploit them for catholic, polemical purposes. At some point in his education, he was probably instructed in the variety of explanations for these natural phenomena. It is likely that he also learned the causes compiled by the likes of Posidonian and Aristotelian physicists, but they do not interest him here. Instead, Irenaeus argues that only God knows the true causes and that faith in this God brings humility and peace. Thus, Irenaeus's discourses on physical subjects ultimately lead him to persevere in a love for God, the all-knowing One.[79]

Literature

In *Haer.* 1.3.6, Irenaeus explains that the Valentinians adapt the good words of the evangelists, apostles, law, and prophets to their own inventions (*adinvenio*). Through their disordered reading of the church's scripture they lead those who are not steadfast in faith away from God. Later in book 1, he claims that the Valentinians attempt to adapt their own system (*argumentum*) of interpretation to the parables, sayings, and words of scripture, but they do so by transferring and rearranging words and passages into a deceptive composition (*Haer.* 1.8.1). He illustrates such illegitimate compositions by describing a skillfully made tile mosaic that a vandal destroys and then reconstructs in a new way. On this analogy, the original mosaic pictures a king (i.e., the literal scripture) but the vandal rearranges this into a dog or fox (*volpecula*). Like this rearrangement of tiles, the Valentinian heretics rearrange the words of scripture to

---

79. See W. C. van Unnik, "Theological Speculation and Its Limits," in *Early Christian Literature and the Classical Tradition: In Honorem Robert M. Grant*, ed. William R. Schoedel and Robert L. Wilken (Paris: Beauchesne, 1979), 33–43.

deceive the simple and ignorant. Though individual pieces of the compositions remain the same (the tiles, on this analogy), the image changes radically because an imposter replaces the original artisan. In another context, he explains the Valentinians' illegitimate use of John's gospel (*Haer.* 1.9.1–3) as the process of taking the words of scripture out of their proper order and transferring (*transfero*) them to their own system (*argumentio*). According to Irenaeus, this process perverts and jumbles scripture in a way that is similar to the violence a Homeric cento does to the works of Homer (*Haer.* 1.9.4).[80] The cento is a pseudo-Homeric poem assembled from a collection of Homeric verses. These verses are scattered throughout the *Iliad* and *Odyssey*, but as brought together in the cento they present a novel poem about Hercules and Eurystheus. As Irenaeus explains, an astute audience recognizes the verses but not the theme, subject, or system (*argumentum*). The simple-minded, by contrast, are snatched away by the familiar verses and mistake the system (*argumentum*) of the poem for the work of Homer. According to Irenaeus, the Valentinians read scripture in just this way: they link disjointed texts to weave their own myth. The resulting Valentinian composition, however, is not Pauline, Johannine, or catholic.[81]

---

80. Only a few Homeric centos have survived, but their importance for the preservation and trajectory of the Homeric tradition and for the production of new texts should not be minimized. See M. D. Usher, "Prolegomenon to the Homeric Cento," *AJP* 2 (1997): 305. On Virgilian centos, see Scott McGill, *Virgil Recomposed: The Mythological and Secular Centos in Antiquity* (Oxford: Oxford University Press, 2005); Karl O. Sandnes, *The Gospel "According to Homer and Virgil": Cento and Canon*, NovTSup 138 (Leiden: Brill, 2011), 107–40. For a brief introduction, see Aaron Pelttari, *The Space That Remains: Reading Latin Poetry in Late Antiquity* (Ithaca: Cornell University Press, 2014), 96–103. As M. D. Usher notes, "the Homeric Centos may be said to stand to the *Iliad* and the *Odyssey* as *parole* does to *langue*." See M. D. Usher, *Homeric Stitchings: The Homeric Centos of the Empress Eudocia* (Lanham, MD: Rowman & Littlefield, 1998), 10; see also Matthew Clark's review of that book in *CP* 96 (2001): 328. Centos both endorse the authority of texts and at the same time violate those norms by deconstructing and reassembling the material (Usher, *Homeric Stitchings*, 11).

81. Jerome also compares misreadings of scripture with Homeric and Virgilian centos. For Jerome, centos reflect private meanings produced by a depraved methodology that bends scripture to the composer's own will (*Ep.* 53.7); see also *Haer.* 1.3.6; 1.8.1; and *Haer.* 1.9.4. I have argued elsewhere (*Irenaeus's Use of Matthew's Gospel in Adversus haereses* [Leuven: Peeters, 1998], 13–32) that Irenaeus's metaphors here are inspired by the language about false prophets and wolves in sheepskins in Matt 7:15.

Irenaeus's presentation of the Homeric cento does not suggest that he composed the cento himself.[82] Much evidence suggests that centos were included in the Greco-Roman curriculum, and Libanius mentions a Homeric cento that was used as a popular classroom text (*Ep.* 990).[83] We can assume that lessons on Homer and exercises involving centos would have equipped Irenaeus as well as the more literate members of his audience to recognize these shorter units from Homer, both as organized in the cento and in their original place in the Homeric corpus.[84] Irenaeus's use of the cento thus shows us something about his own education as well as about the literacy of his readers.[85]

---

82. Opinion on the cento's origin is divided. Jean Danielou argues that it was assembled by Valentinus; Dominic Unger and John J. Dillon hold that it was composed by Irenaeus, but Robert L. Wilken argues that it is the work of neither Valentinus nor Irenaeus but rather an unknown composer; see Jean Danielou, *Gospel Message and Hellenistic Culture*, vol. 2 of *A History of Early Christian Doctrine before the Council of Nicaea*, trans. J. A. Baker (Philadelphia: Westminster, 1973), 85–86; Dominic Unger and John J. Dillon, *St. Irenaeus of Lyons: Against the Heresies, Book 1*, ACW 55 (New York: Paulist, 1992), 181 n. 21; see also H. Ziegler, *Irenäus der Bischof von Lyon* (Berlin: Reimer, 1871), 17; Robert L. Wilken, "The Homeric Cento in Irenaeus, 'Adversus Haereses' I, 9, 4," *VC* 21 (1967): 23–33. Against Unger and Dillon, it seems unlikely that Irenaeus composed it himself. He gives no clear indication that he is personally responsible for the composition and uses vague expressions to introduce it that suggest anonymity. Further, in cases where Irenaeus offers a composition of his own, he tends to clarify this (e.g. *Haer.* 1.4.3–4; 1.11.4). It seems best to conclude, with André Benoit (*Saint Irénée: Introduction a l'étude de sa théologie* [Paris: Presses Universitaires de France, 1960], 60–61) that he learned the cento in school. Irenaeus names Homer or uses the adjective "Homeric" some twelve times (*Haer.* 1.9.4; 1.12.2; 1.13.6; 2.5.4; 2.14.2; 2.22.6; 4.33.3) and, outside of the cento, he cites or alludes to the *Iliad* six times (*Haer.* 1.12.2; 1.13.6; 2.5.4; 2.14.2; 2.22.6; 4.33.3). These uses of Homer are easily explained by the emphasis on the *Iliad* in traditional Greco-Roman education.

83. See Raffaella Cribiore, *Gymnastics of the Mind: Greek Education in Hellenistic and Roman Egypt* (Princeton: Princeton University Press, 2001), 227.

84. Catherine Chin, "Cento," in *The Classical Tradition*, ed. Anthony Grafton, Glenn W. Most, and Salvatore Settis (Cambridge: Harvard University Press, 2010), 189–90; Anke Rondholz, *The Versatile Needle: Hosidius Geta's Cento "Medea" and Its Tradition*, TCSup 15 (Berlin: de Gruyter, 2012), 24.

85. See Rondholz, *Versatile Needle*, 9–10, esp. 7–9, on Irenaeus, and 1–30 on the origin and development of centos. Centos also appear to have been popularly used as entertainment at dinner parties; see Sandnes, *Gospel*, 116–18; Rondholz, *Versatile Needle*, 7.

Irenaeus finds it unthinkable that scripture should be so violently rearranged in ways that do not accord with the church's rule of faith. On this view, John's text is inviolable, to some extent, and any interpretative work must be governed by the church's rule, which is legitimate because it is guided by the love for God. Homeric centos, by contrast, confuse and deceive, and are only appropriate for the learned. Likewise, the Valentinians mislead the simple with illegitimate patchwork compositions.

This gives us insight into how Irenaeus understands the appropriate use of education. Learning is not an end in itself. Rather, literary education such as that represented by the Homeric cento must serve the community by guiding it to the rule of faith and to an enduring love for God.[86]

Conclusion

During his youth in Smyrna, Irenaeus was a disciple of Polycarp and received a typical Greco-Roman education. This education is evident in his discussions of issues familiar from physics, cosmology, music theory, and literature. Thus, having been fed from both the fountains of apostolic tradition and of ancient educational traditions, Irenaeus seeks to circumscribe the value and use of education. His theology makes education foundational, as human history becomes a process whereby God teaches, matures, and perfects the free human creature. These historical-theological assumptions frame his appropriation of the Greco-Roman curriculum. For Irenaeus, God is the teacher, humanity the pupil, history the school, and virtue the end. There is no dualism, however, between sacred and mundane such as we find in the thought of his opponents. The bishop seeks to close any perceived gulf between God's education of his creatures and the more mundane administration of the *paidagōgos* or the school curriculum. At the same time, he reorients the ends or goals of traditional paideia in important ways. This suggests that elegant articulations of the catholic faith require not only training in Greco-Roman paideia but also an education in how it is to be appropriately used.

Three main examples demonstrate these points. First, Irenaeus's training in music theory shapes his conception of the unity and harmony of God and the complex and varied works of God. Against his opponents, he

---

86. For instance, Irenaeus argues against the use of such education for entertaining performances at dinner parties, because they dupe both simple and learned members of the audience (*Haer.* 1.9.4–5).

uses music theory to argue that there is one Creator who presides over a diverse creation. This observation, moreover, is meant to lead the catechumen to love for the one God. Second, Irenaeus appeals to diverse physical theories to argue for a unique divine omniscience. Pluralism in physical theories comes to demonstrate humanity's finitude, its inability to arrive at absolute truth when left to its own devices. Only God knows all solutions. Diverse physical theories, too, should lead the catechumen towards love for God. Finally, he uses his literary training in Homer and Homeric centos to exemplify the misleading hermeneutical practices of his opponents. In contrast to the views of these alleged heretics, he encourages the baptized to recall the interpretations of scripture learned in catechesis, a practice that is meant to secure the rule of faith and lead to a love for God that perseveres. On this view, paideia and the arts are not empty, but they must be appropriately investigated, enjoyed, and made use of in accord with the catholic faith. In general, Irenaeus exploits the education he received in Smyrna to deride the perceived deficiencies of his opponents, to explicate the articles of the rule of faith, and to promote an enduring love for God. This appropriation of Greco-Roman traditions of learning also thoroughly suffuses his theology of redemption. God moves all things toward the goal of humanity's education and maturation so that they might believe in the truth and love him without end.

Irenaeus's polemical treatise thus demonstrates an early and quite robust Christian appropriation of Greco-Roman education. For Irenaeus, God is both heavenly Father and Demiurge, redemptive history is the schoolroom of humanity, and the classical curriculum is a necessary source for articulation of the catholic faith. God the Father uses the mundane within history to educate and bring humanity to perfection. In this process, humanity receives knowledge of both the Creator and the creature. For Irenaeus, the leaders of the church are to master knowledge of the mundane world, particularly the classical curriculum, and exploit this to articulate the church's faith. The goal of this project is to create an enduring love for the one, true God, both Creator and Father.

Bibliography

Andia, Ysabel de. *Homo Vivens: Incorruptibilité et divinisation de l'homme selon Irénée de Lyons*. Paris: Études Augustiniennes, 1986.

Asmis, Elizabeth. "Basic Education in Epicureanism." Pages 209–40 in

Education in Greek and Roman Antiquity. Edited by Y. L. Too. Leiden: Brill, 2001.

Audet, T. A. "Orientations théologiques chez S. Irénée." *Traditio* 1 (1943): 15–54.

Bacq, Philippe. *De l'ancienne a la nouvelle alliance selon S. Irénée: Unité du livre IV de l'Adversus haereses*. SSH. Paris: Lethielleux, 1978.

Behr, John, ed. and trans. *St. Irenaeus of Lyons: On the Apostolic Preaching*. Crestwood, NY: St. Vladimir's Seminary Press, 1997.

Benoit, André. *Saint Irénée: Introduction a l'étude de sa théologie*. Paris: Presses Universitaires de France, 1960.

Berry, Edmund G. "The *De liberis educandis* of Pseudo-Plutarch." *HSCP* 63 (1958): 387–99.

Bingham, D. Jeffrey. *Irenaeus's Use of Matthew's Gospel in Adversus haereses*. Leuven: Peeters, 1998.

———. "Knowledge and Love in Irenaeus of Lyons." Pages 184–99 in *Papers Presented at the Thirteenth International Conference on Patristic Studies, Held in Oxford 1999*. StPatr 36. Edited by Maurice F. Wiles, Edward J. Yarnold, and Paul M. Parvis. Leuven: Peeters, 2001.

Bonner, Stanley. *Education in Ancient Rome: From the Elder Cato to the Younger Pliny*. London: Routledge, 1977.

Brown, Peter. *Power and Persuasion in Late Antiquity: Towards a Christian Empire*. Madison: University of Wisconsin Press, 1992.

Chin, Catherine. "Cento." Pages 189–90 in *The Classical Tradition*. Edited by Anthony Grafton, Glenn W. Most, and Salvatore Settis. Cambridge: Harvard University Press, 2010.

Christides, Johannes. "Education." *BNP* 4:821.

Clark, Matthew. Review of *Homeric Stitchings: The Homeric Centos of the Empress Eudocia*, by M. D. Usher. *CP* 96 (2001): 328.

Clarke, M. L. *Higher Education in the Ancient World*. Albuquerque: University of New Mexico Press, 1971.

Cribiore, Raffaella. *Gymnastics of the Mind: Greek Education in Hellenistic and Roman Egypt*. Princeton: Princeton University Press, 2001.

———. *Writing, Teachers, and Students in Graeco-Roman Egypt*. ASP 36. Atlanta: Scholars Press, 1996.

Curren, R. E. *Aristotle on the Necessity of Public Education*. Lanham, MD: Rowman & Littlefield, 2000.

Danielou, Jean. *Gospel Message and Hellenistic Culture*. Vol. 2 of *A History of Early Christian Doctrine before the Council of Nicaea*. Translated by J. A. Baker. Philadelphia: Westminster, 1973.

Diels, Hermann. *Doxographi graeci*. Berlin: Reimer, 1879.
Drever, J. *Greek Education: Its Practice and Principles*. Cambridge: Cambridge University Press, 1912.
Dueck, Daniela. *Strabo of Amasia: A Greek Man of Letters in Augustan Rome*. London: Routledge, 2000.
Enslin, M. S. "Irenaeus: Mostly Prolegomena." *HTR* 40 (1947): 137–65.
Epictetus. Translated by W. A. Oldfather. 2 vols. LCL. Cambridge: Harvard University Press, 1926–1928.
Frede, Michael. *Essays in Ancient Philosophy*. Minneapolis: University of Minnesota Press, 1987.
Glover, T. R. *The Conflict of Religions in the Early Roman Empire*. Boston: Beacon, 1909.
Grant, Robert M. "Carpocratians and Curriculum: Irenaeus' Reply." *HTR* 79 (1986): 127–36.
———. "Irenaeus and Hellenistic Culture." *HTR* 42 (1949): 41–51.
———, trans. *Irenaeus of Lyons*. ECF. London: Routledge, 1997.
Harnack, Adolf von. *History of Dogma*. Translated by Neil Buchanan. 7 vols. Boston: Little, Brown, 1899–1907.
Hitchcock, F. R. M. *Irenaeus of Lugdunum*. Cambridge: Cambridge University Press, 1914.
Johansen, T. K. *Plato's Natural Philosophy: A Study of the Timaeus-Critias*. Cambridge: Cambridge University Press, 2004.
Jones, Elizabeth M. "Allocating Musical Pleasure: Performance, Pleasure, and Value in Aristotle's *Politics*." Pages 159–82 in *Aesthetic Value in Classical Antiquity*. Edited by Ineke Sluiter and Ralph M. Rosen. MnemosyneSup 350. Leiden: Brill, 2012.
Jowett, Benjamin, trans. *Plato: Protagoras, Philebus, and Gorgias*. Amherst, NY: Prometheus, 1996.
———, trans. *Plato: The Republic*. New York: Vintage, 1991.
Kaster, Robert A. *Guardians of Language: The Grammarian and Society in Late Antiquity*. Berkeley: University of California Press, 1997.
Koch, Hugo. "Zur Lehre vom Urstand und von der Erlösung bei Irenäus." *TSK* 96–97 (1925): 183–214.
Kühnert, F. *Allgemeinbildung und Fachbildung in der Antike*. Berlin: Akademie, 1961.
Lloyd, G. E. R. *Methods and Problems in Greek Science: Selected Papers*. Cambridge: Cambridge University Press, 1991.
Loofs, Friedrich. *Theophilus von Antiochien Adversus Marcionem und die*

anderen theologischen Quellen bei Irenaeus. TU 46.2. Leipzig: Hinrichs, 1930.
McGill, Scott. *Virgil Recomposed: The Mythological and Secular Centos in Antiquity.* Oxford: Oxford University Press, 2005.
McPherran, Mark L. *The Religion of Socrates.* University Park: Pennsylvania State University Press, 1996.
Milton, J. R. "The Limitations of Ancient Atomism." Pages 178–95 in *Science and Mathematics in Ancient Greek Culture.* Edited by C. J. Tuplin and T. E. Rehill. Oxford: Oxford University Press, 2002.
Minns, Denis. *Irenaeus: An Introduction.* London: T&T Clark, 2010.
Mountford, James. "Music and the Romans." *BJRL* 47 (1964): 198–211.
Nautin, Pierre. *Lettres et écrivains chrétiens des IIe et IIIe siècles.* Paris: Cerf, 1953.
Osborn, Eric. *Irenaeus of Lyons.* Cambridge: Cambridge University Press, 2001.
Pelttari, Aaron. *The Space That Remains: Reading Latin Poetry in Late Antiquity.* Ithaca: Cornell University Press, 2014.
Pliny. *Letters.* Translated by Betty Radice. 2 vols. LCL. Cambridge: Harvard University Press, 1969.
Plutarch. *Lives.* Translated by Bernadotte Perrin. 11 vols. LCL. Cambridge: Harvard University Press, 1914–1926.
———. *Moralia.* Translated by Frank Cole Babbit, et al. 15 vols. LCL. London: Heinemann; New York: Putnam, 1927–1969.
Quasten, Johannes. *The Beginnings of Patristic Literature from the Apostles Creed to Irenaeus,* vol. 1 of *Patrology.* Utrecht: Spectrum, 1950.
Reynders, D. B. "La polemique de S. Irénée." *RTAM* 7 (1935): 5–27.
Robinson, James M., ed. *The Nag Hammadi Library in English.* Rev. ed. New York: HarperCollins, 1988.
Rondholz, Anke. *The Versatile Needle: Hosidius Geta's Cento "Medea" and Its Tradition.* TCSup 15. Berlin: de Gruyter, 2012.
Rousseau, Adelin, and Louis Doutreleau, eds. *Irénée de Lyon: Contre les hérésies.* Rev. ed. 5 vols. SC. Paris: Cerf, 1974–2002.
Sandnes, Karl O. *The Gospel "According to Homer and Virgil": Cento and Canon.* NovTSup 138. Leiden: Brill, 2011.
Schoedel, William. "Philosophy and Rhetoric in the *Adversus Haereses* of Irenaeus." *VC* 13 (1959): 22–32.
Sedley, David. *Creationism and Its Critics in Antiquity.* Berkeley: University of California Press, 2007.

Steenberg, M. C. *Of God and Man: Theology as Anthropology from Irenaeus to Athanasius*. London: T&T Clark, 2009.
Tremblay, R. "Le martyre selon saint Irénée de Lyon." *StudMor* 16 (1978): 167–89.
Unger, Dominic, and John J. Dillon. *St. Irenaeus of Lyons: Against the Heresies, Book 1*. ACW 55. New York: Paulist, 1992.
Unnik, W. C. van. "Theological Speculation and Its Limits." Pages 33–43 in *Early Christian Literature and the Classical Tradition: In Honorem Robert M. Grant*. Edited by William R. Schoedel and Robert L. Wilken. Paris: Beauchesne, 1979.
Usher, M. D. *Homeric Stitchings: The Homeric Centos of the Empress Eudocia*. Lanham, MD.: Rowman & Littlefield, 1998.
———. "Prolegomenon to the Homeric Cento." *AJP* 2 (1997): 305–21.
Walsh, Joseph. "Galen's Exhortation to the Study of the Arts, Especially Medicine." *ML* 37 (1930): 507–29.
Wendt, Hans Hinrich. *Die christliche Lehre von der menschlichen Vollkommenheit*. Göttingen: Vandenhoeck & Ruprecht, 1882.
Wilken, Robert L. *The Christians as the Romans Saw Them*. 2nd ed. New Haven: Yale University Press, 2003.
———. "The Homeric Cento in Irenaeus, 'Adversus Haereses' I, 9, 4." *VC* 21 (1967): 23–33.
Wille, G. *Musica Romana: Die Bedeutung der Musik im Leben der Römer*. Amsterdam: Schippers, 1967.
Wisse, Frederik. "The Nag Hammadi Library and the Heresiologists." *VC* 25 (1971): 205–23.
Young, Norman H. "*Paidagogos*: The Social Setting of a Pauline Metaphor." *NovT* 29 (1987): 150–76.
Ziegler, H. *Irenäus der Bischof von Lyon*. Berlin: Reimer, 1871.

Why Did Christians Compete with Pagans for Greek Paideia?

Raffaella Cribiore

In the fourth century CE, Christians and pagans attended the same schools of higher learning.[1] After studying in Caesarea and in Alexandria, Gregory of Nazianzus spent eight years in Athens not only perfecting his rhetoric but also reading poets such as Homer, Pindar, the tragedians, and Callimachus. His turgid Greek teems with allusions that testify to his intimacy with traditional myths about the pagan gods. While he criticized these myths as fictions or ridiculed them, nonetheless he read traditional Greek authors and developed a passion for them. Gregory writes that he attended the lessons of all the teachers who were then practicing in Athens, including the pagan Himerius and the Christian Prohaeresius (Gregory of Nazianzus, *Or. Bas.* 43.22). His love for the λόγοι (traditional culture and philosophy) was strong then and remained strong throughout his career.

In trying to understand why Christians pursued traditional Greek paideia, it is helpful to go to the roots of the question: What were the goals of education in this period? How did they differ from contemporary goals? Should education transmit knowledge and standards of language and style, skills that would function as markers of distinction in society? Or should it communicate, in addition, an attitude or willingness to see life in a certain light and to provide a guide for navigating the world?[2] These questions about the scope and function of education continue to be asked

---

1. In what follows, I will use the term *paganism* throughout. It is a historical construct but is still the most convenient term; see Christopher P. Jones, *Between Pagan and Christian* (Cambridge: Harvard University Press, 2014).

2. Ilinca Tanaseanu-Doebler, "Religious Education in Late Antique Paganism," in *Religious Education in Pre-Modern Europe*, ed. Ilinca Tanaseanu-Doebler and Marvin Doebler, SHR 140 (Leiden: Brill, 2012), 97–101.

today, but they are also ancient. They go back to Plato, Socrates, the sophists, and the conflict between rhetoric and philosophy that began as early as the fifth century BCE and continued throughout antiquity (see Plato, *Republic* and *Laws*).[3]

By the late antique period, there were competing systems of education.[4] After receiving elementary instruction and studying poetry and grammar with a grammarian, a student was exposed to rhetoric; eloquence was the goal of the ἐγκύκλιος παιδεία (circular, complete education) that allowed the wealthy to participate in the spheres of the powerful elites.[5] Some students went on to the study of philosophy.[6] The school of a philosopher was rather informal and comprised of relatively few serious students as well as those who wished to round out their education with a few years of philosophy. Then there were other disciplines such as jurisprudence, and technical skills like shorthand, Roman law, and, in the east, the acquisition of the Latin language.[7] In higher education—that is, after primary instruction—literature was paramount and was seen as a mandatory prerequisite. Synesius of Cyrene, in his discourse *Dio* (4–11), passionately declared that the study of literature had to inform every level of paideia, including rhetoric and philosophy.

It is essential to underline that, for pagans, religion mainly consisted of religious practice (participation in ritual, *orthopraxis*), though scholars now admit that ancient pagans also held religious beliefs, in some sense.[8] Religious practice was strongly connected to myth, and knowledge about

---

3. In works such as *Protagoras* and *Gorgias*, Plato confronted the new education offered by the sophists who imparted a technical, political instruction that aimed at training leading men so that they could participate in politics. They requested large fees that students were willing to pay in order to obtain a political education.

4. In higher education, some stopped at grammar while others proceeded to more demanding disciplines. Those who studied rhetoric and philosophy in particular claimed that their discipline was superior.

5. Raffaella Cribiore, *Gymnastics of the Mind: Greek Education in Hellenistic and Roman Egypt* (Princeton: Princeton University Press, 2001).

6. See Michael Trapp, *Philosophy in the Roman Empire: Ethics, Politics, and Society* (Aldershot: Ashgate, 2007), 18–23.

7. Raffaella Cribiore, *The School of Libanius in Late Antique Antioch* (Princeton: Princeton University Press, 2007), 206–13.

8. For cautions about "belief," see, e.g., Rodney Needham, *Belief, Language, and Experience* (Oxford: Oxford University Press, 1972); within paganism, see Charles King, "The Organization of Roman Religious Beliefs," *ClAnt* 22 (2003): 275–312.

myths was transmitted through different media. Literature, written or performed, and the fine arts communicated this knowledge. For example, the famous mosaics in Antioch, from the second century CE onward, and those from the late antique Near East, both attest to the central role of myths in visual culture, as Glen Bowersock has shown.[9] In some contrast, from the beginning, Christians emphasized the need for early religious education. Baptism was preceded by religious instruction, the catechumenate, which involved ideally three years of instruction, moral formation, and reading of the Bible.

It seems, however, that Christians did not create Christian schools of general learning and did not import their particular religious views into these schools. Pagan and Christian children attended the same schools. The general picture before Julian is that pagans did not begrudge Christians paideia, and Christians taught Greek literature and philosophy at every level and were accepted by their pagan colleagues, their students, and the state, which subsidized them. The emperor Julian's edict of June 362 forbade Christians from teaching the pagan classics and provoked conflict and a competition over the "ownership" of paideia.[10]

Before Julian's edict, Christian students do not seem to have been set apart in the ancient classroom, as demonstrated by Greek and Coptic school exercises from Greco-Roman Egypt. Nathan Carlig's recent work identifies and systematically treats Greek exercises that show Christian signs, basically crosses and chrisms (the Christ monogram similar to a cross).[11] The vast majority of the preserved exercises of Christian provenance are very elementary and testify to the acquisition of a limited

---

9. Glen Bowersock, *Mosaics as History: The Near East from Late Antiquity to Islam* (Cambridge: Harvard University Press, 2006).

10. On the interpretation of the edict as also addressing moderate pagans who were against Julian's extremism, see Raffaella Cribiore, *Libanius the Sophist: Rhetoric, Reality, and Religion in the Fourth Century* (Ithaca, NY: Cornell University Press, 2013), 229–37.

11. The list of the papyri can be found at Université de Liège, Centre de Documentation de Papyrologie Littéraire, "Papyrus scolaires grecs et latins chrétiens," http://tinyurl.com/SBL3548b. See Nathan Carlig, "Recherches sur la forme, la mise en page et le contenu des papyrus scolaires grecs et latins chrétiens d'Égypte," *SEP* 10 (2013): 55–98. Though Carlig's work is very valuable because it is complete, the vast majority of these exercises were already included in my book *Writing, Teachers, and Students from Graeco-Roman Egypt*, ASP 36 (Atlanta: Scholars Press, 1996). This book collected all school exercises of Egyptian provenance and noted in some cases which

literacy. These exercises involve writing individual letters, the alphabet, and syllabaries, which requires only limited technical knowledge. More advanced students in Christian milieus approached whole words, lists of words, and passages of a few lines, but these exercises as they appear in the papyri are largely the same as those in non-Christian schools. They referred to traditional pagan literature even if they bore Christian symbols. Only in a few cases do the exercises show students making up a list with names from the Bible or copying something from the Psalms or the Lord's Prayer. At the level of copying anecdotes and sayings, which was still rather elementary, the pagan tradition prevailed, and there are few examples of Christian adaptations.

A search for longer and more literary Christian exercises produces meager results. Identifiable Christian exercises at this level are extremely rare. A wooden tablet found in Egypt contains a passage from the first book of the *Iliad*, and another has a text from Euripides's *Phoenissae* and part of Callimachus's *Hecale*. Both tablets bear Christian marks, but they stand out in their isolation.[12] The provenance of the elementary Christian exercises is often unknown, a problem that is common to school exercises in general because archaeological excavations in the past were conducted with no attention to context. Archaeologists in Egypt aimed at finding papyri. They did not excavate buildings with attention and did not note down the find places of most texts, though there are some exceptions. Sometimes exercises seem to come from monastic environments in Upper Egypt, especially from the Monastery of Epiphanius and Deir el Bahri in Thebes. Thus it appears that at initial stages of paideia Christian students identified their schoolwork with Christian symbols, as attested by primary education exercises involving alphabets, lists of words, or short passages. When these students moved on to study grammar and rhetoric, however, they appear to have stopped using such signs. The fact that only two upper-level exercises bearing Christian symbols survive seems an indication that advanced students were not required or did not particularly care to distinguish their work in a special way. Their teachers might be pagan (like Libanius in Antioch) or Christian (like Prohaeresius in Athens), but by the time these young men progressed to advanced instruction they seem

---

ones bore Christian signs. The few that were published afterwards do not significantly change the picture of Christian education that appears in the papyri treated earlier.

12. Cribiore, *Writing, Teachers, and Students*, nos. 303 and 310, dating from after the fourth century CE.

to have moved into neutral terrain where religious allegiances mattered little. It is the neutrality of this terrain that Gregory of Nazianzus invokes.

The situation with Coptic school exercises is different in some respects.[13] The elementary exercises correlate almost exactly with the Greek ones in terms of types. Letters of the alphabet, syllabaries, lists of names, and short texts copied as writing exercises correspond to the Greek ones and are distinguished by Christian signs. In terms of content, however, all of the Coptic exercises are religious in nature and consist of passages from the Old and New Testament, prayers, and religious formulas. Another difference is that in Coptic schools, students practiced writing by copying the beginning of personal letters, a practical activity that was unheard of in Greek schools. What is really noteworthy, however, is that the Coptic exercises seem to stop after the initial stages. We know from other contexts that Christian students continued to read Greek literature at higher levels of learning, even if they did not leave traces of their Christian identity. Students of Coptic at higher stages of education, however, are impossible to find. Did Coptic students learn only the rudiments in their schools? This question is most intriguing, and there are no certain answers.[14] Authors like Shenoute and Besa wrote difficult, artificial, and accomplished prose that followed all the rules of rhetoric even though they seem to lack Coptic models for such expertise. Thus we have to suppose that such writers looked to Greek models, probably patristic literature and Greek rhetorical texts. After they achieved an expertise in Greek rhetoric, they must have adapted those rules to Coptic rhetorical prose.

Eric Rebillard's important book about Christians living in late Roman North Africa also sheds light on these issues.[15] Drawing on the works of Tertullian, Cyprian of Carthage, and Augustine, he argues that the Christian/pagan dichotomy that so dominates earlier scholarship simply does not fit with the evidence. Christians in late antiquity did not have single,

---

13. Monika R. M. Hasitzka, *Neue Texte und Dokumentation zum koptisch-Unterricht* (Vienna: Hollinek, 1990).

14. Raffaella Cribiore, "Greek and Coptic Education in Late Antique Egypt," in *Schrifttum, Sprache und Gedankenwelt*, vol. 2 of *Ägypten und Nubien in spätantiker und christlicher Zeit: Akten des 6. Internationalen Koptologenkongresses*, ed. Stephen Emmel et al. (Wiesbaden: Reichert, 1999), 279–86.

15. Eric Rebillard, *Christians and Their Many Identities in Late Antiquity, North Africa 200–450 CE* (Ithaca, NY: Cornell University Press, 2012). See Maijastina Kahlos, *Debate and Dialogue: Christian and Pagan Cultures c. 360–430* (Aldershot: Ashgate, 2007).

monolithic identities but rather situational identities that could change according to the occasion. Thus Christians had fluid and complex identities that allowed them to navigate different alliances and form new allegiances.

Rebillard's arguments about Christian identities are particularly helpful because I independently reached the same conclusions with regard to pagans, or at least one prominent pagan, the sophist Libanius. Libanius had a rhetorical school in fourth-century Antioch and was highly representative of other men of culture in the city.[16] In studying his entire corpus, I hoped to reach conclusions that were less impressionistic than those of other scholars. Constructing theories about an author cannot be based on single works and cannot be confined to works that have been translated.[17] I had considered his activity as teacher of rhetoric in Antioch in a previous study and knew that he had both pagans and Christians in his school.[18] Some of his Christian students followed different paths than those pursued by pagans trained in classical paideia, but they continued to use the rhetorical skills that he taught them and became illustrious in their own right.

If tradition is right, John Chrysostom was the favorite pupil of Libanius, who had expected that he would embark on an academic career. Sozomen (*Hist. eccl.* 8.2.2) reported a charming anecdote, which surely was embellished by Christian sources, which recounted that the sophist had acknowledged John's excellence on his deathbed and had wished for him to become a sophist and a teacher. There are no letters of Libanius that mention John, but it is possible that they were included in the group of letters from the years 365–388 CE that was not preserved. As a student of Libanius, Chrysostom writes with a prose similar to that of his teacher, though easier to understand. He later turned against his master, whom he disdainfully called "the sophist of the city."[19] Others reacted differently.

---

16. Cribiore, *Libanius the Sophist*. My observations come from reading his entire oeuvre (over 1500 letters and 64 orations). My translations of and commentary on twelve of them will appear in *Between City and School: Selected Orations of Libanius*, TTH 65 (Liverpool: Liverpool University Press, forthcoming). In *The School of Libanius in Late Antique Antioch*, I did not take into account the works Libanius wrote for students, *Progymnasmata*, *Meletai*, and *Hypotheseis* to Demosthenes, because these are traditional works that follow set types and did not serve my purpose.

17. Much of what Libanius wrote in fact is still not translated. Because of his intricate Greek, generally scholars do not venture outside of what is available in translation.

18. Cribiore, *School of Libanius*.

19. See Chrysostom, *Bab.* 98–113 for bitter remarks against Libanius. On relations

Amphilochius 4, who became the bishop of Iconium, also attended Libanius's classes (see Libanius, *Ep.* 634; Cribiore, *School of Libanius*, no. 16).[20] After leaving the school, he continued to advance in Greek paideia. He held that the rich traditions of Greek literature could not be ignored and that Christian students needed guidance in approaching them. He also wrote a didactic epistle addressed to one Seleucus, whom he calls "my son," exactly as Libanius addressed his students. Amphilochius's work *Iambi ad Seleucum* recalls the work of another student of the sophist, Basil of Caesarea, who supposedly participated in the classes of Libanius in Constantinople or at Nicomedia. In his last years, Basil left a testimony of his appreciation of classical paideia. His *Ad adulescentes* (*On the Value of Greek Literature*) is a long epistle to his nephews but was probably intended to address other Christian youths attempting to reconcile their religion with their education.[21]

Another Christian student of Libanius, Optimus 1, is less well known. In one of his letters (*Ep.* 1544), the sophist complimented him for the excellence of the Greek displayed in his discourses in school.[22] After he returned home, Optimus continued to write and deliver speeches, but at a certain point was elected bishop of Agdamia in Phrygia and later of Antioch in Pisidia.[23] Optimus was not happy with these appointments but had to obey his superiors. Libanius was pleased that at least his former pupil had the occasion to use rhetoric and advised him, "Make the crowds praise you and let the rhetor be conspicuous there too" (*Ep.* 1544.3). Plato, especially in the *Republic*, had criticized and excised texts from the educational curriculum of his day, and Plutarch in *De audiendis poetis* had also reacted against literary passages he found improper. Both these authors inform the works of Amphilochius and Basil. Amphilochius exhorts the student to read poetry, history, the orators, and the philosophers. He insists

---

with and imitation of the teacher, see Christine Shepardson, *Controlling Contested Places: Late Antique Antioch and the Spatial Politics of Religious Controversy* (Berkeley: University of California Press, 2014), 131–32, 135–36, and passim.

20. The numbers that follow the names of some of the figures who appear in this chapter refer to A. H. M. Jones, John Robert Martindale, and J. Morris, *The Prosopography of the Later Roman Empire, Volume 1: A.D. 260–395* (Cambridge: Cambridge University Press, 1971).

21. N. G. Wilson, ed., *Saint Basil on Greek Literature* (London: Duckworth, 1975).

22. Cribiore, *School of Libanius*, no. 155.

23. See Socrates Scholasticus, *Hist. eccl.* 7.36, 20, who includes Optimus in a list of bishops transferred from one see to another.

that the young man will use his discernment (φύσις) to distinguish what is good and bad. Both Basil and Amphilochius suggest that some parts of literature do not conform to Christian morality and should be avoided, but they do not go as far as forbidding or bowdlerizing texts.

Scholars have acknowledged the relationship between Libanius and these important Christian figures, as well as the letters he exchanged with others such as Gregory of Nyssa. Yet, to date, Libanius has been considered a preeminent pagan, with little subtlety given to this designation. Even worse, he has been regarded as a hypocrite and a flatterer.[24] Isabella Sandwell's recent work attempts to provide an alternative, but it seems too simplistic.[25] To explain people's religious vacillations and conversions from Christian to pagan and vice versa, Sandwell proposes that what she terms "the religious game" pervaded the fourth century. She argues that people changed religious affiliations or started relationships with individuals of different allegiances only to safeguard their interests and to gain material advantages. Yet this scenario is not realistic. This could explain a few individual cases, since hypocrites have always existed, but it is absurd to condemn a whole century for religious opportunism. We cannot use flattery and opportunism alone to explain Libanius's relationship with the aforementioned important Christians (his students) or with others who figure in his correspondence. In this light, it is crucial to understand the complex religious, political, and educational landscape of the fourth century. This can provide a better explanation for why some individuals pursued relationships with friends and relatives of a different religious allegiance, as well as the potential uncertainties and doubts surrounding these relationships. Such an approach also helps to define the relationship between pagans and Christians and will provide a key for understanding the attraction that Christians in the fourth century felt for Greek paideia.

A survey of the works of Libanius shows that he had more than one identity. His works were not all equally public (as other scholars' works usually were), and his orations and his letters do not reveal their author in the same way.[26] Genre is very important for understanding how an

---

24. See Heinz-Günther Nesselrath, *Libanios: Zeuge einer schwindenden Welt*, StAC 4 (Stuttgart: Hiersemann, 2012).

25. Isabella Sandwell, *Religious Identity in Late Antiquity* (Cambridge: Cambridge University Press, 2007).

26. This has always been the interpretation of Libanius's works, including that of

author wanted to present himself to his audience. Genre is not at the forefront of scholarly criticism, particularly in the case of prose, and yet it can illuminate some incongruities in a writer's work. Ancient readers had an intimate knowledge of literary conventions. By trying to understand what their expectations were, we can come closer to understanding an author's intentions.[27] The Libanius of the orations appears coherent in his religious attitude. In these works, he tries to project himself as a spokesman for paganism. All the orations were supposed to be delivered publicly, even though some were not, and they tell us how he identified himself and was identified by others, including the emperor and his courtiers, the people of Antioch, and especially the πεπαιδευμένοι (men of culture) and the parents of his students. In this particular period, when Christians were apparently on the attack and pagans were licking their wounds, Libanius saw one of his duties as rebuilding a collective pagan memory, focusing, for example, on commemorative sites such as temples.[28] In the orations, the sophist consistently mentions all the gods of the Olympian pantheon, whether the speeches are early or late.

The situation is different in Libanius's letters, which consist of a mixture of public and private documents. Many are addressed to relatives, intimate friends, students, and the parents of students. Some letters show only formulaic references to the gods, others contain mythological and scholastic references, and some provide longer and more significant references such as a visit to a temple or a direct communication with Julian.[29] It is not surprising that the letters written during the period of Julian's rule as emperor contain most of the longer pagan references, and yet it is surprising that only a few show Libanius as the spokesman of the new regime.[30] Several deal with the affairs of Christian friends and relatives who had held official posts under Constantius and now had fallen into disgrace.[31]

---

scholars who knew them well, such as A. F. Norman, who is responsible for the translations of his works in the Loeb Classical Library.

27. See H. R. Jauss, "Literary History as a Challenge to Literary Theory," *NLH* 2 (1971): 7–37.

28. Cribiore, *Libanius the Sophist*, 222–28.

29. See ibid., 151–63, on references to religion in Libanius's letters in different periods.

30. References to translations from *Libanius: Autobiography and Selected Letters*, trans. A. F. Norman, 2 vols., LCL (Cambridge: Harvard University Press, 1992) are given as "N." See, e.g., *Ep.* 770 = N92, and *Ep.* 694 = N80.

31. See, e.g., Libanius, *Ep.* 1376 = N107 and *Ep.* 1351 = N10.

The sophist pleads their case vehemently. The letters following Julian's death, moreover, testify to the conflicts that were dividing pagans in that period. Some of them blamed Libanius for his inactivity and regarded him as a lukewarm pagan. One letter, for instance, shows that he responded to the accusation of a friend that he kept silent and did not want to fight on behalf of Julian's memory.[32] Libanius praised the friend for his desire for action but refused to intervene in the polemic, saying that what he had done in the past showed his loyalty.

Libanius's correspondence as a whole also shows a marked unevenness in the sophist's explicit references to Greek gods. Libanius mentions most of the Olympian gods until 365 CE, but when the correspondence resumes in 388 the individual gods have disappeared, except for Zeus and Hermes. Zeus was the god par excellence for him, while the references to Hermes do not show much devotion to him but only mention him as the god of rhetoric, usually in letters to students. The letters also contain several references to a single god, presumably Zeus, who has attributes similar to those of the Christian God.[33] Was Libanius worshipping a single god in his later years? It is difficult to know.

The letters also bring out the sophist's relationships with Christian friends, the most notable of whom was Olympius 3. The rapport between the two friends, the frequency of their encounters, and the intimacy of the letters are so striking that previous scholars concluded that Olympius must have been pagan. My reading of *Or.* 63, never before translated, shows that Olympius was actually a practicing Christian.[34] Not only did he maintain women in his household according to the custom of spiritual marriage, but he was also the brother of Evagrius, who became bishop of Antioch during the schism. Upon his death, Olympius left his entire patrimony to Libanius, a bequest that caused a major uproar in Antioch. These facts speak volumes about the relations between Christians and pagans. In particular, they show that Libanius was a gray pagan, that is, lukewarm, who identified himself to others in a twofold way. He usually performed in the orations as a committed pagan, but in the letters he revealed moderate

---

32. Libanius, *Ep.* 1264 = N133.
33. See Cribiore, *Libanius the Sophist*, 213–22.
34. See ibid., 186–97. So Evagrius, who had disappeared from all writings, apparently reappears only in this oration. On spiritual marriage, see, e.g., Blake Leyerle, *Theatrical Shows and Ascetic Lives: John Chrysostom's Attack on Spiritual Marriage* (Berkeley: University of California Press, 2001).

behavior and close relationships with certain Christians. One can surmise, then, that Libanius did not pay much attention to the religious allegiance of his students, as the evidence also shows.

Appreciating the fluidity of pagan and Christian identities in the fourth century suggests a new appreciation of the causes and consequences of Julian's edict. I have argued in the beginning of this essay that the competition for Greek paideia materialized after Julian's edict. On June 17, 362, the emperor Julian issued an edict that was then followed by a rescript. The edict insisted that the characters of teachers were noteworthy and gave the emperor himself a role in choosing them, which was not previously the case (Cod. Theod. 13.3.5). The rescript was more extreme insofar as it pointed to the inconsistencies of some teachers' behavior (Julian, *Ep.* 61c). In it Julian stated that those who taught traditional Greek texts such as Homer, Hesiod, and others, had to believe in the pagan gods; those who did not were to teach only in Christian churches. Thus Christian teachers of higher education had to resign from their public chairs, though they could teach privately. Some Christians, most notably Gregory of Nazianzus (*Jul.* 4 and 5), reacted very strongly to the edict and the rescript.

Writers from late antiquity to the Renaissance consistently treat Julian's school policy as targeting Christians exclusively. In the twelfth and thirteenth centuries the infamous school edict was still alive in the mind of educators. To give only one example, the rhetor Nicephorus Chrysoberges composed an ἠθοποιία, a speech-in-character practiced in rhetorical schools, which used the figure of a Christian teacher under Julian. He writes: "What might have said a Christian philologist when Julian the Apostate forbade the Christians to read pagan books?"[35] Of course, Julian never forbade Christians from reading traditional Greek books, and Christian children were never barred from pagan schools, as later Christian writers often maintained. The understanding of the spirit of the edict had changed perceptibly immediately after and as an effect of Gregory's raucous accusations, which left many traces on the way others remembered it afterwards.

Scholars have commented on the fact that Libanius did not mention Julian's edict at all, not even in the Epitaph of Julian (*Or.* 18), where he reviewed the life of the emperor. There is no doubt that Christians were

---

35. See J. R. Asmos, "Die Ethopöie des Nikephoros Chrysoberges über Julians Rhetorenedikt," *ByzZ* 15 (1906): 125–36.

the main target of the edict, but were they the only target? Julian must have been aware that there were plenty of moderate "gray" pagans, who did not share Julian's religious preoccupations. The historian Ammianus Marcellinus was one of them. As a dutiful historian, he reports on the school law but mentions it very briefly and unsympathetically, insisting that it needed "to be buried in eternal silence" (Ammianus Marcellinus, *Res gest.* 25.4.20 and 22.10.7). We know that the philosopher Maximus of Ephesus, the emperor's constant companion, poisoned the relationship between Julian and Libanius. Maximus was a fanatical extremist and must have viewed the sophist's friendship with many Christians with suspicion. It may be that Julian's edict also sent a troublesome message to those "gray" pagans, who were told to conform to the emperor's strict guidelines and to verify that they too had "a healthy condition of the mind."[36]

Before recapitulating and coming to some conclusions, I would like to consider students' exposure to Greek myths in school and the presence of traditional stories in people's lives. Myths were available to Christians and pagans through literature, mimes, and the visual arts. But did all pagans understand and use these myths and the stories about the gods with the same intensity as Julian? Julian's extremism was somewhat isolated, and in any case he needed allegorical interpretations to accept them (Julian, *Her.* 221c–223a; *Or.* 5.161c–167b). The pagan Libanius did not accept myths passively as they were traditionally, but at times made polemical observations. He used the myth of the labors of Heracles to incite his students to work harder, but at the same time he refuted that myth and considered it with a smile, even hinting at a possible death of the immortal hero (Libanius, *Ep.* 620).[37] Libanius also declared that the myth of Alcestis's return from the underworld was absurd and, though he strolled in the suburb of Daphne and visited the temple of Apollo, he regarded the myth of Apollo and Daphne as a fairy tale.[38] Even more interesting is the way he encouraged his students to refute myths in his classes. His students learned to ask somewhat irreverent questions such as: how could it be possible that Apollo, a god, could not run faster than

---

36. In the rescript Julian declared that true education consisted "of a healthy condition of the mind."

37. Trans. available in Scott Bradbury, *Selected Letters of Libanius from the Age of Constantius and Julian* (Liverpool: Liverpool University Press, 2004), no. 13.

38. Libanius, *Ep.* 427 = N9 and *Ep.* 1466 = Bradbury, *Selected Letters*, no. 22; see also *Or.* 31.43.

Daphne and catch her? (see Aphtonius, *Prog.* 5). Rhetorical refutations of various elements of myth could threaten traditional beliefs.

In the fourth century, many pagans and Christians discussed the validity of myths and stories about pagan gods. Susanna Elm has shown that Gregory of Nazianzus objected to these myths, insisting that if they were only fiction, they were nonsensical and vain.[39] Even Julian's validation of Greek myths required allegorical interpretations. Did critical discussions about the interpretation of myths continue in the fifth and sixth centuries? Gaza, for example, was profoundly Christian, and yet pagan myth was omnipresent there. It appears that even cultivated people accepted it without the filter of allegory, so myths and stories about the Greek gods became increasingly part of an imaginative world that was embedded in everyday life. In his declamations and in a speech in defense of the mime, Choricius asked his audience to accept myth as part of a world of fiction, neither true nor false (*Decl.* 32).[40] Though John Chrysostom had fought against the immorality of certain spectacles, Choricius underlined the distance between literature, spectacle, and the inner world of a πεπαιδευμένος. These examples show that non-Christian myths were increasingly integrated into Christian tradition. The common paideia of Christians and pagans had effected the change, and mythology could be fully accepted as part of an intermediate domain.

The evidence presented here suggests that generally pagans' and Christians' expectations regarding Greek paideia were different. Pagans looked at ancient texts and myths as important traditions and as means to hone their skills in writing and speaking, but they also expected the ancient myths to help guide them in life. Christians rejected this view and did not presume that the pagan writers had to provide moral guidance. Instead of giving up on those texts, however, they appropriated them. They cherished pagan literature and myths because they were exposed to them in school, but, as Zacharias, bishop of Mytilene, wrote in the sixth century, they could not accept them wholesale; they were treacherous, like the Sirens in Homer who attracted sailors with their sweet voice and then caused their deaths.[41]

---

39. Susanna Elm, *Sons of Hellenism, Fathers of the Church: Emperor Julian, Gregory of Nazianzus, and the Vision of Rome* (Berkeley: University of California Press, 2012), 380–87.

40. In Richard Foerster and Eberhard Richtsteig, eds. *Choricii Gazaei Opera*, BSGRT (Stuttgart: Teubner, 1929).

41. Zacharias Scholasticus, *Ammonio*, ed. Maria Minniti Colonna (Naples: Buona

Traditional paideia was a shared possession of both Christians and pagans. The evidence of surviving school exercises shows that, beyond the elementary stage, Christian students did not identify their exercises in a way that reflected their religious allegiance. This suggests that they had moved to neutral ground and followed a common school curriculum. The classes of the Christian Prohaeresius or of the pagan Libanius included students of different religious allegiances who read the same texts. We have seen, moreover, that often the identities of Christians and pagans in the fourth century were not sharply polarized. In spite of some later polemics, the evidence shows that both groups had a good deal in common. Beyond hard polytheism and extreme Christianity there was a gray territory in which both claimed the texts of the ancient writers as their own.

Bibliography

Asmos, J. R. "Die Ethopöie des Nikephoros Chrysoberges über Julians Rhetorenedikt." *ByzZ* 15 (1906): 125–36.

Bowersock, Glen. *Mosaics as History: The Near East from Late Antiquity to Islam*. Cambridge: Harvard University Press, 2006.

Bradbury, Scott. *Selected Letters of Libanius from the Age of Constantius and Julian*. Liverpool: Liverpool University Press, 2004.

Carlig, Nathan. "Recherches sur la forme, la mise en page et le contenu des papyrus scolaires grecs et latins chrétiens d'Égypte." *SEP* 10 (2013): 55–98.

Cribiore, Raffaella. *Between City and School: Selected Orations of Libanius*. TTH 65. Liverpool: Liverpool University Press, 2015.

———. "Greek and Coptic Education in Late Antique Egypt." Pages 279–86 in *Schrifttum, Sprache und Gedankenwelt*. Vol. 2 of *Ägypten und Nubien in spätantiker und christlicher Zeit: Akten des 6. Internationalen Koptologenkongresses*. Edited by Stephen Emmel, Martin Krause, Siegfried G. Richter, and Sofia Schaten. Wiesbaden: Reichert, 1999.

———. *Gymnastics of the Mind: Greek Education in Hellenistic and Roman Egypt*. Princeton: Princeton University Press, 2001.

———. *Libanius the Sophist: Rhetoric, Reality, and Religion in the Fourth Century*. Ithaca, NY: Cornell University Press, 2013.

Stampa, 1973); on Ammonius, see Jones, Martindale, and Morris, *Prosopography*, 1.158–60.

———. *The School of Libanius in Late Antique Antioch*. Princeton: Princeton University Press, 2007.
———. *Writing, Teachers, and Students from Graeco-Roman Egypt*. ASP 36. Atlanta: Scholars Press, 1996.
Elm, Susanna. *Sons of Hellenism, Fathers of the Church: Emperor Julian, Gregory of Nazianzus, and the Vision of Rome*. Berkeley: University of California Press, 2012.
Foerster, Richard, and Eberhard Richtsteig, eds. *Choricii Gazaei Opera*. BSGRT. Stuttgart: Teubner, 1929.
Hasitzka, Monika R. M. *Neue Texte und Dokumentation zum koptisch-Unterricht*. Vienna: Hollinek, 1990.
Jauss, H. R. "Literary History as a Challenge to Literary Theory." *NLH* 2 (1971): 7–37.
Jones, A. H. M., John Robert Martindale, and J. Morris. *The Prosopography of the Later Roman Empire, Vol. 1: A.D. 260–395*. Cambridge: Cambridge University Press, 1971.
Jones, Christopher P. *Between Pagan and Christian*. Cambridge: Harvard University Press, 2014.
Kahlos, Maijastina. *Debate and Dialogue: Christian and Pagan Cultures c. 360–430*. Aldershot: Ashgate, 2007.
King, Charles. "The Organization of Roman Religious Beliefs." *ClAnt* 22 (2003): 275–312.
Leyerle, Blake. *Theatrical Shows and Ascetic Lives: John Chrysostom's Attack on Spiritual Marriage*. Berkeley: University of California Press, 2001.
Libanius. Translated by A. F. Norman. 4 vols. LCL. Cambridge: Harvard University Press, 1992–2014.
Needham, Rodney. *Belief, Language, and Experience*. Oxford: Oxford University Press, 1972.
Nesselrath, Heinz-Günther. *Libanios: Zeuge einer schwindenden Welt*. StAC 4. Stuttgart: Hiersemann, 2012.
Rebillard, Eric. *Christians and Their Many Identities in Late Antiquity, North Africa 200–450 CE*. Ithaca, NY: Cornell University Press, 2012.
Sandwell, Isabella. *Religious Identity in Late Antiquity*. Cambridge: Cambridge University Press, 2007.
Shepardson, Christine. *Controlling Contested Places: Late Antique Antioch and the Spatial Politics of Religious Controversy*. Berkeley: University of California Press, 2014.
Tanaseanu-Doebler, Ilinca. "Religious Education in Late Antique Paganism." Pages 97–146 in *Religious Education in Pre-Modern Europe*.

Edited by Ilinca Tanaseanu-Doebler and Marvin Doebler. SHR 140. Leiden: Brill, 2012.

Trapp, Michael. *Philosophy in the Roman Empire: Ethics, Politics, and Society*. Aldershot: Ashgate, 2007.

Wilson, N. G., ed. *Saint Basil on Greek Literature*. London: Duckworth, 1975.

Zacharias Scholasticus. *Ammonio*. Edited by Maria Minniti Colonna. Naples: Buona Stampa, 1973.

Contributors

Ellen Bradshaw Aitken (deceased), Dean of the Faculty of Religious Studies, McGill University

C. Andrew Ballard, Adjunct Instructor of Religion, Samford University

D. Jeffrey Bingham, Dean of the School of Theology, Professor of Theology, Southwestern Baptist Theological Seminary

John J. Collins, Holmes Professor of Old Testament Criticism and Interpretation, Yale Divinity School

Raffaella Cribiore, Professor of Classics, New York University

Robert Doran, Samuel Williston Professor of Greek and Hebrew, Department of Religion, Amherst College

Matthew Goff, Professor of Religion, Florida State University

Andrew R. Guffey, Chaplain, Canterbury House, Northwestern University

Karina Martin Hogan, Associate Professor of Biblical Studies and Ancient Judaism, Department of Theology, Fordham University

James L. Kugel, Professor Emeritus of Bible, Bar Ilan University

Patrick Pouchelle, Lecturer in Biblical Exegesis, Member of the Faculty of Theology, Centre Sèvres, Paris

Elisa Uusimäki, Academy of Finland Postdoctoral Fellow, University of Helsinki

Emma Wasserman, Associate Professor of New Testament, Department of Religion, Rutgers University

Jason M. Zurawski, Postdoctoral Fellow, Department of Old Testament/Early Judaism, University of Groningen

Ancient Sources Index

Hebrew Bible/Old Testament		28:3	16 n. 3
		30:11–12	143
Genesis		30:14	143
2–3	172, 186	30:34–35	174
2:9–14	175	36:1–2	16 n. 3
2:15	181		
3:18	181, 186	Leviticus	
3:24	185	6:9	59
8:21	96 n. 38	16:18	101
11:1	41	16:28	101
11:1–9	40	19:14	32
11:26	41	19:16–17	24
12	41	19:17	29, 39 n. 46, 40 n. 46, 48
15:15	298	26:16	203
16	94–95	26:18	121, 128
17:1	41	26:21	128
17:4	138	26:22	203
38:18	97	26:23–24	203 n. 20
49:15	90 n. 17	26:26	121
		26:28	121, 128, 203
Exodus		26:29	203
4:3	97	27:32	97
10:16–21	48		
12:11	97	Numbers	
14:13–15	43	1:2–3	143
14:30	42	6:5	124
15:1	42	6:13	59
15:2	43	6:21	59
15:5	42		
15:10	42	Deuteronomy	
17	42	4	164
17:6	206	4:5–6	59
20:2	45	4:16	115–16
20:12	48	4:26	101
22:22	97	4:36	101 n. 1, 118 n. 57

Deuteronomy (cont.)

4:39–40	116
4:40	66
6:4–9	330 n. 16
7:9	66
8:5	101, 120, 128, 202 n. 17, 206
11:2	120
11:13–21	330 n. 16
12:11	120
13:5	66
16	222
17:19–20	59
21:18	101, 110
22:18	101–2, 115
23:22–24	65
26	222
26:18	66
28:27	21 n. 16
28:58	59
29:19	59
30:2	126 n. 89
31:11–12	59
32:10	103 n. 5, 124 n. 78
32:29	160
33:4	174

1 Kings

3:12	16 n. 3
5:10	16
5:12–13	16
9:7	21 n. 16
10:7	19 n. 9

2 Kings

12:11	115
12:14–15	115

1 Chronicles

24:10	138

2 Chronicles

10:11	120 n. 65
10:14	120 n. 65

Ezra

7	164
7:25	62

Nehemiah

3:5	90 n. 16
8:13–18	67
10:31–32	67

Esther

2:7	124 n. 78

Job

1:13–22	222
2:7–10	222
2:9	223
2:10	225
4:3	126 n. 89
5:17	202 n. 19
11:5–7	18
11:19	33 n. 30
12:25	26
14:9	18 n. 7
28	18 n. 7
28:20–23	18
30:27	26
32:6	16 n. 3
33:16	202 n. 19
36:10	101 n. 1, 202 n. 19
38–41	234
39:14–16	18 n. 7
42:11–17	217 n. 7

Psalms

1	164
1:2–3	175
2:2	121
6:2	120 n. 65
6:12	120
15	160
18:36	122 n. 72
19	69, 74, 164
24	160
36:8–10	176 n. 19
37:38	16 n. 3

38:2	120 n. 65	4:5	16 n. 3
41:6	31 n. 28	4:7	16 n. 3
49:3	21 n. 17	4:13	84
50:17	116	5:12	85 n. 12, 90 n. 17, 115
78	73	6:2	159
78:2	21 n. 17	6:20	85, 330 n. 16
90:10	122	6:20–23	63–64
90:12	125 n. 85	6:23	85–86, 202 n. 19
91	160–61	7	64
92:6–7	17	7:1–2	64
92:12	176 n. 19	7:25	158
94:10	116, 126 n. 89	8	69
94:12	126 n. 89	8:4–5	173
95	314 n. 9, 318	8:10	84 n. 11, 118
104:17–18	18 n. 7	8:10–14	16 n. 3
104:24	17	8:22–31	17
105	78	8:33	84 n. 11, 90 n. 17, 101 n. 1
105:22	122	9:1–6	159
106	78	10	21 n. 15
107:27	26	10–31	91
111:10	16 n. 3	10:4	125 n. 85
119	20 n. 13, 68–69, 160, 164	10:8	28
119:66	122–23	10:14	29
119:94–100	16 n. 3	10:17	23, 85 n. 12, 202 n. 19
141:5	122 n. 72	10:18	24
		10:20–21	30
Proverbs		10:26	25
1–9	74, 156, 162	10:31	19 n. 9
1:1–6	19 n. 9	11:2	31
1:1–7	84	11:10	24
1:2	126 n. 89, 92, 158	12:1	85
1:3	83, 91, 118	12:15	27
1:6	21 n. 17	13:1	330 n. 16
1:8	330 n. 16	13:18	85 n. 12, 90 n. 17, 202 n. 19
1:26	159	13:24	18 n. 7, 86, 97, 117
2:19	159	14:6	25 n. 20
3	64	14:14	23
3:1	64	14:35	18 n. 7
3:11–12	97, 202 n. 17, 316	15:5	85 n. 12, 90 n. 17, 202 n. 16
3:12	85 n. 12, 90 n. 17, 116	15:10	85 n. 12, 202 n. 19
3:13	16 n. 3, 158	15:15	118
3:14–15	159	15:17	29
3:18	85, 158, 174 n. 8	15:32	85 n. 12, 90 n. 17
3:19	17	16:1	29
4:1	85, 116, 330 n. 16	16:16	16 n. 3

Proverbs (cont.)

Reference	Page
16:21	30
16:23	16 n. 3, 30
17:1	18 n. 7
17:16	16 n. 3
17:28	28
18:15	30
18:17	30
19:12	18 n. 7
19:16	33 n. 30
19:18	119 n. 61
19:20	85
19:21	30
19:27	90 n. 17
22:1	22 n. 18, 30
22:2	23
22:7	27
22:15	97, 117, 202 n. 19
23:1–2	18 n. 7
23:12	90 n. 16
23:12–14	86
23:13	97, 117, 202 n. 16
23:13–14	18 n. 7
24:32	256
25:2	18
25:6–7	18 n. 7
25:11	31
26:2	31
26:4–5	49
26:6	16 n. 3
26:9	21 n. 16, 26
26:11	32
26:17	22
26:20	32
26:23	29
26:24	24
26:24–25	29
26:26	24
27:6	26
27:15	32
27:17	32
27:23	16 n. 3
29:9	120 n. 65
29:17	119 n. 61
30:2–3	19 n. 9
31:1–9	116

Ecclesiastes (Qoheleth)

Reference	Page
1:11	31 n. 28
1:16	16, 19 n. 9
2:14	26
2:16	26, 31 n. 28
3:20	65
5:3–4	65
6:4	31 n. 28
7:1	21, 26, 30
7:3	50
7:6	25
7:8	28
7:9	50
7:26	50
8:5	16 n. 3
9:4	50
10:1	22
10:2	16 n. 3
12:11	21 n. 16
12:13	66–67

Song of Songs

Reference	Page
3:2	118

Isaiah

Reference	Page
3:10	208 n. 30
5	183
9:3	90 n. 17
10:27	90 n. 17
14:25	90 n. 17
19:14	26
24:20	26
26:16	203, 208
27:7–9	203
28:26	116–17, 118 n. 57
28:27–28	117
35:3	316
40:4	172
43:5–6	326
50:4	123
51:3	181 n. 38
53:3	204
53:5	209

ANCIENT SOURCES INDEX

Jeremiah	
2:19	325
2:30	118
5:3	118
7:28	116
8	164
10:8	101 n. 1
17	183
27:12	90 n. 16
30:11	101 n. 1, 116–17, 124 n. 78
31:31–34	313
31:33	314
46:28	117, 203 n. 22
49:7	16 n. 3

Ezekiel	
3:3	175 n. 12
5:15	101 n. 1
13:9	123
16:49–50	38
17:2	21 n. 17
28:3	123
31:14	184
36:35	181 n. 38

Daniel	
1:5	124
1:17	17
1:20	124–25
2:18–47	264
9:13	33 n. 30

Hosea	
5:2	115, 121 n. 68
7:15	101 n. 1

Amos	
3:7	123

Habakkuk	
1:12	123
2:6	21 n. 17

Deuterocanonical and Septuagint

3 Kingdoms	
12:11	120, 126 n. 89
12:14	120 n. 65

Judith	
2:2	264 n. 82

Tobit	
1:8	222 n. 21
4:14	125 n. 85
12:7–11	264 n. 82

Wisdom of Solomon	
1:3	204 n. 24
1:4–5	196
1:5	204 n. 24
1:8	204 n. 24
1:9	204 n. 24
2:1–5	208
2:6–11	208
2:11	204 n. 24
2:12	199–200, 208 n. 30
2:14	204 n. 24
2:17	204 n. 24
2:19	204 n. 24
2:20	204 n. 24
2:22	264
3	204
3:1–6	209
3:4	204 n. 24
3:5	204 n. 24, 210
3:6	204 n. 24
3:10	209
3:11	210
3:13–14	210
3:16–17	210
4:2	210 n. 33
4:7–15	210
4:20	204 n. 24
5:1–6a	210–211
5:13	209
6:1–21	197
6:1	198 n. 7

Wisdom of Solomon (cont.)		Sirach	
6:4	197	Prologue	165, 284
6:9–11	197–98	1:4	17
6:12–16	198	1:27	126 n. 89
6:17–21	199–200	3:1–16	18 n. 7
6:22	264 n. 82	3:7	46
6:25	198 n. 7	3:11	47
7:14–22	198–199	4	222 n. 21
7:17–19	296 n. 19	4:11	173
7:25–26	311 n. 3	4:11–19	172
8:1	17	4:17	126 n. 89
8:8	84 n. 9	6:2	84, 119 n. 60
9:1–2	17	6:18–37	172
10:5	40, 48	6:19	181
10:12	210 n. 33	6:20–22	172–173
10:15–21	311 n. 3	6:32	126 n. 89
10:18–21	41	6:34–37	173
10:20	42	6:36	173
11:4	206	6:38	173
11:5	204 n. 24	7:23	119 n. 61
11:6	206	8:8–9	173
11:7	204 n. 24	10:1	126 n. 87
11:8	204 n. 24	11:15	34 n. 33
11:8–10	206	12:16	35
11:9	204 n. 24	14:20–15:10	172
11:10	204 n. 24	15:6	173
11:12–14	207	16:8	38, 38 n. 41
11:15–16	207	16:23–30	38
12:2	204 n. 24, 208	16:24	34 n. 33
12:10	204 n. 24	17:7	180
12:14	204 n. 24	17:8–11	175
12:15	204 n. 24	17:31	35
12:17	204 n. 24	18:3	126 n. 89
12:18–27	207 n. 29	19:12	21 n. 16, 33 n. 30
12:18	204 n. 24	19:13–17	39 n. 46
12:22	204 n. 24	21:19	126 n. 89
12:23	204 n. 24	21:23	125 n. 87
13:1–3	296 n. 19	22:22	264 n. 82
14:15–23	264	24	70, 164, 173–176
16:4–9	207 n. 29	24:1–18	35
16:6	204 n. 24	24:3	164
17:7	204 n. 24	24:8–12	174
18:5	204 n. 24	24:15	174
18:8	204 n. 24	24:17–21	174
		24:23–24	36

24:23	63, 174–75	1 Maccabees	
24:25–27	175	1:11–15	148
24:27	176 n. 23, 184 n. 52	1:15	138, 146
24:28–29	184 n. 51	8:17	138
24:30	176, 184		
24:31–33	176	2 Maccabees	
24:34	177	3:10	222 n. 21
25:24	38	4:9	145
26:14	125 n. 87	4:11–17	138, 147
26:15	126 n. 87	4:18	146
27:16–21	264 n. 82	5:9	146
28:17	34	5:11–6:1	145
30:2	126 n. 89	8:28–30	222 n. 21
30:13	119 n. 61, 126 n. 89		
31:11	119	4 Maccabees	
34:10–12	137	1:15–17	284
34:19	126 n. 87	2:13	39 n. 46
34:25–26	34		
35:5	34	2 Esdras/4 Ezra	179
36:3	34 n. 33	9:32	174 n. 12
36:25	172	14:38–41	175
37:20	34 n. 33		
38:24–39:11	19	Pseudepigrapha	
39:1–5	173		
39:2	84 n. 9	1 Enoch	
39:13	176 n. 21	10:16	179 n. 34
40:29	125 n. 86	48:1	176 n. 18
41:15	119	71:2	229 n. 40
42:15–43:33	69	93:10	179 n. 34
42:8	118–19		
44–50	38–39, 311 n. 3	2 Enoch	
44:16	39 n. 46	22:8–10	229 n. 40
45:1–2	38	42:7	222 n. 21
46:15	34 n. 33		
47:14	177 n. 23	3 Enoch	
50:10	174 n. 8	15	229
51:23	177 n. 25		
51:28	177 n. 25	Martyrdom of Isaiah	
51:30	34 n. 33	4.21–22	52
Baruch		Psalms of Solomon	
3–4	164	8:9	121 n. 68
3:36–4:1	36	12:2	84 n. 84

Testament of Abraham		The Dead Sea Scrolls and the	
11:1–12	229	Damascus Document	
13:2–6	229		
		CD (Cairo Damascus Document)	
Testament of Job		IV,6–10	88
3:3	222	IV,8	92 n. 25
4:6	219	VI,3–10	176
4:10	219	VII,5–8	92 n. 25
9:3–6	222	IX,7	39 n. 46
10:5–6	222	XIII,17–18	89
16:1–7	222	XX,27–34	88
16:3	222		
17:1–18:3	222	1Q26 (1QInstruction)	
18:6–8	224	1 4	179 n. 36
21:3–4	223		
23:1–11	222	1QS (1QSerekh [Community Rule])	
24:1–10	223	II,25–III,1	86–87
25:6	225	III,5–6	86–87
25:9–10	223	V,3	92
25:10	223 n. 22	V,23	92
26:1–2	223	V,24	39 n. 46
26:4	223	VI,13–15	87
26:5	224	VI,15–23	87
26:6	222	VI,21–22	92
27:7	225	VIII,5–6	179 n. 34
32:1–11	228	IX,3–11	87
33:1–4	228	IX,10	92 n. 25
36:3	228	IX,16–17	39 n. 46
37:1–4	228		
37:4	226	1QSa (1QRule of the Congregation)	
38:3–5	228	I,4–5	89
39:11–40:4	217 n. 7	I,6–9	143
47:3	230	I,6–8	87–88
47:8	218, 230		
48:1	230	1QH (1QHodayot)	
49:1	230	V,8	253
50:1	230	IX,12–19	186
52:1–2	230	IX,23	179 n. 36
		X–XVII	182–83
Testament of Levi		XI,20–37	184
18:11	174	XII,28–29	183
		XIII,22–XV,8	183 n. 45
		XIII,27	183 n. 44
		XIII,28	185
		XIV	184

XIV,17–20	184	1 I,11	255
XIV,19	183	1 I,16	255, 271
XV,21–22	184–85	1 I,17	271
XVI	180, 184, 186	1 I,18	178 n. 32
XVI,5–7	184–85	1 I,18–20	268
XVI,5–XVII,36	183 n. 45–46	1 I,19	178–79, 181
XVI,13	185	1 I,27	258
XVI,21	183, 185	2 I,10	178 n. 32
XVI,22	185	2 I,11–12	268
XVI,25–26	185		
XVII,23	185	4Q418 (4QInstruction[d])	
		9+9a–c 13	89 n. 14
4Q269 (4QDamascus Document[d])		43 4–5	178
10 II,2	89	81 1–5	256 n. 51
		81 1–2	257
4Q270 (4QDamascus Document[e])		81 3	180–81
7 I,15	119	81 4–5	179, 271
		81 13	179
4Q299 (4QMysteries[a])		81 17	178, 257
30,4	90	123 II,3–4	179
		169+170,3	89 n. 14
4Q302 (4QAdmonitory Parable)		184 2	179 n. 36
2 II	176 n. 21	221	178
		297,1	89 n. 14
4Q414 (4QRitual of Purification A)			
2 I,1–5	40 n. 46	4Q421 (4QWays of Righteousness[b])	
		1a I,3–6	92
4Q416 (4QInstruction[b])			
2 III,9, 14	178 n. 32	4Q423 (4QInstruction[g])	
2 III,13	89 n. 14	1	180–81
2 III,14	257	1 2–3	181
2 III,15	257		
2 III,15–16	257	4Q424 (4QInstruction-Like Composition B)	
2 III,15–18	45		
2 III,21	257	7,7–9	90–91
2 III,18	179 n. 36		
		4Q425 (4QSapiential-Didactic Work B)	
4Q417 (4QInstruction[c])		1+3	91
1 I,1–4	253–55		
1 I,3	178 n. 32, 271	4Q438 (4QBarkhi Nafshi[e])	
1 I,3–5	179	3 3	90 n. 16
1 I,6–7	178		
1 I,6–8	178–79, 181	4Q525 (4QBeatitudes)	
1 I,8–9	179	1 1–3	91–92
1 I,9	255	2 II–III	156–59

4Q525 (4QBeatitudes) (cont.)

2 II,1	160, 164
2 II,1–7	161
2 II,2–3	160, 163
2 II,3	73
2 II,3–4	164
2 II,4	160
2 II,6	164
5	156, 165
5 6–7	163
5 7–8	160, 165
5 9–13	165
5 14–18	161
6–10	162
13	165
14 II	156, 161, 165
14 II,2	164
14 II,6	160 n. 22
14 II,11	160
14 II,12	160 n. 22
14 II,14–16	166
14 II,18–28	162
14 II,27	159
15	156, 160–61
15 5	160 n. 22
15 7	160 n. 22
16–17	161
16–23	162
21–23	161
23 II,4–6	159
24 II	156
24 II,4–6	162

5Q16

1–2+5	160–61

Hellenistic Jewish Sources

Ezekiel the Tragedian

68–76	229

Josephus, *Contra Apionem*

1.60–68	330 n. 16
2.206	47

Josephus, *Jewish Antiquities*

11.114	144
12.120	138
12.133–153	146
12.142	68
12.156	144
13.275	144

Letter of Aristeas

161	283

Philo, *De Abrahamo*

50–54	94 n. 34
247–251	293 n. 12
251	98 n. 41

Philo, *De aeternitate mundi*

52	93 n. 27

Philo, *De Agricultura*

9	314 n. 10
136	299 n. 29

Philo, *De cherubim*

7–9	290–91

Philo, *De congressu eruditionis gratia*

2	95
9	95
9–10	288–89
11	95
18–19	95
19	314 n. 10
20	289
34–36	303–4
35–36	94 n. 34
36	289
73–79	95
77	290
79	95–96
83–85	96
88	96
94	96
121	96
150	299 n. 29

ANCIENT SOURCES INDEX 387

151–152	290	Philo, *De specialibus legibus*	
154–155	95	2.225	46
158–159	290	2.230	95 n. 37
172–179	97		

Philo, *De vita contemplativa*
3–5	296 n. 19
57	93 n. 27

Philo, *De vita Mosis*
2.48	284
2.52	284

Philo, *De decalogo*
106–107	46

Philo, *Legatio ad Gaium*
16.31	330 n. 16

Philo, *De fuga et inventione*
150	97

Philo, *Legum allegoriae*
1.14	299 n. 29
1.57	340 n. 47
3.121	299 n. 29
3.244–245	95 n. 35, 287–88

Philo, *De gigantibus*
60–63	94

Philo, *De migration Abrahami*
29	314 n. 10
88	289 n. 9
89–94	286 n. 5

Philo, *Quis rerum divinarum heres sit*
63	298
171–172	46
274	298
277–279	298
295–296	96 n. 38

Philo, *De mutatione nominum*
217	328

Philo, *Quod omnis probus liber sit*
13	93
160	314 n. 10

Philo, *De opificio mundi*
126	299 n. 29
143	283 n. 1

Pseudo-Phocylides
8	47

Philo, *De posteritate Caini*
97	97

Sibylline Oracles
3.593–594	47

Philo, *De sacrificiis Abelis el Caini*
63	97
74	299 n. 29

New Testament

Matthew
5:3–12	157 n. 10

Philo, *De sobrietate*
8	303
9	290, 295

6:19–21	225 n. 25
7:15	350 n. 81
10:28	225 n. 25
11:12	333

Philo, *De somniis*
2.9	314 n. 10

13:44–46	225 n. 25

Mark
  10:21   222 n. 21
Luke
  6:20–26   157 n. 10
  7:42–43   333
  23:16   104
John
  1:1–2   17
  1:3   331 n. 19
  15:10   331–33, 334 n. 31
  18:36   228

Acts
  17:26   331 n. 19

Romans
  2:27–29   299–300
  5:20   294 n. 14
  7:4   300
  7:5–6   299
  8:14–17   326
  8:15   326
  10:4   300
  11:25   262 n. 75
  13:10   333
  16:25   262 n. 75

1 Corinthians
  1–4   259, 269
  1:1   261
  1:1–17   260
  1:7   265
  1:11–12   259
  1:13   259
  1:18   260
  1:19   260
  1:20–21   260
  1:22   260, 262
  1:22–25   272
  1:23   271
  1:24   261
  1:25   260
  1:26   261
  1:27   260
  1:28   260, 262
  2:1   262, 273
  2:2   271
  2:3   272
  2:4   272
  2:6   265, 267
  2:7   262
  2:8   271
  3:1–3   314 n. 10
  3:2   267, 325
  3:4   260
  3:5   269
  4:1   262 n. 75, 270
  4:8–13   272
  4:15–16   270
  4:15–21   267
  8:1   334
  9:24–27   333
  10:4   206 n. 27
  11:16   273
  13:2   262 n. 75, 333
  13:13   333
  14:2   262 n. 75
  15:51   262 n. 75

2 Corinthians
  3:5–8   300
  8:13–15   273
  11:6   261

Galatians
  3:1   272, 286
  3:1–18   293
  3:2   293
  3:3   304
  3:5   294
  3:7   294
  3:11   294
  3:13–14   300
  3:18   294
  3:19   294
  3:19–4:2   294
  3:23   294
  3:24–25   286, 294–96

3:25	297	6:1	315 n. 11
4:1–2	295–96	6:2	311 n. 3
4:1–7	326	6:6	314
4:3	296, 300	6:8	311 n. 3
4:4–5	297	8:8–9:5	310, 313
4:4–7	301	8:10–11	313
4:6	326	9–10	313, 318
4:8–9	297, 300	10:4	315 n. 11
4:9	298	10:12–18	314
4:10	297	10:14	315 n. 11
4:11–20	301	10:19	312
4:21–31	304	10:25	311 n. 3, 314 n. 9
4:21–5:1	286	10:26–31	310
4:23	303	10:29–31	311 n. 3
4:24	301	10:32–39	316
4:28	292 n. 11, 303	10:33	317
4:29	303	11:10	311 n. 3
5:1	303	11:16	311 n. 3
		11:19	311 n. 3
Philippians		11:40	315 n. 11
3:8	225 n. 25	12:1–2	315
		12:1–3	317
2 Thessalonians		12:2	320
2:10	332	12:3–12	316–17
		12:12–13	313, 316
Hebrews		12:18–29	317
1:1	319	12:23	315 n. 11
1:2	311 n. 3	12:25	317
2:1	314	12:28–29	311 n. 3
2:5	311 n. 3	12:29	311 n. 3
2:9	320	13:1–3	317, 319
2:10	312	13:1–19	313
2:10–18	313, 316	13:7	313
2:11–13	313	13:22	312
3–4	318		
3:1	312	James	
3:7–4:11	310	1:27	222 n. 21
3:12	312–13		
4:1–11	311 n. 3	Revelation	
4:9	312	10:9	175 n. 12
4:12–13	311 n. 3	22:1–2	176 n. 19
5:7–10	317–18, 320		
5:11–12	313		
5:11–6:3	314		
5:14	315		

Rabbinic Literature

b. Ta'anit
  7a — 176

Genesis Rabbah
  18:4 — 41
  39:2 — 22 n. 18

Hekhalot Rabbati
  4–6 — 230

m. 'Avot
  6:4 — 18 n. 7

t. Ta'anit
  1:18 — 34 n. 33

Targum Neofiti
  Gen 1:1 — 17
  Gen 11:11 — 41

Targum Pseudo-Jonathan
  Gen 11:11 — 41

Early Christian Sources

Clement of Alexandria, *Stromata*
  3.5.3 — 341 n. 51

Codex Theodosianus
  13.3.5 — 369

Gregory of Nazianzus, *Contra Julianum*
  4–5 — 369

Gregory of Nazianzus, *Oratio in laudem Basilii*
  43.22 — 359

Ireneaus, *Adversus Haereses*
  1, Preface — 334 n. 30, 341 n. 51, 342
  1.3.6 — 349, 350 n. 81
  1.4.3–4 — 351 n. 82
  1.6.1 — 333 n. 27
  1.6.2 — 332
  1.8.1 — 342, 349, 350 n. 81
  1.9.1–3 — 350
  1.9.3 — 331 n. 19
  1.9.4 — 350, 351 n. 82
  1.9.4–5 — 352 n. 86
  1.10.1 — 332–33
  1.11.4 — 351 n. 82
  1.12.2 — 351 n. 82
  1.13.6 — 351 n. 82
  1.21.2 — 333 n. 27
  1.23.4 — 334 n. 30
  1.25.1–5 — 341 n. 51
  1.29.3 — 333 n. 27
  1.31.2 — 333 n. 27, 342
  2, Preface — 334 n. 30
  2.5.4 — 351 n. 82
  2.13.6 — 342
  2.14.1–6 — 346
  2.14.2 — 351 n. 82
  2.14.7 — 334 n. 30
  2.15.3 — 342
  2.16.4 — 342
  2.19.8 — 342
  2.20.1–2.25.2 — 345 n. 67
  2.20.3 — 333 n. 27
  2.22.6 — 351 n. 82
  2.25.2 — 342, 345
  2.25.3 — 324 n. 5
  2.25.4 — 334 n. 29
  2.26 — 334
  2.26.1 — 332
  2.28.1 — 333 n. 26
  2.28.1–2 — 346
  2.28.2 — 348–349
  2.28.3 — 324–25
  2.32.2 — 339–40, 341 n. 51
  3.5.2 — 342
  3.6.1 — 326 n. 7
  3.9.1 — 333 n. 28
  3.10.2 — 333 n. 28
  3.11.1 — 334 n. 30
  3.11.9 — 338
  3.12.3 — 333 n. 28
  3.12.12 — 334 n. 30

3.12.5	333 n. 28	5.28.2	332
3.12.9	331 n. 19	5.32.1	332
3.16.4	333 n. 28		
3.16.8	333 n. 28	Ireneaus, *Demonstration of the Apostolic*	
3.18.7	326 n. 7	*Preaching*	
3.19.1	326 n. 7	8	326–27
3.20.1	330 n. 17		
3.20.2	332 n. 22, 333	Jerome, *Epistulae*	
3.25.7	342	53.7	350 n. 81
4.5.5	324 n. 5		
4.9.1	326 n. 7	John Chrysostom, *Homily on St. Babylas*	
4.9.2	326 n. 7, 333 n. 26	98–113	364 n. 19
4.11.2	324		
4.12.2	333	Olympus, *Epistle*	
4.13.2	324 n. 5	63	368
4.14.1	326		
4.14.2	325	Optimus, *Epistle*	
4.14.3–4.16.4	326	1544	365
4.15.2	324 n. 5		
4.16.5	326 n. 7	Origen, *Contra Celsum*	
4.18.6	324 n. 5	1.9	338
4.26.1	333	3.44	338
4.28.3	333 n. 26	3.50	338
4.33.3	351 n. 82	3.55	338
4.33.8	333		
4.33.9	333	Socrates Scholasticus, *Historia Ecclesiastica*	
4.35.4	327		
4.36.7	333 n. 28	7.36	365 n. 23
4.37.7	325, 331, 332 n. 22, 333		
4.38.1	325	Sozomen, *Historia Ecclesiastica*	
4.38.4	330 n. 17	8.2.2	364
4.39.1	330 n. 17		
4.39.4	334 n. 30	Tripartite Tractate (Nag Hammadi Corpus I,5)	
5, Preface	334 n. 30		
5.1.1	324 n. 5, 330 n. 17	109.24–110.24	341
5.2.3	330 n. 17		
5.3.1	330 n. 17	Greek and Latin Authors	
5.12.4	333 n. 28		
5.13.2	342	Aelian, *Varia historia*	
5.14.2	331 n. 19	1.34	111
5.19.2	338		
5.23.3	332	Aeschines, *In Timarchum*	
5.25.3	332 n. 20	11	120 n. 67
5.25.5	333 n. 28		
5.27.2	332 n. 20		

Aeschylus, *Septem contra Thebas*
18   108 n. 25

Alcinous, *Epitome doctrinae platonicae*
  (*Didaskalikos*)
29.2   336 n. 37

Ammianus Marcellinus, *Res gestae*
22.10.7   370
25.4.20   370

Aphtonius, *Progymnasmata*
5   371

Aristophanes, *Vespae*
1297   109

Aristotle, *Constitution of Athens* (*Athēn-aiōn politeia*)
42   142

Aristotle, *Ethica nicomachea*
1103a20   336
1180a29–b23   328
1180b2   112

Aristotle, *Metaphysica*
933b21   340 n. 47
1025b20–21   340 n. 47
1025b23–25   340 n. 47

Aristotle, *Politica*
1310a14   119 n. 63
1342a23–26   337

Aurelius Victor, *De Caesaribus*
9.12   337

Choricius, *Declamation*
32   371

Cicero, *De oratore*
3.23.87   345 n. 68

Cicero, *De natura dorum.*
2.130–136   347 n. 75

Columella, *Res rustica*
Preface   345 n. 68
1   345 n. 68

Diodorus Siculus, *Bibliotheca historica*
1.25.4   263
1.81.1–7   136

Diogenes, *Epistle*
31   219
37   219

Diogenes Laertius, *Vitae Philosophorum*
2.69   109
5.32   348 n. 77
7.87–88   283 n. 1
7.92   336 n. 37
10.144   229 n. 37

Dionysius of Halicarnassus, *De compositione verborum*
25   246

Epictetus, *Diatribai*
2.16.39   314 n. 10
2.17.19   224
2.17.22–26   224
3.22.81–82   328–29
3.24.9   314 n. 10

Epictetus, *Enchiridion*
1   221

Epicurus, *Epistle to Pythagoras*
94   347

Epicurus, *Kyriai Doxai*
17   229 n. 37

Euripides, *Iphigenia taurica*
205–207   108 n. 25

ANCIENT SOURCES INDEX

Galen, *Protrepticus*
  5   340
  14   340

Hippocrates, *Lex*
  2   245
  4–5   244

Horace, *Satires*
  1.10.90–91   345 n. 68

John Chortasmenos, *Epistle*
  23   111 n. 30

Julian, *Epistle*
  61c   369

Julian, *Contra Heraclium*
  221c–223a   370

Julian, *Oration*
  5.161c–167b   370

Juvenal, *Satires*
  7.175–7   345 n. 68

Libanius, *Epistulae*
  427   370 n. 38
  620   370
  634   365
  694   367 n. 30
  770   367 n. 30
  990   351
  1264   368 n. 32
  1351   367 n. 31
  1376   367 n. 31
  1466   370 n. 38

Libanius, *Orations*
  26.10   110
  31.43   370 n. 38

Livy, *Ab urbe condita*
  29.10–14   263
  38.34   145 n. 25

Lucian, *Anacharsis*
  39   144

Lysias, *Epistle*
  3   110

Marcus Aurelius, *Meditations*
  5.8   220 n. 16
  33.4   221

Menander, *Sententiae*
  122   111 n. 32
  384   112
  573   112

Papyrus *BGU* 3.846
  11   113

Papyrus *PSI* 8.972
  18–19   113

Philostratus, *De Gymnastica*
  1   340

Philostratus, *Vita Apollonii*
  1.13   111
  8.7.9   340

Plato, *Crito*
  50e   108 n. 28

Plato, *Leges*
  832d   120 n. 67

Plato, *Phaedrus*
  261b   265

Plato, *Protagoras*
  325c–d   328
  325d–326b   345

Plato, *Respublica*
  401d–e   336–37
  427e   336 n. 37
  430a   108 n. 28

Plato, *Respublica* (cont.)
430d–432b   336 n. 37

Plato, *Symposium*
201c   248
201d   249–50
206c   250, 265
207c   266
209a   250
209e–210a   266–67
210a   250, 265
210a–211e   251, 266
210e   250
211c   250
215b   251
219c   251
222a   252
222b   251

Plato, *Theaetetus*
202e–203a   299 n. 29

Pliny the Younger, *Epistulae*
8.14.6   330

Plutarch, *Alcibiades*
22.3   244 n. 2

Plutarch, *Cato Major*
20.4–5   329

Plutarch, *Dion*
1.4   112

Plutarch, *De genio Socratis*
579c   112 n. 67

Plutarch, *De Iside et Osiride*
377d   263
378b   244 n. 2

Plutarch, *De liberis educandis*
7d   93, 287 n. 7
7d–f   334–35
10e   245

10f   246

Plutarch, *Philopoemen*
16.5–6   144–45

Plutarch, *Quomodo adolescens poetas audire debeat*
14   328

Plutarch, *Themistocles*
15   251 n. 28

Plutarch, *Tiberius et Caius Gracchus*
19   330 n. 15

Propertius, *Elegiae*
1.2, 27–28   345 n. 68
2.1.9–10   345 n. 68

Quintilian, *Institutio oratoria*
1.2.18–20   247
2.18   340 n. 47
5.13.60   247
5.14.27   247
12.2.15–17   335 n. 32

Sallust, *Bellum catalinae*
25.2   330 n. 15

Seneca, *Epistulae*
89.13   329 n. 12
90.19   345 n. 68

Sextus Empiricus, *Pyrrhoniae hypotyposes*
1.18   346

Sophocles, *Ajax*
595   110

Sophocles, *Antigone*
235   122 n. 72

Statius, *Silvae*
3.5.64   345 n. 68

Stobeaus, *Florilegium*
2.31.58   111 n. 30, 112

Strabo, *Geographica*
2.3.8   348

Synesius of Cyrene, *Dio, sive de suo ipsius instituto*
4–11   360

Tacitus, *Dialolgue de oratoribus*
28   330 n. 15

Thucydides, *History of the Peloponnesian War*
1.6   147 n. 33

Vita Aesopi
G.61   110

Xenophon, *De equitande ratione*
10.6   109

Xenophon, *Memorabilia*
1.3.5   109
1.4.1–20   347
4.3.3–14   347

Modern Authors Index

Adams, Samuel L. 19 n. 10, 33 n. 31
Aitken, Ellen 1
Alexandre, Monique 288 n. 8
Amir, Yehoshua 287 n. 7
Anderson, Gary 17 n. 6
Anderson, Graham 107 n. 24
Andia, Ysabel de 333 n. 23
Angus, Samuel 259 n. 59
Arieti, James A. 106–7, 127 n. 92
Asmis, Elizabeth 347 n. 74
Asmos, J. R. 369 n. 35
Assman, Jan 60 n. 7
Attridge, Harold L. 310 n. 3, 312 n. 6, 314 n. 10, 315 n. 12, 317 n. 16, 318–19
Audet, T. A. 323 n. 1
Balch, David L. 272 n. 119
Barbour, Jennie 65 n. 26
Barr, James 105 n. 15
Barrett, C. K. 291 n. 10, 302
Barthes, Roland 320 n. 27
Barzilai, Gabriel 48 n. 66
Bauks, Michaela 187 n. 64
Beaulieu, Paul-Alain 20 n. 10
Belfiore, Elizabeth 248 n. 10, 250 n. 22
Benoit, André 351 n. 82
Berg, Shane 175 n. 14
Bertram, Georg 97, 103–7, 129, 200 n. 14, 202 n. 18
Betz, Dorothea 106–7, 117
Betz, Hans Dieter 270 n. 113, 272, 293 n. 13, 296 n. 19
Bickerman, Elias J. 68, 118, 162
Bildstein, Gerald J. 45 n. 60
Bizzeti, Paolo 195

Black, C. Clifton 312 n. 6
Blenkinsopp, Joseph 117, 216 n. 4
Blinzler, Joseph 297
Bockmuehl, Marcus N. A. 264 n. 87, 284 n. 1
Boer, Martinus C. de 296–99
Bonner, Stanley F. 295 n. 17, 329 n. 13, 330 n. 15, 345 n. 68
Bons, Eberhard 121 n. 68
Borgen, Peder 93 n. 29, 293 n. 12
Bornkamm, Günther 262 n. 74, 264 nn. 83–84
Bourdieu, Pierre 261
Bowden, Hugh 262 n. 76
Bowersock, Glen 361
Boyarin, Daniel 248 n. 11, 249, 268 nn. 100–102
Brändl, Martin 219 n. 14
Branson, R. D. 114–15, 202 n. 16
Bremmer, Jan N. 244 n. 2, 251 n. 28
Brooke, George 73, 157 n. 10, 162, 229 n. 40
Brown, Peter 335
Brown, Raymond E. 258 n. 58, 263–64, 270 n. 110
Brown, William P. 31 n. 29, 176 n. 19
Bruegemann, Walter 216 n. 5
Bundrick, David 296 n. 18
Burkert, Walter 262 n. 76, 263 n. 79, 268 n. 101
Calduch-Benages, Núnia 119 n. 60
Camp, Claudia V. 155 n. 3
Caragounis, Chrys C. 263 n. 81
Carasik, Michael 118
Carr, David 3, 61

Castelli, Elizabeth   234, 270 n. 113, 302 n. 31
Chankowski, Andrzej   139–45
Chazon, Esther G.   182 n. 41
Cheary, John J.   252 n. 29
Cheon, Samuel   206 n. 28
Childs, Brevard   66 n. 29
Chin, Catherine   351 n. 84
Christes, Johannes   330 n. 15
Clarke, Ernest G.   196 n. 5
Clarke, M. L.   345 n. 68
Clemen, Carl   259 n. 59
Clifford, Richard J.   17 n. 4, 21 n. 14, 23 n. 20, 25 n. 22, 31 n. 29
Clines, David J. A.   216 n. 5, 217 n. 8, 218 n. 12, 219
Clinton, Kevin   244 n. 2, 245 n. 4, 250 n. 23, 268 n. 61
Coats, George W.   51 n. 69
Cody, Aelred   312 n. 5
Cohen, Shaye J. D.   266 n. 93
Collins, John J.   36 n. 36, 63 n. 15, 98 n. 42, 156 n. 7, 157 n. 11, 158 n. 15, 163 n. 31, 172 n. 1, 182 n. 42, 199 n. 10, 226, 228 n. 35, 229, 254–56, 261 n. 67, 264 nn. 86–87, 266 n. 93
Collins, Raymond F.   269 n. 106
Colson, F. H.   288 n. 8
Conley, Thomas   288 n. 8
Conzelmann, Hans   262 n. 74, 267 n. 97, 269 n. 106, 270 n. 110
Cook, Johann   83–84
Corrigan, Kevin   250 n. 24
Cosgrove, Charles H.   302 n. 31
Craik, Elizabeth M.   244 n. 1
Cremer, Hermann   104
Crenshaw, James L.   3 n. 6, 51 n. 69, 61, 67, 155 n. 2, 217 n. 8, 256 n. 48
Cribiore, Raffaella   328 n. 11, 351 n. 83
Crouch, Carly L.   62 n. 11
Curren, R. E.   328 n. 10
Danielou, Jean   351 n. 82
Davila, James R.   183 n. 47, 236
Dawson, David   302 n. 31
DeConick, April   227

Deissmann, Adolf   104
Delling, Gerhard   296 n. 18
Di Lella, Alexander A.   33 n. 31, 119 n. 61, 126 n. 89, 165 n. 35, 172 n. 2, 174 n. 9, 177 n. 23
Diels, Hermann   346
Dietrich, Manfried   187 n. 64
Dillon, John J.   351 n. 82
Doran, Robert   62 n. 13, 173 n. 6
Drever, J.   347 n. 74
Driver, Samuel   217 n. 5
Dueck, Daniela   348 n. 77
Dunderberg, Ismo   155 n. 1
Dunn, James D. G.   155 n. 1, 292 n. 11, 294 n. 14
Elgvin, Torleif   92
Elm, Susanna   371
Engberg-Pedersen, Troels   266 n. 93, 269 n. 108
Enns, Peter   40–41 nn. 47–49, 52 n. 43
Enslin, M. S.   323 n. 1
Erichsen, Wolja   136
Eshel, Hanan   145 n. 28
Evans, Nancy   251 n. 26
Fauth, W.   187 n. 64
Fernández Marcos, Natalio   127 n. 93, 215 n. 1
Finsterbusch, Karen   60 n. 2, 68 n. 40, 115 n. 47
Fischer, Georg   117 n. 50
Fishbane, Michael   63 n. 18, 176, 185 n. 53
Fitzgerald, John T.   111 n. 31, 273 n. 122
Fletcher-Louis, Crispin H.   229 n. 40
Foucault, Michael   186–87, 232, 234
Fox, Michael V.   15 n. 1, 20 n. 11, 20 n. 15, 23 n. 20, 25 n. 23, 27 n. 26, 51 n. 69, 64, 66, 83, 158 n. 13
Frede, Michael   348 n. 78
Freedman, David Noel   69 n. 44
Freedman, Kathleen   287 n. 7
Frymer-Kensky, Tikva   98 n. 41
Fujita, Shozo   179 n. 34
Gammie, John G   17 n. 4
García Martínez, Florentino   40 n. 46

Garrett, Duane 256
Geertz, Clifford 217–18
Geva, Hillel 147
Gieschen, Charles A. 229 n. 40
Gilbert, Maurice 175 n. 14, 195
Giulea, Dragos A. 234 n. 53
Given, Mark D. 260 n. 66
Gladd, Benjamin L. 258 n. 58, 262 n. 74, 264 n. 87, 270 n. 110
Glancy, Jennifer A. 272 n. 119
Glazov-Corrigan, Elena 250 n. 24
Glover, T. R. 338 n. 43
Goad, Edwin M. 216 n. 5
Goering, Greg Schmidt 70 n. 51, 174 n. 11, 205 n. 25
Goff, Matthew J. 37 n. 36, 44 n. 56, 45 n. 59, 63 nn. 15–17, 71 n. 54, 72 n. 56, 90–91, 156 n. 5, 157 n. 11, 158 n. 15, 163 n. 31, 252 n. 30, 253 nn. 31–34, 254–56, 258 nn. 56–57, 257 n. 52, 264 n. 87, 267–68, 271 nn. 115–116
Goldin, Judah 173 n. 7
Gordon, Richard L. 262 n. 76
Grabbe, Lester 199 n. 10
Grant, Robert 323, 339 nn. 45–46, 340 n. 48, 341 nn. 50–51, 342 n. 53, 346–47
Green, Deborah 174 n. 9
Greenfield, Jonas 51 n. 69
Grimm, Carl L. W. 195
Gruen, Erich S. 266 n. 93
Gruenwald, Ithamar 231 n. 45
Grund, Alexandra 69 n. 12
Grundmann, W. 269 n. 106
Habel, Norman C. 216 n. 4
Halperin, David M. 249 n. 18, 268 n. 102
Hänsel, Lars 67 n. 37
Harkins, Angela Kim 182, 183 nn. 45–46, 185 nn. 54–56, 186–87
Harl, Marguerite 124 n. 78
Harlé, Paul 104
Harnack, Adolf von 343
Harrington, Daniel J. 44 n. 56, 178 n. 30
Harris, Scott L. 64 n. 20
Hasitzka, Monika R. M. 363 n. 13
Hasselbalch, Trine Bjørnung 182 n. 42
Hatton, Peter T. H. 49 n. 67
Haussoulier, Bernard 140 n. 17
Hengel, Martin 36 n. 36
Henrichs, Albert 287 n. 7
Hermisson, Hans-Jürgen 17 n. 4, 20 n. 11
Hin, Saskia 141
Hitchcock, F. R. M. 324
Hogan, Karina Martin 254
Holm-Nielsen, Svend 183 n. 46
Honigman, Sylvie 127 n. 93
Horsley, Richard 269 n. 107, 284 n. 1
Horst, Pieter W. van der 223 n. 23
Hughes, Julie 183, 186 n. 59
Hunter, Richard 246
Hurtado, Larry W. 229 n. 40
Idel, Moshe 234 n. 52
Jackson, Bernard S. 60
Jaeger, Werner 2, 245 n. 3, 248 n. 12, 249, 316 n. 14
Jassen, Alex P. 176 n. 22
Jastrow, Morris, 216 n. 5, 212 n. 8, 235
Jauss, H. R. 367 n. 27
Jentsch, Werner 106–7
Jeremias, Gert 182
Johanson, Timothy Jay 234 n. 54, 347 n. 75
Jones, Christopher P. 359 n. 1
Jones, Elizabeth M. 337 n. 42
Jonge, Casper C. de 247 n. 7
Joostan, Jan 127 n. 93
Kahlos, Maijastina 363 n. 13
Kahn, Charles H. 266 n. 99
Kampen, John 37 n. 36, 40 n. 46, 44 n. 56, 89 n. 15, 156 n. 5, 157 n. 11, 255 n. 44, 257–58
Kang, Tae Wan 288 n. 8
Kaster, Robert A. 335–37
Kee, Howard C. 226 n. 26, 230-31
Keown, Gerald L. 117 n. 50
Kermode, Frank 176
King, Charles 360 n. 8
Kister, Menahem 40 n. 46

Klauck, Hans-Josef   262 n. 76, 263 n. 79, 264 n. 84
Klawans, Jonathan   34 n. 34
Klein, Anja   68–69
Koch, Hugo   343
Koester, Helmut   283 n. 1, 318 n. 18
Kolarcik, Michael   205 n. 25, 208 n. 30
Kooij, Arie van der   128 n. 95
Koskenniemi, Erkki   3 n. 5
Krüger, Thomas   59 n. 3, 65 nn. 25–27, 66 n. 31, 67
Kugel, James L.   19 nn. 8–9, 21 nn. 15–16, 31 n. 28, 37 n. 39, 38 nn. 41–44, 39 nn 45–46, 41–42 nn. 48–51, 45 n. 61, 47 n. 63, 51 n. 70, 52 n. 72
Kühnert, F.   345 n. 68
Laes, Christian   141 n. 22, 147
Lamberton, Robert   3 n. 4
Lanfer, Peter T.   175 n. 13
Lange, Armin   44 n. 56, 72 n. 55, 163 n. 31, 178 n. 30
Larcher, Chrysostome   196 n. 5, 197 n. 6, 200, 208 n. 30, 210 n. 32
Lee, J. A. L.   39 n. 46
Lefebvre, Michael   60 n. 6
Legras, Bernard   135–37
Lemaire, André   256 n. 48
Lesley, Micahel J.   157 n. 15
Lesses, Rebecca   226 n. 26, 230
Levenson, Bernard M.   65
Levenson, Jon D.   68, 175 n. 13
Levine, Lee I.   266 n. 93
Levison, John R.   269 n. 107
Leyerle, Blake   368 n. 34
Lloyd, G. E. M.   336 n. 38
Loisy, Alfred   259 n. 59
Long, A. A.   220
Longenecker, Richard N.   295 n. 16
Loo, Y. L.   347 n. 74
Loofs, Friedrich   343
Lundbom, Jack R.   117 n. 50
Lutz, Mark J.   271
Ma, John   140, 146 n. 32
Macaskill Grant   163 n. 30
Macatangay, Francis M.   51 n. 69

MacRae, George   155 n. 1, 312 n. 5
Malherbe, Abraham J.   267 n. 98
Margalit, Baruch   29 n. 27
Marriou, Henri Irénée   135 n. 1
Martin, Dale B.   259 n. 61, 260, 261 n. 67, 263, 266 n. 92, 269 n. 108, 270 n. 111, 273 n. 121
Matera, Frank J.   261 n. 69
Matthews, Victor H.   22 n. 18
Mazar, Benjamin   145 n. 28
McGill, Scott   350 n. 80
McPherran, Mark L.   347 n. 75
Meeks, Wayne A.   262 n. 73
Mendelson, Alan   93 n. 28, 94 n. 31, 98 n. 41, 288 n. 8
Metzger, Bruce   262 n. 74
Meyer, Marvin   262 n. 76
Milikowsky, Chaim   41 n. 49
Milton, J. R.   346 n. 73, 347 n. 74
Mitchell, Margaret M.   259 n. 61
Mopsik, Charles   119 n. 61
Morray-Jones, C. R. A.   229 n. 40
Mountford, James   345 n. 68
Murphy, Roland E.   17 n. 4, 174 n. 11
Mylonas, George E.   244 n. 2, 245 n. 4, 251 n. 28
Najman, Hindy   3 n. 6, 73, 93, 157 n. 12, 284 n. 1
Nanos, Mark D.   292 n. 11
Nautin, Pierre   344 n. 66
Needham, Rodney   360 n. 8
Nesselrath, Heinz-Günther   366 n. 25
Newsom, Carol   73, 164 n. 33, 182, 186, 216 n. 3, 217 n. 8, 233 n. 50
Nickelsburg, George W.   163 n. 29, 204 n. 23, 263 n. 81, 310 n. 1
Nicklas, Tobias   105 n. 15
Niehoff, Maren   95 n. 37, 96 n. 38, 287 n. 6
Nikiprowetzky, Valentin   284 n. 1
Nissinen, Martti   177 n. 22
Nock, A. D.   259 n. 54
Nussbaum, Martha   224 n. 37
Ober, Josiah   249
Offerhaus, Ulrich   195 n. 3

Olorsson, Staffan 106–7
Oppenheim, A. L. 187 n. 64
Orlov, Andrei A. 229 n. 39
Osborn, Eric 344
Östborn, Gunner 59 nn. 1–2
Pearson, Birger A. 269 n. 107
Pelttari, Aaron 350 n. 80
Perdue, Leo G. 177 n. 22, 199 n. 10, 216 n. 5, 233 n. 51, 256
Peursen, W. Th. van 118 n. 59
Pfitzner, Victor C. 210 n. 33, 219 n. 14, 221
Pope, Martin 216 n. 4
Pouchelle, Patrick 82–84, 101–3
Pralon, Didier 104
Préaux, Claire 136 n. 3
Prijs, Leo 106–7
Puech, Émile 157 n. 10, 159 n. 17
Punt, Jeremy 302 n. 31
Qimron, Elisha 157 n. 11, 159 nn. 17–18
Quasten, Johannes 343
Quispal, Gilles 229 n. 40
Rad, Gerhard von 17 nn. 4–5, 20 n. 11, 21 n. 16, 36 n. 36, 51 n. 69, 115 n. 45, 155 n. 3
Rea, John R. 113
Reade, Julian 187 n. 65
Rebillard, Eric 363–364
Redford, Donald B. 51 n. 69
Reitzenstein, Richard 259 n. 59, 262 n. 76
Resse, James M. 195
Rey, Jean-Sébastien 3 n. 6, 44 n. 56, 163 n. 31, 178 n. 27
Reynders, D. B. 323 n. 1
Reynolds, Kent Aaron 20 n. 13, 68–69
Rhodes, James 249 n. 17, 251 n. 27
Richardson, N. J. 251 n. 28
Riedway, Christopher 258 n. 58, 265 n. 87
Rist, John M. 220 n. 15
Rogers, Jessie 36 n. 36, 174 n. 12, 175 n. 15
Rondholz, Anke 351 nn. 84–85
Roo, Jacqueline de 157 n. 9
Rösel, Martin 106–7, 128 n. 95
Roth, Martha T. 60
Rousseau, Adelin 331 n. 19, 333 n. 25
Rowland, Christopher 226
Ruiten, Jacques van 175 n. 13
Rusam, Dietrich 297
Russell, Donald A. 247
Sæbø, Magne 115
Sanders, Ed P. 70–71
Sanders, Jack T. 36 n. 36, 216 n. 5
Sandnes, Karl O. 350 n. 80, 351 n. 85
Sandwell, Isabella 366 n. 25
Sattler, Barbara 251 n. 25
Scalise, Pamela J. 117 n. 50
Scarpat, Giuseppe 197 n. 6, 200
Schäfer, Peter 155 n. 1, 226 n. 27, 264 n. 87
Schaper, Joachim 62 n. 14, 66
Schefer, Christina 246 n. 6, 251 n. 26, 265 n. 90
Schiffman, Lawrence 63 n. 17, 257 n. 57
Schipper, Bernd U. 37 n. 36, 44 n. 56, 45 n. 59, 63–64
Schnabel, Eckhard J. 164 n. 32
Schneider, Gerhard 105–106
Schoedel, William 344
Schofer, Jonathan Wyn 173 n. 7
Scholen, Gershom 226–227
Schuddeboam, Feyo L. 244 n. 2
Schüssler Fiorenza, E. 310 n. 2
Schweizer, Eduard 297
Scott, Gary Alan 248 n. 13, 265 n. 91
Scott, James C. 312
Scott, R. B. Y. 17 n. 4, 21 n. 17
Searby, Dennis Michael 111 n. 31
Sedley, David 347 n. 75
Seeligmann, Iaac Leo 106–107
Segal, Moshe T. 35 n. 35, 177 n. 23
Seow, Choon-Leong 66, 216 n. 5
Sharp, Carolyn J. 65 n. 25
Sheffield, Frisbee C. C. 250 n. 21
Shepardson, Christine 365 n. 19
Sheppard, Gerald T. 36 n. 36, 37 n. 38, 66, 174 n. 10

MODERN AUTHORS INDEX 401

Shimoff, Sandra R.   175 n. 13
Shupak, Nili   114 n. 46
Skehan, Patrick W.   33 n. 31, 119 n. 61, 165 n. 35, 172 n. 2, 174 n. 9, 177 n. 23
Smith, Jonathan Z.   259 n. 59
Smothers, Thomas G.   117 n. 50
Snell, Daniel C.   20 n. 12
Steenberg, M. C.   331
Stegeman, Hartmut   183 n. 45
Steinmann, Andrew E.   218, 226
Sterling, Gregory E.   285 n. 4
Stern, Menahem   62 n. 12
Steudel, Annette   90 n. 20
Stone, Michael   226
Stone, Nina   175 n. 14
Stordalen, Terje   175 n. 13
Stowers, Stanley   261, 273 n. 121
Strobel, August   318 n. 17
Strootman, Rolf   146 n. 32
Strubbe, Johan H. M.   141 n. 22, 147
Stuckenbruck, Loren   94 n. 32
Tanaseanu-Doebler, Ilinca   359 n. 2
Tawil, Hayim   115 n. 44
Theissen, Gerd   260, 273 n. 121
Thomas, Samuel I.   179 n. 35, 253 n. 35, 254, 258 n. 58
Thuillier, J. P.   147 n. 33
Tibbs, Clint   269 n. 108
Tigchelaar, Eibert J. C.   3 n. 6, 44 n. 56, 157 n. 11, 158 n. 15, 159 n. 17, 163 n. 34, 175 n. 13, 253 n. 32, 257 n. 51, 264 n. 107
Tiller, Patrick A.   179 n. 34
Too, Yun Lee   109 n. 29
Tooman, William   72–74
Tov, Emanuel   128 n. 95
Tremblay, R.   333 n. 24
Ulrich, Eugene   159 n. 20
Unger, Dominic   351 n. 82
Unnik, W. C. van   349 n. 79
Usener, Knut   106–7, 125
Usher, M. D.   350 n. 80
Uusimäki, Elisa   72 n. 58
Valantasis, Richard   315 n. 13
Vanhoyer, Albert   311 n. 3

VanLandingham, Chris   294 n. 14
Vincenz, Friedrich   37 n. 36
Vries, Hent de   95 n. 36
Wagner, W. H.   288 n. 8
Walsh, Joseph   340 n. 49
Waltke, Bruce K.   23 n. 20
Weber, W.   195
Wedderburn, A. J. M.   259 n. 59
Weeks, Stuart   64–66, 172 n. 1
Weinfeld, Moshe   36 n. 36, 59–60
Weiss, Johannes   266
Welborn, L. L.   259 n. 60, 260, 267 n. 94, 269 n. 106, 273 n. 120
Wendland, Paul   288 n. 8
Wendt, Hans Hinrich   343
Werline, Rodney   218 n. 9
Werman, Cana   255 n.41
Wessels, J. P. H.   51 n. 69
Whybry, R. Norman   163 n. 28
Widder, Wendy L.   115 n. 46, 118, 256 n. 48
Wilken, Robert L.   338 n. 44, 351 n. 82
Williams, Margaret   138 n. 11
Williams, Ronald J.   216 n. 5
Wills, Lawrence   2 n. 2, 234, 312 n. 6
Winston, David   40–41 nn. 47–48, 197 n. 6, 199 n. 8, 203 n. 21, 205 n. 26
Winter, Bruce W.   265 n. 89
Wisse, Friedrich   343
Witte, Markus   215 n. 1
Wold, Benjamin G.   44 n. 56
Wolfson, Elliot   227
Wooden, R. Glenn   124
Woyke, Johannes   298–299
Wright, Addison   195
Wright, Benjamin G.   2 n. 2, 19 n. 10, 38 nn. 40–41, 48–49 n. 66, 70–71, 137, 147 n. 37, 162 n. 27, 166 n. 36, 174 n. 11, 177 n. 26
Young, Norman H.   295 n. 16, 328 n. 9
Zenger, Erich   69 n. 44
Ziegler, H.   351 n. 82
Ziegler, Joseph   196 n. 5, 200 n. 11 223 n. 22

www.ingramcontent.com/pod-product-compliance
Lightning Source LLC
Chambersburg PA
CBHW021928290426
44108CB00012B/767